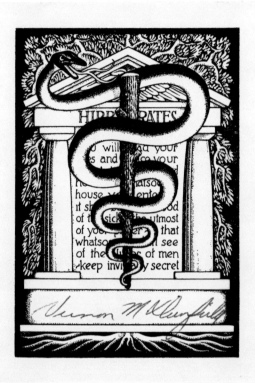

HIPPOCRATES

...u will...ad your
...s and...co your
...
ho...hatso...
house y...ente...
it sh...od
of t...sick...utmost
of you...er... that
whatso...l see
of the...ess of men
...keep inv...y secret

RICHARD THE THIRD

BY PAUL MURRAY KENDALL

Warwick The Kingmaker
The Yorkist Age
Art of Biography

RICARDVS · III · ANG · REX

PAUL MURRAY KENDALL

Richard
the
Third

LONDON
GEORGE ALLEN & UNWIN LTD

First published in 1955
Second impression 1956
Third impression 1957
Fourth impression 1961
Fifth impression 1965
Sixth impression 1968

SBN 04 942048 8

Printed in Great Britain
by Photolithography
Unwin Brothers Limited
Woking and London
(L 2231)

TO
MY TWO CAROLS

Preface

RICHARD THE THIRD is perhaps the most polemical figure in the reaches of English history. Ever since the Tudor historians of the Sixteenth century developed their picture of an arch-villain, he has been the subject of bitter argument by those attacking or defending this view of him, which Shakespeare epitomizes in his popular tragedy, *Richard the Third*.

In the course of this long controversy Richard's career has usually been approached as stuff from which to create a 'case' and his character has been treated as a cardboard counter, black or white, to be pushed back and forth in the struggles of the Great Debate. Is he a villain or is he not? Did he murder the Princes or did he not? Does the Tudor tradition present an accurate likeness, or is it a base slander? The books written about Richard have been largely devoted to arguing the answers to these questions.

The heats of argument are inimical to the art of biography. In this sense, it can be said that no life of Richard has even been written. The object of this volume is to attempt such a life. I have sought to portray what manner of man Richard was, what manner of life he led, and something of the times of which he was a part. Moral judgments I have left as far as possible to the reader.

I have ignored the Tudor tradition, except in so far as it appears to offer bits of reliable evidence; and I have based this biography almost entirely upon source material contemporary with Richard's day.

Since Richard is so controversial a figure, I have provided in the notes an opportunity for the reader to criticize, in the most debated passages of his life, the conclusions which I have drawn from conflicting or ambiguous testimony. Numbers which are asterisked refer to notes in which evidence is discussed or additional information is supplied; the other numbers refer simply to sources.

I have tried to indicate clearly, either in the text or the notes, what is fact and what is my own conjecture; and for conjectures of any importance I have given the reasons or evidence on which the conjecture is based. If the events of Richard's life and the general shape of his character had been previously established, I would probably have given freer rein to speculation. As it is, I have sought to hew him out of the facts, or as close an approach to the facts as I could make.

Nevertheless a biography is a work of interpretation. A succession of facts does not create a life or reveal a character. The accuracy of my portrait of Richard depends, in the last analysis, on the validity of the imaginative judgments that I have drawn from the facts. The notes offer the reader some opportunity of estimating that validity for himself.

To deal with the central mystery of Richard's life—Who murdered the 'Little Princes in the Tower'?—requires an analysis of evidence that is deadly to biography. I have therefore transferred my discussion of this enigma to an appendix (Appendix I). I have also provided, in Appendix II, a brief survey of the vicissitudes which Richard's reputation has encountered since he fell at Bosworth Field.

I owe an especial debt of gratitude to Alec R. Myers, Lecturer in Medieval History in the University of Liverpool, for reading my manuscript and offering suggestions and emendations of the greatest value; I have been able to indicate in the notes only a few of his contributions, and I can by no means indicate my appreciation of his labours and his encouragement.

I am likewise indebted to J. G. Edwards, Director of the Institute of Historical Research; C. H. Williams, of King's College, the University of London; Jack Simmons, the University of Leicester; K. B. McFarlane and C. A. J. Armstrong, of Oxford University; Denys Hay, the University of Edinburgh; and Col. A. H. Burne. I am grateful for the courtesy and help extended to me by the staffs of the London Library; the Students' Room, Dept. of MSS., and the Reading Room of the British Museum; the University of London Library; the Public Record Office; and the Ohio University Library, particularly Miss Catherine Nelson.

For friendly assistance of many kinds I can make only inadequate acknowledgment to Richard Hough; Edward Hodnett, Ohio University; Charles Allen Smart; Edward H. Davidson, the University of Illinois; and Paul Murphy, Ohio University.

My research in England was accomplished during my tenure of a fellowship granted by The Fund for the Advancement of Education. The Research Fund, Ohio University, provided aid in the preparation of the typescript.

June, 1955.   P. M. K.

CONTENTS

A*

ILLUSTRATIONS

MAPS

GENEALOGICAL TREE

LANCASTER AND YORK *

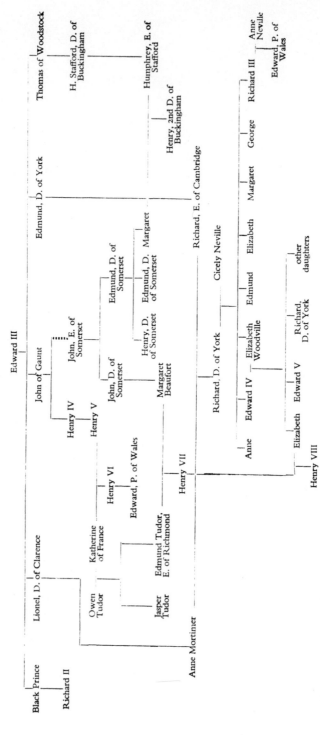

* much simplified

Prologue

Prologue*

WHEN Harry the Fifth descended into the grave in August of 1422, he left a kingdom which seemed to be among the greatest and most fortunate of the earth. The rich provinces of France north of the Loire were in the hands of the English or their Burgundian allies; in the southwest England had long held Guienne, a broad territory fanning out from Bordeaux. At home King Harry had restored the power of the crown, employing the restless energies of the magnates in the sieges of French towns and stuffing gentry and commons with the spoils of victory.

Yet the moment he was dead, this empire began to disintegrate. He had exhausted the credit and the powers of his kingdom. He had taught his lords the habit of war as a way to wealth. He had left behind him only a nine-months-old infant, in whose blood ran the madness of Charles the Sixth of France, father of the Princess Katherine whom Harry had married at the height of his success in 1420.

At once the dead King's cultured and unruly brother, Humphrey, Duke of Gloucester, and his ambitious uncle, Henry Beaufort, Bishop of Winchester and Cardinal, fell into a bitter contest for the supreme authority during the long minority reign. The council of Regency split into quarrelling factions; the retainers of the Duke and of the Cardinal fought in the streets of London; the magnates discovered, to their delight, that they could bicker as they pleased, help themselves to the royal revenue, and manipulate the machinery of justice in their own interests. Meanwhile, John, Duke of Bedford, Regent of France, sought first to extend, then to maintain, and finally to salvage what he could of his dead brother's conquests. In the spring of 1429 the trumpets of the Maid sounded the beginning of the end. After three months of victories she led the Dauphin to Rheims and stood by the altar in white armour while he was crowned Charles the Seventh. She had so stirred the superstitious fears of Englishmen that the council had a desperate struggle to find even meagre reinforcements for Bedford.

Two years later, the Maid's agony at the stake in the market place of Rouen was probably witnessed by King Henry the Sixth himself, a frail and pious little boy of ten. But Joan's work was done. In February of 1435, Bedford was forced to retire from Paris. That summer the Duke of Burgundy at last heeded the voice of the peasant girl whom he had sold to the English. He agreed to forget that his father had been murdered by the courtiers of Charles the Seventh and, counselling his English allies to make peace, he returned to his allegiance as a Peer of France. Without the help of Burgundy the English cause was hopeless.

Twenty years after the death of Henry the Fifth, England still kept a precarious hold upon Guienne, Normandy, Maine and bits of the Ile de France. The chief towns of these provinces were islands beleaguered by a hostile ocean. The French nobles had withdrawn to the territories of Charles the Seventh; the starving peasants hated the English and cut their throats when they could; mercenary bands—the dreaded *Écorcheurs*—took service on either side or ravaged the country on their own. The English dared travel the roads only in armed bodies.

At home, the magnates fought among themselves as they pleased while the court staggered towards bankruptcy and trade was well nigh paralyzed. The feud between Humphrey of Gloucester and the Cardinal continued its wasting course, but the two leaders were yielding to younger men. Cardinal Beaufort, overtaken by age, went into partial retirement. His party was now headed by William de la Pole, Earl of Suffolk, an ambitious nobleman of princely tastes and rapacious habits. Humphrey, though disgraced by the condemnation of his wife as a dabbler in witchcraft, was supported by Richard Plantagenet, Duke of York, the greatest lord in the realm.

On the famous morning of Agincourt, October 25, 1415, Richard Plantagenet was a landless four-year-old orphan. His father, the feckless Earl of Cambridge, younger son of Edmund of Langley, Duke of York, had been attainted and executed on the eve of Henry the Fifth's departure for France, charged with plotting the overthrow of the House of Lancaster. The battle altered the boy's fortunes as much as England's. His father's childless older brother, Edward, Duke of York, fell in the thick of the fighting. The landless orphan was suddenly Richard, Duke of York, a royal ward of immense importance. His wardship was granted to Ralph Neville, first Earl of Westmorland. At Raby castle in Durham, surrounded by the huge family of the Earl—his second wife had borne him thirteen children to supplement the ten given him by his first—Richard passed his boyhood and adolescence. Shortly before he left this household to assume his station in the kingdom, he was betrothed to the Earl's youngest daughter, Cicely, a high-spirited and beautiful girl who was romantically known as 'The Rose of Raby'. In 1430, at the age of nineteen, Richard accompanied his boy sovereign Henry to France and witnessed the empty mummery of his crowning in Notre Dame. Two years later he entered upon his inheritance, the richest in the realm. To the great holdings of the dukedom of York were added not only his father's entailed lands but the vast Mortimer estates which came to him from his mother, Anne Mortimer, whose brother Edmund had died childless in 1425.

For the next fourteen years of his life Richard enacted the roles which his rank and the times demanded: lord of his estates; councillor to the King; warrior and governor in the shrinking empery of France. In 1438, when he was twenty-seven and she a few years younger, he wedded the Rose of Raby—a puzzlingly late marriage for those days. They were rarely afterwards parted. Neither continual pregnancy, the hardships of travel, nor the hazard of dwelling in English France or the Irish Pale deterred Cicely from accompanying her lord. Of the seven children who lived, three were born at Fotheringhay (Anne, Margaret, and Richard), three at Rouen while their father was King's Lieutenant in France (Edward, Edmund, and Elizabeth), and George—from the beginning, a law unto himself—first saw the light of day in Dublin. In their beauty and their quickness of spirit these children resembled their mother. Richard, their father, appears to have been a quiet, solid man whose abilities were moderate but exercised with energy. He was a little below medium height, inclined to stockiness, with a square, forthright countenance which was attractive but not handsome. In France he ruled without brilliance but firmly. In Ireland his fair-dealing would convert that troubled land into a bulwark of the House of York. Excessive greed and ambition—the besetting sins of his contemporary peers—seem to have been largely absent from his character. It would require the unrelenting enmity of a Queen to remind him that he owned a better title to the throne than Henry the Sixth.

While York struggled in the early 1440's to govern France—without enough money, enough supplies, enough troops—the party of Suffolk and the Cardinal, which ruled the King, were turning to a policy of peace. In 1440 Charles d'Orleans, a friend of Suffolk's and a prisoner in England since the battle of Agincourt, was released to use his good offices for that purpose. Negotiations dragged on until 1444, when

Suffolk and Adam de Moleynes, Bishop of Chichester, went to France to arrange a marriage for King Henry which would bring an end to the war.

By this time Charles the Seventh possessed a well-trained army, formidable in its artillery, and he was well aware of the weaknesses of the English. In exchange for the hand of the King of England, Suffolk could secure only a two years' truce. This offer was the sole dowry of the prospective bride, Margaret of Anjou. Suffolk persuaded the royal councillors, however, that the truce could easily be transformed into a treaty of peace which would leave England her chief possessions across the channel.

In early March of 1445 Margaret was married by proxy to Henry the Sixth at Nancy. York met her at Pontoise, the southeast limit of the English lines in France. Accompanied by Suffolk (now a Marquess) and a train of noble ladies, he escorted her across Normandy to Harfleur. She was not yet sixteen, a proud, learned and beautiful girl, daughter of the Duke of Anjou and niece of Charles the Seventh. The bells of Portchester which greeted her ten days later were the first knell of the House of Lancaster. Within fifteen years Margaret was to prove as fatal to her cause as to her greatest enemy.

It was a marriage of fire and milk.

Henry was now twenty-four years old, but no more a ruler than when he lay in his cradle. He was a pathetic prisoner of his darkening mind, his feeble will, and his good intentions. His greatest pleasure was in prayers. His favourite companions were priests—those priests who, his councillors had made sure, would not preach against the ills that ravaged the land. The sight of a low-necked gown would drive him from his chamber, crying, 'Fie! For shame!' Because he sat upon a throne, his virtues had become rods to scourge his country. Credulous and loyal, he nursed a blind affection for his advisers which enabled them to transgress at will against justice. Generous, he cheerfully allowed himself to be pillaged of lands and treasure until the crown was hopelessly mired in debt. In 1450 he owed nearly £400,000; his yearly income had shrunk to £5,000 and the officers of his household spent and embezzled £24,000 a year. The magnates of Cardinal Beaufort's party—all-powerful since 1440—had discovered that it was even easier to rule by the King's favour than by the council. Of the wretched state of his realm Henry was only dimly aware. All would be well, he was sure, if only men would trust and love his ministers as he did. With timorous and maidenly delight he welcomed the bride they had chosen for him as the pledge of peace.

Although Margaret of Anjou was only fifteen years old when she was wedded, she was already a woman: passionate and proud and strong-willed. However humiliating it must have been to her to discover that she was married to a monk, she quickly perceived her duty: she must zealously guard the rights of the Crown; she must crush those who were pointed out to her as its enemies. Awed by her beauty and her strength of will, Henry at once became her humble vassal.

Indomitability was a tradition among the women of her family. Her father, 'good King René', owned glittering titles and small powers or talents to make them good. While he happily passed his time as a prisoner of the Duke of Burgundy in writing poetry and staining glass, his wife struggled to establish his claim to the Kingdom of Naples; and his mother governed Anjou with a man's hand, reducing the province to order and keeping out the English. By family example as by temperament, Margaret was well prepared to become the champion of the Crown. She had no sense of responsibility to England as a nation. Her outlook was personal, feudal, and dynastic. She was as primitive as her father was cultured.

It never occurred to her that the Queen should be above party strife. She quickly discovered her friends: they were the men who had made her marriage and wanted peace with France, the Cardinal's men, the Dukes of Suffolk and of Somerset and their followers.[1] Her enemies were Humphrey of Gloucester and his party. Humphrey not only urged the prosecution of the war, but he was the heir to the throne; and behind the ageing Humphrey stood Richard, Duke of York. 'The Quene,' a correspondent of John Paston's reported a few years later, 'is a grete and stronge labourid woman, for she spareth noo peyne to sue hire thinges to an intent and conclusion to hir power.'[2]

Within a year of her marriage, a tide of public indignation against misgovernment at home and double dealing abroad was beating against her and her favourites. Suffolk, it was discovered, had secretly promised to surrender to the French the province of Maine, the bulwark of Normandy. The Queen was easily persuaded that her unpopularity was due to the machinations of Gloucester and York. In February of 1447 Duke Humphrey was suddenly arrested as he arrived at Bury St. Edmunds for a meeting of Parliament. Five days later he was dead—the victim of a stroke, the court party explained.[3]* As for the Duke of York, who since 1445 had been seeking a renewal of his Lieutenantship of France, he was excluded from the King's councils and finally got out of the way by being appointed Lieutenant of Ireland. France was given to the Duke of Somerset.

In 1449 the Duke of York set out for what the court regarded as his exile in Ireland. Well for him was it that he travelled strong. Royal commands were dispatched to Cheshire, to the Welsh Marches and the seaports in Wales, that the Duke was not to reach his destination. Among those sent to waylay him was Sir Thomas Stanley, of an old Cheshire family, whose sons would repeat the act against York's sons. The Duke evaded all traps and ambushes, however, and passed safely over to Ireland.[4] In less than a year he had converted his exile into a triumph. He made friends of the Irish chieftains; he settled the quarrels of the English who dwelt in The Pale; he not only maintained order but sought to offer justice. His rule was the best that that unhappy island had known in a long time; ever afterward it zealously supported the House of York.

Meanwhile, the final disasters overtook the English in France. Suffolk and Somerset had surrendered Maine in the spring of 1448. The following year, though they knew that their grip upon the Norman towns was feeble, the Dukes wantonly broke the truce in order to sack the rich city of Fougères and compounded their folly by refusing to make reparations.

In the summer of 1449 the French armies fell upon Normandy. Townsmen and peasants seized weapons to aid their countrymen. In a few weeks the thirty-years rule of the English had ignominiously collapsed. By November Somerset was besieged in Rouen. To purchase safe passage for himself and his family, he surrendered not only the city but numerous towns as well. Within six months England had lost all of France save for Calais, hers for a hundred years, and Guienne, which her Kings had ruled for nearly three centuries. By the end of 1451 only Calais remained.

Despite the lands and offices which Suffolk (now a Duke) had swallowed down, the doting affection of the King and the ardent support of the Queen, he could not maintain himself against the storm which the news of these disasters roused in England. His colleague Adam de Moleynes, Bishop of Chichester, was the first victim. On January 9, 1450, he was murdered at Portsmouth by a band of soldiers, whom he had apparently sought to defraud of part of their pay. Seventeen days later, the Commons petitioned for the impeachment of the Duke of Suffolk. He was charged with criminal mismanagement of French affairs, subverting justice to maintain his authority, and antagonizing the King against the Duke of York. Since he did not dare to plead the privilege of trial by his peers, the Queen and he took the only other means of saving him. The King's reputation must be sacrificed for the sake of the minister. On March 17 King Henry, in a humiliating mummery of justice, merely ordered Suffolk to absent himself from England for five years, his banishment to begin on May 1.

But by this time London was howling for the favourite's blood. The next night he barely got away, some two thousand citizens sallying to St. Giles in the hope of intercepting him. On April 30 he embarked at Ipswich. Off Dover his ship was captured by a vessel which had been lying in wait for him. Two days later he was thrust into a small boat and made to kneel above a rough block. Brandishing a rusty sword, a churl took half a dozen strokes to smite off his head. Body and head were then cast upon the sands of Dover.

Though the King might mourn in horror and the Queen seek savagely for revenge, the anger of the people was by no means slaked. England heaved in an earthquake of popular discontent. Ayscough, Bishop of Salisbury, one of the court party, was murdered by his own flock. In June, Kent rose at the call of Jack Cade. Whole districts took arms en masse; many a knight and gentleman sympathized with the rebels. At Sevenoaks, Cade defeated the vanguard of the King's hastily assembled troops. The residue of the royal army melted away. In this crisis the Londoners offered to live and die with King Henry and to pay the expenses of his household for six months if he would but stay with them. Heeding the voice of Queen Margaret, however, he fled shamefully to Kenilworth. But Jack Cade was able to lord it in London for only four days. After a bitter night battle on London Bridge his forces were barred from the city. Offered free pardons, they hastened to accept. Cade was captured in flight and killed.

But the earthquake still shook the realm. There were uprisings in many shires, restlessness everywhere. About midsummer there arrived at court the worst news of all: the Duke of York was returning from Ireland. Panic-stricken, the Queen and her favourites summoned home the Duke of Somerset, who had remained prudently in France, and once more commanded their followers in Cheshire and the Welsh Marches to waylay York. On the way to meet him, Sir William Tresham, a former Speaker of the House of Commons, was ambushed and murdered. But the Duke succeeded in eluding his enemies and came safely to his strongholds in the Welsh Marches.[5]

In the early fall he confronted Henry at Westminster. He swore that he was the King's true liegeman and servant. He demanded his rightful place at the council table in order that he might help to restore order and good government. Finally, he inquired why the King had covertly sent men to intercept him on his journeys to and from Ireland. Henry made a shuffling answer. He had been persuaded that the Duke had unworthy motives. He was now sure, however, that the Duke harboured no such motives.

'We declare you,' said the King hopefully, 'our true subject and faithful cousin.' He agreed to summon Parliament and he piously assured the Duke that he was a lover of good government.[6]

When Parliament met in October, Somerset was accused of criminal misgovernment and reforms were demanded, among them, that the Duke of York be acknowledged as the first councillor of the King. Early in December, however, the Queen and her party regained their courage; Henry, as usual, dotingly did their bidding. Suddenly Somerset was released from prison, appointed Captain of Calais and Comptroller of the Royal Household. Parliament was prorogued until May; in June it was dissolved before it could accomplish anything; for daring to propose that York be formally recognized as heir to the throne, the Speaker of the Commons was thrown into prison.

In disgust the Duke of York retired to his Welsh estates.

The struggle was resumed in earnest in January of 1452. Hearing that the King's heart was hardened against him 'by sinister information of mine enemies', York once again addressed a petition to Henry.[7] It was ignored. In early February, the Duke began to assemble followers. Soon he was at the head of a sizeable army and advancing on London. When his application to enter the city peaceably was refused by the magistrates, he crossed the Thames at Kingston and moved into Kent.

The Queen and the court, meantime, had succeeded in gathering an army even larger than York's. With Henry in nominal command, it moved through London and camped at Blackheath. The Duke had friends among the nobles in the royal army. Through their good offices negotiations were opened. York reiterated his demand that Somerset be brought to trial. King Henry acquiesced, swearing his royal oath that it should be so. At once disbanding his army, the Duke of York came, almost unattended, to Henry's tent. There, to his astonishment and anger, he discovered Somerset, still in power. The Queen's wish had cancelled the King's word. Now helpless, York was hustled to London. His life may have been saved by the rumour that his eldest son Edward, a boy of ten, was marching from Wales at the head of ten thousand men to rescue his father. Or the Queen and Somerset may have feared the storm his murder would provoke. On March 10 at St. Paul's cathedral, in the presence of a great assemblage of lords and commons, the Duke of York was forced to swear an oath to keep the peace, to raise no troops, and to be obedient to the King's command.[8] Despite his popularity with the commons, his desire to strengthen the power and dignity of the Crown, and the support of a considerable portion of the nobility, he had accomplished nothing. Protests and parliaments meant little and the King's word meant less now that Margaret and the court party had ceased to be a government and become a faction. By treating him as an enemy, the Queen had turned York into one.

Shortly after his humiliation, the Duke retired to Fotheringhay, where his Duchess Cicely, great with child, awaited him.

The King's Brother

Richard, Duke of Gloucester

I

RICHARD PLANTAGENET, afterward Duke of Gloucester, and still later King Richard the Third, was born on October 2, 1452, at Fotheringhay castle. He was the last but one of the dozen children whom Duchess Cicely presented to her lord Richard, Duke of York; and he was the youngest of the four sons and three daughters who survived infancy. Nothing is known of his coming into the world and almost nothing of the first seven years of his life. It is probable, however, that before he was many days old he was fondled by a King.

During the month of October, Henry the Sixth made a brief progress to Stamford and Peterborough, one object of which was undoubtedly to pay a call upon the Duke of York at nearby Fothering-hay.[1] Richard's first encounter with royalty must have been an occasion more pathetic than splendid: an undersized, sickly infant being gingerly inspected by a peaked monarch whose mind was already beginning to cloud over. A superstitious retainer of the Duke's might fancy that the feebleness of the child reflected his father's fortunes. The older children were big and handsome and vigorous, born while York's career was advancing. It was when the Duchess was carrying Richard in her womb that her husband had fallen into the power of his enemies.

The world into which Richard Plantagenet had come on October 2 was a broken time, a time between, the disordered ending of many things, a society 'wandering between two worlds, the one dead, the other powerless to be born'. When he was less than a year old, all Europe was shaken by the news that the Turks had finally stormed Constantinople, slaying the last Emperor of Rome as he fought heroically in the breach. Within a few months of Richard's birth, there came into the world four male babies who would variously ring the changes upon these changing times: Ferdinand of Aragon and Savonarola and Leonardo da Vinci and Christopher Columbus. In Germany, men had just begun to print books from movable types. Attempting the reconquest of Guienne, old Talbot, the Terror of the French, was killed and his army blown to bits, in July of 1453, by the artillery of Charles the Seventh. France was struggling at last into nation-hood, while England, the conqueror, slid towards the twilight of anarchy.

From his birth until the summer of 1459 little Richard probably remained at Fotheringhay. So precarious was his health that a versifier, rhyming the family of the Duke, could only report, 'Richard liveth yet.'[2] His first memories were of the great castle, thronged with servants and retainers, which was the earliest home of the House of York—a mass of stone battlements and towers rising, in the shape of a fetterlock, the family badge, from the north bank of the river Nene and protected on its other sides by a double moat. The Norman knight Simon de St. Liz had built it not long after 1100. It was little Richard's great grandfather Edmund, fifth son of Edward the Third and the first Duke of York, who had enlarged and re-edified the castle. Whenever the child was well enough to trot across the drawbridge on his pony, he would see Edmund's shield shining above the north gate. Beyond the bustle and noise of the castle household stretched a quiet world. Nearby to the west rose the spire of the collegiate church which Edmund had begun and which Richard's father was still building. Next it, huddled a small village. From the battlements of the keep little Richard could look far and wide over marshy fens through which wound the Nene until it emptied into The Wash.[3]

Most of his brothers and sisters were probably unknown to him. Anne, thirteen, and Elizabeth, eight, were being schooled, as was the custom, in other noble households. The two eldest boys, Edward and Edmund, dwelt far across England in Ludlow Castle. Richard's playfellows were the children nearest him in age: George, three years older, and Margaret, six. Of his father and mother he saw little. They would arrive with a great train of attendants; hangings were unpacked from carts to blaze upon the walls of the great hall; and sitting in splendid robes on the dais, his father and mother entertained the nobles and gentry of the neighbourhood. Sometimes there were musters of armed men. Then in a little while the Duke and Duchess—with their guard of bowmen, the lords and clerics of their council, their minstrels, trumpeters, heralds, and menials, and a long train of carts carrying beds, tapestries, food—clattered across the drawbridge into the great world of which Richard knew nothing.

In these first seven years it was his sister Margaret who played mother to him, though George was her favourite. Little Richard would accept the unequal division of affection as inevitable, for he himself stood in awe of George. George was not only three years older; he was everything that Richard was not—strong, big for his age, handsome, charming, and spoiled. Richard was never entirely to free himself from the vision of a golden elder brother, whose caprice was instantly to be obeyed, whose casual smile was a dazzling reward.[4]★

At the end of these seven years the unknown world beyond the horizons of the fens suddenly rushed upon him. It was England of 1459, a world of violence.

The nobles fought each other or ranged for prey like beasts in a jungle, unchecked by the royal authority. The Crown was mired in disgrace and impotence because of King Henry's fecklessness and Queen Margaret's savage partisanship. The long wars in France had shivered the dream of chivalry and rent the texture of knightly society. Loyalty, the essential thread, was frayed and twisted. Allegiance was now bought with money and like any other bargain cast aside when a better one appeared. Only the memory of feudalism remained—an outward display, a mask for anarchy. The old ties of obligation based on land tenure had been replaced by a cash-and-power nexus called livery and maintenance. In return for his service in peace and war, a retainer received from his lord wages or favours, protection against enemies, and immunity from the law. Hence, justice went the way of loyalty. The magnates overawed courts and sheriffs, packed juries with their followers, threatened dire reprisals if they themselves or their adherents were convicted. The lord who could not protect his retainers would soon lose them, and perhaps his life as well.[5]

When these forthright methods failed on occasion, the magnates simply helped themselves to the royal prerogative. This procedure took care of John Paston when he had the temerity to bring suit for assault against Lord Moleynes. True, Moleynes had stormed a manor of Paston's as if it were a French village, rudely ejecting Margaret Paston from the premises and threatening Paston with death if he interfered. But Lord Moleynes had friends at court. Before the case opened at Walsingham, Sheriff Jermyn served notice on John Paston that he had received a positive injunction from King Henry to make up a jury panel which would acquit Moleynes.[6]

The chronicler John Hardyng, appalled by what was happening to the realm, cried out to the King:

> In every shire with jacks and sallets clean
>   Misrule doth rise and maketh neighbors war;
> The weaker goes beneath, as oft is seen;
>   The mightiest his quarrel will prefer;
> The poor man's cause is put on back full far,
>   Which, if both peace and law were well conserved,
> Might be amend, and thanks of God deserved.[7]

It was a world harbouring bitter foes of the House of York. While little Richard had been sheltered at Fotheringhay, the fabric of order, crumbling for a generation, had fallen to pieces. Authority had become only a name for the duel to the death between the Duke of York and Queen Margaret.

II*

BEFORE Richard had completed his first year, two events occurred which fatally altered the struggle between the Queen and the Duke of York. In August of 1453, as the result of 'a sudden and thoughtless fright', King Henry at last went mad, even as his grandfather, Charles VI of France, had gone mad.[1] He could neither speak nor understand. With lack-lustre eyes he stared at his frantic Queen, or turned his head aside to look upon the ground. Three months later, Margaret was delivered of a son in the palace of Westminster. She was a dynast. The complex elements of her nature and her breeding became fused in the savage instinct to protect the birthright of her child. Henceforth, she would struggle passionately to annihilate her enemies and to nurse the King into a semblance of sanity so that he might be persuaded to resign the crown to his heir.

When she could no longer conceal the madness of her husband, Margaret and her party were forced to summon a Great Council and to permit the Duke of York to take his place at its head. A little before Christmas of 1453 the Council committed the Duke of Somerset to the Tower. In the spring of 1454 York was appointed Protector and Defender of the Realm with full powers as Regent. Loyally he assembled the nobility to take the oath of allegiance to Margaret's son, Prince Edward, as heir to the crown. By constant labour he managed to suppress the worst disorders in the kingdom. Then, in the Christmas season of 1454, King Henry regained his sanity. On December 30 he happily acknowledged his son, so it was given out. According to another report, he threw up his arms in amazement when the infant was presented to him and declared that he must be the son of the Holy Spirit.[2] In any case, York's regency came to an abrupt end. His ministers were turned out of office. Somerset was released from the Tower and again made Captain of Calais. The Duke of York retired quietly to his castle of Sandal in Yorkshire.

In May of 1455 the Queen and Somerset summoned a Great Council to which no prominent Yorkist was invited. The Council promptly ordered an assemblage of nobles at Leicester 'for the purpose of providing the safety of the King's person against his enemies'.[3] York had no difficulty in realizing that he must fight for his life. With his brother-in-law, the Earl of Salisbury, and with Salisbury's son, the Earl of Warwick, he marched southward, determined to secure a hearing from the King and disprove the slanders of the court party. Surrounded by a quarter of the peers of England, Henry started northward to meet him. The two armies collided at St. Albans. In an hour the forces of York were completely victorious. Somerset, Northumberland, the Duke of Buckingham's eldest son, and Lord Clifford were slain; the Duke of Buckingham, the Earl of Dorset, the Earl of Devon were wounded and taken prisoner; the Queen's favourite, James, Earl of Wiltshire, ignominiously fled. The Yorkists brought King Henry back to London, paying him due reverence.

Within a year the victory of St. Albans had gone for naught. Again, the Queen and her party had achieved control of the King's government, because they controlled the King. Again, they had made York 'to stink in the king's nostrils even unto death; as they insisted that he was endeavouring to gain the kingdom into his own hands'.[4] Again, it had been brought home to the Duke that he could do nothing except when he was backed by armed force. If he took up arms before his enemies moved, however, he would be condemned by many for an aggressor; if he waited until the Queen's party struck an open blow, he was likely to find himself at their mercy. It was impossible to make war on the Queen without seeming to make war on the King; yet unless the Queen's power over the King were broken, neither the realm nor he himself could count upon peace. York's failure to solve this double dilemma would be his destruction.

The state of war was now chronic; the country was split into two irreconcilable factions. Such was the feuding among the nobles that if one lord espoused York's cause, another instantly upheld the Queen. She could also command those barons who enjoyed the climate of anarchy or who, suspicious of York, rallied to the King's banner out of loyalty to the reigning House of Lancaster. York's most powerful supporters were Salisbury, Warwick, and the Duke of Norfolk, all kinsmen by marriage; the men of the Welsh Marches and the southeast counties; and the commons generally, in particular the merchants of London who looked upon the Duke as the only hope of stable government and the revival of trade. The chroniclers of the time, the ballad-makers, were almost all his ardent well-wishers.

The next three years (1456–59) are among the murkiest in English history. While little Richard toddled after George and Margaret within the great castle on the banks of the Nene, the Queen sought furiously to strengthen her following and to establish her small son in the nation's heart; Richard's father moved watchfully from Fotheringhay to Sandal, from Sandal to his strongholds at Ludlow or Wigmore, from the Welsh Marches back to Fotheringhay.

In 1457 the kingdom was shamed and outraged when it learned that Piers de Brezé, one of the great generals of France and a friend of Queen Margaret's, had landed on the coast of England and burnt Sandwich. The Queen became the butt of scurrilous tales and ballads. It was said that Prince Edward was a changeling; it was whispered that he was the son either of the Earl of Wiltshire or the Duke of Somerset. So violent was public indignation that the Queen's government was forced against its will to give the Earl of Warwick a commission to keep the sea for three years. As Captain of Calais, the office he had been granted after the death of Somerset, he had already made a name for himself. Soon England was ringing with his exploits in the channel. In 1458 occurred a token reconciliation between the Yorkist leaders and the sons of those lords who had died at St. Albans. Two by two and hand in hand they went in procession to St. Paul's, the Duke of York escorting the Queen. It was an empty show, a will-o'-the-wisp in the thick night of disorder. There was no government in England. Tense and miserable, the country waited for the worst.

III

In the spring or summer of 1459 Richard was thrust into the world beyond the horizons of the fens. The Queen's party were beginning to prepare for open war. York felt his situation to be so dangerous that he no longer trusted the defences of Fotheringhay castle. Richard and his brother George, surrounded by a strong escort, set out on a journey across the heart of England. From the marshy flats of the Nene they made their way through the great forest of Rockingham to Market Harborough. Then their way lay across the rolling country of the Midlands. There would be a cautious detour around Coventry, with scouts dispatched from the main escort to look out for ambushes. At Coventry an army was gathering beneath the banner of the King. No doubt, Richard spent a night at Warwick castle, home of his cousin, the Earl, whose adventures as Captain of Calais he would know by heart. After passing Kidderminster, the cavalcade took its way through the woods and the river valleys of Shropshire. Past the triple hills of Clee, Richard came at last to the ridge on which stood the village of Ludlow. Beyond, on its western lip, was planted a massive castle. Then the ground fell steeply to the gorge of the river Teme.[1]*

Riding through the eastern gate of the outer fortifications, Richard found himself in a courtyard some five acres square. In the northwest corner rose the castle proper, its moat and wall dominated by an ancient keep with its own walled bailey. Across the castle courtyard a great range of halls and chambers stood against the outer battlements on the northern rim of the ridge.

Little Richard now met for the first time his two eldest brothers, Edward, seventeen, and Edmund, a year younger. They were belted Earls—Edward of March and Edmund of Rutland—and in Richard's eyes, men. Doubtless he often watched, in awe, as they practised the manage of axe and sword. It was likely that their father would soon need their stout young arms. When spring passed into summer, the outer courtyard swarmed with men and horses as the retainers of the House of York came in with armour on their backs. Lord Clinton appeared with his followers and Lord Powis, Sir Walter Devereux, and other knights and squires. Messengers galloped in and out. In late August came word that the Earl of Salisbury was marching to join them with all his power, and that his famous son Richard, Earl of

B

Warwick, would soon arrive with a band of warriors from the garrison of Calais.[2]

On September 25 Richard watched his uncle Salisbury ride into the courtyard at the head of his Yorkshiremen. Pennons waved; clarions sounded a triumphant note. Soon the boy saw, however, that wounded men lay in the baggage carts; gashes showed on armour; the footmen were sweating and weary. It was his first sight of men who had endured the storm of battle. Perhaps from an unobtrusive corner of the council chamber he heard Salisbury tell the tale to his father and mother.

In the preceding May, Margaret and her little Prince Edward had travelled through Lancashire and Cheshire, rallying the gentry to her cause. By early summer the royal standard was set up at Coventry and an army was gathering. When the Queen got word of Salisbury's march, she sent Lords Audeley and Dudley to intercept him.

Finding his way barred at Blore Heath, near Market Drayton, by an army much larger than his own, Salisbury had drawn up his men in the shelter of a wood and grimly awaited the onslaught. His archers and his men-at-arms fought so fiercely that the royal host was thrown back with heavy losses; Lord Audeley was slain and Lord Dudley taken prisoner. When night fell, Salisbury marched around the enemy and came safely to Ludlow. A few days later Richard beheld the arrival of Salisbury's son Richard, Earl of Warwick, and his troops from Calais, which were commanded by a renowned captain and pirate, Andrew Trollope.

Beneath the splendour and excitement of this martial assemblage in the halls of his father, the little boy doubtless felt the tension, lurking in faces and voices, of men confronting a mortal struggle. He would hear harsh words of the Queen, the French woman who was gathering a host to destroy the House of York. At the age of seven he was learning that the world was dangerous, even as, gazing at the bright, confident face of his elder brother Edward, he was beginning to sense the valour and pride of the high blood from which he sprang.

Early in October the news at last arrived that the host mustered at Coventry in the King's name was beginning to move towards Ludlow. When word came that the army had reached Worcester, the Yorkist lords sent a petition to the King protesting their loyalty and desire for peace. The court party countered by publishing the offer of a general pardon to all who would desert York's cause, and with spread banners the King's host continued its westward advance. The Duke, caught on the horns of his dilemma, dispatched a second petition. Ignoring it, the

royal army swept into Leominster and turned north towards Ludlow,
less than thirty miles away.

The road to Leominster left Ludlow by the Broadgate, crossed the
Teme on a fine stone bridge (still standing) and ran south through a
narrow valley of meadows. These are hemmed on the west by rising
ground and on the east by the river—for the Teme, after flowing
eastward past the heights of Ludlow, bends sharply to the south. On
these Ludford meadows the Yorkists had now established their camp,
protected by an earthwork which blocked the valley and the road.

On the afternoon of October 12 the banners of the royal host
appeared down the valley—a force probably twice as large as York's—
and the King's men camped less than a mile away. When night fell,
Andrew Trollope and the Calais garrison provided little Richard with
his first lesson in the bitterness of betrayal. Suddenly they swarmed
across the earthwork and fled to the King and the King's pardon. It was
a dreadful blow: Trollope knew all the plans of the Yorkist leaders; his
men were among the best trained soldiers in the army; this wholesale
desertion chilled the hearts of the rank-and-file.

York, Warwick, and Salisbury held a desperate consultation with
their chief captains—torches flaring in the great chamber of the castle,
servants running to fetch meat and beer at the command of Duchess
Cicely, and Richard and George looking on no doubt from a corner, as
a dozen men in full armour hurriedly debated the issues of life and
death. There was no solution but the hard recourse of flight: Cicely
must be left with her two small boys to the mercy of the court; the
remainder of the army would have to disperse in the darkness as best it
could. The Duke of York, his sons Edward of March and Edmund of
Rutland, Warwick, and Salisbury took horse and with a small escort
galloped westward into the night.

When the troops of the King stormed triumphantly into the un-
defended town the next morning, they found Cicely, Duchess of York,
and her sons Richard and George courageously awaiting them on the
steps of the market cross. If Cicely had hoped to protect her helpless
townsfolk, her effort was vain. She and her boys were hustled off to the
royal camp. Ludlow was pillaged as if it were a French town; after the
drunken soldiery had looted dwellings and outraged women, they
robbed the castle to its bare walls.[3]★

The Duchess and her boys were taken to Coventry, where a
Lancastrian Parliament promptly attainted York, Salisbury, Warwick,
and their chief followers, and declared their estates forfeit to the crown.

King Henry was able to perform one act of kindness, however: he granted the Duchess of York a thousand marks a year to maintain herself and her children. She was put into the custody of her sister, the Duchess of Buckingham. A little before Christmas, Richard and George and their mother took up their life as prisoners of the crown upon one of Buckingham's manors.[4]* One chronicler reports that Cicely was 'kept full straight and many a great rebuke'.[5] Richard was seven years and two months old. Of his father and his brothers he had heard nothing since they vanished into the night, hunted men.

The fugitives, in fact, were doing very well. Somewhere in Wales they had separated. The Duke of York and his son Edmund, Earl of Rutland, struck westward to the coast, found a ship, and sailed for Ireland. York was received at Dublin 'as if he were a second Messiah'. Native chieftains and the English settlers alike rallied to his cause. Royal writs commanding his arrest were ignored; their bearers, often executed. The Irish Parliament recognized York as the virtual ruler of Ireland and declared that only those writs of the English King which were approved by the Parliament would have force.[6]

The Earls of Warwick, Salisbury, and March had fared no less well though their journey was more hazardous. Reaching the Devon coast after many perils, they managed to purchase a ship. On November 2 they were warmly welcomed at Calais, which, under the governance of one of Salisbury's brothers, had remained loyal to its Captain, Warwick.

As soon as the court discovered the whereabouts of the fugitives, it dispatched Richard, Lord Rivers, to Sandwich to prepare a fleet of ships for an assault on Calais. Warwick, however, knew all about Rivers' plans from the men of Kent who daily crossed the channel to swell his ranks. In the early morning of January 7, a small detachment of Warwick's men swooped down on Sandwich, captured the fleet of the King, surprised in their beds Lord Rivers, his wife, and his son Sir Anthony Woodville, and carried ships and captives triumphantly back to Calais. 'As for tidings,' one of the Pastons wrote soon afterwards, 'my Lord Rivers was brought to Calais and before the Lords with eight score torches, and there my Lord of Salisbury rated him, calling him knave's son, that he should be so rude to call him and these other lords traitors, for they shall be found the King's true liegemen when he should be found a traitor, etc. And my Lord of Warwick rated him and said his father was but a squire and brought up with King Henry V, and since then himself made by marriage, and also made

Lord, and that it was not his part to have such language of lords, being of the King's blood. And my Lord of March rated him in like wise.'[7]

In the early spring Warwick dared to sail to Ireland in order to concert measures with York for the invasion of England. The King and Queen moved about the Midlands, harassed and fearful, aware that the Lords of Calais and the Duke of York would soon make a descent upon their shores but, as usual, paralyzed by indecision, incompetence, poverty, and unpopularity. Bills and posters attacking the court appeared on church doors, town walls; ballads were sung in the streets praising the Calais Earls and praying for their quick return; rhymesters appealed to Providence to retore the Duke of York. . . .

> Send hom, most gracious Lord Jhesu most benygne,
> Sende hoom thy trew blode unto his propre veyne,
> Richard, duke of York, Job thy servaunt insygne. . . .[8]

Meanwhile, Edward, Earl of March, young though he was and in the thick of great affairs, had concerned himself for the welfare of his two little brothers. Not long after he had landed at Calais, he sent a message to his kinsman, the Archbishop of Canterbury, begging him to befriend Richard and George. The boys were accordingly taken into the Archbishop's household. Richard would be put rigorously to his books, and it is perhaps here that he began to learn that handsome Italic script that appears in some of his later autographs. If the boy was permitted to read romances, he doubtless found no hero to match his brother Edward and no tale to compare in suspense with the drama of his family's fortunes.[9]*

As spring turned to summer, all England, including a small scholar named Richard Plantagenet, looked for the coming of the Yorkist lords.

In rainy June weather—the worst summer weather in a century—they came.[10] Landing at Sandwich on the 26th with an army of some 2000 men, the Earls of Warwick, Salisbury, and March headed for London, gathering followers as they advanced. On July 2 they were welcomed into the city. Pausing only long enough to establish a siege of the Tower, which held out for King Henry, and to borrow £1,000 from the magistrates, the Earls marched northward to meet the royal army. They found it entrenched in a bend of the river Nene, just south of Northampton. Mistrusting the issue of the day, the Queen and her son had remained at Coventry.

On the rain-soaked afternoon of July 10, the Yorkists assaulted the royal entrenchments. This time it was a wing of the King's army that suddenly changed sides and permitted a flood of men to pour across the earthworks. The Earls won the field in less than an hour. The Duke of Buckingham, who had commanded the royal host, the Earl of Shrewsbury, Lords Beaumont and Egremont lay dead in their smashed armour. Henry the Sixth was captured in his tent. Treated like a King, he was conducted to London on July 16. Two days later the Tower surrendered, and within a week the Yorkist lords had established a government.

It was not until the 15th of September that the Duchess of York, accompanied by Richard and George and their sister Margaret, arrived in the city. Within a few days she received a message from her husband, who had landed at Chester. The indomitable Cicely at once hurried off to join him in a chariot covered with blue velvet and drawn by eight coursers. The children remained in London.

Busy though the Earl of March was with affairs military and political, he now came every day to visit Richard, George, and Margaret in the temporary lodgings he had found for them.[11] It may have been this small domestic idyll which wrought upon Richard one of the master experiences of his life. Edward shone with the blaze of mighty affairs and was the companion of paladins. Yet he took care to watch over his brothers and his sister, regaling them with tales of his adventures, warming them with his affection and his greatness. How could there be anything better than to follow forever and to serve this wonderful brother, so splendid, so kind?

IV

SUDDENLY the wheel of time was speeded up and the wheel of fortune spun dizzily. On October 10 Richard saw his father enter London like a King, the full arms of England inscribed upon his banners, trumpets and clarions proclaiming the triumph of his arrival and a sword borne upright before him. It was indeed with kingly thoughts that the Duke had come. During his past months in Ireland he had found a solution to his dilemma: Queen Margaret could be got rid of only by removing Henry too. Pausing only to greet the city magistrates, York rode through London to Westminster and entered the Painted Chamber where the Lords were assembled. He strode directly to the throne, hesitated, finally put one hand upon it and announced that he had come to claim the crown by hereditary right.

The peers were astonished and dismayed, none more so apparently than Warwick and the young Earl of March. They realized that the realm expected York to reform the government, not to turn out the King. York's action was awkward, politically inept; it was, in fact, alien to his character. His reading of events had forced him into a role unsuited to his plain nature. He had blustered because he was not at his ease. After three weeks of confused debate and legal tergiversation, a compromise was finally effected to which all the lords and the bewildered Henry himself professed agreement. York's claim to the crown as the heir (through his mother) of Lionel, Duke of Clarence, third son of Edward III, was acknowledged to be just—as by lineal right it was, since Henry VI was descended from John of Gaunt, the fourth son. Yet, in virtue of the fact that the House of Lancaster had sat upon the throne for sixty years, Henry was to remain King for the rest of his lifetime. He would be succeeded by the Duke of York, who was named the heir of the realm and Protector as well. Queen Margaret's son Edward was disinherited.

That is, he was disinherited in London. But not in the minds of the Lancastrian lords who had absented themselves from the Parliament, and least of all in the fiery heart of Queen Margaret. When she received the news that her husband had been captured at Northampton, the Queen and her son fled westward from Coventry. After a hazardous journey, at one stage of which she was waylaid and robbed, she reached the safety of Harlech castle. At once she set about recruiting men to her son's cause. The tidings that Parliament had proclaimed York as Henry's heir only spurred her to greater efforts. Sailing to Scotland to beg aid, she offered Berwick, the great frontier fortress, as a reward for Scottish support. Meantime, her followers in the North of England were assembling a formidable host.

To meet these dangers, two small armies left London on December 9. One, commanded by Edward, Earl of March, headed westward for Wales. The Duke of York himself, his son Edmund, Earl of Rutland, and the Earl of Salisbury marched for Yorkshire. Warwick remained at London to maintain the government.

On December 21 York halted at his castle of Sandal, his scouts having brought word that the Lancastrians were gathered in force at Pontefract, only ten miles away. The leaders of the two armies apparently agreed to a truce for the Christmas season. But the Lancastrians were too hungry for revenge to respect oaths. On the late afternoon of December 30 their army suddenly appeared before Sandal castle, at a moment when a portion of the Duke's troops were out foraging. Gallantly but foolishly, York and Rutland and Salisbury rushed forth to the rescue of their men. Their small band was soon surrounded. York was slain fighting manfully; with him fell Sir Thomas Neville, a younger son of Salisbury. Edmund of Rutland, fleeing towards Wakefield, was overtaken by young Lord Clifford whose father had died at St. Albans. As Rutland begged for mercy, Clifford clove him to the earth, hissing, 'By God's blood, thy father slew mine, and so will I do thee and all thy kin!'[1]* Salisbury was captured, only to be executed the next day. The heads of the slain Yorkist leaders were carried to the city of York and impaled on Micklegate Bar, the bloody brows of the Duke being rimmed in bitter derision with a crown of paper and straw. It was now war à l'outrance.

On the morning of January 2 seven-year-old Richard learned that in a moment's swirl of battle he had lost a father, a brother, and an uncle.

Reports soon followed that the victorious Lancastrians, the Queen at their head, were advancing southward to take London and destroy what remained of the House of York. Margaret had promised her motley array of Welsh, Scots, and Yorkshiremen that they might freely pillage the whole South of England. On a front of thirty miles her host marched, leaving ruin in its wake. As if they were conquering a foreign land, her troopers burnt villages, sacked churches, raped women, and murdered all who would protect their goods or who aroused their displeasure.[2]*

About February 10, however, came a piece of good news. At Mortimer's Cross in Herefordshire, young Edward of March had crushed a Lancastrian army under the Earls of Pembroke and Wiltshire. A few days later, the Earl of Warwick left London with the force he had hastily assembled to oppose the advance of the Queen. Experienced in the art of war though he was, Warwick could not match his pupil, the Earl of March. A little beyond St. Albans he drew up his army in three widely spaced wings facing northeast. But the Queen's host, early on the morning of February 17, fell upon his flank from the north, threw his forces into wild disorder and soon routed them. King Henry, whom Warwick had unaccountably taken with him, was found under a tree about a mile from the battle front laughing and talking to himself.

With a shred of his army Warwick fled westward to meet Edward. Fugitives poured pell-mell into London crying that the Lancastrians were at their heels. The great town was thrown into confusion.

Merchants scrambled frantically to hide their valuables, to don harness, to arm their apprentices with clubs, and to join Mayor Lee, now a captain in coat of mail, in patrolling the apparently doomed city. Rumours raced through the streets that, despite her promise to the contrary, the Queen's wild Northerners would sack London.

Soon a detachment of Lancastrian cavalry was pillaging the suburbs. Ships in the harbour began to hoist sail. Though the commons had forced their magistrates to bar the gates and defy Margaret, the Duchess of York hastened to dispatch young Richard and George beyond the reach of the Queen. The Low Countries, she and her advisers hurriedly concluded, would provide the best haven. Philip, Duke of Burgundy, their ruler, had previously shown himself friendly to the Yorkist cause. Richard and George were escorted through the turbulent city to the wharves. That night, accompanied by a squire, John Skelton, and a few attendants, the two boys were tossing on the seas.[3]*

The realm of Burgundy—comprising a broad strip of territory which ran from the French dukedom and county of that name to the great commercial cities of the Low Countries—was then the wealthiest and the most splendid land in Europe. Duke Philip, who liked to think of himself as a medieval crusader but was much more nearly a Renaissance Prince, received Richard and George—after an interval—as if they were potentates and treated them like sons. On April 18 the Milanese ambassador, Prospero Camuglio, wrote to his master Francesco Sforza from Bruges, 'Tomorrow, they say, two younger brothers of March, son of the Duke of York, are coming here, and the Duke of Burgundy has given notice for great honours to be shewn to them.' Later the same day he added, 'Since I wrote today, the two brothers . . . have arrived. . . . The duke, who is most kind in everything, has been to visit them at their lodging, and showed them great reverence.'[4]

Doubtless Richard and George were also greeted by William Caxton, who was then head of the English merchants at Bruges—a successful mercer, as yet untouched by the enchantment of printing. The Duke himself probably showed them his famous library, the finest in Europe, with its gorgeously illuminated manuscripts bound in gem-crusted covers. Perhaps he took them to his country estate at Hesdin, an amazing place in which little bridges collapsed to empty the unwary into garden ponds, books when opened blew dust into the beholder's eye, and in the famous room hung with Jason tapestries thunder and lightning, snow and rain, could be marvellously simulated. Caxton says he saw this chamber, and it is not impossible that Caxton was their guide.[5]

B*

This fine welcome to Bruges, however, came two months after they had reached Burgundy. It appears that at first Richard and George, scions of a family whose fortunes were suddenly very doubtful, had been quietly escorted to Utrecht and there set once more to their oft-interrupted lessons. Hard task it must have been for them to con books, ignorant of what had befallen their kin and their cause, remembering the panic in the London streets as Queen Margaret's terrible host approached. . . .

When tidings finally came, about April 12, they were glorious beyond belief.[6] The brave Londoners had dared to resist the Queen's threats. While she hesitated, Edward of March and the Earl of Warwick entered London ten days after the second battle of St. Albans. Margaret broke her camp and, carrying poor Henry with her, retreated northward. The Yorkist lords now solved the dilemma which had been fatal to the Duke. On March 4, Edward, as the heir of York, was proclaimed King of England. A week later, he and Warwick started in pursuit of the Lancastrians. The Queen and her host turned at bay near Towton in Yorkshire. On March 29, Palm Sunday, in a driving snow storm, King Edward led his outnumbered army to one of the bloodiest victories ever won on English soil. The chief Lancastrian lords were killed or captured; their host was utterly broken; Henry, Margaret and their son fled precipitately into Scotland.

Not only could George and Richard now return safely to England; they were summoned by King Edward to share the pomp of his coronation. The city of Bruges gave the boys a farewell feast. Duke Philip showered them with gifts and had them escorted to Calais by a guard of honour.[7] At Canterbury they were banqueted by the city fathers and sent ceremoniously on their way to the royal palace at Shene (Richmond). Not many hours later they knelt in homage to their brother who had become a King.

In his eight-and-a-half years Richard had experienced rude shocks of fortune, the bitterness of civil strife, the fragility of power, the sting of injustice. One gleam of assurance he had found, the awesome star of his brother Edward. By this time he was old enough to realize how unlike the other young eagles of the House of York he was . . . last and small and weak. Beside the glow of the healthy and assertive George he doubtless felt himself an insignificant shadow. Yet it will appear that out of his early experience he had forged one fierce resolve: to make himself strong in order to serve Edward. His precarious childhood had undoubtedly left scars; it had also lit the first flame of will.

V

KING EDWARD was a month short of his nineteenth birthday when he displayed his prowess at the battle of Towton. His appearance and his charm were no less brilliant than his martial exploits. Standing six feet four inches tall, his zest for life shining in his face, he was regarded by his contemporaries as the handsomest prince—indeed, the handsomest man—in Europe.[1]* Exuberant and convivial, he enjoyed the splendour of his new-won throne as frankly as he enjoyed the pursuit of the girls at court. He seemed content to let the Earl of Warwick consolidate his victory and manage his realm. What, in fact, lay beneath the surface of this remarkable youth, men had not yet learned; Warwick, to his cost, never did learn. It was quickly apparent, however, that Edward meant to associate his brothers unmistakably with his greatness.

On Friday, June 26, Richard tasted the triumph of Edward's state entry into London. With his two brothers the King rode to the Tower, escorted by the Mayor and Aldermen in scarlet and 400 of the principal citizens in green. That evening Richard, along with George and twenty-six other young noblemen, was created a Knight of the Bath. He would undergo the initiation solemnly, too young to realize that the elaborate ceremonial attempted to recapture a vanished chivalry, which had existed largely in the pages of the romances.[2]

He was first of all led to his chamber by two 'governors', who were in charge of his initiation. When a sumptuous bath had been prepared for him, three knights of the Order, accompanied by squires singing and dancing, entered the chamber. Richard having been inducted into the bath, the chief knight sprinkled water on his shoulders and instructed him in the rites and ideals of the Order. Dried and clothed—with the aid of a barber who took the bath as his fee—Richard was now conducted to the chapel. Here throughout the night, in the company of the governors and a priest, he underwent his knightly vigil, which ended at dawn with confession, matins, and the Mass. He was then ceremoniously put to bed for a brief sleep, after which he was even more ceremoniously arrayed for the final rite. Preceded by a youth carrying his sword and spurs, he rode through the courtyard of the Tower to the royal lodgings—a Marshal of Arms leading off the horse as his fee—and presented himself before the King and his lords. At Edward's command two knights fastened Richard's spurs to his heels.

The King himself girded his brother with a sword, kissed him, and said, 'Be thou a good knight'.

Richard returned to the chapel to swear at the high altar that he would maintain the rights of the church and to offer up his sword. Leaving the chapel, he was halted by the Master-Cook who cried, 'I, the King's Master-Cook, am come to receive your spurs as my fee; and if you do anything contrary to the Order of Knighthood, which God forbid, I shall hack your spurs from your heels'. With this warning ringing in his ears he went to dinner, but only to watch others dine: he was not permitted to 'eat nor drink at the table, nor spit, nor look about him, more than a bride'. At last he returned to his chamber and was there clad in a blue robe with a white hood and a token of white silk on the shoulder.

On Saturday afternoon, with the other new Knights of the Bath in like costume, Richard rode in procession with the King from the Tower to Westminster. He assisted on the morrow at the coronation of his brother as King Edward the Fourth. At the Bishop of London's palace next day he watched Edward create brother George Duke of Clarence. William Hastings, the King's dearest friend, who had fought in all his battles, was made Lord Hastings and a number of other faithful followers were awarded titles.

It was fitting that George, the elder brother and heir to the throne, should be honoured before Richard; but Richard's turn came only four months later. On All Hallows day Edward set a cap of estate on his small brother's head and created him Duke of Gloucester.[3] Not many weeks later he and George were elected Knights of the Garter; by early February of 1462 a helm, crest and sword marked his stall among the blazons of the mighty dead in the chapel of St. George.[4] Yet when Richard was made a duke, he was only a few weeks past his ninth birthday and he owned a larger experience of civil strife than of civil learning. It was high time that he should, like all the boys of the nobility, serve his apprenticeship in knightly conduct within the household of a great lord and be tutored in the polite accomplishments of peace and war.[5]

On November 13 Richard and George, along with Warwick and Warwick's brother Lord Montagu, were appointed to call out the levies of Westmorland, Cumberland, Northumberland, and Yorkshire for defence against the Lancastrians and their allies, the Scots.[6] It was the Nevilles, of course, who would actually assemble and command the forces. George of Clarence apparently did not even go north. Now at the ripe age of twelve, he seems to have remained mostly at court, until, in a few years, he was able to persuade King Edward that he was mature enough to have his own establishment.[7]

For Richard, however, the appointment signalled the beginning of yet another new life. The King had arranged that he should enter the household of the greatest lord of all, the Earl of Warwick.

VI

IN November of 1461, or not long after, a small, frail boy who was Duke of Gloucester and Commissioner of Array for the North Parts, rode for the first time beyond Trent and, passing through the city of York, followed a winding, climbing road which brought him, above Fountains Abbey and Ripon, to the swelling moors of Wensleydale. Here, at the Earl of Warwick's castle of Middleham, Richard was to spend the great part of his next three years. Though it was less grand than Warwick castle and though the Earl's household, following the peripatetic habit of the time, moved about from one estate to another, Middleham appears to have been the favourite residence of Warwick's countess and her two daughters and the seat of his 'court'—for the great lords of the age emulated the King in having each his own council and an established, rigid household protocol.[1]*

Its grey stone walls and towers planted solidly on the southern slope of Wensleydale, Middleham castle had already dominated the valley for three hundred years when Richard rode up the steep slope through the marketplace of the village and entered its inner ward by the northern drawbridge and gate. Before him rose one of the largest keeps in England, a massive oblong with walls ten to twelve feet thick which was closely surrounded by the outer fortifications. A flight of stone steps in the east face led up to a covered landing. To the left was the chapel, which had been built out from the keep; to the right, the entrance to the great hall. This occupied the eastern half of the keep; on the other side of the dividing wall were the family solar and the Earl's presence chamber. The keep stood higher than its protective walls, against which, on three sides, were ranged household buildings, offices, living quarters, a mill, a bakehouse with a nursery above it. On the fourth side, the eastern, rose a guard tower from which a drawbridge crossed the moat into a large outer courtyard encircling the stables, smithy, slaughterhouses. Behind the castle, to the south,

the moors rolled upward to the sky; there was yet visible on the slope
the remains of an earlier Norman 'motte and bailey' fortress which
had perhaps been raised on the site of a Saxon or Roman or even an
ancient Celtic earthwork. To the north, the land fell steeply past the
village to the swift-flowing Ure. Beyond, rose the farther slopes of the
dale and the moors.[2]

On special occasions like the Christmas holidays or the spring
festival of Corpus Christi, Richard would ride with the Countess of
Warwick and her daughters and the principal members of the household to the city of York, the metropolis of the region. Lodged in one of
the great religious houses, they would be ceremoniously welcomed by
the Mayor and Aldermen and given fine white bread, wine, fresh fish.[3]
But the heart of Richard's life was the castle and the dale.

The Ure tumbled down from the Pennine ridge, foaming into rapids
and falls at Aysgarth, ten miles west of Middleham. At Aysgarth stood
Nappa Hall, whose owner, James Metcalfe, had served as a captain at
Agincourt. Young Richard must have ridden over to Nappa to hear
tales of the martial exploits of Harry the Fifth; later, Metcalfe's sons
became his faithful followers.[4] Between Aysgarth and Middleham stood
Bolton castle, seat of that doughty fighter, Lord Scrope. A mile and a
half east of Middleham the Ure was joined by the river Cover, emerging
from its smaller dale, and not far beyond rose the walls of Jervaulx
Abbey. The moors, men-at-arms, monks—these were Richard's
neighbours.

Wensleydale was less subdued to man than the softer countryside
which Richard had known in the south: a land of scattered castles
and abbeys, their villages and fields huddled about them amidst the
great wild sweep of moor. The hills seemed to have been rounded by
the stamp of Roman legions and of Celtic Kings. The earth was
gigantic, elemental; leading men's thoughts to God, teaching men the
necessity of human ties; confirming men in their feeling for old ways
and old things. The people were directly swayed by their instincts,
quick to take arms in a quarrel, slow to shift loyalties, earnest in their
convictions. Here young Richard, in those impressionable years
between nine and thirteen, discovered the native country of his spirit,
a country which half created, half affirmed the kind of man he was to be.

There were several lads at Middleham, like himself apprentices
in knightly conduct. Two of them became his dearest friends: Sir
Robert Percy and Francis, later Viscount Lovell.[5]* These boys ate and
slept and trained together. In the great hall they shared the communal

life of Warwick's retainers, officers of the Wardrobe, grooms, esquires of the household, ushers, chaplains, children of the chapel, ladies in waiting upon the Countess, servants. All were under the watchful eyes of the steward, the treasurer, and the comptroller of the household, who maintained order in this bustling hive, according to a detailed code of duties and privileges. King's brother though he was, Richard would have no privacy. Privacy was a luxury whose charms even the greatest lords were only beginning to discover.[6]

In the chamber and in the courtyard Richard and his fellows were tutored in 'the schools of urbanity and nurture of England'. After rising early and hearing Mass, they broke their fasts with a mess of meat, bread, and ale. Studies followed under the direction of a learned clerk or chaplain: some Latin, more French, a smattering of law and of mathematics, music, penmanship. More important still was the subject of knightly conduct. The boys were taught 'to have all courtesy in words, deeds, and degrees [and] diligently to heed rules of goings and sittings'. They conned a variety of tracts on courtly behaviour and Christian doctrine, treatises of knighthood and of war, the accepted code for challenges and the *Acts of Arms,* allegories such as *La Forteresse de Foy,* Froissart's *Chronicles, The Government of Kings and Princes.* In leisure time they developed their knowledge of etiquette by reading romances and by conversing with Warwick's Countess and her two lovely daughters, Isabel, who was about Richard's age, and Anne, four years his junior.

The boys ate dinner at 9.30 or 10.0 in the morning amidst the throng of the great hall. Then, clad in armour, they sallied from the castle to bestride their horses, for they must learn 'to ride cleanly and surely' and to 'wear their harness'. In mock tournaments Richards collected his first scars. He practiced on foot with sword, dagger, and battle-axe. There were lighter exercises too: galloping over the moors, learning to manage a hawk and to hunt stag and boar. Their bones aching, the boys took their supper at four in winter, five in summer, and completed the day's regimen by rehearsing the polite arts of harping, singing, piping, and dancing. Then they retired, their servants fetching the 'livery' for the night: bread and ale for a bedtime snack and, from All Hallows day until Good Friday, the 'winter livery' of candles and firewood.[7]*

It was here that young Richard began the struggle to accomplish his secret resolve. The sickly child who had become a thin, undersized lad drove himself to grow strong, to wield weapons skilfully. Fiercely, grimly he worked at the trade of war. His vitality was forced inward to feed his will. He could not afford to take life as it came; he must prepare himself to serve his magnificent brother Edward. Probably as a result of this rigorous training, his right arm and shoulder grew to be somewhat larger than his left.[8]

Although these three years (1462-64) were the most tranquil Richard had yet known, or for many years to come would know, his sojourn at Middleham castle was not unbroken.

After a generation of growing anarchy, the kingdom was painfully groping its way towards order. King Edward was striving to win over the Lancastrians by a ready clemency, to reassert the force of the royal authority, and by means of an active diplomacy to convince the European powers of the stability of his government. The Earl of Warwick and his brother John, Lord Montagu, were constantly in harness, working to subdue the unruly North. The indomitable Queen Margaret and her adherents, however, kept strife and conspiracy alive: along the coasts, in Wales, and in the marches towards Scotland. Three great Northumberland castles—Bamburgh, Dunstanburgh and the Percy stronghold of Alnwick—were in Lancastrian hands. Leaving her helpless spouse in Scotland, Margaret sailed to France in the summer of 1462 in order to plead her cause with Louis the Eleventh, who had ascended the throne a year before. By mortgaging Calais to Louis— a speculation in futures—she was able to invade Northumberland with a small fleet and army under the command of her old friend Piers de Brezé.

The report of her landing at Bamburgh on October 25 (1462) reached London five days later. King Edward started northward with what forces he could hastily gather. Warwick was already in Yorkshire, where he had spent the summer raising men. No doubt he had come at intervals to Middleham, radiating upon young Richard his glow of fame and great affairs. When Margaret heard that Edward and Warwick were bearing down upon her, she 'broke her field' and took to her ships. A tempest shattered her fleet. With her young son Edward and de Brezé she barely managed to reach Berwick in a small boat; most of her troops were drowned or captured. While King Edward remained at Durham, immobilized by an attack of measles, and the Duke of Norfolk conveyed supplies northward, Warwick and Montagu pressed so vigorously the sieges of the three castles that by early January of 1463 they had all surrendered. Perhaps Richard kept Christmas with his sick brother, for Durham lies less than fifty miles northeast of Middleham. It is possible that the young Duke obtained his first experience of military operations by visiting the sieges.

When, by the middle of January, King Edward moved southward, Richard went with him to share a sacred filial duty. On January 30 at Fotheringhay, Edward and Richard commemorated their father's 'month-mind' (the Duke of York having been slain on December 30, 1460). In the splendid ceremony were borne a hearse powdered with silver roses and golden suns, four great heraldic banners, a 'majesty cloth' depicting Christ upon a rainbow, fifty-one gilded images of Kings and 420 gilded images of angels. Two weeks later the three mighty Nevilles—George, Bishop of Exeter and Chancellor; Lord Montagu; the Earl of Warwick—in a ceremony even more impressive bore the remains of their father and brother to Bisham Abbey in Buckinghamshire. In a triple interment of great pomp the recently deceased Countess of Salisbury was laid to rest with her husband and son. King Edward was represented by Hastings, his Lord Chamberlain, and by John Tiptoft, Earl of Worcester and Constable, as well as by the Duke of Clarence—the first record of George's association with the Earl of Warwick.[9]

In late February, Richard accompanied Edward to London. Though he was too young to be summoned to the Parliament which met at Westminster on April 29, he may have attended some of its sessions. By early June he was on his way back to the moors of Wensleydale.[10]* The Scots and the Lancastrians were again on the rampage; Bamburgh, Dunstanburgh, and Alnwick had once more fallen into Queen Margaret's hands. Warwick, his work all to do again, marched northward from London on June 3, probably taking Richard with him. King Edward set out a month later. Meanwhile Margaret and the Scots had crossed the border and laid siege to Norham castle, but Warwick and his indefatigable brother Lord Montagu soon sent the invaders pelting back across the border. Shortly after, leaving Henry in Edinburgh, Margaret and her son returned to France to await a change in fortune.

The Scots had now had their fill of dying for the House of Lancaster. In early December (1463) they dispatched an embassy to York. King Edward came up from Pontefract on December 3. Six days later, a ten-months' truce was signed. Since the King kept his Christmas at York, Richard probably rode down from Middleham to be with him. Perhaps George of Clarence was there also. To help his brothers make merry, Edward gave them each the Christmas present of two tuns of Gascon wine.

By the end of January, 1464, Edward and Warwick were once again on the march, southward this time. Lancastrians were stirring up trouble in Wales; there was unrest in the Midlands and in Lancashire, rioting in Gloucestershire. It was March before the King and the Earl had sufficiently calmed the country so that they could proceed to London. They now determined upon a great effort to clear Northumberland permanently of Lancastrian arms. Edward scraped together every penny he could lay hands on and he dispatched commissions of array for twenty-two counties, the whole southern half of England.

By these commissions young Richard of Gloucester was suddenly projected upon the stage of great events.

Customarily, a half dozen or more men were appointed commissioners for each county; a great magnate frequently served on the commissions of a number of counties. In this case, however, Richard, Duke of Gloucester, was made sole commissioner for nine of the twenty-two counties: the great belt of western and southwestern lands extending from Shropshire and Warwickshire through Somerset to Devon and Cornwall. If his powers were to have been merely nominal —as they had been in the commissions of November, 1461—he would have been associated with other commissioners. It appears that Richard, at the age of twelve, had been entrusted by his royal brother with the surprisingly responsible charge of levying troops from a quarter of the realm. In this region he had not long before been granted broad lands and offices.[11]

George of Clarence, three years Richard's senior, was not appointed commissioner for a single county.

King Edward had been discovering notable differences in character between his two brothers. He had begun by attempting to balance his favours: George obtained his dukedom four months before Richard; they were made Knights of the Garter at the same time. In February of 1462 George received the Lieutenantship of Ireland for seven years— the office to be administered by a Deputy—and on August 10 enjoyed his first grant of lands, several manors which had belonged to the attainted Earl of Northumberland. Two days later, however, Richard reaped a richer harvest. He was not only granted manors in several counties which had been forfeited by the Earl of Oxford, but he was given the county, honour, and lordship of Richmond and the county, honour, and lordship of Pembroke as well. This marked show of favour to Richard must have thrown George into a fury of jealousy, which blazed the higher when, on September 9, the King bestowed on Richard all the lands and manors of the attainted Lancastrian, Lord Hungerford. Such a fuss did the Duke of Clarence raise that Edward, who loved his ease, felt compelled to transfer the county, honour, and lordship of Richmond from Richard to George, and a few weeks later he cancelled the grant of Hungerford's estates. He soon compensated his younger brother, however. On October 12 of this same year (1462), the quiet, undersized lad practising with weapons in the courtyard of Middleham Castle became Admiral of England, Ireland, and Aquitaine.

Henceforth King Edward made no attempt to disguise the greater trust he reposed in Richard than in George. In December of 1463, while he was keeping his Christmas at York, Edward granted to Richard 'during pleasure' all the estates of Henry Beaufort, Duke of Somerset, who had just turned traitor despite Edward's generous attempt to make him a friend. The Duke's lands were located mainly in the southern and western counties, where, by the grant of August, 1462, Richard was already established in authority as the Constable of Corfe Castle, County Dorset.[12]*

Apparently in February or March of 1464 Richard rode from Middleham into the southwest. His commissions of array arrived early in May. The King had left London on April 28, ordering a rendezvous of his forces at Leicester on May 10. By that date a small figure in full armour had led his county levies northward through Worcester and Coventry to join the royal army, skirting a few miles to his left as he drew near Leicester a village called Market Bosworth.

By the time Edward and Richard reached Pontefract, the Lancastrian hold on Northumberland had already been shattered. On April 25 a small army commanded by Lord Montagu had collided at Hedgeley Moor with a strong force under the Duke of Somerset, the Lords Hungerford and Roos, and Sir Ralph Percy. The Lancastrians were quickly routed; Percy was slain, crying as he fell—so tradition says— 'I have saved the bird in my bosom!' A skittish bird it was indeed, his allegiance to King Henry. Less than eighteen months before he had not only been pardoned by King Edward but given command of the castles of Bamburgh and Dunstanburgh, the former of which he had held for Queen Margaret. Three months later, despite Edward's generosity and his own solemn oath, he had delivered the castles to the Lancastrians. The bird in his bosom was bred in that sorry nest of broken loyalties, the reign of Henry the Sixth.

Three weeks after Hedgeley Moor, on May 15, Montagu had

completed his work: issuing suddenly from Newcastle, he assaulted the remains of the Lancastrian forces at Hexham and speedily crushed them. Somerset, Hungerford, Roos and two dozen of their principal adherents were captured and either beheaded on the field or condemned and executed by sentence of the Constable, the Earl of Worcester. Poor King Henry, hiding nearby at Bywell castle, was forced to flee so precipitously that he left behind him his 'bycocket', or cap of estate.

Save for Harlech castle in Wales and Berwick on Tweed, Edward was now truly King of all England. What seemed the final blow to Lancaster occurred a year later. In July of 1465 the feeble-witted son of Harry the Fifth was run to earth in Lancashire, where he had been wandering for some time with not half-a-dozen attendants. Warwick led the heir of Agincourt on horseback through the streets of London, his feet bound to the stirrups by leather thongs, to a prison chamber in the Tower. He was provided with attendants, treated with kindness, and permitted to see whoever wished to visit him.

Meanwhile, after the battle of Hexham, Montagu rode into Pontefract to report his victory and deliver Henry's bycocket to King Edward. Warwick's brother was promptly rewarded for his great services. On May 27 Richard watched Edward bestow on John Neville the princely earldom of Northumberland. Not long after, the boy probably returned to Middleham and the 'schools of urbanity and nurture'.

That day in Leicester, when Richard came riding in at the head of his county levies, Edward must have smiled at the sight of his small brother, very serious in his martial harness. But it was a smile of more than amusement. Without George's inches, maturity, health, or charm, Richard had already won first place in the affections and confidence of King Edward. He was eleven years old.

In September (1464), England was stunned by a piece of news, which, in effect, brought Richard's boyhood to an end.

Before a meeting of the council at Reading, about September 15, when the Earl of Warwick pressed Edward to approve his scheme of a French marriage, the King announced debonairly that he was already married. He had defied tradition—and the will of the mighty Earl—by secretly wedding Dame Elizabeth Woodville. She was the widow of Lord Ferrers, who had died fighting for King Henry at the second battle of St. Albans, and the daughter of that very Richard Woodville, Lord Rivers, whom Edward and Warwick had rated so insultingly one January night in 1460 at Calais. She was five years older than Edward;

she was the mother of two sons almost as old as Richard. It was believed by some that the King had been bewitched; it was thought by many that Edward had wantonly affronted Warwick only to gratify his lust for the beautiful widow. On Michaelmas day Warwick and George of Clarence—prophetic coupling—escorted Elizabeth into the chapel of Reading Abbey and joined the court in honouring her as Queen. Nevertheless, it was soon widely known that the Earl had quarrelled with the King who had dared to challenge the authority of the Nevilles.[13]*

The rift was in due course patched over and for many months to come the House of Neville appeared to be as portly and as powerful as ever. Warwick's brother George, Bishop of Exeter and Chancellor, was soon elevated to the Archbishopric of York. Yet, whereas Warwick had learned almost nothing from the disasters of King Henry's reign, or the career of Harry Hotspur, Edward had learned a great deal. In marrying his Elizabeth, he had mated his inclination to his policy. 'Warwick,' wrote the Milanese ambassador in 1461, 'seems to me to be everything in this kingdom.'[14] Edward intended to be the ruler as well as the King of England; and the announcement of the marriage was the first article in his declaration of independence.

For Richard, it marked the end of his formal tutelage. The brother of the King could scarcely remain, now, the pupil of the Earl. Besides, he had shown himself ready to take a place in the world, and King Edward knew well that he might soon need all the support he could muster. Abruptly, another stage in Richard's growth ceased. The hard but tranquil regimen of knightly training upon the moors—interspersed by sallies into the turbulent world of the early 1460's—was now permanently broken off. Ahead, stretches a five-year period of mounting tension in the realm, of almost impenetrable obscurity in Richard's history. Only the briefest glimpses of him can be caught and these not of significant moments. Yet in this time of first adolescence he experienced one of the greatest crises of his life, and nothing is known of it save the outward result.

VII

BY the spring of 1465 Richard, a boy not yet thirteen, had left Middleham for his brother's court.[1]* He found it alive with Woodvilles. The new Queen's family was numerous, thriving, and eager to grasp the good things of this world. Richard Woodville, Lord Rivers, had begun his career as a squire. By his marriage to the Dowager Duchess of Bedford (daughter of the Count of St. Pol and descendant of Charlemagne) and by his indefatigable practice of the arts of climbing, he had raised himself to high office and a baronage, while the Duchess was presenting him with seven daughters and five sons who became, most of them, as handsome and pushing as their father.

After the battle of Towton in the spring of 1461, King Edward had paused on his journey south at Grafton Regis, the manor of his old enemy Lord Rivers, whose son Anthony had fought on Henry's side at Towton. For the first time Edward laid eyes on Elizabeth Woodville. She possessed great beauty and she had been well schooled by her parents. Not many days later both Rivers and his son received pardons. In such intervals as he could find Edward pursued the lovely widow hotly. She was adamant: her virtue could be satisfied only by a crown. When the King was on his way to meet his army at Leicester in the spring of 1464, he halted a night at Stony Stratford. The next morning, May day, he rode casually over to Grafton Regis. Returning three hours later, he told his men that he had gone hunting. He had, in fact, wedded Elizabeth with only her mother and two gentlewomen present as witnesses.

By May of 1465, when Richard was with the court at Greenwich, a golden bounty was already showering down upon the Woodvilles. Edward bestowed on his bride lands worth 4,000 marks a year (about £1,300), his 'manor of pleasaunce' at Greenwich, and his manor at Shene (Richmond) as well. She was assigned an establishment in Smithfield, called Ormond's Inn, as her town house, where she promptly set up a menage to outshine the household of Queen Margaret, in which she had once been one of the humbler ladies in waiting. Her family abundantly shared the golden shower. Within two years of her marriage, Elizabeth's sisters had been betrothed to the greatest 'estates' of the realm: Margaret to the heir of the Earl of Arundel; Katherine to the youthful Duke of Buckingham, a ward in the Queen's household; Anne to William Bourchier, son of the Earl of Essex; Elinor to the Earl of Kent's heir; and Mary to Lord Dunster, son and heir of Edward's great friend William, Lord Herbert.

Nor were Elizabeth's five brothers neglected. Anthony, Lord Scales, shortly to be made a Knight of the Garter and Governor of the Isle of Wight, had already become a shining figure at court; Lionel, seeking to rise in the church, would be made Bishop of Salisbury; Edward received military commands; Richard was created, along with his brother John, a Knight of the Bath at his sister's coronation; Sir John Woodville was given a marriage that even in that opportunistic age created a scandal: still in his 'teens, he wedded the Dowager Duchess of Norfolk, a lady venerable enough to be his grandmother but very rich. And by paying 4,000 marks to the Duchess of Exeter, the Queen secured for her elder son, Sir Thomas Grey, the heiress of the exiled Duke of Exeter, who had been promised to Warwick's nephew. Elizabeth's father was likewise cared for. After bestowing 1,000 marks on his faithful adherent, Lord Mountjoy, King Edward asked him to resign the Treasurership to the royal father-in-law. A few weeks later, on Whit Sunday of 1465, Lord Rivers became Earl Rivers, and within two years he was given the high office of Constable of England.

If the greed of the Queen's family had antagonized not only the Nevilles but the older nobility and commons as well, Elizabeth was at least prompt to begin fulfilling her duty to the realm. On February 11, 1466, she gave birth to her first child, Elizabeth; and the little princess was baptized with as much pomp as if she had been the hoped for male heir. The 'churching' of the Queen offered another opportunity for brilliant ceremonial. A procession of ecclesiastics, peers and peeresses, minstrels, heralds, conveyed the Queen to the service in the Abbey and from the Abbey to the banquet at Westminster palace. Four large halls were filled with guests. In a separate chamber bedecked with arras the Queen sat alone at table upon a golden chair, attended by her mother and Edward's sister Margaret, who were required to kneel if addressed. Not until the first course had been served were they permitted to sit down, but the ladies in waiting remained kneeling for the full three hours which the banquet lasted, the Queen not deigning to utter a word to anyone. When the tables had been cleared for merry-making, the Queen's mother resumed her kneeling posture before the Queen, and the Princess Margaret, even while dancing, was careful to make many curtsies to Her Highness.[2]

This vain Queen and the luxury-loving Edward were beginning to create a court not only more lavish but more cultivated than its predecessors. It was elaborate in ceremony, gorgeous in velvet and satin costume, with ladies in linen-covered headresses and men wearing 'pikes' or peaked shoes so long that they were caught up at the knee by a golden chain. Disturbed by this riot of worldliness, the Pope had sent a Bull into England threatening with excommunication any cordwainer who made pikes more than two inches long; but the chronicler Gregory reports laconically, 'Some men said that they would wear long pikes whether Pope will or nill, for they said the Pope's curse would not kill a fly. God amend this. And within a short time after some of the cordwainers got privy seals and protections to make long pikes. . . .'[3]

Through the royal chambers, bright with arras, fresh with strewn flowers and rushes, music was always sounding—trumpeters and clarionists to blazon forth the occasions of state, minstrels singing to shawms and lutes, bandsmen playing viols and rebecks and sackbutts, and a great chorus of sixty voices to sing motets and masses in the royal chapel.

There was some show of learning as well as luxury. Anthony Woodville, Lord Scales, was not only the most accomplished jouster of the day but a gifted amateur of letters, and Warwick's brother George, the Chancellor, found time to be a bibliophile and patron, employing a Greek scribe to copy the works of Plato for him and presenting valuable books to the Universities. By far the most notable aristocratic scholar of the age was John Tiptoft, Earl of Worcester and Constable of England. He had travelled to Jerusalem; he knew Venice, Florence, Rome; for almost two years he had studied at Padua; and he had returned to England with a precious cargo of manuscripts—Lucretius, Suetonius, Tacitus, Sallust, and others. He had himself translated a number of Latin works of which Caxton was later to print two. Bold featured, with protruding eyes, he was, for all his learning, a man of rigour. As Constable he was earning the epithet of 'Butcher of England'. On his way to execution in the fall of 1470 he maintained that he had acted for the good of the state, and while the mob clamoured for his blood, he calmly requested the headsman to perform his office with three strokes 'in honour of the Trinity'. Cold, enigmatic, tinged with cruelty and responsive to the new statecraft of Italy, he was more likely to weep at a torn manuscript than a severed head.[4]

Thus was the sun of the Renaissance rising above the horizon to gild this court with its first rays. The King himself glowed most brightly, perhaps, with the spirit of the coming time—in his zest for living, in the catholicity of his pleasures, in the versatility of his interests and talents, in the adventurous sensuality of his temperament.

Such was the court in which young Richard, fresh from his knightly training on the hardy moors of Yorkshire, had taken up yet another new life.

Meanwhile, what of the House of Neville, once sole occupants of that place in the heavens into which the House of Woodville was so vigorously thrusting itself? Though rumour persisted on the Continent that Warwick had become the enemy of his royal master, the Nevilles seemed to retain their old power over the realm, if not over the King. The Earl, rich in high offices and busy with affairs, still appeared to be what the Scots Bishop of St. Andrews had called him in 1463: 'Conduiseur du royaume d'Angleterre dessoubz le roy Edouart.'[5] The three brothers had recently negotiated a truce with the Scots to endure until 1519; Warwick continued to head embassies to Burgundy and France. After the birth of Princess Elizabeth, it was George Neville, Archbishop of York, who baptized her and the Earl who stood as the only masculine sponsor at the font. Yet an entertainment given about the same time more nearly reveals Warwick's feelings. When, in the early spring of 1466, King Edward impressed a visiting group of Bohemian knights by a fifty course dinner, Warwick immediately after dazzled them with one of sixty courses.[6]

To the Earl, things were not the same. Edward was no longer his protegé; he, no longer the avuncular mentor. He began to doubt—and, what was to him far worse, others including his friend Louis XI began to doubt—that he was still 'le conduiseur du royaume'. His position had become ambiguous, and he had neither the inclination nor quality of mind to study the ambiguity coolly.

The Earl of Warwick lived, more intensely than most men, by his vision of himself and the reflection of that vision in the eyes of others. Heir though he was, in so many ways, to the arrogant, king-rivalling barons of the past, the hazy picture he drew of his place in the world was tinged with the colours of a coming age. It was magnificence he groped for as much as power, a many-faceted excellence which would catch the light of admiration from every direction. Having put Edward on the throne, as he conceived, by his conquering sword, he delighted in clapping harness on his back at all hours to keep him there; he was equally zealous to play the master statesman and let foreign Kings behold his greatness; and he must be bountiful, too, as he hoped to be loved beyond the limits of ordinary acclaim. His castles were thronged with retainers, tenants, suitors. At his London establishment six oxen might be roasted for a breakfast; any acquaintance of his servants was free to bear away from the kitchens so much meat as he could thrust upon a dagger. When the Earl rode through the streets of London or passed through villages on errands of diplomacy or war, crowds of people cried 'Warwick! Warwick!' as if he were a deity dropped from the skies. No one was so splendidly arrayed as he and none bowed so low in courteous salutation to the meanest bystander who would shout a greeting. He perpetually wooed the world and, for a time, won it.

He was indeed genuinely amiable, generous, abounding in energy. Small wonder that he had deeply impressed one frail and earnest apprentice in knighthood who had dwelt for a time in his castle of Middleham. Yet the Earl's charm and *élan*, the grandeur of his estates and offices, and the smile of fortune had hitherto concealed his serious disabilities. His genius was a plant that could flower only in the noonday sun; the wintry touch of adversity caused it to shrivel. At the second battle of St. Albans his faculties had been stunned by Queen Margaret's unexpected flank attack. It appears that he had been badly rattled at the beginning of the battle of Towton.[7*] He possessed indeed scarcely more than ordinary talents and he was both intellectually and emotionally naive. Consequently he was terribly vulnerable to attacks of hurt vanity, being unable to distinguish his desires from his prerogatives. He could imagine himself no other than what he had become and thus he confused his resources with his honours. Because the people of England manifestly admired him, he failed to realize that their devotion might have limits.

Like Hotspur, he could conceive no end to the gratitude which the man on the throne owes to the man who put him there. But it was more than a matter of gratitude. His political horizon was bounded by the reign of Henry the Sixth. Government was an attribute of power. To Warwick, the ills of England had not grown from the fact that a clique of magnates had wielded Henry's sceptre in their own interests but from the fact that they were the wrong magnates.

By flouting the Earl's marriage schemes Edward had wounded Warwick's vanity; by elevating the Woodvilles he had punctured his pride; by asserting his independence he had challenged the foundations of his greatness. To the very quick Warwick felt that he had been monstrously assailed; it never occurred to him that it was the King's right and it was impossible for him to conceive that it might be the King's duty to exercise the royal prerogative. Edward must be taught his place—that was the sum of it.

The crumbling of Warwick's character began almost at once. He sought directly to strike back at the ungrateful King by suborning his brothers—particularly George, for George, now sixteen years of age, was still heir-male to the throne. If Warwick could win over the Dukes of Clarence and Gloucester, the King, supported only by the Woodvilles and a few favourites, would soon be glad to return to the Neville fold, or be forced to return to it.

George of Clarence was an easy conquest. He had become dissatisfied with his lot before Edward married; he hated the Woodvilles as upstart competitors of his greatness; and his shallow nature was quickly captivated by the flattering attentions of the Earl. When Warwick proposed that Clarence marry his elder daughter, the Duke was utterly his. The thought of being allied to the greatest power in the realm as well as standing next in line to the throne unfolded before George's eyes hazy vistas of glory. By the summer of 1466 King Edward had got wind of the scheme. He had long ago taken George's measure and he was of no mind to countenance so potentially dangerous an alliance. He bluntly told his brother to give up all thought of the match. Warwick and Clarence, however, continued to spin plans in secret.

The Earl was also seeking to detach Richard from the King. At a great festival which George Neville held in 1466 to celebrate his enthronization as Archbishop of York, George of Clarence did not appear—perhaps by design—but Richard was there. No doubt the boy wore his splendid garter, which had been fashioned by Matthew Philip, goldsmith and former Mayor of London, and cost three times as much as the one which John Brown later made for Charles of Burgundy. Richard did not dine at the Archbishop's board in the great hall. Instead, he was installed at the head table in the chief chamber of estate, the only male of rank to be seated with ladies. On his right hand sat his sister Elizabeth, Duchess of Suffolk; on his left, his aunt, the Countess of Westmorland; the others at table: Warwick's Countess and her daughters Isabel and Anne. The arrangement savoured strongly of a 'family' grouping. Perhaps it was meant to remind Richard that the Nevilles were happy to consider him one of them and that, though George was to have Isabel and half her mother's inheritance, there remained Anne, a slight girl of ten, who should have the other half.

The banquet itself was one of the most sumptuous of the age, proclaiming the undiminished opulence of the Nevilles and pointedly exceeding the splendour of King Edward. The great Earl himself performed the office of steward and brother John of Northumberland, that of treasurer, while Hastings, Edward's Lord Chamberlain, was comptroller. Sixty-two cooks had laboured to prepare 104 oxen, 6 wild bulls, some 4,000 sheep, calves, and pigs, 500 stags, 400 swans and a galaxy of other meats which were washed down with 300 tuns of ale, 100 tuns of wine, and a pipe of hippocras. Then came 13,000 sweet dishes, climaxed by an array of 'subtleties'—sculptured confections, of which one depicted St. George slaying a dragon of 'marchpane' and another, a pastry Samson pulling down candy pillars. Well might this extravagant display suggest to the guests that the destiny of England lay with the House of Neville.[8]

Perhaps, on the other hand, the Earl of Warwick, beginning feverishly to juggle with the future, was holding out to young Richard quite different but even more glittering marital prospects.

The man who had caught George of Clarence in a web of promises had himself fallen victim to the very Father of Flattery, Louis XI of France. It was that monarch's settled policy to win over—by bribes, favours, or honeyed words—the chief officers of his neighbours' realms. Not long after he mounted the throne in 1461 he had set his cap for the all-powerful Earl. He ventured to send to him for a dog; he did favours for his Lieutenant at Calais; soon he was writing letters to Warwick, informal and artlessly admiring. The Earl found them a heady draught: they helped stimulate him to the conclusion that since France was the perpetual springboard for Lancastrian assaults, England must make a treaty of peace which would put an end to Queen Margaret's hopes. With Louis' enthusiastic concurrence he had arranged the preliminaries, in the spring of 1464, for a marriage alliance between Edward and Louis' sister-in-law, Bona of Savoy. When the ungrateful Edward announced his marriage to Elizabeth Woodville, King Louis, sensing that this apparent reverse might open up promising possibilities, continued to protest his friendship and show his esteem for the injured Warwick.

Now, in the spring of 1467, Louis was writing to the Duke of Milan that by the help of Warwick he had reached a secret agreement with the King of England. Edward would renounce his claims to France and become Louis' brother-in-arms in a war to exterminate the Duke of Burgundy and his son Charles, Count of Charolais. Warwick's reward was to be the marriage of Isabel to the Duke of Clarence; Edward's sister Margaret would wed Philip of Bresse; while Richard, Duke of Gloucester, would receive the hand of Louis's second daughter, whose dowry would be Holland, Zealand, and Brabant—spoils of the extermination of the House of Burgundy! The work of a master tale-spinner, it was a fantastic yarn, except in so far as it doubtless reflected something of Warwick's grandiose visions and Louis' eagerness to let the world know that the mighty Earl was his devoted friend.[9]

Of Richard's actual involvement in the web which Warwick and Clarence were weaving, there exists only the testimony of a lurid rumour which reached France about this time.[10]* George and Richard, so it ran, skipped away from court to visit Warwick at Cambridge and concert plans for George's marriage to Isabel. Penetrating their whereabouts, the King commanded his brothers instantly to appear before him. He rated them severely and then ordered four knights of his household to put them under arrest.[11]* If there shines any gleam of truth in the murk of this gossip, it is that Richard, cherishing a deep admiration for the radiant and martial Warwick, had been happy to find himself courted by the Earl and by his brother George—until he discovered what they were about.

In the Woodville court Richard could not have been at ease. Edward doubtless gave him tasks—when he remembered—and warmed him with his dazzling smile of affection, his exuberant habit of clasping round the shoulders,[12] an occasional word of approbation. But the sun of York was usually withdrawn these days into soft clouds of luxury; the martial hero whose campaigns Richard must have known by heart spent his hours tilting, hunting, carousing, dancing, charming pretty faces—except when, suddenly all business, he closeted himself with his advisers to grapple with the problems of policy.

In the halls of Westminster palace, on the terraces of Greenwich and Shene, young Richard could not find, amidst the laughter and the whispers and the innuendo of intrigue, the means of making a home for himself. The North was in his blood. He knew that he was meant for service and not for pleasure. He was not subtle of mind nor malleable of temperament. He could not bring himself to enjoy the company of the Woodvilles, whose arrogance shone as bright as the newness of their fortunes. The Queen's elder son, Sir Thomas Grey (later, the Marquess of Dorset), a lad of about Richard's age, was already in training to become a boon companion of the King. In the tilt-yard the talk was all of Anthony Woodville, Lord Scales, who dominated the tourney well nigh as much by the ingenuity of his harness as by the skilful play of his weapons. The Queen, beautiful and rapacious, would know how to show her haughtiness to the undersized lad from Yorkshire with the awkward torso and solemn face. She viewed the King's two brothers only as rivals of her family for the favours of her lord. Woodvilles surrounded Edward like a glittering hedge, barbed with glances, insinuations, and the small, icy manœuvres of ambition.

Would Richard not eagerly welcome what measure of companionship he was offered by George of Clarence, to whose golden attraction he had long ago succumbed, whose petulant charm still hid from him the hard and heedless egotism beneath? Clarence was not only three years older now; he was a man, old enough to talk of marriage, to busy himself with important affairs and have important friends. Clarence despised the Woodvilles. Clarence was the companion and ally of the Earl of Warwick.

The geniality and splendour and virile energy which had won the admiration of the world could not have left young Richard unmoved. Middleham had been his home; Warwick, his lord. The Nevilles were deep-rooted in the North. Richard and John and George were his mother's nephews. Warwick would know how to enchant the lad, to play upon his distaste for the Woodvilles and his unease at court.

When the companion of his childhood and the great Lord of the North were poised against the Queen and her kindred, the scales of Richard's mind could register only one choice. Gradually Clarence and Warwick drew him, flatteringly, into their confidence. Under the benevolent auspices of the Nevilles, Clarence would marry Isabel and Richard too would make a great marriage; the Woodvilles, the unlovely intruders, would be sent away, and King Edward and his two brothers would live happily ever after with the Earl of Warwick and *his* two brothers, as was obviously intended by Providence for the weal of the kingdom. It was a vision which Richard, groping for stability, harbouring deep loyalties, was ripe to appreciate. Only . . . a small part of the vision remained blurred. For Richard, however, that part was the centre. When it began to clear, he instantly rejected the whole dream. Mining facilely the ore of Richard's simplicity, Clarence and Warwick suddenly ran against adamantine.

Richard had realized that they aimed at forcing the King to do their will and acknowledge their power. Neither his affection for them nor his dislike of the Woodvilles could corrode his loyalty to Edward.

To the pair of schemers this defection was doubtless of small moment. Shutting the lad out of their confidence and their company, they pressed on with their plans. Richard could only endure his misery in silence, remembering, perhaps, the contemptuous voice of Clarence calling him a Woodville-lover or a milksop.

Thus, while the kindred of the Queen saturated the court with the glow of their new-minted greatness and Edward moved to free himself from the domination of the Nevilles and Clarence and Warwick assembled their power to manage the King, Richard grew towards manhood, an obscure figure, mute and no doubt lonely.

It appears that Edward had no difficulty in divining his younger brother's choice. In February of 1467 he confidently put Richard, Warwick, and the Earl of Northumberland together on a commission of *oyer and terminer*** to inquire into some trouble at York.[13] By this time Warwick and the Duke of Clarence were secretly negotiating at Rome to secure the necessary papal dispensation for the marriage of Clarence and Isabel, who were cousins.

VIII

THE Earl of Warwick's pride was soothed and—so it then seemed—his hand was strengthened by his conquest of the Duke of Clarence. Early in 1468 he could not resist boasting to Louis XI that he had 'drawn over' Edward's elder brother.[1] But this was only a beginning. He must answer Edward's challenge; he must make clear to the world that he was master still of the realm. The issue to which his emotions drove him was the direction of England's foreign policy. This, in the 1460's, had reduced itself to an essential choice: Burgundy or France?

The ageing Philip the Good and his son Charles, Count of Charolais, who in 1465 took over the conduct of affairs and in 1467 succeeded to the ducal coronet, were rulers of an anomalous state. As Duke of Burgundy, Philip was, theoretically, a Peer of France and vassal of Louis XI; as suzerain of the Low Countries he reigned in his own right. Philip, indeed, considered himself an independent sovereign; his son Charles the Rash would spend his life striving ardently to erect the dukedom into a kingdom. It was the dearest object of Louis XI, on the other hand, to round out his northern frontiers at the expense of the Low Countries and to return the Duchy and County of Burgundy to the fold of France.

Since Edward's accession, England, France, and Burgundy had been dancing a wry diplomatic pavane, each state dreading the alliance of the other two against it. At first sight, Edward's choice seemed easy. There were traditional ties of friendship and vital ties of trade between England and Burgundy; and only an alliance with Duke Philip would

---

* A commission conferring the power to hear and determine indictments on specific or general offences and, often, to investigate and punish riots or other disorders.

make possible a renewed assault upon Normandy. France was the 'adversary'; the English still expected their monarch to make good Harry the Fifth's pretensions to the French throne, or at least to regain some of the lands across the channel which they had so humiliatingly lost. But there were complications. The Duke of Burgundy had outraged English opinion when he made peace with Charles the Seventh in 1435; in 1464 he had given fresh cause for offence by prohibiting the importation of English cloth into his dominions; and the Count of Charolais, who traced his descent from John of Gaunt, was avowedly sympathetic to the House of Lancaster and sheltered at his court the Duke of Somerset (younger brother of the Somerset slain at Hexham) and the Duke of Exeter. And for England's friendship Louis XI seemed willing to make a high bid: advantageous marriages, the partition of Burgundy, trade concessions to English merchants, a promise to abandon Margaret and the Lancastrian cause. During the first years of his reign Edward had moved with prudent caution, despite pressure from Warwick to rush into the arms of Louis. He had taken short truces with Burgundy and with France; and even after he had dashed Louis' hopes by marrying Elizabeth Woodville, he had left the door open for further negotiations.

Now, Warwick, in a swirl of injured feelings, was determined to refurbish his pride by forcing Edward to make an alliance with France. He and the Count of Charolais, meeting for the first time in the spring of 1466, had instantly hated each other. His vanity was increasingly warmed by Louis' flattering regard. And it was in his negotiations with France that Edward had dared to humiliate him. As for Edward, though Warwick's pointed counter-challenge no doubt inclined him to look the more favourably upon Burgundy, he was too shrewd a King to turn his foreign policy into a joust with a disgruntled baron, however powerful he was. Edward would drive the best bargain that he could.

After he had quarrelled with Charolais at Boulogne in the spring of 1466, Warwick returned to Calais to meet Louis' ambassadors. Both parties being of one mind, Warwick soon returned triumphantly to England with a truce for twenty months, a fine offer for the hand of Margaret of York, and a variety of inducements to turn the truce into a permanent treaty of peace. Edward gladly accepted the truce and promised to consider the inducements. In the meanwhile, the Count of Charolais, alarmed by Louis' plans of 'extermination', had brought himself at last to swallow his Lancastrian prejudices and bid earnestly for Edward's support. He made a tentative offer to marry Margaret

2 HENRY VI 1421–1471. Artist Unknown

himself, he talked of removing the restrictions on English cloth, and he signed a treaty of amity and mutual defence. Edward, happy to exploit his advantage, encouraged both parties to pursue their negotiations with him. Consequently, the early spring of 1467 witnessed the arrival in London of an imposing embassy from Burgundy and an equally imposing embassy from France. With all the weapons of diplomacy the rival envoys proceeded to do battle, the French actively aided by Warwick. Edward did not yet openly commit himself. The French ambassadors departed with high hopes, for Warwick with a magnificent train of attendants accompanied them to consult with Louis himself, who for years had been trying to meet the Earl face to face—the spider eager to weave his silken web of flattery about this splendid fly.

Edward had been content to give Warwick his head in order to get him out of the way. As the Earl left England, a jocund fleet, bedecked with pennons and banners, sailed up the Thames, bearing Antoine, the Bastard of Burgundy, to joust with Anthony Woodville, Lord Scales, and also an embassy from Charolais to conclude a firm alliance with England. Philip's son was now prepared to make an outright offer for Margaret's hand. Edward, for his part, had come to the conclusion that, however much his subjects might grumble against Philip and Charles, they were of no mind to imperil their commerce with Burgundy and they could not stomach an alliance with Louis XI.

London was at its gayest: bright with a thousand banners and tapestries, thronged with lords and commons come for a meeting of Parliament, and throbbing with anticipation of the tournament, which was to become the most famous of the century. On Saturday, May 30, the Bastard was accompanied up the river by barges blazing with arras and the gowns of knights and ladies. Taking horse at Billingsgate, he rode in a splendid procession through Cheap and Cornhill, past St. Paul's, to his lodging in the Bishop of Salisbury's palace in Fleet Street, where his chambers had been 'hanged with beds of cloth of gold'. On the following Tuesday, June 2, King Edward entered London in great state, Lord Scales bearing his sword before him, in order to greet the Bastard and attend the opening of Parliament on the morrow. The tournament would not begin until Thursday, June 11. Under the eye of the Earl of Worcester—the Constable being also the Arbiter of Chivalry—the sheriffs were finishing the construction of the lists at Smithfield, an arena ninety yards long by eighty yards wide.[2]

c

On Wednesday the Bastard and his knights were the King's guests at the opening session of the Lords* in the Painted Chamber. They did not hear, however, the customary address by the Chancellor. Angrily suspecting that the warm welcome given the Burgundians portended something more, George Neville, Archbishop of York, dared to show his displeasure by absenting himself under the thin excuse of illness. King Edward was probably already aware that the Archbishop was covertly intriguing for a Cardinal's hat and for the dispensation which would permit Clarence and Isabel to marry. On Monday, June 8, the King took horse and rode to his Chancellor's palace near Charing Cross. Coolly he demanded that Warwick's brother fetch at once the Great Seal, waited till it was placed in his hands, and rode away to bestow the Chancellorship upon Robert Stillington, Bishop of Bath and Wells.

Four days later, all London streamed out to Smithfield to witness the great tourney. Two 'lodges', or grandstands, had been erected facing each other across the lists, the larger for the court, the smaller for the Mayor and city magistrates. The Burgundian chronicler, Olivier de la Marche, was there to report that King Edward 'was clothed in purple, having the Garter on his thigh, and a thick staff in his hand; and truly he seemed a person well worthy to be King, for he was a fine Prince, and great. . . . An Earl held the sword before him . . . and around his seat were twenty or twenty-five counsellors, all with white hair; and they resembled senators set there together to counsel their master.' Below him sat ranks of knights, esquires, and archers of the Crown.

Lord Scales rode first into the field, two helmets borne before him by George of Clarence and the Earl of Arundel. Doing his reverence to the King, he went to his pavilion to arm himself. After the Bastard had performed the same ceremony, the two ran a course with lances but neither scored a hit. Then discarding much of their armour and taking swords, they again thundered upon each other. The Bastard's horse rammed its head against Scales's saddle, reared and fell dead, pinning the Bastard to the ground. After Scales proved that he had used no illegal armour and the Bastard had been extricated, Edward asked the shaken Burgundian if he wished another mount. The Bastard replied that 'it was no season' and went to his chambers. Grimly he

*Since the terms 'House of Lords' and 'House of Commons' were not employed until the 16th Century, I have used 'Lords' and 'Commons', as they were called in Richard's day.

remarked to Olivier de la Marche, 'Doubt not: he has fought a beast today, and tomorrow he shall fight a man.'

Next day they were to fight on foot with spears, then axes, but 'the King beholding the casting spears right jeopardous and right perilous, said, in as much as it was but an act of pleasaunce, he would not have none such mischievous weapons used before him.' So Scales and the Bastard laid on with their axes, Scales striking with the head and his adversary with the small end of the blade. Fiercely they hacked at each other, axes clanging on armour, until the combat became so violent that 'the King . . . cast his staff, and with a high voice, cried, "Whoo!" Notwithstanding, in the departing there were given two or three great strokes' but at the King's command, they took each other by the hand, and promised 'to love together as brothers in arms.'

During these days of merrymaking and feats of chivalry, the diplomats in the Bastard's train had held very satisfactory conferences with Edward and his council. More jousts and feasting were scheduled, but when news came that Duke Philip had died on Monday, June 15, the Bastard hurried home to his father's funeral.

It is to be remarked that young Richard, Duke of Gloucester took no part in the tournament, save no doubt as an onlooker. Neither as a boy nor man did he display an interest in the mock-heroics of the lists. To him, the manage of weapons was a duty, not a sport. The artificiality of the tournament, its flamboyance of self-display, he had neither the exuberant personality, the playful imagination, nor the gamesome temperament to enjoy. He was apparently too earnest to see in jousting, with its formula of tutoring knights to wage war against the Infidel, much else but a pointless unreality.[3]

The Bastard had been gone only a week, when the Earl of Warwick returned, flushed with the triumph of his reception by the French King. As the Earl sailed up the Seine, Louis had rushed down from Rouen to greet him. They had walked together in a stately procession to the cathedral to make an offering and then had retired to a Dominican convent, so that, Louis explained, they could talk intimately without interruptions or eavesdroppers. When they parted a week later, Louis poured streams of gold upon Warwick's attendants, bade each man take what pleased him from the great textile shops of Rouen; to the Earl himself the French King gave a cup of gold worth 2,000 livres and a hint that might prove to be even more valuable: if perchance Warwick ever decided to restore Henry VI to the throne, his devoted friend and admirer, Louis, would do all in his power to help. At the moment,

however, Warwick was interested only in bringing Edward to heel
and dictating the French alliance. An embassy accompanied him to
England, armed with an array of seductive promises and Louis'
injunction to prevent at all costs the marriage of the new Duke of
Burgundy with Edward's sister.

When he reached London, Warwick's first discovery was that his
brother had been deprived of the Chancellorship; the next, that though
Edward received the French envoys civilly enough, the talk at court
was all of Burgundy. Though the ambassadors were invited to follow
the King to Windsor—the plague having broken out in London— and
remained in England for six weeks, all they brought back to Louis was
Edward's empty promise to send another embassy and a few hunting
horns, leather bottles, and mastiffs. Meanwhile, King Edward had
concluded an alliance with Henry of Castile, which was aimed against
France; and in renewing their treaty of amity and mutual defence,
both he and Duke Charles now bound their heirs and successors to
respect the league. At this very moment their envoys were drawing up
the marriage treaty. Such was Edward's answer to the Earl of Warwick.

The Mayor of London had had some difficulty with one of *his* chief
ministers this year: 'John Derby, alderman, for so much as he refused
to carry or to pay for the carriage away of a dead dog lying at his door,
and for unfitting language which he gave unto the mayor, he was by a
court of aldermen deemed to a fine of £1, which he paid every penny.'[4]
King Edward did not have so easy a time as the Mayor.

In naked rage at his defeat, Warwick retired to his Yorkshire strongholds, summoning his brothers to a council and communicating with
his ardent follower, the Duke of Clarence. George, Archbishop of York,
hurried to Warwick's side; he was clever and ambitious, a zestful
intriguer, fluid as quicksilver. John of Northumberland, however, the
blunt and brilliant soldier of the family, gave his brothers cold comfort:
he would stand by the King and that was that.

When Edward moved to Coventry to keep his Christmas of 1467 and
investigate a ripple of discord in the Midlands, he took with him a
bodyguard of 200 archers and he also took with him George of Clarence,
scarcely for the pleasure of his company. Yet Edward soon indicated
that he cherished the Earl of Warwick—as the first *servant* of the
crown. Early in January the King bade Warwick come to a council
meeting. The Earl replied with open hostility that Edward would not
see him as long as the Woodvilles and Lord Herbert were at court; but
the Archbishop of York, judging that the time was not yet ripe for

fomenting trouble, patched matters up with Earl Rivers at Nottingham and persuaded Warwick to go to Coventry. The King greeted him warmly, reconciled him with Lord Herbert and kept the Woodvilles pretty well out of sight. But Warwick had come only to make Edward see the error of his ways and that he failed utterly to do. By the end of March, 1468, not only was the marriage treaty with Burgundy finally approved, but the King signed an alliance with Francis, Duke of Brittany against the King of France.

Yet Warwick was offered, and did not refuse, the honour of escorting Margaret of York on the first stage of her wedding journey. On June 18 she set out from London with the Earl and a train of lords and rode to the monastery of Stratford Langthorne in Essex. Here she lingered for several days of feasting with her three brothers, with Edward's Queen, and with Warwick—an inflammable company whose merriment must have covered many an incendiary glance and bitter whisper. There sat young Richard in their midst—having turned his back upon Warwick and Clarence whom he loved because he could not turn his coat against his brother Edward whose Woodville court he could not like. This is our only glimpse of him throughout the year of 1468. He and the King, Warwick, and Clarence accompanied Margaret to Margate, whence, on June 23, she sailed to become the bride of Charles, accurately called the *Téméraire,* Duke of Burgundy.[5]

Then the royal party galloped back to London, for the realm was stirring uneasily and the Spectre of Lancaster was again raising its head. Some weeks before, a captured agent of Queen Margaret's, when his feet were burned with hot irons—it was the Tudors who made torture an art—implicated many persons, including one Hawkins, a servant of Warwick's friend, Lord Wenlock. Hawkins, in turn, accused Lord Wenlock and Sir Thomas Cook, a former Mayor and one of the wealthiest merchants of London, of treasonable correspondence with Queen Margaret.[6] Cook had been released on bail at the request of Margaret of York, for he had been instrumental in arranging the bond which guaranteed her dowry. Edward not only took no action against Wenlock but appointed both Clarence and Warwick to the commission of inquiry investigating the case as a sign of his confidence in them.

At this moment, Louis XI, eager to do Edward any mischief, launched the Lancastrian Jasper Tudor, still calling himself Earl of Pembroke, upon the coast of Wales. Though he burned Denbigh, he was soon routed by Lord Herbert's brother; and Lord Herbert himself shortly afterwards captured Harlech castle, the last foothold of Lancaster in Britain, for which feat Herbert received the earldom of Pembroke. This uprising in Wales, however, convinced Edward that Hawkins' accusations had some foundation in fact. Earl Rivers was therefore able to persuade the King that Sir Thomas Cook was guilty, and the unfortunate merchant was rearrested. Rivers' motives of cupidity and personal revenge were nicely balanced. Rivers' wife, the Dowager Duchess of Bedford, 'ever was extremely again [against] ... Sir Thomas, and all was because she might not have certain arras at her pleasure and price belonging unto ... Sir Thomas.' Under the guise of seeking evidence Rivers and his relative by marriage, Sir John Fogge, Treasurer of the royal Household, spoiled Cook's town and country houses. Besides valuable plate and other goods, Rivers and Fogge seized 'the aforesaid arras which the Duchess of Bedford desired, wrought in most richest wise with gold of the whole story of the Siege of Jerusalem which ... cost in barter when [Cook] ... bought it £800.' Yet when Sir Thomas was brought before Chief Justice Markham, famed for his honesty, Markham ordered the jury to return a verdict of misprision of treason only. Rivers promptly had Cook committed to King's Bench prison to exact the dreadful fine of £8,000, and then Elizabeth Woodville, by the archaic right of 'Queen's gold' mulcted him of 100 marks for every £1,000 of fine. Rivers crowned his victory by driving from office the Chief Justice who had dared to cross him.[7]

Much earlier in the year, it seems that Queen Elizabeth had compassed a long-sought revenge of her own, according to a story which may be coloured in some of its details but is fundamentally credible. About the time of the Queen's coronation, in May of 1465, the Earl of Desmond, Deputy Lieutenant of Ireland, had come to England in order to clear himself of some charges brought against him and to pay homage to the King. Desmond was a man after Edward's own heart: cultivated, brave, convivial. One day when they were out hunting, Edward, in his direct and merry way, inquired of Desmond what he thought of the royal marriage. Desmond replied frankly: he esteemed the Queen's beauty and virtues but he thought the King would have done better to marry a Princess who would have secured him a foreign alliance. Edward accepted this answer in the spirit in which he had asked the question and sent Desmond back to Ireland loaded with presents. A little later, in casual jest, he reported the Earl's words to Elizabeth— being not yet well schooled in his Queen's character. Coldly furious, she dissembled her feelings and grimly awaited an opportunity to settle accounts with Desmond. When, in 1467, the Earl of Worcester became Deputy Lieutenant of Ireland, he agreed to give the Queen her revenge. Desmond was indicted on a flimsy charge, and when he bravely came in to face his accusers, he was cast into prison and condemned to be beheaded. Shortly after he suffered on the block, two small sons of his were cruelly murdered. It is said that the Queen stole the King's signet to seal the death warrant; there is evidence that the King was not pleased with the news of Desmond's execution.[8]*

Edward had shown no lack of wisdom in choosing to make a marriage which would help him to break the baronial domination of the crown. The trouble lay with the particular family whom he had touched with his golden sceptre. Their abuse of greatness probably harmed him as much as he was aided, in his work of strengthening the royal power, by their utter dependence upon him.

The uneasy year of 1468 drew to an end in comparative quiet, but tension was in the air. Richard of Gloucester, young though he was, must have realized that the choice of allegiance he had had to make might soon be forced upon the nation as a whole. Clarence and the Nevilles were a hive of secret plans, from which, now and then, came an ominous buzzing. Small comfort would it have been to the King's subjects if they had realized that Edward and Warwick seriously misunderstood each other. The Earl was blind to the King's great abilities; the King failed to appreciate the limitations of the Earl's intelligence.

IX

THE beginning of the trouble seemed relatively trivial: in the early spring of 1469 an agitator calling himself Robin of Redesdale stirred a small rising in Yorkshire. John Neville, Earl of Northumberland, promptly put it down. Almost immediately a new Robin, Robin of Holderness, popped up in the East Riding to lead what seemed at first only a riotous airing of local grievances, but soon the rioters were shouting for the restoration of Henry Percy as Earl of Northumberland. Again John Neville sprang to arms and at the gates of York defeated the rebels, killing their leader. By this time, however, Robin of Redesdale had reappeared in Lancashire and was raising a more formidable head of insurrection.

When he received this news, King Edward decided to come north himself to investigate and punish these persistent disturbances. The southern coasts were safely guarded against Lancastrian or French attack by the Earl of Warwick, whose fleet was cruising in the channel. Edward ordained 'stuff for the field'—artillery, tents, a thousand jackets of blue or murrey—to be carted to Fotheringhay. He sent out a few calls for troops. But the risings seemed no more dangerous than others which had been easily taken in hand, and the King did not seek to raise a large army nor to hurry northward. Had he been a connoisseur of prognostics, he might have adopted a less leisurely pace. Months before, a shower of blood had stained grass and drying linen in Bedford-shire; elsewhere a horseman and men in arms were seen rushing through the air. 'A certain woman, too, in the county of Huntingdon, who was with child and near the time of her delivery, to her extreme horror, felt the embryo in her womb weeping . . . and uttering a kind of sobbing noise.'[1]

Edward took with him two of his best captains, Sir John Howard and Louis de Bretaylle, his faithful Knight of the Body Sir Thomas Mongomery, and a swashbuckling Portuguese Jew, Edward Brampton, who, as was the custom, had been godfathered at his ceremony of conversion by the King himself and had gratefully adopted the royal name;[2] but the King's chief companions were kindred of the Queen: Earl Rivers and two of his sons, Lord Scales and Sir John Woodville. Perhaps Edward was not entirely happy to find himself surrounded by Woodvilles; perhaps it occurred to him, after much persuasion by Richard himself, that his younger brother, now in his seventeenth year, was ready for a mild taste of campaigning. Just before he departed, he ordained that Richard was to go with him. Hastily making what preparations he could, Richard set off, eager to 'wage' men for his service but sorely lacking in money. Among those in his train were his boyhood friend Robert Percy and John à Parr, one of his squires.[3]*

Leaving London the first week in June, the royal party proceeded into East Anglia to visit the shrines of St. Edmund and of Our Lady of Walsingham and to gather men. *En route* they called briefly on George Neville, Archbishop of York, at his manor of The Moor in Hertford-shire. Thinking that it might be well to keep an eye on the slippery Archbishop, King Edward suggested that he come north to look into these troubles in his diocese, and George Neville readily promised that he would join the King a little later. About the 18th of June the royal cavalcade rode into Norwich.

Here Edward and Richard found themselves in the middle of a

serious land dispute between the Dukes of Norfolk and Suffolk and the Paston family. Norfolk claimed the castle of Caister; Suffolk, the manor of Hellesden—portions of the estate of the late Sir John Fastolfe which had come into John Paston's hands as Fastolfe's chief executor. Paston's elder son, Sir John, now head of the family, was engaged to a relative of the Queen's. Therefore Sir John's brother applied to the three Woodvilles to help him bring his case to the King's attention. They were all profuse with promises 'that the matter should do well enough', but in the end young Paston wrote with some bitterness to Sir John that 'for all their words of pleasure, I cannot understand what their labour in this country hath done good'. Of his own volition, however, King Edward warned the Duke of Norfolk's council to abide by the law's decision; and the fact that the King's route to Walsingham lay through the manor of Hellesden, some two miles northwest of Norwich, provided a means of letting Edward see with his own eyes the lawless violence that Suffolk had used. In 1465 his men had invaded the estate, stripped the house of its valuables, and wrecked the lodge. Thomas Wingfield, a member of the royal household, promised Sir John's brother 'that he would find the means that my lord of Gloucester and himself both should shew the King the lodge that was broken down, and also that they would tell him of the breaking down of the place'.

Richard and Wingfield duly pointed out the ruins of the lodge to the King, but Edward told Sir John's uncle that if Suffolk had indeed done the damage, the Pastons should have complained to the commission of *oyer and terminer* which sat at Norwich shortly after; he added that he would not do special favours for the Pastons or anybody else. Though Richard was not successful in his intercession, he did succeed in 'waging' four men of young Paston's acquaintance to take arms under his banner: 'Bernard, Barney, Broom, and W. Calthorp.' He did better than Lord Scales who was unable to persuade young Paston to enter the King's service.[4]

By June 21 Edward and Richard had left Norwich for Walsingham. When they reached Castle Rising on the 24th, Richard found himself so short of money that he was forced to dispatch to a follower of his an urgent plea for a loan, the earliest letter of Richard's that is extant. 'Right trusty and well beloved', he dictated to his secretary in the customary style of the day,

we greet you well. And forasmuch as the King's good grace hath appointed me to attend upon his highness into the North parties of his land, which will be to me great cost and charge, whereunto I am so suddenly called that I am not so well purveyed of

C*

money therefore as behoves me to be, and therefore pray you as my special trust is in you, to lend me an hundred pound of money unto Easter next coming, at which time I promise you ye shall be truly thereof content and paid again, as the bearer hereof shall inform you: to whom I pray you to give credence therein, and show me such friendliness in the same as I may do for you hereafter, wherein ye shall find me ready. Written at Rising the 24 day of June.

R. GLOUCESTR.

Seizing a pen, Richard wrote the superscription, 'The Duke of Gloucester' and added an anxious postscript: 'Sir I say I pray you that ye fail me not at this time in my great need, as ye will that I show you my good lordship in that matter that ye labour to me for'.[5]*

By June 26 King Edward and Richard had reached Lynn with a party of some 200 horsemen; pushing through the watery fen country, they spent a night at Croyland abbey. The next morning the brothers took ship and sailed up the Nene to Fotheringhay castle.[6] Here they passed a week in the company of Queen Elizabeth, while contingents of troops and their military supplies came in. On July 5 the King's little army set out northward for Stamford. On the 7th it passed through Grantham and came to Newark. . . .

Suddenly the King wheeled his force about and headed with all speed for the safety of Nottingham castle. At Newark he had learned that Robin of Redesdale was rapidly advancing southward with a larger army than his own, and one of Robin's proclamations had fallen into his hands. A glance was enough to show that the Earl of Warwick had inspired it. The Woodvilles, Herbert Earl of Pembroke, Stafford Earl of Devon, Sir John Fogge, and others were damned as avaricious favourites who preyed upon the realm and led the King to ignore the lords of his own blood (meaning, of course, Warwick and Clarence). Edward himself was ominously likened to Edward II, Richard II and Henry VI, all deposed monarchs.[7]

At once Edward ordered—or permitted—the Woodvilles to seek their own safety. Lord Scales galloped off to go in hiding on his Norfolk estates near Lynn. Earl Rivers and his son Sir John fled westward. The King sent word to the Earls of Pembroke and Devon and Lord Hastings to come in haste with whatever forces they could muster. Then with his own hand he wrote almost identical notes to Warwick, the Archbishop of York, and brother George cordially requesting them to join him in a peaceable manner. To Warwick's note he added the hope that the Earl was not 'of any such disposition toward us, as the rumour here runneth.'[8]

But rumour, as the King well knew, had not outrun the facts; it was

Clarence and Warwick who had outrun the King. On July 6, three days before Edward dispatched his notes, they had slipped across the channel to Calais, accompanied by the Archbishop of York, the Earl of Oxford and a host of followers. Five days later, Isabel Neville was married to George of Clarence by the Archbishop in the presence of Warwick and five other Knights of the Garter. Clarence had obtained the precious dispensation by bribing Edward's own agent at the papal court. A few days after, preceded by manifestos supporting the 'petitions' of Robin of Redesdale, who was none other than Warwick's cousin by marriage, Sir John Conyers, the Earl and his party crossed the channel. Gathering forces in Kent, they entered London about July 20 and shortly moved northward to meet the Yorkshire insurgents.

Three armies were now converging upon the area around Banbury. The Earl of Pembroke with a force of Welsh pikemen and the Earl of Devon, supported by West Country archers, were marching northeast to Edward's aid. Robin had skirted Nottingham to the west in order to cut the King off from London. Warwick, having heard of Pembroke's and Devon's advance, was hastening north, pushing out cavalry detachments ahead of him. When Pembroke and Devon reached Banbury on July 26, they quarrelled about billets, and the Earl of Devon angrily pulled back his troops about ten miles. At this moment Robin of Redesdale's rebel host fell upon Pembroke. Though he was badly outnumbered and had no archers, William Herbert fought like a lion to save the day; but before Stafford of Devon could reach him, an advance party of Warwick's horse arrived to clinch the victory. Pembroke and his brother, Sir Richard Herbert, were haled to Warwick's and Clarence's headquarters at Northampton and next day beheaded. Before he died the valiant Pembroke was permitted to write a hasty farewell to his Countess: 'Wife,' he concluded it, 'pray for me and take the said order [of widowhood] that ye promised me, as ye had in my life my heart and love'.[9]

Edward, Richard, and Lord Hastings were still at Nottingham waiting for reinforcements. Three days after Pembroke's defeat, of which they remained in ignorance, they began to move slowly southward. At Olney they met fugitives from the battle panting out their tale of disaster and crying that the host of Warwick and Clarence was at their heels. The small army of the King melted away; Edward apparently dismissed most of those who remained staunch. He had been outmanœuvred, but not daunted. Bold and resourceful, he abandoned the lion's role for the fox's.

Not many hours later the Archbishop of York, resplendent in full armour, galloped up at the head of a strong party of horse. Blandly he suggested that the King accompany him and blandly Edward agreed. On August 2 the royal captive arrived at Coventry to confront Clarence and Warwick. They seem to have prepared only the rough outline of their drama. Edward proceeded to transform it into high comedy by the impeccable style with which he played his part. He gave them fair words, he smiled, he signed whatever they put before him. About the 7th of August he was removed to the stronghold of Warwick castle. A few days later, Earl Rivers and Sir John Woodville, taken somewhere near Chepstow, were beheaded outside the walls of Coventry. Thomas Herbert, another of Pembroke's kinsmen, went to the block in Bristol, and the Earl of Devon met the same fate in Somersetshire.

About the middle of August the Duke of Clarence and the Archbishop of York arrived in London in order to see that the royal council kept up the appearance of government. Warwick had caused the King to summon a Parliament, the business of which would be to legalize and confirm the triumph of the Nevilles. Suddenly, Edward was conveyed by secret night marches to Middleham castle in far-off Wensleydale, and, shortly after, the meeting of Parliament was cancelled.[10]*

The news that Edward was a prisoner had run like wildfire and the kingdom was ablaze. Popular though Warwick was, the people of England were shocked and dismayed by the capture of their King. London hovered on the brink of mob violence. The Duke of Burgundy, promising all aid, threatened the city with dire consequences if it deserted his brother-in-law; and the magistrates made no bones about pledging their loyalty. John Neville, Earl of Northumberland, would not lift a finger to help his brothers. In East Anglia, the Duke of Norfolk chose this time of confusion to besiege Caister castle, and despite the Archbishop of York's and Clarence's good will to the Pastons, Norfolk maintained the siege until young Paston and his tiny garrison surrendered. No wonder Edward had been hurried northward beyond easy reach of rescue. The country was out of control.

At this propitious moment, Humphrey Neville of Brancepeth, a distant kinsman of Warwick's, stirred up a Lancastrian rising along the Scots border. Warwick confidently set about gathering men in Yorkshire to put it down. On the 8th or 9th of September, however, the Archbishop of York hurried northward from London, having received very disquieting news. Warwick could muster no troops. Not until they knew that the King was at liberty would men answer the call to arms. When he had conferred with his brother, the Archbishop rode on to Middleham. Soon after, King Edward showed himself to his people of York and was then permitted to go to Pontefract. Now Warwick had no difficulty raising men. Humphrey Neville, quickly captured, was beheaded at York on September 29, the King coming up to the city in order to witness the execution.

Where was Richard in these critical days? The records and the chroniclers are silent. There is no reason to suppose he accompanied King Edward in his captivity. Apparently, when the Archbishop of York appeared at Olney, he complacently allowed Richard and Hastings to depart where they pleased. Hastings, going into Lancashire, quietly began to gather followers. Richard, it seems probable, likewise went north and in concert with the Lord Chamberlain set to work to rescue his brother.[11]

During these September days, King Edward, at Pontefract, was appreciating to the full the alterations which the people of England had made in Warwick's drama; and he now adroitly prepared his own script for the denouement. When he learned that Richard and Hastings, and perhaps Northumberland, had gathered a force, he suddenly took action. Without consulting the Nevilles, he summoned the chief lords of his council to come at once to Pontefract. They obeyed with alacrity. Richard and Hastings arrived with several hundred men horsed and armed. Smiling, the King informed the Archbishop, Warwick, and Clarence that these men had come to escort him and his lords to London. The Nevilles could only acquiesce. To keep up appearances and discover what yet might be salvaged from the debacle, the Archbishop of York trailed southward in the royal wake. At his manor of The Moor he was joined by the Earl of Oxford. The pair of them then spurred on to join the King for his entry into London. They had not gone three miles, however, when they received a message from Edward. Come when we send for you, he told them bluntly. There was nothing for them to do but turn back.

With Richard and Hastings at his side and accompanied by the Duke of Suffolk and young Henry Duke of Buckingham, the Earls of Essex and Arundel and faithful Northumberland, Lords John of Buckingham, Dacre, and Mountjoy, and a thousand horse, the King of England was heartily welcomed to his capital by the Mayor and Aldermen in scarlet and 200 of the chief citizens in blue.[12]*

X

THE Woodvilles would again dominate King Edward's court, but he would never again look to them as the bulwark of his power. He had discovered, these past weeks, a stouter prop to his throne in his brother Richard. Not only was Edward eager to reward his brother's services; he was compelled by his dangerous position to pile responsibilities upon the rewards. Hitherto, Richard's life has been the story of events and people impinging upon him; now, though only just turned seventeen, he begins to impinge upon events. His brief adolescence, itself severely tried by the impending conflict between Edward and Warwick, was abruptly cut short by his brother's need for him to play a man's part.

Less than a week after he reached London, Richard found himself appointed Constable of England for life—even though in the letters patent conferring the office upon the late Earl Rivers it had been expressly given to his son Lord Scales in reversion. King Edward had greatly augmented the Constable's traditional powers. Not only was he the President of the Court of Chivalry and of Courts Martial; he had the immense authority of determining treasonable acts by simple inspection of fact and of meting out punishment. Edward had made him the spearhead in his campaign to reduce the realm to order.[1]

While, in the next six weeks, Richard was receiving rich grants or estates and lands, including the great manor and castle of Sudeley, trouble had begun to stir in Wales; a region always sensitive to weakness of the crown, strong in Lancastrian sympathies, and, along with Northumberland, the chief breeding ground of disorder. The unrest began in North Wales. Pembroke, its Chief Justice, was dead and Hastings, its Chamberlain, was needed at the King's side. People refused to pay their yearly dues to the royal officers, the Sheriff of Anglesey setting an example by his bold defiance. The disaffection spread. Soon the bards were muttering in their mountain valleys and Welsh gentlemen looked to their arms and their followers. The times seemed propitious to defy the Saxon King at Westminster.[2]

The Saxon King called upon his young brother, the Constable, to restore the royal authority. As early as October 29 he had received commissions to array men in Shropshire, Gloucester, and Worcester. On November 7 he was appointed for life Chief Justice of North Wales

and not long after rode westward to begin assembling a force of men.
Three weeks later he was made 'during pleasure' chief steward,
approver, and surveyor of the entire principality of Wales and the
earldom of March. By this time, the bards were chanting and armed
men galloped in the mountains. Two Welsh gentlemen, Morgan ap
Thomas ap Griffith and Henry ap Thomas ap Griffith, having gathered
a considerable following, boldly assaulted and captured the King's
castles of Carmarthen and Cardigan in South Wales, which were in
the charge of the Earl of Warwick. From these bases the insurgents
began raiding the whole country round. As soon as the news reached
Edward, he dispatched Richard full authority to recapture the castles
and imprison or pardon the rebels.[3]*

It was Richard's first independent military command. He no doubt
took it as seriously as if he were leading the chivalry of England against
the French. The result confirmed King Edward's judgment of his
brother. The castles were recaptured; the rebels were apparently content
to swear an oath of fealty and to receive pardons.

So promptly indeed did Richard accomplish his task that he was
able to return to London during the Christmas season to report his
success and to confer with the King regarding a fresh outbreak of
disturbances. The result was that he shortly returned westward to head
a great commission of *oyer and terminer* for both North and South
Wales. A month later he was appointed Chief Justice and Chamberlain
of South Wales and Steward, during the minority of Pembroke's son,
of all the King's lands in the counties of Carmarthen and Cardigan. Not
only had Richard, by this accumulation of powers, become the virtual
Viceroy of the principality of Wales, but he had displaced the man who
had once sought to win his allegiance from Edward. During the King's
captivity the previous August, these very offices had been appropriated
by Warwick. Now Edward felt himself strong enough to augment his
loyal brother's power at the Earl's expense.[4]*

Throughout these winter months the King had been vigorously
taking every means to restore his position. Polydore Vergil, the Tudor
historian, cannot resist praising the sagacity he displayed in this crisis:
'not to omit any carefulness, travail, nor counsel that meet was for his
avail in this troublesome time, he regarded nothing more than to win
again the friendship of such noble men as were now alienated from him,
to confirm the good will of them who were hovering and unconstant,
and to reduce the mind of the multitude, being brought by these
innovations [Warwick's capture of the King] into a murmuring and

doubtfulness what to do, unto their late obedience, affection, and good will towards him'.[5]

Edward's most pressing problem was how to handle Warwick and Clarence. Despite the vengeful urgings of the Queen and his own private feelings, he played the ruler rather than the man. To bring peace to his uneasy realm, he realized that he must seek an accommodation with his recent captors. After much negotiation, Warwick and Clarence consented to attend an assembly of all the peers and arrived in London early in December. It was a feast of peace and forgiveness. The King and the Earl agreed to sink their past differences in oblivion. Edward issued a general pardon to all who had been guilty of riot or insurrection. The reconciliation was sealed when the King betrothed his eldest daughter to John Neville's young son, who, on January 5, 1470, was created Duke of Bedford. Since the Earl of Northumberland was, however, the one Neville who had remained faithful to him, Edward was rewarding his own follower rather than making a concession to Warwick.

Yet the Earl of Warwick and the Duke of Clarence had reason to feel satisfied with themselves. They had demonstrated their ability to dominate and humiliate the King; they had disposed of two Herberts and two Woodvilles with impunity; and they had forced Edward to make the first overtures of peace.

But Warwick was not happy. He had begun to discover the weaknesses of his son-in-law, and he had failed to regain his power over the King. Before the council meetings were over, Edward published that failure to the world by accepting the honour of the *Toison d'Or* (the Order of the Golden Fleece) from the Duke of Burgundy and by dispatching an embassy to invest his brother-in-law with the Order of the Garter. Not long after, he took back from Warwick, as has been shown, the offices which the Earl had wrung from him in his captivity. Clarence was probably even less happy than Warwick. He lacked the intelligence to be content with, or to comprehend, the emptiness of his victory.

In the middle of the winter there occurred in Lincolnshire a disturbance which seemed no more serious than others which had been besetting the kingdom.[6] Lord Willoughby and Welles, aided by his brothers-in-law Sir Thomas de la Lande and Sir Thomas Dymmock, had plundered the manor of Sir Thomas Burgh. King Edward took a special interest in the outrage, however, for Burgh was his Master of the Horse and Lord Welles, an old Lancastrian. When disorder began to spread through the county, the King determined to investigate the trouble himself. He sent out a summons for men, ordering his army to assemble at Grantham on March 12; he proclaimed a general pardon for all offences—even high treason—committed before Christmas; and he ordered Welles and Dymmock to appear before him. Although they promptly obeyed the royal writ and, after affirming their loyalty, as promptly received the King's pardon, Edward kept them in light custody; for by this time Lincolnshire was rioting in behalf of Henry the Sixth. Warwick left London for the Midlands, promising to support the King in his campaign; Clarence's last word to Edward was that he was going westward to meet his wife but soon after he wrote that he would join Warwick in helping to stamp out the Lincolnshire rising.

Following his interview with Clarence, on the afternoon of Tuesday, March 6, 1470, King Edward rode from London to Waltham Abbey with a noble company including the Earl of Arundel, Lord Hastings, and Henry Percy, who had lost the earldom of Northumberland by attainder and had only been released from prison the previous October. The next morning Edward received serious tidings: on the preceding Sunday, March 4, Lord Welles' son Sir Robert had caused to be announced in all the churches of Lincolnshire, in the name of the Duke of Clarence, the Earl of Warwick, and himself, that every man must be at Ranby Hawe on Tuesday in readiness to resist the King who was coming to destroy the people.

Sending to London for Welles and Dymmock, King Edward moved swiftly northward. At Royston he received Clarence's letter; and so determined was he to give Clarence and Warwick no cause for complaint that he dispatched to them the commissions of array which he had dictated at Waltham abbey and then withheld after hearing the news from Lincolnshire. It was a shrewd gamble. The previous summer they had persuaded many that they were the injured parties; Edward forecast that if they assumed the role of aggressors and conspirators they would not fare so well. Happy in the loyalties he had won back during the winter and in the knowledge that Wales was firmly held by his brother Richard, he was prepared to test Warwick's and Clarence's intentions.

Welles and Dymmock, under guard, overtook the King at Huntingdon. Confident in their pardons, or their hopes, they declared boldly that they themselves were 'the very provokers and causers' of the insurrection. Edward told them tersely that unless Welles persuaded his son to submit, he and Dymmock would die the death. Their pardons covered only offences committed before Christmas. In terror

Welles rushed off to write a letter to his son, while Edward thrust his army forward. When he arrived at Fotheringhay, he learned that Sir Robert with a great host had passed Grantham and seemed to be making for Leicester. Reaching Stamford on Monday, March 12, the King received word from Clarence and Warwick that they were on their way from Coventry to join him and that they would halt at Leicester that night. Almost at the same moment scouts galloped in with news that Sir Robert Welles and his forces lay at Empingham, only five miles west of Stamford. It was obvious that Sir Robert, abandoning his design of cutting the King off from London, had wheeled about to surprise the royal army and rescue his father.

King Edward instantly sent Welles and Dymmock to the block and flung himself upon the rebels. Sir Robert and his companions tried to rally their forces by shouting 'à Warwick! à Clarence!' but the rebels broke and fled, shedding their jackets as they ran, to give the battle its name of Lose-Coat Field. In the victorious pursuit papers were discovered on a slain servant of the Duke of Clarence and shortly after Sir Robert Welles was captured and confessed all. The Lincolnshire rising had been the work of the Duke of Clarence and the Earl of Warwick. Their object: nothing less than to depose Edward so that Clarence himself could mount the throne.

The King began to move warily northward, summoning his two 'great rebels' to disband their forces and come to him at once. Even as he was receiving their ready promise to obey, however, news arrived that Warwick's friends in Yorkshire had fomented a rising. Edward sent hasty word to the Earl of Northumberland to deal with these insurgents. In this critical and complicated situation the King needed the services of his Constable. Richard, however, was holding down Wales. On March 14 Edward gave warning to prospective rebels that he was in no mood for mercy by appointing the harsh John Tiptoft, Earl of Worcester, Constable for life.[7] Continuing to move northward towards Doncaster by Grantham, Newark and Retford, he was receiving from Warwick and Clarence—who were proceeding on a parallel course some thirty-five miles to the west—a stream of increasingly fervent messages in which they protested their loyalty, asked for safe-conducts, and reiterated their promise to join the King soon.

At Doncaster on Monday, March 19, Sir Robert Welles, publicly reaffirming the guilt of Clarence and Warwick, was beheaded in the presence of the entire army; and when, at this moment, the King was bombarded by yet another demand for safe-conducts from his 'great rebels', he sternly ordered them to appear before him at once or abide the consequences. Next morning 'at 9 of the bell, the King took the field, and mustered his people, and it was said that were never seen in England so many goodly men, and so well arrayed in a field'.[8] Launching his army southwestward, Edward set out in pursuit of Warwick and Clarence; but upon reaching Rotherham he learned that the pair had that morning fled westward from Chesterfield intending to join Lord Stanley at Manchester. Forced to turn back in order to replenish his supplies of food and horse-fodder, Edward made his way to Pontefract and then to York.[9]

He discovered that Warwick's brother had crushed the Yorkshire rising and brought in its leaders to receive the King's pardon. Yet on March 25, the day after he formally proclaimed Warwick and Clarence traitors, King Edward took the earldom of Northumberland from John Neville and restored it to Henry Percy. Edward's object was to bring peace to the north parts which had so often clamoured for Percy's return; the trusty John he hoped to content by elevating him to the Marquisate of Montagu; but to the man who had rejected his brothers to support his King the new title and an annuity of £40 seemed small recompense for the loss of a princely earldom.[10]* Though Edward's decision would soon cost him dear, its full consequences would be inherited by Richard, Duke of Gloucester—who just a few days before had delivered, it seems, an effective stroke in his brother's behalf.

Richard's part in this campaign remains obscure; the service he performed is reflected in but a single document. From such scanty evidence must his movements be reconstructed.[11]*

Three or four days after the battle of Empingham, Richard, in Wales, received the news of Clarence's and Warwick's treachery and of the King's decision to continue his northward march. He determined to give his brother what aid he could, and, hastily assembling a small band of men, he headed north on the Hereford–Shrewsbury road. As he was riding through Cheshire, Richard suddenly found his way blocked by followers of Lord Stanley. He scattered them and moved on warily, dispatching a warning to the King of Stanley's hostility.

Richard's intervention had come at an opportune moment. Lord Stanley, who was married to Warwick's sister, had given Warwick and Clarence assurances that he would support them. As they moved northward, temporizing with the King, Stanley, at Manchester, was gathering his retainers. The news of the Duke of Gloucester's approach took him by surprise. At almost the same moment he learned that

Warwick and Clarence were galloping westward from Chesterfield, expecting him to succour them. Stanley's nerve deserted him. He sent messengers riding in hot haste: one, to Clarence and Warwick with word that he was unable to help them; the other, to the King, protesting righteously that the Duke of Gloucester had attacked his people. Abandoning all hope of raising a following, Clarence and Warwick wheeled about and fled south.

By this time King Edward, discerning the true state of affairs, had sent word to Richard thanking him for his prompt action and requesting him to stay his march. Lord Stanley he ordered to disband his retainers and keep the peace. On March 25, at York, Edward commanded proclamation to be made that no man was to stir up trouble because of 'any matter of variance late fallen between his right entirely beloved brother the Duke of Gloucester and the Lord Stanley'. Two or three days later Richard received commissions to array the men of Gloucestershire and Herefordshire in order to join the King in the pursuit of his rebels.[12]

With only a small escort the Duke and the Earl hurried first to Warwick castle; then, with their wives and Warwick's daughter Anne, they headed for the Devonshire coast. Richard and the King, meeting somewhere in the Midlands, reached Wells on April 11 and Exeter by the 14th; but the fugitives had found ships and got safely away. Anthony, Earl Rivers, beat them off from Southampton; Calais refused to admit them; finally they landed at Honfleur and were given a warm welcome by officers of Louis XI.[13]

XI

THERE now followed in Richard's and Edward's life a twelve months, span which can scarcely be rivalled in the annals of history for crowding events, reversals of fortune, perils by land and sea, betrayals and double betrayals, bloody battles, and dazzling victories. It is as if fact, charmed by the verve of King Edward, had resolved to outdo the fertile inventions of romance.

Not long after his great rebels had fled the kingdom, Edward began to receive a stream of warnings from his brother-in-law, the Duke of Burgundy, and from his own officers at Calais that Warwick and Clarence would surely and shortly attempt an invasion. Well aware of his danger, Edward spent the summer in an effort to meet it. While a Great Council was being held at Canterbury in June to concert measures for defence, Richard rode into the western Midlands to ready men. A little later he was sent by Edward to the city of Lincoln to investigate some troubles in that touchy region.[1] Meantime, the King inspected the channel ports, loosed spies to watch the Earl of Warwick, and sent Earl Rivers to sea with a fleet that joined Lord Howard and a Burgundian armada in blockading the French coasts. The new Marquess of Montagu and the new Earl of Northumberland were raising forces in Yorkshire. One other defensive means Edward took: he dispatched a lady across the channel, ostensibly to join the entourage of the Duchess of Clarence but actually to entreat the Duke to return to his family allegiance.

In the middle of the summer news reached London of a rising in Yorkshire fomented by Warwick's friends. Percy, Earl of Northumberland reported that it was too powerful for him to put down; the Marquess of Montagu sent no word at all. Early in August, King Edward set forth, accompanied by his brother Richard, Lord Hastings, and a small force. By the time they reached York, the rising had collapsed. But at York the King lingered uneasily. The city and the county seemed so restless that Edward made Richard head of a commission of *oyer and terminer* to restore order.[2]

Yorkshire was the land which Richard loved and of which he had seen little since his boyhood days at Middleham. It had been in Wales that the King had established him in authority because it was there that Edward had needed a loyal and zealous lieutenant. Now his own desires and the King's needs marched hand in hand. Weighing the enigmatic silence of Northumberland and Montague with the insurrections which Yorkshire had so often raised against him, Edward appointed Richard, on August 26, to an office the Nevilles had long held: the Wardenship of the West Marches towards Scotland.[3]

Early in September King Edward received strong warnings that Warwick was preparing to set foot in England. He dispatched orders to the men of Kent to ready themselves, but he continued to stand guard in Yorkshire in order to cut the Earl off from his strength there and in the Midlands. Warwick, however, had other plans and Edward was threatened by dangers he had not foreseen.[4]

The Earl of Warwick had experienced a profitable summer.[5] Arriving on the shores of France a fugitive, he was received by King Louis as a prince. In early June they met at Amboise and came to a quick agreement upon a project that Louis had long entertained in his agile mind: the French King would use his good offices to reconcile Warwick and Queen Margaret; Warwick would restore King Henry to the throne; Louis' reward would be an alliance of England and France against Burgundy; Warwick's, the marriage of his younger daughter Anne to Margaret's son, Prince Edward. Clarence, a rather embarrassing piece of excess baggage, would be taken care of, somehow. Warwick and the Duke retired to Normandy to allow Louis to exercise his arts upon Margaret. It turned out that, though cast down from Olympus and eager to reascend its slopes, Juno remained Juno. King Louis had to employ all of his extensive repertory of charm to persuade her even to set eyes upon the hated Earl.

On July 22, the Queen and Warwick—Clarence having been left in Normandy—met under Louis' auspices at Angers. For fifteen minutes the haughty Margaret kept the haughty Neville upon his knees begging for forgiveness. At last she consented, grudgingly, to pardon him so that he could place her again upon the throne; but the marriage of Warwick's daughter to her son she would not hear of. King Louis was there, however, to perform prodigies of tact; and in the end Margaret swallowed the marriage too, though she would not have it solemnized till the Earl had reconquered England. On July 25, Anne Neville, a delicate girl of fifteen, was betrothed to Prince Edward, now sixteen years of age. In a regal ceremony staged in the cathedral of Angers, the Earl and the Queen swore on a piece of the True Cross an oath of mutual fidelity, and Louis the Matchmaker promised to uphold the House of Lancaster. Warwick brought back to his son-in-law—who had just been listening to the persuasions of a clever lady—the feeble consolation that Clarence would succeed to the throne if Anne bore Edward no heir.

A month later, on September 9, a storm having providentially broken the Anglo-Burgundian blockade, Warwick and Clarence and their followers embarked in a fleet of ships provided by King Louis. Landing at Dartmouth and Plymouth on September 13, they marched eastward, gathering many adherents in Lancastrian Devon. The race for London was on.

The moment he received the tidings, King Edward summoned the Marquess of Montagu to join him at once and hastened southward with about 3,000 men. He halted at Doncaster to spend the night. Not long after Edward had retired, a serjeant of his minstrels burst into his bedroom crying that enemies were 'coming for to take him'. The unruffled King scouted the news until fugitives began pouring into his camp. The enemy was the Marquess of Montagu. Declaring that Edward had forfeited his allegiance by fobbing him off with a marquisate and 'only a pie's nest to maintain it with', John Neville had persuaded most of his army, which outnumbered the King's, to espouse with him the cause of Warwick.

Leaping on their horses, Edward, Richard, Hastings, and Earl Rivers rallied followers and galloped eastward through the night. When the fugitives reached the northern shore of the Wash, they could find no better transport than small boats. Boldly they pushed off for Norfolk, were almost drowned when a tempest battered their little craft, but managed, steering through the night, to reach Lynn on Sunday, September 30. Fortunately, several fishing ships lay in the harbour. Taking with them what men they could stuff into their tiny fleet, King Edward and his brother Richard, accompanied by Hastings and Rivers, set sail on Tuesday, October 2, for the shores of Burgundy.[6] Their perils were not yet over. Vessels of the Hanseatic League sighted the flotilla and crammed on all sail for the pursuit. To the very beaches of Alkmaar they chased the King's little ships and only just in time Edward's old friend, the Seigneur de la Gruthuyse, Governor of Holland, appeared to warn off the Easterlings* and welcome Edward warmly to the domains of his brother-in-law. For the second time in his life Richard found himself a fugitive in Burgundy.

England showed few signs, for the moment, of regretting the precipitate departure of the House of York. On Saturday, October 6, Warwick and Clarence, with a train of nobles that included Lord Stanley, entered London in triumph, extracted a shambling and feeble-witted Henry from the Tower and proceeded to establish the govern-ment of what was called the 're-adoption' of Henry the Sixth.[7] Clarence was noticeably subordinate to his father-in-law. Warwick made few changes in office, the most notable being the return of George Neville, Archbishop of York, to the chancellorship. A Parliament was summoned and obediently confirmed the verdict of fortune, reversed the attainders of the Lancastrians, and reluctantly approved Warwick's policy of peace with France. It was unaware that the Earl had promised King Louis an aggressive alliance against Burgundy. Twice during the winter Queen Margaret was expected in England. The Queen's fleet was ready, but the Queen was not. In the past she had often acted rashly when she should have considered; now she hesitated when she and her son should have been in England winning hearts.

* The name by which the English usually designated the men of the Hanse towns.

Meanwhile, the sanctuaries were crowded with Yorkists; London made no pretence of being overjoyed by the change in rule; the Yorkist Duke of Norfolk sued as humbly to the Lancastrian Earl of Oxford as, young Paston reported gleefully, he himself had sued to the Duke of Norfolk.[8] Clarence's mother and sisters secretly laboured to persuade him to return to his allegiance. On November 2 in the sanctuary of Westminster Abbey, Queen Elizabeth succeeded, in dire adversity, in producing that which had been denied her during her splendid days: a male heir, who was hopefully christened Edward. Many an Englishman was gladdened by tidings of this event and looked the more confidently for the return of the infant's father.

These loyal hearts had not long to wait. For a time Charles, Duke of Burgundy, temporized, thinking that he might come to terms with the House of Lancaster; but when Louis' ambassadors opened negotiations with England and Louis himself brusquely declared war on Burgundy, Charles's illusions slipped from him and he realized that, for his own preservation, he must help his brother-in-law. Now for the first time, a week after Christmas, he openly received Edward and Richard, who had been enjoying the hospitality of the Seigneur de la Gruthuyse. Edward soon persuaded Charles to part with 50,000 crowns, to hire Burgundian and Hanse ships for him, and to recruit several hundred Flemish gunners. Richard probably divided his time between Gruthuyse's fine mansion in Bruges and the port of Flushing, where the fleet was beginning to assemble. He spent a few days in February, however, with his sister, Duchess Margaret, at Lille, Margaret no doubt recalling their childhood days at Fotheringhay and hopefully prophesying the return to the fold of her favourite brother Clarence. Richard almost certainly renewed acquaintance with William Caxton, who had by this time resigned the Governorship of the English merchants at Bruges to take service with the Duchess Margaret. By the middle of February he would be at Flushing, supervising with Hastings and Rivers the victualling of the fleet and the equipping of the little army. The English exiles embarked on March 2, but weather held them in port for nine days.[9]

On March 11, King Edward, ordering his pilots to make for friendly East Anglia, set sail for the 'enterprise of England' with an army of some 1,500 men—about 1,000 English and 500 Flemings. Next morning a landing party which he sent ashore near Cromer in Norfolk was promptly beaten back to its boats. Edward decided to try a more hostile shore which might be less well guarded. Northward he steered for

Yorkshire. A storm fell upon his navy and scattered his ships. The vessels Richard commanded were driven ashore a few miles above Ravenspur, the now vanished port at the mouth of the Humber at which, seventy-two years before, Henry Bolingbroke had landed to take the crown from Richard II and establish the House of Lancaster.[10]*

It was the evening of March 14: a ticklish moment for a young captain with darkness coming down on unfriendly territory, the wind howling over a grey sea, his men shaken by their narrow escape from death, and no sign of the rest of the army. On leading his band southward next morning, however, Richard found King Edward and his little host at Ravenspur. Through a threatening countryside they marched resolutely northwestward towards York. Kingston-upon-Hull shut them out. Beverley opened its gates. York, it turned out, would not admit Edward until, taking a leaf from Bolingbroke's book, he swore that he had come only to reclaim his Duchy of York! Then, cheering lustily for Henry and mounting the ostrich plumes of Lancaster, Edward and Richard, with only a handful of followers, walked boldly through the city streets. A few hours later, the whole army was permitted to come within the walls to spend the night. York was probably more cautious than hostile; if things went ill with Edward, his oath would perhaps enable the city fathers to make their peace with Warwick.

The next morning King Edward cheerfully marched his little band southward, even though he had learned that the Earl of Northumberland and Marquess Montagu, poised in Yorkshire and sworn to take him, had each a larger army than his own. This much gratitude did Henry Percy now show to Edward: his retainers gathered about him, the Earl remained motionless upon his estates, prepared to accept whoever emerged the victor in the coming struggle. The only cause which the once great-hearted House of Percy would henceforth support was its own interest.

The Marquess lay in strength at Pontefract, to block the road south. Undismayed and marching with great speed, Edward slipped around him and drove onward to Sandal castle, scene of his father's death, where a band of retainers awaited his coming. Yet John Neville could not have been ignorant of the invaders' movements nor afraid to attack them. At the supreme touch, his old loyalty to Edward and Richard proved deeper than his allegiance to his brother or fears of his own safety. Unable to bring himself to assault the gallant little band led by two brothers he had loved, the Marquess, sick at heart, slowly trailed southward after them.[11]*

All over England now, men were donning harness and arraying followers to hunt down 'yonder man Edward'[12] or to espouse his quarrel or to sit watchfully at home and await the arbitrament of other swords. Onward Edward rolled to Doncaster and then to Nottingham, his army swelling its ranks as men-at-arms and yeoman archers hastened in to join him. At Nottingham scouts brought him the first sure word of the mighty forces which were gathering to crush his daring venture. Warwick had set up his standard at Coventry and was rapidly gathering an army by appeals and menaces. Clarence was levying troops in the southwest counties. The Bastard of Fauconberg hovered in the channel with a powerful fleet. Queen Margaret and her son were momently expected in England. The most immediate danger threatened from the east: the Duke of Exeter, the Earl of Oxford, and Viscount Beaumont had reached Newark with a 'great fellowship'. With Montagu coming up behind, Warwick to his front, and Oxford on his flank, Edward and his force appeared to be doomed. The King possessed, however, three intangible resources: his own peerless generalship, the zealous service of his brother Richard, and his brother George's discontents.

Quickly estimating the situation, Edward made a sudden feint to the east in such ostensible force that Oxford beat a hasty retreat. Then, hurrying his army southward to Leicester, where he was joined by some 2,500 men, the King marched directly on Coventry. Warwick took shelter behind the walls of the city. On March 29, only two weeks after his landing, Edward proclaimed himself King and offered the Earl of Warwick the choice of pardon for life only or the hazard of battle. Warwick, waiting for Montagu, Oxford, and, above all, Clarence, accepted neither offer but remained behind the battlements of the town.

Clarence was coming up from the southeast. As soon as he had heard of Edward's landing, he had hastened to assemble all the men he could lay his hands on. He stayed at Wells until the 23rd of March, sending to his friend Henry Vernon of Derbyshire to supply him with the latest news. On the 30th he was at Malmesbury. By April 2 he had reached Burford and was making for Banbury.[13]

Next day, he marched out of Banbury towards Coventry. As if to oppose him, Edward broke his camp, now situated at Warwick, and moved about three miles south. When the two forces were less than a mile apart, Edward and Richard rode confidently forward. Clarence cantered towards them with a few followers. A family reconciliation followed. Throwing himself on his knees, Clarence was instantly raised and kissed by the King. Then while Hastings and Rivers fraternized with Clarence's friends, Richard and George embraced and conversed apart for a little. Finally, after trumpeters had sounded joyous fanfares, Clarence addressed Edward's army with the golden eloquence for which he was already noted,[14]* and then Edward paid his respects to Clarence's men, promising them his abounding 'grace and good love'. The following day Edward permitted brother George to ease his honour by offering his father-in-law a pardon 'with divers good conditions'; the furious Earl spurned the offer but still refused to come out and fight, though Montagu and Oxford had just joined him.

Early the next morning, Friday, April 5, King Edward suddenly hurled his army southward for London. On Sunday he was at Daventry, on Tuesday at Dunstable; Wednesday night he spent at St. Albans, having sent orders to the London magistrates to arrest King Henry and keep him in good custody. But on that very Wednesday the distracted city council, and George Neville, the Archbishop, received urgent commands from Warwick to hold London until he arrived. They were also expecting hourly word of the landing of Queen Margaret and her son, whom two days before the Duke of Somerset and the Earl of Devonshire (Courtenay, the Lancastrian Earl) had gone south to meet. Tension mounted in the city. The sanctuaries were crammed with Yorkist adherents; the Tower was full of Yorkist prisoners. Warwick's followers were still in apparent control, but the citizens were beginning to stir. Mayor Stokton had prudently taken to his bed. In an attempt to rally the city for Lancaster, the Archbishop of York mounted poor King Harry on a horse and had him led through the streets surrounded by a thin shell of armed men. At the head of the procession a staff was borne, from which dangled two fox-tails—once the ensign of the mighty Henry the Fifth but now only two fox-tails, drooping like the half-witted heir of Agincourt.[15] The council quickly decided that the city could not oppose King Edward. When news came that evening that he had reached St. Albans, the slippery Archbishop dispatched him a humble request to be taken into favour.

At noon on Maundy Thursday, April 11, the gates of London flew open and young Richard of Gloucester entered the city at King Edward's side to the blowing of trumpets and the rolling surf of cheers. In the eyes of most Londoners, Edward was 'their' King. He had revived their trade and was himself a dealer in wool; he spent freely among the victuallers, vintners, drapers, and goldsmiths and at the moment owed large sums; and he was ardently championed by the ladies and merchants' wives of the city, many of whom had apparently received from him favours which were never engrossed upon the patent rolls. Besides, there were not many who believed that Richard Neville, whatever the odds in his advantage, could ever defeat Edward Plantagenet in battle.

Edward went first to St. Paul's to make an offering. He halted briefly at the Bishop of London's palace to see that Henry VI and his smooth-tongued keeper, the Archbishop, were packed off safely to the Tower. Then he rode to Westminster and pausing only long enough to utter a brief prayer and let the Archbishop of Canterbury touch the crown to his brows, he strode into the sanctuary. . . .

> The kyng comforted the quene and other ladyes eke,
> His swete babis full tendurly he did kys,
> The yonge prynce he behelde and in his armys did bere.
> Thus his bale turnyd hym to blis;
> Aftur sorow joy, the course of the worlde is.
> The sighte of his babis relesid parte of his woo;
> Thus the wille of God in every thyng is doo.[16]

When Edward brought his wife and children to Baynard's Castle, the old Duchess of York's house on the bank of the Thames, Richard and George of Clarence completed the family reunion.

Next day, while the bells of London tolled for Good Friday, Richard attended a great council of war and afterwards looked to the supplies and equipment of his men. Stout warriors came in to the King's aid: Lord Howard, a brother of Lord Hastings, and Sir Humphrey Bourchier and his brother leading a troop of Kentishmen. The best news of all, however, came from the scouts, who reported that the Earl of Warwick was approaching the city with all his forces. One of the principal reasons Edward had marched for London was to tempt Warwick to battle before Queen Margaret and the Bastard of Fauconberg arrived.

At midday on Easter Eve the royal captains—Richard of Gloucester, George of Clarence, Lord Hastings, Earl Rivers, Lord Howard, Lord Say—mustered the army in St. John's fields under Edward's eye. Scouts brought fresh tidings that Warwick had taken the Barnet road out of St. Albans. As Edward's chief commanders took up their stations in marching order, the throng of citizens who were watching must have been startled. The ever-faithful Lord Hastings commanded the rear-guard; the King himself, assisted by Clarence—well to keep an eye on Clarence—led the centre wing; but the critical charge of commanding the van Edward had bestowed upon his brother Richard, who was but eighteen years old and had never fought a major battle.[17]

XII*

AT four o'clock in the afternoon Edward ordered his army to set forth, taking King Henry with him for safe keeping. As it grew dark, Richard was leading the van of the host up the long hill towards Barnet, ten miles north of London. A messenger reported that Edward's 'afore-riders' had collided with Warwick's 'afore-riders' in Barnet, had driven them from the town and were pursuing. By the time Richard entered Barnet, perched on the southern edge of a great plateau 400 feet above sea-level, the Yorkist scouts were pouring back into the town from the St. Albans road: Warwick's whole army lay not more than a mile ahead, astride the road, and sheltering behind a thick line of hedges. Halting his men in the town, Richard sent word to the King, who soon galloped up to survey the situation. It was now full night, but after a brief conference with his commanders, Edward decided to press forward. Under cover of darkness the army was to form a line so close to Warwick's host that the Earl must needs fight on the morrow. It was an exceedingly difficult manoeuvre, which reveals the King's confidence in his captains and his men.

Bidding his troops to show no lights nor make undue noise, Richard warily led them several hundred yards up the St. Albans road and swung off to the right on to the treeless, heathery flat which is now the placid park of Hadley Common. While he and his officers struggled in the dark to form a line, King Edward was bringing his centre into position astride the road, and finally Hastings, turning off to his left, extended his wing along the western slope of the plateau. Richard and his men could hear, somewhere ahead of them, the thousand noises of a great host. To their left sounded the intermittent boom of Warwick's cannon. Aware that the King's army had approached, the Earl 'shot guns almost all the night, but . . . they always overshot the King's host, and hurted them nothing, and the cause was the King's host lay much nearer them than they deemed.'[1] To keep his position hidden, Edward refrained from replying with his artillery. Like the other commanders, Richard strove to settle his men for the night as quietly as possible. Soldiers stretched out on the damp ground to get

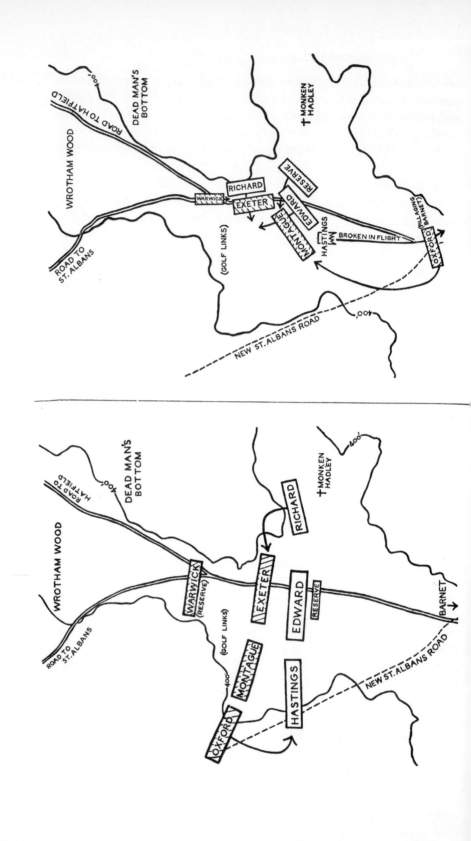

what sleep they could; men at arms in their iron harness, archers in padded leather 'jacks'. A dense mist began to roll up from the valleys and settled over both the hosts, making armour clammy to the touch, muffling sounds.

By four o'clock in the morning of Easter Sunday, Richard's captains had waked their men. Grimly munching the cold meat they had brought with them in their wallets, they moved with stiff joints into their positions of battle. Like Edward and Hastings, Richard had placed on each flank a clump of archers. Between them stretched a line of dismounted men-at-arms. Even the greatest lords, and the King himself, fought on foot, cavalry being used only to reconnoitre or pursue.[2] An opaque, watery greyness proclaimed the coming of dawn. Thick fog blanketed the field. Though it was impossible to see ten yards, the King's trumpets suddenly sounded the alert. Richard ordered his archers to fire blindly. Cannon boomed up and down the line. Beyond the wall of mist, Warwick's trumpets replied.

As Richard was discovering that no enemy fire of arrows or artillery came from before his front, Yorkist trumpets sounded again. His test was upon him. He lacked the physique to be a warrior, the experience to command an army corps, and the eloquence of a Clarence to stir the imagination of followers. For two years he had actively shared Edward's turbulent history, and Edward, appraising what his young brother had accomplished, had now given the precious right wing of the host into his hands. He owned only the hard-won resources which his will had forged, and whatever he had learned of the ways of battle, and his courage.

The slight and youthful Duke of Gloucester tersely gave his captains the word to advance banner.

With his squires at his side and his household knights gathered about him, he led the royal vanguard forth through the mist to close with the enemy. To his left he heard a crash of steel as two lines of fighting men collided. But still he encountered nothing except an endless milk-grey opacity. Only when he found himself advancing down a steep slope into marshy bottom land did he realize why he had met no resistance. Warwick must have anchored his left wing on the edge of the plateau overlooking this bottom. In the darkness Richard had far outflanked the enemy's position.

Hurriedly he and his captains swung the line about so that it was heading west instead of north. Up the slope Richard and his men clambered. With a shout they burst onto the plateau and fell upon

Warwick's flank. The Lancastrians recoiled. Confusion spread down their line. Up from the bottom the Yorkists continued to swarm. But the going was laborious and slow for men encased in steel. By the time Richard had enough men to establish a foothold, the enemy captains had been able to make a new front running north and south. Heavy reinforcements streamed out of the mist to bolster them.

Richard was in the thick of the conflict, swinging a heavy battle-axe. One of his squires went down.[3]* The numbers of the enemy swelled. At intervals his household warriors closed a steel wall in front of him so that he could consult with his captains. On either side of him the writhing battle-line faded away into the fog. His men were out-numbered now. The Lancastrian reinforcements were pressing hard to hurl his whole wing from the plateau. Desperately Richard and his men struggled to hold their positions. The issue was doubtful in the extreme.

Warwick had brought 15,000 men to that field, adherents of the Nevilles and Lancastrians cheek by jowl. The Duke of Exeter commanded the left wing, which was stationed between the St. Albans road and the marshy hollow, today called Dead Man's Bottom. Montagu held the centre, the bulk of which extended west of the road; the Lancastrian Earl of Oxford, the right wing. It was Oxford's men who were sheltered by a line of hedge, perhaps the same which can still be discerned running northwestward across a golf links to the new Barnet-St. Albans Road. Warwick took up his command post with the reserve. Though this host outnumbered the King's forces, probably by a third, it had been stung by Edward's unopposed march through the realm, oppressed by the loss of London, and infected with doubts by the treachery of Clarence and the ambiguity of Montagu. Yet many of these men must have come to the field like Sir John Paston and his younger brother, with right good hope of victory. The Pastons were not fighting out of loyalty to King Harry or intense political conviction but because the Earl of Oxford had taken their part against the Duke of Norfolk; and doubtless it was such local ties and special interests that drew many of the combatants to the heath north of Barnet on this fog-wrapped Easter Sunday.[4]

When the Duke of Exeter discovered that a strong force, storming out of the marshy hollow, had thrown his flank into disorder, he dispatched an alarming message to Warwick; and as he laboured to form a new line he sent further urgent appeals for help. Warwick, nervously jumping to the conclusion that Edward had thrown the bulk

3 EDWARD IV 1442–1483. Artist Unknown

(National Portrait Gallery, London

of his army into this surprise attack, hurriedly committed most of his precious reserve to the Duke. He was soon relieved to learn that Exeter's line was now holding, and in a moment he received glowing good news.

Like Richard, the Earl of Oxford had discovered that his right wing far outflanked the enemy; but, unlike Richard's, his men had easy going. They swung eastward, crashed into Hastings' flank and began to roll up his line. Most of Hastings' wing was swept away. With the Earl himself at their head, the Lancastrians pelted towards Barnet in hot pursuit, poured into the town, and began plundering. Some of the Yorkists, finding horses, fled all the way to London, crying that the day was lost and King Edward and his two brothers slain.

The rank-and-file of the King's army were not disheartened, however, for the mist providentially hid this disaster from them; and Hastings managed to form the wreck of his wing into a front to hold off the right side of Montagu's centre. Richard's flank attack and the collapse of Hastings' force had wrenched the battle line about so that it now ran roughly north and south.[5]*

In the centre of the field the fighting raged fiercely. The King himself 'valiantly assailed [his enemies], in the midst and strongest of their battle, where he, with great violence, beat and bore down afore him all that stood in his way, and, then, turned to the range, first on that one hand, and then on that other hand, in length, and so beat and bore them down, so that nothing might stand in the sight of him and the well assured fellowship that attended truly upon him.'[6]

Yet, though Warwick had comitted almost all his reserve to the struggle on Exeter's wing, his hopes were high. When Oxford returned from the pursuit of Hastings' broken force, he would fall upon Edward's rear; and Exeter had sent word that he was thrusting Richard's men towards the fatal trap of the hollow. Edward, in his turn, sensed that victory depended upon his reserve, which he had grimly husbanded even after the collapse of his left. If his brother Richard could hold out—— Messengers came and went through the mist. The answer was always the same: Richard would hold, without reinforcements. Suddenly the King glimpsed a confused movement in Montagu's right centre. Horsemen appeared, recoiled. Men were shouting 'Treason! Treason!'——

It had taken the Earl of Oxford some time to rally his men, happily looting in Barnet, and to reform their ranks. Hastening up the road to strike Edward's rear, he collided with Montagu's flank instead: the

D

fog had hidden from him the fact that the line of battle had swung round. In the poor visibility, Montagu's men mistook Oxford's banner of a star with streams for King Edward's emblem of a blazing sun. Thinking they were being attacked on the flank by the enemy, they promptly delivered a stiff volley of arrows. Oxford's force was thrown back in confusion. Somebody cried 'Treason!' The cry was taken up by both parties. Panic spread to Montagu's troops. The smouldering resentment between Neville followers and old Lancastrians had done its work. Thinking that they had been betrayed, Oxford and his men fled from the field, and the Earl galloped northward for the safety of Scotland.

Ignorant though he was of the cause of this commotion, King Edward realized that his opportunity had come. With the whole of his reserve he smashed at the centre of Warwick's line.

Of all this Richard, far out on the eastern edge of the plateau, knew nothing. Dangerously his line swayed back and forth, his soldiers fighting bitterly to maintain themselves atop the hill. He possessed no fresh troops. Edward's precious reserve he could not bring himself to deplete. He was grimly staking everything on the men who, a lifetime ago, had charged with him out of the hollow. His second squire had now been killed at his side; he himself was slightly wounded.

Suddenly, there was a swirl in the mist to the left of and behind the enemy's position. A shiver ran down the Lancastrian line. Exeter's men began to give way, stubbornly at first, then faster. Warwick's centre must be crumbling. Richard signalled his trumpeters. The call to advance banners rang out. The weary young commander and his weary men surged forward. The hedge of steel before them began to fall apart. Then the enemy were in full flight, casting away their weapons as they ran.

Out of the mist loomed the great sun banner of the House of York. A giant figure strode forward. Pushing his visor up, Richard saw that the King was smiling at him in brotherly pride. The right wing, driving westward across the Lancastrian rear, had linked up with Edward's centre to bring the battle to an end. It was seven o'clock in the morning; the struggle had lasted almost three hours.

The men of Montagu and Warwick had not been able to withstand the shock of Edward's great blow. After a brief, bitter resistance, they had broken and fled. The Marquess fell slain—fighting bravely for his brother, some said; others, that the Lancastrians, detecting or suspecting his treachery, had killed him; still others, that though he gave battle under Warwick's banner, he wore beneath his harness the colours of the King. It is quite probable that John Neville, caught in a hopeless conflict of loyalties, had determined not to survive the field. Only thus, perhaps, could he save the bird in his bosom. When Warwick learned that Oxford was fled, his brother slain, and his line crumbling, he lumbered from the battle in his heavy armour towards Wrotham wood, where his horses were tethered. Overtaken by pursuing Yorkists, he was killed before the King could intervene.[7]

Early in the afternoon Edward led his army in triumph back to London, his brother Richard riding by his side. Next morning, the bodies of the King-maker and the Marquess, naked but for loin-cloths, were conveyed to St. Paul's cathedral, where they lay for two days upon the pavement that the end of the House of Neville might be known to all.[8]*

XIII

ONLY just in time had Edward and Richard settled accounts with Warwick. On the very day of Barnet, Queen Margaret had landed at Weymouth with Prince Edward and his wife, Anne Neville, and gone to Cerne abbey. There the Duke of Somerset and the Earl of Devon met her shortly after with the news of Warwick's overthrow.

When the Countess of Warwick, who had sailed to Portsmouth, heard the tidings, she fled at once to sanctuary in Beaulieu abbey; but Queen Margaret, though at first terribly shaken by the blow and filled with fear for the safety of her son, was at last persuaded by Somerset that King Edward had been fatally weakened and that victory was hers for the taking. As the Queen's party moved to Exeter and then to Taunton and Wells, her hopes rose, for the gentry of Devon and Cornwall came streaming in and Somerset, Dorset and Wiltshire likewise rallied in numbers to her banner.

Two days after Barnet, on Tuesday, April 16, word of the Queen's landing reached London. Richard and the other commanders set instantly to work to assemble a fresh army; the King summoned men from far and wide to meet him at Windsor and borrowed money from his loyal Londoners. While he was celebrating the Feast of St. George (April 23) at Windsor Castle with his brothers and his captains, Edward learned from his scouts that though Margaret had made a feint in the direction of London, she was probably on her way to join Jasper Tudor in Wales. The King set off next day in wary pursuit. On Tuesday, April 30, at Malmesbury he was informed that the Lancastrians, marching north from Wells through Bath, had turned westward to enter Bristol. Margaret's commanders had, in fact, underestimated the King's speed of advance. On Thursday, May 2, they issued hastily from Bristol. Making a pretence of preparing to give battle on Sodbury Hill, they marched as fast as they could up the Severn valley. To escape into Wales, they must reach the bridge at Gloucester before the King overtook them.

Edward arrived on Sodbury Hill that same afternoon. Finding no enemy, he encamped his army and anxiously sent out scouts. At three o'clock on Friday morning they galloped into the sleeping camp to report that Margaret's army was racing through the night towards Gloucester. Edward dispatched word to the governor of the town that he must hold out at all costs against the rebels. Richard and Hastings and the other commanders roused their men. Through the darkness the army started in pursuit of the fleeing enemy.

When the Queen reached Gloucester at ten o'clock on Friday morning, she discovered the gates of the city barred and soldiers manning the walls. Not daring to pause for an assault—for she now knew that Edward was on her trail—Margaret frantically drove her weary host northward towards Tewkesbury, the next possible crossing of the Severn.

A grim race now ensued. The day was hot. The Queen's footsore and dusty soldiers struggled through 'a foul country, all in lanes and stony ways, betwixt woods, without any good refreshing'. Not far behind and a little to the east of them in the rocky upland, Edward, Richard, and Hastings urged their army forward, on roads no less difficult. The men could 'not find, in all the way, horse-meat, ne man's-meat, ne so much as drink for their horses, save in one little brook, where was full little relief, it was so soon troubled with the carriages [carts] that had passed it. And all that day was evermore the King's host within five or six miles of his enemies; he in plain country and they amongst woods; having always good espials upon them'.[1]*

When the Lancastrians reached the outskirts of Tewkesbury about four o'clock in the afternoon, the foot soldiers threw themselves upon the ground in utter exhaustion. The Queen's commanders informed her that neither men nor horses could go another step. In an agony of fear for her son, Margaret was forced to turn at bay.

As the modern road from Gloucester to Tewkesbury passes Gupshill Inn, less than a mile south of the town, it cuts through the heart of the Lancastrian position. The Queen's forces dragged themselves into battle array on an irregular line of high ground, bounded on the left by a stream called Swillbrook and on the right by a wooded knoll. The position ran roughly east and west 'in a close even at the town's end; the town, and the abbey, at their backs; afore them, and upon every hand of them, foul lanes, and deep dykes, and many hedges, hills, and valleys, a right evil place to approach, as could well have been devised'. Though this position appeared to be as formidable in its way as the massive Norman tower of Tewkesbury Abbey rising directly to the rear, it was exposed to one ominous hazard: not far behind the right wing, northwestward down a slope of meadow, the river Avon flowed to its confluence with the Severn.

So hot were the Yorkists upon the trail that when they reached Cheltenham, but nine miles from Tewkesbury, Edward learned that 'his enemies were come to Tewkesbury, and there were taking a field. Whereupon the King . . . a little comforted himself and his people, with such meat and drink as he had done [caused] to be carried with him . . . and, incontinent, set forth towards his enemies . . . and lodged himself, and all his host, within three mile of them'.

Early next morning Richard of Gloucester, again commanding the vanguard, marched northwestward across this inhospitable country to take up a position facing the Duke of Somerset on the Lancastrian right wing. The King followed his brother into the centre of the line, opposite Prince Edward, the son of Margaret, and Lord Wenlock, the friend of Warwick. Hastings with the rearguard filled up the position to the right until his flank touched the Swillbrook.

Richard at once led an assault, but the 'foul lanes' and many hedges made it impossible for him to get at the enemy. There followed a fierce exchange of arrows, with some cannon fire. Then Somerset, perceiving that his foes were checked, decided upon a bold stroke. Concealed by the hedges and thickets, he led his army westward to the slope of the wooded knoll and charged down upon the Yorkist left flank. Coolly Richard rallied his men. Though they gave some ground they did not fall into panic. Once he and his captains had reformed their line to face Somerset, they pressed the attack so vigorously that the Lancastrians began to fall back. At this moment a small band of spears, whom King Edward had stationed on the knoll for just such an emergency, descended upon Somerset's rear shouting as if they were an army.

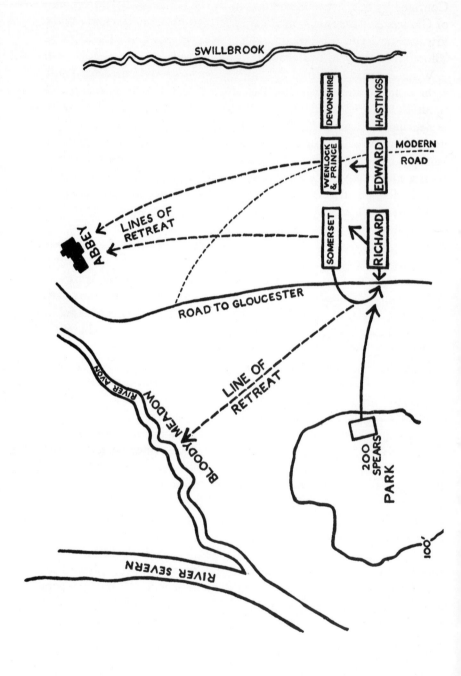

Confused by this diversion and shaken by the fierce assault of the Duke of Gloucester, Somerset's men wavered, then broke in headlong flight towards the Avon. The pursuit which followed has given the name of 'Bloody Meadow' to this ground.

When Edward perceived that his brother had routed the Lancastrian right wing, he himself attacked the centre, while Richard swung round upon its now unprotected right flank. As Prince Edward was experiencing his first bitter taste of battle, the Duke of Somerset rode up to Lord Wenlock in a fury, cried that Wenlock had deliberately betrayed him by not supporting his flank attack on Richard's wing, and with a single blow of his battle-axe cleft Wenlock's skull. Beholding their leaders butchering each other as King Edward and the Duke of Gloucester splintered their line, the Lancastrian centre crumbled into flight. Many were drowned trying to cross the Avon; many fell beneath the swords of the closely pursuing Yorkists; some hid themselves in the abbey or the town. Swept away by the rout and spurring towards Tewkesbury in terror, Prince Edward was overtaken by a detachment commanded by the Duke of Clarence. Though the youth cried for succour to the man who had shortly before been his ally, he was immediately slain. Clarence was no doubt eager to assert his new-found loyalty.[2]*

A few moments later the King came storming up to the abbey doors. The abbot confronted him, pleading that he not defile a holy place. Regaining his temper, Edward not only consented but in a hasty moment offered his pardon to the soldiers who had sought shelter there. When he discovered, however, that Somerset himself and his chief captains were within, he determined to seize them. After he had generously tried to make a friend of Somerset's brother in 1463, the ungrateful Beaufort had betrayed him at the first opportunity. The abbey was not a specially privileged sanctuary. By the standards of the century the rebel leaders had no reason to expect anything but death; and policy dictated to the King that he must break his hastily given word in order to rid the realm of these inveterate troublers of the peace. On Monday, May 6, Somerset and about a dozen others were taken from the abbey, and tried before Richard of Gloucester, Constable once again, and the Duke of Norfolk, Marshal of England. Sentenced to death, the rebel leaders were immediately beheaded in the market place of Tewkesbury.[3]*

King Edward and his army now proceeded to Coventry, where both good news and bad greeted them. A rising in the North had been easily quelled, but the Bastard of Fauconberg was attacking London. At this moment Queen Margaret, captured in a house of religion not far from Tewkesbury, was brought in. It was only a husk they had taken, the shell of a woman and the shadow of a Queen. That dauntless spirit had been crushed at last by the news of her son's death, which had been broken to her by her captor, Sir William Stanley, with brutal relish. Lifelessly, she was borne along in King Edward's train as he took his way rapidly towards London to meet the final Lancastrian threat.

It was less serious than it first appeared. Having assembled a mob of Kentishmen, the Bastard bombarded the city with artillery placed on the south bank and attacked some of the gates; but the Earls of Rivers and Essex drove his men back by sudden sallies, the Londoners defended themselves valiantly, and when a small advance guard of the King's army arrived, Fauconberg fled to his fleet at Sandwich.

On Tuesday, May 21, King Edward entered his capital in the full panoply of victory—trumpets and clarions sounding, battle flags streaming above his troops. The honour of heading this triumphal procession was bestowed upon Richard, Duke of Gloucester. He was followed by Lord Hastings and then by the King himself; towards the rear came the Duke of Clarence and finally the drooping figure of Queen Margaret seated in a chariot.

That evening the King held a conference of his advisers, at the conclusion of which he sent the Constable of England, his brother Richard, with a delegation of noblemen to bear an order to Lord Dudley, Constable of the Tower: that feeble candle, the life of Henry the Sixth, was to be snuffed out. His death must bring to an end, it seemed, the convulsions of civil strife which had so long shaken the realm. The next night Henry's body, surrounded by torches and a guard of honour, was borne to St. Paul's where it lay upon a bier, the face uncovered. Shortly after it was transported up the Thames to be entombed in the Lady chapel of Chertsey abbey.[4]*

Meanwhile, the morning after his visit to the Tower, Richard set off in pursuit of the Bastard of Fauconberg. Edward soon followed with reinforcements, but when he reached Sandwich the Bastard had already submitted himself and his fleet to the Duke of Gloucester and been promised pardon. The King and his brother returned to London. The campaign was over.

In the space of twelve fierce months, Richard had become the King's first general, the chief prop of his throne, and his most trusted officer. He was not yet nineteen.

The Lord of the North

WHILE the great actors in these events shook the kingdom with their struggles, there were others who received buffets but gave none, who had no ambition to seek conquest but would suffer grievously in defeat. Such were the women of these passionate combatants; and of these none was more violently tossed upon the sea of strife than Warwick's frail daughter, Anne Neville.

She was not yet fourteen years old that March day in the spring of 1470 when her father and her brother-in-law rode away from Warwick castle to unseat King Edward and make Isabel Queen of England. With her mother and her sister, who was expecting a child in about six weeks, she endured a month of anxious days. Then Warwick and Clarence, shorn of most of their followers, galloped into the castle courtyard, fugitives. The women learned that they too must flee; in a few hours the party set out southward in hot haste. At Exeter, the ladies of the House of Neville were hastily packed aboard a small vessel. As it was approaching Calais, Isabel's labour began. Guns cracked; the ship swung about—Calais refused to admit Warwick's fleet. In a rude cabin Anne and her mother did what they could for Isabel. Wine might ease her labour a little but there was no wine. Alarmed for his daughter's safety, Warwick sent to Lord Wenlock, deputy governor of Calais. Wenlock obligingly dispatched wine for Isabel, but informed the Earl that the harbour would remain closed to him. Isabel's baby was born dead, or died within a few hours. Anne helped her mother prepare the little body for burial and the sailors then slipped it into the sea.[1]

Not long after Anne found herself in Normandy, her fortunes underwent a bewildering change. On Warwick's return from his interview with King Louis, she was informed that she might become the wife of Prince Edward, son of her father's greatest enemy, Margaret of Anjou. A month later, she learned that her betrothal had been ceremoniously announced at Angers and that, as soon as her father reconquered

England for Henry VI, she would wed the Prince. She was coldly welcomed into the household of Margaret of Anjou at Amboise, and here for the first time she met the arrogant and boastful youth of sixteen who was to be her husband. Prince Edward's disposition reflected the schooling in hatred and revenge which his passionate mother had given him. 'This boy,' the Milanese ambassador had written three years earlier, 'though only thirteen years of age, already talks of nothing else but of cutting off heads or making war, as if he had everything in his hands or was the god of battle. . . .'[2]

About December 13, Anne was wedded to Edward by the Grand Vicar of Bayeux, who had secured a dispensation for the marriage from the Patriarch of Jerusalem. It was something of a hole-and-corner affair. Queen Margaret, perhaps under pressure from Louis XI, fulfilled her bargain, but left herself as free as possible to disavow or annul it later. In all probability, Anne never shared a marriage bed with the Prince. The day after the ceremony the young couple and their mothers set out for Paris.[3]

Four months later, on Easter Sunday, Anne returned, with her husband and mother-in-law, to the land of which her invincible father was now master. She was smitten the next day with the news that even as she had been disembarking, her father and her uncle Montagu had been slain at Barnet Field. In the midst of Lancastrians feverishly planning to attack King Edward, she was alone with her grief. Borne along with Margaret's growing army, she was doubtless too stricken to be aware that she was no longer regarded as of any consequence. Early on the morning of Tewkesbury, as trumpets presaged the opening of the battle, she was hurried into a boat with the Queen and her attendants. On the other side of the Severn the ladies took shelter in a house of religion. That afternoon a fugitive brought the crushing word that the day was lost and King Edward harrying the vanquished; the man had no news of Prince Edward. They heard nothing more till Sir William Stanley found them three or four days later. With the others Anne was brought to Coventry, a bewildered and despairing girl.

Doubtless Richard of Gloucester saw her, briefly. Clarence took her in charge and sent her to Isabel. When Richard returned from Sandwich to London, he probably sought out Anne in the household of the Duchess of Clarence. In childhood they had known each other well. Now Richard was the mightiest subject of the kingdom, the conqueror of her father and her husband. She was only the landless daughter of a dead rebel; her father's estates were the prize of the

Crown; her mother's estates were being seized by George of Clarence. Richard doubtless had small opportunity to offer her comfort. However sympathetic Anne's sister may have been, her brother-in-law would treat her with scant state and keep her out of sight as much as possible—he had no wish to remind the world, or his brother Richard, that if the Countess of Warwick was to be deprived of her property, Anne was the legal heiress to half of it.[4]*

Richard, for his part, was busy helping the King to pick up the reins of government and was preparing to go north against the Scots. He was again Constable and Admiral of England. While Edward was marching from Coventry to London, he had given his brother Warwick's office of Great Chamberlain and soon added the Stewardship of the Duchy of Lancaster beyond Trent. Still other grants and powers flowed from the grateful King. Though Richard had become, in 1469–70, the virtual viceroy of Wales, it was in the North that his heart lay; and since the Lancastrians were still capable of stirring up trouble there, the Scots were 'furrowing' the borders, and Northumberland, whose allegiance was ambiguous, held the greatest strength in the region, Edward was happy to transfer his brother's seat of power from the Welsh Marches to Yorkshire.

Richard resigned the offices of Chief Justice and Chamberlain of South Wales to the youthful Earl of Pembroke.[5] In return, he obtained in the North the lands and the supreme command which had once been Warwick's. Already Warden of the West Marches towards Scotland, he was given authority over the Earl of Northumberland, Warden of the East and Middle Marches.[6] A few days before he set forth on his campaign against the Scots, he received Warwick's estates of Middleham, Sheriff Hutton, and Penrith; and two weeks later the grant was enlarged to include the whole of the Earl's holdings in Yorkshire and Cumberland. Richard had won his way back to Middleham castle.[7]

Anne Neville had once been happy at Middleham, too; now she was helpless and miserable; she had been a companion of Richard's childhood; she might lay claim to half her mother's great estates. Before he left London, Richard secured the King's permission to make her his wife.

His work on the border was quickly accomplished. Though the Bastard of Fauconberg, who had gone northward with him, deserted his new-found allegiance and had to be executed, Richard apparently taught the Scots a sharp lesson. By early August, James III was expressing his great willingness to negotiate infractions of the truce.

In late September, Richard hurried south. When he sought Anne at Clarence's London house, Clarence declared angrily that the affairs of the Nevilles were entirely in his hands and that Anne Neville was not for the Duke of Gloucester.

It was a nasty blow, coming from the elder brother who still, it seems, cast something of his old spell despite his recent treason. But Richard had no intention of relinquishing Anne. He took the quiet way of appealing to the King for justice. Edward informed Clarence that he was not to interfere with Richard's suit. On returning to his brother's town house, Richard found that Clarence was ready for him. Anne Neville, George declared, was not in his household. When Richard, having satisfied himself that the statement was true, demanded to know where she was, Clarence had his answer pat: since he was supposed to hold no right of wardship over Anne, he could not consider himself responsible for her whereabouts. He neither knew nor cared where she was.

Grimly Richard set to work to find her. And find her, he somehow did. Disguised as a cook-maid, she had been hidden in the kitchens of a dependent or friend of Clarence's. Richard escorted her to the sanctuary of St. Martin le Grand. It was the only refuge which would protect her from her brother-in-law without placing her under obligation to himself. If any other motive besides a delicate and honourable consideration for her feelings prompted him to this solution, it is not evident.[8]*

King Edward showed his attitude in the matter by conferring on his younger brother, on December 4, a vast grant of lands and manors forfeited by the Earl of Oxford and other rebels.[9] Yet, though he could not help revealing his affection and gratitude towards Richard, the King was anxious, for the peace of his realm, to reconcile his two brothers. Clarence was in a spiteful and dangerous mood. His anger at the prospect of losing Anne Neville's inheritance had been sharpened by Edward's granting the northern estates of Warwick to Richard as well as giving him three great offices to George's one, the Lieutenantship of Ireland. In an attempt to placate Clarence, the King requested his two brothers to appear before his council in order to debate Clarence's claim of guardianship over Anne. 'So many arguments,' says the Croyland Chronicler who witnessed the scene, 'were, with the greatest acuteness, put forward on either side . . . that all present, and the lawyers even, were quite surprised that these princes should find arguments in such abundance by means of which to support their respective causes.'[10] Since Richard was no match for his eloquent and florid brother in the art of persuasion, it was probably the cogency of his plea which balanced the charm of his brother's tongue. Clarence's claim was, in fact, neither legal nor equitable.[11]* The King's council cautiously suspended judgment; Edward continued to look for a way of mollifying George without injuring Richard.

It was no happy season that Richard spent at court this Christmas. Anne was still in sanctuary. Woodvilles seemed as numerous and as assertive as ever. And always there was brother George, glowering and implacable. Some two months later, Sir John Paston reported that, on February 16 (1472), the King and Queen, accompanied by the Dukes of Clarence and Gloucester, had gone 'to Sheen to pardon, men say not all in charity.' Paston added, the King 'entreateth my lord of Clarence for my lord of Gloucester, and, as it is said, he answereth that he [Richard] will have my lady his sister-in-law but they shall part [share] no lyvelode [estates].'[12]

This surly rejoinder Richard, to the King's great relief, was ready to accept as a basis for reconciliation. Soon after, an agreement was reached. Clarence signified his willingness for Richard to marry Anne, and, at the King's special request, grudgingly agreed—on condition that no grant of lands made to himself would ever be cancelled by Parliament or any other authority—that Richard should have Middleham and some of Warwick's other Yorkshire estates, which Edward had already given him. Richard, for his part, relinquished to Clarence the remainder of Warwick's lands and property, including the manors Warwick had held in his wife's right; he surrendered to Clarence the Great Chamberlainship of England in exchange for the much more modest office of Warden of the Royal Forests beyond Trent; and he agreed that Clarence should be given the earldoms of Warwick and Salisbury. If he was seeking to marry Anne Neville merely in order to augment his estate, he had made a remarkably poor bargain.[13]

Richard sought out Anne in St. Martin's sanctuary. She came forth at once to be his bride. Since they were cousins they needed an ecclesiastical dispensation to wed, but Richard was in no mood for waiting. Without the dispensation and, apparently, without any ceremony, they were immediately married.[14]* Then turning their backs on the splendours of London and Westminster, they speedily retired to the castle in Wensleydale which spelled home to them both. The arrogant presences of the Woodville tribe and the surly company of George of Clarence could stir only painful memories for Warwick's daughter; and Richard, oppressed by the acrid hostility of one brother and the relapse of the other from magnificent leader into sybaritic King, chafed to breathe the free air of the moors. In their feeling for the past and their shrinking from the life of court, the twenty-year-old bridegroom and the sixteen-year-old bride seem to have been thoroughly compatible.

By the late spring of 1472, Richard and Anne had established themselves at Middleham to begin the task of maintaining order and of winning hearts in the North. The summer passed tranquilly. In the late fall Richard had to journey to London to attend Parliament. If he returned to Middleham for Christmas, he was probably again in the capital for the parliamentary session which lasted from February to April. During this year of 1473, Anne gave birth to a son, who was named Edward, doubtless in honour of his royal uncle. By this time Richard's and Anne's domestic happiness had been darkened by a familiar shadow. George of Clarence was again seeking to trouble them, and the rest of the realm as well.

Clarence had been born with the taste of the world sour in his mouth, and no amount of goods or honours could sweeten it. Before Richard and Anne had left London, he was dabbling in conspiracy with that habitual intriguer, George Neville, Archbishop of York, whom Edward had pardoned and set at liberty as soon as he recovered his kingdom. The Archbishop, in his turn, was in touch with that unquenchable Lancastrian, the Earl of Oxford, who was making futile raids against Calais with the French King's help. To lessen Clarence's temptations, King Edward arrested the Archbishop at the end of April and sent him for safe-keeping to Hammes castle, one of the fortresses protecting Calais. Clarence subsided only momentarily. Mistily there hovered before him a golden crown. Since the Lancastrian Parliament of 1470 had declared him heir to the throne after Prince Edward and since Prince Edward and Henry VI were both dead, was he not in very fact King of England? Though Clarence's jealousy of Richard's favour with their elder brother was real enough, he was using it to mask his designs against the 'usurping' Edward.

In the spring of 1473, the political weather in England grew tense and threatening. Clarence and the Earl of Oxford were in the thick of a new conspiracy with Louis XI. While the former stirred Lancastrian hopes in a number of shires, the latter was hovering off the coasts with a small fleet. In a letter of April 16, Sir John Paston expressed the general uncertainty and suspense. 'The Earl of Oxford was on

Saturday at Dieppe and is purposed into Scotland with . . . twelve ships. I mistrust that work. Item, there be in London many flying tales, saying that there should be a work, and yet they wot not how.' But it was to England that Oxford sailed, landing on the coast of Essex on May 28. He had only a small force and his reception was cold. When he learned that the Earl of Essex and Lords Dynham and Duras were marching against him, he hastily took to his ships and resumed his hovering in the channel. 'Men look after they wot not what,' Paston wrote from London shortly after, 'but men buy harness fast; the King's menial men and the Duke of Clarence's are many in this town.'[15]

While Clarence was stirring mischief this late spring, Richard came to Nottingham to consult his brother Edward on political and family business. He had realized that it was of first importance to his mission in the North that he establish with Henry Percy, Earl of Northumberland, a relationship which would harmonize their respective jurisdictions and encourage Percy to work loyally and happily with him. On May 12 he and the Earl appeared before the royal council at Nottingham and swore to a compact, in which Northumberland recognized Richard's superior authority, and Richard agreed to respect all of Percy's rights and be to him 'a good and gracious lord'.[16]

Richard's private business concerned the Countess of Warwick. She was still immured in the sanctuary of Beaulieu abbey; for the King had dispatched officers of the crown to keep strict watch upon her. Why Edward, who was usually lenient enough with the wives of rebels, chose to treat the Countess so harshly remains a mystery. Perhaps he had hoped to avoid antagonizing brother George, who had seized all her lands. When Richard now requested Edward to permit him to assume responsibility for the Countess so that she might be given a home in the North, the King was in no mood to oppose Richard's wishes for the sake of appeasing Clarence. Before the end of May, Richard had dispatched his follower, Sir James Tyrell, to the Countess. She promptly accepted her son-in-law's offer. 'Item,' Paston added to a letter of June 3 reporting the landing of Oxford, 'how that the Countess of Warwick is now out of Beaulieu sanctuary, and Sir James Tyrell conveyeth her northward, men say by the King's assent, whereto some men say that the Duke of Clarence is not agreed.' By this time King Edward was so wroth with Clarence, he declared openly that he was thinking of restoring to the Countess all her estates so that she might bestow them upon the Duke of Gloucester.[17]

Richard had rescued his mother-in-law from virtual imprisonment not only, it seems, out of regard for his wife's happiness but because of his own compassion for her plight. When Warwick challenged the King, Richard had fought him fiercely; but now that the Nevilles were beaten and impotent, he actively befriended them. Little cause as he had to cherish the slippery George Neville, he was pleading with the King for his release. 'Item,' Sir John Paston jotted in the fall of 1473, 'I hope by the means of the Duke of Gloucester that my Lord Archbishop shall come home.' The following year, he was able to effect the Archbishop's deliverance from prison. When the Marquess of Montagu's son was stripped of his dukedom a few years later, Richard secured his wardship and brought the boy into his household. Later still, he bestowed an annuity on the Earl of Oxford's wife, who was a sister of the King-maker, though Oxford was his enemy.[18]

Throughout the summer of 1473 Clarence's anger simmered; Oxford cruised off the coasts taking merchantmen; the King moved watchfully from place to place in the Midlands. On September 10 Richard received a commission to array the men of Yorkshire and lead them south at the King's call.[19] Twenty days later, the Earl of Oxford with a small force seized St. Michael's Mount, sought to arouse Cornwall, and sent to the King of France for aid. Clarence's hopes blazed up. He stirred his followers and tenants, giving out that he was about to revenge himself on the Duke of Gloucester; but Edward, and others, were not deceived. Sir John Paston wrote from London that most men about the King had sent 'for their harness, and it is said for certain that the Duke of Clarence maketh him big in that he can, showing as he would but deal with the Duke of Gloucester; but the King intendeth . . . to be as big as they both and to be a stifler atween them. And some think that under this there should be some other thing intended and some treason conspired; so what shall fall can I not say'. Even the usually cautious Sir John dared hint that Clarence's eye was upon the crown.[20]

As it turned out, nothing befell. Neither Cornwall nor Louis XI responded to Oxford's call; it speedily became clear that the venturesome Earl had trapped himself on the rocky mount. By the middle of February, 1474, he was forced to surrender for pardon of his life only. Even Clarence realized that, for the time being at least, he would have to bow to brother Edward and make the best bargain he could for the Neville lands. Sir John Paston was soon recording the hope that 'the two Dukes of Clarence and Gloucester should be set at one by the award of the King'. The record of Clarence's follies has survived; his winning charm can only be guessed at.[21]

Patiently Richard agreed to reopen the whole question of the division of lands between himself and George; Edward set to work to pacify his recaltitrant brother, who was all the more difficult to placate since in the preceding fall Parliament had passed an act of resumption of Crown lands, from which Richard had been exempted but which had cost Clarence the 'noble demesne of Tutbury and several other lands'.[22] Edward determined that, in order to establish the settlement between his brothers as solidly as possible, it must come into being by a bill of Parliament. In the spring of 1474 there was passed an enactment that 'in like manner and form as if the ... Countess [of Warwick] were dead', her property was to be partitioned between her co-heiresses, Anne and Isabel, and their respective husbands; the sharing itself was left to the arbitrament of the King. In July Clarence's feelings were soothed by a vast grant of estates, which a like gift to Richard fell somewhat short of matching. The settlement was completed in February of 1475 when Parliament confirmed the division of Warwick's estates which Edward had already made. Richard was to keep Middleham, Sheriff Hutton, and Warwick's other lands in Yorkshire; Clarence, the manor of Clavering in Essex and the Earl's London mansion, 'le Herber'.[23]*

From this tedious strife of Clarence's making Richard had emerged with great estates and the heightened affection and trust of his royal brother, with the wife and home of his choice and a young son. But the contest had been grim and wearing. Once again he had been caught in the recurring pattern of sundered allegiance. Perhaps it was in defiance of this pattern, in a dogged clinging to the elemental defences of his childhood, that he had chosen the motto, 'Loyaulté me lie'— Loyalty Binds Me. If it is primarily a pledge to King Edward, it is also a revelation of his own need. In the North, at least, he could offer, and hope to enjoy, loyalty. Middleham was his refuge as well as his home.

Scarcely had he seen the end of his difficulties with Clarence, however, than he was summoned forth from Wensleydale by his duty to the King. In the spring of 1475 he was making preparations to do battle once more at Edward's side.

Edward had been eager to placate brother George because he was about to invade the realm of France.

II

KING EDWARD had persuaded Parliament to make him large grants of money. He had cajoled many of his wealthier subjects to offer him substantial contributions, wryly called 'benevolences'. He had made peace with Scotland and the Hanse Towns, secured the goodwill of the Duke of Brittany, and renewed his treaty with the kingdom of Castile. The Duke of Burgundy was the eager partner of his enterprise. At the desire of his subjects, in whom the Agincourt fever still burned, and by the advice of his council, who thought that foreign war would drain off the energies that kicked up strife at home, Edward was prepared to assert Henry V's claim to the French crown, or at least to reconquer some of the provinces from which the English had been evicted a quarter of a century before.

His army was to be raised by indentures: the magnates of the kingdom contracted to supply bodies of soldiers at so much a head. The two largest contracts were those signed by the Dukes of Gloucester and of Clarence, each of whom agreed to bring into the field 120 men-at-arms, including himself, and 1,000 archers.[1]

When Richard's call to battle sounded across the dales and moors, the warriors of the North willingly looked to their weapons and readied their tenants. Richard's chief officers of arms, Gloucester Herald and Blanc Sanglier Pursuivant, supervised the making of banners for the host and of 'cognizances', or badges; each man of Richard's contingent would wear a badge displaying his emblem, the White Boar [Blanc Sanglier]. The origin of this heraldic sign is uncertain. It possibly derived from the honour of Windsor, with which it may have become associated through the legend of Guy of Warwick: 'But first, near Windsor, I did slay / A boar of passing might and strength. . . .' On the other hand, the boar—often spelled in those days 'bore'—may have been an anagram of Ebor(acum), York.[2]

Whatever the provenience of the emblem, the White Boar had proved so valiant in combat and Richard had so established himself in the affections of Yorkshire, that men flocked to his colours. When, in May, he led his troops to Barham Downs near Canterbury, the mustering place of the army, he had brought with him at least 300 men more than he had indented for. King Edward was so pleased with his young brother that he presented him with the great Yorkshire castle of

Skipton in Craven and added additional powers and perquisites to the office of Sheriff of Cumberland, which, in February, he had granted Richard for life.[3]

With the coming of June, the host began to pour across the channel into Calais from all the Kentish ports. Numbering some 1,500 men-at-arms and 11,000 archers, supported by a great train of artillery and fifteen surgeons, it was 'the finest army', says Commynes, 'that ever King of England led into France'. With Edward and Clarence, Richard crossed to Calais on July 4. Two days later, their sister Margaret, Duchess of Burgundy, arrived to wish them well and bring them handsome presents. Richard and Clarence escorted her back to St. Omer, where they apparently remained for some days, awaiting the arrival of Margaret's erratic husband.

The fact was, instead of preparing his forces these past months for the grand assault on Louis XI, Duke Charles had marched eastward in a fit of anger to besiege the insignificant city of Neuss. Charles was not called 'The Rash' for nothing. Even Commynes, who knew him intimately, could only explain this fantastic blunder by suggesting that God had troubled his senses. It was not until the 14th of July that he appeared at Calais, and then, in place of a great army, he was accompanied only by a bodyguard. He eked out his resources, however, with enthusiasm. Edward's host was magnificent enough, he declared, to march not only through France but to the very gates of Rome. Edward had but to sweep across Normandy to Champagne and there Charles would join him with his forces, which had just broken off the siege of Neuss to pillage the dukedom of Lorraine.[4]

King Edward maintained his cordiality to the Duke but ignored his grandiose suggestions. He took counsel with Richard and his other commanders. It was decided finally that since the Count of St. Pol had offered to deliver up St. Quentin, the army had best begin its campaign by establishing a base in that city. Charles proved perfectly agreeable. As Edward marshalled his great host and set out towards Doullens and Peronne, Charles rode over to St. Omer to rejoin his Duchess, and Richard, as well as a number of other English lords, went with him—perhaps it would still be possible to salvage something from the Duke's promises besides enthusiasm. Edward marched the army very slowly, feeling his way, thinking about his situation. Two nights the English spent upon the field of Agincourt: whatever martial hopes that sojourn inspired in his soldiers, Edward knew that Louis XI would never be manœuvred into such a disaster as had befallen the French sixty years before. Duke Charles was paying one of his frequent brief visits to the English army when, on August 11, it approached the walls of St. Quentin. No sooner had the first troops come into range than the guns of the town opened fire. St. Pol had turned his coat again. Word arrived, in the meanwhile, that King Louis had advanced from Beauvais to Compiègne at the head of a powerful army.

Next morning, Duke Charles rode away to resume command of his forces. Edward had lost all faith in him. The English King probably had no doubt that he could win a victory, perhaps a great victory, but without the aid of Burgundy he knew that he could not exploit it; and since he had almost run out of money and Louis had ruthlessly laid waste the countryside, it was even possible that he might not be able to recover from it.

Deciding to test Louis' desire for peace, he had some of his councillors drop a hint in the ears of a captured nobleman who was then returned to the French King. It was all that Louis needed. 'Ah Holy Mary', he had cried in desperation on learning that Edward and Charles were about to descend on him, 'even now when I have given thee 1,400 crowns, thou dost not help me one white'.[5] Leaping at the opening Edward had given him, he proposed that ambassadors from both sides meet halfway between the armies and he assured Edward that he would make him a very attractive offer for peace. The English King summoned a great council of his commanders and councillors—the Dukes of Gloucester and Clarence, Norfolk and Suffolk, the Marquess of Dorset, the Earls of Northumberland, Pembroke, and Rivers, Lords Hastings, Stanley, Howard, and others.

A considerable majority favoured making peace with France. But the Duke of Gloucester was not among them. In speaking against the abandonment of the war, Richard was, for the first time, opposing a policy of his brother. Doubtless he nursed no illusions about Edward's ability to conquer France; he probably contended that after so many taxes imposed and so many hopes aroused, the English should seek battle with Louis XI in order to treat with him as victors.

Edward, however, had made up his mind. On the morning of August 15 his ambassadors met with those of Louis at a village not far from Amiens. The terms the English brought with them were accepted at once: in return for the immediate withdrawal of the English army from France and a seven years' truce and intercourse of merchandise, Louis XI agreed to pay King Edward 75,000 gold crowns at once and 50,000 crowns a year; to marry the Dauphin to Edward's eldest daughter Elizabeth; and to sign a private amity which bound both Kings to take the part of the other against rebellious subjects.[6] Three days later, having heard the rumour of what was going forward, Charles of Burgundy came storming into Edward's camp. Furiously he accused Edward of perfidy and taunted him with the victories won by other English Kings in France. Then he flung away, declaring that he would have no part of Edward's peace.

But King Louis was now the very monarch of hospitality. He threw open the town of Amiens to the English troops. Outside the city gates he planted an array of tables adorned with venison pasties and the finest potables. After the English troops had quenched their martial ardours in Louis' wine, they marched to the village of Picquigny, where a bridge had been thrown across the river Somme. On this the two Kings met face to face, each accompanied by a dozen attendants. With Edward were the Duke of Clarence and other peers, but not the Duke of Gloucester. Having resolutely opposed the treaty, Richard would not be a party to its signing. Far from valuing his younger brother the less for his opposition, Edward pointedly bestowed on him a fine grant of estates.[7]

The English King strode on to the bridge at Picquigny a magnificent figure, displaying a black velvet cap gleaming with a jewelled fleur-de-lys and a gown of cloth of gold lined with red satin. Louis . . . Louis cared nothing for the accessories of power. He wore a motley costume of everything and nothing—like a mountebank, some said. His trusted adviser Commynes had been given the doubtful honour of dressing in precisely the same costume in order to halve the danger of assassination. The two Kings advanced to the wooden barrier which had been erected in the middle of the bridge, half bowed to each other, embraced through the bars, spoke some words of greeting, and, with their hands on a piece of the True Cross, signed the treaty. Motioning their attendants to draw back, they then talked together for some minutes with great cordiality, before making their farewells.

Louis was eager to win as many friends at the English court as he could. With Edward's knowledge and consent, the chief councillors of England accepted handsome pensions from the French King, which they preferred to call tribute. The largest pension, 2,000 crowns a year, went to the King's most intimate friend, William Lord Hastings.

Any who looked upon the peace with unfriendly eyes, Louis anxiously sought to placate. When Commynes reported that Louis de Bretaylle, a favourite captain of Edward's, had remarked that though his King had won nine victories, his present defeat was a disgrace which outweighed them all, Louis hastened to invite de Bretaylle to dinner and made him a splendid offer to enter the service of France. When this was refused, he bestowed on him 1,000 crowns, promised to favour his brother, and bade him a warm farewell, Commynes whispering in his ear a plea to work for the continuance of peace.

With what eagerness, then, did Louis seek to exercise his arts upon Richard, Duke of Gloucester, the King's martial brother who had so strongly opposed the treaty. Richard politely accepted an invitation to dine with Louis in Amiens and 'received from him, as a courtesy when it could not be taken as a bribe, a present of plate and fine horses suitable to his rank and station'.[8] But Richard was too plain and inflexible a personality to respond in kind to Louis' easy camaraderie. Louis felt that he had failed to make an impact upon the Duke of Gloucester. Henceforth, Richard was marked in his mind as an enemy of France—an impression which, to Richard's cost, he would pass on to his successor.

In early September Richard recrossed the channel. It is unlikely that, before leading his forces back to Yorkshire, he paused in London. Edward's affection had not been lessened by Richard's opposition, nor Richard's loyalty by Edward's disregard of his advice. Yet a residue of feeling was doubtless left in Richard's mind. It represented not a rift but a shadow, a portent, a symbol of the alteration Richard had begun to sense in his brother's character, of an alienation it was impossible to arrest. The distance between the moors of Wensleydale and the Woodville court was measured in more than miles.

By the time Richard reached Middleham, the last of Edward's great army, its mettle untested, had returned to England.

Passing and repassing through Calais in their pride of plumes, banners, and armour, almost all the men of this host have forever faded; whereas one quiet merchant dwelling in the town, a man with a gentle heart and a lively humour, has preserved, fresh and blooming against time's decay, a single moment of his life—when, composing a letter to the thirteen-year-old girl he will subsequently marry, he hears his friends impatiently calling him to come down to dinner and smiles and finishes his missive. . . .

'And if ye would be a good eater of your meat alway', Thomas Betson tells his little Katherine, 'that ye might wax and grow fast to be a woman, ye should make me the gladdest man of the world, by my troth: for when I remember your favour and your sad [sincere] loving dealing towards me, for sooth ye make me even very glad and joyous in my heart: and on the other side again [i.e., the reverse of joyous] when I remember your young youth. And therefore I pray you, even as you love me, to be merry and to eat your meat like a woman. . . . I pray you, greet well my horse, and pray him to give you four of his years to help you with all: and I will at my coming home give him four of my years. . . . Tell him that I prayed him so. . . . Commend me to the Clock, and pray him to amend his unthrifty manners: for he strikes ever in undue time, and he will be ever afore. . . . I trust to you that he shall amend against my coming, the which shall be shortly with all hands and all feet, with God's grace. . . . And Almighty Jesus make you a good woman, and send you many good years and long to live in health and virtue to His pleasure. [Written] at great Calais, on this side on the sea, the first day of June, when every man was gone to his Dinner, and the clock smote nine, and all our household cried after me and bade me come down; come down to dinner at once! And what answer I gave them, ye knew it of old'.[9]

As Thomas Betson, Merchant of the Staple, watched the soldiers of King Edward's army re-embark in Calais harbour, he doubtless heard many a disgruntled mutter. They brought home with them neither booty nor glorious scars. The men who had stayed in England grouched also. Though Edward put as good a face as he could upon the truce, the taxpayers grumbled that they had paid for victories, not truces; and they were soon angrily protesting to the King that his disbanded troops were working off their martial spirits by robbery and murder on the highways.

Edward took prompt and thorough action. He journeyed watchfully about his kingdom with his judges 'and no one, not even his own domestic, did he spare, but instantly had him hanged if he was found to be guilty of theft or murder'.[10] In a short space he had reduced the realm to order by these vigorous measures, and it was not long before his subjects were regarding him with as deep an affection as ever.

In truth, the King had brilliantly solved the dilemma which Henry V had bequeathed to the fifteenth century. By invading France only to sell a truce at an immense price, Edward accomplished two ends: he had set off on the military expedition his subjects demanded and had humbled France; but instead of burdening his people with the immense taxes and inevitable futility of a partial conquest, he secured to himself an annuity which enabled him to dispense with parliamentary grants and to strengthen the powers of his government. The Kings who came after him could do no better than to emulate this policy.

Shortly after he reached home, Edward extracted 50,000 additional crowns from King Louis as a ransom for Margaret of Anjou. When she finally returned to the land of her birth in the following March, she had not only to relinquish all her pretensions in England but resign to Louis—as payment, he said, for all the help he had given her—her rights of inheritance from her father. With the small pension he doled out she retired to one of her father's estates, on which she lived, brokenhearted, until her death in August of 1482. As soon as Louis heard of her demise, he wrote to demand all her dogs: 'She has made me her heir, and . . . this is all I shall get. I pray you not to keep any back, for you would cause me a terribly great displeasure'.[11]

If the magnates of the kingdom of England had lost the opportunity of displaying their bravery on the fields of France, bravery of quite a different sort one of the sheriffs of London had had occasion to witness not long before. Though it was more than half a century since the Church, with the fanatical encouragement of Henry V, had carried on a campaign of persecution and fire to extinguish the followers of Wyclif, lollardry still persisted, particularly among the humble artisans in towns and villages, and on occasion a victim was still seized by the ecclesiastical authorities. John Goos, a lollard sentenced to be burnt at Tower Hill for heresy, 'before dinner was delivered unto Robert Byllydon, one of the sheriffs, to put in execution the same afternoon; where he, like a charitable man, had him home to his house, and there exhorted him that he should die a Christian man, and renounce his false errors. But that other, after long exhortation heard, required the sheriff that he might have meat, for he said that he was sore hungered. Then the sheriff commanded him meat, whereof he took as [if] he had ailed nothing and said to such as stood about him, "I eat now a good and competent dinner, for I shall pass a little sharp shower ere I go to supper". And when he had dined, he required that he might shortly be led to his execution'.[12]

It was some such fate as this which many of Edward's subjects wished for the royal councillors who had gone to France; for though the people could not help taking the King again to their hearts, they nursed anger against the men who had advised him to make a truce with Louis and who had taken the French King's gold.[13] The popularity of Richard of Gloucester, on the other hand, grew the greater for his refusal to be a party to the treaty.

For a year and a half he now stayed clear of the court and devoted himself to his family, his estates, the Marches, and the men of the North.[14]*

When he journeyed to London early in 1477, it was at the urgent summons of the King, who required his counsel. Out of the sudden misfortune of Burgundy, the guile of Louis XI, the intrigues of the Woodvilles, was developing the train of circumstances which would induce the explosion of that brilliant and unstable star, the Duke of Clarence.

III

IT is hard to be the brother of a King. To share the blood royal, but not the throne. To be almost everything, and therefore nothing. The French title suits him best: 'Monsieur'. A delicate irony plays in that title, the shadow of amusement. Monsieur must be otherwise nameless because he bears the royal name. King's brother is an occupation without duties but with a thousand temptations. Ambition is his birthright, and conspiracy is the only refreshment of his envy. The pages of history are crowded with his trouble-making and his treacheries. Even now the brothers of Louis XI and of James III of Scotland were playing their own spirited variations on this pregnant theme, which George of Clarence so furiously and fertilely embellished.

To the inevitable disabilities of King's brother, Clarence added a remarkably shallow character. Some of it must have been inherited from his shadowy grandfather, that feckless Earl of Cambridge who indulged in a foolish plot to overthrow Henry V and was promptly beheaded at Southampton in 1415. Clarence was almost as handsome and striking a figure as his brother Edward; he was unusually eloquent; he was capable of radiating a golden charm; and he was incapable of forgetting that a Lancastrian Parliament had once passed a bill regulating the succession in terms of which he could now look upon himself as King.

When Clarence returned from the expedition to France, he was, for the time being, quiescent. But he was only readying his lance to tilt at the first windmill, and it was soon flashing on the horizon. His Duchess, Isabel, died on December 22, 1476, not long after giving birth to a son who very shortly followed her to the grave. Two weeks later there occurred a more spectacular death, one that startled the monarchs of

Europe. On January 5, 1477, in the snow before the walls of Nancy, which in fury and despair he had been besieging, was finally snuffed out that fiery particle, Charles the Rash, Duke of Burgundy. He left behind him a daughter Mary, the greatest heiress of Europe. And who was happier to receive this news than Louis XI? He promptly announced that the County and the Duchy of Burgundy had reverted to the Crown of France; and he prepared to launch his armies, not only to overrun those territories but to claim as many of the rich towns lying north of the river Somme as he could put his hands on.

For King Edward, the news was extremely grave. The cities of Flanders were the keystone of English trade. Burgundy was the traditional ally of England, the means of ensuring that Louis gave no trouble and continued to pay his 50,000 crowns a year. As soon as the King received these unpalatable tidings, he summoned a Great Council to meet on February 13. Richard and Clarence both arrived 'in all haste' a day or two after the meetings had begun.[1] What advice Richard offered the King is unknown; in view of his previous attitude towards Louis XI, it is likely that he spoke for taking a strong stand against Louis' determination to dismember Burgundy. Edward and his council, however, temporized. They would support Duke Charles' heiress as best they could without openly opposing the King of France. Messages were hastily sent to Edward's sister Margaret, Dowager Duchess of Burgundy. Negotiations were opened with the heiress Mary. Envoys were also dispatched to Louis XI, but their object was only to suggest that the seven years' truce be extended to endure the lifetime of both Kings. Meanwhile the Duke of Clarence had grown ripe with secret hopes and private visions.

The Dowager Duchess Margaret, it turned out, had very definite proposals to make. Her favourite brother George represented, in her eyes, the solution to the problem. Having been conveniently widowed, he could now wed Mary. The marriage would keep Burgundy firmly in the English orbit, and Clarence could at last experience the bliss of wearing, if not a crown, the most splendid coronet in Europe. This was the substance of Clarence's visions. But there were breath-taking extensions to this substance, of which Edward and his ministers remained as yet unaware. Clarence, and possibly Duchess Margaret, looked upon the marriage to Mary as but a stepping stone. Clarence would use the splendid resources of his new dukedom to achieve his rightful position as King of England.

What Richard thought of his sister Margaret's proposal has not been recorded. King Edward, however, at once quietly quashed it. Mary herself was of like mind. What she needed was a great prince to defend her dominions against Louis XI and she had no inclination to give her hand to an English Duke who could bring her nothing except trouble. So Edward's refusal was unnecessary. But Clarence's cup of bitterness spilled over; for he persuaded himself that Mary would certainly have married him if his spoil-sport brother had not ruined everything.

He proceeded to make himself as unpleasant as possible. He rarely appeared at court in the succeeding weeks; when he appeared, he ostentatiously refused meat and drink, as if he suspected poison. From noblemen such as Lord Dynham he was extorting money for his schemes by threats and intimidation.[2] He glowered upon everybody, but particularly upon the Woodvilles. For by this time he had got wind of the fact that King Edward had put forward as a candidate for Mary's hand the Queen's brother Anthony, Earl Rivers. Mary refused the Earl even more peremptorily than she had refused the Duke, and Edward no doubt was content enough. He had proposed Rivers only at the entreaties of his Queen, who was almost always able to persuade him to gratify her insatiable ambitions for her family.

To Clarence this proposal was the pitch of the intolerable. On April 12, at Layford in Somersetshire, two of his bravos, backed by eighty armed men, smashed into the dwelling of Ankarette Twynyho, who had been an intimate servant of the Duke's dead wife, and forcibly carried her off to Warwick. Here Clarence had judges and jurors in his pocket. Ankarette was hailed before the Justices of the Peace, charged with having poisoned the Duchess of Clarence, and promptly condemned by the jury, 'for fear and great menaces and doubt of loss of their lives and goods'. Protesting her innocence to the last, she was hustled to the gallows and hanged; and hanged with her was one John Thuresby of Warwick on the charge of having poisoned the Duchess's infant son. Though the windings of Clarence's mind are obscure, his principal motive was obvious: to suggest that Ankarette Twynyho had been suborned by the Woodvilles or by the King to strike a dastardly blow at the noble Duke of Clarence. Beyond its terrible brutality, this deed of Clarence's had a sinister connotation which Edward could not miss. Clarence had taken the King's justice into his own hands, as if indeed he were King.[3]

The last shreds of Edward's amazing patience were gnawed away by the Woodvilles. The blood of the Queen's father and her brother John still glistened on Clarence's hands. Now the opportunity for the long deferred revenge had at last arrived. Elizabeth and her kindred had their servants everywhere, their agents, their tale-bearers. The King's ear was assaulted by stories of Clarence's evil ambitions, by rehearsals of the injuries he had done the Woodvilles. The Queen feared, reports a contemporary, 'that her offspring by the King would never come to the throne, unless the Duke of Clarence were removed'.4*

Clarence's downfall began obliquely. An Oxford clerk, John Stacey, was accused of sorcery. In his confession he in turn accused another Oxford clerk, Thomas Blake, who was of no importance, and one Thomas Burdett, who was of immense importance because he was a trusted member of Clarence's household. Arraigned on a charge of disseminating treasonable writings and of attempting to procure the King's death by necromancy, Burdett was tried before a commission of lords and condemned to death on May 19. Before he was hanged the following day, Burdett passionately protested his innocence.

Thus had King Edward given his brother a stiff warning. But warnings were lost on the Duke. As soon as Edward went to Windsor, he burst in upon the King's council at Westminster, bringing with him Dr. John Goddard—the very minorite preacher who had proclaimed Henry VI's title to the throne at Paul's Cross in September of 1470—and forthwith ordered Goddard to read Burdett's last protest. From this rash defiance Clarence soon rushed into wilder acts. He gathered followers in his halls, he sent his servants about the land to declare that the King resorted to the Black Art and poisoned his subjects by craft, he cried fiercely that the King meant to consume him 'as a candle consumeth in burning, whereof he would in brief time quyte [requite] him'. To season his own claim to the throne, he spread the tale that Edward was a bastard and he struck at the Woodvilles by impugning the validity of Edward's marriage. Finally, having ordered his retainers and followers to 'be ready in harness within an hour warning . . . to levy war against the King', he managed to stir up a small rising in Cambridgeshire and Huntingdonshire, which soon flickered out.5*

At this moment, early June of 1477, Edward received further confirmation—if more was needed—of his brother's treason. It was Louis XI who completed the downfall of Clarence. Out of pure friendship—Louis enjoyed making Edward miserable—he reported to the King of England what his spies had learned in Burgundy—that Clarence had sought the hand of Mary only as a means of seizing the English crown.6

Edward summoned Clarence to appear before him in the palace of

Westminster. In the presence of the Lord Mayor of London, he accused his brother of subverting the laws of the realm and presuming to take justice into his own hands. Then abruptly calling his guards, he consigned the malcontent Duke to the Tower.

Richard had returned to Yorkshire before Clarence was committed to prison. By October he had again journeyed to London on the King's business, and on a more poignant mission.[7]* For him, and for Edward too, the approach of the Christmas of 1477 offered little cheer. Its festivity was haunted by a live ghost, their brother George, who lay miserable in a stone chamber while the Woodvilles made merry.

The gaiety of court was heightened by the imminent marriage of Edward's second son Richard and given a new flavour by a recent venture of Anthony, Earl Rivers. At the sign of the Red Pale—a building which stood in a court of almshouses some yards west of Westminster abbey—William Caxton had printed on November 18 *The Dictes and Sayings of the Philosophers*, a translation by Rivers of a French manuscript which Louis de Bretaylle had given him during a pilgrimage to St. James of Compostella. When Caxton, not many months before, had finally returned to the land of his birth, he had been recommended by Duchess Margaret of Burgundy not only to the King, who was to become his patron, but to her favourite brother, to whom he had already dedicated an edition he had printed in Flanders of *The Game and Play of the Chess*—a pastime requiring precisely those qualities of mind which Clarence lacked. But Caxton had found the Duke in no position to help him and the talented Earl Rivers ready with a manuscript which he was pleased to offer. The volume that the court was now curiously inspecting was probably the first book printed in England.

Meanwhile, against the mumming and the music of the Christmas entertainments, Richard pleaded with King Edward for George's life. That the Duke of Clarence was the prime architect of his own ruin, Richard must have recognized; but he was moved by a loyalty spun in childhood, the force of a primal affection. Bitterly moved, too, by his knowledge that it was the omnivorous Woodvilles—the tribe that had shut him off from his royal brother and stained Edward's greatness—who were triumphantly pushing Clarence towards the abyss of death. But Edward, touched though he must have been by Richard's pleas and his own pangs of regret, remained curiously inflexible. Though forgiving brother George had become well nigh a habit with him, some action or word of Clarence's had enabled the Woodvilles to hold him to his resolve—perhaps the Duke's dangerous assertion that the royal marriage, and hence the royal heir, were illegitimate.[8]*

The Christmas season was crowned on January 15, 1478, by the marriage festivities of the Duke of York, aged four, and Anne Mowbray, aged six, the heiress of the House of the Dukes of Norfolk. After the ceremony in St. Stephen's chapel, Richard, Duke of Gloucester, dipped into golden basins filled with coins and threw a largesse to the onlookers. Then he and Henry, Duke of Buckingham, escorted the little bride to the King's great chamber for the wedding banquet. A week later, a joust was held at Westminster. The chief challengers were the Queen's eldest son by her previous marriage, the Marquess of Dorset (formerly, Sir Thomas Grey), and the Queen's brother Anthony, Earl Rivers (formerly, Lord Scales), first knight of the tourney. One of the three principal prizes was won by Richard Haute, a relative of the Queen's, and the most splendid figure of the day was Earl Rivers, 'horsed and armed in the habit of a white hermit' complete with his hermitage 'walled and covered with black velvet'. This gorgeous spectacle, Richard took no part in, nor even attended. Tournaments, like everything else, had become the special preserve of the Woodvilles.[9]

The day after Anne Mowbray's wedding, January 16, Parliament convened to try George of Clarence on an attainder of high treason. It proved to be a terrible occasion—the House of York rending its own flesh in public. Nobody accused the Duke except the King. Nobody answered the King's accusations except the Duke. Edward rehearsed the story of Clarence's repeated treacheries and of his own repeated acts of forgiveness. Even now, he declared with feeling, he would have pardoned his brother if Clarence had made due submission; but Clarence had proved incorrigible and he was therefore forced to act for the safety of the realm. There was no question of the Duke's guilt. On February 7, the Duke of Buckingham, who was appointed High Steward for the occasion, passed the sentence of death upon Clarence.[10]

Yet now Edward's heart failed him; or perhaps Richard's pleas held his hand. Torn by doubts, he hesitated for ten days. But the Woodvilles had their way.[11] On February 18, the Speaker of the Commons came to the bar of the Lords and requested that whatever was to be done should be done at once. On the same day, George, Duke of Clarence, was privately executed in the Tower, none knows how. The execution was a formal one, however; Clarence was informed of his imminent end and accorded the usual rites of the condemned. He was extinguished— or his body afterwards immersed—in a vat of his favourite Malmesey wine. Perhaps this bizarre ending was at his own wild, desperate, contemptuous request.[12]*

The King preserved the earldom of Warwick for Clarence's heir and carefully supervised the welfare of his daughter Margaret. On Richard's little son Edward was bestowed the dignity of the earldom of Salisbury. Richard himself was given the office of Great Chamberlain, which he had relinquished to Clarence in 1472. He gained, however, no benefit of lands from Clarence's death. True, he received the fee-farm and castle of Richmond, which fifteen years before he had resigned to his envious brother, but this grant came to him merely in exchange for the manors of Sudeley, Farley and Corff, which he relinquished to the King. Edward kept most of Clarence's estates in his own hand. The Marquess Dorset received some toothsome tit-bits of offices and profits.[13]*

Three days after Clarence was executed, Richard secured a license to found two colleges, one at Barnard castle and one at Middleham. Their purpose was to house priests and choristers who would pray for the King and Queen, for Richard and Anne and their little son, and for the souls of the King's deceased brothers and sisters, of whom Clarence was now one.[14]

IV

IT is hard to be the brother of a King. . . .

The Duke of Gloucester was an anomaly.

During these years of strife with brother George, the invasion of France, and unhappy and enforced journeys to Westminster, Richard had been transforming the unruly North—rife with intermingled Lancastrian sympathies, memories of the House of Neville, and habitual subservience to the Percies—into a land of comparative peace and order, reconciled to the House of York and devoted to himself.

He left Westminster soon after Clarence's execution. He was back at Middleham before the end of March.[1] With all speed he had withdrawn into his own country and would remain there as long as he was able. The North was the touchstone of happiness and fulfillment; the South meant trouble, unease, division of spirit. So, to Richard's undoing, would it always mean.

During the next four years he rode to London only twice: once to pay a brief visit to his sister Margaret, Dowager Duchess of Burgundy, who came to England in the summer of 1480, and again in the early spring of 1481 to advise with the King concerning the Scots war.[2] Yet, hidden though he was from the gaze of the kingdom his work in the North became a byword. An Italian visitor, Dominic Mancini, who arrived in England in 1482, recorded what he was told about the Duke of Gloucester. After the death of Clarence, says Mancini, 'he came very rarely to court. He kept himself within his own lands and set out to acquire the loyalty of his people through favours and justice. The good reputation of his private life and public activities powerfully attracted the esteem of strangers. Such was his renown in warfare, that whenever a difficult and dangerous policy had to be undertaken, it would be entrusted to his direction and his generalship. By these arts Richard acquired the favour of the people, and avoided the jealousy of the queen, from whom he lived far separated'.[3]

When his duties permitted him to be at Middleham, Richard lived with his wife and son the life of a country lord. In his great hall minstrels and players performed for his guests; there were mummings to delight little Edward; he looked to the management of his estates; he encouraged the trade of Middleham by securing a licence from the King for the village to hold two fairs a year.[4]*

Most of the judicial work of his two greatest offices, the Constableship and the Admiralty of England, he delegated to experienced jurists. Dr. William Godyer heard admiralty cases at Horton quay in South-wark or 'in the principal court of Admiralty of England', probably in the White Hall. Godyer also heard cases in the Court of the Constable in the White Hall, as did Master John Aleyn, Doctor of Laws, described, like Godyer, as 'lieutenant or commissary' of the Duke of Gloucester.[5]

Even so, Richard was often called from home by his manifold affairs. As steward of the Duchy of Lancaster north of Trent, he held official residence at Pontefract castle; and a variety of business brought him frequently to his estate of Sheriff Hutton, which was conveniently close to the city of York and the principal manors of the Earl of Northumberland. His most demanding office, however, was the Wardenship of the West Marches, with its supervisory authority over Northumberland's Wardenship of the East and Middle Marches. Though there was a truce with the Scots throughout the 1470's, the borders were often troubled by armed forays and casual hostilities. Richard spent much of his time seeing that the frontier fortresses were properly garrisoned and victualled; he was responsible for the repair of fortifications; he conducted conferences with the Scots regarding breaches of the truce;

he arranged for the exchange of prisoners and the reception of envoys.[6]
Two generations after his death, his accomplishments on the border
were still used as a standard of excellence by which to measure the work
of a warden of the Marches.[7]*

Yet Richard's greatest service and the principal source of the devotion
which he inspired did not lie in his official achievements but in the
pervasive influence he won by his labours as friend and justicer to the
people of Yorkshire. His brother the King had given him, through the
bestowal of powers and estates, pre-eminence beyond Trent. It was by
his own efforts, however, that he became Lord of the North. As the
years passed, men of all classes came increasingly to avail themselves of
his justice and to seek his aid. Richard's council, whose primary function
was to help him govern, developed into a great judicial body, a court of
requests to hear poor men's petitions, a court of equity and arbitration.

Among these councillors were Richard's neighbour, Lord Scrope of
Bolton, who had fought for Warwick against Edward but was now
Richard's devoted adherent; Baron Greystoke, who like Scrope was
related by marriage to the Nevilles; Sir Francis Lovell, Richard's
boyhood friend; Sir James Harrington and Sir William Parre; Sir
Richard Nele, Richard Pygott, and Miles Metcalfe, who were lawyers;
and probably some of the Justices for the Assize of the northern circuit.
For his military affairs and other services demanding bold action,
Richard called upon men like Sir James Tyrell, Sir Ralph Assheton, and
probably Richard Ratcliffe. His secretary was a man of vigorous talents
named John Kendall, the son of a John Kendall who had spent his life
in the service of the House of York.[8]

In these times the lesser gentry and yeomen and peasants who held
manor land by lease or custom were often at the mercy of the baronage,
of neighbours enjoying the protection of a magnate, or of greedy
landlords who found ways to get around the law. The practice of
evicting tenants was beginning its ruthless course; the common law had
grown too rigid, or royal officers were too intimidated, to offer relief
in many cases. Richard's council appears to have acted as a court of
appeal, in which these oppressed classes were able to obtain some relief
of their grievances. Poor tenants, whose only claim to the land they
worked was the immemorial custom of the manor, were upheld against
landlords seeking to dispossess them in order to convert their holdings
from arable into pasture. But the work of the council was not confined
to rectifying economic hardship. Richard 'offered good and indifferent
justice to all who sought it, were they rich or poor, gentle or simple'.

E

He served as arbiter of disputes between individuals, towns, between factions within a town. His decisions were obeyed because he held the chief authority north of Trent; but his verdict was sought because he offered a sympathetic hearing and fair dealing. He was a bestower of aid as well as judgment, aid to all manner of men and causes. In even so relatively minor a matter as the decay of Holy Trinity Priory at York, he was confidently appealed to, since the priory 'without your abundant grace and due reformation will be utterly extinct and expired for ever'.[9]

In almost all his labours, whether on the Marches or in Yorkshire, Richard found it necessary to pay careful heed to Henry Percy, Earl of Northumberland, whose family had once been lords of the North and who was the dominant magnate of the region. The official form of their relationship had been developed by the supreme authority Richard held over all the Marches; by the compact to which Richard and Northumberland had sworn before the King's council in 1473; and by a personal indenture Richard negotiated with the Earl a year later whereby in return for Northumberland's promise of faithful service, he undertook to be his 'good lord'. Royal commissions indicated a rough division of authority: Richard's special domain was Cumberland and Westmorland; the Earl's, the county of Northumberland; both were appointed to commissions for Yorkshire, in which, sometimes, Richard appears only for the West Riding and Northumberland for the East Riding.[10]

Such a parchment partitioning scarcely represented the realities of power, especially since Richard's council had become, by its sheer effectiveness, the first judicial authority of Yorkshire. Richard, therefore, sought to maintain harmony, to associate the Earl with him in judicial cases, to favour his interests and be his friend. In disputes among the gentry he made Northumberland joint arbiter with himself; he saw to it that the city of York consulted him in its affairs; and in the wars against the Scots, Northumberland was always his second-in-command.[11]*

Yet Richard never touched Henry Percy's heart, which was apparently impervious to the sentiment of gratitude. Though the Earl did good service of war on the borders and avoided any overt indication of dissatisfaction or jealousy, he could not forget that the writs of the House of Percy had once run supreme in Yorkshire. It is in his dealings with the city of York that his discontent most clearly appears. His repeated failures to assert the dominance his family had once held over the town he charged to the account of the Duke of Gloucester. Yet for his own sake as well as the King's, Richard could not afford to let Northumberland treat the metropolis of the North as his private preserve; Edward pointedly bade the citizens to do Richard's bidding;[12] and the citizens, in any case, were so whole-heartedly won to Richard by his benevolent dealing that they had no wish to be at the command of the Earl of Northumberland.

It is this intimate association with the city of York which, preserved in the municipal archives, most vividly reveals Richard's life and work in the North.

York, second only to London in dignity and population, was then and for some years to come at the zenith of its medieval greatness. Built upon the ruins of the Roman Eboracum and enjoying its profitable outlet to the sea by the river Ouse, the capital of the North was a thriving city of some 13,000 inhabitants, enclosed in a wall of white stone which was broken by four battlemented and barbicaned gates. Outside the walls nine churches, and three score within, thrust their towers into the air, dominated by the magnificent Minster which had just been brought to completion in 1472. The castle, crowned by a mighty citadel, was beginning to fall into ruin; but numbers of great buildings proclaimed the city's importance: the abbey of St. Mary's, Holy Trinity Priory, friaries of the Four Orders, St. Leonard's Hospital and fifteen smaller hospitals, twelve chantry chapels, Guildhall and the spacious halls of the Merchant Adventurers and Merchant Taylors, and Ouse bridge, with its great arch, its chapel, and its council chamber. Proud of its charter of liberties, the city was governed by a Mayor, a Board of Aldermen and a Council of Twenty-Four. Men like Richard York, who had served as adviser to the King, and Miles Metcalfe, a councillor of the Duke of Gloucester's, were happy to be elected officers of the municipality. Well nigh one hundred different trades offered their wares and services; the Merchant Adventurers of York, founded more than a century before, carried on a lively trade with the Baltic and the Continent, sending their goods down the Ouse for trans-shipment at Kingston-on-Hull, and still other merchants belonged to the powerful fellowship of the Wool Staplers. Traders from the Hanse towns, whose noses were proverbially unrivaled at smelling out profits, were now flocking to the city in order to hawk their Teutonic wares, to the great bitterness of the local merchants. The Easterlings were not quite so unpopular, however, as the Scots. Not infrequently the Mayor was called upon to certify that a citizen 'defamed of the children of iniquity' by being called a Scot was indeed a proper

Englishman. John Harrington, clerk of the city, was so exercised by this ghastly slander murmured against him by Thomas Wharfe that he hastened to solicit testimonials from Sir John Ashe, Lady Fitzhugh, Sir John Conyers, and Sir Robert Harrington that he was no 'false Scot'. 'If this slanderous report', Ashe wrote fiercely, 'come to the ears of some young men of the blood that he [Harrington] is of, it will grieve them, I doubt not, which I pray you desire the said Thomas Wharfe to remember'.

When Richard of Gloucester paid one of his frequent visits to the city, he usually stayed at the house of the Augustinian friars in Lendal. He could always count on a warm welcome from the Mayor and Aldermen, expressed in gifts of tench and pike, wine by the gallon, and 'demain' bread, i.e., *dominus* or lord's bread, a fine milk loaf. Richard and Anne sometimes visited York to enjoy the pageantry of Christmas and Easter; but as friends of the city they were particularly interested in its famous celebration of the festival of Corpus Christi, which, falling on the first Thursday after Trinity Sunday, came in the fine season of late spring. On this day the great cycle of mystery plays was staged by the guilds of the city—some fifty sacred scenes acted by five or six hundred performers. Beginning at dawn, the waggons, marshalled on Toft Green, wound slowly through the streets, pausing to exhibit their Biblical stories before the principal public places from Holy Trinity Priory to the towering Minster and before the homes of those who were rich, or pious, enough to pay a fee for the privilege. The dramas were distributed among the guilds by a certain logic: the shipwrights, fishmongers, and mariners drew on their experience to play the tale of Noah; the goldsmiths made splendid the Three Kings coming from the East; while the vintners handled the miracle at Cana.

The day after Corpus Christi was reserved for the more solemn and stately ceremonial of the Corpus Christi Guild, which had been founded almost three quarters of a century before. During the festival of 1477 Richard and Anne became members of the Guild—twenty-one years after the induction of Richard's mother Cicely. They walked in the procession of ecclesiastics, Guild members, officers of the city and the companies, which, in a dazzle of torches and tapers and crosses and banners, moved from the Priory of Holy Trinity to the Minster. Glittering in their midst was borne the shrine of silver gilt crusted with gems which housed a beryl vase containing the sacred elements. Along the route the fronts of the houses were hung with arras and the doorways strewn with rushes and flowers.

That the Lord of the North and his wife were happy to become members of this Guild of citizens illustrates the intimate relation which Richard had established with the men of York. If they found themselves in trouble or in need, they inevitably turned to the Duke of Gloucester; and the blaze of his great affairs did not blind him to their hopes and anxieties.

When, in 1476, the city fathers desired to sack their clerk, Thomas Yotten, for various peculations, they ran into serious difficulties. Yotten promptly appealed to the Earl of Northumberland for protection, and the Earl showed himself very willing to interfere in the case. The city now turned to Richard, explained the matter to him, and begged him to use his good offices to secure the King's permission for them to dismiss their clerk. At once Richard wrote to Lord Hastings and to Lord Stanley, recounting the dispute at length and asking them to do him the favour to 'move the King's good grace on my behalf'. When the King's serjeants of the law had investigated the case, Edward approved the dismissal of Yotten and gave the city liberty to choose whom they would for the office.

Even in so seemingly trivial a matter as fishgarths, Richard was indefatigable in his service to the magistrates of York; for he recognized that in their eyes the matter was not trivial. Fishgarths were weirs or systems of nets and wicker 'rooms' erected in rivers to trap fish, especially salmon. They were hated by the people because they impeded navigation of the rivers and because they diminished the number of fish a poor man might catch by hook and line. Though for centuries Parliament had sought to limit their size and numbers, powerful elements had always been able to circumvent the law, particularly abbots and bishops who needed plentiful supplies of fish for their clergy. In January of 1463 the corporation of York had been granted the power to supervise fishgarths and remove illegal ones from the rivers Ouse and Humber and their navigable tributaries. But this authority could not cope with vested interests. When, however, in 1475 Parliament strengthened the magistrates' hand, they began to take vigorous measures. They started by showing their commission to Richard of Gloucester. He demonstrated his respect for their authority by dispatching letters to his bailiffs and tenants commanding them instantly to remove all fishgarths that they might have erected. With this powerful support the magistrates proceeded to approach one of the most highly placed offenders, the Bishop of Durham; and they did not fail to point out to the bishop that the Duke of Gloucester had granted to them 'his gracious aid and assistance, and over that' had sent 'his full honourable letters unto his bailees and tenants'. How the Bishop of Durham responded is not on record.

In the autumn of 1477 the city of York became very eager to do something about a weir in the river Aire called Goldale garth, which belonged to the Crown lands of the Duchy of Lancaster. They applied first to the council of the Duchy and then to the King himself; but it was in their good friend Richard that they put their hopes. 'Right high and mighty prince', they wrote to him when he was at London, 'and our full tender and especial good lord, we your humble servants . . . having a singular confidence in your high and noble lordship afore any other, beseecheth . . . your high and good grace to be a mean to the King . . . in these premises, and we, your said humble servants, shall evermore pray to the single "almyfluent" god for your prosperous estate'.

Burdened though he was, not only with councils of state but thoughts of Clarence's impending doom, Richard replied, within a few days of receiving the letter, that he had mentioned the matter to the King, that the King had commanded him, at his next homecoming, to see that all illegal garths were pulled down, and that 'any . . . thing that we may do to the weal of your . . . city we shall put us in our uttermost devoir and good will by God's grace, who keep you'.

As soon as Richard had returned to Middleham after the execution of Clarence, a delegation from York rode to confer with him about fishgarths. Probably at Richard's suggestion, the party then called upon the Earl of Northumberland to discuss the same subject. An elaborate investigation was organized. Richard appointed three representatives— Sir William Redeman, Lord Hastings' brother Ralph, and the escheator of the chamber of York—and Northumberland appointed two, who, with the Mayor and Aldermen and twenty-four attendants, spent four days and nights surveying on horseback and by boat the fishgarths in the Ouse, the Aire, and the Wharfe. Though this outing cost the city £19 4s 3d, it appears that by 1479 many fishgarths had been cast down and public discontent much allayed. But the problem was perennial. Five years later Richard was authorizing a commission to cast down all fishgarths in fresh waters within the county of York.[13]

Richard was no less a good friend to the city in times of real crisis. Not many months after he had returned from the expedition to France, a spirit of restlessness developed in Yorkshire and there were disturbances in York itself, which probably stemmed from the disbanding of the army that had fought no battle. In March of 1476, Richard and Northumberland arrived in the city with 5,000 men to restore order and mete out justice. King Edward apparently desired severe measures to be taken, but Richard effectually interceded for his friends and persuaded his brother not to withdraw the city's charter. As soon as the grateful council learned that the Duke would visit York during Christmas of that year, they decided that 'the Duke of Gloucester shall, for his great labour now late made unto the King's good grace for the confirmation of the liberties of this City be presented, at his coming to the City, with six swans and six pikes'.

When they found themselves entangled in a serious dispute over the mayoralty election of 1482, the men of York again turned to Richard. On St. Blaise's day, January 3, those citizens eligible to vote had chosen between Richard York and Thomas Wrangwysh. As soon as the city government announced that Richard York had won the election, the supporters of Wrangwysh vehemently protested that their candidate was the victor. The quarrel began to assume alarming proportions. When the city magistrates went to the pains of sending a delegation of officials to carry to the King the certification of York's election, Wrangwysh's adherents promptly aired their grievances to the King also. On March 7, Alderman Tong, Miles Metcalfe, the city Recorder, and the rest of the delegation returned from London, bearing the King's command that, until the election had been investigated, York and Wrangwysh were to cease their strife and Robert Amyas was to continue in office as Mayor. Two weeks before, the magistrates had sought to strengthen their position by sending further certificates to the King, the Lord Chancellor, Hastings the Lord Chamberlain, and the Earl of Northumberland, and it was then that they had appealed to Richard of Gloucester to exert his influence in their behalf, in order to secure royal confirmation of York's election. Richard acted so promptly to win Edward's approval that on March 12 the Mayor and Aldermen received notice from Westminster that York was confirmed as Mayor. Two years later Wrangwysh was duly elected to the office. He was apparently the best soldier in the city. It was known to all that he stood high in the favour of Richard of Gloucester. Richard's fondness for Wrangwysh had not deflected him from upholding the dignity and supporting what he must have considered to be the just case of the city government.

On Richard's next visit to York, its officials spared no pains to show their appreciation for what 'the high and mighty prince the Duke of

Gloucester have at all times done for the weal of this city'. First the three chamberlains and the esquire to the Mace rode to the 'Austin' friars and presented Richard with gifts of wine, fish, and demain bread. Then the Mayor and Aldermen in scarlet and the Council of the Twenty-four in 'murry' [mulberry] led a procession of citizens to the friary in order to give their friend 'a laud and a thank of his great labour good and benevolent lordship done before-time for the honour and common weal of this city'.

Yet immediately after Richard left York, a disturbance of some sort occurred in which the alarm bell was rung. It may have sprung from the disputed election or a factional quarrel or have been a manifestation of the general restlessness which seemed to afflict England in the early spring of 1482. The offence committed at York was apparently slight, but on March 21 the city fathers sent a message to Richard explaining the disorder and asking what his pleasure was regarding the culprits whom they had clapped in jail. Richard replied a few days later that in his view they should be delivered from prison. This gentle solution of the problem so delighted the Mayor and his brethren that instantly they decided on Richard's next coming to the city to load his table with two dozen rabbits, six pheasants, one dozen partridges, wine, and demain bread.

Two weeks later Richard gave another demonstration of the respect he felt for the dignity and rights of York. Having learned that Thomas Redeheid, a servant of his treasurer, had bullied and insulted a citizen of York who was on a visit to Middleham castle, Richard took the trouble to send Redeheid to the city in the custody of Sir Ralph Assheton so that he might be punished according to the judgment of the Mayor and Aldermen.

Shortly afterwards, a tailor of the city named John Davyson, who was bitterly at odds with Roger Brere, saddler, could think of no better way of getting his enemy in trouble than to spread the report that Brere had made a jibe against the Duke of Gloucester. The chief men of York were so much disturbed by this gossip that William Melrig, who was falsely alleged to have heard Brere's jibe, was summoned before the Mayor, sheriffs, chamberlains, and a concourse of citizens to make his emphatic denial.

That the language of affection and devotion which the men of York addressed to Richard sincerely reflected their feelings is eloquently demonstrated by the way in which they subsequently dared to brave and defy Henry the Seventh. They were proud of their right of self-government and not afraid to speak their minds. In January of 1483, for example, there occurred a spirited political conversation when a group of citizens were 'sitting at the ale at Eden Berrys, in Gothyrngate'.

The discussion was opened with a lively question: 'Sirs, whom shall we have to our mayor this year?'

One Steven Hoghson answered, 'Sirs, one thing and it please the commons I would we had Master Wrangwysh, for he is the man that my lord of Gloucester will do for'.

Robert Rede, a 'gyrdeler', was quick to retort, 'That may not be, for the Mayor must be chosen by the commonalty, and not by no lord'. It appears that he added, 'My Lord of Gloucester will not be displeased whomsoever it pleases the commons to choose for their Mayor'.[14]

When the time came, in 1480, for Richard to lead the forces of England against the Scots, none served him with more devoted loyalty than the men of York.

V

THE conduct of the war against Scotland was the last of the many services which Richard performed for his royal brother.

Louis XI, eager to keep Edward occupied while he finished off Burgundy, had finally persuaded James III, in the winter of 1479-80, to violate his truce with England and rouse his country to arms. Weak in character as in authority, James was something of a Richard II, with his lowborn favourites, his penchant for the arts, and his disdain of an unruly nobility.

When the Scots began to indulge in large-scale border raiding in the early spring of 1480, King Edward perceived that they meant to make serious trouble and on May 12 appointed Richard as his Lieutenant-General in the North, authorizing him to call up the men of the Marches and adjoining counties. This was a defensive measure; commissions of array for the northern shires only could not produce an army capable of invading Scotland. Yet after the Earl of Angus had penetrated into Northumberland and burned Bamburgh, Richard determined on a limited offensive effort which might check the ardour of the Scots. Early in September he led across the borders a raiding party, which included a stout band from the faithful city of York; and so successful was this brief, sharp campaign that it not only put an end to Scottish incursions for this year but gave Edward an accomplishment

E*

of which he was quick to make use in his attempts to raise money for the war by asking for 'benevolences'.[1]

Before the middle of October, Richard had returned to Yorkshire and was at Sheriff Hutton. He was immediately confronted with a problem that threatened to disturb his relationship with the Earl of Northumberland. The Earl had apparently received word that the Scots might attempt retaliation. On October 13, Northumberland wrote to the magistrates of York from his manor of Wressell, charging them to prepare an armed force 'to be ready to attend upon me . . . as soon as ye have warning, without delay or tarrying, as you will answer at your peril'. The men of the city liked neither the hard-handed peremptoriness of the tone nor the implication that they were at Northumberland's command. They instantly sent an alderman to Sheriff Hutton in order to seek the advice of the Duke of Gloucester. It appears that Richard was able to reassure the city without giving Northumberland cause for complaint. In the following April, King Edward upheld the citizens' desire to look to Richard as their leader by telling them to put their complete faith in his 'entirely beloved brother'.[2]*

Meanwhile, Richard and Northumberland were working together in apparent harmony to prepare the great campaign which Edward and his council had determined to launch against the Scots in the summer of 1481, and which the King himself would command. During the winter Richard was overseeing the repair of the walls of Carlisle, recruiting a large body of men to reinforce the garrisons of the border strongholds, and, with Northumberland, conducting a military census to determine how many men the baronage, gentry, and towns of the North could bring to the field. Towards the end of March, Richard and a number of his councillors arrived in London to perfect the plans for the invasion. He was also concerned, as usual, with befriending the men of the North. When King Edward found the yield from benevolences insufficient to defray the enormous costs of raising an army by indenture, he took the unpopular step of exacting the payment of a parliamentary tax which he had remitted upon his return from France more than five years before. He agreed to exempt, however, the county and city of York because of what they had done the previous year and 'this year trusted to be done'. And because of his brother's plea that the citizens of York were making as great a military effort as their finances allowed, he agreed to be content with the contingent they promised of a captain and 120 archers.[3]

The first blow of the campaign was struck at the beginning of the summer by the fleet, commanded by Lord Howard. Boldly he sailed into the Firth of Forth, captured eight large ships, destroyed many smaller ones, and burned Blackness. But the great attack by land which was to complement this brilliant victory was never launched. Everything waited upon the King's leading his army north to join Richard and his second-in-command, Northumberland, and the King did not come. His health and his energies were failing and the restlessness of his realm made him reluctant to turn his back upon it. His system of extracting benevolences was resented by the well-to-do; his high-handed attempt to collect the parliamentary tax he had years before relinquished was resented by everybody. It was 'adverse turmoil', he confessed in a letter to the Pope, which kept him in the south.[4]

Very little is known of the campaign which Richard waged this summer. He possibly had under his command a few thousand men that the King had raised by indenture, but he was mainly dependent upon the forces of the border garrisons. James the Third, on the other hand, had raised a great army. That it failed to make a serious incursion into northern England indicates the success that Richard and Northumberland achieved in an irregular war of sudden sallies and defensive operations.[5]*

They had returned to Yorkshire when, early in September, there suddenly came word that three Scottish hosts were about to invade England simultaneously. On Friday, September 7, the Earl of Northumberland dispatched messages to his friends and retainers and to the city of York, bidding them hastily assemble men and meet him on the following Monday morning at Northallerton. Next day the men of York were busily arraying a force to answer Northumberland's call, when they received a message from Richard of Gloucester informing them that the Scots were threatening all the Marches and requesting them to meet him with what forces they could muster on the following Thursday at Durham. Instead of setting forth early Monday morning to keep the rendezvous with the Earl, they delayed their departure until Tuesday in order to march as an independent contingent until they put themselves under Richard's banner at Durham. Either the report of the Scots' invasion proved to be false or else Richard's forces quickly repelled it; for nothing more is heard of trouble from the north for the remainder of this year.[6]*

In October Richard rode down to Nottingham to confer with King Edward, who had finally managed to journey that far north. Though the King insisted that in the coming year he would take personal command of an invasion of Scotland, Richard probably realized, even then, that he might have to manage that great effort himself. Upon returning to the North, he laid a foundation for the enterprise by establishing a dogged siege of Berwick, the frontier fortress on the sea which two decades before Margaret of Anjou had surrendered to the Scots.[7]*

As Richard laboured in the first months of 1482 to prepare a powerful offensive he was plagued with difficulties that threatened to wreck the whole campaign. The harvest of the preceding fall had been the worst that England and Europe had known for many years, and the winter which followed had been unusually severe. With all his frontier garrisons running desperately short of food, Richard was forced in February to secure a licence from the King permitting him to purchase grain and vegetables anywhere they might be found in England, Wales or Ireland and at any price he had to pay. Though Wales and Ireland themselves were complaining of starvation, Richard apparently somehow found the means of victualling his forces and maintained his siege of Berwick.

Even more serious was the restlessness which afflicted the country in waves of disorder or discontent. Men with half-filled stomachs were the readier to show their dislike of the King's failure to support Burgundy, their anger against the King's persistence in extracting benevolences and in demanding the payment of the tax. When, late in the winter, disturbances broke out in Northumberland, Richard was empowered to offer the royal pardon to all persons in Tynedale who would duly make submission. Later, a commission of *oyer and terminer* was issued for the city of York itself; but since the commissioners were mostly drawn from the members of Richard's council, with a few from Northumberland's, it seems likely that the commission was called into being mainly to provide a central authority for the North while Richard and Northumberland were leading the warriors of the region against the Scots. In the Duchy of Lancaster, however, affairs were so bad that its council admitted on May 4 that the 'great strifes, variances, controversies, debates' could be remedied 'by no person but only by the King himself'.[8]

Despite these difficulties, Richard was able to push forward his preparations; the people of the North, whatever their discontents, would follow the banner of the Duke of Gloucester. When the fine weather of May approached and the King still showed no signs of moving northward, Richard determined to commence operations himself. His call for men met with a hearty response. The citizens of York at once decided that 'for so much as the said Duke at all times have been benevolent, good and gracious lord to this city, it was thought . . . that it were spedeful and also thankful to his said grace to send unto him a certain people, well and defensibly arrayed. . . .' Though they were already committed to supplying 120 archers later at their own expense, they were able in a few days to send Richard eighty well armed horsemen.[9]

Richard quickly thrust his force across the border, took and burned Dumfries and many a lesser town, then coolly retired before an army could be raised against him. His purpose was doubtless to feel out the preparations of the Scots and to anger them into putting a large army in the field, which he hoped later to bring to a decisive battle.

By the beginning of June he was hastening southward to meet King Edward, who was promising action and who had found a new ally for him. The Duke of Albany, a Clarence in kilt, had three years before fled to France after plotting against his brother King James. In April of 1482 Edward, dangling a crown before his eyes, persuaded Albany to come to England; but he put off making any definite promises until he had conferred with his brother. By this time Edward had admitted to himself that he could not lead an army northward; he must depend upon Richard for the invasion of Scotland.

Richard met Albany and King Edward within the familiar walls of Fotheringhay castle. Though he probably had small confidence in Albany's chances of supplanting James III, he readily approved Edward's plan. On June 11 an agreement was concluded, in which Albany promised, when he was set upon the throne by Richard, to do homage to the King of England for his crown, to sign a treaty of peace, and to give up the fortress of Berwick and certain border lands in the West.

With anxious eyes King Edward watched his loyal, vigorous brother set out northward with the Duke of Albany. His health was now too precarious for campaigning.[10] He had given Richard a pliant traitor, for what the gift was worth; he had provided him with some contingents raised by indenture. Harried by the discontents in the realm and by his realization that the failure to support Burgundy might soon cost him dear, he could only return wearily to London hoping that his brother would somehow provide him with the victory he so badly needed to recover his prestige. He had renewed Richard's commission as Lieutenant General; he now sent him £200 for the transport of his ordnance, £100 for draught horses, and 200 marks with which to pay for 2,000 sheaves of arrows.

Meanwhile, the magistrates of York, undaunted by the early hour at which, they had learned, Richard planned to reach the city, made great preparations to show the brother of James III the esteem in which they held the Duke of Gloucester. On June 17 they agreed that 'all the aldermen, in scarlet, and the Twenty-four, in crimson, and every other man of craft in the city in their best array shall be [ready the following morning]—the aldermen and Twenty-four by four of the clock, and every other of the city by three of the clock—at Miklyth Barr, to attend of my lord's of Gloucester good grace, and of the Duke of Albany, upon the pain of every alderman that make default 12d and every commoner that make default 6d. And that my said lords shall be presented with demain bread, ten gallons of wine, two great pikes, two tenches, and six bremes'.[11]

Soon after this hearty reception, the municipal contingent of armed men was moving northward under Richard's banners. The Earl of Northumberland had tried a new tactic this time in his attempt to bring the citizens within the orbit of his power. He had made a request that in addition to the force which they were supplying to the Duke of Gloucester at their own expense, they should send him as many men as they could, who would receive the King's wages. Since the city, because of the contribution it had made to Richard's raid in May, had secured permission from him to reduce its quota to 100 archers, it is doubtful if there were any extra men available for the Earl.[12]

Before the end of July, Richard stood at the gates of Berwick with an army that perhaps numbered 20,000 men, including nine surgeons headed by the King's own physician, Master William Hobbes. The town was speedily forced to yield, but the citadel of the castle continued to hold out. Meanwhile, James the Third, stung by the burning of Dumfries, had gathered a large army and was advancing southward. As he reached Lauder, he was suddenly seized by his discontented magnates. After they had hanged his favourites from Lauder bridge, they clapped him into Edinburgh castle as their prisoner.

The moment he got word of the Scots' approach, Richard, with Northumberland as second-in-command, led the English host to meet them, leaving Lord Stanley with a force to continue the siege of Berwick castle. The Scots lords had no stomach, however, to fight a pitched battle. As Richard swept northward, burning towns and villages in his attempt to provoke an engagement, the enemy retired to Haddington, eighteen miles east of their capital. By the last day of July, Richard had captured Edinburgh without the loss of a man, and so firm was his authority over the army that neither goods nor inhabitants were molested.[13]* The moment he had brought the city under full control, he set out to attack the enemy army at Haddington; but on August 2 the Scots lords sent a message confessing that so far as they were concerned the war was over and asking his terms for a truce and a renewal of the marriage treaty, in which Edward's daughter Cicely had been pledged to the heir of James the Third.

In the present anarchical state of Scottish affairs, however, a treaty could mean little; Edward had already half promised Cicely to the Duke of Albany; and whatever their differences, the men of Scotland, Richard had become aware, would not accept Albany as their King. He therefore replied that before there was talk of a treaty the lords must return all the money which Edward had paid towards Cicely's dower and must pledge to leave Berwick castle to its fate. At the same time, he permitted Albany to seal a bargain with the Chancellor of Scotland, whereby, in return for a full pardon and restitution of his estates, he agreed to swear allegiance to his brother James. Accurately forecasting that the fickle Duke would soon be stirring up more trouble, Richard contented himself with having Albany sign an oath to keep faith with the King of England! On August 4, the magistrates of Edinburgh made their conqueror an offer: if he would withdraw peaceably from the city, they promised that in case King Edward no longer wished Cicely to marry James' heir, they would themselves refund every penny of the dowry money in yearly instalments.[14]

By this time Richard's supplies must have been running low, his men becoming restless, his communications imperilled; the Scots would not fight a battle and were in no condition to sign a treaty. On the other hand, Scotland had now been taught a convincing lesson of English superiority in arms. Deciding to accept the city's offer as an acknowledgment of his triumph, Richard speedily led his army back to Berwick, where Lord Stanley was still pushing on the siege of the citadel. Before the assembly of his whole host 'in Hutton Field beside Berwick', Richard on August 12 bestowed knighthood or the dignity of knight banneret on a number of officers who had especially distinguished themselves and distributed suitable rewards to the rank-and-file.[15] Then with an eye to King Edward's mounting expenses, he dismissed most of the men to their homes, keeping only a force sufficient to press the assault of the castle. A band of Scots made a show of descending upon him to raise the siege, but he coolly stood his ground and they retired with alacrity. On August 24 the castle fell. The great fortress which King Edward had so long yearned to repossess, was at last won back.

The happiest man in the kingdom was the King. So starved was he for good news that, copying an innovation of Louis XI's, he had established a system of express couriers along the 335 mile route from London to Berwick 'to do us service in our messages between us and our brother. . . .' The moment he learned of the capture of Edinburgh, Edward jubilantly published the news of Richard's accomplishment. The Lieutenant of Calais ordered a procession, a firing of the guns, and 'at night bonfires to be made at every man's door as was on midsummer night'. When the crowning word came, the day after its fall, that Berwick was his, the King not only spread the tidings among his subjects but immediately wrote a long, exultant letter to the Pope, in which he thanked 'God, the giver of all good gifts, for the support received from our most loving brother, whose success is so proven that he alone would suffice to chastise the whole kingdom of Scotland'.[16]

In the middle of November, Edward sent out writs for a Parliament to convene on the following January 20. Some time before Christmas, Richard arrived in London to receive the thanks of his brother and to lay plans for the future.[17] Well was it for Edward that Richard had provided a great victory; during the Christmas season the King received from across the channel the evil tidings he had been dreading.

VI

THOUGH Richard must have been pleased by the acclaim which greeted him in London and moved by the almost pathetic gratitude of his brother, he was a man in an alien land. Edward's court he could not stomach; and Edward himself—the happy-valiant Prince whom he had followed as his lodestar—had slipped away, had altered, had been sundered from him. It was more than age which had weakened Edward, and the coarsening of his once magnificent figure represented a subtler deterioration.

He had come to a throne enfeebled and discredited to rule over a realm racked by a generation of baronial irresponsibility and sunk in habitual disorder. Within fifteen years he had freed the crown from the domination of the lords, and in invigorating the power of the monarch, he had infused new strength into the monarchy. He paved his way to this success by solving brilliantly four great problems of government. Wales, that father of troubles, he had brought under control by creating the Council of the Welsh Marches; the loyalty of the turbulent North he had won by making his brother Richard lord of the region; and the solution he had found for the dilemma of France aided him in solving that domestic dilemma of finances which had confounded his predecessors for more than two and a half centuries. His subjects expected him to govern strongly and yet were unwilling to give him the means to maintain his government. 'Money,' remarks Thomas More, 'is the only thing that withdraweth the hearts of Englishmen from the Prince.'[1] The 50,000 crowns which arrived yearly from King Louis helped to make Edward independent of parliamentary grants. His shrewd managing of his resources did the rest. Customs regulations were stringently enforced. Fines were promptly collected. Having long dabbled in trade, Edward became a merchant on a great scale, exporting wool and woollen cloths at a handsome profit. Thus he built up the treasure which fortified his strength and assured his independence.

His diplomacy had been alert and usually shrewd; he sought to advance the interests of his merchants as well as the security of his state. He had signed treaties of amity with Denmark, the Hanse towns, Castile, and Portugal. For years he had maintained good terms with Scotland and kept Ireland quiet. By his support of the weak and wavering Duke of Brittany and by his alliance with the Duke of Burgundy, he had—until the late 1470's—shown himself a match for the wily Louis himself, the wizard of the age. In the community of European nations he had restored England to a place in the first rank.

Now, though his slackening grip upon affairs and his increasing severity were causing his subjects to grumble, he did not lose his hold upon their hearts. He was familiar with them as no King had ever been before. He admired and made full use of the learned accomplishments of men of common rank; he shared his table and his society with his fellow merchants of London; he was easy of access and frank of speech; he had the politician's knack of remembering names and faces; and, at bottom, he was loved because he loved. When his great-granddaughter, Queen Elizabeth, boasted that she was 'mere English', she was talking in Edward's vein.[2]★

Like Antony, Edward revelled long o' nights, but he had often laboured long o' days. His gigantic capacity to enjoy life had masked his industry. Thus it was that in his great years he had established, by his solutions to master problems and with the indefatigable support of his brother Richard, the foundations of the proud national state governed by a strong monarch which would come after. But the particular edifice which Edward had reared upon this base was no longer being kept in tight repair. There had begun to appear, after his reconquest of the realm, an alteration in his character and in the texture of his government, an alteration which was accelerated following his return from France in 1475. His will to rule greatly and his splendid energies were increasingly sapped by his pursuit of pleasure; and this immersion in self-indulgence and a hardening grip upon his kingdom were both signs of the disillusionment which had been born of his long struggle for mastery.

This was the change which had afflicted Richard with the sense of loss and alienation. The generous, undaunted, sunny-hearted prince determined to give justice to all had turned into the monarch who wearily and grimly permitted himself to be satisfied with keeping order. The brother unmatched in war and triumphant in the arts of peace had become too shaky in health to lead a campaign and too weakened in will to break out of the net which Louis XI was weaving for him.

It was the unchecked greed and arrogance of the Woodvilles, it was the habitual debauchery into which Edward had sunk in the company of the genial, brave, and corrupt Lord Hastings, it was the enervating tension of intrigue in the royal Household—these were the thieves, Richard felt, that had robbed him of his brother and his brother of his greatness.[3]*

It was the court.

The court was like a tropical garden not altogether reclaimed from jungle: overheated, luxuriant in blooms of pageantry and the vari-coloured plumage of tilting knights, rustling with the endless whisperings of faction, dense with suspicions and half-hidden hatreds.

Though the Queen and her kindred gave the court its dominant tone, Edward had long since ceased to be faithful to his wife. He took delight in jesting that he had three concubines 'which in three diverse properties diversely excelled, one the merriest, another the wiliest, the third the holiest harlot in the realm'. The last two moved from the King's bed into oblivion. The first was the woman who captured not only the King's fancy but the King's heart: Mistress Jane Shore, wife of a prosperous London mercer. 'For many he had, but her he loved.' She gladdened the last years of his life and it may even be that to her he remained faithful. Their liaison began, apparently, about a year after Edward's return from France—if any significance can be attached to an entry on the Patent Rolls for December 4, 1476, which bestowed the King's protection upon William Shore, citizen of London, and his servants, with all his lands, goods, and possessions in England and elsewhere. It was by her charm as much as by her body that Jane Shore held him. She was intelligent, witty, merry of temper, and very warm-hearted. 'Where the King took displeasure she would mitigate and appease his mind; where men were out of favour, she would bring them in his grace ... either for none or very small rewards, and those rather gay than rich.' It appears that Lord Hastings and the Marquess of Dorset loved her too; but out of loyalty, or discretion, they for the time being kept their passion secret. To the light-hearted Jane, Richard must have appeared a stern and doubtless fearful figure; as, to him, she was a bawd and thus a part of what had diminished his brother's glory. At Westminster, the man of the moors was an Israelite in Babylon.[4]*

That which made rank the smouldering Italianate atmosphere of court was the bitter, covert feud between the Woodvilles and the old nobility, who hated their insolence and scorned their pretensions. Young Henry Stafford, second Duke of Buckingham, loathed the Queen because as a stripling under her guardianship, he had been forced to marry her sister Katherine and to continue living for some years in her household. It was Lord Hastings, however, who led the opposition to the Queen and her kindred, mostly because he found himself menaced by their enmity. On one occasion, by means of an accusation Earl Rivers brought against him, he was, according to More, 'for a while (but it lasted not long) far fallen into the King's indignation and stood in great fear of himself'. Rivers hated Hastings because in 1471 the King had taken the Captaincy of Calais from him and given it to the Lord Chamberlain; Marquess Dorset hated Hastings because they were strenuous competitors to be the King's chief boon companion and quarrelled and deceived each other over their mistresses; the Queen hated Hastings because he was 'secretly familiar with the King in wanton company', and because he wielded great influence as Edward's dearest friend. Round these un-Homeric combatants whirled a cloud of time-servers and tale-bearers, haughty retainers and spying servants. It was in the deadly tangles of this silken web that the King was being parted from his greatness and Clarence had been parted from his life.[5]

As Edward's health worsened, the severity of his rule and the deterioration of his will increased; his inability to take decisive action in the conduct of the Scots war was matched by the irresolution of his ·diplomacy. Louis XI had caught him on the horns of a dilemma from which he longed to extricate himself, but instead he remained fretfully passive while time inexorably slipped away. The heiress of Burgundy, Mary, had married Maximilian, son of the German Emperor. Young and vigorous, Maximilian was a general of talent, but he had no money of his own and his father could spare him no soldiers. Already King Louis had swallowed up the Duchy of Burgundy, overrun much of the county of Artois; he continued to press remorselessly upon the crumbling frontiers of Flanders, even threatening Calais. Racked by misgivings, Edward watched the unequal contest, anxious to help Burgundy, his greatest ally and the bulwark of English trade, but unwilling to lose the 50,000 crowns a year which Louis paid him. While Maximilian pleaded with growing desperation for aid, Louis used honeyed words, extended his truce with Edward to last one year beyond the demise of whichever of them died first. Edward did nothing, feebly hoping that Louis, who had had two attacks of apoplexy, would soon die or that he could be persuaded to accept reasonable terms from Maximilian.

While Edward was entertaining Richard during the Christmas season of 1482, tidings from across the sea confirmed his worst fears. Beaten to his knees, Maximilian of Burgundy made peace with Louis XI on December 23. By this treaty of Arras, Maximilian agreed that his daughter Margaret should marry the Dauphin of France and bring Louis as her marriage portion the counties of Artois and Burgundy. Not only was England's surest friend enfeebled, its Prince committed to give no more aid to English pretensions to France, but before the world Louis had flouted the Princess Elizabeth, who, he had promised and sworn again, was to have become the Dauphin's bride. Edward knew that he would never again see the colour of Louis' money, and he would soon learn that French corsairs were boldly thrusting into the channel. His diplomacy had collapsed.

In his agony of mind, Edward turned, as he had so often turned before, to the faithful brother, whose recent victory had providentially given him the means of palliating his subjects' discontent and his own frustration. With Burgundy helpless, it was, for the time being, impossible to attempt retaliation against Louis. Richard conselled his brother to press the war in Scotland to a triumphant conclusion. A firm peace would not only secure the border and end a serious drain on the resources of the kingdom, but it might even lead to enlisting the Scots as allies against France.[6]★

Shaken in health, humiliated, leaning upon his brother for assurance and support, Edward was happy to accept Richard's counsel. When Parliament met on January 20, it immediately showed itself ready to follow Richard's counsel too. He seemed, in fact, to bear the weight of the kingdom upon his shoulders. The Commons chose for their Speaker John Wode, under-secretary of the Treasury and a friend of Richard's. On February 18, after praising the martial exploits of the Duke of Gloucester, Northumberland, Stanley, and other captains, they approved a tax on aliens for the defence of the realm. Three days before they had granted the King a tax for the prosecution of the war, excepting from it, at Richard's request, the counties of Westmorland, Cumberland, Northumberland, and York because these had borne so heavy a share of the late campaign. The most remarkable enactment of the Parliament, however, was the guerdon it bestowed upon Richard of Gloucester.[7]

He, and his heirs after him, were granted permanent possession of the Wardenship of the West Marches. To support this great hereditary authority, Richard received the castle, constableship, and fee-farm of the city of Carlisle and all the King's lands and manors, the King's customary fines, fees, forfeits, profits, wreck of sea and the like, and the right to appoint the sheriff and escheator, in Cumberland county. Furthermore, since Richard, 'by his manifold and diligent labours and devoirs' had subdued more than thirty miles of Scots border lands, much of which he had brought under Edward's obeisance, and since more of such lands 'he intendeth, and with God's grace is like, to get and subdue hereafter', he was to enjoy possession of these lands and all others he could win from the Scots above the West Marches, and he was given the power to make Scots 'denizens' of England 'by writing under his seal'.

It was nothing less than a great county palatine Richard was given, created out of Cumberland county and the Scots marches, a heredity *appanage,* which, though it owed obedience to the English Crown, was well nigh an autonomous principality.

Such a grant must undoubtedly prove, in the long run, detrimental to the interest of the kingdom. For Richard, however, it represented the crown of his long labours in the North and the final resolution of that fundamental problem, how a King's brother can create a life of his own that offers scope for his talents and occupation for his energies. The hard experience of his whole lifetime had shaped his desire for this gift. It was impossible to be safe without being strong. He wanted to make himself and his little son independent of the fierce jealousies of court and secure against the power of the Woodvilles, who already controlled the Prince of Wales and might someday, therefore, attempt to control the realm. This imposing grant clearly represented Richard's ambition; it also clearly defined the limit of his ambition.

Not long after Parliament concluded its business on February 20, Richard bade his brother farewell and set out for the North. It was the last time he ever saw King Edward. On March 6 he reached York, to be welcomed by the Aldermen in violet and the Council of the Twenty-four in blue and heaped with the usual gifts of wine and food.[8] He was a Prince of the Blood and they were but commoners, these merchants and artisans, and yet perhaps they were his best friends—sober like himself and hard working; responsible governors of men.

He left them soon and rode northward towards the swelling moors of Wensleydale. Despite his great offices and his triumphs, he appears a lonely figure as he travels across the sweep of Yorkshire land and sky. During his thirty years he had endured a lifetime of violence and known but little rest. Much that was dear to him had been lost: the invincible young warrior named Edward . . . Warwick . . . faithful Montagu . . . Clarence. . . . Gazing into the faces of the Woodvilles during the recent Christmas mummings, how could he help remembering his wild, rash brother, mouldering now behind the altar of Tewkesbury abbey?

Upward into the hills Richard rode, a figure slight of build and a little less than normal height; his face more memorable than handsome, a rather thin face of strongly marked but harmonious features: eyes direct and earnest, shadowed by care; a forthright nose; a chin remarkable for the contrast of its bold structure with its delicate moulding. The face suggests the whole man, a frail body compelled to the service of a powerful will.[9]* There is a veil of darkness upon him. With half his deeds a man of vivid personality like Clarence or Warwick would have created twice the blaze of fame. Though the kingdom resounds with his praise, he remains, to most of it, unknown. He has no brilliant smile to make hearts beat high. What he gets, he earns. The men he has won are the men of the North, who have served with him in battle and known his justice in times of peace.

Only, perhaps, when he has ridden into the courtyard of Middleham and mounted the steps of the great keep will his face light up, as he catches his first glimpse of Anne and his delicate little Prince.

The King

Protector and Defensor

I

ON Wednesday, April 9, 1483, news came coursing from Westminster to Ludgate and then raced through the narrow ways of London: Edward the King had breathed his last. Soon the bells of the great Abbey began to toll. Their funeral clangour was caught up by the hundred churches within and without the city . . . by St. Dunstan-in-the-West and St. Martin-in-the-Fields and the Priory of St. John at Clerkenwell . . . by St. Olave's from across the river in Southwark . . . by the parish churches within the walls, St. Andrew Undershaft and St. Peter in Cheap and St. Vedast and St. Mary Woolchurch . . . and by the brazen strokes out-tonguing them all of St. Paul's on Ludgate Hill. Citizens had clustered along the streets to talk, the low-voiced talk of grave and anxious men. Aldermen in fur-trimmed gowns of scarlet made their way solemnly to the Guildhall. On the river, splendid barges moved upstream: the magnates and the princes of the Church then in the city were being rowed to Westminster.

The King had been ill only about a week. A day or two after Easter (March 30) he had accompanied a party of courtiers going a-fishing. Over-exerting himself in the damps of the fickle spring weather, he had apparently collapsed, perhaps from a stroke of apoplexy or an attack of acute indigestion. Though a false report of his death had reached York as early as April 6, the King had rallied from his seizure, and those about him found no reason to think that he was mortally stricken. Yet his illness lingered; daily he grew weaker; he quietly told his intimates that he was dying. Somehow, his once-magnificent constitution had at last failed him.[1*]

Men were stunned. Suddenly, they had lost the strong and affable *genie* who had held them safe in his great hand. He had of late years grown stout, but on his mighty frame this corpulence was not unseemly; he had become less active than formerly and suffered periods of ill health or debility, but all had hoped that the King had before him a mellow middle age in which to enjoy the quiet he had won for his realm and to oversee the coming to manhood of his elder son and heir. On the day of his death he was three weeks short of being forty-one years old.

His feast of Christmas past had exceeded in opulence the entertainments of former years. To lutes and viols the court danced. There were 'disguisings' . . . ancestor of the Elizabethan masque. Actors thrived, for the King called for plays and surrounded by his courtiers watched the antics of the Vice Titivillus, the agony of Mankind besieged by World, Flesh, and Devil, the coarse horse-play which flickered about the grim spectre of Death. Trumpets and clarions summoned a richly dressed throng to banquets of royal length. Edward's beautiful daughters, shining like angels in their Christmas gowns, cast a glow of innocence upon the revelry. Presiding over the festivities like a genial wizard, in a new fashion of very full sleeves which were rolled across the shoulders, King Edward entertained with affection and pride his victorious young brother Richard, Duke of Gloucester.[2]

Yet neither the faithful service of Richard nor the merry devices of his court could rescue him from the grip of a profound melancholy. He was not a professional monarch like Louis XI or Henry VII: he could not sink the man in the King nor squeeze the juice of life from a grim pursuit of destiny and dynasty. The Treaty of Arras burned in his blood like a fever, but not simply because he regretted his failure to shore up Maximilian against the French. King Louis' triumph was a fateful pointer, underscoring the inaction of his later years, the loss of youth, the emptiness of pleasure, the end of his bright vitality . . . quenched by nights of sensual indulgence crowded upon the labours of statecraft. Touched by the passion of the Renaissance, he had reached out avidly for experience. But were not his carouses, like his Christmas revelling, in part a groping to escape the pangs of memory? He could not sink the man in the King. He could not, in contemplating the greatness of his accomplishment, forget what it had cost. The past was crowded with lost illusions and the faces of men dear to him whom he had had to crush; the present was dominion that had lost its savour; the future, a weary bickering with fate and his own mistakes. Even the amplitude of his might, the loyalty of his brother Richard, the wit of Mistress Shore, and the love of his subjects could not comfort him. Once an illness laid him a-bed, the conqueror of Warwick let death take him, apparently without a struggle. When he lost his ebullience, he lost everything.

As his last hours approached, the King's thoughts coiled uneasily about his twelve-year-old heir Edward, who had dwelt most of his life far off at Ludlow on the border of the Welsh Marches. At the age of three he had been sent there, with his council, to win the loyalty of Wales. The council which governed in his name was the chief of Edward's administrative innovations that the Tudors and their successors copied. Almost two hundred years later, a masque *Comus*, written by young John Milton, was first performed at Ludlow Castle for the induction of the Earl of Bridgewater as Lord President of the Council of Wales.

With an eye to the future—less prudent, as always, than ambitious,— the Prince's mother had seen to it that her son was surrounded by Woodvilles: 'in effect,' More remarks, 'everyone as he was nearest of kin unto the Queen, so was planted next about the prince . . . whereby her blood might of youth [i.e., from his childhood] be rooted in the prince's favour.' Though John Alcock, Bishop of Worcester, was titled President of the Council, its ruling power was Earl Rivers, the Queen's brother, who held the office of Governor of the Prince; Lord Richard Grey, her younger son by her first marriage, was one of the Councillors; and Richard Haute, a relative of the Woodvilles, was Comptroller of the Household. The council owned a dual function: to supervise the upbringing of the Prince and to exercise jurisdiction not only over his lands in Wales, Cornwall, and Chester but also over the Marches and the border shires of Shropshire, Hereford, Gloucester, and Worcester. By the standard of the times, it was a sheltered existence that young Edward led: removed from the main current of life into the placid backwater of Ludlow; padded by an elaborate regimen of 'virtuous learning', daily orisons, literary edifica- tion, and manly sports; and nurtured by his mother's kin, whose view of politics and personalities was the only one he ever knew.[3]

To the dying King, the peaceful succession of his son was now his one worldly preoccupation. There pressed upon him the awful realization that he was leaving his boy threatened by perils that he him- self, with forethought, might have extinguished. Two shadows in particular he had allowed his reign to cast upon the future. One, very large and ominous, was rooted at the heart of his government. The other represented a loose end of statesmanship which he had not quite tied up and which the now triumphant Louis XI might pounce upon, to England's cost.

This second shadow emanated from the figure of a young man whose only name was Henry Tydder or Tudor but who persisted in calling himself the Earl of Richmond, a Lancastrian refugee at the court of Francis, Duke of Brittany. The lineage of Henry Tudor was high, mysterious, and flawed: it was blazoned with royal colours which were everywhere criss-crossed by the bar sinister. In his mother's descent, his great-great-grandfather was John of Gaunt, fourth son of Edward III. Gaunt had a mistress, Catherine Swynford, who was the daughter of a Flemish herald named Payn Roet. She bore him four children while her husband, Sir Hugh, and Gaunt's second wife, Constance of Castile, were both alive. After the demise of their respective spouses Gaunt married her. A protégé of the Duke's, one Geoffrey Chaucer, had married her sister. Despite the buzz of scandal, Richard II was kind enough to legitimate Gaunt's bastards by patent and act of Parliament, to bestow upon them the impressive name of Beaufort (derived from the castle in France where they were born), and to set them on the path to high station. John, the eldest, became Earl of Somerset; his brother Henry, Bishop of Winchester and Cardinal. In 1407 Gaunt's son Henry IV, half brother to the Beauforts, confirmed their patent of legitimacy but added the limiting phrase *excepta dignitate regali*. Whether, in the light of present day constitutional studies, he had the right so to alter an act of Parliament matters little; most people of the fifteenth century took it for granted that the legitimating patent barred the Beauforts from the throne.

The Earl of Somerset's grand-daughter, sole heir of his eldest son John, Duke of Somerset, was a shrewd, pious, learned girl named Margaret Beaufort. In 1456, at the age of thirteen, she was married to Edmund Tudor, Earl of Richmond. Some two months after his death, on January 28, 1457, she gave birth to Henry Tudor. She was twice more to marry, but Henry was the only child she brought into the world—as if, the historians of the Tudor dynasty would one day unblushingly declare, after she had produced so great a gift for England, Providence decreed that she had richly fulfilled her destiny.

On his father's side, Henry's ancestry was far more mysterious than on his mother's; it was equally illustrious and flawed. A generation before Henry's birth there had appeared at the English court an adventurous Welshman named Owen Tudor. So far as anyone knew, he came of an Anglesey family of no great pretensions; his father Meredith had been butler to the Bishop of Bangor and escheator of Anglesey. Later, much later, the Tudors were traced back to dizzy heights in the dimness of the ancient past; they were sprung, it would be solemnly averred, from the loins of Cadwallader himself and were thus vessels of the royal blood of Celtic Wales. Owen managed to become a clerk of the Wardrobe in the household of Queen Katherine, Henry V's widow and daughter of the mad Charles VI of France. She lived remote from court, forgotten. No doubt she was lonely. Owen Tudor would be handsome and sympathetic and he would know how to sing sad Welsh songs to the sad Katherine. Soon he had sung himself into her bed. She bore him three children: Jasper, Edmund and Owen. So obscure was Katherine's household, so unheeded by the court, that not, apparently, until she died in 1437 did the council of Henry VI discover her *amour*.

They were furious. The Queen meant nothing to them but the slight upon the memory of their hero, Henry V, meant a great deal. Owen protested that he and the Queen were truly married. No proof of the wedding was ever forthcoming, however; and, since Owen had not troubled to apply for letters of denization, the marriage would have been illegal. Cast into Newgate prison by the outraged council, the dashing Welshman pursued his adventures. 'This same year [of 1437],' records *The Great Chronicle*, 'one Owen no man of birth neither of lyflode [property] broke out of Newgate against night at Searching Time through help of his priest and went his way hurting foul his keeper. But at the last blessed be God he was taken again. The which Owen had privily wedded Queen Katherine and had three or four children by her unwyting [unknown to] the common people till that she were dead and buried.'[4]*

Eventually, the weak and kindly Henry VI made all well. He recognized his half-brothers, welcomed them at court, and in 1453 created Jasper Earl of Pembroke and Edmund, Earl of Richmond. Owen, the third son, had become a monk at Westminster. Perhaps the taint of madness in Queen Katherine's veins, which clouded the mind of King Henry, had passed mainly, in the children of her second connection, to the monk Owen, of whom nothing is known; perhaps it appears in Jasper's childlessness; perhaps, in the suspicions which smouldered in Henry Tudor's mind in his later years.

Not long after the birth of her son, Margaret Beaufort married Sir Henry Stafford. She relinquished Henry to his uncle Jasper to be reared in Wales at Pembroke Castle. In February of 1461 Jasper managed to escape after the crushing defeat at Mortimer's Cross; but young Edward of March, soon to be Edward IV, captured and condemned to death Henry's grandfather. Even when the scaffold was erected in the market place at Hereford, the jaunty Owen hoped to circumvent death as he had circumvented so many obstacles in his adventurous life, 'weening and trusting alway', Gregory reports of him, 'that he should not be headed till he saw the axe and the block; and when he was in his doublet, he trusted on pardon and grace till the collar of his red velvet doublet was ripped off. Then he said, "That head shall lie on the stock that was wont to lie in Queen Katherine's lap" and put his heart and mind wholly unto God and full meekly took his death'. Then his head was 'set upon the highest grice of the market cross, and a mad woman kemped his hair and washed away the blood of his face, and she got candles and set about him burning, more than a hundred'.[5]

For several months young Henry Tudor was a fugitive, hiding in the bit of Welsh territory still held by the Lancastrians. When Lord Herbert captured Pembroke castle in September of 1461, he found Henry within it. Herbert was granted the castle and, on the payment of 1,000 pounds, the custody and marriage of the four-year-old captive. The Herberts took the boy to their hearts, reared and educated him like a son, and fondly looked forward to his becoming the husband of their daughter Maud. Their hopes were bloodily ended by the field of Edgecot in August, 1469: Herbert of Pembroke was captured and immediately executed by Warwick and Clarence. When, a year later, Jasper Tudor accompanied this pair on their successful invasion of England, he found his nephew Henry living quietly in the household of the Countess of Pembroke.[6]

After the final defeat of the Lancastrian cause at Tewkesbury, Jasper and Henry fled to Pembroke castle and then, perceiving that England held no safety for them, took ship for France. The master of the vessel, however, was a Breton. Through his treachery or the unkindness of the elements, they were put ashore at Brest. They found themselves the uncertain guests of Francis, Duke of Brittany and pawns in the game of European politics. King Edward, whose aid against Louis XI the Duke of Brittany was constantly seeking, made offers for their return. King Louis, whom Francis feared above all mortals, demanded that Jasper and Henry be surrendered to him or at least be prevented from passing into the hands of anyone else . . . meaning Edward. Counters so valuable Duke Francis would not relinquish—until, that is, the price was right. When, a few months after the fugitives had reached Brittany, Edward IV renewed a thirty-years' treaty with Francis, the most the Breton duke promised was that Jasper and Henry would be kept under strict surveillance.

As, with the passing years, the die-hard adherents of the House of Lancaster, deprived of their root of allegiance, turned to the spurious or doubtful graft upon the stock, King Edward became increasingly concerned about this remote but not necessarily trivial threat to his dynasty. The year after he had returned from his French expedition Edward made a vigorous effort to secure Henry Tudor, offering Francis a handsome subsidy for his delivery and promising that he would not only treat Henry honourably but provide him with a marriage in the royal family. Edward had small reason to fear Henry himself; it was the nuisance value that the ingenious Louis XI might discover in Henry that motivated Edward's generous, and doubtless genuine, offer.

Only Polydore Vergil, Henry Tudor's own historian, reports the sequel: At last, he tells us, 'wearied with prayer and vanquished with price', Duke Francis delivered up Henry Tudor to King Edward's ambassadors, who 'departed with great joy to St. Malo . . . there to have taken shipping. . . .' The natural suspiciousness of Henry's character having been aggravated by his experience, he was so sure death awaited him that 'through agony of mind [he] fell by the way into a fever.' So says Vergil, following, no doubt, the reminiscence of Henry himself. It is likely this illness was, partly at least, counterfeited in a desperate hope of gaining time. The child of circumstance must throw himself upon the succour of circumstance. Now, as later, Henry showed himself to be the white-headed boy of fortune. While the English ambassadors kindly paused at St. Malo, Duke Francis changed his mind and sent his clever treasurer Pierre Landois posting hotfoot to get the Tudor back. While Landois made a pretence of conferring with the ambassadors, his men conveyed the feverish Henry to a sanctuary. To the bitter protests of Edward's outwitted envoys Landois replied coolly that it was by their own negligence their charge had escaped! Duke Francis promised Edward, however, that both the Tudors would be carefully watched. He treated Henry well and apparently grew fond of him; but he kept his promise as long as King Edward lived.[7]

Now, lying anxious of heart in the shadow of death, Edward could take small comfort from contemplating the shifting vagaries of Francis's character and the dangerous humiliation which Louis XI had dealt him. The shadow of Henry Tudor was cast upon Edward's mind by the ominous lightning that glared upon the south-eastern horizons.

Far more menacing, however, were the apparitions that lurked in his own palace.

The worm of discord within the court gnawed agonizingly upon his thoughts. As his strength ebbed, he summoned the leaders of the two factions to his chamber and bade his attendants prop him in the bed with pillows. His Queen he did not summon. Elizabeth held small meaning for him, dying, and no more hope for the realm when he was dead.

The courtiers gathered about him. On one side stood the kindred of the Queen—her two sons by her first marriage, the profligate Thomas, Marquess of Dorset, and young Lord Richard Grey; two of her brothers, Lionel, Bishop of Salisbury and the martial Sir Edward Woodville. On the other side stood representatives of the old nobility headed by William, Lord Hastings, the King's Chamberlain and dearest friend. Between the parties hovered the shadow of the King's brother Clarence, done to death, all believed, by the insatiable Queen whom he had dared to scorn. Between them yawned the bitter gulf of covert insult, intrigue, and feud.

Looking into their faces, Edward spoke with unwonted earnestness. He was no preacher, he told them, but let them remember that he was soon going to the place the preachers talked about and that he addressed them with the authority not of kingship but of the dying. Unless they loved one another, his son and the kingdom and they themselves would all be brought to ruin. . . .

Exhausted, perhaps having no hope in the power of his words, he rolled over on his right side, face against the pillows, and stared at them. They were moved to tears. The Marquess and Hastings clasped hands and swore to love one another; the rest of the lords and gentlemen followed suit.[8]*

Edward sighed, dismissed them. The strength which his son and the kingdom needed did not lie in these men. There was only one man capable of ordering the realm and subduing the factions which split the court. It was a man he loved well and who, he knew, loved him. . . .

At last he summoned his executors: five great prelates and three lords, not precisely the same group he had appointed for the will he made before he invaded France in 1475. Lord Stanley had been added; Queen Elizabeth had been dropped. With real humility the fast-weakening King begged these men to pay all his just debts, to rectify any extortions of which he might be found guilty, and to distribute a generous portion of his goods to the poor. Then, aware that his minutes on earth were numbered, he added the all-important codicil to his will; he bequeathed his boy heir and his realm to the protection of his brother Richard, Duke of Gloucester. After that, the priests came bearing the Eucharist. Now but a weary son of Holy Church, Edward turned his final thoughts wholly to God.[9]*

Not many hours later, while the bells tolled, the magnates who happened to be in the city gathered at Westminster, among them Lord Howard who only the day before had arrived in London from his Essex estates.[10] Having assembled at the Guildhall, the Mayor and his brethren, too, made their way to the palace. The citizens talked or prayed or grieved in silence—perhaps as much for themselves who had lost a good and great master as for the King now facing the dread judgment of Heaven. In the minds of some already stirred the old saw which the bad days of Henry VI had too eloquently affirmed: 'Woe to that land whose ruler is a child'.

In his chamber the dead King lay upon a board, naked save for a cloth which covered him from his navel to his knees. Before the body passed the lords spiritual and temporal and the Mayor and Aldermen of London that they might look upon their master for the last time and witness that he was indeed dead. The next morning he was borne into the chapel of St. Stephen's and the solemn obsequies were begun. Eight days they lasted, as if men were loath to let him go. After a final ceremony in the Abbey, the funeral procession left London for Windsor on April 18. On April 20, in the pomp of regal dominion and the solemnity of Holy Church, King Edward the Fourth was laid at last to rest in the chapel of St. George, gorgeous in its fan vaulting, which he himself had edified.[11]

It was a beginning as well as an ending. The Bishops in their albs and chasubles, the magnates and courtiers in flowing black moved through the ritual unaware that they were characters in the prologue to a high and bloody drama . . . their concord soon to be broken, their vestments to be stained or rent. Some then present had not long to live and would not die quietly. Many who lived would stand in peril of their lives or their honours. For the moment, the Woodvilles—Sir Richard and Sir Edward, the Bishop of Salisbury and the Marquess— offered the mass penny and knelt in prayer with Hastings and Stanley and Audley and Howard. Lord Ferrers of Chartley was present, who would die in battle; and a gentleman usher, William Colyngbourne, who would die horribly, but not for a rhyme; and the gigantic Sir John Cheyney who would be cut down by a King's hand; and John Morton, Bishop of Ely, who would end a cardinal, much hated.

The leading actors of this drama were not, however, present. Some-

F

where in the palace of Westminster Queen Elizabeth was feverishly
arranging the future to suit her heart's desire. At Ludlow castle in the
Marches of Wales dwelt Prince Edward, now Edward the Fifth, a boy
of twelve, and his maternal uncle and governor, Anthony Woodville,
Earl Rivers. Henry Stafford, second Duke of Buckingham and of the
blood royal, was on his Welsh estates. Oversea, at the court of Francis,
Duke of Brittany, a young man with a pale, wedge-shaped face, thinning
yellow hair, and wary grey eyes waited and watched. And far off at
his castle of Middleham lay the dead King's sole surviving brother
and the new King's uncle, Richard, Duke of Gloucester.

II*

It was mid-April when a messenger galloped into the courtyard of
Middleham Castle bearing the stunning news that King Edward had
died on April 9. Barely two months had passed since Richard parted
from the King. Though his brother's health had not been good, he had
no surmise that Edward stood near the edge of death. His thoughts
were upon bringing the Scots to heel and upon establishing the county
palatine by means of which he and his heirs might live safely withdrawn
from court in Edward's declining years. The King's death abruptly
ended all prospects of such a withdrawal. It ended other things too.
In the first words of the messenger, the pole-star of Richard's life had
fallen from the sky.[1]*

A chaplain said requiem masses in the chapel of the castle. The
household assumed black. Anne doubtless tried to explain to her frail
little prince, Edward, now ten years old, why his father looked so pale
and stern. Richard had small time for the outward show of grief. The
world beyond the southward upthrust of the moors had suddenly
turned dangerous. Middleham lay well over two hundred miles from
London and Edward had been dead a week.

The messenger had not been dispatched by the Queen or the Chan-
cellor. He was a man of the Lord Hastings, and he brought more than
tidings of Edward's death. Hastings' message had been curt and urgent:
'The King has left all to your protection—goods, heir, realm. Secure
the person of our sovereign Lord Edward the Fifth and get you to
London.'[2] No formal notice of this new authority having arrived,
Richard decided to dispatch a query to Earl Rivers at Ludlow: As
Protector and uncle of Edward V, he wished to honour his sovereign

by entering London with him. When and by what route would the young King travel to his capital?[3]*

Before many days had passed, a second messenger in the colours of Lord Hastings clattered across the drawbridge. The Woodvilles, wrote the Lord Chamberlain, had usurped the direction of affairs. Only by a desperate effort had he succeeded in limiting the escort which would bring Edward up to London to 2,000 men. Richard should not fail to come strong and secure the King.

There was still no official word from Westminster. Weighing this silence with Hastings' news, Richard composed a letter to Queen Elizabeth, commiserating with her and promising to serve her son. Then he addressed himself to the dead King's council.

He had been loyal to his brother Edward, he began, at home and abroad, in peace and war. He would be equally loyal to his brother's heir and all his brother's issue. He desired only that the new government of the kingdom be established according to law and justice. By his brother's testament he had been made Protector of the realm. If the council were debating the disposition of authority, he asked them to consider the position rightfully due him according to the law of the land and his brother's ordinance. Richard added one warning: nothing which was contrary to law and King Edward's will could be decreed without harm.[4]*

The letter was far from eloquent, except in its massive plainness and its moderation. Richard's reference to law is to be understood, in modern terms, rather as 'recognized precedent'. In that day there was no body of legislation which defined even the rights of the succession, much less the forming of a regency government. During the minority of Richard II, his uncles had assumed charge of affairs. Henry V had bequeathed the regency of France to his brother Bedford, the regency of England to his brother Humphrey of Gloucester. In leaving the kingdom to the protection of his sole surviving brother, King Edward had followed—Richard was reminding the council—a custom approved by over a century of practice. But the wishes of a deceased monarch, Richard knew, had not always prevailed. Jealous magnates had limited Humphrey's protectorship to a nominal authority which the party of the Beauforts had frequently thwarted.[5]

Not long after this letter was dispatched, there arrived at Middleham a courier in the livery of Henry Stafford, second Duke of Buckingham, dusty with the long miles he had ridden from Brecon in South Wales. Buckingham wrote that in the new world that was a-making, he put himself entirely at the Duke of Gloucester's service, with 1,000 men if need be. What would Gloucester have him do? The messenger, on his master's behalf, begged to have an immediate answer.

Richard had had small opportunity to know Buckingham well. It was clear that the young Duke had written immediately he heard of Edward's death and that he was not averse to stirring in troubles. He was, after Richard himself, however, the noblest blood in England and he seemed genuinely eager to offer his support. While the courier had his bread and meat and ale, Richard wrote a reply: He was shortly coming south to join the King's progress to London. He would be pleased to have Buckingham meet him on the road—but with a small escort only, not more than 300 men.

Richard himself had already determined to limit his company to a similar number.[6] These tenants, retainers, and friends he had requested to meet him at York. About April 20 he bade farewell to Anne and his son and began a journey, about which he could forecast little but that it was likely to be dangerous. Before he set forth from York, he administered to the men who were accompanying him and to the magistrates of the city the oath of fealty to King Edward V. Northumberland, Warden of the East and Middle Marches, was not there. It may be that Richard had asked the Earl to remain at Berwick in order to watch the Scots: it is possible that Henry Percy used his duties as an excuse to discover how affairs would shape before he put himself at Richard of Gloucester's side.[7]*

As Richard's cavalcade moved southward towards Nottingham, he encountered a courier from Earl Rivers. Sending courteous greetings, Rivers wrote that the King and he would leave Ludlow on April 24. They should reach Northampton on the 29th, where, perchance, it might please the Duke of Gloucester to join them. Richard sent back word that he would fall in with this proposal.

The cavalcade now moved at a slow pace, pausing a day or two at Pontefract. Not until April 26 did Richard arrive at Nottingham. Here a second messenger from Buckingham brought him word that the Duke was *en route* from Wales. Richard bade the man ask his master to join the rendezvous at Northampton.[8]

By this time he had received further messages from Lord Hastings, each more pressing and ominous than the last: The Woodvilles had ignored Richard's appointment as Protector. They were moving to crown the King at once in order to keep power in their hands. Richard must secure young Edward at all costs. In his latest communication the usually debonair Lord Chamberlain had written wildly that he stood alone, that his very life was in danger because he had espoused the Protector's cause.[9]

It must have been clear to Richard, as he and his troop slowly approached Northampton, that if King Edward had had no brother to assume the protectorship, the two hostile factions of court would by this time be stirring civil strife. Hastings had leaped to identify his party with the Protector. Buckingham, who loathed the Queen and her kindred, was obviously chafing to triumph over them. The Wood-villes, on the other hand, had momentarily captured the council in order that they might capture the King. Richard had come to only one decision: to hold himself uncommitted to anything, except his dead brother's ordinance. Precisely what was happening in the capital he could not tell; precisely what attitude Earl Rivers and his 2,000 men would take at Northampton he did not know. He did know that the authority of the protectorship was rightfully his, and he trusted to his abilities and to the will of the realm to make good that authority. There is something at once naïve and formidable about Richard's rigorous confidence, in the face of opposition so aggressive and a political situation so complex and explosive.

What was happening in London might have been predicted by measuring the known character of the Queen and her kindred against the dangers and opportunities which, in their view, the death of Edward opened to them. They were at the nadir of their unpopularity: detested by the commons for their extortions and for the profligacy of the Marquess, Lord Richard Grey and Sir Edward Woodville; hated by the nobles as arrogant upstarts who had monopolized the royal favour; and held by all to have encompassed the death of the Duke of Clarence. Sustained only by the power of the King, they considered that his death must imperil their fortunes and their lives, if anyone besides themselves assumed control of Edward V. Driven by their avidity for power, they reached for the first means of circumventing the protectorship of Richard of Gloucester, in order to bring the new King, and thus the realm, under their sway. Their motives were a mesh of self-defence and ambition.[10]

The Queen was the impelling spirit of the Woodville Clan. She was the greediest and the most wilful; neither her triumphs nor humiliations of the past two decades had taught her anything. Her brother Sir Edward, soldier and court gallant, and her brother Lionel, the haughty bishop of Salisbury, would follow her lead. Her eldest son by her first marriage, the Marquess of Dorset, now in his early thirties, was her lieutenant and colleague in conspiracy. The grain of his character cannot now be discerned. The actions of his life spell out a man of little solidity or acumen. His ignorance of politics would make him the more ready to plunge into his mother's schemes. Because he was a favourite of the dead King's idle hours and because as a Marquess he outranked all but the few dukes of the kingdom, he could pretend to considerable authority in the uncertainties of an *interregnum*.

As soon as it was clear that King Edward was dying, the Queen and the Marquess began developing their hopes. Their first object must be to win to their cause a majority of the royal councillors then at West-minister. With the Marquess himself and the Queen's two brothers they already had a nucleus of three. Hastings would bitterly oppose them, and he would doubtless have other barons, like Lord Howard, on his side. And perhaps Lord Stanley, though this pliant and cautious opportunist might be touched on the sensitive nerve of his self-interest. Most of the men of common birth, elevated to the council through ability and prudence, could be counted on, however; Dominic Mancini, who for well nigh a year had been observing affairs at court with his sharp Italian eyes, reports that the Queen 'attracted to her party many strangers and introduced them to court, so that they alone should manage the public and private business of the crown . . . give or sell offices, and finally rule the very King himself'. It was the high ecclesiastics—the Archbishop of Canterbury; Rotherham, Archbishop of York and Chancellor; Russell, Bishop of Lincoln and Keeper of the Privy Seal; Morton, Bishop of Ely; Story, Bishop of Chichester and an executor of the King's will; and a few others—who would form the decisive group in the council and must therefore be made sure.[11]*

The rising tide of anti-clericalism provided the Woodvilles with a potent means of persuasion. Edward IV had confirmed the privileges of the clergy; the first care of Holy Church must be that Edward V follow in his father's footsteps. How alarmed the prelates at this very moment were, is cried aloud in an oration written to be delivered at the Convocation on April 18 which the death of Edward indefinitely postponed.

Let the clergy reform their morals, the author urgently demands. But above all, let them cease to quarrel among themselves and to criticize the Church in the hearing of laymen. 'These things provoke the laity of our time, to attempt such unbridled enormities against the hurch. Fearing no censure, they even indict clergymen for fictitious rimes . . . throw them into squalid prisons to make them empty their barns. . . . There are scarcely ten in any diocese who do not yearly suffer either in their person or their purse!'[12]

Richard of Gloucester's views of the church establishment had probably never been canvassed. Many of the barons were doubtless hostile. In its need, the clergy must cling to the royal power. That power seemed now to be represented by the Woodvilles. The new King, as well as the sinews of government, was theirs. As soon as Edward were crowned, the protectorship would mean nothing.

Another passage in the oration, written not many hours after Edward's death, points the directions affairs were taking. The author—perhaps one of the bishops—offers a bidding prayer for 'our new prince . . . our dread king Edward V; the lady queen Elizabeth, his mother; all the royal offspring; the princes of the King; his nobles and people.' The Protector is not even mentioned. The very position of Elizabeth's name suggests 'Queen Regent'. This is scarcely a slip of the pen, for such a dignity was clean contrary to custom. Joan of Kent, mother of Richard II, found herself—popular though she was—completely excluded from power when her son succeeded to the rule. Katherine, Henry V's queen, was ignored by the council which governed for the infant Henry VI.[13]

While, in St. Stephen's chapel, a mist of incense drifted above gorgeous vestments as the soul of Edward was wafted on its way, in secret conferences within the palace Queen Elizabeth and the Marquess had gained the majority voice among the dead King's officers and advisers. The Marquess, as Constable of the Tower, likewise controlled the greatest armaments depot of the realm and the mighty treasure which Edward had amassed. Earl Rivers held the young King himself.

Not until they believed they had grasped the threads of power did the Queen and the Marquess dispatch the first news to Rivers: his nephew, now King, must be brought to London for his crowning in all speed and with a strong escort; Gloucester had been nominated Protector but the Queen was safely in charge of the realm.[14]

Soon afterward, the Queen and the Marquess summoned a meeting of the dead King's councillors, doubtless in the name of Edward V and under the colour of transacting necessary business. The first proposal was innocuous—that in order to keep the wheels of justice turning, the judges of the King's Bench and Common Pleas be reappointed to their offices. This having been readily accepted, the Marquess next urged the immediate need of providing for the defence of the realm.[15]

French freebooters had been harrying the channel for many weeks. More recently, Lord Cordes—the most aggressive and able of Louis XI's commanders—had been vigorously prosecuting this undeclared war at sea. The news of Edward's death would likely stir him to greater efforts. Therefore, proposed the Marquess, a fleet must be equipped at once to protect the coast towns as well as merchant shipping. This measure, too, was quickly approved.

Dorset was then able to attain his real objective: he succeeded in appointing as Commander of this fleet his uncle Sir Edward Woodville, who at once set about gathering ships and filling them with his own followers. The Marquess, apparently without consulting the council, provided his uncle with a portion of the treasure in the Tower; the rest of it he promptly divided with his mother. The need of protecting the coasts was genuine enough, but the Woodvilles had turned it into a means of securing themselves by force. Sir Edward was assembling a Woodville fleet. Ostensibly directed against the French at sea, it could easily be directed against the Queen's enemies in England. Neither Hastings nor anybody else had forgotten how in May of 1471 the Bastard of Fauconberg had led his sailors to assault London itself. Nor could Hastings and his friends be unaware that the Woodville fleet might attempt to win Calais, the keystone of England's overseas trade and her only permanent garrison. Hastings himself, its governor, would then be cut off from his stronghold.[16]*

Had the Woodvilles gone no further, they might have defended their actions on the grounds of necessity and the good of the state. But they had only begun. The council they had called into being was, in fact, as unlawful as their own pretentions. In the fifteenth century, a King's council was simply whatever men he summoned to give him advice and help him govern. It had no independent existence; with the death of a King it ceased to be. When the new King chose his advisers, there was again a royal council. From the moment Edward died, there could be no official council until, by virtue of his authority, the Protector gathered a group of advisers in the name of Edward V. Everybody knew this. Everybody also knew that if the Woodvilles got the King crowned at once, the lawlessness of their methods would not matter a straw.[17]

The Queen and the Marquess now felt themselves so secure that they proceeded, not only to appoint county commissions to collect the tax on aliens voted by the late Parliament, but boldly to proclaim by their choice of commissioners in whose hands the government lay. Hastings, it is true, headed seven of the commissions—doubtless, an attempt momentarily to placate him. The names of the Marquess and his uncle Rivers were liberally scattered through the patents under the style of 'uterine brother' and 'uterine uncle' to the King. In the styling lay the claim to power. No mention was made of a Protector; the name of Richard, Duke of Gloucester did not appear.[18]*

The moment had come for the decisive move. Having bidden the councillors to assemble in the presence of the Queen, as if she were Regent, the Marquess blandly exposed his hand. In order to avoid all ambiguities that might disorder men's minds, he asserted, the King should be crowned as soon as possible. He suggested Sunday, May 4, as the date for the coronation, a date less than three weeks away.

This time, the council baulked. Opposition had begun to develop in other quarters than the faction of Hastings. Several councillors— the more prudent members, says the Croyland Chronicler who was himself probably present—had become alarmed by the naked ambition of the Woodvilles and their reckless attempt to ignore the ordinance of the dead King's will. They had come to the opinion 'that the guardian- ship of so youthful a person [the King], until he should reach the years of maturity, ought to be utterly forbidden to his uncles and brothers by the mother's side.' The chronicler adds dryly that the possibility of effecting such a separation would not be increased if young Edward were brought to London by a large force of Woodville troops. This issue was now raised. What manner of escort, somebody asked, could be deemed sufficient for the prince?

The intimate supporters of the Woodvilles attempted to glide over the question, either by keeping their answers vague or by declaring that the size of the escort must be left to the King himself—which would mean, to the decision of Earl Rivers.

This was too much for Hastings, who, whatever his anger and his fears, had hitherto kept himself under control. Passionately he declared that if a moderate escort were not agreed upon, he himself would instantly retire to Calais. A heated debate ensued. At last the Queen proposed, with a show of graciousness, that she request her son to limit his escort to 2,000 men. To this figure Hastings agreed, believing that as a result of his pressing messages, the Duke of Gloucester would not come south with fewer men than that. By means of this concession the Woodvilles were able to secure a majority in the council for the all- important proposal that the coronation should take place on Sunday,

F*

May 4. According to custom, a Protector's authority ceased as soon as the King was crowned, however young he was. The government devolved upon the King's councillors; in effect, upon a council of regency whose composition would be dictated by whoever managed the mind of the King. It might even be that Edward could be anointed in the Abbey before the Duke of Gloucester reached London. Then, the Queen and her kindred would hold the Tower, the treasure, the sea, and the consecrated King.[19]

It is one thing to win a majority; it is another to satisfy men's minds. The councillors were growing progressively more nervous. At the next meeting Hastings, or another, felt that the time had come to expose the real issue. The council was reminded that Richard of Gloucester was the lawful Protector of England. What, came the pointed question, was the extent of the Protector's powers?

Ignoring the actual terms of Edward's will, Dorset and his chief adherents sought to play the same game upon the absent Richard which magnates with no less ambition but with at least some colour of justification had played, to his face, upon Harry the Fifth's unstable brother Humphrey. Gloucester was indeed Protector, declared the Marquess, but that office should be considered to confer on him no more than first place in the council which would carry on the government till the King was crowned.

The speciousness and unreality of this contention alarmed those prudent councillors mentioned by the Croyland Chronicler and they were well nigh as vigorous in their opposition as Hastings. They declared flatly that the present council lacked any right to discuss, much less to settle, so high a matter. Since the Protector was lawfully entitled to annul any such decision taken in his absence and since he was not likely to be pleased by a proceeding so inimical to him, the Marquess's proposal was illegal, futile, and dangerous.[20]*

At this moment of conflict, the council received Richard's letter. It swept through the chamber like a gust of air from the moors. Hastings and his party were cheered. The councillors who had begun to move away from the Woodvilles took heart. It was probably Hastings who saw to it that Richard's declaration was published abroad. Mancini was struck by the impact it made: 'This letter had a great effect on the minds of the people, who, as they had previously favoured the duke in their hearts from a belief in his probity, now began to support him openly and aloud, so that it was commonly said by all that the duke deserved the government.'[21]

It was the voice of the council which, however, counted, at the moment. The Marquess played upon the timorousness of his wavering followers. He talked of the dangers of committing the government to one man; he hinted that if Richard held supreme authority, none who had ever supported the Woodvilles would be safe. Forcing a vote on the resolution that Richard's protectorship should be shorn of real power, he still managed to command a majority. Doubtless a number of councillors felt that if the King was to be crowned on May 4, the rights of the Protector in the brief interval that remained were of small moment. Others, however, could not help murmuring their fears to the Marquess. He laughed them away. 'We are so important,' he was heard to boast, 'that even without the King's uncle we can make and enforce these decisions.'[22]*

He dispatched a letter to Rivers, telling him that the King must reach London no later than May 1, three days before the coronation. There was possibly a touch of asperity in the message. It may be that Rivers had not displayed much enthusiasm for the proceedings of the Queen.

Yet, upon the governor of the prince now rested the fate of the glittering edifice erected with such bravado at Westminster. Perhaps the Marquess had some cause to be peremptory. Anthony, Earl Rivers was, in fact, the changeling of the Woodville clan. London was not farther from Ludlow than he from the world of his kin.[23]

Pilgrim and knight, worldling and ascetic, Anthony Woodville was moved both by the vision of the Grail and of the Good Life. He was the most famous jouster of the age. Patron of Caxton, he translated three devotional works which Caxton printed, and he was given to penning ballads against the Seven Deadly Sins. In a mist of quasi-contradictions, he eludes us. Though he counted himself a staunch son of Holy Church, he seems to have developed an intimate and special piety, half mystical, yet learned. The blows that fell upon his family, the perils he himself suffered, and the violent reversals of fortune in the course of Warwick's attempt to reseat Henry VI upon the throne, produced in him a profound religious experience. Thenceforth, he told Caxton, he had resolved to dedicate himself to the cause of God. He perused the philosophers and devotional exercises like those of Christine of Pisa; he went on pilgrimage to the shrine of St. James of Compostella and talked of fighting the Infidel; he was appointed by Pope Sixtus IV defender and director of papal causes in England; and, as he uneasily prepared to set forth from Ludlow with his nephew, he was wearing, beneath the rich robes of an earl, a hair shirt.

The contrast of garments is representative, for Rivers was also very much a man of the world. He paid heed to the surfaces of living: gorgeous clothes, an impressive retinue, splendid ceremony. Striving to maintain his reputation in jousting, he dazzled all beholders by his skill in arms, the opulence and originality of his costume, and his gracious deportment. In the work-a-day world, he had commanded military expeditions and gone on diplomatic missions in the service of King Edward at the same time that he held the governorship of Edward's heir and first place in the council of Wales. If he could not claim the erudition of a John Tiptoft, Earl of Worcester, he was none-theless a genuine lover of books and a scholar. When he journeyed beyond the Alps, he seems to have sought inspiration equally from the holiness of famous shrines and from the golden reawakening of the cities of Italy. None could say whether he was more moved by the culture or the sacred authority of the papal court. Among the people he was famed for his ceremonious feats of arms; among the élite, for his accomplishments of mind.

Yet, though he blazed bright upon his times, he exerted curiously little force upon them. Perhaps he was too versatile, or too sensitive, to achieve a notable success. His ambition seems to have been flawed by doubts, by a certain slackness of will or unsureness of purpose. Despite his prowess with weapons, he was undistinguished in battle. On the eve of Morat he prudently withdrew from the camp of the Duke of Burgundy. He was apparently not indifferent to the prize of office, but neither the hurly-burly of politics nor the hard responsibility of authority much appealed to him. King Edward held him, for a time at least, in some contempt: suddenly angered when Rivers, after the defeat of Warwick and Queen Margaret, asked leave to go off on pilgrimage, Edward roared that he was a coward thus to think of leaving the realm when it was not yet fully restored to order.

Still, if Rivers shrank from laborious tasks of governing, he showed no wish to remain quietly on his estates or at Ludlow and be a petty King of country acres. A court was his *milieu*, but a Renaissance court; thus, he was a man half out of touch with his times. It is when he is viewed as a prototype of the Earl of Essex that he comes to life. Yet Essex was not his equal as a man of letters or even of affairs, nor so serious about either tilting or praying. If Elizabeth's favourite had worn a hair shirt, it would rather have represented a flamboyant gesture of melancholy than a pledge of faith.

Such was the man who was now making hasty preparations to bring his nephew up to London that he might be crowned in the interest of his mother's family. The time the Queen had prescribed was short. Rivers must make temporary arrangements for maintaining the Council of Wales; the gentry and soldiers who were to compose the King's escort had to be mustered; and there were the thousand tasks of breaking up a great household and procuring provisions and armament for the journey. These matters, however, did not lie at the heart of Rivers' thoughts. Two days after he had received the Queen's first message, on April 16, he caused the new King to write to the burgesses of Lynn a letter which was buoyant enough. After reporting the death of his father, young **Edw**ard gave notice that he intended 'to be at our city of London in all **conv**enient haste by God's grace to be crowned at Westminster'. He **concl**uded by commanding the magistrates to show their zeal by keeping peace and good order. Why should Earl Rivers be at pains to inform the insignificant town of Lynn of the great change which fortune had suddenly wrought? His favourite manor lay but eight miles from the town; in the first glow of the news he had remembered to communicate his happy prospects to his old friends and retainers.[24]

Since then, however, he had received further messages from Westminster; he had read, and courteously answered, an inquiry from Richard of Gloucester. The communications from the capital and the communication from Yorkshire did not rest comfortably together in his mind. On April 23 Rivers, a Knight of the Garter, superintended a splendid ceremony in which the new King honoured St. George. The next morning, at the head of 2,000 men and a long train of carts stuffed with household goods, supplies, and barrels of armour, the King and his uterine uncle left the lovely heights above the river Teme and rode eastward through the green and shapely hills of Shropshire. Rivers probably paid small heed to the scenery: he was still wondering, uneasily, what course he should follow when he reached Northampton.[25]*

III*

ON the afternoon of Tuesday, April 29, Richard of Gloucester rode into Northampton with his cavalcade of northern gentry. There was no sign of the King and Rivers. From his harbingers Richard learned that they had already passed through the town with their little army and continued southward towards Stony Stratford. He also learned from out-riders of Buckingham that the Duke would shortly reach

Northampton. Ordering the harbingers to assign the quarters they had arranged for, Richard prepared to spend the night at the inn which had been bespoken for himself and Buckingham.[1]*

Shortly after, the beat of horses' hooves in the street outside sounded the arrival, not of Buckingham but of Anthony, Earl Rivers, accompanied by a train of attendants. Readily he hailed Richard with the name of Protector. He had come, he said, at the behest of their new sovereign lord to convey young Edward's greetings to his uncle. Saluting him with equal courtesy, Richard took him into mine host's best parlour. Servants were commanded to arrange lodging for the Earl at a nearby inn and billets for the Earl's men.

Rivers quickly came to the heart of his errand. The King had pushed on to Stony Stratford for the night, he informed Richard with all the nonchalance he could muster, because it was feared that Northampton and the surrounding villages lacked sufficient accommodations both for the royal train and that of his uncle.

Richard acknowledged the explanation without asking questions; the Earl and he drank together and fell into genial conversation. While he listened to Anthony Woodville, however, Richard must have been turning over in his mind the possible significance of this cordial embassy. The Earl's greeting chimed oddly with Hastings' reports of what was happening in London. The excuse for the King's failure to await him was scarcely convincing. Necessary though it might have been for the greater part of Edward's train to move on southward, why had the King himself—if he was so eager to greet his uncle—not remained at Northampton? Did the answer lie in the fact that Stony Stratford was fourteen miles closer to London?

In the midst of supper the Duke of Buckingham arrived. Perceiving that the evening was merry, he at once matched his spirits to the occasion. When the meal was cleared away, the three noblemen lingered over wine in animated talk. Henry Stafford was ready of tongue; Anthony Woodville was a man of imagination who had seen much of the world; it was undoubtedly Richard of Gloucester who said least. So ironically convivial were these idle hours, precariously perched upon the edge of sudden action and great events, that this age, usually careless of recording itself, remembered the moment well. The cultivated Italian, Mancini, the grave ecclesiastic who wrote the 'Continuation' of the *Croyland Chronicle*, sometimes omit affairs of prime importance; but this bubble of life they were both at pains to report.

It was late evening by the time the three men rose from the table.

Casually they had agreed to ride together in the morning to Stony Stratford. After genial farewells, Rivers with a few of his intimates left the inn to seek his bed. Within the chamber where Richard and Buckingham had resumed their seats, the atmosphere of gaiety instantly disappeared. Rushlights flickered upon the serious faces of their advisers drawn close about them. Before the Dukes decided upon a course of action, they had to explore each other's minds. It was Buckingham who, by a single message, had suddenly thrust himself into Richard's affairs, and it was undoubtedly Buckingham who now did most of the talking. As a result of what he said this late night in a Northampton inn, he leaped from obscurity into the light of high events. Seldom has a man so little known become so important so quickly.

By his blood he was endowed with great place. He was descended from Thomas of Woodstock, youngest son of Edward III. Twenty-three years before this meeting with Richard, his grandfather had been killed, on the outskirts of this very town, fighting for King Henry against Richard's brother and Warwick. His father had been mortally wounded at St. Albans in 1455, fighting against Richard's father. His mother was the daughter of Edmund, duke of Somerset, who likewise perished at St. Albans holding the house of York in deadly hatred. At the age of twelve he had become the ward, and very valuable property, of Queen Elizabeth. She reared him in her household and while he was still not much more than a boy she wedded him to her sister Katherine. For a number of years thereafter the couple had lived in the Queen's shadow, while Buckingham nursed his hatred of the family he had been forced to marry into. He took no part in the tumultuous events of 1470-71; in the last decade of Edward's life he made no mark at court or in government. He was appointed seneschal of England to pronounce sentence of death upon the Duke of Clarence probably because he was, after Richard, the premier duke of the realm. He occasionally appears as a name in the record of court ceremonies. Upon the screen of history he had in his first thirty years cast but a faint image.

Now, suddenly, out of nowhere, propelled by the moment and by whatever dreams he had been dreaming in remote Brecon, he had appeared at Richard of Gloucester's side to make fervent offers of his service and swear his love for the Protector's cause. He talked on, flushed and animated; sober and musing, Richard listened. Untested though Richard knew him to be, Buckingham made a remarkable impact. He was everything that Richard was not—eloquent, volatile, buoyant. What better ally could the Protector wish than the man who, after himself, was the first peer of England?

Still, impressed though he was, Richard himself shaped the course of action on which they finally agreed: his character is stamped upon its simplicity and decisiveness. He had spent his life dealing with conspiracy and disorder. His experience had taught him that a single violent stroke may prevent widespread violence, that a potential enemy should be immobilized first and his intentions examined later. He made his decision out of what he had learned from being the hardy prop of his brother's throne. Before the Dukes retired to a very brief rest, they had drawn up a set of orders for their lieutenants.

As the dawn of April 30 broke over Northampton, Earl Rivers' inn was quietly surrounded by armed men, and his people were forbidden to issue forth. The Earl's escort was similarly confined to its quarters. Guards posted on the Stony Stratford road allowed none to pass. Abruptly awakened to this unpleasant situation by his frightened servants, Earl Rivers decided to put a good face upon the matter. He was permitted to leave his inn in order to confront the Dukes, whom he greeted with his wonted courtesy. When, affecting bewilderment, he inquired the reason for this incomprehensible proceeding, he was at once committed to custody. Then, in the first light, Richard and Buckingham rode hard for Stony Stratford.

They found the town crowded with mounted men in the act of departing. One detachment was already moving southward. The young King, surrounded by the officers of his household, had just mounted his horse. Ceremoniously, the gentlemen of Wales and Yorkshire alighted and did reverence to their boy sovereign. Between the kneeling ranks, Richard and Buckingham advanced to the King's presence, paid him the homage of their knees, and rose to greet him with grave respect. There was no doubt a quaver in young Edward's voice as, searching in vain for the sight of Rivers and beholding instead the sober features of an uncle he knew little of and had not been taught to love, he returned the greeting.

Close by Edward were his aged chamberlain, Sir Thomas Vaughan, and his half brother, Lord Richard Grey. The latter had the day before joined the King, having ridden out from London with a number of Woodville followers. Possibly, he had carried orders from the Queen and the Marquess that Rivers must, at all costs, get his nephew to London before Richard of Gloucester overtook them. Behind the royal party stretched ranks of armed men. Behind the Dukes stood their company of attendants. With calm authority Richard informed the King that he had serious tidings to relate. Vaughan, Grey and a few others surrounded Edward as he retired to his lodgings accompanied by the Dukes. After Richard had condoled with his nephew for the loss of his father, he announced his purpose in plain terms. Certain ministers about the dead King, he said, had ruined his health by encouraging him in his excesses. These men must be removed from power in order that they might not play the same game with the son as with the father——

Lord Richard Grey started to protest, was imperiously silenced by Buckingham.

In fact, Richard pursued, these very men had not only openly conspired to deprive him of the protectorship, lawfully his, but they had laid a trap for his life. Lord Richard here and Earl Rivers and the Marquess were the leaders. For his own safety he had been forced, at Northampton, to arrest Rivers.

The young King stammered that the Marquess and Lord Richard and his uncle Rivers were his friends and he trusted them. As for the governing of the realm, he was certain that his nobles and the Queen——

The ruling of the land, Buckingham interposed, was for men, not women. The Queen had no rightful authority. Edward had been deceived, the truth hidden from him.

Angry and frightened, the twelve-year-old monarch listened. Learned though he was, he was not much more than a child. In a single moment his world had collapsed. Perhaps he had not even been informed of the protectorship. Quietly Richard told the pale boy that for many years he had served his father in council and in battle. Because of his experience, his reputation and his nearness of blood, he had been appointed by King Edward the Protector of the realm and the heir. Would His Highness be content with his father's ordinance?

Edward realized that his only course was to acquiesce with what dignity he could muster. He would indeed be content, he said falteringly, with the government his father had arranged for him. Richard explained that for safety's sake they must return to Northampton until word came that all was well in London. The King nodded helplessly. When he had been escorted to his chamber, Lord Richard Grey and Sir Thomas Vaughan were promptly arrested. Then Richard dealt with the royal escort. He proclaimed that since the King had now been safely received into his protectorship, the servants and soldiers who had accompanied him from Ludlow were immediately to quit Stony Stratford and disperse in orderly fashion to their homes. Though they outnumbered the Duke's followers, they were now leaderless; and they had no heart to oppose the stern command of the first general in the kingdom. In small groups they quickly melted away.[2]*

On the return to Northampton, Richard and Buckingham were at pains to pay Edward every mark of honour due a King, but they severed all his connections with his Woodville past. When the boy was lodged, he found his personal attendants replaced by men of the Dukes' choosing. Probably he shed a few tears. At dinner that night Richard doubtless sought to comfort the unhappy boy. To Edward's uncle Rivers he sent a dish from his own table, praying him to be of good cheer, that all should be well enough. The courtly Rivers returned his thanks to Richard but requested the servant to bear the dish to his nephew, Lord Richard, who unused to adversity, needed comfort the more. He himself was well acquainted with the fickleness of fortune.

Richard prepared to remain at Northampton until he had word from Hastings what effect his *coup* had produced upon affairs in London. He seems to have felt little anxiety. After all, he had done no more than to assume the office of Protector which his dead brother had willed him. Before he retired that night, he dispatched an explanation of his action to the lords and citizens.

Meanwhile, on the road which ran southward through St. Albans and Barnet, messengers of the Duke of Gloucester and friends of the Woodvilles were already galloping headlong for London with the momentous news.

It was nearly midnight of the same evening, April 30, when the tidings reached the Queen and the Marquess at Westminster. Enraged and terrified, they rushed frantically into action. Trusted advisers were tumbled from their beds. It was hastily decided that the King must be wrested from Gloucester and Buckingham by force. Late night or no, the Marquess dispatched appeals to the chief lords from whom he might expect support. Their answers sent the façade of power crashing about the Woodvilles' ears. Some were evasive; some, openly hostile. Nobody, it appeared, wanted to fight for the Queen and the Marquess; few were disposed to identify the Woodville cause with that of the young King.

Mother and son fell into a panic. Lacking either the innocence or the courage quietly to await the King's arrival, they could think only of flight. Ironically, Sir Edward Woodville and his fleet had sailed only the day before, Sir Edward taking his share of Edward IV's treasure with him. The Marquess now hurriedly sent an escort to fetch the remainder of the treasure from the Tower. Then he, the Queen, and the Queen's brother Lionel, Bishop of Salisbury, retired precipitately to the sanctuary of Westminster Abbey, taking with them the royal princesses, the little Duke of York, brother to the King, and the more nervous of their followers. The rest, surrounded by their armed retainers, remained uneasily in the shadow of the Abbey and the palace.[3]*

Meanwhile, Richard's messenger had roused the Lord Chamberlain. Jubilantly Hastings heard the news. Then, realizing that the city, crowded with nobles come up for the coronation, would soon be shaken by rumours, he sent off a message of reassurance to Thomas Rotherham, Archbishop of York, the Chancellor.

Rotherham was not without ability, but he was ageing and timorous and he was committed to the Queen's cause.[4] Jerked from sleep and confronted with this shocking news, he was in no mood to hear from Hastings' servant that all would be well. 'Well!' he cried out, his hands trembling. 'It may be well enough but it will never be as well as it has been!' Wildly bidding his attendants take weapon, he seized the Great Seal of England and, riding in the midst of his armed household, he hastened to the Queen. At Westminster he came upon a scene of torchlit confusion. Crates and boxes, furniture, plate, tapestries were being carried and dragged from the palace to the sanctuary. Men were ripping a great hole in the sanctuary wall so that the Queen's goods and the coffers containing the dead King's treasure might more quickly be stowed within. Rotherham found the Queen sitting 'alone, a-low on the rushes all desolate and dismayed'. When he attempted to comfort her by using Hastings' assurances, she cut him short with the fierce cry that Hastings was 'one of them that laboureth to destroy me and my blood'. The Chancellor lost his head, spoke of crowning little York if any mischief happened to Edward, and finally, as an earnest of his zeal for her cause, deposited in her hands the Great Seal.[5]*

In the first light of dawn Rotherham betook himself back to his palace. Boats were already upon the river. The iron ring of harness could be heard in the streets. Men stirred abroad, armed, wary, harkening to the flying tales that raced through London like wildfire.

As it grew lighter, two movements could be discerned in the restless city. Some men made their way to Westminster and the Queen's party. Others were drawn to the powerful pole of the Lord Chamberlain. Many waited prudently in their inns and homes for some gleam of truth to shine through the fog of rumours. Those courtiers who were moved only by self-interest were caught in a painful dilemma; which-ever party they chose, they were ready, at the first indication of the shape of the future, to change sides.

Hastings was up early this morning to greet the lords and gentlemen who flocked to his standard in order to offer support, seek counsel, or gain protection. The most popular nobleman in the realm and the late King's dearest friend, he was, in fact, the man of the hour. He doubtless felt himself to be, not so much the representative of the Protector as, in spirit, the very custodian of King Edward's intentions. The Wood-villes, whose success he identified with his own destruction, had been crushed with a single blow. True, he may have been a trifle chagrined by the sudden prominence which Buckingham had assumed in the Protector's affairs; but the two Dukes had accomplished precisely what he had begged them to do. Despite the momentary threat of disorder, the future looked secure.

Having assembled the lords in an informal gathering, Hastings warmly defended Richard's action. The case of Rivers, Grey, and Vaughan, he promised, would be submitted to the decision of the King's council. His words satisfied almost all the magnates. They, and the city magistrates, were further reassured when the Protector's letter arrived.

He had not captured his nephew the King, Richard wrote, but had rescued him and the realm; both had fallen into the hands of those who, having tainted the honour and the health of the father, could not be expected to show more regard for the youth of the son. For his own safety and the safety of the kingdom he had arrested Rivers, Vaughan and Grey. He would soon bring the King up to London to be crowned.[6]★

This message completed Hastings' work. By the end of the day, the Lord Chamberlain was able to send Richard word that the Woodville cause had collapsed, that the Protector's action was approved, and that the city eagerly awaited his entrance with the King. The Chancellor, he added, had on first hearing the news given the Great Seal to the Queen but, repenting of this flagrant illegality, had hurried to Westminster to take it back again; in consequence, the lords had removed the Seal from his possession. The only bad news Hastings had to report was that on April 29 the Woodville fleet had sailed and that the Marquess had apparently rifled the royal treasure.

By May 2, Richard at Northampton was plunged into the thick of decisions. Satisfied though he was by Hastings' declaration that he could enter the capital at once, he hastened to dictate, in the King's name, two requests to the Archbishop of Canterbury:

Most reverend father in God and right entirely beloved cousin. We greet you heartily well, and desire and pray you to see for the safeguard and sure keeping of the Great Seal of this our realm unto our coming to our city of London. Where by your good advice and others of our council the same further may be demeaned for the weal of us and our said realm; and that it will like you to call unto you the lords there and provide for the surety and safeguard of our Tower of London, and the treasure being in the same, in all diligence, and our faithful trust is in you: given under our signet at our town of Northampton, the second day of May.[7]

Richard wrote to Hastings and to the Mayor and Aldermen of the city that the King and he would enter London two days hence, on Sunday, May 4. Rivers, Grey and Vaughan he had no wish to see brought prisoners in his train, and the times were too unsettled for any judgment yet to be passed upon them. He decided to transfer them to the safest place he knew, Yorkshire. Rivers was sent under guard to Sheriff Hutton; Grey, to Middleham; and Vaughan, to Pontefract. Next day Richard and Buckingham and their train of gentlemen rode southward with the King, halting for the night at St. Albans.[8]

Of Richard's attempt, in these first hours of their relationship, to comfort and gain the confidence of his royal nephew only two hints survive. One of these is a piece of parchment, the record of an idle moment. At the top appears in a regally large, though rather stiff, hand the signature EDWARDUS QUINTUS. Next is inscribed in clear Italic script, neater than his usual writing, 'Loyaulte me lie', and directly beneath 'Richard Gloucestre'. Sprawled broad and careless at the bottom appears 'Souvente me souvene' and below, 'Harre Bokingham'. This playful scribbling doubtless represents an occasion when Richard and Buckingham were attempting to establish an easy relationship with their far from friendly young sovereign. The signatures, as well as the mottoes, are not without symbolic value.[9]

The second hint is plainer. It is the first grant made under the new King's signet and it was given on Saturday evening at St. Albans. Apparently Richard discovered in conversation with Edward that the boy had had a favourite chaplain at Ludlow, or a tutor, whom it would give him pleasure to reward. At once Richard summoned his secretary, John Kendall. A royal command was dispatched to the custodian of the seal of the earldom of March that he should send a writ to the Bishop of Hereford asking that one John Geffrey be appointed to the rectorship of the parish church of Pembrigge. The new monarch probably enjoyed his first exercise in power; whether he was grateful to his uncle who was so quick to do him pleasure is another matter.[10]*

Very early on the morning of Sunday, May 4, the royal cavalcade departed from St. Albans. The sun was not yet high in the sky as they rode across the rolling land north of Barnet. Perhaps Richard described to the King that desperate battle he himself had cause to remember so well, in which Edward's father had conquered the mighty Warwick. Not long after they had wound down the great hill south of Barnet, the King was greeted by the Mayor and Aldermen of London and a train of leading citizens. Men were thick upon the city walls as Edward passed through the gates into his capital. Cheering crowds packed the narrow streets. Church bells clanged and pealed.

The twelve-year-old sovereign appeared in blue velvet. On his right rode the Protector and on his left, Buckingham, both in coarse black cloth. The city fathers were gay in scarlet trimmed with fur. Behind, the five hundred gentlemen of Wales and Yorkshire, in black, made a sombre contrast to the bright violet gowns of five hundred of the most eminent burgesses. Of military force there was no sign, save for four wagons heaped with barrels of harness. These rolled at the head of the procession, escorted by criers who, at thronged street corners, paused to bellow that this armour—some of it labelled with the Woodville arms—had been gathered by Earl Rivers for use against the Duke of Gloucester. Most of the crowd were indignant, cried that it were alms to hang the rascals! But some were moved to doubt or distrust by this display.

On through the narrow streets towards Ludgate hill and St. Paul's the procession wound its way, cheered by lords and commons alike. Perhaps the noise of welcome could be heard even in the sanctuary at Westminster. Around the mighty pile of the cathedral the procession moved to the palace of the Bishop of London, where the sovereign dismounted to enter his temporary lodgings. The lords of his realm followed him in to pay him homage. Richard went on to Crosby's Place, his town house in Bishopsgate street. Thus, on the morning on which he was to have been crowned by the Woodvilles, was King Edward the Fifth brought to his capital city by the Lord Protector. The coronation had, of course, been postponed.[11]

IV*

RICHARD moved at once to restore confidence in the government. Assembling all the lords spiritual and temporal and the city magistrates, he administered to them in a solemn public ceremony the oath of fealty to King Edward the Fifth. A thrill of joy ran through London. Men lost their fears, looked forward to a prosperous reign. Lord Howard sent home thirty of his servants, and no doubt other barons who had surrounded themselves with bristling retinues did likewise.[1]

In this atmosphere of hope Richard summoned his first council. He ignored what was past; he did not exclude those who had most strongly supported the Woodvilles. The lords had taken the Great Seal away from Rotherham, but the Archbishop of York was called to the meeting. So was John Alcock, Bishop of Worcester, who had been president of the Prince's council at Ludlow and who had possibly accompanied young Edward to Stony Stratford. The men whom Richard welcomed to the council board were those who had served as the advisers and ministers of his brother.[2]

They immediately caused Richard to be proclaimed Protector and Defensor of the Realm. It does not appear that they elected him to this office; rather, they registered and confirmed the rights which King Edward's will had given him. They then proceeded to define the dimensions of the Protector's authority, but since the will is no longer extant, it is impossible to tell whether they again only approved what the dead King had ordained or whether the document was couched in general terms on which they now stamped their own interpretation. 'With the consent and goodwill of all the lords', reports the Croyland Chronicler, '[Richard] was invested with power to order and forbid in every matter, just like another king. . . .' He was also given the 'tutele and oversight of the king's most royal person'. As Regent of the kingdom and Governor of the Prince, he owned an authority most nearly like to that which the Duke of Somerset was to exercise three quarters of a century later during the minority of Edward VI. Though the royal council thus became an advisory body to the Protector, Richard well knew that his power depended upon the goodwill of the lords; and, as they doubtless had expected, he immediately promised that he would be guided in all things by their decisions. Writs and commands issued in the King's name soon began to bear the formula, 'by thadvise of oure derest oncle the duc of Gloucester, protectour and defensour of this our royalme during our yong age', to which was sometimes appended the phrase, 'and by thadvise of the lordes of our counsaille'.[3]*

Richard and the council quickly organized their government. Rotherham was formally rebuked for having given the Great Seal to the Queen, and the chancellorship was bestowed, to everyone's entire satisfaction, upon John Russell, Bishop of Lincoln. He was, says More, 'a wyse manne and a good and of muche experyence, and one of the beste learned menne undoubtedlye that England hadde in hys time'; and Mancini says, 'a man of equally great learning and piety'. One of the late King's most distinguished diplomats, Russell had been Keeper of the Privy Seal. This office was now conferred upon Master John Gunthorpe, Dean of Wells, who had likewise long served King Edward in council and on embassy and whose erudition was probably even more remarkable than Russell's. A number of minor appointments were made but no other noteworthy changes. John Wode, the former Speaker of the Commons and friend of Richard's, was appointed Treasurer; even here the Protector could scarcely be accused of favouritism since Wode had formerly served as under-treasurer. The judges, the barons of the exchequer, were all confirmed in their offices. Richard sought to make the transition from the old regime to the new as unobtrusive as possible.[4]

The council now turned their attention to the needs of their sovereign lord. It was felt by all that the Bishop of London's palace was no proper lodging for a King; no doubt its chambers called to mind the miserable weakness of Henry VI, who had more than once sought refuge there. Some councillors proposed the Hospital of St. John as a suitable abode; one or two even suggested Westminster, though its proximity to the sanctuary certainly did not recommend it. It was the one new voice in the council, the Duke of Buckingham, who made the obvious nomination: the Tower. This held, then, no such dark and bloody connotation as the reign of the Tudors conferred upon it. Previous Kings had frequently used it as a residence; it was thought of as a secure fortress in time of trouble. After some discussion, Buckingham's proposal was unanimously approved. Sometime between the ninth and the nineteenth of May King Edward was installed in the apartments of state at the Tower. With equal harmony Richard and his council discussed the question of the King's coronation. So quickly had the realm settled into quiet that it seemed safe to hold the ceremony within a few weeks; the date was tentatively set for Tuesday, June 24. Not long after, it was decided that Parliament should be assembled to confirm the establishment of the new reign. Summonses were dispatched on May 13 for a gathering of Lords and Commons on June 25, and three days later the Archbishop of Canterbury was requested to assemble his clergy in convocation at St. Paul's.[5]

A matter of less importance, executing the provisions of the late King's will, had, however, proved impossible to manage. On May 7 the executors, meeting with the council at Baynard's Castle, near Paul's Wharf, the town residence of Richard's mother, had unanimously declined to administer the will. How, for example, could Edward's bequests to his children be honoured while the Queen held them fast in sanctuary? The late King's goods were accordingly put under ecclesiastical sequestration by the Archbishop of Canterbury; on May 23 he appointed a commission to sell sufficient of them to pay the costs of the royal funeral which had amounted to the resounding sum of 1,496 pounds, seventeen shillings and twopence.[6]

The Woodvilles, indeed, constituted the most pressing problem which confronted the new government. Honouring his promise, Richard had at once submitted to the council's scrutiny his action in arresting Rivers, Vaughan, and Grey. His temper had been much sharpened, however, since he had sent Earl Rivers a dish from his table. There was some evidence that the Woodvilles had been preparing to use force against him; Sir Edward was even now defying the government with his powerful fleet; and the Marquess had managed to escape from sanctuary. It was thought that he had fled to his uncle Edward but he had actually gone into hiding, where, no one ever learned. Richard proposed that a charge of treason be brought against Rivers, Vaughan, and Grey. Buckingham, Hastings, and probably the rest of the barons hearily concurred. A number of the spiritual lords, however, demurred. Richard's swift action, they pointed out, had forestalled his adversaries. Even if it could be proved that the Woodvilles had prepared an ambush, it was highly doubtful that their conspiracy could be called treason since Richard had not yet been officially proclaimed Protector. At last the council agreed upon a compromise. No specific charges were brought but all were of one mind that Rivers and his associates must be kept in prison. As for the Queen herself, she presented a problem concerning which there was no disagreement but only a very cloudy prospect of success. How could she be persuaded to abandon the role of foiled conspirator and assume the honourable, but powerless, office of Queen

Dowager? Richard appointed a committee to negotiate with her; it made no headway but persisted in its efforts, exposing itself to throbbing scenes of scorn, tears, and indignation.[7]*

The fleet of Sir Edward Woodville was the most pressing danger, however; and here, on the familiar field of action, Richard, with the concurrence of the council, came swiftly and surely to grips with the problem. He was not long in London before he discovered that Sir Edward's navy was anchored in the Downs, that favourite rendezvous for ships situated between the Goodwin Sands and the east coast of Kent. Believing that a speedy offer of forgiveness would make force unnecessary, he decreed that all soldiers and sailors who deserted the Woodville fleet would be given full pardon; Sir Edward, the Marquess, and their staunch adherent Robert Ratcliffe were denounced as enemies of the state and a price put upon their heads. On May 9 Richard dispatched men to take command of fortifications on the Isle of Wight and at Portsmouth and to provide stores and armament for the ships which were hastily being readied. Lord Cobham, a retainer of Lord Howard's, was sent with a small force to Dover and Sandwich to see that the ports were prepared to resist a surprise attack. On May 10 Richard ordered Sir Thomas Fulford and one Halwelle 'to rig them to the sea in all haste and go to the Downs among Sir Edward and his company in that they may'. Four days after, Edward Brampton, John Wellis, and Thomas Grey received writs 'to go to the sea with ships to take Sir Edward Woodville'. It was an audacious and ticklish venture—with only a few craft to approach close enough to Sir Edward's vessels in order to spread the news of the offer of pardon. Richard had been able, however, to find audacious men. Perhaps Lord Howard, who was well acquainted with both Fulford and Brampton, had suggested them to the Protector.[8]

Thomas Fulford was the son of Sir Baldwin Fulford, that ill-fated Lancastrian knight from the West Country, who in the early spring of 1460 had sworn that, 'on pain of losing his head, he would destroy the earl of Warwick and his navy, if the king would grant him his expenses'. Warwick's navy never felt his steel, but he indeed lost his head; for after Towton it was cut off and sent to be hung up in the market-place of Exeter. Though Thomas had sailed with his father, he dared two years later to thrust himself upon King Edward's attention by petitioning for permission to bury Sir Baldwin's head. Not long after he thrust himself even more vigorously upon the attention of John Staplehill, who had captured Sir Baldwin and been given some of his lands as a reward.

With an armed company Thomas stormed one of these manors, plundered it of £300 worth of goods, beat the servants, and 'so menaced, affrayed, and disturbed' Staplehill's wife that 'she was . . . in despair of her life', having been told plainly that if her husband 'had there then been founden, there should no gold have redeemed him'. Nothing came of Staplehill's vehement complaint; Sir Thomas had, in fact, already received a pardon from the King. Edward found it difficult to dislike a bold man. Yet when Warwick reseated Henry VI briefly on the throne, Sir Thomas sallied forth for the old cause. Even after Tewkesbury had ended the last Lancastrian hope, he broke out of sanctuary to go down to the West Country and stir up commotions. Again, though, he managed to make his peace with Edward, and in 1481 this hardy sea-dog had commanded the fleet which threatened the west coast of Scotland.[9]

On the east coast at this same time Edward Brampton held a command in the victorious navy of Lord Howard. Far from being the mere English that his name suggests, he was an exotic: a tough and swash-buckling Portuguese Jew, doubtless the same Brampton who had accompanied young Richard into Norfolk in the disastrous summer of 1469. There were few Jews in the England of this day and only a handful who at any one time accepted Christianity. Like these, Brampton had lived in the 'House of Convertites', had been god-fathered at his baptism by the King himself and taken the King's name; but unlike the rest, he had sallied forth, sword in hand, to do his god-father any kind of service that needs a hardy fellow. He had wielded a doughty blade at Barnet and Tewkesbury. When the attempt to dig the Earl of Oxford out of St. Michael's Mount had bogged down in December of 1473, King Edward sent Brampton and William Fetherston with four ships to assault the Mount by sea and cut off the Earl's supplies, and not much more than a month later Oxford was the King's prisoner. In Lord Howard's naval expedition of 1481 Brampton had commanded one of the largest warships, 'the great carvel of Portingale', which carried 160 sailors and 240 soldiers.[10]

Such were the men, Fulford and Brampton, whom Richard picked to send against the Woodville fleet. They brought the mission off as well as anyone could expect, with the aid of a couple of sea dogs as hardy and resourceful as themselves. After they had somehow managed to spread the offer of pardon through the fleet, Sir Edward Woodville in alarm planted a knot of trusted men in each of the ships whose masters or officers he doubted; he took special care to set a picked troop aboard two great Genoese carracks which he had chartered for his service. It was the Italian commanders, however, who, determined to avoid offending the government, ruined Sir Edward's hopes. Having first filled their guards with drink and then overpowered them one by one, the Genoese captains blew up trumpets, broke out their colours, and, declaring for the Protector and council, set sail for London. After a moment of confusion, all but two of the fleet followed suit. In these two vessels Sir Edward and a troop of his adherents fled to Brittany, bearing a portion of Edward the Fourth's treasure to line the future enterprises of one Henry Tudor, calling himself the Earl of Richmond.[11]

While Richard was working to dispose of the Woodville fleet, he had moved to halt the undeclared war which the French were waging at sea. On May 11 he sent to the aggrieved Lord Cordes an envoy empowered to discuss a mutual restoration of ships and goods as prelude to a renewal of the truce, and he had requested Lord Dynham, Hastings' deputy at Calais, to further the negotiations as best he could. Happily, Maximilian of Burgundy soon sent messages of friendship to the new government, to which Richard quickly replied, pledging a continuance of their old peace and amity. He also sent more ships to sea, one of which was commanded by John Davy, a servant of Lord Howard's.[12]

In these first days of his protectorship, then, Richard was moving quickly on a wide front of action. This range of measures reveals almost nothing, however, about the political complexion of the council, about what was going on in the minds of these councillors who on May 5 had rushed with such happy unanimity to harness themselves to the chariot of the protectorship. Before May ended it began to appear that there had been some misunderstandings concerning who was driving and who was pulling.

Though most of the spiritual lords in the new council had been far from hostile to the Woodvilles, they could be counted on to accept Richard's government, or any government which was clothed in the appearance of law or traditional right. As bishops, these men were for peace and continuity and royal dominion. They were also—indeed, primarily—civil servants, learned though they were in theology and conscious though they remained of being churchmen. Bishoprics were the rewards they had received for being successful ministers of state. The English Church did not supply the King with officers; the officers of the King staffed the English Church: denizens were they of Westminster, not of their sees. Hence, public servants like John Russell, Bishop of Lincoln, or John Gunthorpe, Dean of Wells, or John Morton,

Bishop of Ely, did not possess power but were its servants. Their force lay in the abilities they exercised in their dual roles of executives and advisers. They administered policy which they created only to the extent to which power heeded their counsel.

The sudden eclipse of the Queen and the Marquess had left a kind of political vacuum. The Woodvilles had been for years the only check, so it seemed, upon Hastings' will. Within the frame of the protectorship, he and the barons were the one discernible party. In supporting Richard, they were acknowledging their own triumph. When Hastings had come from Calais in the fall of 1482, five hundred gentlemen in white gowns had met him at Dover to escort him in honour to the King.[13] His intimacy with Edward, his services to the royal house, his unparalleled popularity with nobles and commons alike gave him a position of indefinite but immense power. How could he help seeing himself as the guardian of the cause of York? The protectorship entitled Richard to the form of complete authority because Edward had so willed it and because Richard was the King's only brother. As for the fact of power, that was to be wielded harmoniously, through the Protector, by Hastings and his friends. The future looked no less bright than the immediate present. Surely the young King, now effectively separated from his maternal kindred, would not forget the services nor withstand the charm which had so captivated his father. In the race for the favour of the boy who within a few years would rule in his own right, whose chances were brighter than Hastings'?

The inner baronial group of which Hastings was chief was in fact very small, numbering only Lord Stanley, Lord Howard, and—of much lesser weight—William FitzAlan, Earl of Arundel and Warden of the Cinque Ports. With these must be considered the Earl of Northumberland, who, though exerting small force at the centre of authority, represented another kind of power as Warden of the East and Middle Marches and, next after Richard, chief of the North. During these first weeks of May he probably stood beyond the periphery of Hastings' interests. Richard, it seems, had not found reason to be sure of his loyalty. Therefore the Protector renewed Northumberland's appointment as Warden for one year only, carefully guaranteeing him the payment of his expenses, and extended his captaincy of Berwick for no more than five months. This provisional grant invited Northumberland to declare his allegiance unequivocally.[14]

The barons who had welcomed him so warmly to the capital Richard, in turn, heeded and honoured. Hastings kept all his offices:

the governorship of Calais, the sinecure of the mastership of the mint and the exchange, and the Lord Chamberlainship which gave him ready access to the young King's ear. Richard and Buckingham made much of him, deferred to his opinions and sought his company. A protégé and agent of his, a rising young lawyer named William Catesby, he recommended to Richard's attention. Richard obligingly appointed Catesby Chancellor of the earldom of March and made him a member of the council. Hastings' deputy at Calais, Lord Dynham, was given the stewardship of the Duchy of Cornwall. Thomas, Lord Stanley, second in importance to Hastings, also fared well enough: he seems to have retained the prominent position in the Protector's council which he had held in the late King's as well as the stewardship of the royal Household. Lord Howard was made Seneschal of the Duchy of Lancaster south of Trent; and the Earl of Arundel became Master of the Game of all the King's forests, chaces and parks south of Trent.[15]*

Yet upon the fair prospects of Hastings and his friends a mighty shadow had fallen. It was cast by Henry Stafford, second Duke of Buckingham. They could not have foreseen his sudden leap to Richard's side, nor, immediately after, what the leap might portend. When Buckingham rode into London, they doubtless supposed that he would slip quietly into their ranks: there was nowhere else to go. It was not long before they were undeceived. From the very first, Buckingham's voice sounded often and weightily in the council chamber. Without as well as within the chamber he made no bones about the fact that he was the Protector's ally, the Protector's friend, the Protector's man. It was Buckingham who rushed in to fill the political vacuum left by the collapse of the Woodvilles. He created, he was, the party of the Protector.[16]

Nor did Richard look askance at his enthusiastic adherent. His motives for so willingly accepting Buckingham's service were mixed and perhaps not altogether conscious, and perhaps they shifted and changed shape with the passage of time. In this uncertain and unsettled May he could scarce have helped appreciating so zealous a supporter. Furthermore, Buckingham the man of state was new-born. In the feuds of Edward's court he had assumed no positive role; he was entangled in no old commitments nor moulded by previous political partisanship; though his family was Lancastrian, he had been reared in the bosom of the House of York; though he was married to a Woodville, his antipathy to the tribe was known to all. Since, in addition, he was, after Richard, the first peer of the realm, and therefore born to greatness, none of the barons should be offended if Richard showed him high favour. His strength and his chief lands, too, lay in the very region in which, Richard realized, his government was weakest, Wales; for Wales and the Marches had been ruled by Earl Rivers. Yet part, at least, of the explanation for the tremendous hold which Buckingham, in a matter of days, had secured upon the Protector lay in the depths of Richard's character. He had plucked the dominant string of Richard's sense of loyalty. First to put himself at the Protector's side, he had been a rock of dependability in that anxious, slippery situation at Northampton and Stony Stratford which afterwards looked so simple only because it was so adroitly handled. He had become, indeed, a friend, to a man who lacked the flexible and easy temperament to be a maker of friends. It is not uncommon for men without the radiance of a vivid personality to over-value that radiance, to mistake a will-o'-the-wisp for a genuine fire. Such doubtless was Richard. And such a prismatic man was Buckingham, catching the light of public attention and reflecting it intensified and flashing in a thousand glints and coloured sparkles. Probably he reminded Richard of his brother George, sounded in Richard's heart a tone like that which long ago within the walls of Fotheringhay castle George had sounded for the first time. If this be so, Richard would not let himself remember that the radiance of George of Clarence had been only a mask for dreams that were ego-ridden, irresponsible, and, in the end, fatal.[17]★

On May 15 Richard signalized Buckingham's pre-eminence in the protectorship by two vast grants of concentrated authority and patronage. In one he was given the power of supervision and array of all the King's subjects in Shropshire, Hereford, Somerset, Dorset, and Wiltshire, and in the same counties he was made constable of all the royal castles, as the offices should fall vacant, and steward of all the royal demesnes and manors. The second grant was yet more opulent: he was appointed Chief Justice and Chamberlain in both North and South Wales; supervisor and governor of the King's subjects in those regions; constable, steward, and receiver of the most important Welsh castles and lordships, with power to appoint all the chief officers of the counties; and keeper of all the royal forests and chases therein. He had the right to stuff castles with as many soldiers as he pleased, to take for his own use whatever armaments were on the royal lands and other goods as well, to dispose of great sums of royal income with very little accounting. That not even a few islands of land might remain which

were not subject to his sway, he was a few days later made constable
and steward of the castles and manors within Wales which belonged
to the duchy of Lancaster and the earldom of March. These grants, it
must be noticed, were not of possessions but of authority. They did not
increase Buckingham's baronial holdings at the expense of the Crown;
they did not create a great hereditary *appanage*. What they did, however,
was to make Buckingham the ruler, virtually the viceroy, of Wales and
the Marches and a good slice of the West Country.[18]

By the middle of May other men had gathered about the Protector,
developing the political organism which Buckingham had created at
one startling bound. It was hardly a party. It had been called into being
by the fusion of unique circumstances and particular personalities; yet
it represented, generically, the accretion of ambitions and devotions
and hopes and loyalties mixed with self-interests which attaches itself
to any leader of known capacity. In the eyes of certain councillors,
however, it began to take on the colour of a party. The men of this
accretion were alike only in their general allegiance to Richard; they
were separated from the baronial group, at first, only by their belief,
in most cases vague, that the protectorship possessed substance and
meaning as well as form.

Francis Lovell, created Viscount Lovell shortly before Edward's
death, was one of them, a man of whom little is known save that he was
probably Richard's oldest and dearest friend. He was destined to perish
mysteriously—by starvation, probably, as a consequence of being walled
up in what he thought was a safe refuge—after an adventurous life,
through which runs the one decisive theme of his devotion to Richard
of Gloucester. Richard now appointed him Chief Butler of England, an
office Earl Rivers had held, and gave him the ruling of the honour of
Wallingford and the lordship of Thorpe Waterfelde. Another adherent
from among the nobles was the young Earl of Lincoln, son of Richard's
sister Elizabeth and the Duke of Suffolk and great-great grandson of
Geoffrey Chaucer. Two prelates of the council soon identified themselves with the Protector's circle: Robert Stillington, Bishop of Bath
and Wells, who had once been Chancellor to King Edward and an
intimate friend of the Duke of Clarence and was no lover of the
Woodvilles; and Thomas Langton, whom Richard elevated to the
bishopric of St. David's on May 21 and who, like Gunthorpe and
Russell, was an experienced diplomat and a man of the New Learning.
Some of Richard's northern followers had been added to the council
or to his household, men like Sir Richard Ratcliffe and Sir James Tyrell

and Robert Brackenbury. And William Catesby, Hastings' man, was more and more becoming the Protector's man.[19]*

Except for the unexpected prominence of Buckingham, what most keenly flicked Hastings was the quiet shift in allegiance of John, Lord Howard. Howard had been one of the small group of barons at the heart of King Edward's government, a pack-horse, like Hastings, in the great affairs of the 1460's and 1470's. Howard had served under Hastings, had deferred to him. It was only when he dined at Lord Hastings' house that he honoured the master in sending generous tips to the cooks. For the Christmas of 1481 he had given 'my lord chamberlain a double silver dish to put hot water in' which cost 12 pounds, a handsome and expensive present. Two months later Howard gave him a pipe of fine wine costing three pounds, six shillings, eight pence. After the King's death he had stood with Hastings against the Woodvilles; along with Lord Stanley he was the nucleus of Hastings' party. Some time during the month of May, however, it became clear that Howard now looked to Richard of Gloucester for leadership. What may well have galled Hastings most was that Howard could be considered to represent—second only to himself among the barons—the true interests, the authentic tradition of the royal house.

John Howard was, indeed, of the essential stuff from which the triumph and dominion of York had been fashioned. Bred out of a union of the gentry with the high peerage, he sprang, on his father's side, from an old East Anglian family, while his mother was the daughter of that Mowbray Duke of Norfolk who had been exiled for life by Richard II. Some thirty years old when Edward assumed the crown in 1461, he made his first notable appearance in history as the new King marched towards Towton. Sir John Howard joined young Edward with a sword in one hand, a bag of gold in the other, the gold being a gift of £100 sent by the abbot of Bury St. Edmunds. The moment symbolizes the pattern of Sir John's subsequent life: devotion to Edward's cause and readiness to fight for it, a strong sense of the practical, the habit of being on hand at critical moments. Fortune and his abilities raised him to consort with princes; he came to know the lavish hospitality of Louis XI as well as the luxury of Edward's court. Yet he seems always to have remained the Essex man—plain, solid, tough, a careful householder with a generous heart, a lover of Colchester oysters and of the sea from which they are ripped. The sea was his element. He traded in ships; he fought in ships; ships were his dearest substance. But like most captains of his time he fought on land as well.

G

In the summer of 1462 he was besieging the Lancastrians in Alnwick castle; three or four months later he was commanding part of a fleet which harried the French coast. He served a time as sheriff of Norfolk and Suffolk. He engaged in the rough and tumble of East Anglian politics . . . and cooled his heels in prison a short while because of a fierce bout with the Pastons, in the course of which his wife remarked—with his own bluntness—that if Sir John's men found Paston, his life would not be worth a penny. Soon, however, it was John Paston's turn to taste prison life and Sir John Howard was set at liberty. In the unruly world of the 1460's Edward well realized his need of men like Sir John.[20]*

It was Howard who pursued Warwick's fleet in the spring of 1470 and, before the Earl slipped into Honfleur, wrested prizes from it. Taking sanctuary when Edward fled to Burgundy, he managed to reach London on Good Friday of 1471, the day after the King re-entered his capital, and thus he fought at Barnet and Tewkesbury. By this time he had been created a peer; he was soon after elected a Knight of the Garter. With Lord Hastings, his companion in arms and fellow member of the King's council, he entered, in 1471, into a closer relationship when he was appointed the Lord Chamberlain's deputy at Calais. The 1470's being a decade of peace, Howard became a diplomat. He helped weave a web of treaties between Duke Charles of Burgundy and Edward which led to the invasion of France in 1475—but he was not becalmed of adventure. On one of his missions the ship in which he was sailing to Calais was attacked by three Hanse vessels, driven on the sands, and in the fierce fight sixteen of Howard's men were hacked to death by the Easterlings. Lucky as well as handy with his sword, Howard escaped without a wound.

On the expedition to France he was one of the four commissioners who negotiated the treaty with Louis XI. After accompanying King Edward on to the bridge at Picquigny, he was dined the same evening by King Louis. With the exception of Hastings, he received the handsomest of the French pensions, 1,200 crowns a year, and many a fine piece of plate to boot. Subsequently, he became Edward's chief envoy to the court of France. It was the war with Scotland which gave him his greatest opportunity as an independent commander, and on the element he loved. In 1481 all England rang with his exploits after he had steered boldly up the Firth of Forth to destroy the pride of Scotland's navy.

The sketch of the man which his career draws—the outlines of a man of action—is transformed into a living portrait by his account books. For all his honours, his scars, and his service at courts, he yet remained essentially the country lord, concerned with the welfare of his tenants and neighbours, immersed in the business of his estates, knowing every detail of his household affairs. At home, on his manor at Stoke Nayland in Essex, he sat down with his steward every Saturday and went over the accounts, annotating them copiously with his own hand. Yet his purse was always open. He enjoyed pleasing children with little gifts; he was constantly bestowing alms wherever he went; 'item', reads the account book for October 13, 1482, 'to the young man of the stable that is sick, 4d.' Several promising youngsters around the countryside he supported, wholly or in part, at Cambridge University, and he encouraged other talents as well. On October 18, 1482, 'my Lord made covenant with William Wastell, of London, harper, that he shall have the son of John Colet, of Colchester, harper, for a year, to teach him to harp and sing, for the which teaching my lord shall give him 13s 4d and a gown. . . .' Howard, in fact, dearly loved music, music of all kinds: the earnest drone of a village bagpiper, the martial airs of my lord of Gloucester's trumpeters, the lovely polyphony of trained voices. He kept in his household 'Thomas the Harper', a singer, Nicholas Stapleton, and at least four children to sing in his chapel, for whom he bought masses and anthems and doubtless provided schooling. Wandering musicians and the minstrel bands of the magnates alike found a warm welcome in his hall; the 'waytes' of London caroled for him when he visited the capital. Plays he took great pleasure in too; the strolling companies in noble livery and the humbler players of neighbouring towns visited him often and fared well. And when he sailed to fight the Scots, he took with him not only calthorpes and serpentines and steel harness but French romances and French treatises on dice and chess and *Les Dits des Sages*.

Though for two decades John Howard had done service of peace and war with Richard of Gloucester, relations between the two men seem to have become more intimate after the Scots war broke out. On the naval expedition of 1481 he and Richard had conferred about operations at Newcastle or Scarborough; the success that each achieved in the North itself provided a fresh tie. In the course of 1481 Richard sold to John Howard his East Anglian manor of Wysnowe for 1,100 marks. The following February John Kendall arrived at Stoke Nayland to deliver the 'evidences', i.e., the title, of the property. He returned to Yorkshire with a generous amount of Howard's silver jingling in his

purse and in his baggage Howard's gift to his master of seven crossbows
of wood and one of steel. What more fitting present from the first
admiral to the first general of the realm? That summer Howard was
entertained by Richard's players on the shawmes and at Christmas
by a travelling quartet of his actors.[21]

Music and armour. . . . The two men had interests in common. There
were other reasons why Richard and Howard might develop a relationship different from that which existed between Richard and the other
great barons of the King's council. Unlike Hastings, Howard was not
a boon companion of the King's idleness; unlike Stanley's, his hard
service to the cause of York was flawed by no lapses in allegiance.
There were affinities of temperament as well; plainness of mind, hardi-
hood developed by a long experience of action, a mutual sense that
each was a man deeply rooted in his own 'country' and touched by
the spirit of the feudal past.[22]★

Despite his association with Hastings and Stanley, John Howard
chose to regard the Protector as the stable and meaningful centre of
the new regime. On May 15, the day after he had been granted the
stewardship of the Duchy of Lancaster south of Trent, Lord Howard
presented to Richard a cup with a cover, weighing 65 ounces of gold.
When Anne, Duchess of Gloucester, arrived in London three weeks
later, she sent, that very day, a box of 'waffers' to John Howard's
wife.[23]

Despite the differences in interest and allegiance that were beginning
to develop among the councillors, the government of the Protector
functioned in harmony and with confidence throughout the month of
May. Still, men's minds were very sensitive to the future. Edward the
Fifth was King right enough, but, in the view of the times, he would
not be utterly and finally enthroned until he received the chrism and
the crown in Westminster Abbey. Recognizing this feeling, Richard
had pushed on preparations for a splendid coronation. Under the
direction of Peter Curteys, Keeper of the Wardrobe, tailors were busily
fashioning satin and velvet and cloth of silver and of gold into ceremonial costumes for the young King and his household.[24] The date of
the event had been moved forward from Tuesday, June 24 to Sunday,
June 22, though the change had probably not yet been announced.[25]★
The sheriffs of all shires and great towns had been ordered, on May
20, to submit the names of all those, not knights, who for the past three
years had enjoyed an annual income of at least £40 a year from land

in order that they might be called to receive knighthood at the King's crowning; three weeks later the royal summons went out to fifty men—sons of the gentry and of the peerage, except Henry Colet, alderman of London—to appear at the Tower by June 18.[26] The counties and towns were electing men to represent them in the Parliament, and at the coronation too. Richard's friends, the magistrates and chief citizens of York, had chosen Thomas Wrangwysh, who was high in the Protector's favour, and William Wells, and, with their usual shrewd eye to business, had decided to pay their representatives for two extra days in order that they might attend the coronation 'to commune with such lords as shall be there for the weal of the city'.[27]★

The men of power, however, did not view the coronation in the same sentimental light as did most of the commons. In the councillors' view, far from stabilizing affairs, it would offer a terrible challenge to order ... and also to ambition. To Richard the problem was most urgent because most dangerous. In the council which after the coronation must inevitably govern for Edward while he was a minor, there would exist neither a leadership nor a relation with the King prescribed by law. How could government fail to become an arena of savagely competing interests, a bitter struggle to gain the ear of the young King who would soon be the fountain-head of power?

About mid May—either at the same time that the council decided to summon Parliament (before May 13) or only a little while after—Richard raised the question of the future. In answer, a proposal was put forward that the protectorship be continued until Edward the Fifth became of age to rule. The clerics of the council, the party of peace, supported it strongly; Hastings and his friends apparently approved also, either because they had not yet become seriously uneasy about their interests or because they found it impossible to defeat, and therefore impolitic to oppose, so popular a measure. The policy of extending the protectorship, the council agreed, should be presented for the sanction of Lords and Commons as the chief business of state which had required the summoning of Parliament.[28]

Richard well realized that there was no 'made law' or custom which dictated—or even acknowledged—such a proceeding. Like men of former times, he solved this problem of government for which the past offered no solution by consulting the Law of God and the Law of Nature. These, the fifteenth century knew, were written plain in the divine order of the world. It was left for later centuries to invent the idea that the sum of such solutions was something called the English

Constitution. By the Law of Nature, Richard recognized that political order and the rights of his own power could only be secured upon the goodwill of the realm. By the Law of God, he recognized that justice would be truly observed if the Lords and Commons, assembled with the King in his own High Court of Parliament, gave their assent to a bestowal of authority that the King himself, being a minor, was not able, and that no one else was entitled, to make. That Parliament would so assent, Richard, like the rest of the council, took for granted. The commons too knew the Law of God, wanted peace, and approved of the Protector. The most influential among the lords spiritual and temporal were already committed.[29]

So passed the month of May and the first days of June, 1483. What was to be feared and hoped from the future dominated the thoughts of men, as would poignantly appear before the protectorship was six weeks old. John Russell had begun to draft the speech which as Chancellor—and Richard's spokesman—he would deliver at the opening of Parliament. Taking for his theme, as was customary, the text from Holy Writ appropriate to that date—in this case, the text for the Nativity of St. John the Baptist which fell on June 24, the day before—Russell was shaping it by the tortuous scholastic method of the time into an appeal for harmony among the lords and orderly obedience in the commons, these to be nurtured by Parliament's confirming the continuation of the protectorship. Even by the standards of modern rhetoric, Russell had hit upon two moving and dramatic touches—one, in which he was going to picture the youthful King as standing between two royal brothers of high renown, his dead father and his uncle the Protector; the second he was working up as his peroration, in which, speaking as if in the King's own person, he would declare, 'Uncle, I am gladde to have yow ... confirmed in this place [,] you to be my protector in alle my [affairs] and besenessez. *Ita fiat,* amen'.[30]

Russell's future audience was already beginning to arrive in London; in the narrow streets lords and their retinues jostled knights of the shires and burgesses from the towns. How the government conducted itself from now until the coronation would be under the scrutiny of the whole realm. Busy with plans for the coronation and the Parliament as well as routine affairs, the council moved about rather bewilderingly, however, and often split into groups charged with special duties. At times the whole council met formally in the Star Chamber, the famous *camera stellata* at Westminster. More often, at the Tower Richard

drafted in council, a smaller administrative council, the writs and bills
through which business was dispatched, and the King then affixed his
signature or sign manual by way of commanding that the bills be
executed under the Great Seal or the Privy Seal or the Signet Seal, as
the particular bill or writ warranted—that is, by John Russell's office,
if it were an important patent that must blaze with the full authority
of red wax and linen; or by John Gunthorpe's office, if it were a routine
command; or merely by Richard's secretary John Kendall, if it were
business which demanded great haste or did not need to be formally
registered.

The committees of the council had divers meeting places. At Westminster a committee headed by Chancellor Russell seems to have had
charge of coronation arrangements. Another set of councillors—
particularly Hastings, Stanley, Rotherham, Morton and their staffs—
gathered at the Tower for official consultations about the conduct of
Parliament and spoke frequently with the King; less officially, they had
also begun to meet at each other's houses. Still another group, Richard's
intimate circle of advisers clustered at Crosby's Place. Functioning in
this maze of conciliar business were three various centres of govern-
mental or court activity. The most formal consisted of the justices,
the heads of the exchequer, the officers of the chancery and of Privy
Seal, who carried on their work at Westminster. The apartments of
the boy sovereign in the Tower had become the haunt of a variety of
men, some of whom came openly in dutiful homage while others
made more covert visits as friends of the Woodvilles, as the King's
sympathizers and adherents. The third centre was Crosby's Place, the
court of the Protector, thronged with his household staff, a growing
body of supporters, and the daily procession of men with suits,
grievances, hopes of place or favour.

Amidst increasing tension generated by the approach of the coronation and the Parliament and by the unacknowledged differences which
smouldered in the council, Richard carried on the labours of government, weighed the counsel of his friends, and, talking little himself,
listened to the minds of many men. Buckingham was the talker and
Buckingham was everywhere. When Richard rode through the streets,
Buckingham was at his side. In council Buckingham dominated the
discussion. Buckingham was working enthusiastically at being a great
man.

So passed the days of May. On June 5 Richard welcomed his wife
Anne to Crosby's Place: he must have besought her to join him as soon

as he reached London. Their little son, however, she had left at Middleham; his health was too delicate for such a journey. In the first hours
of their reunion Anne reported to Richard that his friends the citizens
of York were growing anxious about their suit for the reduction of the
city fee-farm.[31]* They could not be expected, Richard now realized,
to understand that the moment was unpropitious for such a grant on
his part. When Anne retired to her chambers, Richard summoned
John Kendall and, despite the pressure of greater affairs, earnestly
sought to make clear to the men of York that he had not forgotten
them:

Right trusty and well beloved, we greet you well, and where, by your letters of
supplication to us delivered by your servant John Brackenbury, we understand that,
by reason of your great charges that ye have had and sustained, as well in the defence
of this realm against the Scots as otherwise, your worshipful city remaineth greatly in
poverty, for the which ye desire us to be good mean unto the King's Grace for an
ease of such charges as ye yearly bear and pay unto His Highness, we let you wit that
for such great matters and businesses as we now have to do for the weal and usefulness
of the realm, we as yet can not [ne can] have convenient leisure to accomplish this
your business, but be assured that for your kind and loving dispositions to us at all
times showed, which we can not [ne can] forget, we in goodly haste shall so endeavour
us for your ease in this behalf as that ye shall verily understand we be your especial
good and loving lord, as your said servant shall show you, to whom it will like you
herein to give further credence; and for the diligent service which he hath done to our
singular pleasure unto us at this time, we pray you to give unto him laud and thanks,
and God keep you.[32]

V*

With the beginning of June there comes a change. A feeling of
unease, restlessness, doubt gathers like mist at Westminster and the
Tower. It is a thing of dark corners and the rustle of whispers, insub-
stantial but pervasive. Some do not perceive it or have no inkling of
its meaning.

Writing on Monday, June 9, to an acquaintance in the country,
Simon Stallworthe, a servant of the Lord Chancellor's, reports that
there is nothing new since he has last written, some time before May 19.
The Queen is still in sanctuary with the little Duke of York, Lionel,
Bishop of Salisbury, and others and will not yet depart. Wherever
they can be found, the possessions of the Marquess are seized; the Prior
of Westminster is in great trouble on account of certain goods [part
of the royal treasure, no doubt] which the Marquess had delivered to

him. Anne, the Lord Protector's wife, arrived in London on June 5. There is great business over the approaching coronation. The Protector, Buckingham, and all the other lords spiritual and temporal have been at Westminster in the council chamber from ten till two. None spoke with the Queen. . . .[1]

Only the last sentence points to any change in the political situation; negotiations with Elizabeth had been, at least temporarily, broken off. It is a pity that Stallworthe did not know or was not moved to report what happened in this formal session of the council, which apparently took place on the same day he wrote his letter; for on the following day the Protector set in motion a policy which abruptly altered the complexion of the protectorship.

The gatherings of Hastings and his friends had not gone unnoticed, nor the occasions they found to speak together with the young King. The very composition of the group suggested its reason for being. While Richard had remained afar off in Yorkshire, while Buckingham had been only a courtier and Howard, a follower of Hastings; Rotherham, Morton, Stanley, and Hastings had sat at the heart of Edward's government. Now they, the centre, felt themselves relegated to the periphery, while the periphery had presumed to become the centre. Well before May had run its course, Richard must have realized that this group had grown into a settled dissatisfaction with the new shape he had given the world, resented the pre-eminence of Buckingham, and considered themselves bereft of power they had taken for granted they would enjoy.[2]

Richard was already on guard against counter movements by the Woodvilles; men had been appointed to investigate and subdue any troubles they might foment. Perhaps it was such men who had first detected something suspicious in the activities of Hastings' party; perhaps these activities had been betrayed to the Protector by one of Hastings' followers. Buckingham set himself to probing their designs covertly, while he consorted with them in order to sound their intentions. To the Protector he certainly did not minimize the danger of an incipient conspiracy.[3]

Richard listened to the reports of his men and to Buckingham's warnings. He must have realized that Buckingham's tale lost nothing in the telling. He knew that Buckingham himself was the chief cause of the disaffection. The tendrils of his life were intertwined with Hastings'; they were the two men the mighty Edward had looked to before all others; they had shared the flight to Burgundy and the

G*

mist-wrapped, bloody journey of Barnet; and the genuine affability of the Lord Chamberlain had warmed Richard as it had the rest of the world. But to win back Hastings, Richard must, in some measure, sacrifice Buckingham. Yet, if he followed this policy, he would deflate his partisan in order to placate a man who was beginning to act like his rival; and he was tied to Buckingham now by a bond of loyalty which it was not in his nature to break. The chief men who whispered with Hastings, furthermore, had each already stirred distrust or dislike in Richard's mind.

When he was but seventeen years old—in the spring of 1470—he had experienced Stanley's capacity for disloyalty, when that shifty lord had been the husband of Warwick's sister. Now Stanley was the husband of a Lancastrian Pretender's mother. Thomas Rotherham, Archbishop of York, had all too recently shown where his heart lay; it was obvious that, resenting his loss of office and hankering after the Woodvilles, he looked sourly upon the protectorship. By far the most formidable in ability of the malcontents was John Morton, Bishop of Ely. He had served Edward well but only after the cause of Lancaster had finally expired. In ardently supporting the fortunes of Queen Margaret, he had hazarded his life in the field of action and been un-daunted by danger or disaster. Captured after the battle of Towton, he had escaped from the Tower to rejoin Margaret in France, and he had marched with her the dusty miles to the fatal field of Tewkesbury. Like many another man of the century, he had espoused the Church in order to rise. His *métier* was the manipulation of power, not the service of God. He was formidable because his fertile mind was driven by prodigious energy and will and an unflickering ambition, and because, having a vast experience of men and affairs, he knew when to be bold as well as prudent. Mancini describes him as a man 'of great resource and daring . . . trained in party intrigue since King Henry's time. . . .' It says much of him that, afterwards, he would serve Henry VII as first minister, to the entire satisfaction of them both, and that he would be mainly remembered as the wielder of Morton's Fork, a device to extract money for his master. To one who spent much, Morton declared that obviously he could give much; to one who spent little, the Cardinal pointed out that therefore he could give much. Whether or not he actually invented this remorseless stratagem, its popular ascription to him reflects the esteem in which he was held when he at last achieved his ambition. Now, in the spring of 1483, though in his sixties, he was the master plotter of England.[4]*

Perhaps Morton had hoped to receive the post of Privy Seal or even Chancellor, or saw no love for himself in the Protector's eyes, or distrusted the Protector's intentions; perhaps, offered by the discontents of Hastings and Stanley the opportunity of weaving the threads of secret, weighty affairs, he could resist no more than a land-locked mariner resists the chance of putting to sea; and perhaps, remembering Henry Tudor in Brittany and beholding at last the first rift in the House of York, he was moved by an intuition that he might yet help Lancaster to regain the realm.

Richard, for his part, probably found neither Morton's past nor his character congenial; Richard's taste in ecclesiastical statesmen ran to men of genuine learning like Russell and Gunthorpe. He could sense that the wily Bishop of Ely might be dangerous—as he was well aware, for example, that the even more wily Louis XI was dangerous—but not that it might be wise to make use of him. There was little in common between the chieftain of the House of York and the ambitious ex-Lancastrian partisan who was deeply, subtly versed in the ways of power.

Such was the quadrumvirate of the dispossessed who, sometime in May, had moved from the private airing of their grievances to the more clandestine stage of seeking means to alleviate them. As this duel, hidden from all except Hastings' and Richard's intimates, was beginning to develop, Richard was suddenly put in possession of an old but highly inflammable secret—one which had, perhaps, previously brushed his mind, but only as a fleeting rumour of what his brother Clarence had once whispered or was said to have whispered.

Robert Stillington, Bishop of Bath and Wells, one day sought out the Protector in order to inform him—on what grounds will shortly appear—that the King and the little Duke of York had no rightful claim to the throne because Queen Elizabeth had not been Edward's lawful wife. At first, Richard probably communicated this startling and dangerous information to no one; then, after some days, only to Buckingham, and one or two other trusted intimates. He well knew that the continuation of the protectorship itself was becoming doubtful enough, without his violently shaking an already explosive mixture. As he turned the revelation over tensely and gingerly in his mind, his energies were bent to the double load of carrying on the government and discerning the purpose and the pace of Hastings' plans. The stringency of time gave an obvious edge to both. If the Protector were to be undone, the deed almost certainly must be accomplished before

Parliament met on June 25 to give the protectorship the tremendous reinforcement of its confirmation. Even at Crosby's Place there were certain to be men of Hastings' following. If they detected, as sooner or later they must, the rustle of a weighty secret being discussed *in camera* by the Protector's advisers, the Lord Chamberlain's suspicions would undoubtedly increase the urgency of his plans.[5]★

Meanwhile, the iron circle of necessity had closed upon the quadrumvirate of the dispossessed, and they had realized that there was but one direction in which they could move. Having supported Richard in order to drive out the Woodvilles, they must now turn to the Woodvilles in order to unseat the Protector. Such a reversal is a classical rhythm of politics. The Queen was no more distasteful to Hastings than Margaret had been to Warwick. The present impotence of the Queen's friends was more than balanced by their relation with the King. Hastings must win young Edward; therefore he must unite with those the King held most dear. This policy was urged upon the Lord Chamberlain by more than reason. The bright voice of Jane Shore was in his ear. At Edward's death, if not before, she had become the mistress of the Marquess of Dorset. When Hastings got rid of the Marquess he had taken over from that rival his dead master's woman, as he hoped to take over from Richard his dead master's son. Though she was hardly beloved of the Queen, Jane's warm heart, and perhaps her troubled conscience, made her an active champion of the Woodvilles. When Hastings revealed to her the direction of his thoughts, she begged him to succour the Queen and become the protector of the young King. She herself, she declared, would act as intermediary— who would be less suspected? Once Hastings and his friends determined to join forces with the Woodvilles, Jane Shore was chosen to deliver their messages to the sanctuary.[6]★

Either she was closely watched and her purpose discovered or the new alliance was brought to light by the men who had previously revealed Hastings' disaffection. Buckingham now possessed a powerful argument to drive the Protector to action. Richard listened to him and to other advisers and weighed the news.

With the King accessible, with this new combination creating redoubtable strength and opportunity, with a man like Morton at Hastings' elbow, and London crowded with nobles and their retainers, to delay until the plot was consummated or the conspiracy driven into the open might easily be fatal. Again, a problem of state assumed a military shape in Richard's eyes. One sudden stroke at Stony Stratford had undone the Woodvilles without jarring the web of peace and order. Was not the same strategy called for here, in a situation strikingly similar, a strategy condoned by the lawfulness of the power it preserved and the evil of disorder it averted? If, suddenly appropriating the King, Hastings' party sought to govern in his name, Richard must either lose his protectorship and perhaps his life, or conduct a civil war to regain Edward V as his father had been forced to conduct a civil war in order to approach Henry VI.

Powerful emotions swirled among these thoughts. The moment Hastings and Morton and Stanley and Rotherham touched hands with the Woodvilles, they had recreated, in Richard's eyes, the evil circle of Edward's court. They were seeking to revive a bitter pattern of estrangement and corruption. This political fusion probably struck deeper as an affront to his feelings than as a threat to his government; it fired in him a decade's accumulation of hurt and anger. Any thought of frankly exploring with Hastings their differences was blocked by the shadow of the dead King, the presumption of Mistress Shore, and the tongue of Buckingham. Richard's urge to retaliate against the past not only marched with his determination to safeguard the future but darkly marked out the course suggested to him by Stillington's revelation. A rush of passion swept him alike beyond the calculation of political expediency and the control of his conscience.

Perhaps, deepest of all, there stirred in Richard the sense that Hastings was disputing his dearest loyalty, that Hastings dared to consider himself truer to Edward than Richard was. With Stillington's secret lying unresolved in his mind and Jane Shore sharing the Lord Chamberlain's bed, it was a challenge Richard could not endure.

On June 10, the day after the full meeting of the council mentioned by Stallworthe, Richard abruptly took action. He appealed to the North for military aid against the Woodvilles and called upon the Earl of Northumberland, who must have previously sent assurances of his loyalty, to take command of the expedition. 'Right trusty and well beloved,' he addressed the Mayor, Aldermen, and Commons of the city of York,

we greet you well, and as ye love the weal of us, and the weal and surety of your own selves, we heartily pray you to come unto us to London in all the diligence ye can possible after the sight hereof, with as many as ye can defensibly arrayed, there to aid and assist us against the Queen, her blood adherents, and affinity, which have intended, and daily doth intend, to murder and utterly destroy us and our cousin the duke of Buckingham, and the old royal blood of this realm, and as it is now openly known, by their subtle and damnable ways forecasted the same [i.e., plotted the same], and also the final destruction and disinheriting of you and all other inheritors [i.e., men of property] and men of honour, as well of the north parts as other countries, that belong to us; as our trusty servant, this bearer, shall more at large show you, to whom we pray you give credence, and as ever we may do for you in time coming fail not, but haste you to us hither.[7]

It is at this moment that Sir Richard Ratcliffe, a Yorkshire knight and brother-in-law of Richard's neighbour Lord Scrope of Bolton, enters upon the stage of history. He was 'this bearer'. Leaving London on Wednesday, June 11, with a saddlebag of Richard's letters, he galloped northward at a punishing speed. He halted at Leconfield, one of Northumberland's Yorkshire manors, to deliver messages to the Earl, who only the day before had returned from York; then he lashed his horse onward to reach the city on Sunday, June 15, only one day after John Brackenbury had arrived with the letter of June 5. The instant the Mayor had scanned Richard's request, he sent his servants running to summon the members of the council. What explanation Ratcliffe made of the political situation in London, the council clerk did not record, but he did record the Protector's verbal instructions which Ratcliffe relayed to the Mayor and his fellows: 'The credence of the which letter is that as much fellowship as the city may make defensibly arrayed, as well of horse as of foot, be on Wednesday at even next coming [June 18] at Pontefract, there attending upon my lord of Northumberland, and so with him to go up to London, there to attend upon my said lord's good grace.' The burgers of York wasted no time. They at once had Richard's appeal published through the city and on the following day they determined to send southward no less than 300 men, under the joint captaincy of their parliamentary represen-tatives, Thomas Wrangwysh and William Wells.[8*] Meanwhile, Sir Richard Ratcliffe had galloped on to deliver the remaining messages to Richard's adherents, of which the surviving letter, addressed 'To My Lord Nevill, in haste', is doubtless a typical example:

My Lord Nevill, I recommend me to you as heartily as I can; and as ever ye love me and your own weal and security, and this realm, that ye come to me with that ye may make, defensibly arrayed, in all the haste that is possible; and that ye give credence to Richard Ratcliffe, this bearer, whom I now do send to you, instructed with all my mind and intent.

And, my Lord, do me now good service, as ye have always before done, and I trust now so to remember you as shall be the making of you and yours. And God send you good fortunes.

Written at London, 11th day of June, with the hand of your heartily loving cousin and master,

R. GLOUCESTER.[9]

In his 'credence' to the Mayor and to Lord Neville, Ratcliffe doubt-less enlarged on the combination of the Woodvilles with Lord Hastings' party. For the commonalty of York, however, a simple rallying cry was obviously desirable; hence the appeal directed solely against the Queen and her kindred who had already demonstrated their opposition to the Protector and had long been unpopular. Yet this call for aid probably did not spring from Richard's fear of the present conspiracy, against which he had already determined on a course of action. He was anticipating the need of armed force to check the counter-blow which might follow or some other upheaval which lay hidden in the now uncertain future.

The remarkable terms of this sudden pressing appeal shed some light on its purpose but even more upon the character of its author. In the moment of urgency Richard does not, as well he might, demand support for the government against rebels, emphasizing his authority as Protector to secure troops; he reverts to the primitive seignorial obligation. It is as their 'good lord' that he stirs the men of York; to Neville he writes as 'cousin and master'. He invokes the theme of loyalty and personal feeling which animated his relation with the men of the North. It was a feeling that his brother Edward understood but was too sophisticated to depend upon and that was as alien to the earlier Tudors as it would have been comprehensible, both to the victor and the vanquished at Hastings.

There are lesser touches of interest in the letters. The prominence of Buckingham in the message to York suggests the acceleration of his influence; the theme of 'the old royal blood' reflects basic Yorkist doctrine, here raised against the Woodvilles, which Richard's father had used against Lancaster and Beaufort. Of a piece with the dominance of instinct and feeling in this appeal is its destination. It was not good politics for the Protector of the whole realm to remind people, by asking for help from one quarter only, that he was still essentially Lord of the North.

Many hours before Ratcliffe reached York, Richard had moved to crush the conspiracy of Hastings and the Woodvilles. On Thursday, June 12, he appointed two meetings of councillors for the following morning. One group, headed by Chancellor Russell, was to discuss at Westminster certain matters relating to the coronation. The second group was requested to attend in the council chamber of the Tower at ten o'clock in the morning. It consisted of Hastings, Stanley, Morton, Rotherham, and Buckingham, Howard and other intimate advisers of the Protector. On Friday morning, June 13, these lords and prelates came from their various abodes in the city to assemble in the large chamber in the White Tower that they knew well. For different reasons, they were all doubtless very conscious of the presence, in the nearby apartments of state, of young Edward their sovereign lord. Perhaps Hastings was still a little under the spell of Mistress Shore's embraces. Not six weeks ago he had been fond of remarking at any opportunity that the government had been transferred from two of the Queen's kindred to two more powerful persons of the King's without causing so much blood to be shed as would be produced by a cut finger.[10] This elation had long since evaporated; on this morning he nursed other thoughts. The councillors took their seats about the table with a rustling of rich gowns and a cross current of greetings. The usher shut the chamber door. Sitting stern of face at the head of the table, Richard opened the meeting.

There had just been detected, he declared abruptly, a conspiracy against the government. The Queen and her adherents were among the ringleaders. And Shore's wife. There were others however. . . . After an instant of strained silence, Richard directly accused Hastings and Stanley and Morton and Rotherham of plotting with the Woodvilles against the protectorship. Hastings tensely denied the charge. Richard flung on the board the dreaded word *Treason*. The Lord Chamberlain made a hot rejoinder. Men sprang to their feet. Perhaps Hastings and Stanley reached for a weapon. The usher flung open the door, bawling, 'Treason! Treason!' A band of armed men rushed into the room. There was a scuffle. . . .

In a moment it was all over. Morton and Rotherham were escorted to prison quarters in the Tower. Stanley was put under special detention in his own lodgings. Hastings, in the grasp of guards, was summarily informed that he was to be executed at once, and at Richard's order was hurried from the chamber. A priest was found so that the Lord Chamberlain might briefly be shriven; then he was led to the green by the Tower chapel. On a square piece of timber intended for building repairs, William, Lord Hastings was beheaded forthwith.[11]*

By this time the cries of treason in the Tower had roused the city. Rumour galloped in a thousand tongues. Down Tower street raced the flying tales, along Bishopsgate, through the goldsmiths' shops in the Poultry and Cheapside. Citizens poured into the streets or apprehensively looked to their weapons. A yeoman of the Protector's household galloped to the home of Edmund Shaa, Mayor and goldsmith of

London, bidding him repair to the Tower at once. The City hummed and buzzed.

It was not long, however, before a royal herald appeared in the streets, a trumpet commanding silence for his proclamation. Lord Hastings had been executed—he read from his parchment—by the authority of the royal council, after being detected in a plot to destroy the Lord Protector and the Duke of Buckingham so as to rule King and realm at his pleasure. He had been immediately punished for his treason in order to forestall riotous attempts to deliver him. The government was secure. There was no cause for alarm. The city was to go peacefully about its business. Hastings, the herald concluded, had been an evil councillor to Edward the Fourth, enticing the King to dishonour and setting him an example of vicious living. This very night past he had lain with Shore's wife, who was herself one of the plotters.[12]

Men went back to their homes, put up their weapons. Apprentices resumed their labours. On his return from the Tower, the Mayor assured the principal citizens that a dangerous outbreak had been happily prevented. The city quickly resumed its accustomed mien. Many accepted, or thought it best to accept, the explanation of the Lord Protector. A number, however, were sceptical. Henceforth, there grew a creeping surf of whispers that the King's uncle would assume the crown.[13]*

Richard could hardly have denounced Hastings' licentious living under the supposition that it was an issue ripe for exploitation. The rivalry of the Lord Chamberlain and the Marquess in procuring the King's pleasures, the royal *amours* themselves—even when they touched the wives of citizens—were rather looked upon with complacence by Edward's subjects than endured with shame.[14]* It is the feelings of Edward's brother rather than a calculated propaganda of the Protector which this passage reveals. Richard's urge to justify to others what he could not reconcile to his own conscience resulted in a plea which had little appeal for anyone except himself. The speed with which Hastings was hustled to the headsman was perhaps prompted by Richard's fear that if he paused to reflect, he would be unable to commit the deed.

The body of the Lord Chamberlain was borne to Windsor and, by the Protector's order, interred in the unfinished chapel of St. George close to the tomb of Edward the Fourth, who in his will of 1475 had expressed the wish that Hastings be buried near him. Not many weeks later, Richard sealed an indenture, swearing to take Katherine, Hastings' widow, directly under his protection and to secure for her the enjoyment of her husband's lands, goods, privileges, and the custody not only of their heir until the boy came of age but also the wardship of the young Earl of Shrewsbury who was married to their daughter Anne. Hastings, he promised, would never be attainted; Katherine would be defended against any attempt by intimidation or fraud to deprive her of her rights. Though, in a moment of doubt, Richard soon removed Hastings' brother from the captaincy of Guisnes castle, he thereafter wooed his support and treated him generously and eventually permitted him to repurchase the reversion of the office he had lost.[15] Thus did he seek to atone for what, clearly, he could never forgive himself; but the act represented, nonetheless, a breach in his character, forced by the pressures of an unhappy past which had not been of his making and the insidious demands of a complex, subtle present with which the plain and earnest and strong-willed lord of the moors could not deal without corroding his nature.

Hastings' colleagues got off very lightly. Two of them were, after all, bishops. The ineffectual Rotherham suffered only a brief imprisonment. At Buckingham's request, John Morton was dispatched to the Duke's favourite castle of Brecknock, where he was comfortably lodged. Stanley's art of landing on the winning side had not deserted him. In a few days he was not only released but restored to his place in the council. To forgive Stanley was a kind of twisted expiation for the execution of a better and a dearer man. Besides, Stanley was a time-server. With Stanley, Richard felt no competition in loyalties.[16]*

Not many hours after the death of Hastings, Richard assembled a full council in order to explain and justify his act. The evidence of conspiracy he exhibited may not have reconciled by any means all of the councillors to that violent stroke, but there is no reason to doubt that many of them were convinced of the Protector's need to take action of some kind. Though Richard, and Buckingham, had certainly overawed the council, the power of the Protector was still supported only by men's wills.

He now rode the momentum of events to deal with the Woodvilles, proposing to the council that if the Queen herself could not be induced to come forth from the sanctuary, the little Duke of York must be secured. The King needed his brother's companionship; the coronation ceremony would be maimed by his absence; the spectacle of the Dowager Queen hiding her children under the wings of the Church cast an intolerable obloquy upon the government. Was not the Queen, in fact, holding little York as a political hostage? Buckingham eloquently developed the theme, affirming that, since the child neither needed nor was capable of wanting sanctuary, he could be removed without rupture of the holy right. The lords spiritual were divided. Some held with the horrified Archbishop of Canterbury that to fetch the child, no matter what arguments might be marshalled, would violate a refuge that St. Peter himself had sanctified. Other bishops, however, and all the temporal lords agreed that if the Queen would not relinquish the little Duke, he must be fetched.

On Monday morning, June 16, the councillors assembled at the Tower and then, accompanied by a body of armed men, were rowed up river to Westminster. The armed men surrounded the sanctuary. Richard, Buckingham, and a part of the council retired to the Star Chamber, while the rest, headed by the Archbishop of Canterbury and Lord Howard, proceeded into the abbot's quarters to seek the Queen. Appalled by the thought of force, the old Archbishop pleaded hard with the beleaguered Elizabeth. At first she was adamant in her refusals, but the grim faces of Howard and the other lords shook her resolution. After the Archbishop had renewed his assurances that her son would be most respectfully and carefully tended, the Queen consented, with apparent goodwill, to let him go. That her feelings did not match her words is probable enough.

The Archbishop took the nine-year-old boy by the hand and led him forth, followed by the train of councillors. Standing alone in the vast space of Westminster hall, Buckingham welcomed the lad and conducted him to the door of the Star Chamber. Here Richard greeted him affectionately, talked with him a little, and returned him to the care of the Archbishop, who escorted him to his brother in the Tower. About this same time Richard had taken into his own household another scion of the House of York. Young Edward, Earl of Warwick, Clarence's ten-year-old son, had been brought up from the country and placed in the care of Richard's wife, his aunt.

Meanwhile, Richard had decided that Rivers, Vaughan, and Grey must be executed.[17]*

In his prison at Sheriff Hutton on Monday, June 23, Anthony Woodville, Earl Rivers, is informed that, as a result of his sister's plotting, he has been sentenced to death by Richard of Gloucester, Constable and Protector. He is given spiritual consolation. He is given pen, ink, paper. In a maelstrom of all moods he desperately gathers his thoughts and sets himself to make his will:

He earnestly desires that his debts be paid. He prays that sufficient of his goods be allowed to his executors so that bequests to the poor and to the Church will be honoured. Struggling to cleanse his soul, he recalls some recent transactions in property in which he may have acted with a high hand and begs that the matter be looked into and justice done. Uncertain of where he will die, he nominates resting places for his body both north and south of Trent. He names five executors, among them, Chancellor Russell and William Catesby. Finally, he begs Richard, Duke of Gloucester, to oversee the carrying out of his wishes. Then he is informed that he will be conveyed to Pontefract castle and there, with Sir Thomas Vaughan and Lord Richard Grey, beheaded. He adds a last sentence to his will, asking to be buried at Pontefract with the Lord Richard.[18]

He is a man of letters and he has writing materials; he seeks to order his throbbing mind at this terrible moment by the discipline of composition, to crowd upon paper some final reckoning with the world. It takes the form of a little ballad, genuinely pathetic in its accents, but in form a surprisingly typical medieval plaint upon the mutability of life:

Somewhat musing
And more mourning,
In remembering
    Th'unsteadfastness;
This world being
Of such wheeling,
Me contrarying,
    What may I guess?

With displeasure,
To my grievance,
And no surance
    Of remedy;
Lo, in this trance,
Now in substance,
Such is my dance,
    Willing to die.

I fear, doubtless,
Remediless
Is now to seize
    My woeful chance;
For unkindness,
Withoutenless,
And no redress,
    Me doth advance.

Methinks truly
Bounden am I,
And that greatly,
    To be content;
Seeing plainly
Fortune doth wry
All contrary
    From mine intent.

My life was lent
Me to one intent.
It is nigh spent.
    Welcome Fortune!
But I ne went [never thought]
Thus to be shent [ruined],
But she it meant:
    Such is her won [custom].[19]*

On Tuesday, June 24, Rivers was escorted to Pontefract. Grey had been brought from Middleham castle; Vaughan was already there. Next day the three men went in silence to the block. The execution was officially supervised by the Earl of Northumberland, Warden of the East and Middle Marches; it was carried out by Sir Richard Ratcliffe; it was viewed by the men of York and the rest of the little army which was about to march southward to London. Rivers' will was never to be proved, but the priests of the chapel of Our Lady of Pewe, at Westminster, for whom Rivers had done much, would keep his obit on the 25th of each June. The hairshirt which, it was discovered, the Earl wore to his death, was hung up in a church at Doncaster as a holy object.[20]*

Anthony Woodville's father was a rapacious adventurer; his mother, so formidable and devious a woman that she was held to be a witch. His brother Lionel was a type of their father in the gown of a bishop. His sister the Queen—beautiful, suffering, brought from nowhere to the highest place and cast down again to misery and friendless death— owned a destiny presenting the grand outlines of 'tragedie'[21]* which disintegrates upon inspection because it was developed by a mean, stupid, and cruel character. So unlovely was his family that even Anthony, for all his accomplishments, could not be loved, save perhaps by his immediate followers and by Caxton. In Richard's mind, the renewed plotting of the Queen justified his execution. Yet, in a broader view, he perished because nobody spoke for him and because he was the ablest, not the most guilty, of a family which had long exacerbated the feelings, and now threatened the stability, of the realm. Richard had no such struggle to reconcile to his conscience the dispatching of Rivers as he had of Hastings; the claims of Rivers upon his heart were shadowed by the figure of George of Clarence. Besides, the breach had been opened.

VI*

WHEN he sat down on Saturday, June 21, to report events to his friend in the country, Simon Stallworthe, servant of the Lord Chancellor, could scarce hold the pen, he was so ill. And sick at heart. 'Worshipful Sir, I commend me to you and for tidings,' he begins abruptly, 'I hold you happy that ye are out of the press for with us is much trouble and every man doubts other.' After giving the news of the beheading of Hastings and the delivery of little York from sanctuary, he reports that

Lord Lisle, the Queen's own brother-in-law, has sought the favour of the Lord Protector and attends upon him. It is thought that 20,000 of the Protector's and Buckingham's men will arrive in London this week —for what purpose Stallworthe does not know, except to keep the peace. The Lord Chancellor is very busy—busier than he would wish to be, Stallworthe adds cautiously, 'if any other ways would be taken'. Morton, Bishop of Ely, and Rotherham, Archbishop of York, are still in the Tower, along with Oliver King [former secretary to King Edward and one of Hastings' party]. 'I suppose they shall come out nevertheless,' Stallworthe writes, then draws a line through the words. For safe keeping, he goes on, the Protector has stationed men in their London houses; and he supposes that the Protector will also send men to their manors in the country. Morton, Rotherham and King are not likely to come out of prison yet.[1]* Mistress Shore is in prison; what shall happen to her, he does not know. Concluding with an apology for not writing more because he is so ill, Stallworthe adds a postscript that all of the Lord Chamberlain's men have entered the service of the Duke of Buckingham.[2]

London was now in the grip of rumour, doubt, fear, speculation. Though the young King could be seen shooting at butts with his brother on the Tower greens, whispers ran more strongly that he should not be King much longer.[3] The Lord Protector often rode through the city these days with a great train of lords and attendants. He now divided his time between Crosby's Place and his mother's home on the river, Baynard's Castle. It was noted that he entertained at dinner increasing numbers of guests. In view of the troubled times, the council had postponed the coronation and ceased to make preparations for the meeting of a Parliament.[4]* Buckingham, his retinue swelled by the men of the dead Lord Chamberlain—what better illuminates the decay of loyalty and the vanity of the Duke?—was more than ever acting like a king-maker.

There were no disturbances in London or elsewhere. No demonstrations against the Lord Protector. None of the lords or gentry gathered their retainers about them and bolted for the safety of their castles. No plots were hatched. London and the lords waited. Whatever emotion they felt concerning the succession to the throne, their first concern was for the safety of the realm and for order. The two months' reign of Edward V had already forecast disaster and recalled the bad old days of Henry VI. The Protector was a man few knew well and a number, in consequence, feared, a man of the distant and rugged North; but he was also the mighty Edward's brother and the first general of the kingdom and it was said that in his own country he ruled with justice and humanity.

Meanwhile, at York on June 21—the day Stallworthe wrote his letter—the magistrates decided that their force of three hundred men should wear the city's cognizance, or emblem, but take with them to Pontefract cognizances of the Duke of Gloucester and consult with the Earl of Northumberland whether they should wear both on their march south. For though their troop had originally been ordered to reach Pontefract by June 18, they had not left York on Saturday, the twenty-first, and did not, indeed, arrive at Pontefract until the following Monday or Tuesday, in time to witness the execution of Rivers on the twenty-fifth. The rumours Stallworthe had heard were mistaken: no troops would enter London this week, or even the following week. Richard of Gloucester had sent word to delay the appearance of his northerners: he wanted no show of force in the capital during these critical days.[5]*

The most noteworthy piece of news Stallworthe was unaware of or chary of mentioning directly: on the day he penned his letter and during the days that had elapsed since the delivery of the little Duke of York, the Protector and his inner council had been discussing with a variety of lords, prelates, and influential commoners the revelation of Bishop Stillington.

The Bishop of Bath and Wells had declared to Richard that the children of Elizabeth Woodville and King Edward were illegitimate because the King had been affianced to another when he married Elizabeth. In the eyes of the Church, the essence of marriage was consent, a mutual interchange of personal vows; therefore, betrothal had the force of a legal tie and the sanction of a sacred obligation. It was not infrequently abused in these times. Men seeking release from marriage could secure a divorce from the papal court by raking up some evidence of a previous engagement to marry. Henry VIII obtained an annulment of his marriage to Anne Boleyn—as he was cutting off her head—on the grounds that she had once been betrothed to the Earl of Northumberland. In humbler circumstances, the sanctity of troth-plight had enabled one Richard Calle to marry Margery Paston, daughter of the family he served, despite the furious attempts of the Pastons to prevent the match.[6] Stillington's avowal, then, was of the utmost seriousness.

It is doubtful if he was able to produce proof . . . a letter from the lady, a scrap of writing from the King. It had been a most secret under-taking, he explained to Richard, known but to himself. He alone had witnessed, or transmitted, the King's oath to the lady of his desire. Only then had she been willing to surrender to her sovereign, who, however, had sworn troth but to have his use of her. Richard well knew that his brother had seduced ladies of the court both before and after his marriage.[7] Commynes remarks that courtiers frequently use troth-plight only to deceive.[8]

And who was the lady? Richard demanded. He doubtless expected Stillington to name one of the light-of-loves of Edward's early court, about which he himself knew little. The bishop's answer was consider-ably more impressive. Edward's victim was no less than the Lady Eleanor Butler, widow of Sir Thomas Butler and daughter of the old Earl of Shrewsbury, the great Talbot himself. Though by this time she had been dead for fifteen years, she would be readily remembered. A meagre outline of her life still survives in the public records.

The Lady Eleanor was apparently the daughter of Talbot's second marriage. In 1449 or 1450 she was married to Sir Thomas Butler, son and heir of Ralph Butler, Lord Sudeley. She had become a widow by the time Edward assumed the crown in March of 1461. Her death occurred in June of 1468. Though she was seemingly married at a time when Edward was only eight years old, it is quite likely that she herself was no more than thirteen or fourteen, and Edward's passion for Elizabeth Woodville indicates that he was disposed to find older women attractive.

A passage in the Patent Rolls indicates that the Lady Eleanor was newly widowed when Edward became King and hints at the circum-stances under which she may have come to the young monarch's attention. In the last disturbed months of Henry's reign, after the Yorkist victory at Northampton, Eleanor's father-in-law, Lord Sudeley, succeeded in getting into his hands one of the two manors which he had jointly settled on her and his son when they were married. Since he had not bothered, however, to secure a royal license for the transfer, the King seized both manors. It is possible that Edward first laid eyes on the still youthful widow when she directly appealed to him to restore her lands. Thus, the tradition that Elizabeth Woodville met her sovereign in just these circumstances may preserve an actual happening, which, after Elizabeth's elevation to the throne, was transferred in the careless channels of rumour from the Lady Eleanor to the Queen by way of romanticizing a royal courtship about which little was known. In any case, it is on record that the Lady Eleanor died possessed of the two manors which the King had taken into his keeping.[9]

As an obvious precaution before further considering the matter, Richard must have made sufficient inquiries about the lady to discover that what was known of her life tallied with Stillington's disclosure. A mysterious passage in the bishop's own life tallied with it too—as Richard must have realized, whether or not Stillington avowed it.

As early as the winter of 1470–71, the bishop had been closely concerned with the fortunes of the Duke of Clarence. His diocese, after all, lay in the very heart of Clarence's great manorial holdings. While Warwick ruled at Westminster and Richard and Edward were refugees in Burgundy, Stillington was secretly pleading with George of Clarence to return to his family allegiance. Perhaps it was due in part to Clarence's influence that after Edward reconquered his kingdom, the Bishop of Bath and Wells became Chancellor once again. Removed from this office in 1475, he soon resumed his intimate connections with Clarence. On February 18, 1478, the Duke was executed. Three weeks later, on March 6, Elizabeth Stonor wrote her husband, 'Ye shall understand that the Bishop of Bath is brought into the Tower since you departed.' After he had paid a heavy fine, Stillington, on June 20, received a royal pardon, in which his offence is named: he had uttered words prejudicial to the King and his state.[10]

Richard had been in Yorkshire when Clarence was arrested in the early summer of 1477. Less than two weeks after his brother's execution he had left London for Middleham. Hence, though he must afterwards have learned that Stillington had been imprisoned for being in some way implicated in Clarence's treason, it is likely that he remained unaware—until the bishop approached him—of the precise role Stillington had played.

The Bishop of Bath and Wells had probably let slip to Clarence the secret of the pre-contract. It helped to engender Clarence's misty dream that when he had married Mary of Burgundy he could use her power to win for himself the English Crown. In his last furious months of reckless plotting and spreading tales against the King, Clarence . . . even Clarence . . . doubtless realized that he dare not raise the issue of the pre-contract until he had achieved sufficient strength to defy Edward. But apparently he blabbed it to a few. An informer of the Woodvilles, or a trusted adherent of his own, reported the words. They were Clarence's death warrant. Thus may be explained what many men of the time found inexplicable. No one doubted the Duke's guilt; the puzzle was, why, at this particular occasion, did Edward proceed against his brother when, in so many other instances, what seemed like more overt treason had been forgiven?

The King knew at once where Clarence had got the story, but he had no wish to bring Stillington's revelation into the open. A fine and a few months imprisonment, on a general charge of defaming the King, was sufficient to secure from the bishop a private oath that he would henceforth be silent and an open declaration to the few who had learned the secret that it was arrant and malicious nonsense. Stillington did not regain Edward's favour, and ever after he was held in intense enmity by the Woodvilles.

He comes down to us but the shadow of a man. Little more is known of his life, up to this time, than has been indicated; nothing is known of his character save what can be guessed by a precarious triangulation of scattered facts. In May of 1483 he was something more than sixty years of age. Ten years before, he had briefly relinquished the chancellorship apparently from ill health; why he was dismissed in 1475 remains unknown. The Croyland Chronicler casually remarks of him during these years that he 'did nothing except through his pupil, John Alcock, Bishop of Worcester. . . .' Alcock seems to have stood high in the favour of the Woodvilles; perhaps he dominated Stillington as the watchdog of the Queen. Stillington's accomplishments as Chancellor appear to be undistinguished. A Doctor of Civil and Canon Law, he rose unobtrusively in the government service; the chancellorship was suddenly thrust upon him in 1467 when Edward took it away from Warwick's brother George. In the faint and untrustworthy light of surviving information, Stillington stands as a man of rather mediocre talents, not remarkable for strength of character. Pious King Henry, it is true, had once praised him for his 'great cunning, virtues, and priestly demeaning.'[11]

Resentment against Edward for the loss of his high office, a desire for revenge upon the Woodvilles, may have urged him to make his declaration. No discernible reward did he receive from Richard, unless it be found in a minor enactment of the Parliament of 1484, the approval of a petition from the masters of the collegiate chapel which Stillington had established out of his own property at Nether Acaster near York to enclose forty acres of land the bishop had given them. Men of weak or unworthy character can foster schools as well as more blameless folk. Still, it is perhaps something in the bishop's favour that he used whatever credit he had with Richard to advance the cause of his foundation, which provided 'three masters to teach grammar, music, and writing and such things as belong to the scrivener's art'.[12]

No doubt, the pressure of events and Buckingham's voice in his ear and his own ambition sharpened Richard's will to accept Stillington's disclosure; but, that brooding upon the available evidence, he came genuinely to believe in the truth of the pre-contract is indicated by the openness with which he proclaimed its terms. Had there been grave doubt in his mind, he would not likely have reiterated, as late as in his Parliament of 1484, that Edward had stood troth-plight to the Lady Eleanor Butler.[13] A generalization would have sufficed, as such generalizations had so often sufficed in the Parliaments of the preceding century. The relentlessness with which, afterward, Henry VII sought to destroy all trace of the pre-contract and hounded the Bishop of Bath and Wells, the unanimity with which Tudor historians perverted or suppressed mention of it, support the surviving evidence that, in all probability, Richard had very good reason to conclude that Stillington's secret was true.[14]*

When Richard made the momentous disclosure to Buckingham and the inner council, they were quickly agreed that he must claim his rights. Buckingham had already been hinting at every opportunity that the realm needed a man and not a boy, that men dreaded a minority reign, that the Lord Protector was popular and powerful enough to achieve the highest destiny, and finally that his humble vassal, brilliant adviser, entire well wisher, and valiant cousin, Harry Buckingham, burned to serve him.[15]* In urging Richard to make use of the pre-contract, Lord Howard and Catesby and Stillington and Langton, Bishop of St. David's, and others of the inner council were doubtless, like most men, motivated by self-interest as well as by considerations of principle and the public weal. Howard, for instance, could have claimed, through his mother, the dukedom of Norfolk, except that King Edward, by marrying his second son to the little heiress of the last Duke, had vested in him the dignity and the estates of the Mowbrays. But Lady Anne Mowbray was now dead. Howard had considerable interest in seconding Buckingham's eloquent pleas. Forces well nigh as strong as hope of personal gain, however, impelled him in the same direction. Richard was of a mettle his own temperament had taught him to admire and trust; his long experience of affairs counselled the need of strong government; in a quaking present which foreshadowed an ominous future Richard probably represented, to his forthright mind, the only assurance of order.

Now, what a number of men had been privately thinking on the subject of political expediency and the public good suddenly appeared in the guise of lawfulness and right. After listening to his advisers, Richard would only go so far, however, as to propose that the chief men of the realm be informed of the secret and their advice sought. He had chosen to regard the pre-contract as establishing a rightful opportunity rather than a solemn directive.[16]*

Hence the veiled, intensive activity during the days which followed the delivery of little York from sanctuary, the streams of visitors to Crosby's Place and Baynard's Castle, the splendour of the train with which Richard, having relinquished black, now rode in purple through the city. To an ever-widening circle of lords, prelates and influential gentlemen the secret of the pre-contract was disclosed. Their responses convinced the Protector and his council that most men would support, or acquiesce in, Richard's assumption of power now that it could be justified. When Stallworthe wrote his agitated letter on Saturday, Richard had come to his fateful decision.

The very next day, Sunday, June 22, the tension which racked the capital was suddenly released. The Lord Protector, accompanied by Buckingham and a great train of magnates, rode to Paul's Cross—where in the past preachers Yorkist or Lancastrian had often made political exhortations—to hear Friar Ralph Shaa, brother of the Mayor and a man famous for his learning and eloquence.

The friar announced to the throng of citizens and nobles a provocative biblical text: bastard slips shall not take root. After lauding the Duke who had founded the fortunes of York and remarking that of his three sons Richard only had been born in England and was therefore the most truly English, the friar reminded his hearers of the Protector's character and career, which made him a man worthy of sitting upon the throne itself. In very fact, he went on, it had just been discovered that by God's law as well as by worth, Richard was entitled to the crown. When Edward the Fourth had married Elizabeth Woodville, he had been solemnly contracted to another. The children he had begotten upon her were illegitimate. Thus, the offspring of King Edward set aside, the son of the Duke of Clarence disabled in blood by Clarence's attainder, Richard of Gloucester was the true heir of York and therefore rightful King of England. . . .

The citizens quietly melted away to their homes. Few can have been entirely surprised that the Protector had laid formal claim to the throne. In other quarters of the city, meanwhile, lesser preachers were stirring other issues besides the pre-contract. Buckingham had no reason to love the House of York; neither scruple nor his own interest put any brake upon the means he thought appropriate to use in Richard's behalf. Not content to expound only the decisive argument, he and his lieutenants primed a number of preachers to declare the illegitimacy of Edward himself. It was no invention of the moment. The scandalous tale had been whispered for years and widely diffused. Curiously enough, Mancini states categorically that when the Duchess of York learned that her son Edward was married to Elizabeth Woodville, she 'fell into such a frenzy, that she offered to submit to a public inquiry and asserted that Edward was not the offspring of her husband the duke of York, but was conceived in adultery, and therefore in no wise worthy of the honour of kingship'. After the Duke of Burgundy and Edward had fallen out over Louis XI's peace offers in 1475, Duke Charles began scornfully calling him 'Blayborgne', in token that he was the son of an archer of that name; Louis himself also knew the story. In 1477 Clarence, of course, had made wide use of it. There is no reason to suppose that Richard countenanced the raking up of this scandal. It constituted an attack upon his house and it was unnecessary. Possibly one of the reasons why he shifted his residence to his mother's home was to dissociate himself from the lengths to which his lieutenants had gone in promoting his cause.[17]*

On the morning after Friar Ralph had delivered his sermon, the nobles and high prelates assembled in what was actually a preliminary session of the Lords. This time it was Buckingham who played the orator in urging Richard's right to the throne. Virtually all of his audience not only knew what he was going to say but had themselves helped to shape the decision. Next day, Tuesday, June 24, Buckingham addressed the chief citizens of the city in the Guildhall to the same purpose and awed them by the splendour of his delivery. So fluent was he, Fabyan records, that he did not once pause to spit; and *The Great Chronicle* is driven to report that his words were 'so well and eloquently uttered, and with so angelic a countenance . . . that such as heard him marvelled and said that never tofore that day had they heard any man learned or unlearned make such a rehearsal or oration as that was'.[18]

On Wednesday, June 25—the day on which, weeks ago, Parliament had been summoned to meet—a gathering, which was in all but legal name a Parliament, assembled at Westminster. Directly after the execution of Hastings, the chancery had begun sending out writs of postponement, mainly to the towns; but Richard soon decided, as the movement to make him King accelerated, that the Lords and Commons must be consulted, and the dispatching of the writs was discontinued. The Lords appeared virtually in full strength; gaps in the Commons were filled by a sizable delegation of London citizens.[19]

A roll of parchment engrossing Richard's title to the throne was brought before a joint session of Lords and Commons. In customary style, it embroidered the Protector's precise claim with a variety of other reasons, some of which were not very relevant and others, not susceptible to proof. This was the legislative vernacular of the day; we have our own, scarcely less discursive, and denser. The evils which the Woodvilles had wrought upon the realm were rehearsed as showing, in its fruits, the falseness of Edward's marriage. The ceremony itself had been performed without the assent of the lords, under the influence of Elizabeth's and her mother's sorcery, and in a profane place contrary to God's laws. Finally, 'at the time of contract of the same pretensed marriage . . . the said King Edward was and stood married and troth plight to one Dame Eleanor Butler, daughter of the old Earl of Shrewsbury. . . .' In consequence, the petition declared to the Protector, 'ye be the undoubted son and heir of Richard late Duke of York . . . wherefore . . . we humbly desire, pray, and require your said noble Grace, that, according to this election of us the three estates of this land, as by your true inheritance, ye will accept and take upon you the said crown and Royal Dignity. . . .'[20] After the reading of this petition, Lords and Commons recorded their unanimous approval and determined on the morrow to present the roll of parchment to the Lord Protector.

Consequently, on Thursday, June 26, a great concourse of nobles, prelates, gentry, and citizens thronged to Baynard's Castle. Once more Buckingham played the orator, reading the petition and calling upon the Protector to assume the sceptre. Appearing on a battlement or stairhead before the great assemblage, Richard acceded, with a show of modesty, to the wishes of Lords and Commons and was forthwith hailed as King Richard the Third. He descended then to take horse and ride at the head of a princely train to Westminster Hall. He formally assumed the royal prerogative by seating himself in the marble chair of King's Bench, the traditional seat of the King as Justicer and by taking the royal oath. At his right hand stood John Howard, heir of the Mowbrays; at his left, the Duke of Suffolk, husband of Richard's sister and father of the Earl of Lincoln. Before him were assembled the Justices of King's Bench and of Common Pleas and the Serjeants of the Law, and the massive hall beyond was crammed with spectators.[21]*

Richard insisted on treating the occasion as more than a ceremony. Earnestly he delivered a lecture to all his judges and legal officers, straitly charging them to dispense justice without fear or favour and declaring that all men, of whatever degree, must be treated equally in the sight of the law. To drive home the sincerity of his words, he summoned from the sanctuary where he had taken refuge Sir John Fogge, a relative of the Woodvilles and a deadly enemy—the man, in fact, who had so ruthlessly helped the Queen's father to plunder Sir Thomas Cook in 1468. In the sight of all, Richard took Sir John by the hand and swore to be his friend. Not many hours later Fogge was appointed a Justice of the Peace for the county of Kent. After thus demonstrating his determination to rule without malice or partiality, Richard departed from Westminster Hall to make offering at the shrine of Edward the Confessor while the monks of the abbey sang 'Te Deum'.[22]

From this day he dated the beginning of his reign. At the cost of four men's lives, without employing military force, he had mounted the throne by a title of inheritance and the election of the Lords and Commons of the realm. A number of men were opposed to his elevation; many accepted it as right, or necessary, or inevitable; not a few regarded it as fortunate. In assuming the crown, Richard had been as much impelled, it appears, by the political and social forces of the moment as by his own will.

VII*

so marched events, as diversely and confusingly reported by the chroniclers, who could only sketch outward shapes and effects. The heart of the drama, the conflict within Richard's mind, is well nigh shut from our sight; and what we can glimpse comes to us distorted by the lens of what-happened-after. The opacity of the future is the dominant dimension of any moment of choice. In order to view Richard in the arena of decision, we must attempt to enter by the entrance, not the exit.

Neither Richard's past, nor his government as Protector, nor his subsequent reign indicates that he was inordinately ambitious. Before the emergence of the pre-contract he may have experienced twinges of desire for the throne, but there is no evidence that he aspired to it. The pre-contract made it possible for him to aspire to it, if he chose.

A lineal right to the crown was indispensable, but it was not decisive. Henry IV had usurped the throne as a leader of reform. York's title had enabled Edward to claim the sceptre, but it was bad Lancastrian government which impelled the nation to endorse his claim. When Warwick reseated Henry VI, he asserted the validity of Henry's title as a matter of course, but he knew that the only real means of keeping Henry on the throne was to make his rule popular.

As Richard struggled with the problem, he was pressed by the will of others and borne along on the rapid movement of events. The silvery voice of Buckingham was in his ear—Buckingham, who was so zealously loyal, and so like Clarence in his charm. His other advisers surrounded him with their convictions. Yet they did not speak distinctly to his conscience nor light up the murky dilemma of his conflicting loyalties. His wife Anne was with him to share, at brief moments, his troubled musings. She was a gentle lady: she would say little; but she was the daughter of Warwick and the mother of a prince who could become heir to the throne. There was the young King himself. When Richard entered the royal apartments, Edward's face stiffened and his eyes went blank and he spoke with the obvious wariness of a precocious twelve-year-old. Richard could find no point of contact, no means to establish communication with this frail youth of scholarly bent. He had no affection for the Duke of Gloucester, to begin with. He had been deeply shocked by the arrest of Rivers, the flight of his mother to sanctuary, the downfall of his party. Since his upbringing had made him impervious to the lawful rights of the Protector, he held Richard directly responsible for all these calamities, When Richard tried to find a nephew, he met only with a Woodville. The boy's rearing had drained out of him the blood of his father.

Meanwhile, the rhythm of events themselves sounded an ever more insistent beat in Richard's mind. Perhaps his course had already been determined, blindly, by the wills of men who had been hostile to him. The Woodvilles' attempt to seize power, the conspiracy of Hastings, his own counter-blows, now the disclosure of the pre-contract—had not the gathering momentum of these circumstances swept him past the point of choice? Public opinion took the answer for granted. Most men assumed, whether angrily, cynically or hopefully, that he would mount the throne; he could read the expectation in their eyes. Perhaps there was no decision to seek; perhaps he was simply struggling to justify what had somehow already been decided.

His thoughts swung restlessly between the poles of the past and the

LIZABETH VXOR
DWARDVS IIII

4 ELIZABETH WOODVILLE, wife of Edward IV. Artist Unknown

(Queens' College, Cambridge; photo Edward Leigh)

future. As a child he had been tossed by the storms which Henry VI's reign had brewed; before he was nine years old he had lost a father and a brother and been forced to flee the kingdom. England had sunk to her knees in a mire of quarrelling magnates. Yet Henry's minority had begun more auspiciously than Edward's. Hidden in sanctuaries or in refuges abroad, the King's mother and her numerous kindred awaited only the opportunity to stir up strife in the King's name. There were still partisans of Lancaster ready to make capital of any conflict within the House of York. Surrounded by Woodville exiles, Henry Tudor was eagerly scanning events from the court of Brittany. And there was no reason to suppose that the nobles had forgot how to exploit the weakness of a protectorship.

Richard well knew that his office was a slippery eminence, a vulnerable authority. Had not Richard II precipitated his own ruin by turning savagely on those who had governed during his minority? Had not Humphrey of Gloucester, once Henry VI's Protector, been done to death, as it was said, by men who had turned the King's heart against him? Richard realized that if the protectorship continued, there would inevitably develop a King's party to whom the future would belong. On the day that young Edward assumed the sceptre for himself, where would the former Protector of the realm find protection against the long meditated revenge of the King?

In Richard's mind all these elements of feeling, confused by moral misgivings, swam beneath the surface of political considerations and the immediate promptings of the hour. Soon he was driven back upon his only certainty: he would do nothing without the assent of the nobles and commons of the realm. Though he must have recognized that the very act of relinquishing the solution to them half proposed their answer, he set about consulting their wills in all sincerity. Even Polydore Vergil, creator of the official Tudor portrait of Richard, admits that 'not withstanding that many of his friends urged him to utter himself plainly and to dispatch at once that which remained, yet, lest his doings might easily be misliked, his desire was that the people might earnestly be dealt with, and the whole matter referred to the determination of others. . . .'

The opinions of the Mayor and the chief citizens were canvassed as carefully as those of the lords. London was not only the heart of the realm; it was the nurse and guardian of the fortunes of the House of York. London had supported Richard's father; London had been the first to acclaim Richard's brother Edward; London had joyfully

H

opened its arms to Edward and Richard in the spring of 1471 when their cause looked far from hopeful. Furthermore, Richard's relations with the men of York had schooled him to respect the intelligence and value the support of the rising middle class. Yet the prominent role which the Londoners played in the events of his elevation also represented a deeper working within his mind. The sermon at Paul's Cross, the appeal to the citizens, the thronging of the three estates to Baynard's Castle, the ceremony of Richard's seating himself in the marble chair of King's Bench and afterwards making an offering at the shrine of St. Edward, the claim of hereditary rights confirmed by 'popular' election—these events imitate a pattern from the past. It was by such steps that Edward, in March of 1461, had ascended to the throne. Thus did Richard seek to identify himself with the authentic tradition of his House; thus did he grope to regain the brother he had lost to Dame Elizabeth Grey, Hastings, and Mistress Shore, and to redefine his loyalty to the Edward he had worshipped as a boy by mentally divorcing him from the monarch who had fathered a Woodville child. Was it not possible for him to set aside Edward's heir and yet be truer to Edward than Edward had been to himself?

This pattern which Richard had imposed upon events hints at the ultimate means by which he had justified to himself the assumption of the throne. He would succeed his brother to redeem his brother's rule, to return it to its true track, from which it had been deflected by the greed and vanity of the Woodville court. He was deeply religious, but his mind was rigid and unsubtle. Good works, said Holy Church, must be the fruit of faith, the proof of faith. Good works, too, should be his proof. He must stand upon his merits. By the justice and goodness of his rule he would seek to satisfy his conscience and his subjects that he had rightly ascended the throne. All, he now saw, must turn on that. Hence it was that on the first day of his reign he so earnestly lectured the judges and took Sir John Fogge by the hand. He had set himself a task dangerous for any King, doubly dangerous for him who takes a crown another is already wearing. Richard perhaps failed to consider that in the England of 1483 it might be easier to find some colour of justification for assuming the throne than to hold it; as he certainly ignored that it would be easier for a monarch to keep the crown by the uses of power than by the merits of his rule.

VIII*

ONCE he had assumed the crown, Richard pressed on his affairs with dispatch. The date of the coronation·was immediately set for Sunday, July 6. The day after he had seated himself in the marble chair, he appointed John Russell to be his Chancellor and at Baynard's Castle delivered the Great Seal into his keeping in the presence of Buckingham, Stanley, John Gunthorpe, who had been confirmed in his office of Privy Seal, and other lords and prelates. The fast-rising Catesby was made Chancellor of the Exchequer. Peter Curteys, Keeper of the Wardrobe, plunged into the heavy task of providing garments and all manner of rich stuff for the coronation; he sent hastily for skinners and tailors, promising them bonuses, and began to assemble an array of costly materials, including no less than 68,701 'powderings' [to ornament gowns] made of 'bogy shanks'* at twenty shillings the thousand. On Saturday, June 28, Richard girded swords on Thomas, son of Lord Howard, and on Viscount Berkeley, co-heir with Howard of the House of Mowbray, which made them the belted earls respectively of Surrey and Nottingham. Upon John Howard himself the King bestowed the cap of maintenance, the coronet and the golden rod which marked his elevation to the dukedom of Norfolk. In order to secure the speedy adherence of Calais, Richard appointed a commission to acquaint Lord Dynham, the deputy governor, with the change of rule and to supervise the taking of the oath of allegiance to the new King. As a token of his confidence, he empowered Dynham to continue negotiations with Lord Cordes.[1]

Within a few days, Richard's forces from the North, accompanied by a scattering of Buckingham's men, finally arrived under the command of the Earl of Northumberland. They were mustered in Moor Fields, some three or four thousand of them, in their rusty sallets and well-worn gear.[2]* Londoners trooped out to see the show. Some, who had heard tales that a huge army was marching upon the capital, mocked their own foolish fears in jibing at the make-shift harness of the band; others took it for granted that the men had been summoned to guard against a Woodville outbreak while London was thronged for the coronation.[3] When Richard rode out to greet them, they were drawn up in a huge circle on the fields. Around their ranks he passed with bared

* A sort of fur made of lamb's wool clipped from the animal's legs; later called 'budge'.

head, thanked them for their loyal service, and then led them through the city to Baynard's Castle. He had decided to employ them as auxiliary police for the coronation, perhaps as much to give them something to do as for any other reason. Immediately after the ceremony they were dismissed to their homes with thanks and rewards.

Meanwhile, seventeen gentlemen had been summoned to receive the order of knighthood. Nobles and gentry were still crowding into the already crowded city. Mindful of disturbances that had broken out during such occasions in the past, Richard issued a proclamation for the keeping of the peace in London and the vicinity. Men were strictly forbidden to stir up old quarrels, make affrays or challenges, or break into the sanctuaries in order to attack followers of the Woodvilles. Under penalty of death, no one was to harm aliens or strangers, from whom many commercial benefits flowed. The problem of lodgings had become so serious that all new arrivals were required to make application to the royal harbingers, who would find them quarters. Finally, Richard imposed a ten o'clock curfew on the city and forbade all, but those duly licensed, to carry weapons abroad.[4]

On the day before the coronation, Richard rode in a gorgeous procession of magnates, prelates, knights, and household attendants through cheering crowds of Londoners as he took the traditional journey from the Tower to Westminster. Above a doublet of blue cloth of gold 'wrought with nets and pine-apples' he wore a long gown of purple velvet, furred with ermine and enriched with 3,300 powderings of bogy shanks. His seven henchmen, or pages, were gay in doublets of crimson satin and short gowns of white cloth of gold. Richard's frail Queen, borne in a richly adorned horse-litter, was attended by seven ladies on horseback and by five henchmen wearing doublets of crimson satin and short gowns of blue velvet. None outshone the Duke of Buckingham, however, who had encased his handsome person in a gown of blue velvet blazing with a design of golden cart-wheels.[5]★

On the morrow it was Buckingham who supervised the assembling of the great coronation procession in the White Hall. John Howard had been granted the traditional honour of the Mowbrays, the Earl Marshalship, and been created High Steward of England for the crowning of the King; but having, in his own opinion, created a monarch, Buckingham was determined that nobody but himself should be in charge of his enthroning. He had forced Richard to set him above Norfolk as first officer of the Coronation.[5]★

On a broad ribbon of red cloth the procession made its way to Westminster Hall and then, with the King and Queen walking barefoot, moved towards the Abbey, led by the royal musicians and heralds. A great Cross was born before a line of priests, abbots, and bishops. Then came the principal magnates with the regalia: Northumberland exhibiting the pointless sword of mercy; Stanley with the Lord High Constable's Mace; the Earl of Kent and Viscount Lovell with the pointed swords of justice; the Duke of Suffolk, carrying the sceptre; the Earl of Lincoln, the cross with the ball; the Earl of Surrey, the sword of state held upright in its scabbard; and finally the Duke of Norfolk bearing the jewelled crown between his hands. King Richard walked in a gown of purple velvet with a bishop on either side of him and a cloth of estate borne over his head by the wardens of the Cinque Ports. His train was held by the Duke of Buckingham, who grasped the white wand of High Steward. A troop of earls and barons preceded the lords who carried the Queen's regalia; then came the Queen, with Stanley's wife, the Countess of Richmond, holding her train. She was followed by the Duchess of Suffolk, the King's sister, walking in state by herself, the Duchess of Norfolk at the head of twenty noble ladies, and a long line of knights and squires and gentlemen.

As they approached the West Front of the Abbey, Richard and his lords could glimpse, in the courtyard of the almonry, the sign of the Red Pale, where William Caxton, the former mercer, was producing quantities of books by means of his amazing machine. A burst of singing rang against stone arches: the procession was entering the nave.

After hearing a special service of 'latin and prick song', the royal couple walked from their seats of estate in St. Edward's shrine to the high altar. Divested of their robes, they stood naked to the waist to be annointed with the sacred Chrism. Then they were arrayed in cloth of gold, Cardinal Bourchier set crowns upon their heads, and music burst from the organs. 'Te Deum' having been sung, the consecrated King and Queen resumed their seats of estate in St. Edward's shrine to hear High Mass. On either side of King Richard stood Buckingham and Norfolk, while Surrey held upright before him the sword of state. The Queen was attended by the Duchess of Suffolk and the Countess of Richmond, with the Duchess of Norfolk and other ladies kneeling behind. When the *Pax* had been given, Richard and Anne returned to the high altar to receive communion. Then, after the King had offered up the crown of St. Edward and other sacred relics at the Shrine, trumpets and clarions and the organs sounded and the procession returned upon red cloth to Westminster Hall.

Leaving their robes of estate upon the dais, Richard and Anne retired for a little to their private chambers. It was perhaps in this domestic interlude that Anne presented to her husband the coronation gift which Peter Curteys had agreed to make for her: a long gown of purple cloth of gold embroidered with insignias of the Garter and white roses and lined with white damask. Perhaps, too, they commented to each other on certain minor aspects of the ceremony, which must have struck many who saw it. Buckingham had blazed in solitary splendour: his Woodville wife had not attended, or had not been permitted by her lord to attend. Lord Stanley's lady, on the other hand, like Stanley himself, had been specially honoured. While many an earl had merely walked in procession, Baron Stanley had borne the Constable's Mace, though he was not Constable,[7]* and while numerous countesses and even the Duchess of Norfolk took stations behind the Queen, it was Stanley's wife, the mother of Henry Tudor, who carried Anne's train and stood on the left hand of her seat of estate.

Meanwhile, the Duke of Norfolk had ridden into Westminster Hall on a charger trapped to the ground in cloth of gold to dismiss the throng of spectators so that the coronation banquet might begin. Buckingham busily supervised the setting up of four great tables in the lower part of the hall and one on the dais. At four o'clock in the afternoon the King and Queen made their appearance. When the lords and ladies had done their homage, they retired to their respective boards: one for the bishops, one for the earls, one for the barons, and a board for the ladies who sat all on one side with their carvers kneeling before them. At the table on the dais Richard was seated in the middle with Anne on the left end. Whenever the royal couple touched food, cloths of estate were held over their heads. Two squires were stretched prone at Richard's feet. Norfolk, Surrey, Lord Audeley the carver, and the King's boyhood friends Sir Robert Percy and Viscount Lovell served him with dishes of gold and silver. At the beginning of the second course Sir Robert Dymmock, the King's Champion, rode into the hall in pure white armour astride a steed trapped in red and white silk. After he had delivered his traditional challenge and the hall had resounded with the single, massive cry, 'King Richard!' the Champion was served red wine in a covered cup. He drank, cast the rest of the wine to the floor, and retired with the cup as his fee.

It was growing dark now. For the third course the attendants served only wafers and hippocras. As men appeared bearing clusters of flaming wax torches and torchets, the noble company gathered round the dais to make obeisance to their new-crowned sovereigns. To the music of the trumpets and clarions, Richard and Anne walked from the hall, and the lords and their ladies departed into the summer darkness.

Never before had the Abbey witnessed so gorgeous a coronation.[8]* With the exception of three earls who were minors and a handful of other nobles, the entire peerage of England had assisted at the enthronization of King Richard. By comparison, the coronation of Edward IV and, even more, the coronation of Henry VII were rump affairs. Richard had reason to think that the realm had accepted him with good heart.

If he stood musing at an open window in his chamber, he would hear the murmur of the tide, and see, beyond the great, dark curve of the Thames, the glimmer of lights. So had the Plantagenets who had gone before him gazed upon the river and the town, moved by the glory of St. Edward's diadem. So too had his brother gazed. Edward had loved London. Edward had been as comfortably at ease in this palace as if it were a favourite cloak. Yet Edward too had taken the crown. . . . A thousand problems loomed in the darkness. But they were all one problem—to reach the hearts of men and satisfy them that he was their sovereign. Only thus could he hope to satisfy his own conscience and to endure the eye of God. Had God withheld His Presence from the chrism? In his own works he must seek an answer. He was a King.

Richard, by Grace of God ...

THOUGH the walls and spires of London stood in Richard's sight as they had for centuries, new forces and transformations, decay and fresh growth of which Richard could only sense the first effects, coursed in the blood of the giant that, beyond the east windows of Westminster palace, lay sprawled beside the tidal water that gave it life.

The London of King Richard more nearly resembled, perhaps, the town of Edward the Third than the city of Elizabeth, since the daily pageantry of the church was to be shorn and suburbs would blot out environing fields and farms; but in its riches, energy, and self-esteem London was far more like what it was to become under Gloriana than what it had been. It was the principal home of the King: it was now the seat of Parliament, which at the bidding of the House of York had ceased to wander from town to town; it housed the great lawyers in their inns, courtiers, bishops, foreign merchants, and envoys dispatched by the European princes. All the highways of the island led to the capital; its broad estuary enticed the traffic of the channel and the seas; around it lay some of the most fertile lands in the kingdom. To the marvel of continental visitors, London blazed on the far perimeter of civilization the Queen City of the Oceans. If Paris was the largest and Rome or Venice the grandest, London was the richest and busiest of towns.

It was a filthy, crowded, clamorous hive of human activity—its narrow streets, many unpaved, running all hugger-mugger, darkened by the leaning upper storeys of gilt and gabled houses and thick with refuse which was left to be scavenged by flocks of kites and ravens. Erasmus, a few years after this time, permitted himself to be appalled by the stench and the dirt; but his nose, it must be remembered, had been thrown somewhat out of joint by his failure to find preferment and by an unfortunate argument with the royal customs which had left him £20 the poorer. Yet, dirty the city certainly was. It was also an architectural hodge-podge. So thought Italian visitors, accustomed to their sharply defined cities of stone. They found the houses quaint and crazy, comfortable and often opulent on the inside but built every which way as fancy and convenience dictated—houses with ground floors of stone supporting wooden eaves and 'pentices'; houses of half-timber and white-washed plaster; here and there a building of brick or a thatched roof or a stone mansion. London architecture was like the English law: traditional, eccentric, and mysterious. Yet, despite themselves, these visitors were impressed, even awed. A double wonder transpires their comments: their marvelling at London and their marvelling at their own enchantment.

The heart of the city—its chief highway and its means of life—was the clear-flowing river. Small boats plied up and down like restless water-bugs. The barges of the great glided westward to Westminster or down to Greenwich, floating caravans of carved wood and gilding, gay with banners, the liveries of the oarsmen, with burnished armour or scarlet gowns. The barges slid between the traffic of the seas. The greatest vessels—carracks of Genoa or the Flanders galleys—had to tie up five miles below the city; but ships of 100 tons—and many whose prows split the oceans were no larger—sailed up past the Tower to the city's heart. On many of these the old leg-of-mutton sail had given way to a rigging of several sails which permitted them to navigate closer to the wind and to hold their courses in heavy weather. A forest of masts and tackle grew thick along the river bank. Great cranes—amazing to the Italians—swung bales from ship to shore. From the Tower to Black-friars stretched the wharves and warehouses, broken by the battlements of Baynard's Castle and by the stone bulk of the Steelyard, the shop-warehouse-legatine compound of the Easterlings which stood where Cannon Street Station stands now.

The crown of the river was The Bridge, known throughout Christendom as one of the wonders of the world. It was grander, longer and more exciting than the Rialto, the Ponte Vecchio, the Pont Neuf. With stone gates at both ends and a towered gate in the middle from which the drawbridge was worked (kept permanently lowered after 1481), London Bridge supported on its twenty pillars of bright white stone a piece of the city itself. Its ancient roadway was hemmed on both sides by the ground-floor shops of mercers and haberdashers who dwelt in the storeys above. Underneath, the current rushed with a low roar through nineteen arches: 'shooting the bridge' was only for the experienced waterman. The dwellings and the drawbridge still bore scars of the great night battle the citizens had fought with Jack Cade's

H*

rabble in the summer of 1450 and of the Bastard of Fauconberg's attack in the spring of 1471.

By present-day standards London was neither large nor populous. It housed between 50 and 75 thousand inhabitants—four times the number of its nearest rivals, York or Bristol, and, in the opinion of an Italian visitor, no fewer than Florence or Rome. It stretched little more than a mile along the river and less than that from the river to its northern walls. Its extent is remembered to-day in the names of streets and Underground stations. From the Tower, its eastern boundary on the river, the city wall—marked by its gates—ran in a rough semi-circle northward to Aldgate, then westward past Moorgate and Aldersgate and so south by Newgate and by Ludgate, on the hill west of St. Paul's, to Blackfriars on the river.

Dominic Mancini presents the only surviving description of the city as it looked on the day that Richard was crowned. 'London might complain of us for ignoring her,' he says, 'as she is so famous throughout the world.' He distinguishes three principal paved streets, 'the busiest in the whole city and almost straight. Of these three, the one closer to the river and lower than the rest, is occupied by liquid and weighty commodities: there are to be found all manner of minerals, wines, honey, pitch, wax, flax, ropes, thread, grain, fish and'—adds the refined Italian, dead to the romance of commerce—'other distasteful goods.' This was Thames Street, still traceable, skirting the wharves, warehouses, Fishmonger Hall and the Steelyard, in almost a straight line from the Tower to Blackfriars. In the second street, part way up the slope from the river, 'you will find,' Mancini reports, 'hardly anything for sale but cloths.' Actually far from straight and to-day not so easily discerned, this street ran westward from the Tower as Tower Street, became East Cheap, broadened into lines of mercers' and drapers' shops on Candlewick (Cannon) Street, and then twisted its way by Budge Row and Watling Street into St. Paul's churchyard. 'In the third street, which touches the centre of the town and runs on the level, there is traffic in more precious wares such as gold and silver cups, dyed stuffs, various silks, carpets, tapestry, and much other exotic merchandise.' Commencing as Aldgate Street on the east, this thoroughfare first became Cornhill; from the Stocks Market it continued as The Poultry until it was transformed into West Cheap or Cheapside, the most splendid roadway in the city, often called simply 'The Street'. Earlier in the century Lydgate had mentioned the rich wares of Cheap; travellers from Bohemia marvelled, in 1466, to learn that London

boasted 200 master goldsmiths; 'Chepe' was their glittering domain.
A few years after Mancini's visit, another Italian found here 'fifty-two
goldsmiths' shops so rich and full of silver vessels great and small, that
in all the shops in Milan, Rome, Venice, and Florence put together I
do not think there would be found so many of the magnificence that
are to be seen in London. And these vessels are all either salt cellars or
drinking cups or basins to hold water for the hands; for they eat off
that fine tin, which is little inferior to silver. . . . [pewter].' Mancini
declares that 'there is no where a lack of anything. . . . There are in the
town many other populous quarters with numerous trades, for whatever
there is in the city it all belongs to craftsmen and merchants.' At booths
and stalls capped apprentices showed their masters' wares. 'Yet their
houses are not'—as in other cities—'encumbered with merchandise only
at the entrance: but in the inmost quarters there are spacious depositories,
where the goods are heaped up, stowed and packed away as honey
may be seen in cells.'

The Italian who looked at London not many years after Mancini
noted that the merchants were no less proud and no less esteemed than
the merchant-nobles of Venice itself. The edifices these men reared in
stone and wood reflected their wealth: the cloth market of Blackwell
Hall (Basinghall Street), the Leadenhall, the Stocks Market (on the site
of Mansion House), Guildhall, and the handsome halls of the Merchant
Taylors, the Grocers, the Goldsmiths, the Skinners, the Haberdashers,
the Vintners. Edward the Fourth was happy, in 1467, to demonstrate
the prosperity of London to the Bastard of Burgundy by feasting with
him in Grocers Hall. Nor did the merchants fare less well by themselves. At a Lord Mayor's banquet, a thousand guests would spend four
hours consuming, with punctilious etiquette, a choice of fifty or sixty
courses served on plate of silver or silver gilt. The homes of these men
of trade were now beginning to keep pace with their means. Crosby's
Place is the best surviving example. Built in Bishopsgate Street by Sir
John Crosby in the first years of Edward the Fourth, it was purchased
or rented by Richard to serve as his town house. Its great hall, with
richly carved ceiling and musicians gallery and high walls and spacious
windows—designed like the hall of an Oxford or Cambridge college—
stands today in Chelsea on the river bank. These merchants were
royally cherished by the House of York. Edward, himself a trader,
made them his familiars, borrowed money from them which he repaid
by valuable customs concessions, spent lavishly in their shops, steered
his foreign policy in their interest and shaped his domestic legislation

by their counsel. Richard followed his brother's example. He canvassed their support and was sensitive to their opinions, he took their advice in Parliament, he sought to keep the seas safe for their shipping and to negotiate with foreign powers to their advantage.

London was, however, more than a city of merchants. No less than 97 parish churches thrust their steeples into the air, dominated by the spire of St. Paul's rising 500 feet from the cathedral on Ludgate Hill, and a score of great religious houses sheltered within their walls cloisters, gardens, hospitals, chapels, shrines, and chantries. The city resounded with the clangour of bells and the voices of singing clergy; the city shimmered in the colours of church pageantry. On feast days processions of choristers wound through the streets bearing banners, lighted candles, and crosses. Funerals were almost as grand, with more singers, heralds, torch bearers, and poor men bearing white staves. Bishops and mitred abbots, often in London on business, rode as stately as peers at the head of trains of liveried servants, clerics, and men at arms. In parish churches and monastic houses glowed many a silver or jewel-crusted reliquary. The Bohemian visitors of 1466 were dazzled upon viewing, in London alone, 'twenty golden sepulchres adorned with precious stones'. They were no less moved by the beauty of English singing. After hearing the chorus of sixty voices in the King's Chapel, they decided that 'there are no better singers in the world'.

London was also the city of the King and his court; besides the palace at Westminster, there were three royal residences within the walls, the Tower and Baynard's Castle and the Wardrobe. It was the court which provided the most thrilling pageantry of London: scarcely less spectacular than coronations were the tournaments, royal weddings and christenings, victorious entries into the city, the reception of foreign potentates, the welcoming home of the King. On these occasions the Mayor and Aldermen donned scarlet gowns trimmed with fur; the chief citizens rode in violet or green. Tapestries fluttered from windows; trumpets and clarions sounded above the shouting of the crowd; tableaux were staged in the principal places of the city.

As colourful as any spectacle were the costumes of the age. During the reign of Edward the Fourth the attire of courtiers had grown ever more gorgeous, and the rest of the world followed the lead of court. Lords emulated the King; squires and gentlemen, the lords; citizens, even priests, could not resist the quickening impulse to go as richly clad as their means allowed—this, despite Edward's sumptuary laws which sought to confine men to costumes appropriate to their several stations in life. What the present age vaguely pictures as medieval dress is the court costume of Richard's day: men in robes of velvet or brocade and black velvet caps with turned up edges, or in doublets (tunics) of green or scarlet with padded shoulders and slashed sleeves, and long hose ending in shoes with pointed 'pikes'; women wearing the steeple head-dress or 'hennin', which trailed a mist of fine linen, and low-necked gowns with full trains. These garments were enriched by a profusion of rings, bracelets, necklaces, and, for the men, honorific collars of suns and roses.

This medley of colour and life which was London had long ago begun to push beyond its walls. Along the chief roads it reached thin tentacles towards the neighbouring villages of Islington, Clerkenwell, Hoxton, Kennington. Southwark, Mancini noted, 'is a suburb remark-able for its streets and buildings, which, if it were surrounded by walls, might be called a second city'. So populous had the district from Ludgate to Westminster now become that to Mancini's eye it was a 'suburb continuing uninterruptedly from the metropolis and differing in appearance very slightly from it'. This was really only a ribbon of buildings, however, pursuing the line of Fleet Street and the Strand—lined with the palaces of bishops—and at Charing Cross turning south to follow the river to Westminster.

A metropolis it was, and yet redolent of the countryside: girdled by farms, by fields where youths practiced archery, and harbouring many a green garden. On May Day the May pole was still set up in Cornhill. Maidens danced in the streets for garlands on summer evenings while boys armed with make-shift shields and staves hacked at each other in mimic warfare. And on the bosom of the river, green-banked, floated the white swans. 'London,' sang the Scot William Dunbar, enchanted by what he saw, 'thou art of Townes A *per se*!'

> Strong be thy wallis that about thee standis;
>   Wise be the people that within thee dwellis;
> Fresh be thy ryver with his lusty strandis;
>   Blithe be thy churches, wele sownynge be thy bellis;
> Riche be thy merchauntis in substaunce that excellis;
>   Fair be their wives, right lovesom, white and small;
> Clere be thy virgyns, lusty under kellis:
>   London, thou art the flour of Cities all.

Through the gates of the city ran roads to all the quarters of the kingdom. In wet weather patches of mire made for slow going; some of the lesser roads were well nigh impassable in winter, but they were on the whole not nearly so bad as they are usually thought to have been. Causeways carried them above marshy river banks or across swamps; bridges were often built solidly of stone. It was not uncommon now for men to leave bequests of money to keep the local stretch of highway in repair. The arrow-straight stone roads of the Romans, Watling Street running northwest and Ermine Street running northeast, still bore their burden of carts and horsemen. It is doubtful if the highways of the eighteenth century were much better.

Even as London, the countryside looked other than it does to-day. To the Bohemian visitors, who saw only the southern counties, it was remarkably thickly populated; but French and Italian travellers, perhaps venturing farther, thought the land sparse of inhabitants. They were struck by the great forests, like those of Dean and Rockingham and Nottingham which spread, each of them, across almost 1,000 square miles. Swamps there were in plenty too and lonely expanses of heath and moor and waste and abundant streams. In the valleys and by the rivers nestled towns and villages, still surrounded by their open fields and common pastures of an earlier day. By modern standards the lot of the peasant was hard, narrow, often brutish. But to foreigners the prosperity of the country was no less remarkable than that of London. Not only did the nobles surround their manor houses with splendid parks and well-kept enclosures. Everywhere one met thriving franklins; the tenant farmers, who held by copyhold or leasehold from an abbey or manor, seemed to live well; and the peasants had plenty to eat, stout clothing, and a few acres of their own. Serfdom lingered, especially in the remoter parts, but it was already an exception and an anachronism. Sir John Fortescue complacently contrasted the misery of the French peasant with the independence and well being of his English counterpart.

'The riches of England,' affirms the Italian observer who followed Mancini, 'are greater than those of any other country in Europe. . . . There is no small innkeeper, however poor and humble he may be, who does not serve his table with silver dishes and drinking cups and no one who has not in his house silver plate to the amount of at least £100 . . . is considered by the English to be a person of any consequence.' Under King Richard, England owned a balanced prosperity she would not see again for a long time. In just a few years a hard and unhappy era would commence for the lower classes, enforced by rising prices, widespread enclosure of lands and eviction of tenants, the Tudors' tendency to ignore the suffering of the politically impotent levels of society, and Henry the Eighth's wanton debasement of the coinage. In alliance with the House of Tudor the ambitious burgesses and gentry would claw their way to wealth across the face of the poor. 'Sheep ate the men,' says Thomas More, referring to the conversion of arable land to pasture. 'These decaying times of charity,' Stow called the sixteenth century.

The prosperity of Yorkist England had wrought few changes upon the face of the countryside. Dominant upon the skyline stood yet the castle or the abbey, built three centuries before by the magnificent energies of the Normans. Castles no longer had much utility as fortresses. When the Lancastrians tried to defend Bamburgh against King Edward in 1464, the royal artillery so battered the walls that great blocks of masonry went flying into the sea and Sir Ralph Grey's chamber toppled down on his head. Though Edward and Richard had kept the strongholds in the Welsh and Scottish marches up to the mark and accomplished notable repairs at Windsor, Warwick, Nottingham, Middleham, Barnard Castle and a few other places, a number of castles, it appears, would soon be abandoned or were already being allowed to fall into ruin. No new ones were being built. Noblemen deserted their dark keeps to dwell in more comfortable apartments erected within their courtyards, and cut windows in forbidding walls, as Richard had done at Middleham; but manor houses, galleried and oriel-windowed, were still almost a generation distant. The increased ease of living which marked the Yorkist period is mainly to be found in a greater profusion and richness of carpets, cushions, tapestries, chests and beds; and in the growing desire for privacy which the lord and his family found in privy chambers and solars, retreating from the hurly-burly of communal life in the great hall.

The religious houses, too, stood outwardly unchanged from Angevin days, except for their accumulation of precious adornments. An impression of their size, their opulence, and their stateliness still lingers in the mighty ruins of Glastonbury, Tintern, Fountains. 'The abbeys,' poor, betrayed Robert Aske said in the hard days of their dissolution, 'was one of the beauties of this realm to all men passing through the same.' The Italian visitor thought that 'the great monasteries are more like baronial palaces than religious houses. Many of these monasteries possess unicorns' horns of an extraordinary size.' Not even St. Martin of Tours could compare with the richness of Edward the Confessor's tomb; but the shrine of St. Thomas à Becket at Canterbury 'surpassed all belief', plated as it was with pure gold; and yet the gold was 'scarcely visible for the variety of precious stones with which it is studded, such as sapphires, diamonds, rubies . . . and emeralds . . . but everything is left far behind by a ruby, not larger than a man's thumb, which is set to the right of the altar.' This was the famous 'Regal of France' given by Louis VII.

But within their walls, the great abbeys and nunneries showed a sad decline from the ages when they had stood as fortresses of Christian devotion and of civilization as well. There were now only about 7,000 monks and 2,000 nuns, scarcely enough in many establishments to maintain the offices of the Church. The world outside the cloister had grown brighter, more hopeful, safer. These survivors of another time were more lazy than evil, leading humdrum lives, clinging to their privileges and, out of habit, continuing their rites and their charitable works. Their worldliness sprang partly from an invasion of the world which they had encouraged. In return for a lump sum of money, called a 'corrody', a man or woman might pass the rest of his days in a religious house, bringing with him his secular way of life and, often, his dogs and servants as well. These speculative annuities not only lamed the spirit but, in the case of long-lived folk, lightened the purse of the abbey.

The monks had long ago resigned spiritual leadership to the friars; but the friars, despite their reputation for learning and preaching, had now grown lethargic and fond of worldly possessions. The secular clergy were no better. Many churches were served by ignorant and ill-paid vicars who could hardly mumble a Paternoster; priests sought the well-paid, easy posts of officiating in a chantry or of being 'retained' by a guild or of serving as secretary and adviser to a lord or gentleman. While bishops accumulated benefices, they stayed far from their sees, serving as the royal officers of state.

Monks, friars, bishops, deans—such as they were—were symbols of the time. The vast, rich, complex, massive institution of the Church lay upon the land, rather like a fat whale stranded in a lagoon abounding in its food—not uncomfortable enough and too well fed, too inert, to try to move in any direction at all. Though pricked by the Lollards and stung by hostile criticism from the laity into holding tight to its privileges, the Church was not sufficiently challenged to attempt or even imagine reform. It held a third of the land, exacted a tenth of men's income, and charged exorbitant fees for burials, christenings, proving of wills. Yet the powerful demands of a century before that it be made to disgorge its wealth were now seldom heard. This acquiescence probably reflects the growth of prosperity in Yorkist days; men had discovered that they and the kingdom could thrive without looting the ecclesiastical establishment.

The slide from ardent faith was lay as well as clerical, a mutual move-ment; if ecclesiastics no longer waged flaming battle for souls, numbers of souls had been distracted by new interests from the fear of eternity and the hunger for grace and an unthinking dependence upon Holy Church. Our Italian visitor was puzzled by a seeming paradox: though the English faithfully attend mass, say many paternosters in public, and do not 'omit any forms incumbent upon good Christians; there are, however, many who have various opinions concerning religion'. The bite of the comment lies equally in the phrase 'omit any forms'. Obser-vance was often habitual rather than urgent; it also offered the means for a conspicuous consumption of goods. The lovely parish churches built, re-edified, or adorned in this period—the 'wool' churches of East Anglia, the towered churches of Somerset, that jewel of stone built by William Canynges at Bristol, St. Mary Redcliffe—represent, in part, ways of spending money—in an age which did not possess many such ways—in order to display power and command esteem. Now was occurring the last great surge in ecclesiastical building and it is the one artistic glory of Edward's and Richard's time: perpendicular architec-ture. This cannot match the spiritual aspiration, the daring, the haunting wonder of earlier Gothic; but in sheer power of loveliness is it not pre-eminent? It is, in any case, the end of something. After, long after, comes Wren and stone grows monumental and mute. Though per-pendicular architecture has not forgot the spirit, it revels in the physical beauty of shapes and colours. The gorgeousness of its fan vaulting, the dazzling ostentation of its glass, the proud assertion of its straight lines sing man's exultation in his power to create a thing goodly to look upon. There are four supreme examples: Eton College Chapel, King's College Chapel at Cambridge, the chapel of St. George, and Henry VII's Chapel at Westminster Abbey. The first three were founded between 1450 and 1485; the last is their child and closes the story.

As the Church lost touch with men's sense of awe, the unknown became more fearsome and superstition burgeoned. When people cease to believe in God, Carlyle remarks, God pays them back by making them believe in Cagliostro. People had not ceased to believe in God, but throughout the century there seems to have been an increasing preoccupation with witches and the forces of darkness. In 1441 Humphrey of Gloucester's wife Eleanor had been condemned to life imprisonment for dabbling in the black art; Elizabeth Woodville's mother was formally accused of witchcraft in 1469; Clarence became enmeshed in the alleged wizardry of his follower Burdett. Politicians had discovered that men were quick to believe any tale of necromancy. There was a growing fear of the world which could not be apprehended by the senses. Men's minds had become less satisfied, less secure. To these gnawing uncertainties were mated a sharpening curiosity about life and a fresh political and social awareness.

But the means of communicating knowledge had not kept pace with these intellectual hungers, printing being as yet but a whisper. From this unslaked need was generated the writhing crop of rumours which plagued men's minds, which had caused many of King Edward's troubles, and which, under the artful manipulation of Henry Tudor's followers, would poison King Richard's hopes. The marvellous, fading from the Church, grew a new head in the market-place. Credulity was nourished by suspicion and ignorance. Carried by pedlars, disbanded soldiers, itinerant friars, the menials of the great, rumour sifted through the kingdom like a contagious disease. The food it battened on was the affairs of the great; above all, the mystery which hedges a King. When Edward the Fourth died, the word 'poison' rode a foam of whispers. Soldiers fleeing from Barnet after Hastings' wing was crushed outstripped pursuit to retail the hideously toothsome news that Edward and his two brothers had been butchered by Warwick. In 1461 tales had been wafted across the channel that Queen Margaret and Somerset had murdered King Henry to gratify their guilty passion and their ambition.

With superstition and rumour ran their stablemate, prophecy, mysteriously wise after the event and often pungently ironic. During the unrest provoked by Clarence in the early 1470's, King Edward dared not summon a popular prophet named Hogan, lest people take it for a sign that the King endorsed Hogan's powers. Folk believed that Edward had condemned George of Clarence because of a prophecy which said that one whose name began with G would supersede Edward's heirs—though it seems likely that the prophecy was not invented until after Richard of Gloucester had assumed the throne. Following this event, says Mancini, the pat prognostication circulated that within a space of three months three Kings would reign. Commynes remarks that the English are never unprovided with prophecies. Superstition, rumour, and prophecy were powerful, and could be dangerous, forces in the England of King Richard. And the fat whale of the church establishment fed well and lived on until, half a century later, it was suddenly dispatched by a harpoon.

·   ·   ·

The three quarters of a million or so inhabitants of the realm of England struck foreigners as being so different from other Europeans as to require considerable interpretation, laudatory and derogatory by turns. There was no doubt in these visitors' minds that the English were an entity, a nation; and there are plenty of indications that the English heartily agreed with them. If the swan of an enlightened patriotism had not yet spread her wings, the unprepossessing cygnet of insularity and xenophobia was in lusty growth. The conclusions of the Bohemian knights who came to England in 1466, of Mancini who recorded the events of the protectorship, of Nicolas von Poppelau who had journeyed the length of Europe to meet King Richard at Middleham in 1484, and of the Italian diplomat who set down his impressions some fifteen years later must be considered with a good deal of caution. They looked through the special aperture of their own customs and prejudices and they too were not uncritical of foreigners; but their reports often jibe and their strongest impressions are the ones in which they show most agreement.

Your Englishman of Richard's day knew that no other land or folk could hold a candle to his people. The Island Race lumped aliens together as a conniving lot who 'never came into their island but to make themselves masters of it and to usurp their goods'. As to their own virtues—'The English are great lovers of themselves and of everything belonging to them; they think that there are no other men than themselves and no other world but England; and whenever they see a handsome foreigner, they say that "he looks like an Englishman", and that "it is a great pity that he should not be an Englishman"; and when they partake of any delicacies with a foreigner, they ask him, "whether such a thing is made in *their* country?" . . . It is not unamusing to hear the women and children' of former sanctuary men who have been forced to leave the kingdom 'lament . . . that "they had better have died than go out of the world", as if'—the Italian adds scornfully—'England were the whole world.' Perhaps part of this insularity sprang from a deep-grained conservatism, jarring to an Italian diplomat of flexible mind: 'If the king should propose to change any old established rule, it would seem to every Englishman as if his life were taken away from him. . . .' The events of the succeeding generation, however, told a somewhat different story.

Englishmen were amazingly hardy and robust fellows—'their bodies are stronger than other peoples', for they seem to have hands and arms of iron.' Naturally, they are prodigious trenchermen. 'They have a very high reputation in arms . . . but I have it on the best information,' the diplomat confides, 'that when . . . war is raging most furiously, they will seek for good eating and all their other comforts, without thinking of what harm might befall them.' Dinner is indeed an important occasion. The English 'think that no greater honour can be conferred or received than to invite others to eat with them, or to be invited themselves; and they would sooner give four or five ducats to provide an entertainment for a person, than a groat to assist him in any distress'. Their chief virtues, von Poppelau thought, were their wealth and hospitality, but he found their cooking poor. Baffling to the Italian mind were the rough and ready humour, the careless dispositions, the rudiments of a sporting instinct: the English 'have no idea of the point of honour. When they do fight it is from some caprice, and after exchanging two or three stabs with a knife, even when they wound each other, they will make peace instantly, and go away and drink together'. Yet men of breeding could be very civil too, even by Italian standards. They 'are extremely polite in their language. . . . They have the incredible courtesy of remaining with their heads uncovered, with an admirable grace, whilst they talk to each other'.

Foreign travellers were titillated by the discovery that English women insisted on being people too and were very much a part of the scene. They were enthusiastically commended as 'the greatest beauties of the world, and as fair as alabaster'—but amazingly bold and free: following the hunt like men, preferring to ride horseback than to go sedately in a carriage, and thus often showing a tantalizing glimpse of limb. Very beautiful, von Poppelau also conceded them to be, but 'astoundingly impudent'. And how familiar they were! An English-woman, Erasmus notes with favour, by way of salutation kisses every man she knows at all well. This warmth of greeting had amazed the Bohemians: on the arrival of guests, 'the hostess comes into the street to receive them with all her household and they all kiss'.

Yet there was a darker side to English character, which in the hard days of the earlier Tudors would grow yet grimmer, until under the last Tudor of all hidden sweetness would find its way into the light. With varying emphases, almost all of the foreigners found the English grasping, cold, materialistic. Von Poppelau was impressed by the virtues of King Richard, but his subjects were another matter: 'they surpassed the Poles in ostentation and pilfering, the Hungarians in brutality, and the Lombards in deceit. . . . The avarice of the people made everything in England dear'.

To the Venetian diplomat, the English showed so little feeling that he thought them either 'the most discreet lovers in the world or . . . incapable of love. They keep a jealous guard over their wives, though anything, in the end, may be compensated by the power of money'. They are equally wanting in affection for their children; 'for after having kept them at home till they arrive at the age of seven or nine years at the utmost, they put them out, both males and females, to hard service in the houses of other people, binding them generally for another seven or nine years. And these are called apprentices and during that time they perform all the most menial offices; and few are born who are exempted from this fate, for everyone, however rich he may be, sends away his children into the houses of others, whilst he, in return, receives those of strangers into his own. And on [my] inquiring their reason for this severity, they answered that they did it in order that their children might learn better manners. But I, for my part, believe that they do it because they like to enjoy all their comforts themselves, and that they are better served by strangers than they would be by their own children. [These] never return, for the girls are settled by their patrons, and the boys make the best marriage they can and, assisted by their patrons, not by their fathers, they . . . strive diligently . . . to make some fortune for themselves.'

The widow of a merchant or a rich man, the Venetian continues, usually bestows herself on the apprentice in her house who is most pleasing to her and who was probably not displeasing to her in the lifetime of her husband. When her children are of age, 'their fortunes [i.e., what they inherited from their father] are restored to them by their mother's [second] husband, who has enjoyed them for many years, but never [restored] to the full amount. . . . No Englishman complains of this corrupt practice, it being common throughout the kingdom'. Wardships of rich or highborn orphans were, indeed, bought and sold like any other commodity; what could be made out of the particular marriage arranged for the orphan and out of the use of his money while he was a minor constituted the buyer's profit.

The Italian's generalization is, of course, over-large and no doubt he mistook undemonstrativeness for lack of feeling; but while the Paston letters and other sources reveal instances of strong domestic affections, the usual behaviour of the Pastons towards their children supports the Italian's general view. When Elizabeth Paston, for example, returned home, unmarried, from service in another household, her mother made life such a hell for her that her cousin wrote her brother begging him quickly to find Elizabeth a marriage because she was beaten weekly or oftener and so severely that on the last occasion her head was broken in two or three places. A widower appeared on the horizon, middle-aged and disfigured, so unpalatable that even the family had its doubts. Elizabeth, a girl of twenty, indicated that she was willing to have him—'if his land be sure'. Again, the Paston letters in general confirm the observation that Englishmen were preoccupied with gain and often harsh and suspicious in their methods of dealing. They had not yet quite perceived that life need not be so hard and that a man could prosper without ruthlessness. At its best, this arrant materialism shows as a forthright insistence on reality, an expression of prodigious, though unenlightened, energy.

There is yet another side to the Englishman of King Richard's day, a sensibility and a capacity for simple delight as yet only haltingly articulate. Look at his gardens and his parks. He has learned to enjoy 'flowers white and red' and the green of fields, dogs and horses, the sea, the grace of swans, 'and the young rabbits that in a sunny morning sit washing their faces'. The loveliness of spring shines in his songs and carols; his ballads are bright with the brave poignance of star-crossed love. Though he thinks himself an unmoved, no-nonsense sort of fellow, he has a child's love of colour—in his dress, his house, his church, and the court of his King. Witness his fondness for pageantry which will pop out at a funeral as well as a marriage. Give him any excuse and he will have braying trumpets, flickering torches, cloth of gold, singing, actors posturing on stages, banners, minstrelsy and whatever else he can devise of 'gorgeous ceremony'. He has not yet found his full voice or mined his genius or harnessed his energies by his imagination. But he is vigorously alive, a lusty and complex fellow not too easily penetrated by foreigners.

It is a changing, trans-shifting, restless time. The seeds of still richer and greater changes in men's minds have already begun to burgeon. In the year of 1483 a crop of marvellous boys were nursing thoughts and visions that their elders did not suspect. John More, the witty butler of Lincoln's Inn, was the father of a youngster of seven named Thomas. In Ipswich dwelt another Thomas, three years older, son of a dealer in meat. Of the same age as this Thomas Wolsey was a lad, now in school at Cracow, destined to make a far deeper impress on men's imaginations, a Polish boy who would someday be called Copernicus. Michelangelo and Raphael and Niccolo Machiavelli were growing into their 'teens in far-off Italy. The bastard son of a priest, a young man of about seventeen named Desiderius Erasmus was stuffing into his head all the learning he could find in the religious house in which he was immured. In the insignificant German town of Eisleben there was born this year a child christened Martin Luther, while at Florence, Lorenzo the Magnificent, poet and prince and patron, fed with his taste and his generosity a blaze of Greek learning, philosophical speculation, painting, architecture, sculpture. Between the bronze doors of Ghiberti and Giotto's campanile walk Florentines whose heads are singing with Plato and whose eyes are fixed upon a misty dream of the Full Life. Pico della Mirandola has this year defended against the frowning doctors of the church the 900 theses into which he has compressed all knowledge. One hundred and thirty-seven of them having been declared heretical or suspect, Pico flees to France, is arrested at the instigation of the papal legate, is permitted to escape, and hastens to Florence and a triumphal welcome by Lorenzo. Rome herself will soon be driven to a sudden frenzy by a glimpse of the loveliness of the pagan world. On April 18, 1485, some workmen dug up a statue of Julia, daughter of Claudius. As the tremendous news spread through the city, the statue was hurried to the Capitol. Thronging from all quarters, a wild procession of pilgrims passionately adored *Julia antiqua* as a revelation of the classic age. Pope Innocent the Eighth so feared for the True Faith that under the cover of night he had Julia removed from the Capitol and secretly buried.

Meanwhile, across the channel, a master builder is dying as Richard begins his reign; the old fox with the shrewdest brain in Christendom, now terror-stricken at the approach of death, is holed up in his impregnable den at Plessis-les-Tours. Death is terrible to King Louis the Eleventh because it will part him from the great passion of his life, France, because it will break the web of those darting thoughts and subtle schemes it has been his heart's delight to weave. Five days before Richard was crowned, Louis gave his last public audience, to delegates of the towns of France. In health he had cared nothing for dress; on this occasion he sought to beguile his mortal illness by wearing a long gown of crimson velvet lined with martens and two scarlet caps. Afterward, he disappeared from view into his gloomy stronghold. Grown morbidly suspicious, he had preserved himself against earthly dangers by iron spikes and Scots guards, but against the advance of death his frantic efforts were less successful. He had tried to buy the intercession of saints: 200,000 francs he gave for a silver screen for St.

Martin of Tours; St. John of the Lateran, at Rome, was placated by a golden chalice; St. Eutropius of Saintes and the Three Kings of Cologne, by precious reliquaries. Having sent far and wide in search of holy men, he had finally persuaded Francis of Paola, who ate roots and lived under a rock in Calabria, to make the long journey to the banks of the Loire. But Francis refused to taste the luscious fruits Louis had ordered for his delectation; he scorned the couch provided in the specially built hermitage, preferring to sleep on a mat of reeds woven by himself; and he bluntly told the King that he must trust in God. In desperation, Louis turned to one last expedient which seemed more accessible. Having secured the Pope's permission, he caused the Holy Ampulla, whose sacred chrism had never been removed from Rheims, to be brought to Plessis-les-Tours. He had promised to use but a single tiny drop of the oil and to return the Ampulla after he had worshipped it. On a sideboard which he could see from his bed it stood between the Staff of Moses and the Cross of Victory. Even news of the death of Edward the Fourth had given him no pleasure: it was but a horrible reminder that Kings perish like other men. Clawing at the slippery sides of life and faith, King Louis slid inexorably towards his end.

What of that quartet of men who had been born at the same time that Richard had opened his eyes upon the grey stone of Fotheringhay castle?

In the year of 1483 Leonardo da Vinci departed from Florence to take service under Ludovico Sforza, the ruler of Milan. His teeming brain—infinite riches in a little room—had not yet dazzled the world. He had left behind him, unfinished, the first of his great paintings, *The Adoration of the Magi*. Savonarola, the monk with the tongue of fire, had recoiled into obscurity after failing to move the citizens of Ferrara and Florence. Preaching to gaping villagers, he was perfecting that thunderous voice of doom which would one day drive out the Medici and soon after deliver his own body to the stake. The weaver's son with the sea in his blood, Christopher Columbus, had taken service with the Portuguese. During Richard's first months upon the throne, he was sailing down the shore of West Africa to Mina, the fort which Portugal had built upon the Gold Coast. By night and day his gaze swept the vastness of water to the west. Already, the plan of reaching the Indies by sailing into the setting sun lay matured in his mind; in another year he would make his first effort to persuade the King of Portugal to give him ships and money. The rulers who would finally listen to him, Ferdinand the Aragonese and his consort Isabella of Castile, were beginning the last stage in forging a

Spanish nation from the domains of Leon, Aragon, and Castile. Since 1478 the figure of the Grand Inquisitor had been expressing the grip of their power and the dynamics of their orthodoxy.

The rival hues of the long past and the quickening future which coloured King Richard's mind shine clear in the lives of these four contemporaries: da Vinci and Savonarola charging opposite poles of men's thinking; King Ferdinand calling into being the Inquisition and nurturing the vision of Columbus.

In England, Edward the Fourth had given a new meaning to the monarchy by bringing to an end the turbulent dominion of the nobles and by setting the kingdom on the road towards a more fruitful release of its energies than it had hitherto achieved. Richard recognized the essential greatness of his brother's accomplishment; but, in his estrangement from court, he had become more sensitive to Edward's weaknesses than to the political realities by which Edward had steered his course. Moved by his love of older and more parochial ways, Richard would seek to transform the pattern of government Edward had bequeathed him into a shape which might yield justice as well as order and rest upon loyalty rather than fear. In a time between, he was a man between. He was more like his father than like his brother; but it was his brother's understanding touch upon the pulse of the age which he needed.

II*

UNDER the rains, under the sunlight of July, the kingdom of England lay waiting and wondering. Only London and the lords had any understanding of the events which had brought King Richard to the throne. Only London and the lords had heard the new King's pledge to nourish peace and to govern justly. It was therefore politic for Richard to show himself to the rest of the realm; he was, in fact, eager to demonstrate in his kingly person the kind of rule he meant to give. There were more intimate considerations. He wanted to behold his frail little son who was now the precious vessel of his dynasty. He wanted to be beheld by the men of Yorkshire, who, being his friends, would feel themselves elevated by his greatness.

Soon after the coronation he retired with his councillors to the quiet of Greenwich to settle his affairs.[1] To the rulers of Europe he sent word of his assumption of the crown. The three chief props of his throne—

Buckingham, Norfolk, and Northumberland—he had determined to establish, virtually as his lieutenants, in Wales, East Anglia, and the North.

Buckingham came first. Confirmed in the great powers which had been granted him under the protectorship, he proceeded to reap a fresh harvest. Perhaps Richard had in mind the trouble which the Percies had caused Henry IV, the attempt of Warwick to unseat Edward: he who considers himself a King-maker is triply sensitive to ingratitude in the monarch he has made. Besides, none had been so zealously loyal as Buckingham—and, in his volatility and eloquence, he was so like Clarence. On July 13 Richard gratified a wish the Duke had long cherished. Buckingham possessed half the great estate of Humphrey de Bohun, Earl of Hereford, which had descended to him from one of Humphrey's co-heiresses. The rest of the estate had gone to King Henry IV, who had married Bohun's other daughter, and thus was merged in the Crown holdings. From the death of Henry VI and his son Edward, Buckingham had considered himself heir-general to the whole estate. Apparently he had tried, without success, to press his claim on King Edward. Richard now restored to him the other half of the Bohun lands, some fifty manors worth more than £700 a year. He made the grant provisional, however—'till the same shall be vested in him by the next Parliament'; but there was a sound reason for the delay. Henry VI having been attainted in 1461, his share of the Bohun estate, like all his other lands, had come to the Yorkist crown by parliamentary confiscation. Therefore Buckingham could not become the heir of property which Henry VI had forfeited long before his death. Whatever a Parliament had done, only a Parliament could properly undo. It must pass a bill reversing so much of the attainder of Henry VI as applied to the Bohun lands so that Buckingham could be held to have inherited them upon Henry's death. Since the Duke seems to have insisted upon receiving the grant as his lawful due rather than a gift, he must have been satisfied with this provision. New powers came to him on the same day as these long desired lands. Richard gave him the highest military post in the kingdom, the Constableship, and then made him Great Chamberlain of England. Even Warwick had scarcely held such concentrated might.[2]

This excessive outpouring was obviously intended to reward Buckingham's services and satiate his ambitions; but it also, no doubt, expressed Richard's now intensified craving for loyalty and his need to share the responsibility for a decision which filled him with unease.

Buckingham had urged him to the deed and Buckingham deserved to enjoy, but must also help to bear, its consequences.

To John Howard, Duke of Norfolk, Richard granted the authority of supervision and array of the King's subjects in a third of the counties of England, rewarded his exploits at sea by appointing him Admiral, and enlarged his purse to support his new powers by presenting him with the yearly income of twenty-three royal estates and the outright gift of almost half a hundred manors. The Earl of Northumberland received the Wardenship of the entire Scots border: East March, Middle March, and Richard's palatinate in the west—but the patent ran for a year only. Richard had not yet made up his mind how the North should be governed.[3]

There were other appointments of interest. Robert Brackenbury, an old Yorkshire adherent, was given the lucrative office—which had belonged to Hastings—of Master and Worker of the King's Moneys and Keeper of the Exchange and was also made Constable of the Tower. Francis, Viscount Lovell, became Lord Chamberlain and Chief Butler of England. And on July 19, King Richard gave to his son Edward the Lieutenantcy of Ireland.[4]

The King now chose one group of his councillors, headed by the Chancellor, John Russell, Bishop of Lincoln, to carry on the government at Westminster. The others, among whom was Lord Stanley, would accompany him on his progress. Stanley he decided to keep with him not only for that baron's experienced advice but as a measure of prudence.[5*] He took no company of archers with him nor any armed escort. He had other hopes for safeguarding his position on the throne. In dismissing his chief lords to their estates after the coronation, he had given 'strait commandments that they should see the countries where they dwelled well guided and that no extortions were done to his subjects'.[6] Earnestly he adjured them to uphold the rights of 'our holy mother the church', to protect people 'of what estate, degree, or condition so ever they be' against robbery and oppression, to keep the highways free of crime, and to rule in such a way that each 'may appear and be named a very Justicer'.[7]

About two weeks after his coronation King Richard set out from Windsor on his progress, accompanied by a great train of lords, bishops, justices, and officers of his Household. Halting at Reading on July 23, he went next day to Oxford. William Waynflete, Bishop of Winchester and Founder of Magdalen College, had arrived two days before in order to prepare a worthy reception. The royal party were met by the Chancellor and the regents of the University and escorted to the gates of Magdalen, where the Founder and his scholars greeted them in solemn procession. That night the King and his chief lords were lodged in the college. On the morrow Richard, at his express desire, was treated to two scholastic disputations in the great hall, one in moral philosophy and the other in theology. The University, lethargic in spirit and declining in numbers, clung to the thinking of its long past; yet the disputant who opposed Dr. John Taylor, Professor of Sacred Theology, was Master William Grocin, now in his late thirties, who would soon go to Italy and return to inspire Colet, Erasmus and More with his learning, particularly his knowledge of Greek. John Colet himself, son of Henry the London alderman, had just this year entered the University. Pleased by what he had heard, the King rewarded each of the disputants with game and money, bestowing a buck and one hundred shillings upon Dr. Taylor and a buck and five marks upon Grocin; and refreshed the tables of the college with venison and wine. After dinner the King rode on to Woodstock, but he returned the next day to inspect the University and linger several more hours in the congenial atmosphere of Latin and learning.[8]

The royal progress then wound through the Cotswolds and came to Gloucester. Here Richard encountered the Duke of Buckingham, who had apparently remained in London a few days after the King's departure and was now riding home to Brecon by the main road, which led through Gloucester and Hereford. This brief meeting was, in fact, the last time that they were destined to see each other.[9]*

After delighting the citizens of Gloucester by granting them a charter of liberties, King Richard moved along the Severn to Tewkesbury, following the same road up which, a dozen years before, the harried host of Queen Margaret had fled. He passed through the great Norman door of the abbey church in order to stand in meditation by the tomb of George of Clarence and his wife, who were buried behind the altar. Somewhere beneath the stones of the choir lay the body of Prince Edward, the former husband of Anne Neville. On August 4 Richard made the abbot the munificent gift of £310 out of the rents of Clarence's estates.[10]

From Tewkesbury, King Richard went to Worcester and then turned eastward to Warwick, which he had reached by August 8. After spending a week at the great castle that had once been the King-maker's, he proceeded northward by Coventry, Leicester, and Nottingham—passing two or three days in each place—and lingered several days at

Pontefract before his entry into York. The reception he was everywhere accorded answered his most sanguine hopes, and the demonstrations he gave of the spirit in which he meant to rule won him golden opinions. Richard's secretary, John Kendall, wrote the magistrates of York that the King had been 'worshipfully received with pageants, and other etc., and his lords and judges in every place sitting, determining the complaint of poor folks with due punishment of offenders [against] his laws'. The writer is scarcely unbiased, but the Warwickshire antiquary John Rous, who in the reign of Henry VII would reveal to the world that Richard had monstrously lain two years in his mother's womb, gives even more glowing testimony. At Woodstock, he reports, Richard graciously eased the sore hearts of the inhabitants by disafforesting for their use some lands which King Edward had for his own pleasure annexed to Whichwood Forest. London, Gloucester, and Worcester had each offered the King a benevolence to help defray his expenses; but he had declined all the offers, saying he had rather have their hearts than their money. In early September, Dr. Thomas Langton, Bishop of St. David's, who had been one of King Edward's most experienced diplomats, wrote to his friend the Prior of Christ Church that 'I trust to God soon, by Michaelmas, the King shall be at London. He contents the people where he goes best that ever did prince; for many a poor man that hath suffered wrong many days have been relieved and helped by him and his commands in his progress. And in many great cities and towns were great sums of money given him which he hath refused. On my truth I liked never the conditions of any prince so well as his; God hath sent him to us for the weal of us all....'[11]

At Warwick, Richard had been joined by Queen Anne who came directly from Windsor, bringing with her a Spanish envoy. He must have expected to find an Edward V upon the throne, but he was content to negotiate with Richard III. In his first formal audience Graufidius de Sasiola declared that his Royal Mistress, Queen Isabella, desired peace with England and stood ready to give assistance against Louis XI. He then made a curious disclosure. Isabella's heart, he said, had been turned against England because Edward IV had refused the offer of her hand to marry Elizabeth Woodville. Therefore she had made a league with the French King. But now that Edward IV was dead and that Louis XI had failed to live up to the treaties he had signed with her, she wanted to ally herself with England against France. Richard had no wish at this moment to be drawn into an active war with France, but a treaty of peace with Spain he was eager to make, both for the security and prestige it would bring. Therefore, welcoming Sasiola warmly, he proposed a renewal of the amity and league which had existed between Edward IV and Henry of Castile. Sasiola promised that this would suit Isabella very well. Losing no time, Richard wrote his council in London next day to inform them of the proposal he had made and to request the Chancellor, if this policy met with the approval of the council, to draw up a Treaty of Amity as quickly as possible and seal it with the Great Seal.

A month before, he had appointed Bernard de la Forssa, who had performed many such missions for Edward IV, to go to Spain on this very business. Since Forssa had apparently not yet sailed, Richard dispatched him further instructions in which he outlined his reasons for desiring a renewal of the previous league but made clear that he was willing to agree to a new treaty if Queen Isabella so wished. He wrote a very friendly letter to the Queen herself, announcing the arrival of the Spanish ambassador and telling her that Bernard de la Forssa was on his way to complete negotiations.[12]

Other foreign affairs occupied him on this progress. There was not much he could do at the moment to strengthen the alliance with Burgundy, for Duke Maximilian and his Flemish subjects were quarrelling with one another. The Scots, however, were now showing signs of tiring of the warfare which had brought them little but hard knocks. On August 16, James the Third sent Richard a proposal for an eight months' abstinence of war with a view to permanent peace—'a courteous and wise letter', Bishop Langton called it. Richard showed his willingness to negotiate by offering to provide safe-conducts for a Scots embassy. Still, none knew better than he how weak and vacillating King James was. He confirmed Earl Douglas's annuity of £500 and he supported at his court the Duke of Albany, who had once again betrayed his brother, delivered Dunbar to the English, and fled across the border. If the Scots continued to make trouble, Douglas and Albany would be sent north to keep them busy.[13]

Irish affairs also demanded Richard's attention. By coining silver money similar in appearance to that of England but worth much less because it was heavily alloyed, the Irish were visiting serious financial losses on English merchants. Richard therefore ordered that money was to be minted only at Waterford and Dublin and that the coins must be clearly differentiated from those of England. He wisely avoided tampering with the government of Ireland, however. The Earl of Kildare was re-appointed Deputy Lieutenant for a year, and further at the King's pleasure; all other officers were confirmed in their posts. Richard was careful to recognize also that other powerful peer, the Earl of Desmond. Desmond was requested to take an oath of allegiance to the King, and to renounce the wearing of Irish clothing. As an inducement, Richard sent him gowns, doublets, hose and bonnets and also the King's livery: a collar of gold worked in roses and suns with a white boar appended. One part of the instructions for Desmond casts an interesting light upon the past. The services of the Earl's father to Richard's father were, Richard assured him, warmly remembered. Further, the King and Desmond were bound by a common tie of sorrow, for those who had murdered the Earl's father [i.e., the Wood-villes] were the very ones who had encompassed the death of the Duke of Clarence. If the Earl so desired, Richard promised to give him opportunity to prosecute the guilty parties at law. Brother George still cast a long shadow.[14]

As for France, Richard's efforts this summer to redeem the dangerously ragged and uncertain situation his brother Edward had bequeathed him came to little. His ally Maximilian was busy fighting against rebellious subjects; the King of France was busy with heaven. Richard's and Louis' minds touched once. Struggling to keep his grip on affairs even though he knew he was sinking to his end, King Louis replied to Richard's announcement of his assumption of the throne with a very informal, almost offhand, note: 'Monsieur mon cousin, I have seen the letter that you sent me by your herald Blanc Sanglier and thank you for the news you've given me and if I can do you any service, I'll do it very willingly for I want to have your friendship. Adieu, Monsieur mon cousin'.

This cool and cavalier communication the King of England answered from his castle of Leicester on August 18 in a letter which contains the only gleam of Richard's wit that has survived. The wit is grim enough, but unmistakable. He lets Louis know that if France doesn't give a hang about the relations between the two countries, neither does England; he directly questions Louis' intentions; and he well nigh parodies Louis' casual style. Louis need not think that Richard, though newly seated on the throne, is panting to be recognized by Louis! 'Monsieur, mon cousin', he writes,

I have seen the letters you have sent me by Buckingham herald, whereby I understand that you want my friendship in good form and manner, which contents me well enough; for I have no intention of breaking such truces as have previously been concluded between the late King of most noble memory, my brother, and you for as long as they still have to run [i.e., till April 9, 1484]. Nevertheless, the merchants of this my kingdom of England, seeing the great provocations your subjects have given them in seizing ships and merchandise and other goods, are fearful of venturing to go to Bordeaux and other places under your rule until they are assured by you that they can surely and safely carry on trade in all the places subject to your sway, according to the rights established by the aforesaid truces. Therefore, in order that my subjects and merchants may not find themselves deceived as a result of this present ambiguous situation, I pray you that by my servant this bearer, one of the grooms of my stable [no more impressive envoy being called for!], you will let me know in writing your full intentions, at the same time informing me if there is anything I can do for you in order that I may do it with good heart. And farewell to you, Monsieur mon cousin.

Richard had a clear understanding of the temper of Anglo-French relations, and of King Louis XI. But Louis never saw this communication. He died at Plessis-les-Tours on August 30, leaving his heir, Charles VIII, and his realm to the regency of his shrewd daughter, Anne de Beaujeu. In the meantime, Richard had managed to send a small fleet to sea for the summer to operate against the French privateers.[15]*

Difficulties with France inevitably dictated a friendly approach to Francis, Duke of Brittany, who for almost two decades had been the wavering and timorous ally of Edward IV. On July 13 Richard appointed Dr. Thomas Hutton, 'a man of pregnant wit', to negotiate with the Duke for a diet which would arrange for mutual redress of grievances—arising from piratical depredations on both sides—and re-establish the old league of friendship and intercourse of merchandise. Hutton was also instructed to 'feel and understand the mind and disposition of the Duke anempst [in regard to] Sir Edward Woodville and his retinue, practicing by all means to him possible to ensearch and know if there be intended any enterprise out of land upon any part of this realm, certifying with all diligence all the news and disposition there from time to time'. Richard made no mention of Henry Tudor doubtless because he did not want Duke Francis to suppose that he regarded the Tudor as of any importance. He would soon learn, however, that Francis was not impressed by this omission.[16]

Meanwhile, in his progress King Richard had at last entered Yorkshire. After pausing from August 20 to August 23 at Nottingham, he seems to have reached Pontefract next day, where he had summoned to meet him seventy knights and gentlemen of the North. His purpose was doubtless to inquire into the state of local affairs and to read them the same lecture on administering justice which he had delivered to the lords in London.[17]

SOWENT ME SOWIENT

5 LADY MARGARET BEAUFORT 1443–1507.   Artist Unknown

(National Portrait Gallery, London)

At York the citizens had been busily preparing for a month to welcome their new King in a style which would show their love and uphold his honour. As soon as the news of his accession had reached the city, the Mayor and four aldermen rode to Middleham to pay their homage to little Prince Edward and to present him with demain bread, a barrel of red and a barrel of white wine, six cygnets, six herons and twenty-four rabbits. Not long after, they entered into exhaustive discussions concerning arrangements for the official welcome of their sovereign, sending for priests and men of the guilds who were expert at devising pageantry. Richard himself was no less eager that the chief men of his court be impressed by the reception he received at York. On August 23 John Kendall, Richard's secretary, penned an exuberant letter from Nottingham to the magistrates of the city. King Richard, he wrote, cherished them dearly. Though he himself knew they were preparing a welcome better than any he could devise, he could not resist expressing his hope that the King and Queen would be received with pageants, speeches, and arras and tapestry hanging in the streets—'for many southern lords and men of worship are with them and will greatly mark you receiving their Graces'.

About the 19th of August Prince Edward left Middleham to join his parents at Pontefract. At York he probably tarried for a day, during which he spent 13s 4d for a primer and a total of 7s 10d for black satin cloth to cover it and for a psalter. The boy's health was so poor that, instead of riding a horse, he had to be conveyed in a chariot. He was probably reunited with his parents on August 24, for on that date he was formally created Prince of Wales and Earl of Chester.

Either on Saturday August 30 or the day before, Richard, Anne and Prince Edward made their state entry into York, accompanied by their splendid retinue which included the Bishops of Worcester, Coventry, Lichfield, Durham, St. Asaph's and St. David's, the Duke of Albany, the Earls of Northumberland, Warwick (Clarence's young son), Surrey, Huntingdon, and Lincoln; the Lords Stanley, Dudley, Morley, and Scrope, as well as Viscount Lovell the Lord Chamberlain, the Chief Justice of England, and many officers of the Household. The royal cavalcade had been met at Tadcaster by the two sheriffs of the city, who now rode at the head of the long procession each bearing his rod of authority. The King and Queen were greeted at Brekles Mills, outside the walls, by the Mayor and Aldermen in scarlet and the council, the bridgemasters, and other chief citizens in gowns of red; as the royal couple came past St. James' church and passed into the city by the

I

Micklegate, they were cheered by a mass of citizens clad in blue velvet and vari-coloured mustersdevelers. Then unfolded the array of pageants: one staged just within the gate, another at the bridge over the river Ouse, and a third at Stayngate. After a speech of welcome the Mayor presented King Richard with a hundred marks in a cup of gold and the Queen with a hundred gold pounds in a piece of rich plate.[18]

So delighted was Richard by this reception that he and his councillors decided next day to appoint a ceremony at York for the investiture of young Edward as Prince of Wales. Orders were hastily dispatched to the Keeper of the Wardrobe in London to deliver a great variety of raiment: doublets, gowns, cloth of gold, gilt spurs, four religious banners, three coats of arms beaten with pure gold for the King himself, coats of arms for heralds, a thousand pennons, and 13,000 costume badges of the white boar. To Sir James Tyrrel, now Master of the King's Henchmen, and seven of the henchmen themselves were given many yards of Holland cloth and other goods for the ceremony. The ensuing week was occupied by a round of state occasions. The Mayor upheld his dignity by entertaining the chief officers and lords of Richard's court at two dinners. On Sunday, September 7, the 'Creed play', a favourite drama in the possession of the Corpus Christi Guild, was acted before the King and Queen in the municipal hall.

The ceremony of investiture took place next day, and so impressive was the report of its splendours that a number of people in other parts of the kingdom supposed that Richard and Anne had celebrated a second coronation. In the solemn grandeur of York minster the Prince of Wales was given a golden wand and a golden wreath was fitted upon his brows. The King took the occasion to knight the Spanish ambassador and place a gold collar about his neck. Then, in state procession, Richard and Anne and their son walked from the Minster with their crowns upon their heads, to the 'great honour, joy, and congratulation of the inhabitants, as in show of rejoicing they extolled King Richard above the skies'.

He displayed his gratitude ten days later when he called before him in the chapter house of the cathedral the Mayor, Aldermen, and chief commoners of the city. Thanking them for their past services and their present show of goodwill, he granted them a relief of more than half the taxes which they yearly paid the crown.

In the course of this happy sojourn, Richard established a royal household at the castle of Sheriff Hutton, the purpose of which was to provide a residence for two of the chief scions of the House of York.

Clarence's son, the young Earl of Warwick, who had been taken into
the retinue of Queen Anne, went now to Sheriff Hutton to live under
the care of his cousin John, Earl of Lincoln, son of Richard's sister, the
Duchess of Suffolk. It was from this household that Richard's chief
innovation in government, the Council of the North, would
develop.[19]★

Shortly after the middle of September the King and Queen parted,
Anne apparently accompanying her son to Middleham castle, while
Richard began to retrace his steps southward, conscious that he had
been long away from London and that there were signs of restlessness
on the political horizon. As a result of warnings he received from his
council at Westminster he had appointed in late August a commission
of *oyer and terminer* for the capital and one for the belt of counties
surrounding it. Probably while he was still at York, he had heard
unpleasant tidings from the lips of Georges de Mainbier, envoy of
Francis of Brittany.[20]

Though Mainbier was full of the Duke's loving protestations of
friendship, the proposals which he set forth were arrant blackmail.
Francis had nothing to say about so inconsequential a figure as Sir
Edward Woodville, but he had a great deal to say about Henry Tudor.
Since the death of Edward IV, King Louis had made many offers for
the custody of the 'Lord of Richmond' and, Francis having virtuously
refused these for fear that Louis was meditating mischief, the French
King was now uttering violent threats to make war on Brittany. Such
a war Duke Francis could not survive without help. Therefore if
Richard did not wish Henry Tudor to be delivered to Louis XI, he
must be prepared on a month's notice to send Francis 4,000 archers at
his own expense and, if required, another two or three thousand at the
Duke's expense. Furthermore, since the Estates of Brittany were to
meet towards the end of September, an immediate answer to these
proposals was requested. Clearly, Duke Francis meant to make all the
capital he could out of the fact that Richard was but newly seated in a
throne by no means yet secure.

Richard, however, probably had no inclination and he was certainly
in no position to make even a gesture of assenting to Francis's demands.
Though his reply has not survived, subsequent events indicate that
Francis did not get what he wanted. Richard realized that he would
gain nothing but trouble by giving the Duke of Brittany the idea that
the King of England was afraid of Henry Tudor.

After pausing for several days at Pontefract, Richard moved

southward towards Lincolnshire at the beginning of October. Spending the night of the 10th at Gainsborough, he came the next day to the city of Lincoln. Here he was greeted by the tidings that a rebellion had broken out in the southern counties and that his greatest ally and most powerful minister, Henry, Duke of Buckingham, had risen in revolt against him.[21]

III

IT had begun as a movement in the southern and southwestern counties to restore Edward V to the throne. Soon two other conspiracies, animated by quite different motives, were in the making. By the end of September the three centres of insurrection had coalesced into a single, but by no means single-minded, effort to end the rule of Richard III.

Scarcely had the King departed from Windsor in July when 'the people of the southern and western parts of the kingdom began to murmur greatly and to form meetings and confederacies in order to deliver the two princes from the Tower. Soon it became known that many things were going on in secret, and some in the face of all the world, to promote this object, especially by those in sanctuary'. Queen Elizabeth was urged to smuggle her daughters in disguise from Westminster and send them beyond sea so that if anything happened to the princes, one of these girls might find a husband who would help her to restore King Edward's blood to the throne. But the plan was anticipated or speedily discovered, and the council set John Nesfeld to guard the sanctuary at Westminster. Still, conspiracy continued to burgeon.[1]

Even this first movement was motivated by a diversity of interests. A few of its leaders were undoubtedly men who were loyal on principle to the line of Edward IV. Others had been dispossessed by the redistribution of offices which the new regime had put into effect. Sir John Cheyney of Wiltshire, for one, who was Master of the Horse to King Edward, found himself replaced by Sir James Tyrell. There were a number of men among the gentry, particularly in Kent and Devonshire, who for a generation had ever shown themselves ready to seek advantage from troubled times. Most of these were old Lancastrians, like the Courtenays—Peter, Bishop of Exeter, and his kinsman Edward —who from their Devon strongholds were eagerly sniffing the air of unrest and gathering their followers. It was the Woodvilles, however, who dominated the movement, provided most of its strength, and directed its energies.

When the first intimations of a rising reached the Marquess of Dorset, apparently hiding somewhere in Yorkshire, he made his way south to Wiltshire and went to work with his uncle Lionel, Bishop of Salisbury who had slipped away from the sanctuary at Westminster some time before and was fomenting trouble in his diocese. In Kent and Surrey, Richard Guildford, whose father had been a friend of Earl Rivers, assumed the leadership of the conspiracy. His principal lieutenants were his own kin, relatives of the Woodvilles, and men, like Sir John Fogge, connected with the Woodvilles by marriage. A few adherents seem to have been friends of John Morton, Bishop of Ely. In Berkshire, Sir Richard Woodville was seconded by supporters of his family like Sir William Stonor, who had found favour with the Marquess and had been hostile to Richard when he was Duke of Gloucester. Among the chief plotters at Exeter was Sir Thomas Saint Leger, who was hoping to marry his daughter to the Marquess's son. Aimed at restoring Edward V to the throne, this Woodville conspiracy attracted other elements of discontent by its promise to overthrow King Richard III.[2]

Suddenly, some time in September, the leaders of the movement disclosed to the rank-and-file the amazing and wonderful news that the Duke of Buckingham himself, repenting of his past conduct, would rise to their support at the head of all his mighty forces. Within a few days, however, the leaders as well as the rank-and-file were thrown into confusion and dismay by tidings from the Duke of Buckingham—and who could be better informed?—that the sons of King Edward had been put to death, none knew how.[3]

It is with the entry of Buckingham that the scene grows murky; the shape of the rebellion is lost in a fog of contrarieties, gross errors of fact, and palpable distortions. This umbrageous confusion radiates from two inter-linked centres of darkness: the motives of the Duke of Buckingham and the perplexed enigma of the little Princes' fate. The two principal contemporary sources of information are reliable enough but reflect only the surface of events: the bill of attainder passed by King Richard's Parliament does little more than list the names of the chief rebels and the areas in which they operated; the Croyland Chronicler supplies only a scant, terse outline of what happened. Writing a generation later, Thomas More concentrates upon the fascinating alteration in Buckingham's allegiance, but abruptly breaks off his narrative at the crisis of the Duke's transformation; and Polydore Vergil either deals disingenuously with accurate information or has been victimized by tales which have taken on the colour of Tudor opinions. Still later, Grafton and Hall work the story up into elaborate accounts, vividly punctuated by dialogue and intimate glimpses into Buckingham's mind, which, like jungle snakes, reveal themselves for what they are by the brilliance of their hues.

In Hall's narrative, when Buckingham parts from Richard at Gloucester, he is outraged by the King's irascible and arrogant refusal to grant him the Bohun lands and shocked at the discovery that the sons of Edward have been put to death by royal command. He first decides to claim the throne for himself and for two days he meditates upon this enticing idea at Tewkesbury. But as he proceeds through Worcester towards Bridgnorth, he happens to meet on the road the Countess of Richmond, wife of Lord Stanley and mother of Henry Tudor. This chance encounter momentarily dashes his hopes by causing him to recollect that Henry Tudor, being descended from John, Duke of Somerset, has a better claim to the throne than he, the grandson of Duke John's younger brother Edmund. His better nature soon asserts itself, however, and he determines to promote the marriage of Henry with one of Edward's daughters and stir up a rebellion to place the crown upon Henry's head.[4]

An interesting story it is, but only a story . . . a Tudor tale. In the first place, the Countess of Richmond undoubtedly remained in London after the coronation, for she was soon busy there spinning an intrigue of her own. In the second place, if Buckingham had taken the road through Tewkesbury and Worcester, he would not have parted from King Richard at Gloucester, because that was the very route that Richard himself followed; but nobody on his way to Brecon, which lies west of Gloucester, would ride northwest to Bridgnorth. Third, Richard, as we have seen, had not refused Buckingham the Bohun inheritance; and fourth, More and the later Tudor writers all date the murder of the princes as occurring days after Buckingham had reached Brecon.

Polydore Vergil tells a simpler but scarcely more credible story, which is disfigured at the very outset by the fact that he places Buckingham's rebellion a whole year late, in 1484. He reports the tale that Richard had harshly upbraided the Duke for demanding the Bohun inheritance and that, in consequence, Buckingham decided, when he had brooded at Brecon for a little, to seat Henry Tudor upon the throne if Henry would agree to marry one of Edward's daughters. This plan he disclosed to his prisoner, the Bishop of Ely, who enthusiastically set about putting it in operation by sending word to the Countess of Richmond in London. According to Vergil, this lady had already hit upon the idea, had persuaded Queen Elizabeth to give her consent, and won to the cause such men as Richard Guildford and John Cheyney. Not only is this story set awry by the confusion in time and the feebleness of Buckingham's motivation, but the Countess of Richmond is made to assume so prominent a role that the Woodville conspiracy, the generating force of the rebellion, disappears altogether.[5]

It is also absent from Thomas More's *Richard the Third*, but More is much franker than Vergil about the conflicts and the dubious assertions in the sources of information available to him. He mentions the report that Buckingham and the King had quarrelled over the Bohun property but rejects it as contrary to common sense. He rather vaguely indicates his belief that it was the Duke's insatiate ambition which made him ripe for revolt and in a wonderfully comic scene sets about showing how the artful ministrations of John Morton, Bishop of Ely, turned Buckingham into a rebel. Easily penetrating his captor's shallow mind, John Morton—says More—'found the mean to set this Duke in his top. [His] wisdom abused . . . [Buckingham's] pride to his own deliverance and the Duke's destruction'. More breaks off his narrative, however, at the very moment when the wily Bishop is entangling Buckingham in his web.[6]

It is the contemporary Croyland Chronicler who provides the only trustworthy foundation on which to attempt a reconstruction of the course of Buckingham's rebellion. Unfortunately, he gives but a terse summary: 'At last, it was determined by the people in the vicinity of the city of London, throughout the counties of Kent, Essex, Sussex, Hampshire, Dorsetshire, Devonshire, Somersetshire, Wiltshire, and Berkshire, as well as some others of the southern counties of the kingdom, to avenge their grievances before-stated [i.e., to rescue Edward's sons from captivity]; upon which, public proclamation was made, that Henry, Duke of Buckingham, who at this time was living at Brecknock in Wales, had repented of his former conduct, and would be the chief mover in this attempt, while a rumour was spread that the sons of King Edward before-named had died a violent death, but it was uncertain how. Accordingly, all those who had set on foot this insurrection, seeing that if they could find no one to take the lead in their designs, the ruin of all would speedily ensue, turned their thoughts to Henry, Earl of Richmond. . . . To him a message was, accordingly, sent, by the Duke of Buckingham, by the advice of the lord Bishop of Ely, who was then his prisoner at Brecknock, requesting him to hasten over to England as soon as he possibly could, for the purpose of marrying Elizabeth, the eldest daughter of the late King, and at the same time, together with her, taking possession of the throne'.[7]

Though even this statement is by no means entirely clear, the outline of events which it gives is supported in general by the evidence of the parliamentary act of attainder, the family connections of the chief rebels, and a few letters and documents. The sum of this evidence, taken with what can be discovered of the intentions of the Duke of Buckingham, indicates that the Duke and John Morton, with the aid of the Countess of Richmond, impinged upon a conspiracy to free the Princes and by exploding its motive for action diverted it to the radically different purpose of overthrowing King Richard, in order to seat Henry Tudor on the throne.

The rumour of the Princes' death which was spread among the Woodville rebels played a decisive part in shaping the insurrection; the actual fate of the Princes, however, was immaterial to the movement and is not illuminated by it. In the view of the Lancastrians who were rousing themselves at the call of Morton and the Countess, it would not matter whether the Princes were discovered to be alive or dead, once Henry Tudor was seated on the throne. Polydore Vergil himself inadvertently reveals this attitude when he reports that after the Countess had heard of the Princes' death she 'began to hope well of her son's fortune, supposing that that deed [the killing of the Princes] would without doubt prove for the profit of the commonwealth. . . .'[8] The Duke of Buckingham likewise had no interest in the Princes, beyond the use to which the rumour of their deaths could be put.

There are, roughly, three possibilities regarding the situation of Edward's two sons at the time that Buckingham, at Brecon, was beginning to take the Bishop of Ely into his confidence. They may have been alive, in which case they were probably either dwelling in the Tower or had been conveyed northward to take up a secret residence at Sheriff Hutton in the custody of the Earl of Lincoln. Should this conjecture be true, then Buckingham and Morton devised the report of the Princes' deaths, knowing that it would find ready credence and that if they accomplished their end, no one would be in a position to produce the Princes in any case. There is the second possibility that Buckingham, for reasons unsuspected by the King, persuaded Richard to snuff out the lives of the two boys by convincing him that the deed was necessary to the safety of his throne. It is also possible that, after Richard had begun his progress, Buckingham remained briefly in London in order to murder the Princes himself. Being Constable, he could open all doors and command what he would. Perhaps he justified his act under the colour of solicitude for his sovereign's security or left Richard to learn of it as best he might, in either case knowing that the King could do nothing except conceal what had happened.

Only thus far does the fate of the Princes enter the story of the rebellion. This thrice perplexed mystery which stands at the heart of Richard's reign requires so extensive an analysis that, in order to maintain the flow of Richard's life, I have been forced to remove it from the context of the biography.*

There remain to be traced the intentions of the proud and volatile Duke of Buckingham. Although Vergil plumps for the grotesque story that Henry Stafford rushed to abandon all that he had gained from King Richard for love of the grey eyes of an unknown young man in Brittany, Henry VII's historian does give another version of Buckingham's motives, only to discount it in terms which suggest that it is indeed a true one. On at least two other occasions when Vergil is forced to make a choice between two different versions of an event— his accounts of Warwick's break with King Edward and of Friar Shaa's sermon on Sunday, June 22—he chooses the inaccurate version and dismisses the truth as being mere common rumour. Similarly he discounts as only vulgar report the information he has gathered 'that the duke did the less dissuade King Richard from usurping the kingdom, by mean of so many mischievous deeds upon that intent that he afterward, being hated both of God and man, might be expelled from the same, and so himself called by the commons to that dignity, whereunto he aspired by all means possible, and that therefore he had at last stirred up war against King Richard'.[9] All the available evidence which seems trustworthy supports precisely this explanation.

Portents of Buckingham's ambitious dreams had appeared years before. In 1474 he had sought and received permission to bear the arms of Thomas of Woodstock, son of Edward III and his own great-great-grandfather, without any other arms to be quartered with them. He is also reported to have got in his possession an exemplification of the act of Richard II's parliament legitimating the Beauforts, which did not contain the clause later inserted by Henry IV that barred them

* See Appendix I, p. 393. Some readers may wish to turn now to this mystery. Others may find more satisfaction in bringing to it the judgments they have formed as a result of following the whole course of Richard's life.

I•

from the throne.[10] Thus did he cultivate the precious memory of his double descent from Edward the Third—through his Beaufort mother from John of Gaunt, in which doubtful lineage he was preceded by the Countess of Richmond and her son, but also from Edward's youngest son Thomas, of whom he was the unchallenged heir and in which lineage there was no flaw. A step which Buckingham took while Richard was still Protector suggests the burgeoning of his secret ambitions in the sunlight of his suddenly achieved greatness. After Hastings' conspiracy was crushed, the Duke requested and was given the custody of the Bishop of Ely. Why should Buckingham wish to become John Morton's gaoler except that he was already visioning the use to which he could put the mind of that master plotter?

It appears that when the Duke of Buckingham parted from his King at Gloucester, he was not only gorged with honours but dazzled by the heights to which he had so quickly and so facilely climbed. Clearly, he had only to aspire in order to achieve, and a single leap would now waft him to the summit of his dreams. He had openly boasted that he would have as many Stafford knots as ever did Warwick have ragged staves.[11] Like the great Earl, he was a King-maker; but, unlike Warwick, he would not fail to be more. Once Warwick had deposed Edward IV, he could offer only a Clarence or a Henry VI, whereas the Duke of Buckingham could offer himself. 'I have heard of some that say they saw it', reports More, 'that when the crown was first set upon King Richard's head, the Duke of Buckingham could not abide the sight but ried his head another way'.[12] To enthrone a King only to pluck him from the throne and seize his crown—that was a design whose grandeur might presume to express the imperial scope of Buckingham's character! The word 'motive' is too weighty to express the mating of impulse and opportunity, the exuberant assumptions, the prompting of illusions and caprices which drove Duke Henry, as they had driven Clarence, to whatever lay at the end of the enchanting rainbow.

As soon as Buckingham reached Brecon, he set about hungrily to consume the convenient talents of his prisoner, the Bishop of Ely. In no time John Morton saw through him to the bottom, and the vague hopes he himself had nursed of a Lancastrian restoration now rapidly took form in his agile mind. When the Bishop applied a little flattery, Buckingham opened up like a flower in the morning sun. The grave, black-gowned prelate and the ebullient Duke went earnestly to work to uncrown King Richard. At Morton's suggestion, a messenger was dispatched to the Countess of Richmond, who at once sent to Wales her shrewd man of affairs, Reynold Bray. From him Buckingham and Morton learned that an insurrection was already brewing in the southern counties and that the Countess had been in touch with a number of Lancastrian friends. In discussions of which the Duke was undoubtedly kept in ignorance, Bray and Morton developed their plans. Then, well aware of his host's ambitions, the Bishop of Ely exerted all the force of his mind to mould Buckingham to his own ends. Regretfully he pointed out that though Henry Stafford, Duke of Buckingham, clearly deserved the crown, another seemed to have—not a better claim, oh certainly not!—but a better chance. Circumstances, alas, appeared to point to Henry Tudor, his cousin, as the man. For one thing, Henry Tudor was unmarried and was therefore free to marry, as a sop to the Yorkists and a bid for Woodville support, the eldest daughter of Queen Elizabeth and Edward IV. For another, the Countess of Richmond could command a large Lancastrian following and had connections with some of the leaders of the plot which was already hatching. Obviously, however, everything depended upon that thrice noble and all-powerful lord, the Duke of Buckingham. He could with a breath seat Henry on the throne, if he were willing. . . .

Buckingham's hopes must at first have been sadly jarred. Successively to bestow a crown, by the mere exercise of his fancy, upon two monarchs within a short span of months had some savour in it, but this was not the regal adventure he had dreamed. Yet he had committed himself so far, he realized, that he dared not recoil into the bosom of King Richard. The memory of his past success, however, soon gave him new heart. He signified his assent to Morton's plans. He would indeed join with Henry Tudor, encourage him to invade the kingdom in order to support the assault upon the crown. But when Richard was crushed —that would be another matter. Then perhaps it would be the man with the greatest army at his back, then perhaps it would be Buckingham, the legitimate descendant of Thomas of Woodstock, rather than Henry Tudor, the illegitimate descendant of John of Gaunt, who would snatch the fruits of victory and assume the crown. This comedy of cross purposes entered its critical phase of double deception. Brecknock became a castle of visions within visions, humming with the counterpoint of common aims expressed aloud and secret thoughts buzzing in the brains of Morton and Buckingham.

As for the sons of Edward IV, either the Duke was able to give the Bishop assurances that they were out of the way, or else this pair of plotters now devised the rumour of their deaths as a means of capturing the rebellion already being fomented. Thus it was that the Countess of Richmond succeeded in winning the Dowager Queen's promise to give her eldest daughter to Henry Tudor, that the marvellous news came to the southern rebels of Buckingham's decision to lead them, and that, when these same rebels had been thrown into despair by the report which quickly followed of the death of the Princes, they soon after agreed to find their revenge in elevating Henry Tudor and Edward's daughter Elizabeth to the throne.

Buckingham was now secretly assembling his tenants and retainers; all the bailiffs and stewards of his Welsh lands had been straitly charged that at their master's call they must bring to the field every man they could lay hands on. Through Morton the Duke was in close communication with the Countess of Richmond and a stream of messengers linked him with Richard Guildford, Sir John Cheyney and Sir William Stonor, with the Marquess Dorset and the Courtenays at Exeter. By September 28 he was writing directly to Henry Tudor. Very early in October the grand design was finally forged. Insurrections would break out simultaneously in the southern counties from Maidstone and Guildford through Newbury and Salisbury to Exeter. The men of Kent and Surrey would seize, or at least threaten, London. The men of Devon and Dorset would march eastward. Henry Tudor, with a stout force supplied by the Duke of Brittany, would land on the south coast. And the Duke of Buckingham would cross the Severn at the head of his host and advance southeastward to close a mighty vice upon the hapless King Richard. The date on which each of these multiple actions should begin was set for Saturday, October 18.[13]

But the conspiracy was too big to remain a secret, and there were many men in the southern parts loyal to the King. Before the end of August, mutterings of revolt and mysterious disturbances had prompted the royal government to appoint commissions of *oyer and terminer*. And a good ten days before the agreed date, the Duke of Norfolk and the council at Westminster were apprised of the rebellion, when the impatient rebels of Kent rose prematurely, began an advance on London and proclaimed that the mighty Duke of Buckingham was the leader of their cause.[14]

Until then his plotting had gone unsuspected. It was he who headed the commissions of *oyer and terminer*. As late as September 16 the King had dispatched writs, in the name of Prince Edward, to the royal officers in North and South Wales, ordering them to pay their accounts to the Duke of Buckingham.[15] Not until Richard reached Lincoln on October 11 did he learn that Buckingham had betrayed him.

IV

RICHARD had no armed forces with him. Many of the lords and councillors who had gone on his progress had departed to their homes. The defection of his Constable and chief ally and friend, Harry Buckingham, shook the foundations of his authority and must have lacerated his pride. In his thirty-one years, however, he had engrossed a large experience of betrayal, insurrection, and the making of war.

Within a few hours of receiving the news, Richard had issued his first commands to the council at Westminster and set the rendezvous for his army at Leicester on October 20 and 21. The clerks of John Kendall, his secretary, were inscribing the summonses to arms which a hastily assembled corps of messengers had begun bearing to the quarters of the kingdom. The lords and gentlemen of the King's household sent urgent appeals to their followers; Viscount Lovell requested Sir William Stonor of Oxfordshire to come wearing the Lovell cognizance, unaware that Stonor was committed to the rebellion.[1]

Next day, Sunday, October 12, Richard dictated another letter to his Chancellor, thanking him for the reception which the Bishop's servants had provided at Lincoln for the royal entourage and bidding him, since illness prevented his coming himself, to send the Great Seal at once. In a rush of feeling the King seized pen to add a poignant postscript:

We would most gladly ye came yourself if that ye may, and if ye may not, we pray you not to fail, but to accomplish in all diligence our said commandment, to send our Seal incontinent upon the sight hereof, as we trust you, with such as ye trust and the Officers pertaining to attend with it; praying you to ascertain us of your News. Here, loved be God, is all well and truly determined, and for to resist the Malice of him that had best Cause to be true, the Duke of Buckingham, the most untrue Creature living; whom with God's Grace we shall not be long till that we will be in those parts, and subdue his Malice. We assure you there was never false traitor better purveyed for, as this bearer Gloucester shall show you.[2]

On October 15 Richard issued his first public proclamation, declaring Buckingham to be a rebel, bidding all his subjects be ready to take arms, and straitly charging that no one was to hurt or despoil any of the Duke's followers who had held aloof from his treason. Three days later, Robert Blackwell, one of the clerks of the chancellery, delivered the Great Seal into the hands of the King at the Angel inn in Grantham.

Viscount Lovell had gone the day before to Banbury to meet his men, and of Richard's chief officers there remained with him at the moment only four bishops, the Earl of Northumberland, who had accompanied him from Yorkshire, and Thomas, Lord Stanley. There survives no clue to Stanley's motives for supporting the King, or seeming to support the King, when his wife, the Countess of Richmond, was playing a major role in preparing the invasion of her son, Henry Tudor. It seems likely that either the Countess found it impossible to communicate with her husband, whom Richard had kept with him, or that Stanley could find no means to detach himself from the King's side. It is also quite possible that the slippery Stanley had found it expedient to keep a foot in both camps.[3]

On October 18, the day that widespread insurrections broke out in the southern counties and Buckingham unfurled his banners, the secretary of Stanley's son, Lord Strange, wrote from Aldcliffe in the county of Lancaster to a relative of his that 'People in this country be so troubled, in such commandment as they have in the King's name and otherwise, marvellously, that they know not what to do. My Lord Strange goeth forth from Latham upon Monday next with 10,000 men, whither we cannot say. The Duke of Buck: has so many men, as it is said here, that he is able to go where he will; but I trust he shall be right well withstanded and all his malice: and else were great pity. Messengers cometh daily, both from the King's grace and the Duke, into this country'. The letter may be straightforward enough, but there are hints of ambiguity, particularly in the phrases 'whither we cannot say' and 'else it were great pity'. Stanley's son finally decided to come in on the side of the King, but he certainly did not bring 10,000 men.[4]

Meanwhile, King Richard had been heartened by news from John Howard, Duke of Norfolk. After accompanying the King to Windsor early in July, the Duke had returned to London, where he busied himself, among other things, in overseeing certain alterations in the house and garden of Crosby's Place. He had left London on August 11 to go a progress of his own through East Anglia, in order to greet the tenants of his newly granted manors and, as the King's justicer in this region, to seek the goodwill of its inhabitants, most of whom he knew well. He returned to London at the beginning of September to investigate, as one of the commissioners of the *oyer and terminer*, the first rumblings of trouble; on Friday, September 12, he commenced a brief tour of Surrey and Sussex, halting at Reigate and at Horsham. After returning to London about a week later, he saw to it that he had a sizable body of retainers and tenants ready at hand. When he received word on October 10 of a rising in Kent, he swept into action. On the same day his messengers were riding hard with summonses to arms to the chief men of East Anglia, including one addressed to 'my right well beloved friend, John Paston, be this delivered in haste':

Right well beloved friend, I commend me to you. It is so that the Kentishmen be up in the Weald, and say that they will come and rob the city, which I shall let [prevent] if I may.

Therefore I pray you that with all diligence ye make you ready and come hither, and bring with you six tall fellows in harness, and ye shall not lose your labour, that knoweth God, who have you in His keeping.

Next day Norfolk was able to send out several reconnoitring parties, including a body of about 100 men under Sir John à Medellon and Sir John Norbery which occupied Gravesend to hold the passage across the Thames. The Duke was also busy advising the council at Westminster and doubtless helping the citizens prepare the defences of London. By October 18, he had assembled such strength that he was able to send a force to Reigate, and the next day he was throwing out another screen of men to protect the city. As a result of these prompt and vigorous measures, the rebels of Kent and Surrey, their links with East Anglia almost entirely severed, were quickly reduced to impotence. Though they had moved from Maidstone down the Medway to Rochester, the Duke of Norfolk blocked their way at Gravesend. Forced to abandon their attempt upon the capital, Sir John and Richard Guildford, Sir John Fogge, Sir George Brown, Sir Richard Haute, Sir Thomas Lewkenor and a few other gentry retired with their men to Guildford to await news from the West.[5]

By the time King Richard was making his way to Leicester, on October 21, he had decided that, as a result of John Howard's resolute activity, he need not detach any large body of troops for the defence of London. At Leicester he found a goodly army assembling, including a contingent of 300 men from the city of York under the captaincy of his friend Thomas Wrangwysh. On October 23 he judged that the muster of his host was as complete as time permitted. He drew up a second proclamation but, having perceived that the rebellion was localized in the southern counties, the West country, and the southern Midlands, he had it dispatched only to those regions. After reminding his subjects that, in accordance with his coronation oath to rule by mercy and justice, he had first begun 'at Mercy in giving unto all manner persons his Full and General Pardon', trusting thereby to secure their allegiance, and that he had 'dressed himself to divers Parties of this his Realm for the indifferent Administration of Justice to every Person', the King announced the treachery of the Marquess Dorset, Sir William Norris, Sir George Brown, Sir John Cheyney, and several others who had risen in the cause of that 'great Rebel and Traitor the late Duke of Buckingham, and Bishops of Ely and Salisbury'. Denouncing them for their 'damnable maintenance of vices'—doubtless with the Marquess Dorset principally in mind—as well as for their treason, the King promised not to proceed against any yeoman or commoner 'thus abused by these Traitors, Adulterers, and Bawds', who withdrew at once from their cause. A price was put on the heads of the chief rebels: 1,000 pounds or lands worth £100 a year, for the capture of Buckingham; 1,000 marks or lands worth 100 marks a year, for the Marquess and the two bishops; and for the knights, 500 marks or lands worth £40 a year. Finally, all men were urged to spring to arms in order to subdue the rebellion. Although it appears that by this time Thomas Hutton had hurried back from Brittany to warn the King—if Richard had not already received this intelligence from the council in London—that Henry Tudor was preparing with active assistance from Duke Francis to invade the kingdom of England, the royal proclamation made no mention of this threat.[6]

Next morning, October 24, King Richard opened his campaign by leading his army to Coventry. Since the Constable of England was also the chief rebel, Richard here appointed Sir Ralph Assheton as Vice-Constable 'for this time'. Then he launched his army southward. He had determined, first to drive a wedge between the Duke of Buckingham and the rebels in the West country and the southern counties, and then to turn his whole force against Buckingham, the most formidable head of the rebellion.[7]

Or so he had seemed. King Richard had not been many hours on the march before he learned that the menacing pyrotechnics of the Duke of Buckingham had ignominiously fizzled out in the foulness of the weather, the disgruntlement of men who had been forced to join his army against their will, the brilliant guerilla tactics of bands loyal to the King, and the general incapacity of the shallow-minded Duke himself.

Even as Buckingham duly spread his banners on October 18 and began to move eastward from Brecon, he had been harassed by a force under the command of a family of Vaughans, chieftains in the region, who cut off his communications with Wales, hung upon his flanks, and boldly raided the lands of Brecknock castle. Ahead of the Duke's host, Humphrey Stafford was systematically wrecking bridges and blocking passes and posting bodies of men in narrow defiles from which even an army could not dislodge them. It was a miserable and frightening march that the mighty Duke made from Brecon into Herefordshire. In perturbation he halted momentarily at Weobley, appropriating the manor of Lord Ferrers.[8]

Great numbers of men had not flocked to his cause. He had been able to bring to the field only his own tenants and retainers and such Welshmen as his officers could assemble by force or threats. The attacks of the Vaughans and Humphrey Stafford shook what little morale the troops possessed. And it appears that the elements themselves were fighting on the side of the guerillas. Great storms of rain had washed out roads and flooded river-crossings. By the time Buckingham halted at Weobley his army was disintegrating. He was accompanied by a curious quartet of advisers: John Morton, Bishop of Ely; John Rush, a London merchant; Sir William Knyvet of Norfolk; and Thomas Nandik, of Cambridge University, an astrologer. While the Duke helplessly watched his host melting away, John Morton, perceiving that Buckingham's cause was hopelessly lost, found means to abandon the captor who had become his tool. He fled first to the fen country around Ely and then escaped to Flanders. The terrible realization struck Buckingham that he had been duped by the Bishop and ruined by his own illusions. In a panic he donned rough clothing and galloped wildly northward into Shropshire to seek a hiding place.[9]

King Richard learned of the collapse of Buckingham's revolt not long after he had left Coventry and therefore headed his army due southward for Wiltshire. When Sir William Stonor and Sir William Berkeley and Sir Richard Woodville at Newbury, Sir John Cheyney, Sir Giles Dawbeney, Walter Hungerford and Bishop Lionel at Salisbury got word that Buckingham was a fugitive and the King was rapidly approaching, they instantly abandoned all thought of resistance. Some sought sanctuary or hiding places with friends; others fled south to the seaside and escaped to Brittany. About October 28, King Richard entered Salisbury without having fought so much as a skirmish.[10]

A day or two later the Duke of Buckingham was brought a captive to that city. He had sought shelter with a servant of his, one Ralph Bannaster, who dwelt near Wem. Prompted by fear or the attractive reward, Bannaster had turned him in to the Sheriff of Shropshire who conveyed him promptly to Salisbury. As a rebel taken in arms, he was summarily tried by a commission under Sir Ralph Assheton, the Vice-Constable. Volubly the Duke of Buckingham confessed, poured out the whole story of the conspiracy, in the desperate hope of securing one favour—permission to speak with King Richard. Like the coquette who cannot believe that her fascination will ever fail, Buckingham conceived that, in spite of all, he might yet exercise his charm upon the man he had sought to destroy. It is possible that he was counting upon some secret revelation to save him, perhaps a disclosure concerning the sons of Edward IV. His prayer, however, was denied. He was sentenced to be executed. Losing all dignity, he begged and pleaded, feverish, abject, terror-stricken. But Richard would not see him. The wound had gone too deep. And the likeness to Clarence, turned bitter now, was borne out in their common fate. On Sunday, November 2, upon a newly erected scaffold in the market place of Salisbury—the noble spire of the cathedral pointing the way to heaven—Henry Stafford, second Duke of Buckingham, was beheaded as a traitor.[11]*

The next morning King Richard set out for the West country. He had just been informed by one of the detachments of troops which he had dispatched to guard the southern coasts that Henry Tudor, appearing off the Dorset harbour of Poole with only two ships, had quickly sensed the danger in which he stood and sailed away westward. By November 5, the King was at Bridport and by the 8th he was established at Exeter. Without attempting to strike a blow, the Marquess of Dorset, the Courtenays, and most of their chief followers, had taken ship and escaped to Brittany. Sir Thomas Saint Leger and two of his confederates, however, were captured; though large sums of money were offered to ransom Saint Leger's life, Richard saw no reason to spare the second husband of his eldest sister who had chosen to become an agent of the Woodvilles, and all three men were executed. Now came word that the Tudor's two ships had hovered off Plymouth only long enough to learn of Buckingham's death and the collapse of the rebellion and had then sailed off eastward.[12]

Though Henry Tudor's venture had fared no better than the others, it had begun promisingly if somewhat tardily. Provided by Duke Francis with no less than fifteen ships and some 5,000 Breton soldiers, Henry had sailed from Paimpol, it seems, on October 31. On the first night of the voyage his fleet had been scattered by a tempest; most of the vessels were driven back to Normandy or Brittany and the next morning Henry found himself off the Dorset coast with only two ships.

Perceiving that the shores around Poole were lined with troops, he sent a small boat to make inquiries. The soldiers shouted that the rebellion had prospered and that they themselves had been dispatched by the Duke of Buckingham to conduct the Earl of Richmond to the Duke's camp. This rude stratagem did not entice Henry, however, whose uncertain life of exile had engendered in him the suspicious wariness of an animal. When he had sailed on to Plymouth and learned that the King had already reached Exeter in unopposed triumph, he at once abandoned his enterprise and returned to Brittany. By November 22 he was at Nantes, receiving a loan of 10,000 crowns from his friend Duke Francis, by means of which he might for a while maintain himself and his flock of exiles while he tried to weave the web of a new conspiracy.[13]★

Within two weeks of his setting forth from Leicester, King Richard had disposed of the great rebellion. He remained in Exeter about a week, appointing commissions to take into the King's hands the estates of the chief rebels and to restore order in the western and southern counties and the Marches of Wales. The last knots of insurrection in Surrey and Sussex fell apart; there was a show of resistance at Bodiam castle but it was quickly extinguished by John Howard's son, the Earl of Surrey. According to the London chroniclers, Sir George Brown, a man named Roger or Robert or William Clifford, and four yeomen of the crown who had betrayed their master were captured and arraigned at Westminster. All were condemned to death for treason and immediately executed.[14]★

King Richard's return from Exeter was not so much a military expedition as a progress. He was in Salisbury by November 18 and so made his way through Winchester and Farnham to the Kentish coast towns. Lord Cobham, one of John Howard's lieutenants, headed a delegation of citizens to welcome him to Canterbury. He was back in London on November 25, four months after he had departed from the city.[15]

The rebellion had collapsed partly because of its internal weaknesses, partly because of Richard's generalship, partly because of the loyalty, or apathy, of the English people. Except for Richard Beauchamp, Lord Seintmount, not a single baron or earl had deserted his allegiance to join the rebels. No town of any consequence had been won over. Not a great many of the commons had been attracted to the cause, and those who had sprung to arms were quick to desert. The rebellion had found almost no partisans north of the Thames and east of the Severn.

Except for Buckingham, the Marquess, and the two bishops, its leaders had been country gentry of Lancastrian persuasion or Woodville sympathies.

The principle upon which King Richard dealt out punishment resembles the precept that his brother Edward had ordained on the field of battle: seek out the leaders; spare the commons. Apparently, only ten men were executed for treason, all of them fomenters as well as captains of the rising. The King did not harass ordinary folk, impose heavy fines on them, or permit them to be plundered; they were encouraged to sink back peaceably into their daily occupations. In the Parliament which was soon to meet 96 men were attainted of treason and their goods confiscated, but at least a third of these were eventually pardoned. Even such prime movers of the rebellion as the Bishop of Ely, the Marquess Dorset, and Sir Richard Woodville were offered the royal clemency. Men like Walter Hungerford and Sir John Fogge, who had showed his gratitude for Richard's kindness by promptly joining the conspiracy, were not only pardoned but promised a partial restoration of their estates. Reynold Bray, who had worked so diligently for the Countess of Richmond, was not even included in the act of attainder but received a pardon two weeks before Parliament met, doubtless through the good offices of Lord Stanley. As for the Countess herself, who had been the Athena of the rebellion, she was stripped of her titles, but her lands were given to her husband to enjoy for his lifetime and the punishment of attainder was 'remitted'. This generosity was gracefully ascribed by Richard to the good service of Lord Stanley.[16]

Yet, though the speedy suppression of the rebellion had impressively demonstrated the King's strength, it was to have less happy consequences. As a result of the disappearance of Buckingham, Richard improvised a piece-meal supervision of the Welsh Marches, a problem in government for which, as will be seen, he never sought a broad and permanent solution. Richard Huddleston, a Knight of the Body, was made constable of the castle of Beaumaris, captain of the towns of Beaumaris and Anglesey, sheriff of Anglesey 'during pleasure', and master forester of Snowdon; Thomas Tunstall, an Esquire of the Body, became constable and captain of the castle and town of Conway; and a parcel of similar offices was bestowed upon the Master of the Royal Henchmen, Sir James Tyrell. A more serious consequence of Buckingham's extinction was that Richard felt compelled to reward and cherish the Stanleys, who—from what motives it is uncertain—had remained at least outwardly faithful to him. On the day that Buckingham was executed Lord Stanley was granted his castle and lordship of Kymbellton; on November 18 he was made Constable of England with an annuity of £100; and broad grants of land were to follow. His brother, Sir William, was appointed Chief Justice of North Wales and, soon after, Constable of the Castle and Captain of the town of Caernarvon with a retinue of twenty-four soldiers. Of Buckingham's other principal offices, the Chief Justiceship of South Wales went to William Herbert, Earl of Huntingdon, and on the last day of November the Great Chamberlainship of England was bestowed upon the Earl of Northumberland, who had accompanied Richard on the campaign. Next day Percy received a large grant of estates and, a few weeks later, the lordship of Holderness in the East Riding, which had belonged to Buckingham. King Richard scattered a number of lesser rewards for good service: some twenty-five small annuities, half of them to Welshmen, and an annuity of 40 marks to the native chieftain Rhys ap Thomas.[17]

On November 25, the Mayor and Aldermen of London in scarlet and 500 of the chief citizens in violet met their victorious King at Kennington and escorted him through Southwark and across London Bridge to the Wardrobe beside Blackfriars, where he temporarily lodged. Next day in the Star' Chamber at Westminster, Richard re-delivered to Chancellor Russell the Great Seal in its white leather bag. The ceremony was witnessed by the men who enacted the chief roles in his reign: Thomas, Archbishop of York, forgiven and restored to royal favour as a councillor; three eminent scholars of the New Learning: John Sherwood, Bishop of Durham, Thomas Langton, Bishop of St. David's, and John Gunthorpe, Keeper of the Privy Seal; the Bishops of Bath and Wells and of St. Asaph's; Thomas Barowe, Master of the Rolls; John Howard, Duke of Norfolk; William Fitzalan, Earl of Arundel and Warden of the Cinque Ports; Henry Percy, Earl of Northumberland; Thomas, Lord Stanley; Sir Richard Ratcliffe, Knight of the Body; and William Catesby, Esquire of the Body. Of the secular men, all but one would be present at the supreme crisis of Richard's life; but two of them would not be at his side.[18]*

V

THE King and Queen kept a ceremonious Christmas. Anne had not brought with her from Middleham, however, the little boy who gave meaning to it all; his health remained too precarious for him to travel.

The King was running short of ready money, but it does not appear that his financial position was serious. Although he possessed, as yet, no revenues beyond the yield of the Crown lands and the usual royal perquisites, he had apparently been able to defray the heavy costs of putting an army in the field by at last making use of the treasure his brother had accumulated. To meet current expenses and the demands of the Christmas season, he turned to the London merchants. Sir Edmund Shaa, goldsmith and late Mayor, purchased 275 pounds of silver plate for £550. A number of royal treasures were used as pledges for loans. Stephen Gardiner advanced £66 for a salt cellar of gold crusted with precious stones; other merchants offered from 40 marks to £100 for such valuables as a helmet of King Edward's embellished with gold, gems, and pearls, gold cups garnished with gems, 'and the twelve apostles of silver and overgilt'. The King was so pleased with the ready response of the London merchants that he presented to the city a flat cup with a cover of gold, encrusted with rubies, diamonds and pearls. To brighten their own wardrobes and provide gifts for the court, the King and Queen ran up a bill of £1,200 with a mercer; and Richard probably presented Anne with the latest fashion in jewels, for on December 9 he had licensed a merchant of Genoa to bring precious gems into the kingdom provided that he himself was given the first opportunity to buy. The speedy extinction of the rebellion gave obvious cause for celebration; and if Richard sensed that he was straining too hard to reknit the bonds of allegiance to the Crown, there would be the more reason to conceal his cares under the sort of elaborate ceremonial to which his brother had accustomed the kingdom.[1]

Across the channel in Brittany there was performed another kind of ceremony. In the cathedral of Rennes on Christmas morning, Henry Tudor swore an oath to marry Elizabeth, daughter of Edward IV, and thus unite the red rose and the white. His followers knelt and did him homage as if he had been crowned.

For the men on the dark waters between Rennes and London there was little Christmas cheer. Defying the winter storms, the hard-bitten mariners of Brittany and England prowled the seas in battle array and fought each other on plunging, icy decks. The moment Richard returned to London, he had bent his energies on forcing Duke Francis to realize his mistake in supporting Henry Tudor and to sue for peace. The channel had become so dangerous for English shipping that a wool fleet bound for Calais had been compelled to return to London in order to avoid capture.[2]

Though Richard had never fought at sea, he had been Admiral for twenty years, and his present Admiral, the Duke of Norfolk, was a master of naval warfare. In a matter of days English men of war were setting forth to engage the Bretons. The port towns were stirred to actions. Vessels were refitted, victualled and manned. Writs were dispatched empowering captains and ship-masters to secure supplies and armour at reasonable prices. As Breton prizes were brought into the harbours, agents of the Crown readied them to take to the sea with English crews and supervised the disposal of their cargo for the benefit of those merchants who had suffered losses in the naval war. By the middle of December an English fleet, commanded by Thomas Wentworth, was scouring the channel, seeking to bring the fleet of Brittany to battle. As soon as Richard got word that Duke Francis's flotilla had been located, he quickly dispatched commissions to the magistrates of the port towns 'to man out their small boats and help the English fleet in case they shall see them engaged with the fleet of the Bretons, now lying in Flanders'. No record survives of a full-scale engagement, but a few days before Christmas the King was issuing letters 'for certain Bretons taken prisoner to go into Brittany to fetch money for ransome of themselves and their fellows'. Still, he did not relax his efforts. The magistrates of London were ordered to seize all Breton goods within the city and deliver them to the Exchequer. When he could, Richard purchased foreign ships to swell his navy; and he took pains to see that merchant vessels were given protection. Learning that a number of East Anglian fishing craft and trading ships were about to make the dangerous voyage to Iceland, he sent them strict warning to follow the convoy system he had established:

For as much as we understand that certain of you intend hastily to depart towards Iceland, not purveyed of wafters [not supplied with convoying vessels] for your surety . . . we . . . straitly charge . . . that . . . none of you severally [separately] depart out of any of our havens . . . without our license first had so to do; and thereupon, that ye gather and assemble yourselves in such one of our havens or ports . . . as ye shall think most convenient, well harnessed and apparelled for your own surety, and so for to depart all together toward Humber, to attend there upon our ships of Hull as your wafters, for the surety of you all; and that ye dissever not without tempest of weather compel you. . . .

The convoy reached Iceland safely and in July was ordered to use the same system on the return voyage. Long before then, however, King Richard's vigorous campaign at sea had accomplished its object and Duke Francis was happy to make a treaty with England.[3]

King Richard's deepest concern during this Christmas season was with the state of his own realm. As King Edward had done before him, he wrestled with the evil of livery and maintenance, which had enabled the rebel leaders to raise a following against him. The Chamberlain of North Wales and the Sheriff of Staffordshire were ordered to administer the oath of allegiance to all the inhabitants within their jurisdictions and to warn them against giving or taking 'any liveries, clothings, badges, or cognizances'. The same admonition was dispatched to the citizens of Gloucester, Bristol, Canterbury, and perhaps to other towns and counties as well.[4]

Richard was particularly troubled by the rising in Kent, a shire which owned a long record of unrest, which contained some of the most important ports of the kingdom, and which lay at the very door of London. Early in January he went on a progress through the county, seeking means to secure the loyalty of its inhabitants. On the 10th he was at Canterbury; from Sandwich on the 16th he issued commissions to several lords, knights, and gentlemen to administer the oath of allegiance throughout the hundreds of Kent. He established one of his Household knights, Sir Marmaduke Constable, as his lieutenant or deputy in the honour and town of Tunbridge and the lordship of Penshurst and commanded the inhabitants to attend upon Sir Marmaduke, 'whom the King has deputed to make his abode amongst them; and that they in no wise presume to take clothing or to be retained by anybody'.[5]

Richard likewise issued a proclamation to the citizens of the county, which reveals the anxious cares of the King who must be always earning his right to the crown. Briefly he commended those of his subjects who had remained loyal or had quickly forsaken the rebellion, and announced rewards for the taking of rebels still at large. These practical considerations were but a prologue to what was most on the King's mind: he earnestly emphasized his determination

to see due administration of justice throughout this his realm to be had, and to reform, punish, and subdue all extortions and oppressions in the same. And for that cause with all, that at his coming now into this his said county Kent, that every person dwelling within the same that find himself grieved, oppressed, or unlawfully wronged, do make a bill of his complaint and put it to his highness, and he shall be heard and without delay have such convenient remedy as shall accord with his laws; for his grace is utterly determined that all his true subjects shall live in rest and quiet, and peaceably enjoy their lands, livelodes, and goods, according to the laws of this his land, which they be naturally born to inherit. And therefore the King chargeth and commandeth that no manner man, of whatsoever condition or degree he be, rob, hurt, or spoil any of his said subjects in their bodies or goods, upon pain of death; and also that no manner man make, pick, or continue any quarrel to other for any old or new rancour, hate, malice, or cause, or offers made, upon pain of death, nor also take man's meat, horse-meat [i.e., fodder], or any other victual or stuff, without he pay truly therefore to the owners thereof, upon pain of losing of his horse, harness, goods, and his body to prison at the King's will. . . .[6]

Perhaps the greatest consequence of the rebellion lay in its effect upon King Richard. Instead of warning him to make himself as strong as possible, it drove him with ever increasing strain to labour in the quest of allegiance. But the class of men who would have most reason to appreciate the offer of justice did not represent the political or military might of the kingdom.

It was his High Court of Parliament, however, upon which Richard was principally depending to express to the whole realm the kind of rule he meant to exercise. During these weeks while he was pressing on the naval warfare against the Bretons and going his progress in Kent, the King and his councillors were preparing an *agenda* for the forthcoming sessions unlike any that had been known since Parliament began, perhaps a century before, to think of itself not only as the King's High Court but also as the nation's representative legislature.[7]

Originally summoned to meet on November 6 but postponed by the outbreak of the rebellion, Parliament assembled in the Painted Chamber at Westminster on Friday, January 23. Chancellor Russell delivered the opening address, based as usual on the gospel text for the day: 'We have many members in one body, and all members have not the same office'. Russell took as his theme the urgent necessity of restoring the health of the commonweal. Each must do his duty—'the prince to give equal justice with pity and mercy and to defend his land from outward hostility, the subjects to do their true labour and occupations whereby his royal and necessary charges may be supported'. The security of the realm has been shaken by the faithless French—'our old new-reconciled enemies'—who have broken oaths and treaties; worse yet, the kingdom has been led into darkness by those who recently rebelled against their King, an act contrary to the commandments of God Himself. This darkness can be remedied only if the people of England employ the light of reason for 'the advancing of the common weal'.[8]

On the following Monday the Commons showed their goodwill toward the King by presenting as their Speaker, William Catesby, one of his most trusted councillors and Esquire of the Body; and the Parliament then set to work upon bills similar to those which its predecessors had been passing during the past three decades of rebellions and uncertainties regarding the succession to the throne. It enacted a settlement of the crown upon King Richard—the *Titulus Regis*—and ordained his son Edward as heir apparent, by confirming and re-capitulating the bill which had been promulgated in the informal Parliament of the previous June. It passed an act of attainder against the chief fomenters of the late rebellion and authorized the King to make grants of lands forfeited by attainder; the three traitorous bishops of Ely, Salisbury and Exeter were only disabled from enjoying any possessions, and the property rights of rebels' wives were solicitously safeguarded. The King asked for no imposition of taxes, but on the last day of the session the Speaker announced that the Commons had voted the customary royal subsidies of tunnage and poundage—a duty on merchandise imported and exported—and the tax on the exportation of wool and hides. In addition there were the usual 'private' acts. Viscount Lovell and Sir James Tyrell were granted certain lands to which they made claim; and a petition of the Earl of Northumberland's was approved that all attainders and confiscations of land which had been enacted against the House of Percy since the days of Henry IV be annulled. Some petitions from religious establishments were also granted, and humbler interests had their hearing. At the request of the inhabitants of Croyland, in the fen country, who from time immemorial had reared swans 'from which a great part of their relief and living hath been sustained', a bill of the previous Parliament was annulled which declared that no one not a lord's son or possessing lands worth five marks a year should possess 'any Marke or Game of his own Swans'.

The remarkable work of the Parliament lay in a series of statutes directly sponsored by the King and his council. Three of these are aimed at correcting economic injustices; three, at safeguarding the rights of the individual against abuses of the law itself.

The wholesale confiscations of property during the Wars of the Roses and the failure of the common law to keep pace with various tricks that had been invented for fraudulently disposing of estates had thrown the traditional methods of conveying land into confusion. Men found their property rights contested by titles they had never heard of and, as the Paston Letters eloquently testify, could be brought to the brink of ruin by endless lawsuits. The first of Richard's statutes took action against 'privy and unknown feoffements', a practice by which a seller of land concealed from the buyer that a part of the property had already been disposed of to somebody else. It was enacted that henceforth every estate feoffement, gift of land and the like 'shall be good to him that it is made unto and against the sellers and their heirs'. Another statute sought to prevent the concealment of property transfers called 'fines', which were made in the Court of Common Pleas, by providing that such fines must be proclaimed by the court and notices of the transaction sent to various officials. A statute of limitations makes its appearance in this act: persons wishing to take action because of the proclamation of a fine were given five years in which to bring suit. The third statute abolished an economic injustice which had been visited upon the realm by the royal power itself. Edward IV's direct demands for money, euphemistically called 'benevolences', were condemned, and the right of the King to make such exactions was 'dampned and annulled forever'.

The other three statutes sought to refine and reform the machinery of justice, so that forms of law might no longer be used as instruments of extortion and oppression. One statute was aimed at correcting abuses in the courts of piepowder, that is, courts which sat only to determine offences committed at fairs and which were usually under the direction of the bailiff or steward of the land on which the fair was held. One of King Edward's parliaments had authorized these officials to rule in matters which did not originate at fairs; but since this statute had resulted in a variety of oppressions practiced by bailiffs and stewards, it was now enacted that they have jurisdiction only over cases which arise at fair time. Much more important were the other two statutes, designed to protect innocent men against the perversion of legal forms by their predatory or malicious neighbours. One was an act for 'returning of sufficient jurors'. Officials who impanel juries were forbidden to choose any juror who was not 'of good name and fame' and who did not possess freehold land worth twenty shillings a year or copyhold land worth twenty-six shillings, eight pence. Sheriffs and bailiffs who failed to obey the law were to be fined forty shillings, and all indictments brought by unqualified juries were declared void. This act was promulgated because 'it daily happens' that men of no substance were finding means of being elected to jury duty in order to force indictments of innocent men or to quash indictments of guilty ones. The last statute was designed to protect men who were arrested and kept in prison without bail on accusations 'of light suspicion' or of malice. Justices of the Peace were given the power, on arrests for suspicion of felony, to give bail, just as if the accused had been indicted before these Justices in their sessions. Of equal importance was the provision that the goods of persons arrested for suspicion of felony should not be seized before conviction.

To the commons and the gentry these laws offered a prospect of fair dealing in the courts which they had not seen for decades; but they undoubtedly were one of the chief reasons why Richard did not retain the support of a number among the nobility and upper gentry. For these laws were aimed directly at curbing the practices by which this class had overawed and preyed upon its weaker neighbours throughout the past century. By striking at evils which were mainly the result of the system of livery and maintenance, Richard was serving justice at the risk—a risk he must have realized—of alienating the men whose military power he would need in the day of battle.

Examples of government-sponsored legislation may be found in the parliamentary enactments of King Edward's reign, but seldom before had a King presented to his High Court a coherent programme of statutes for the reformation of the machinery of law. Though Richard had certainly profited by the advice of such enlightened statesmen as John Russell, John Gunthorpe, and Thomas Langton, this programme clearly springs from the principles by which he had sought to rule from the first day of his reign.

The Commons too originated a number of statutes, which reflect the mercantile interests and concerns of the age; similar ones had been passed by the parliaments of Edward IV and a great many more would be enacted in Tudor days. Like some kindred measures of our own time, this legislative tinkering with the economy by means of minute regulation met with indifferent success. One of these acts, for example, attempted to abolish certain deceitful devices for stretching cloth, the practice of exporting the finest wools from the kingdom to the hardship of native cloth manufacturers, and the use of cheap dyes that fade. The statute sounds reasonable enough, but on the following October 25 King Richard, at the earnest request of the merchant class, proclaimed the annulment of the act because it hurt more than it did good.[9] There were also acts prohibiting the importation of silk lace and ribbands and of such hardware as scissors, bells (except hawks' bells), nails, leather purses, painted glasses, and the like; defining the contents of a butt of Malvesey wine as 126 gallons; requiring the Italian merchants, who have outrageously driven up the price of bow-staves and fraudulently sold them 'ungarbled'—i.e., ungraded—to import with each butt of Malvesey or Tyre wine ten good bow-staves.

One of these acts is memorable, because of a provision which King

Richard inserted in it. This was the statute 'touching the merchants of Italy', a lengthy piece of legislation, the principal terms of which were that Italian merchants bringing goods into the realm must sell them wholesale, that within eight months of the sale they must buy native commodities with the money received rather than ship it out of the kingdom, that they must not sell wool or woollen cloth in England, that aliens are not to set themselves up as handicrafters except as servants to native manufacturers of certain fancy goods, and that no merchant stranger may be a host except to a stranger of his own nation since at present the houses of merchant strangers are overflowing with aliens from all lands busy making secret bargains.

To this measure, animated by xenophobia, Richard attached the following limitation: 'Provided alway that this act or any part thereof, or any other act made or to be made in the present parliament, in no wise extend . . . any let, hurt or impediment to any artificer or merchant stranger of what nation or country he be . . . for bringing into this realm, or selling by retail or otherwise, of any manner books written or imprinted, or for the inhabiting within the said realm for the same intent, or to any writer, limner, binder, or imprinter of such books, as he hath or shall have to sell by way of merchandise, or for their abode in the same realm for the exercising of the said occupations. . . .' To Richard and his councillors belongs the honour of having devised the first piece of legislation for the protection and fostering of the art of printing and the dissemination of learning by books.

When Parliament came to the end of its short but fruitful session on February 20 and the King bade farewell to his Lords and Commons, he must have experienced one of the rare moments of content which his reign afforded him. In the grave and enduring pigment of parliamentary authority he had painted large for the whole realm to see his principle of rule by desert, his offer of peace and justice in exchange for a national allegiance to the Crown.

But in a land so wearied by the turbulence of the past fifty years that subjects could aspire to no more than order and were readier to respond to a demand for obedience than an offer for goodwill, this message could not exert the quickening power on which he had set his hope.

VI

ABOUT ten days after Parliament was dismissed, King Richard secured the capitulation of one of his bitterest enemies. Not many yards from where the Commons assembled for their deliberations in the Chapter House of Westminster Abbey, King Edward's Queen and her five daughters remained still in sanctuary. There, at the very heart of his kingdom, they maintained themselves, a potent source of conspiracy, a living reproach to his rule. While Parliament was in session, Richard sent to the Queen 'grave men'; the Woodville matriarch who had desperately sought to dispossess the Protector was 'strongly solicited' to come to terms with the man who had dispossessed her son. Yet, though her presence in the sanctuary was acutely uncomfortable, if not dangerous, Richard made her no glowing promises. Indeed, while the negotiations were in progress, Parliament enacted a statute which deprived her of her property and annulled all her letters patents.[1]

The accounts appeared to be incompatible. She had conspired against Richard the moment her husband was dead; her kindred had fomented the recent rebellion; her daughter she had promised in marriage to Henry Tudor in order to bring him to the throne, and her son the Marquess and her brothers were even now in Brittany at his side. She could retort that her brother Anthony had been executed and her son Lord Richard Grey, her family attainted, her children bastardized, her two princes bereft of the crown and—as she had certainly been persuaded to believe the preceding fall—of their lives as well.

Yet the accounts proved not to be incompatible, after all. She sent her five daughters forth from sanctuary into Richard's care, on terms which the King, in a public ceremony, swore to abide by. On March 1, 1484, before an assembly of lords spiritual and temporal and the Mayor and Aldermen of London he took his oath:

I Richard . . . promise and swear, *verbo regio*, that if the daughters of Elizabeth Grey, late calling herself Queen of England . . . will come to me out of the Sanctuary of Westminster, and be guided, ruled, and demeaned after me, then I shall see that they shall be in surety of their lives and also not suffer any manner hurt . . . nor them nor any of them imprison . . .; but I shall put them into honest places of good name and fame, and them honestly and courteously shall see to be founden [supported] and entreated [treated], and to have all things requisite and necessary for their exhibitions and findings as my kinswomen; and that I shall do marry [arrange for the marriage of] . . . them to gentlemen born, and every of them give in marriage lands and tenements to the yearly value of 200 marks for term of their lives. . . . And such gentlemen as shall hap to marry with them I shall straitly charge lovingly to love and entreat them, as wives and my kinswomen, as they will avoid and eschew my displeasure.

And over this, that I shall yearly . . . pay . . . for the exhibition and finding of the said Dame Elizabeth Grey, during her natural life . . . to John Nesfeld, one of the esquires of my body, for his finding to attend upon her, the sum of 700 marks . . .; and moreover I promise to them that if any surmise or evil report be made to me of them by any person . . . that then I shall not give thereunto faith nor credence, nor therefore put them to any manner punishment, before that they or any of them so accused may be at their lawful defence and answer. . . .[2]

These terms were far from being extravagantly attractive; they indicate that Richard was offering no concession out of fear or reparation out of guilt. Why Queen Elizabeth, for her part, was induced to this startling acquiescence presents a problem so obscured in the mystery of the princes' fate that it must be discussed in the chapter dealing with that subject.*

Did the Queen herself come forth from sanctuary? The Croyland Chronicler, Polydore Vergil, and the oath itself say only that she delivered up her daughters. There is no further light upon the enigma. John Nesfeld, who had been set to guarding the sanctuary in the late summer of the preceding year, would shortly be fighting at sea for the King, his task at Westminster presumably finished. It seems unlikely that if Elizabeth were willing to trust her daughters to Richard, she would herself choose to remain in the wearisome confines of the sanctuary or that Richard himself would be willing to strike a bargain that did not include her coming forth. It seems reasonably probable that she had secretly agreed to retire to a country house, under the nominal wardenship of Nesfeld, where she could, in seclusion, support a modest state on her annuity of 700 marks. Richard had, in fact, provided the Queen, his enemy, a handsomer stipend and a greater liberty than one day Henry Tudor would allow her when she was his mother-in-law. Neither Elizabeth nor her daughters ever complained of the treatment they received at Richard's hands—had they done so, the Tudor chroniclers would scarcely have failed to make use of the story. Not only did the Queen take Richard at his word and accept his modest offer, but not long after, she began sending secret messages to her son the Marquess, urging him to abandon Henry Tudor and return to England where he should find favour with the King. Whatever the vagaries of a much tried woman, it might be supposed that the Marquess would

* See Appendix I, p. 413.

ignore the pleas and scorn the promise. Not so. Determining to seek his peace with Richard, he fled one night from Paris and made for Calais or Burgundy. He was, however, overtaken at Compiègne by emissaries of the outraged Henry and 'persuaded' to return. For all his travails and his family's pains, he had considered Richard's word better than the Tudor's hope.[3]

While King Richard was occupied during this winter and early spring with these weighty matters, the registry book of his writs and grants—Harleian MS 433—reveals that he and his council were also concerned, as usual, with the affairs of humbler folk.

Aware of the hardships of the innocent creditors of the Duke of Buckingham, the King had commissioned Sir William Husee, Chief Justice of King's Bench, and William Catesby and a few others to administer certain of the Duke's forfeited lands in order to pay his debts; he even made an outright payment of some £27 to Richard and Roger Baker of Brecknock for bread and ale delivered to Buckingham's household. Having learned that the Prior of Carlisle was hard pressed to meet the £8 fee he was charged by the chancery, as was customary, for a royal licence, Richard ordered the clerk of the Hanaper to return the Prior's money and further instructed him not to charge the bailiffs of Huntingdon for letters patent he was granting to the town. Provisions to ecclesiastical livings came under his eye too: when he was informed of unfair dealing in the diocese of Exeter, he bluntly bade the Vicar-general, Master John Combe, to promote Master Rauf Scrope to the vicarage of Paynton, 'which the said Mr. John Combe hath presented himself unto by crafty means'.

Misfortunes, needs, good services were likewise noticed. On February 7 there was issued 'a protection for requiring of alms by Edmund Filpot of Twicknam . . . Bricklayer, who by infortune and negligence had his dwelling house and place, with thirteen small tenements to the same annexed, and all his goods therein then being, suddenly burnt, to his utter undoing; who before, kept after his degree a great household, by the which many poor creatures were refreshed'. To the Abbot of Creyke, county Norfolk, who had suffered the same disaster, Richard, two weeks later, sent a contribution of £46 13s 4d towards the repair of his church. A few days after, he presented an annuity of £4 to Master John Bentley, clerk, to help defray his expenses at Oxford. To two of his minstrels who pleased him well, Robert Green and John Hawkins, he granted, about the same time, annuities of ten marks each. The registry book likewise reveals the King's affection and esteem for his faithful secretary, John Kendall. Sometime during the winter he was given an extra wage of 6d a day and an annuity of £80 during the life of the attainted Sir William Stonor's mother; in March of 1484 he not only received £100 out of the sum that had been realized from confiscated Breton goods but he also shared with Thomas Metcalfe, Chancellor of the Duchy of Lancaster and one of the Yorkshire Metcalfes who had long been devoted to Richard, the considerable grant of 500 marks yearly 'during pleasure' from the temporalities of the bishopric of Ely.

As the first spring of Richard's reign approached, John Brown, the King's bear-ward or 'Master-Guider and Ruler of all his bears and apes' set off along the roads of England, protected by a royal letter bidding mayors and bailiffs not to vex or molest him or his charges. Throughout the shires, men and women were anticipating journeys to the shrine of St. Thomas à Becket or to Our Lady of Walsingham. It would not be long before Richard's officers were issuing licenses for ship-masters to sail with boatloads of pilgrims to the famous tomb of St. James of Compostella in Spain.[4]

During the first week in March, Richard and his Queen once again set forth from London. Henry Tudor would make another descent upon England whenever he was able; spring would bring weather suitable for an invasion. Richard felt himself best able to meet the threat by making his headquarters at Nottingham, in the heart of his kingdom. Middleham, too, was much in his thoughts, and the eleven-year-old boy in whom dwelt his and Anne's hopes for the future. Though Edward's health had apparently never been good, his father and mother probably took heart from remembering that Richard himself had been a sickly child. While Parliament was still sitting, the King had assembled in a palace chamber not far from the Queen's apartments the principal lords of his realm, his councillors, and the chief officers of his Household in order to administer to them a special and solemn oath that if anything happened to him, they would be true to his son.[5] Voices less articulate also called him northward as the first breath of spring quickened the air. To move from town to town, to spend hours a day in the saddle, better sorted with his temper than to continue holding court in the palace at Westminster. His fragile body housed a will fed by remarkable energies and a valiant but unquiet heart; his earnestness to bring peace to the realm and the remorseless gnawing of his need for justifying his

K

rule drove him forth to grapple at first hand with the issues that confronted him.

But when Richard and Anne reached Cambridge, they tarried happily for a few days in the congenial cloisters of the University. Perhaps Richard discussed ecclesiastical politics with learned doctors, for he was now about to send to Rome Thomas Langton, Bishop of St. Davids, to join Dr. John Sherwood, the Bishop-elect of Durham, in representing England at the Vatican. The King had chosen the two men, of those he could spare, who would best reflect, at the Renaissance court of Sixtus IV, the lustre of the New Learning in their native land. Richard and Anne bestowed a variety of endowments and gifts of money upon the University. To express its thanks for this bounty Cambridge hastened to procure a decree from the Archbishop of York that whereas Queen Anne had endowed Queens' College with great rents and the King had founded scholarships and 'bestowed not a little money for the strength and ornament of the University, both in ratifying the University's privileges and founding and erecting the building of the King's College—the unparalleled ornament of all England——' therefore in gratitude the mass of Salus Populi, falling on May 2, should be celebrated by the University for the happy state of the King and Queen. Their stay at Cambridge was a serene interlude, brief and never to be recaptured. By March 15 they had moved on to Buckden, an episcopal manor of Chancellor Russell's. A few days later they rode across the hills encircling Nottingham and ascended to the massive fortress which towered above the town on its upthrust of dark rock.[6]

About the middle of April a messenger from the North brought the news that their little son was dead. 'You might', records the Croyland Chronicler, 'have seen his father and mother in a state almost bordering on madness, by reason of their sudden grief'.[7]

Anne did not outlive her boy a year. For her was the sorrow, doubly poignant, of a bereaved mother who can have no more children. For Richard, there might be something worse. Had God dispossessed him of a son because he had dispossessed his brother's son of a crown . . . if not of more? Was he the striker of the blow by which his child had been extinguished, his delicate wife stricken? According to tradition, he henceforth called the gloomy rock of Nottingham the Castle of his Care.

But a King must have a successor. There were two possibilities: Clarence's son, the Earl of Warwick, and the Earl of Lincoln, son of

Richard's sister Anne and the Duke of Suffolk. Clarence's descendants had been disabled by attainder but this could be reversed. Warwick, however, was only a boy of ten and he appears to have been what in the present age would be called a retarded child. Lincoln was a man, married, who had already demonstrated his martial spirit during the rebellion. For four months Richard could not bring himself to make any public announcement regarding the succession. Then, on August 21, he appointed Lincoln as Lieutenant of Ireland, a post which the House of York had come to bestow upon the heir apparent. This appointment did something to repair the disaster to his dynasty, but there was nothing which could retrieve the disaster to his spirit.[8]*

VII

GRIEF was a luxury that a King so placed as Richard could not long indulge. As summer weather approached, the Scots were beginning their border forays, and the chaotic warfare at sea grew in intensity. The fabric of foreign affairs, unravelling during the last year of King Edward's reign, remained to be knit up. The threat of Henry Tudor and his followers swelled like a thunderhead on the southeastern horizon. Whatever the loss of Prince Edward had meant to the father and the dynast, the King summoned his experience of affairs, his vitality, and his courage, to fight where he must and negotiate when he could.

Against the exiles in Brittany, records the Croyland Chronicler, he 'took all necessary precautions for the defence of his party. . . . The King was better prepared to oppose them in the present year than at any time afterwards, both by reason of the treasure which he had in hand . . . as well as particular grants which had been . . . distributed throughout the kingdom'. To speed his communications, he re-established the system of posts which King Edward had introduced during the campaign against the Scots in 1482, whereby a message could be dispatched two hundred miles within two days; and to keep watch on Henry Tudor he sent agents into Brittany 'from whom he learned nearly all the movements of the enemy'.[1]

If his system of posts looks towards the future, so too did his interest in ordnance. By temperament, King Edward had not been much disposed to pay attention to gunpowder, though he had made some use of it in battle and accumulated a number of guns in the Tower. Warwick the King-maker appears to have caught a glimpse of its true possibilities. He had experimented with Flemish hand-gunners at the disastrous second battle of St. Albans in 1461 and had effectively employed cannon to reduce Lancastrian castles in 1462–63. During the years Richard spent in Warwick's household he possibly acquired his first respect for this weapon. Gunpowder had been used, gingerly, for over a century, but outside of France, where Charles VII and Louis XI had developed a strong corps of artillery, there was little confidence in it. Had not an exploding cannon blown James II of Scotland to bits? Did not a soldier often find his hand-gun more dangerous to himself than to the enemy?

During the early months of 1484, Richard set about developing an arsenal of artillery in the Tower. One Roger Bykeley was appointed to hire carpenters and 'cartwrights' and other workmen to help in assembling 'cannons and necessaries for the King's ordnance'. William Nele, gunner, was granted a life annuity of 6d daily for his good service in making cannon within the Tower of London and elsewhere. Richard also relied upon the skill of Flemish artisans: Patrick de la Mote was made chief cannoner and master founder of all the King's cannon, and Theobald Ferrount and Gland Pyroo, gunners, were taken into Richard's service. At a cost of £24 the King purchased twenty new guns and two serpentines, which were perhaps imported from Flanders.[2]

Ordnance, however, was still secondary to men-at-arms and archers. On the first of May, Richard issued commissions of array for most of the counties of England, the name of the dead Prince Edward still appearing in them. For foreign war this levy of arms had long ago been abandoned in favour of indentures but it remained the only practicable means by which forces could be raised on short notice for the defence of the realm. As the conflict between Edward and Warwick revealed, the royal levy had come, in this century, to represent such allegiance of the most warlike nobles and gentry as the King could depend on in his hour of trial.

The names of Richard's commissioners suggest the web of loyalties he had sought to weave. The North would be raised by the Earls of Northumberland and Lincoln, the increasingly influential Yorkshire knight Sir Richard Ratcliffe, Lord Scrope of Bolton, and Gervase Clifton, Knight of the Body; the Midland counties by Richard's Chamberlain Viscount Lovell, his councillor William Catesby, and another Knight of the Body, Sir Marmaduke Constable, who was

Lord of the Manor of an obscure village called Market Bosworth; East
Anglia and the southern counties were the charge of the Duke of Nor-
folk, his son the Earl of Surrey, the Comptroller of the royal Household
Sir Robert Percy, and the Earl of Arundel, Warden of the Cinque
Ports. The southwest, however, had to be left largely to men from
other parts such as Morgan Kidwelly, the Attorney-General, Scrope of
Bolton, and Lord Zouche of the Midlands. There were no commissions
of array for Wales; various royal officers, like Sir James Tyrell and Sir
Richard Huddleston, who commanded the chief castles and towns,
would summon to the field the Welshmen under their jurisdiction. Nor
were there commissions for Cheshire or Lancashire: the Stanleys, who
wielded an archaic feudal power in these regions, were sworn to rally
their men to the King's support. Sir William Stanley was, in addition,
the chief commissioner for Shropshire.[3]

Richard issued no proclamations against Henry Tudor, for by the
end of July it appeared that he would be unable to invade the realm
during the present summer. Still, except for excursions into Yorkshire
to take action against the Scot and to direct the fleet which he had based
in Northern waters, and one visit to London, the King kept his watch
at Nottingham, high on the great thrust of rock in the Castle of his
Care, until early November.

These were months of harassing problems and constant labours. At
the same time that he was preparing his defences against invasion,
Richard had been forced to find means of combating the Breton fleet,
the Scots fleet, and French corsairs and men of war and to take action
against English pirates who were exacerbating his relations with friendly
powers.

The vigorous naval campaign which he had waged against Brittany
during the winter soon bore fruit, however. Before the end of April,
Duke Francis had called home his battered warships and promised to
observe for a year the truce and commercial agreement which he had
concluded with the late King Edward.[4] Against the pirates, too, Richard
took active measures. These hard-bitten freebooters of East Anglia and
Devon and Cornwall not only plundered Breton and French vessels,
but ever since the last years of Edward IV they had been falling with
equal zest upon the merchantmen of Spain and Burgundy. The ships
of their own countrymen they usually spared—as long as foreign game
was in sight. As soon as Richard came to the throne he had been
confronted by claims for reparation brought by English merchants
against Burgundian pirates and by claims of Burgundian and Spanish

traders against the men of Fowey and Plymouth, claims which in some instances reached back several years.[5]

To check piracy, Richard used all the means at his command. The energies of his ship-masters and his mariners he enlisted for his naval campaign; on receiving complaints of piratical depredations, he dispatched officers to the port towns to investigate the trouble and arrest the malefactors; he developed the office of the Admiralty; he required owners and captains of vessels to post ample security that they would attack no ship of a friendly power, and he ordained that town magistrates who permitted unbonded ships to leave harbour would be liable for any damages they did; he negotiated with Burgundy to settle past claims and injuries by means of a diet; he satisfied Spanish traders with customs concessions. These measures seem to have done much in the course of the year to restore the confidence of merchants and bring piracy under control.[6]

In order to meet the haphazard naval challenge of the French and to cool the ardour of the Scots, who were preparing for battle by land and sea, Richard recruited a force of Northern men to watch the borders, and, commissioning every ship he could come by, he managed to assemble a powerful fleet off Scarborough to deal with both the French and the Scots. The former did not offer themselves for a large-scale engagement; but in a skirmish two of his bravest captains, John Nesfeld and Sir Thomas Everingham, were captured and held for a ransom, which was immediately paid by the King. About the same time as this minor reverse occurred, however, his navy finally brought the fleet of Scotland to battle and gave it a decisive beating. In June, Richard had come to Scarborough to supervise the outfitting of his ships; he had again hurried to that port in July to take active charge of their re-arming and re-victualling. Since the Croyland Chronicler records that the victory over the Scots was gained 'by means of his [Richard's] skill in naval warfare', it is quite possible that the King had taken personal command of his fleet and directed its triumphant engagement. Meanwhile, on the borders his Northerners won a great victory over a marauding army of Scots. These defeats by land and sea had the effect for which he had been hoping: King James the Third sent word that he wished to treat for a genuine peace.[7]

Such was Richard's prime purpose during this summer, to fight with all the strength he could command in order to convince his enemies of the wisdom of treating with him. Both the swirl of warfare from which he extricated himself with such success and the difficulty he was encountering in diplomatic negotiations sprang not so much from the determined hostility to his regime of other European powers, but from the consequences of Louis XI's victory over Edward IV and the wave of internal weaknesses by which most of the countries happened to be assailed at the very time when Richard came to the throne. It was his peculiar misfortune to find himself ringed by states which lacked the stability to offer meaningful alliances and—in the case of France, for example—the discipline to control their freebooters. Even his relations with the papacy were haunted by this evil chance. Before Richard's impressively erudite envoys, Thomas Langton and John Sherwood, could do much more than establish themselves at the Vatican, Sixtus IV died; and in December, Richard had to commission Langton, Sherwood, and an English officer of the Order of St. John of Jerusalem to offer his spiritual obedience to Innocent the Eighth.[8]

Spain was far from weak, but Ferdinand and Isabella's chief interest in England seems to have been centred in the hope that by making war on France, she would leave them free to complete their conquest of the Moors. No record survives of any response they made to Richard's embassy. It may be that they considered his offer to renew the treaty of amity an insufficient inducement, or thought his position still too uncertain to make negotiations worthwhile. When Bernard de la Forssa returned to England, however, his services were rewarded by an annuity of £40. With the other power of the Iberian peninsula, Portugal, Richard was more successful; in June he concluded a treaty reaffirming the pact of friendship which had been established in the time of Richard II.[9]

But England's most important ally, Burgundy, was still torn by Maximilian's struggle to recover the rebellious cities which held his son Philip and carried on a government in Philip's name. As a result of his difficulties, Maximilian pressed on Richard a series of proposals which he could not accept because they were contrary to his interest. Early in 1484 Maximilian had asked to arbitrate the quarrel between England and Brittany—his object being to free Richard for the adventures that *he* wanted the King of England to undertake. Richard had replied that there could be no arbitration until Duke Francis gave an undertaking to keep Henry Tudor and his followers in protective custody. Later, Maximilian sent an embassy armed with a set of requests and promises that were patently the product of wishful thinking. Richard should not make a treaty with France, for that would lose him the glowing opportunity of conquering that country

If, instead, he would cut off all trade with the rebellious cities and supply Maximilian with 6,000 archers and a navy to help reduce them, then Maximilian would provide a great army to help Richard to win France, or, if the King should chance so to prefer, to overwhelm Scotland. Richard not only realized the absurdity of these promises but he knew that the prosperity of his merchants depended upon trade with the cities of Flanders. He had no alternative but to persuade Maximilian to be content with the existing treaty of amity and mercantile intercourse and to dispatch an embassy to make a separate commercial treaty with the cities. This treaty was signed on September 25, and on October 6 the men of Ghent and the other towns agreed to the holding of a diet in London on the following January 20 to settle the claims of the merchants of both parties.[10]

France, there was no dealing with. She, too, was weak and divided, suffering the greedy dissensions of a minority reign. The conflict between the houses of Orleans and Bourbon was threatening to deprive the boy-king Charles VIII of his throne. Though the Estates General, meeting at Tours in January, 1484, had sought to avert open war by appointing a council of twelve, representing all interests, to carry on the Regency, the Princes were still intriguing against the Regent, the Lady of Beaujeu, and preparing to stir up strife. Ostensibly, this weakness would seem to work to Richard's advantage. The French, however, appeared to be united in harbouring the conviction, bequeathed by Louis XI, that the English King was an enemy of France and would revive when he could the claims of Henry V. They were neither in a position nor in a mood to offer a firm truce. Then, in this summer, fortune suddenly placed in the hands of the French court a weapon which might be used to cause the English King, at the very least, a good deal of trouble. That weapon was Henry Tudor and his followers.

Consequently, Richard found it impossible to come to an understanding with France. It is possible that the protracted negotiations with Lord Cordes for mutual redress of grievances bore some fruit, for Richard authorized a payment of £150 to two traders of Rouen and nothing more is heard of Lord Cordes' depredations; but the state of undeclared hostility persisted. In March, Richard had instructed Bishop Langton to present himself, on his way to Rome, at the French court and had given him the power to conclude a truce with the government of Charles VIII and arrange a diet for settling claims and injuries. As a result of Langton's mission, the French informed Richard that they wished to send an embassy, and on September 13 he dispatched the safe-conducts for it. Apparently, it was this embassy of which Maximilian had got word; there is no record, however, that it ever reached England. The court of France, fearing civil strife, hoped that it might distract its neighbour by the same spectre.[11]

One way of bringing France to terms was to support Brittany, the last province which still maintained an independent existence; and before the end of April Richard had succeeded in bringing the Bretons to seek an alliance. But Brittany also was distracted at this time, and her internal troubles would cost the King of England dear. Duke Francis was suffering from bouts of insanity. His Treasurer and chief officer, Pierre Landois, was hated by the nobles. It was Landois' government that, having abandoned the sea war and hastily promised to observe the existing truce, sent an embassy to England towards the end of May. When Richard met the Breton envoys at Pontefract at the beginning of June, they quickly came to terms. On June 8 Richard signed a truce and abstinence of war to endure until the following April 25. It appears that there was a secret codicil to the treaty: in return for the aid of 1,000 archers against France and probably for a grant of the revenues of the chief rebels' estates, Pierre Landois agreed to return Henry Tudor to the same careful custody in which he had been kept until the death of Edward IV. The archers were recruited by indenture; John, Lord Powis was appointed their captain; a commission was empowered, in the latter part of June, to take muster of the forces at Southampton. If the expedition sailed, however, it soon returned to England. Brittany was in no condition to conduct military operations against France; besides, it was no longer possible for Landois to fulfil the conditions on which the archers had been promised.[12]

Henry Tudor was well served, by friends and by fortune. While negotiations were going on between Richard and Landois' envoys, John Morton, living in Flanders, got word of what was afoot. He sent Christopher Urswick to warn Henry of his danger. As soon as Henry, who was staying at Vannes with some 300 followers, heard the news, he dispatched Urswick to the French court to seek permission for the English exiles to take refuge in France. This being readily granted, Henry put into immediate execution the plan he had concocted with his chief supporters. These, headed by Jasper Tudor, left Vannes, ostensibly as an embassy riding to consult Duke Francis, who happened to be staying in a town close to French territory. When the 'embassy' neared the border of Brittany, they suddenly turned south and galloped

K•

safely into Anjou. Two days later Henry Tudor rode out of Vannes with only five servants, saying he was going to visit a friend who lived not far off, 'and because an huge multitude of English people was left in the town, nobody suspected his voyage'. When he had left Vannes well behind him, he turned into a wood and quickly changed clothes with one of his servants; then he rode hard for the border, frequently altering his route in order to throw off pursuit and halting only when it was necessary to feed and rest the horses. Scarcely an hour after he had crossed into Anjou, the men Landois sent in pursuit arrived at the frontier town through which he had passed. The rank-and-file of the exiles who had been so ruthlessly abandoned fared better than might have been expected. When Duke Francis temporarily recovered his wits, he reprimanded Landois for his action, and supplied the English at Vannes with the means of rejoining their master. By the time the French court removed from the Loire valley to Paris in the fall, Henry Tudor and his band of exiles were in hopeful attendance upon it.[13]*

Whatever disappointment Richard felt at Landois' failure, he did not permit it to affect his diplomacy. When, a few months later, Duke Francis sent an envoy to seek a more permanent agreement, Richard willingly extended the truce to endure until 1492.[14] Allied to Brittany and maintaining a friendly neutrality as regards Maximilian and his rebellious Flemish cities, he was able to strengthen the sinews of English trade and concentrate his naval power against the sporadic challenges of the French.

Richard's greatest diplomatic success during this year lay in inducing the Scots to seek a genuine treaty of peace and amity. Scotland presented the most pathetic spectacle of the European scene—a political landscape as murky and barren as the Hebrides in November: weak King, perpetually squabbling nobles, paralysis of policy. Scotland was ineluctably sliding towards Flodden Field and John Knox. In the summer of 1483, King James had made conciliatory overtures but permitted hostilities to continue. Both the overtures and the warfare were renewed in 1484.[15] But the reverse which Richard's men administered to their northern neighbours this summer, coming atop the defeats Richard had been inflicting upon them for the past three years, finally drummed into the hardest-headed Scots that they must make peace.

When, in July, James III sent his counsellor, Lord Lyle, to seek terms, Richard commissioned only a squire to go to Scotland; but once he was certain that the Scots were in earnest, he made clear his eagerness to set the two kingdoms at peace. He proposed an honourable treaty to be cemented by a marriage alliance; and, this offer being at once accepted by King James, he prepared to greet the Scots envoys with all courtesy and dignity. It was an impressive embassy which rode down from Edinburgh at the beginning of September: the Earl of Argyll, Chancellor of Scotland, the Bishop of Aberdeen, Lords Lyle and Oliphant, and a long train of officers and attendants. They were met on their journey by a delegation of English lords and royal councillors escorted by a body of knights, and on the afternoon of Friday, September 11, the splendid cavalcade entered Nottingham.[16]

In the same vein of pomp Richard received the Scots next morning before High Mass. He was enthroned on a dais in the great hall of Nottingham castle. Over him blazed his canopy of state. The greatest powers of his kingdom were grouped around him—Norfolk, Northumberland, and Stanley, Chancellor Russell, the Earls of Shrewsbury and Nottingham, the Bishops of St. Asaph's and Worcester, the Comptroller of his household, Sir Robert Percy, his councillors William Catesby and Sir Richard Ratcliffe, and the Chief Justices Bryan and Husee. Beyond them in ranks stood the knights and squires of the King's Body and the royal henchmen captained by Sir James Tyrell. The Scots ambassadors walked through this splendid assemblage to make their obeisances before the throne, presented their credentials, and Master Archibald Whitelaw, King James' secretary—a man who twenty-five years before had been an envoy from James II to Richard's father—stood forth and delivered a Latin oration resounding in praise of the King of England. Then he knelt before the dais to deliver up the commissions for the treaty of peace and the marriage, crusted with the wax and tape of the Great Seal of Scotland. These Richard graciously received and handed over to Chancellor Russell, who brought the ceremony to an end by pronouncing an address of welcome to the Scots.

On Monday, September 14, the negotiators set to work. Their task was light, for the parties were in hearty agreement; and it remained only to establish the machinery for redress of future grievances and to arrange the terms of the marriage settlement. Shortly thereafter King Richard made proclamation that a truce of three years had been signed with Scotland and that the amity of the two nations was sealed by an agreement that Anne, Richard's niece, daughter of the Duke and Duchess of Suffolk, should wed James, Duke of Rothesay, heir to the Scots throne. If they wished, the friends of both parties were to be included in the truce. Richard nominated the Kings of Spain and

Portugal, the Dukes Maximilian of Austria, his son Philip of Flanders, and Francis of Brittany. The Scots likewise named Brittany as well as the Kings of France and Norway.[17]

This firm accord with a neighbour who had been troubling the northern counties for five years was the best fruit of this laborious summer. The very movements of the King suggest the intensity with which he applied himself to his problems. Leaving Nottingham at the end of April, he spent the first days of May at York. From there he went sadly with his Queen to Middlcham. He could not afford, or perhaps endure, to linger long. He would never see Middleham again. On May 16 he was at Durham, whence he journeyed to Scarborough to supervise the fitting and manning of his fleet. By June 8 he was at Pontefract to meet the Breton ambassadors. The middle of the month found him at York. Then he returned to Scarborough where he remained throughout the first part of July, perhaps in this interval taking command of the naval expedition which defeated the Scots. By July 21 he had gone back to York and was establishing the Council of the North, a governing body which would endure for almost two centuries. Then towards the end of the month he went south by Buckden and Stamford to London, where he remained throughout most of August.[18]* By the 26th he had started northward again to meet the Scots envoys at Nottingham, and here he continued to hold his court throughout September and October. Then he came south once more by Melton Mowbray and Peterborough and Buckden. It was November before he finally returned to the palace of Westminster. In the first year and a half of his reign he had spent less than eight months in his capital.[19]

About a month later royal officers laid their hands upon two traitors to the Crown whom they had long been hunting, John Turburvyle and William Colyngbourne. Of Turburvyle little is known. The fate of Colyngbourne, however, received much attention, probably because of the impudent lampoon he composed against King Richard's government. Subsequent to Buckingham's rebellion, the trial of Colyngbourne is the only arraignment for treason of which the London chroniclers give any notice.

Colyngbourne was a Wiltshire gentleman who had been an officer of the King's mother. Early in 1484, if not previously, he had gone into hiding when it was discovered that he was an agent of Henry Tudor. The indictment now brought against him—the particularity of which seems to indicate his guilt—charged that he had committed two treasonable offences in London during the month of July. On the 18th he had fastened to the door of St. Paul's a seditious rhyme:

> The Cat, the Rat, and Lovell our dog
> Rule all England under an Hog.

The publicity this mocking doggerel attained, obscured the second charge, which was far more deadly, that on July 10 he had offered one Thomas Yate £8 to bear a message to Henry Tudor urging him to land in the south of England in the fall and advising him to tell the French court that the English King would only trifle with their envoys since he meant to make war on France.

On November 29 Richard appointed to hear the case a commission of great dignity: the Dukes of Norfolk and Suffolk, the Earls of Nottingham and Surrey; Viscounts Lovell and Lisle; three barons including Lord Stanley; Sir William Husee and four other justices of King's Bench. The trial took place at Guildhall in early December. John Turburvyle was sentenced to prison. Colyngbourne was convicted of treason and condemned to death. He was executed in the fashion which this age, and the next, reserved for traitors. First he was hanged, at Tower Hill, on a new pair of gallows and then, Fabyan records, 'cut down, being alive, and his bowels ripped out of his belly and cast into the fire there by him, and lived till the butcher put his hand into the bulk of his body, insomuch that he said at the same instant, "O Lord Jesus, yet more trouble", and so died. . . .'[20]*

About the time that Colyngbourne and Turburvyle were arrested, Richard's mind had been further troubled by news from across the channel. Apparently he had been receiving conflicting reports during the late summer and fall—that Henry Tudor had been warmly welcomed by the court of France, that the court was so divided by rival interests that he could get no promise of aid. But now came the unpalatable tidings from Calais that the greatest Lancastrian leader yet alive had escaped from custody and joined the Tudor.[21]

John de Vere, late Earl of Oxford, had been imprisoned since 1474 in Hammes castle, of which James Blount was Lieutenant. Henry Tudor's reception at the French court had caused Richard to become concerned for the safety of Calais and its protecting forts, Guisnes and Hammes. In August he bade the Cinque Ports be ready to assist in their defence. Knowing that Oxford would deliver Hammes to the Tudor's French friends if he had an opportunity, and, perhaps, being informed that

Blount was on suspiciously cordial terms with his prisoner, he gave orders on October 28 that the Earl was to be conveyed to England by William Bolton, a yeoman usher of the Chamber. But Oxford had indeed persuaded Blount to join his cause; and the pair of them now fled to Paris. When Lord Dynham sent a detachment from Calais to investigate the situation at Hammes, they were refused admittance. By the middle of December, the men of Hammes, fearful perhaps of being held responsible for Oxford's escape, were withstanding a siege by Dynham's troops. After Richard offered a full pardon to the garrison and to Blount's wife, however, it appears that the soldiers willingly resumed their duties. But he hastened to replace the men of Guisnes with a fresh force and to supersede its ailing Lieutenant, Lord Mountjoy, who was James Blount's brother, by that trusted Knight of the Body, Sir James Tyrell.[22]*

Stung by Oxford's escape and the treachery of Blount and Colyngbourne, chafing to take action against his enemies, Richard, on December 3, ordered his Chancellor to publish a proclamation against Henry Tudor and his followers, in which all the King's subjects were commanded to be ready to resist the rebels. On December 8 he issued fresh commissions of array, most of them to the same men who, the preceding May, had been appointed commissioners. Ten days later he dispatched further commissions ordering a military census of the lords and gentry, which was to record how many men each could call up at half a day's notice.[23]

It was mid-winter. No invasion could be expected for months. By his proclamations and commissions Richard only reminded his realm— a land grown weary in the last decades of summonses to arms—that his throne was not secure and that peace was not yet to be hoped for. Rumours were whispered that the Princes had been done to death; Henry Tudor was working upon old discontents and Lancastrian leanings; allegiance and justice were proving to be elusive game. There were facts, consequences, that even willingness and will could not circumvent as readily as the anxious heart desired. The King who would rule by desert rather than hold his throne by the most expedient way was becoming a hostage to his own feelings.

VIII

so approached the Christmas season of 1484, with yeomen of the crown riding in all directions from London bearing martial commissions, proclamations against the rebels, and sundry warnings to the coast towns to ready their defences; with King Richard at Westminster, unquiet of heart and straining to slake his frustration in action; with the King's council so busy that until the beginning of the new year it could not spare one of its clerks, John Harrington, to York, where he was also clerk of the corporation. The King covered his cares with a mantle of splendour for the celebration of Christmas; the opulence and power of his estate were certified in richness of gowns and gorgeousness of ceremony. True to his oath, he saw to it that the daughters of Edward IV were worthily entertained and apparelled. The eldest, Elizabeth—tall, with long golden hair—was attired in robes as magnificent as the Queen's.[1]

No revelry could long distract the sober King, however. His anxieties reached deeper than Henry Tudor and the state of his kingdom. His wife Anne, for all the gaiety of her dress, was fast failing. The tireless, robust King-maker had brought forth two delicate daughters. Isabel had died before she was twenty-four, probably of tuberculosis. It was this same disease which was ravaging Anne, crushed in spirit by the death of her son. Richard could not look at her without realizing that she was doomed. The strains under which he laboured began to be intensified now by a despair for which there was no remedy.[2]*

Meanwhile, outside the palace of Westminster the hum and buzz of human existence sounded in its accustomed way, whatever the sorrows and problems of Plantagenet. The shops in Cheapside were bright with silver goods, gold cups, Italian necklaces, Flemish tapestries. The Wayts of London serenaded gentry and merchants with carols. Men and women on country manors prepared to entertain neighbours with games of cards, backgammon, with harping and playing on the lute by talented servants, and with communal singing.

Not many yards from Westminster palace, at the sign of the Red Pale in the western precincts of the Abbey grounds, William Caxton, now in his sixties but still vigorous of mind, must have been looking upon the Christmas season with satisfaction. During the past year his press had dressed in the fine uniformity of type, among other treasures, the *Canterbury Tales* and the *Troilus and Cressida* of Master Geoffrey Chaucer, the English poet he admired above all others. With his assistants he would be planning further triumphs, the clatter of metal resounding from the composing room, the good bite of wet ink in his nose, and a puff of monkish song drifting from the Abbey doors to the east.

Up in York, one John Stafford was in trouble. His boy Richard was in trouble too and that was what John minded most. He had been 'noised for a coiner' and on Thursday, December 17, he was arrested by order of the Mayor, Thomas Wrangwysh, who ordered his officers to search the suspect. One hundred counterfeit crowns were found on him—French crowns—and other coins of 'laton', a soft alloy, 'which he thought to have gilt and uttered [passed] within the city and other places, in the great deceit and hurt of the King's people'. Though Stafford protested anxiously that his boy Richard had no part in his counterfeiting, both of them were committed to prison.[3]

The next morning the Mayor, aided by Thomas Aske, the city attorney, and a few of the aldermen, secretly examined Stafford. Having been caught in the act, he made a full confession, doubtless hoping at least to save his son if he could not manage to save himself. It was a grave business. False coining, by statute of Edward III, had been declared high treason; the punishment was death in its direst form. The city now turned to the Council of the North, which King Richard had established the previous July. Wrangwysh wrote to the Earl of Lincoln at Sandal, recounting the coiner's confession and requesting the Earl, who was president of the council, 'to show your commandment by our servant this bearer how I shall deal with the said John and with his son'.

The city's message reached Sandal the same day; the Earl at once composed a reply which Wrangwysh received the next morning. 'You have', wrote Lincoln, 'not only done unto me a right singular pleasure but for the same have deserved of the King's grace a great and special thank not be be unremembered; nathless [nevertheless] I pray you for sundry considerations on Monday next to do [cause] the said Stafford to be sent hither unto me, keeping with you his son'. He added that before Christmas day he would be sending dispatches to the King 'amongst which your faithful diligence and acquittal in this behalf ne shall be forgotten. . . .'

On the 20th the Mayor read Lincoln's answer to the city council. They were pleased but slightly uneasy, for the Earl's request to examine the coiner touched a tender spot—the prerogatives of the corporation of York. After some debate it was agreed that the Mayor should accede to Lincoln's wish, but remind him of those prerogatives. Consequently, Wrangwysh wrote frankly to Lincoln that, though the council was pleased to send him the coiner to be examined 'after your high pleasure and wisdom', John Stafford was then to be remitted to York 'to be punished after his demerits, according to the rights of the said city. . . .'

So, a week before Christmas, with his boy languishing in York gaol, John Stafford was taken by John Sponer and John Nicholson to face the questioning of the Earl of Lincoln and his fellow councillors of the North. Here Stafford drops from the pages of history as abruptly as he entered them. There is reason to suppose, however, that he and his son lived to give thanks at the Mass of Christ. For the confession that he had made was also a defence, which was certainly ingenious and may very well have been true.

John Stafford told the Mayor that while dwelling on the late Earl of Shrewsbury's manor of Wynfeld in Derbyshire he had found certain coining irons, 'one bearing the print and coin of the French King called the crown, and the other bearing the print of the Dutch coin called St. Andrew, with which irons he hath coined and set the prints of the said irons upon laton gilt, by the space of a year or more, and thought to have uttered them to such as he might'. But he had a trump card to play. Indicted for coining in Derbyshire, he had obtained a special charter of pardon 'under the King's broad seal of England'. This he probably had with him and produced before the Mayor and the city attorney. He had been pardoned for the reason that though counterfeiting English coin was treason, counterfeiting the coin of any other kingdom was not even a felony; it would not become so till the reign of Henry VII. Stafford's story of how he came by the coining irons is convincing, for the 'late Earl of Shrewsbury' was the grandson of that John Talbot, first Earl, who, in 1452 while King's Lieutenant of the Duchy of Aquitaine, was granted the power to coin French money of gold and silver as often as he thought fit. This circumstance neatly accounts for the presence of the irons on the manor of Wynfeld. So perhaps John Stafford and his boy Richard had a happy Christmas, after all.

To a family in Norfolk the season was presenting an age-old problem: how much gaiety is to be permitted in a household recently bereaved? On Christmas eve Margery Paston ceased her tasks to take up pen and report to her husband what she had discovered on this vexed subject, which had arisen because of the death of her mother-in-law early in

November. This girl Margery, married to John Paston the younger, was not known to that Italian diplomat who a few years later recorded that he had never observed a sign of love among the English. Before they were married Margery had boldly let her John know how much she longed to be his bride, had signed herself his Valentine, and had worked hard to secure her father's consent to the marriage settlement.[4]

'Please it you to know', she wrote John, who was away in London, 'that I sent your eldest son to my Lady Morley to have knowledge what sports were used in her house in Christmas next following after the decease of my lord her husband, and she said that there were no disguisings, nor harping, nor luting, nor singing, nor no loud disports, but playing at the tables [backgammon], and chess, and cards. Such disports she gave her folks leave to play and none other.

'Your son did his errand right well as ye shall hear after this. I sent your younger son to the Lady Stapleton, and she said according to my Lady Morley's saying in that, and as she had seen used in places of worship where she hath been. . . .

'I am sorry that ye shall not at home be for Christmas. I pray you that ye will come as soon as ye may. I shall think myself half a widow, because ye shall not be at home. . . . God have you in his keeping. Written on Christmas even. By your M.P.'

So arrived, within and without the King's palace, the Christmas of 1484.

On Epiphany, Richard and his dying Queen, wearing their crowns, presided over a courtly revel. At this moment he was handed an urgent message. 'While he was keeping this festival with remarkable splendour in the great hall', records the Croyland Chronicler, 'news was brought him . . . from his spies beyond the sea, that, notwithstanding the potency and splendour of his royal state, his adversaries would, without question, invade the kingdom during the following summer. . . . Than this, there was nothing that could befall him more desirable. . . .'[5]

IX*

RICHARD had reigned for only eighteen months, but whatever shape and meaning his government possessed was now developed. Ahead, lay preparations for defence, a span of strained waiting, and a journey into despair.

Much of Richard's policy was aimed at fulfilling the work of his great brother; much, however, turned away from what Richard conceived to be the errors into which Edward had been led by the distractions of his court. But it was fused into a whole by the heat of his convictions. Seldom has a rule so brief been so impregnated by the character of the ruler; seldom has a ruler spoken with so personal an accent. Both the government and those it governed he conceived in intimate terms. He wore the machinery of the Crown like a coat of his own making: it contained and represented and expressed him. Thus, he was unusually sensitive of his self-imposed duties to his subjects, but he was also unusually vulnerable to the attacks of his conscience.

Richard was accessible, earnest, concerned. The King was not remote and awe-ful, as he was to become in Tudor times—ascended into a state above mortality, addressed no longer as 'Your Grace' in common with Dukes and Archbishops but uniquely as 'Your Majesty', perceptible in his acts only through his officers, perceptible in his person only from a distance, perceptible in his thoughts and feelings never, during the secretive reign of Henry VII, and, during the last half of Henry VIII's reign, mostly in vindictive punitions and the harsh *fiats* of an ailing, suspicious nature.

The governor preoccupied with justice has no rest, and in the fifteenth century, could have small comfort. Viewed as a social phenomenon, Richard's reign can be seen as an ironic comedy of justice: ironic because he offended against justice in securing the authority by which to pursue it and because his subjects preferred something else, namely, stability. Viewed as the history of a man, his reign shows elements of true tragedy because the protagonist cannot resolve the conflict within himself and he cannot win his conflict with the world, with which he refuses to compromise.

Richard pursued justice into thickets of trivial matters as well as through the forest of high affairs. This preoccupation stands four-square in the series of parliamentary statutes designed to free the individual from oppressions of his person and his purse. In the proclamation he published in Kent shortly after Buckingham's rebellion, Richard shows himself more anxious to persuade the citizens to be just to one another than to seek out concealed rebels and to demand public order. Similarly, when local grievances provoke a riot in the city of York in the early fall of 1484, Richard's concern is not with punishing the rioters but with lecturing them on the proper means for them to seek redress of their wrongs.[1] The burden of his exhortation to the lords and gentry, following his coronation, is not that they uphold his government but that they be very justicers to those they govern. In the detailed instructions which Richard gave Sir Marmaduke Constable for the efficient managing of the royal honour of Tutbury, his first command is for Sir Marmaduke to root out the evils of livery and maintenance; his next, to discharge all county bailiffs who have been practising oppressions and extortions upon the common people. Intent upon understanding the machinery of justice, he summons his judges to the Star Chamber in order to question them earnestly about his laws.[2]

When Richard hears that a Vicar-general has defrauded a parson of his living, he is quick to send a warrant demanding restitution. Upon learning, even as he is busy stamping out the last embers of Buckingham's rebellion, that one of the under-clerks in the office of Privy Seal has, despite markedly good service, been passed over in the promotion list, he sends a warrant to John Gunthorpe, Keeper of the Privy Seal, 'to discharge Richard Bele from his place in the office of the said Privy Seal, to which he had been admitted contrary to the old rule and due order, by means of giving of great gifts and other sinister and ungodly ways in great discouraging of the under-clerks, which have long continued therein, to have the experience of the same—to see a stranger, never brought up in the said office, to put them by of their promotion'. In Bele's stead Richard granted the place to Robert Bolman, for his 'good and diligent service . . . in the said office, and specially in this the King's great journey and for his experience and long continuance in the same'. Though a reorganization in the office of Privy Seal reduced the number of clerks to six and thus left Bolman an under-clerk, the King gave him an annuity of 100s and later granted him a clerkship at the first vacancy.

Richard conceived the King's relationship with the realm to be that of the Duke of Gloucester with the North writ large, in so far as he meant to make his rule personal, accessible, and paternal. But recognizing that it would be impossible for the King to establish so close a bond with the entire kingdom, he chose to make use of the few great magnates who remained after decades of civil strife in order to create in the regions of England something like the government he had given Yorkshire. Thus it was that he conferred lands and powers upon Buckingham in the west, Norfolk and Surrey in East Anglia, the Stanleys in Cheshire, Lancashire and North Wales, and Northumberland in the North and upon the Marches. These great lords were granted commissions of array, of the peace, and of *oyer and terminer*, which gave them broad powers of rallying men for defence, maintaining order and enforcing the laws. Richard meant their authority as lieutenants of the King to replace, or transcend, their personal sway as inheritors of the feudal tradition, and he hoped that the opulence of their endowments would remove all motive for aggrandizement against their neighbours, injustice to those they governed, or disloyalty to the King. Thus did he seek to reinterpret the old function of the King as head of the feodality, to work a transmutation upon moribund feudalism whereby men of lands and lineage were to reassert their primitive roles as active leaders, doers, but as agents, now, of the King's law and the King's peace. Thus did he seek to maintain the strong central government his brother had created, and yet to make it parochial in its sensitivity to local issues and grievances while it remained national in its final authority. But to these magnates he had given a feudal-like governance that was not circumscribed by the old feudal dues and ideas. In this age between, they were no longer bound by obligation arising out of land tenure but they had not yet been securely subdued to the royal power expressed as law. It was on the doubtful cement of loyalty that Richard must needs depend.

Still, though he tried to reanimate traditions of the past, he was thoroughly aware of the rising power of the middle class, as represented by the merchants of the towns, and he exerted great efforts to establish a bond of trust between them and the crown. His relations as Duke of Gloucester with the men of York had given him a deep respect for the worth and importance of this class. He granted governing privileges, presents of money, partial remission of royal fees to no less than eighteen towns in all quarters of the kingdom during the first year and a half of his reign. Their well-being spelled prosperity for the country; their devotion to the King foretold an alliance of the stable middle class with the throne against baronial irresponsibility or recalcitrance; the increasing importance of townsmen encouraged the spread of those virtues which they were beginning to exemplify: sobriety, industry, piety. That they might not be drawn into the quarrels of nobles or be distracted from their direct allegiance to the King, Richard repeatedly exhorted municipal officers to see that no citizens accepted liveries or retainders. In May of 1485 he addressed a long letter to the Mayor of Coventry which represents the concern he felt for the good governance of his towns, and is also a remarkably able piece of prose. The opening sentence strikes the theme of the whole document:

. . . It is come unto our knowledge how that ye have late full laudably with great diligence applied you to the observing and executing of such sad [serious] directions and substantial ordinances amongst you according to our writing late directed unto you in that behalf as thereby love and unity is enhanced amongst you, and dissensions, variances and discords set apart to the honour and weal of our city there: for the which we greatly laud and commend your sadness and circumspect wisdoms, and thank you heartily for the same, willing and exhorting you that like as ye have begun and done ye will diligently ensure the perfect continuance of the same.[3]

To the lower classes—peasants, yeomen, urban artisans—Richard sought to give the protection of justice, not only under his law and through his officers, but by making himself accessible to appeal, particularly through the medium of his council. King Edward had apparently established a committee of his advisers to hear the causes of men who had not the means to seek their rights in the courts or from those in power. In order to foster this service Richard formally created the institution (though not the name, which came later) of the 'Court of Requests', which was to endure for many a year. John Harrington was appointed, in December of 1483, to the clerkship of a special branch of the council sitting in the White Hall whose duty it was to hear the 'bills, requests, and supplications of poor persons'.[4] In addition, the council as a whole functioned as a final tribunal of appeal to which the King's subjects might prefer complaints of oppression or extortion or other injustice. Sometimes the council took action; sometimes it referred a case to an appropriate court; sometimes it requested local authorities to investigate. This latter course it took, for example, in the case of a woman of York, about whom the King dispatched a communication to the Mayor in September of 1484,

letting you know that grievous complaint hath been made unto us on the behalf of our poor subject Katherine Bassingbourne of an injury to be done unto her by one Henry Faucet, as by a bill of supplication which we send unto you herein enclosed more at large it appeareth. Wherefore we willing in that behalf the administration of justice whereunto we be professed, and also trusting in your wisdom and in-differency, will and desire you that ye—taking the contents of the said bill in due and mature examination—will, calling the parties before you, set such final direction in the same as shall accord with our laws and good conscience. . . .

In selecting his councillors, Richard emulated the achievement of his great brother. For more than a century preceding Edward's coming to the throne, the magnates had dominated the King's council, often exercising their influence in it to thwart the King; and in the long disaster of Henry VI's reign they had used the council as an instrument for entirely usurping the royal power. After Edward had freed himself of the House of Neville and crushed the power of the barons, he maintained a council which was completely the servant of his will, composed largely of gifted commoners in holy orders who were his personal advisers and diplomatic emissaries.

For his council Richard chose the ablest men that England could then boast; they had all served his brother at home and abroad and the chief of them were the first Renaissance scholars which England had yet produced, men who had studied in Italy (with the exception of John Russell), collected classical manuscripts, and written Latin works: Russell, the Chancellor; John Gunthorpe, Keeper of the Privy Seal; Thomas Langton, Bishop of St. David's and then of Salisbury; John Sherwood, Bishop of Durham and Richard's representative at the Vatican (for whom he had tried to secure a Cardinalate in recognition of his abilities and of his erudition). Other clerics on the council included Edmund Chaderton, Treasurer of the King's Chamber and Royal Chaplain; Rotherham, Archbishop of York; the Bishops of Worcester, St. Asaph's, Bath and Wells; Thomas Barowe, Master of the Rolls, and Dr. Thomas Hutton; and there were three influential commoners, John Kendall, the King's Secretary, the lawyer William Catesby, and Sir Richard Ratcliffe. Two other commoners served as the principal legal advisers, Thomas Lynom, the King's Solicitor, and Morgan Kidwelly, his Attorney General. Only a few lords sat, on occasion, at the council table and these because Richard sought their advice: John, Lord Audeley, who in December of 1484 became Treasurer of the Exchequer; Lord Stanley, Steward of the royal Household; Viscount Lovell, the Chamberlain; John, Lord Scrope of Bolton, Richard's friend and neighbour from Wensleydale. Richard meant the nobility to be the agents of policy, not its creators.

He had his own agents too, men who were constantly employed in carrying out the council's decisions and who, so far as their personalities can be conjectured, were of an entirely different stamp from the learned, deliberate, and sedentary councillors. These were ready men of action, captains on land or sea, officers capable of executing dangerous errands, of maintaining peace in the wilder portions of the Welsh Marches, of holding master strongholds for the King, supervising lands of the royal demesne, or taking charge of estates forfeited by rebels. Prominent among these men were Sir James Tyrell, Master of the Horse and of the Henxmen; Sir Robert Brackenbury, Constable of the Tower, called 'gentle Brackenbury' by one chronicler[5] and evidently a man of wide popularity and some learning, to whom the Italian poet, Pietro Carmeliano, seeking his fortune in England, had dedicated one of his Latin works; and that doughty adventurer Edward Brampton, who received many gifts from Richard for his services and finally a knight-hood—the first ever conferred in England upon a convertite Jew. For a number of these trusted men of his Household Richard found a special employment as sheriffs. The office of sheriff, a yearly appoint-ment, had once represented the authority of the King in each county; by the first years of Edward IV, however, he had lost almost all his powers to the Justices, or Commissioners, of the Peace. Richard, it appears, sought to revive his importance as a means of strengthening the power of the central government in the shires; for the principal lords and gentry of a county were usually its Justices of the Peace. Sir Robert Brackenbury became Sheriff of Kent for life; Sir Richard Ratcliffe, Sheriff of Westmorland for life; Sir Thomas Wortley, Knight of the Body, Sheriff of Staffordshire; Sir Robert Percy, Comptroller of the Household, Sheriff of Essex and of Hertfordshire; Sir Edmund Hastings, who had been a member of Richard's ducal council, Sheriff of Yorkshire.

There were other governmental reforms and innovations which Richard found the time to institute. Much concerned with the develop-ment of English sea-power, he offered as an inducement towards the building of ships the attractive bounty of a first voyage free of customs duties; and since Norfolk, the Admiral, was busy with many affairs, he created by commission an Admiralty Office with Sir John Wode and the indefatigable Brackenbury as Vice-Admirals, a staff of three under them, and a notary to keep official records. After a study of govern-mental finance, he inaugurated a rigorous reform which transferred many functions from the inefficient and tradition-bound Exchequer to an officer of his Household, the Treasurer of the Royal Chamber. This reorganization, which gave the King a more direct and flexible control of his revenues, was so successful that it was copied, in detail, by Richard's successors.[6]

His most important and enduring creation was the Council of the North, established in July of 1484, which lasted, almost precisely as Richard instituted it, for more than a century and a half. In general, this council functioned for the northern regions as the council at Westminster functioned for the entire kingdom; its places of residence, Sandal castle and Sheriff Hutton, were called the King's Household in the North; John, Earl of Lincoln, Richard's heir and the President of the council, signed its decrees *per consilium Regis*; and for the operation of the household as well as for the proceedings of the council Richard drew up detailed sets of instructions.

Essentially, the council extended the accessibility of the King as the redresser of grievances and the maintainer of harmony. Its chief objects were to give justice and promote tranquillity. It possessed both civil and criminal jurisdiction, the power of investigating, commanding the presence of witnesses by sub-poena, ordering by decree, giving verdict, punishing.

Only a few of its members are known. With its President, the Earl of Lincoln, was nominally associated—he was still a boy—Clarence's son the Earl of Warwick. Lord Morley, Lincoln's youthful brother-in-law, and Henry Percy, Earl of Northumberland, were also members. No register of the council's activities has survived; but its work is illustrated in the story of John Stafford, the coiner, and the municipal records of York indicate that less than three months after its establishment the council dealt effectively with a riotous protest against certain enclosures of land. This success aroused, however, the resentment of the proud Henry Percy, whom the city had ignored in making its appeal to the council.[7]

Even though the treason of Buckingham had left Wales without a central government, it is not difficult to perceive why Richard chose to institute this council in the North rather than to revive the Council of the Welsh Marches, which King Edward had inaugurated years before. It was in the North that King Richard's heart and his strength lay. The loyalty which the region had accorded him as Duke of Gloucester he wished to retain for the crown; it was the most instinctively feudal and conservative quarter of the realm and it was remote from Westminster; presumably, it would offer a lively, but not harsh, school of government for the Earl of Lincoln; and it was a region over which the Earl of Northumberland patently longed to reassert the sway which his ancestors had enjoyed. Mindful of the resentment which the Earl had shown signs of cherishing in the 1470's because of the uncertain division of their powers, Richard tried to establish a clearer separation of authority. Northumberland enjoyed the military jurisdiction of Warden-General of the Scots Marches, with the Captainship of Berwick; he was appointed Sheriff of Northumberland for life, Constable of all its royal castles, and Bailiff of Tynedale; and he received grants of manors that made him the greatest landowner in England. The Council of the North exercised authority only in Yorkshire, Cumberland, and Westmorland. Yet, even though he was himself a member of the council, Northumberland was not content. That body represented a continuance of Richard's hold upon the North, which sat ill upon

Henry Percy's haughty stomach, dieted though it was with mighty offices and opulent possessions.

The dominant tone of Richard's government, ringing through these institutions, was created by his own preoccupations and attitudes, the reach and stress of his character to express himself as King. Such was his concern with justice; such, too, was his hope of effecting an amelioration of men's morals. In the coils of circumstance and high place, of opportunity in the guise of duty, of warped memories of the past and cloudy urgencies of the present, Richard had seized the throne and then, very possibly, had done a far more grievous wrong; yet, though these acts cast an ironic shadow they need not cast doubt upon the intense sincerity of his moral feeling. This sincerity is demonstrated not only in deeds and documents but also by the strain under which he laboured precisely because he could not reconcile some of his acts committed in the arena of power with his view of himself as a responsible human creature balanced upon the awful enigma of God's hand. He must rule by merit because such rule was good in the judgment of Heaven and because it might even be good enough to mitigate his transgressions.

Richard's concern for morality, like his quest for justice, fused his character and his politics. He was a rudimentary Puritan, as were many of the townsmen to whom he felt himself so warmly bound. It was the vices particularly repugnant to 16th and 17th century Puritans from which he wished to turn men's habits—lechery and arrogance and dishonesty and blasphemy and ruthless greed. Hence, in part, his antagonism to his brother's court, his attack upon the dead Hastings' reputation, his insistence that Jane Shore do public penance for harlotry. Hence his disregarding political expediency to attack the Marquess of Dorset, in the proclamation of October, 1483, as a lecher, and his rather wishful assumption, in his proclamation of December, 1484, that Henry Tudor represented a rabble of extortionists and adulterers.

On the other hand, a positive determination to encourage good living and to seek men of good character for offices pervades documents, letters, instructions, from his hand. None more succinctly expresses his feeling than the communication which he sent to each of his bishops in March of 1484.

The Convocation of the clergy, meeting during the sessions of Parliament, had supplicated Richard, first to confirm the rights of the Church, as King Edward had done, and then to enforce those rights, painting a lurid picture of clerics 'cruelly, grievously . . . troubled . . .

and arrested', dragged to prison from the very altar by impious secular hands or so threatened by the laity that they dare not reside on their benefices. Richard granted the Church its liberties, including the traditional privilege of trying erring members in its courts;[8] but he seized the occasion to address to the bishops a plea of his own. 'Our principal intent and fervent desire', he begins directly, 'is to see virtue and cleanness of living to be advanced . . . and vices . . . provoking the high indignation and fearful displeasure of God to be repressed and annulled; and this . . . put in execution by persons of high estate . . . not only induceth persons of lower degree to take thereof example . . . but also thereby the great and infinite goodness of God is made placable and graciously inclined to the exaudition of petitions and prayers'. Since in every diocese there are men, spiritual as well as secular, leading evil lives, Richard wills each bishop to reform such persons, 'not sparing for any . . . favour . . . or affection, whether the offenders be spiritual or temporal'. In return for diligent obedience to this behest, he promises that clerics will be punished only according to the laws of Holy Church. 'And thus proceeding to the execution hereof, you shall do unto yourself great honour, and unto us right singular pleasure'.

This exhortation provides an ironic commentary on the stagnation which had settled upon the Church—once the single great force making for righteousness in a society ignorant and often brutal; now having to be implored by a King, and bribed with the promise of retaining its immunities, to set a decent moral example to the world!

The pattern of Richard's many grants and gifts also mingles the policy of the ruler and the predilections of the man. To the great seignorial personalities—Buckingham, Norfolk, Northumberland, the Stanleys—went the largest endowment in lands. In order to fill vacancies in the Knighthood of the Garter, Richard's chapter elected his friend Viscount Lovell, the Lord Chamberlain; Thomas, Earl of Surrey, Norfolk's heir, who enjoyed a cash annuity of £1,100; that influential councillor, Sir Richard Ratcliffe of Yorkshire; Thomas, Lord Stanley, whose allegiance Richard was seeking so hard to win; and three of the Knights of the Body—Sir Thomas Burgh, Sir Richard Tunstall, and Sir John Conyers.[9]

His intimate servants he could not resist loading with presents. The diligent and much-employed Robert Brackenbury received grants and rewards providing an income of at least £400 a year, a sum which probably equalled the revenue of many a baron; Sir Richard Ratcliffe was given in 1485 a vast array of lands with a rent roll of some £650;

about forty other royal servants, Knights and Esquires of the Body most of them, shared grants of forfeited estates yielding more than £2,500 annually. On John Kendall, Secretary, Richard bestowed a rich variety of presents and perquisites worth some £450 a year and advanced his official status from Yeoman of the Crown to King's Councillor. Kendall's father appears to have been that John Kendall who had spent his life in the service of Richard's father and brother and whom King Edward had appointed to the office of Controller of the King's Works and later made an Alms Knight attached to the Chapel of St. George. He died sometime during Richard's reign, having lived to see his son play the most important role in the government which a King's Secretary had yet achieved. The career of John Kendall the younger anticipates the elevation of Thomas Cromwell, as Henry VIII's Secretary, to the position of first minister formerly held by the Chancellor.[10]*

In numbers, these various grants represent but one arrow in the full quiver of gifts which Richard sent winging among all sorts and conditions of men. Puritan though in many ways he was, he could not forgo the self-indulgence of liberality. Much of his giving is calculated upon no expectation of political increment. Sometimes the motive of honourable obligation appears, but often Richard scattered small gifts like a benevolent agent of Providence. The record of his grants is peppered with annuities of a few marks or pounds to humble folk, many of whom were widows. He is sensitive of his duty to old servants: he continued an annuity of £20 to Joan Peysmarsh 'for her good service to the King in his youth and to his mother'; he revived a £10 annuity which Warwick years before had bestowed upon a faithful follower; to Anne Caux, 'once the nurse of Edward IV', he gave £20 yearly 'in consideration of her poverty'; Katherine Vaux, the faithful Lady in Waiting to his old enemy Queen Margaret of Anjou, received an annuity of 20 marks. He relieved the distress of wives of rebels whose property had been forfeited: he granted an annuity to the Duchess of Buckingham, ordered Lady Rivers' tenants to pay her their dues, gave the Countess of Oxford a pension. 'For her good and virtuous disposition' he took Florence, wife of the rebel Alexander Cheyney, into his protection and granted her the custody of her husband's lands. For his times, Richard reveals a surprising sense of women as people in their own right, and it appears that he liked to compliment those whose character or domestic virtues moved his admiration. In gifts of small annuities he frequently couples the wife's name with the husband's;

to Alice Shipwarde, wife of a Bristol merchant, he gave a handsome
annuity of £40; Viscount Lovell's sister, Frideswide, wife of Edward
Norris, received on one occasion a 'reward' of 50 marks, on another an
annuity of 100 marks; Joanna Mountfort, one of the daughters of Sir
Thomas Mountfort, enjoyed a bounty of 10 marks yearly.

This structure and texture of Richard's rule are not without weaknesses. The *Croyland Chronicle*—probably in the person of the censorious
monk who edited the 'Second Continuation' rather than the learned
statesman who provided much of the information—makes two specific
complaints against Richard's government. The King, he says, favoured
Northerners to the displeasure of the men of the southern counties, and
he was extravagant in his expenditure.[11]

In the first accusation there is much truth. Of his chief temporal
advisers and officers, Lords Stanley and Scrope of Bolton, Viscount
Lovell, Brackenbury, Ratcliffe, Sir Robert Percy, John Kendall were
all Northerners and William Catesby was a man of the Midlands.
Possibly a considerable number of minor posts—those of bailiffs,
parkers, wardens, rangers, stewards, porters and the like—went to
Northern men also. No less than seven members of the Metcalfe family
of Wensleydale, for example, received offices or annuities, the latter
very small. Certain royal demesnes, lands forfeited by rebels, and
supervisory authorities in the southern and southwestern counties were
given into the hands of royal servants who were mostly from the North.
Scrope of Bolton and Lord Zouche of the Midlands held commissions
of *oyer and terminer* for Cornwall and Devon; George Neville was made
keeper of parks and chaces in Dorset; Robert Brackenbury became
Sheriff of Kent; Sir Marmaduke Constable, of the Midlands, was given
charge, after Buckingham's rebellion, of the honour and town of
Tunbridge and its neighbouring lordships.

Richard had not come to the throne, however, at the head of a party.
He had for years been associated with one region of the kingdom,
where he had won a great following. It was almost inevitable that he
should often turn, in his exigencies, to the men of that region for trusty
service and feel moved to reward their loyalty. The pronounced
northern influence upon the heart of his government was undoubtedly
a greater source of dissatisfaction than the moderate infiltration of
Northerners into positions of authority in the southern counties. On
the whole, this animus does not appear to have been sufficiently
widespread to undermine Richard's hold upon the obedience of his
subjects.

The second accusation, of extravagance, seems more significant. Richard's munificence had deprived the Crown of much of the great lands forfeited by rebels, and saddled his regular sources of income with many charges for annuities; by the beginning of 1485 he had apparently consumed the treasure which his brother had accumulated; and by diminishing his resources, he diminished his power of levying the sinews of war to meet the impending challenge of Henry Tudor. To such criticism Richard might have replied that it becomes a King to reward good service, even good conduct, that the grants he had made to his followers gave the them greater means to maintain his authority in peace and back his quarrel in battle; and that without asking Parliament for a grant of taxes, he had put down Buckingham's rebellion and carried on a successful campaign against the Bretons, French, and Scots. Perhaps he also believed that through his financial reforms, the Crown lands and other sources of revenue would be made to yield a markedly increased return. Still, even though his grants sprang from generous motives, they did not contribute greatly to the strength of his rule and they threatened to shake the structure of his credit.

A subtler weakness derived from the earnestness of his character; he was, in a sense, the victim of the terms on which he was determined to govern. He lacked the sustained and purposive ruthlessness which, though it would not have enhanced the happiness nor probably even the tranquillity of the realm, would doubtless have assured his grip upon it. Had there existed no concentrated, external threat to his rule, his generous behaviour to the Stanleys and Northumberland might have proved a wise policy of conciliation; but in the circumstances and on their political records, the power Richard allowed them to exercise cannot be justified by any standard of *realpolitik*. As a consequence of his incapacity to sink the man in the King, he betrayed a feeling of insecurity; a mounting strain which gave him sleepless nights, a careworn look, and an uneasy manner; an almost feverish preoccupation with affairs large and small; a haggard pursuit of his subjects' goodwill —all of which must have tended to make men suspicious of his intentions, doubtful of the solidity of his rule, and troubled, or wearied, by the intensity with which, like a bird circling its nest of young, he hovered over the kingdom and all within it.

Yet Richard's government was not only well intentioned but appears to have been, in general, fairly popular. According to the testimony of Commynes, who disliked him—perhaps because he was acquainted only with Henry Tudor's version of English events—and from what may be discerned even in Vergil, Richard's authority and the beneficence of his rule were acknowledged by the mass of his subjects. The esteem which he afterwards retained among the followers of the House of York is reflected in a proclamation of Perkin Warbeck, who, even while he had to maintain the role of younger son to Edward IV, felt compelled to declare that 'though desire of rule did bind [King Richard], yet, in his other actions, he was noble, and loved the honour of the realm, and the contentment and comfort of his nobles and people'. More reliable testimony to his hold upon the kingdom can be descried in the quick collapse of Buckingham's rebellion, the comparative peace and order that lapped the country, and the paucity of charges which his enemies could find to rumour against him. Whatever numbers of people may have suspected concerning the fate of King Edward's sons, however much sentiments were at first offended by the sudden seizure of the crown, Richard's subjects had apparently become content, by the time the second Christmas of his reign arrived, to leave to heaven's judgment his transgressions in assuming the purple and to accept a rule which augured well for themselves and the realm. Thomas Langton, one of England's few ornaments of the New Learning, had declared enthusiastically that 'God hath sent him to us for the weal of us all'; though Langton was a favoured councillor of Richard's, he was so able a man that only his sudden demise prevented his elevation, by Richard's successor and foe, to the Archbishopric of Canterbury.

When the picture of Richard's government is viewed in the frame of its actual brevity, the remarkable dimensions of his achievement leap into focus. Even though it was not so much a reign in being as a reign in defence of its being, Richard vigorously translated the idiom of his character into the language of kingship. In the course of a mere eighteen months, crowded with cares and problems, he laid down a coherent programme of legal enactments, maintained an orderly society, and actively promoted the well-being of his subjects. A comparable period in the reigns of his predecessor and of his successor shows no such accomplishment.

The metal of Richard's character must be mined from his acts and his rule. Little evidence survives of his private life, his personality, the colour of his mind. The record of his official behaviour does, however, reveal a marked dualism that also seems to be discernible in his nature. For his advisers he chose the most learned clerics of his time, but as the servants of his will he apparently had a liking for brave, hardy, venturesome men. He showed a sensitivity to the feudal past and was attracted to the traditional ways of the North, and yet he energetically forwarded the interests of the rising middle class and experimented with the machinery of government. Though he was a lord of the moors, a great captain, a doer, he admired the New Learning and seems to have been introspective, though not subtle, of mind. Elements of this antithesis are symbolized in Richard's founding and incorporation of the Heralds' College—the movement towards organization and systematization pointing to the future and the interest in crests, coats of arms and ancestral lineage suggesting a love of the past. This dualism is likewise symbolized in a work, the *Order of Chivalry*, which William Caxton dedicated to King Richard, probably in 1484. The printer, harbinger of the coming day, looks to the King to revive the knightly spirit of a former age, hoping that he may 'command this book to be had and read unto other young lords knights and gentlemen within this royaume that the noble order of Chivalry be hereafter better used and honoured than it hath been in late days passed. . . . And I shall pray almighty God for his long life and prosperous welfare and that he may have victory of all his enemies. . . .'

There is a trace of this dichotomy even in Richard's faith. His religious feeling is conventionally expressed in his foundation of chapels, colleges, chantries, a hospital, and gifts for the repair of churches. But the supposition that Richard was something of a Puritan in temperament is complemented by an extant manuscript which bears what appears to be his genuine autograph: it is a copy of Wyclif's translation of the New Testament.[12] Richard was no secret lollard—a number of 'good catholics' in this age apparently owned such volumes, simply in order to read the Bible in English—but that he perused a lollard Testament suggests a religious experience more powerful and more private than conventional piety.

Little is known of Richard's domestic life; nothing, of his relationship with his mother. There survives only one letter of his to that old woman, once the lovely Rose of Raby, who, having seen and suffered much, now followed the strict regimen of a religious in her castle of Berkhamsted. 'I recommend me to you as heartily as is to me possible', he writes; 'beseeching you in my most humble and effectuous wise of your daily blessing to my singular comfort and defence in my need. And, Madam, I heartily beseech you that I may often hear from you to my comfort. . . . And I pray God send you the accomplishment of your noble desires. . . . Your most humble son. . . .' Though the letter is cast in a customary form, its tone of filial devotion seems to transcend

6 HENRY VII 1457–1509. Artist Unknown

(*National Portrait Gallery, London*)

the merely conventional expression of the times, when sons, even sons of high estate, were expected to be dutiful to their mothers.

It appears that Richard's marriage was happy, that he gave Anne Neville his heart as well as his name. Even the Tudor historians, for all their zest in elaborating monstrous legends of Richard's wickedness, cast no slur upon his marital fidelity, and Mancini gives positive testimony that the purity of his private life was well known to the public. Since he acknowledged, and was at pains to make honourable provision for, two bastard children, it seems likely that they were born before his marriage—the bastards of a bachelor being then regarded as the natural, and therefore unreprehensible, consequence of human frailty. The girl, Katherine Plantagenet, was, in fact, of sufficient age to be married in 1484 and the boy, called John of Pomfret or John of Gloucester, was old enough, though still a minor, to be appointed to high place. Katherine became the wife of William Herbert, Earl of Huntingdon, Richard settling on the couple property worth 1,000 marks a year and a further annuity of £152 10s 10d.

He possessed, so far as they can be descried, cultivated tastes and interests. Both Queen Anne and he had a troupe of minstrels; his choirmaster combed the kingdom for voices of suitable beauty for the royal chapel; even when he was travelling, his daily mass was sung so elaborately as to be admiringly remembered by a foreign visitor who heard it. He was a princely builder. He re-edified numerous castles and palaces, sending on occasion across the sea for the best stone of Caen. He made handsome contributions to the two architectural wonders of his day: an annuity of 250 marks for the finishing of St. George's chapel, and several gifts, crowned by a present of £300, for the building of King's College chapel, Cambridge. Only the scantiest record remains of the books he must have owned—an English version of Renatus's *De re militari*, a French chronicle, a folio volume of tales, including two of Chaucer's, on a leaf of which is written in Richard's hand 'tant le desieree R. Gloucestre'.[13]

Of the man himself, the impact that his personality made upon observers, the tone and texture of his daily behaviour, very little direct evidence is available. Sir William Stanley, no friend of his—what man who hopes to betray another with impunity is not contemptuous of his intended victim?—provides the merest gleam of light in a letter to a friend who had invited him to come hunting. He replies regretfully that he is too pressed by his duties—there is no hope of getting leave at present from 'old Dick'.[14] Now Sir William was quite a few years older

L

than King Richard. The epithet 'old Dick' suggests, perhaps, a disdain of tedious earnestness, of Richard's plain, dull devotion to work. On the other hand, the diary of a German traveller of noble family records an entirely different impression. Nicolas von Poppelau's account of a nine days' sojourn in the King's household provides the most intimate picture of Richard and his daily life that has been preserved.[15]

Arriving in London on April 16, 1484, von Poppelau set out northward to meet the King and finally came up with him early in May at Middleham castle. After presenting Richard with letters of introduction from the Emperor, von Poppelau delivered a Latin oration, which, he notes, elicited the admiration of all—the King taking him graciously by the hand and ordering a chamberlain to conduct him to his lodgings. Next morning he attended a magnificent singing of the Mass and was then admitted to the royal entourage in order to watch Richard at dinner.

'Afterwards the King spoke quite alone with von Poppelau, and asked him a great deal about the emperor and the princes of the empire. Finally he came to speak of the Turks, and when Nicolas told of the victory over the Turk gained by the king of Hungary before St. Martin's day 1483, Richard was delighted and cried out, "I wish that my kingdom lay upon the confines of Turkey; with my own people alone and without the help of other princes I should like to drive away not only the Turks, but all my foes".' During the remainder of his visit von Poppelau dined every day at the royal table and was honoured by Richard with the present of a golden necklace, 'which the king took from the neck of a certain lord'. Though von Poppelau found nothing good to say about the English people, he admired their King. The epitome of his praise was that Richard had a great heart.

Yet the testimony of these moments, the isolating of qualities and parts, do not approach the sum of the man. It appears that few in his own day understood or were intimate with Richard, and he eludes us too—a blurred figure, dark. . . . Not an obscurity deriving only from the paucity of records; there is a darkness within as well as upon him.

The passionately loyal brother who was Constable of England and commander in his 'teens, who indefatigably bolstered Edward's throne and won the devotion of the North, may readily be traced in the King earnestly seeking to dispense justice to his subjects and exerting a prodigious vitality to deal with the problems of his government. But between these lives stands the Protector who usurped the throne, the brother who thus doomed, if he did not murder, the boy King who was

Edward's son. The dislocation of this middle moment can be divined, it is true, in the progressive corrosion worked upon Richard's relation with his brother by the direction of Edward's later life; and its consequences plainly show themselves in the King's labour to atone for his rupture of the succession, in his compulsive reliance upon loyalty rather than force, and the haunted and feverish pursuit of welldoing that wore out his heart. Yet it is a fractured life, and the man who lived it must also have been, obscurely, fractured.

His early years had pressed harshly upon him; the sickliness of his body, the violence surrounding his childhood, had thrown him in upon himself; unresilient and unexuberant, he met force of circumstance by force of will. He found a master outlet for his emotions and his instinct to aspire, loyalty to Edward; and this drove him to a bare and simple organization of his life, to grow strong and to serve. The responsibilities so early thrust upon him and never afterwards lightened worked only to harden the fibres of his character. Thus it was impossible for him to communicate himself easily and warmly to the world. The austere landscape of his spirit, ribbed with the rock of will, faithfully supported its burdens but it could not bloom; and thus it somehow intimidated or repelled even as it served.

The earnestness with which Richard applied himself, the stiff restraints of his character, the formidable impact of his control—these sometimes lamed what they accomplished by the unease which they stirred. What his brothers could command with a smile, he could win only by effort. It may be that the tense and passionate and sudden choice which propelled him to the throne represented a cracking of this bleak restraint, the explosion of a spirit too tightly confined. Perhaps he briefly persuaded himself that he could be other than he was or finally rebelled when the urge to retaliate against the past became irresistible. But the marble chair of King's Bench pressed hard and inexorable, forcing him back into the prison of his conscience and the habit of his duty.

He seems to have emerged from an earlier world . . . ruder and more naïve and simpler. He has in him something of the first martyrs and something of the Germanic chieftain. An elemental fierceness, subjugated to duty, once broke loose: a grim sense of moral responsibility sat in harsh judgment upon the outburst. If we cannot see his portrait clearly, we can at least choose its painter—not Holbein or even Rembrandt, but perhaps El Greco. Yet though his will was edged with iron and his mind was rigid, he was delicately aware of the feelings of others and sought unwaveringly to work the welfare of those he governed. The harmony he never achieved within himself he did not cease to desire for his fellows. That harmony had been denied him first by circumstance, then by his brother's deterioration, and finally, cumulatively, by the compulsions of his own character.

One flash of that character, a moment of self-revelation, is transmitted in an undated letter which he addressed to his Chancellor, probably when he was on his progress in the summer of 1483.

While Mistress Jane Shore lay in Ludgate prison after doing her public penance for harlotry, a report reached Richard that his Solicitor, Thomas Lynom, was actually on the verge of marrying the woman whose hostile plotting with Hastings he had so recently been investigating. Politically and morally, Richard took a harsh view of Mistress Shore and he might well persuade himself that he was acting for Lynom's good in prohibiting the match. But this is the letter which he wrote to John Russell:

> Signifying unto you, that it is showed unto us, that our servant and solicitor, Thomas Lynom, marvellously blinded and abused with the late wife of William Shore, now being in Ludgate by our commandment, hath made contract of matrimony with her, as it is said; and intendeth, to our full great marvel, to proceed to effect the same. We, for many causes, would be very sorry that he should be so disposed; and pray you, therefore, to send for him, in that ye goodly may exhort and stir him to the contrary.
>
> And, if ye find him utter set for to marry her, and none otherwise would be advertised, then, if it may stand with the law of the church, we be content (the time of marriage being deferred to our coming next to London) that, upon sufficient surety being found of her good a-bearing, ye do send for her keeper, and discharge him of our commandment by warrant of these; committing her to the rule and guiding of her father or any other, by your discretion in the mean season.

Lynom decided not to marry Mistress Shore; he apparently continued to serve Richard faithfully, and to enjoy Richard's favour.

X

WITH the beginning of the new year (1485), a murky shadow seems to descend upon the King. His writs and grants decline in number. Immobile, his life all but hidden, he remains for months immured in his palace. This is the longest sojourn in his capital he is ever to experience. True, the country is quiet; there is no need for the King to stir abroad. Since Buckingham's rebellion the realm has known internal peace, and as a consequence of Richard's diplomacy and generalship it now enjoys stable relations with most of its foreign neighbours. Richard has appointed some commissions of *oyer and terminer* to investigate treasonable activities; but these, like Colyngbourne's plotting, have apparently been the schemes of Henry Tudor's scattered partisans, representing no real disaffection in the nation at large.

Yet a cloud has descended upon Richard. It is a period of suspension the man turned inward upon himself. Except for a few forced and painful sallies into the world, these months represent a withdrawal, a lonely wrestling with the shapes of the past and the mocking, amorphous images of the future. King Saul has retired within the cave of the Witch of Endor. He will return to the demands of life with only his courage and his resolution unravaged.

Richard lay at his palace of Westminster, waiting. In expectation of Henry Tudor's descent, he could ease his heart a little by commanding his officers to prepare against invasion and the lords and gentry to hold themselves ready to answer his summons. But against the fast-approaching death of his Queen there was nothing he could do. As January gave way to February, Anne took to the bed from which she would not rise again. While she wasted away, her physicians declared to Richard that her illness was not only mortal but contagious; he must not share her chamber. At least once, the tide of his despair rose beyond his control. To his former enemy whom he had since treated as a friend and a familiar, Thomas Rotherham, Archbishop of York, he cried out in agony that he had lost everything—his son had been taken from him—Anne had been able to bear him no more children—and now she too was slipping away, leaving him barren, alone.

With the coming of March it was clear that she was dying. Groping for a gleam of light in his darkness, for some thread of meaningful continuity in his life, Richard, on March 11, appointed his bastard son John, Captain of Calais, calling him in the patent, the writ for which he doubtless wrote out with his own hand, 'our dear son, our bastard John of Gloucester whose quickness of mind, agility of body, and inclination to all good customs give us great hope of his good service for the future.'[1]

Five days later, while the people of England gaped at a great eclipse of the sun, Anne died. With high ceremony her body was borne to Westminster Abbey and interred near the south door leading into St. Edward's chapel.

She was scarcely in her grave—perhaps not even yet dead—when

Richard discovered that a fog of rumour had crept over the palace walls to envelop him.

It was whispered that he was planning to marry his niece Elizabeth, and the gossip was tricked out with dark hints that he was far from unhappy to see his wife descend into the tomb. The very kindness with which Richard and Anne had treated the Queen's daughters, the position of princely dignity they had accorded Elizabeth during the Christmas festivities, were now turned against the King.

The rumours may have had a slender foundation in actuality. It is probable that in his wretchedness Richard had given vent to his longing for an heir, had desperately or grimly tossed out a mention of the Princess Elizabeth, whom Henry Tudor had sworn to marry in order to hold the Woodville faction to his side. He said enough to alarm two of his most intimate advisers, William Catesby and Sir Richard Ratcliffe, who were touchy on the point for reasons of their own. He said enough to enable a treacherous councillor to set in motion the machinery of gossip. That he ever seriously contemplated marrying his niece is unlikely. To deny her to the Tudor, he had only to wed her to any man of his choosing. To marry her himself would be tacitly to acknowledge that the pre-contract was an invention and he, a usurper. It did not require the cunning of Louis XI to read this elementary lesson in polity.[2]* Polydore Vergil himself has revealed the secret enemy in whom Richard by favour and friendliness had sought in vain to kindle loyalty. It was Thomas Rotherham, Archbishop of York, who had wrought the words Richard had spoken in confidence into a morsel of malicious gossip.

These rumours about Elizabeth were but a new stage in the campaign of slander which the partisans of Henry Tudor had begun waging the year before. In the previous December Richard had written to the Mayor of Windsor about the false reports, invented by 'our ancient enemies of France' [a reminder that Henry Tudor was now an instrument of French interests], which were being circulated by seditious persons to provoke discord and division between the King and his lords; the Mayor was commanded to examine 'the first showers and utterers thereof' and commit them to prison as an example to others.[3] The employment of rumour and broadsides for political purposes was not new, as has been shown, and Henry VII would find himself attacked by this same weapon. But the campaign carried on by the Tudor's partisans seems to have been more deliberately organized than any which had preceded it. It was undoubtedly Rotherham who had betrayed Richard's negotiations with Brittany to John Morton in Flanders and who kept that consummate intriguer in touch with events. Morton was probably one of the directors of the campaign as Reynold Bray, the shrewd, energetic servant of Stanley's wife, whom Richard had pardoned despite his prominent role in Buckingham's revolt, was unquestionably another. Since there was little they dreaded more than that the King might marry off the girl on whom depended much of Henry's support, it seems likely that, whether genuinely alarmed or not, they seized the advantage of the Queen's death to prevent, by slanderously mooting it, a marriage that would play havoc with their hopes. Both the intensity and the frail substance of this guerilla warfare-by-rumour suggest that the Tudor partisans were experiencing some difficulty in finding authentic injustices or severities on which they could capitalize.

Meanwhile, in these gloomy March days of his grief, Richard turned to hunting, a pastime in which he had showed no marked interest. Toward the end of Anne's illness and after her death he called for hawks and falcons, and men were sent into Wales and even beyond the sea to secure them for the King, who sought in the open air of field and forest and in the clean plummet of the bird of prey some release from the arena of his emotions.[4] This reflex of pain availed little. Soon he was goaded into denying to his own council the rumour that he intended to marry his niece. So fearful were Catesby and Ratcliffe of the revenge which Elizabeth might seek because they had urged the execution of her uncle Rivers and her half-brother Richard Grey, that they belaboured the King with arguments of Doctors of Divinity affirming the marriage to be incestuous and with their own declarations that the North would never accept such an insult to the memory of Warwick's daughter. Distracted by his grief and his impotent anger and the clamour of these advisers, Richard impetuously assembled within the great hall of the hospital of the Knights of St. John in Clerkenwell the Mayor, Aldermen and chief citizens of London, the lords spiritual and temporal then at the capital, and the officers of his Household. He stood before them to deny 'in a loud and distinct voice' the gossip which had been spread against him and to charge all public officers with the duty of apprehending seditious rumour-mongers.

A few days later he informed his friends, the men of York, of his public denial and reiterated his command that the bearers of false tidings be apprehended and their tales traced. The opening of his letter shows signs of wear and strain. 'It is so,' he wrote, 'that divers seditious and evil disposed persons (both in our city of London and elsewhere within this our realm) enforce themselves daily to sow seed of noise and disclaundre against our person, and against many of the lords and estates of our land, to abuse the multitude of our subjects and avert their minds from us . . . some by setting up of bills, some by messages and sending forth of . . . lies, some by bold and presumptuous open speech and communication one with another, wherethrough the innocent people which would live in rest and peace, and truly under our obeisance . . . be greatly abused, and oft times put in dangers of their lives, lands and goods, as oft as they follow the . . . devices of the said seditious persons, to our great heaviness and pity. . . .'[5]

Henceforth there grew in Richard's heart an anger against Henry Tudor, who used the arrow which flies by night to attack his honour and flung poisoned barbs to prick the skin of England's peace.

Meanwhile, Henry was 'pinched by the very stomach', as Vergil puts it, at the thought of King Richard's marrying Elizabeth. The report had arrived at a critical moment in his affairs. After taking hasty counsel with his chief followers, he pitched upon a substitute bride, the sister of Sir Walter Herbert, a man of influence in Wales. Since the Earl of Northumberland's wife was kin to Sir Walter, Henry sought, according to Vergil, to open communications with the Earl by sending him two messengers, both of whom were intercepted by men loyal to the King. It was soon clear, however, that Richard was not going to marry Elizabeth, and Henry resumed the military preparations which not long before he had been able to begin.

Henry had had no easy time since he had passed into France. For a man pretending to a royal destiny to play humble suitor to a King is bad enough; Henry had to sue to divers lords and councillors as well. The court of France was still a battleground of factions, none of which Henry could afford to neglect. Hat in hand, supple of mind and of smile, he must needs beg of them all. It was the moment of his exile which would require many years of absolute rule and the proud Spanish marriage—of his son Arthur to Katherine of Aragon—to wipe out. He had effective resources, however. He was himself of the royal line of Valois, his father and Louis XI being first cousins; he had been so long on the Continent that his language and his manner, no less than his blood, must have made him seem half a Frenchman to the court of Charles VIII; and though, afterwards, he would be very sparing of his charm, he was able now to speak so movingly of his 'wrongs' and so persuasively of his 'rights' that Commynes was much impressed.[6] The

Regent, Charles VIII's sister, feared Richard's intentions towards France and had her father's dealings with Edward to guide her. To weaken England, she must encourage pretenders to its throne. If they succeed, they may be grateful; at least, they will be too shallowly rooted to offer trouble for some time. If they fail, they may nonetheless provoke a period of civil strife; at worst, the aid given them—never very much—can be disavowed.

Before the coming of spring, Henry's begging had succeeded. And none knew better than he that it was high time. The escape of Oxford had been a great stroke of fortune; but the Marquess of Dorset's attempt to steal away cast an ominous light upon the future. He could not for long sustain the hope of his followers in England or of his band of exiles. He must go forward, or decline into the precarious desuetude of a French pensioner, which might be no less dangerous than the invasion which he contemplated. Having finally extracted from the court of Charles a promise of money, ships, and some troops, he was setting up his headquarters at Rouen when he was distracted by the report of Richard's marriage plans.

Richard, meanwhile, was kept informed by his agents of Henry Tudor's preparations, and, in his outward life, he applied himself to the task of countering the blow.

The heavy costs of suppressing Buckingham's rebellion and of conducting military operations on land and sea during 1484 and the liberality of his grants and gifts had now seriously depleted his treasury. Seldom, if ever, had a King undertaken such prolonged employment of fleet and army without the financial support of a parliamentary grant. To find the ready money he needed for the defence of the realm, he was compelled to resort to loans. He made it clear that these requests were not the benevolences which his Parliament had outlawed. For the loans which he floated among the merchants of London he provided, as he had done the year before, 'good and sufficient pledges', and the invitations to subscribe money which the royal commissioners—carefully coached in the courteous language they were to use—delivered to the wealthy gentlemen and abbots of the shires, bore a specific promise of repayment in two instalments spread over a little less than a year and a half. Only a few loans of as much as £200 were asked; most were from £40 to £100 or 100 marks. A number of the 'charters' were issued bearing the names of men to be approached; others were to be filled in at the discretion of the commissioners. The solicitation lasted from late February until April 1, Good Friday, and seems to have brought in

L*

about £20,000—a heartening amount, considering that the customary parliamentary tax of a Fifteenth and a Tenth netted only some £31,000 (after a deduction of £6,000 for the relief of decayed towns). Benevolence or not, however, the measure was obviously far from popular.[7]

As the season of sea storms and bogged roads gave way to the sun of spring, Richard learned that Henry Tudor's fleet was rigging at Harfleur and that the government of Charles VIII was providing men and money as well as ships. When the blow would come and where it would strike, the King's agents had been unable to discover.

There was small chance that the exiles would attempt to land in the North or in East Anglia, districts loyal to the King in which they had developed no following. The south and the southeastern coasts had seen successful invasions in the past and would be the more vulnerable since Richard meant to go northward again in order to station himself at Nottingham. In 1461 the Yorkist lords of Calais had entered the Kingdom through Sandwich; eleven years later, Queen Margaret landed at Weymouth; and in 1483 Henry Tudor had touched at Poole in Dorset. All these ports were not much more than a day's march from London, and London seemed to be the touchstone of the fortunes of the House of York. Hence, in April, Richard dispatched Sir George Neville to sea with a fleet to watch the channel and guard the harbours of Kent.[8] Viscount Lovell was set to strengthening the coast defences and mustering the forces of the southern counties. As for the capital itself, a good store of ordnance had been accumulated in the Tower, and the Duke of Norfolk would remain in East Anglia to guard the approaches to the city, as he had done at the outbreak of Buckingham's rebellion. In the West, Richard took no precautions beyond the ones addressed to the whole kingdom. A few of his northern friends like John, Lord Scrope of Bolton held positions of authority in Devon and Cornwall.[9] The chief supporters of Henry Tudor or the Woodvilles had fled to Brittany, and the rebuff Henry had encountered at Plymouth was not one he was likely to risk again. The West was no hotbed of Yorkist sympathies but neither did it appear to be propitious soil for invasion.

There remained Wales. Henry Tudor was half a Welshman; his followers boasted that he was descended from the misty line of Welsh Kings; and though the men of Wales were not given to uniting in a cause, he offered them an expression of national pride and national aspirations which had been stifled for three-quarters of a century. His uncle, Jasper Tudor, still styled himself Earl of Pembroke and had been a great lord of the land. In the 1460's he had held Harlech castle for the cause of Lancaster long after the rest of England was Edward's. The disappearance of Buckingham had left a gap in the royal government. Wales was controlled piece-meal by officers of the King and native chieftains like Rhys ap Thomas. James Tyrell, Knight of the Body and one of Richard's most trusted servants, ruled Glamorgan and Morgannok; but Tyrell had to be sent to hold Guisnes castle, and the charge of these lordships must needs be left to his deputies.[10]

Richard was not without resources in Wales, however. Fifteen years before he had had a brief experience of governing the Marches, and since becoming King he had shown favour to the Welsh. Many had proved themselves loyal during Buckingham's rebellion and a number had been rewarded with small annuities. Morgan Kidwelly, Richard's Attorney-General, was a Welshman. Rhys ap Thomas, the principal chieftain of South Wales, protested that Henry Tudor would have to pass over his belly to penetrate that country. The Chief Justiceship was in the hands of William Herbert, Earl of Huntingdon, Richard's son-in-law and scion of a family which had long been identified with the region. Finally, on the eastern border of Wales stretched a great demesne of Mortimer and York lands, now united to the Crown, which, along with the Severn river, formed a stout barrier against an incursion from the Marches.

In the northeast of England, however, lay the power of the Stanleys. Sir William owned most of East Denbighshire, was the Chief Justice of North Wales, and wielded great influence in Shropshire. His brother Lord Stanley and Stanley's son Lord Strange dominated Cheshire and Lancashire. If Henry Tudor landed on his ancestral shore and struck north, the Stanleys would hold the position of critical importance. What manner of men they were, none had better reason to know than Richard the King.

The coming of May found him still in London. Not until the middle of the month did he bid farewell to his capital and ride to Windsor accompanied by the Knights and Esquires of his Household, by Lord Stanley, John Kendall, William Catesby and other advisers. A body of councillors remained in London to carry on the government, headed by Chancellor Russell. Viscount Lovell was stationed at Southampton to see to the refitting of the fleet and to lead the forces of the southern counties against an attempted landing in that neighbourhood. John, Duke of Norfolk and his son the Earl of Surrey stood ready in Essex.

The immediate defence of the capital was committed to Sir Robert Brackenbury, the Constable of the Tower.

From Windsor, Richard moved to Kenilworth, where he lingered for at least two weeks. It was probably the middle of June when he took up his watch upon the great rock which towered above the town of Nottingham. He had come home to the Castle of his Care.[11]

At this time he sent the eldest daughter of Edward IV to reside in the household of the Council of the North, which now lay at Sheriff Hutton, not far from the city of York. This castle was become a stone chalice, holding much of what was left of the blood royal of York: the Princess Elizabeth and doubtless one or more of her sisters, the Earls of Warwick and of Lincoln, Lord Morley, husband of one of Lincoln's sisters, and perhaps Richard's bastard son, John of Gloucester.

Richard continued with the customary measures of defence. On June 21 he ordered his Chancellor to issue another proclamation against 'Piers Bishop of Exeter, Jasper Tidder son of Owen Tidder calling himself Earl of Pembroke, John late Earl of Oxon, and Sir Edward Widevile, with other . . . rebels and traitors . . . [who] have chosen to be their captain one Henry Tidder, which of his . . . insatiable covetousness . . . usurpeth upon him the name and title of royal estate of this Roialme. . . .' Except that the Marquess of Dorset's name was now omitted and the bastard descent of Henry 'Tidder' was traced, this proclamation is almost identical with the one Richard had published the previous December. The kingdom was warned that Henry had surrendered all English claims in France and had promised the great lands, offices, and Church dignities of England to his followers; and all subjects of the King were called on 'to be ready in their most defensible array, to do his Highness service of war. . . .'[12]

Next day Richard sent instructions to his commissioners of array in all the shires. They were commanded 'first that they, in the King's behalf, thank the people for their true and loving disposition showed to his highness the last year, for the . . . defence of his . . . person and of this his realm against his rebels and traitors; exhorting them so to continue'. Next, they were to review the levies 'and see that they be able men, and well horsed and harnessed, and no rascal'. Lastly the commissioners were to 'show all Lords, Noblemen, captains, and other, that the King's noble pleasure and commandment is, that they truly and honourably—all manner quarrels, grudges, rancours, and unkindness laid apart—attend and execute the King's commandment, and everyone be loving and assisting to other in the King's quarrels and cause'. At the same time the sheriffs of the shires were ordered to remain at their posts that they might be ready for instant action as soon as the invasion was reported.[13]

These precautions represented—save for the characteristically intimate and earnest tone of the instructions to commissioners—the ordinary machinery of defence in this age. Richard apparently did not—or would not—consider Henry Tudor a mortally dangerous threat to his crown. To make such an admission to his kingdom, to confess it to himself, would be an acknowledgment that government by desert was a failure or that he had failed in the measure of his desert. The heart of his proud disdain for the pretensions of the Tudor was contained in his refusal to marry off Elizabeth and her sisters. The promise of marriage to a daughter of Edward IV was the very pith of Henry Tudor's strength, the scaffolding of his claim, the sole means of projecting himself as a national figure rather than a factional chieftain. When Elizabeth Woodville sent forth her daughters from sanctuary, she had dealt Henry a deadly blow, of which Richard refused to take advantage. Was there an archaic residue of chivalric feeling in his refusal? In the case that Heaven chose to bless the Tudor's enterprise, finding him, Richard, wanting in its enigmatic scales of justice, did Richard conceive it to be the part of honour and the way of God's will to leave Princess Elizabeth's destiny to be decided by the ordeal of battle? Or did the thought flicker across his mind that she might escape beyond the sea, if he were defeated, and one day restore in its own right the blood of his brother Edward to the throne? Only the fact itself speaks clearly: he did not give Edward's daughters in marriage in order to put them beyond the reach of the only enemy who threatened his rule.[14]*

Below these outward manifestations of his life there flowed a profounder compulsion, a deep and undeviating stream on which his daily acts floated in eddies and superficial currents which masked the ineluctable course beneath. He moved now like a man walking under the postulates of a dream, half fulfilling and half creating the direction of his life. Forward went the search to discover in him who had taken the throne from his brother's son the lineaments of the man he had thought himself to be. Rigidly continued the testing of his own actions, and the estimating of others', by the assumptions on which his conscience had permitted him to become King. Yet his grip on life had been progressively undermined by emotional disasters. He had recreated Clarence in Buckingham and Buckingham had promptly fulfilled the recreation by betraying him. He had taken the throne from Edward's son and Heaven had soon after taken his own son from him. The woman to whom he had given the life of his heart had sunk into the grave, stricken by despair as much as disease. His effort to rule well had been mocked by rumour, the quiet of the realm and his own peace poisoned by conspiracy. His courage had not diminished; his will to pursue the path he had marked out did not falter. But he could not sink the man in the King. The tide of hope had drained away from his resolves, leaving them exposed as barren and stony absolutes. Perhaps there flickered within him an inarticulate feeling that to follow the trail straight off the map might provide some ultimate confirmation of its validity.

Not long after Richard reached Nottingham, he made the choice which signalled the direction of his course. To him came Thomas, Lord Stanley with his thin, shrewd face[15]—full of years and gravity and exemplary sentiments and prudent counsel and exudations of loyalty— to ask leave to retire for a time to his estates, from which he had been long absent, in order to rest and refresh himself. Should the invasion occur during this interval, he was quick to point out, he would be the better able, at home, to rally his men to the King's cause.

Richard listened, studying Stanley's face—had he not always known that this request would be made? From the day he had taken the man into his favour after the execution of Hastings, there is no record that Lord Stanley had ever left his side. This baron had great experience of affairs both military and civil, had for more than a decade been an assiduous servant of King Edward's, and proved himself a worthy captain in Richard's great campaign against the Scots. As Steward of Richard's royal Household,[16] he must needs be in close attendance upon the King; and the business of his estates, his local authorities, he had his energetic brother Sir William and his son Lord Strange to look after for him. Yet both Richard and he knew—each aware that the other must be likewise aware—that there could be a more compelling motive, on Richard's part, for asking this constant service and, on Stanley's, a prudent reason to refrain from seeking leave to depart from court. As long as Stanley was in attendance, Richard did not have to recognize the possibility of his disloyalty.

In a century of civil strife, fierce partisanship, betrayals, broken causes, in which many among the lords and gentry had been brought to ruin or extinction, Lord Stanley and his brother Sir William had thrived. They thrived by daring to make politics their trade, by sloughing off the encumbrances of loyalty and honour, by developing an ambiguity of attitude which enabled them to join the winning side, and by exploiting the relative facility with which treason in this age might be lived down, provided it were neither too passionate, overt nor damaging.

In 1459 the Stanleys had begun the operations which were to bring them great lands and high place. Sir William joined the cause of the Duke of York and following the disaster at Ludlow was attainted by the Lancastrian Parliament which met soon after. Thomas delayed and temporized, ignoring several royal summonses, and when he at last appeared at Blore Heath with 2,000 men at his back, he stood idly by while the Earl of Salisbury defeated the Lancastrian army sent to crush him. The Commons petitioned for his attainder, but Stanley had sufficiently developed his arts to persuade King Henry's lords to forgive him. Though he duly took his place in the army which opposed the Yorkists at Northampton in 1460, he apparently fought with little heart, for the victors promptly made him Chief Justice of Cheshire and Flint. The appointment is the more remarkable considering that a decade before his father had been one of the Queen's emissaries who attempted to ambush the Duke of York on his journeys to and from Ireland.

He espoused Warwick's cause in the late 1460's; but just as Warwick and Clarence, in March of 1470, were fleeing to him for the succour he had promised, he was given a fright by Richard of Gloucester, and, hastily deciding that the Earl's chances were dim, he refused to stir. Yet, on Warwick's invading the Kingdom the following October, Lord Stanley rode into London at his side, having managed to excuse his previous desertion. When Edward and Richard returned from Burgundy, the Stanley brothers again divided their allegiance. Sir William is reported to have joined Edward at Nottingham with 300 men. Lord Stanley was besieging Hornby castle for King Henry.[17] He apparently lay low until Barnet and Tewkesbury had unmistakably demonstrated the triumph of the House of York. Then he reappeared before King Edward, and so convincing was his self-exculpation that he was not only forgiven the betrayal of his oath to Edward—cancelled by the betrayal of his oath to Henry—but Edward made him one of his intimate advisers and Steward of his Household. Thus his success in extricating himself from the collapse of Hastings' conspiracy was but a further manifestation of an accomplished political agility; and his ambiguous position during Buckingham's rebellion—when the speedy ruin of his wife's cause and his being caught at Richard's side made it inexpedient for him to show his colours—represented the familiar juggling with allegiance which he had ever been able to manage to the increase of his fortunes. If his wife lost her estates, he became Constable of England, received huge grants of lands, as well as possession for life of the Countess's property, and bounded into a position of the greatest influence with the King.

Granted his smooth pliancy, his shrewd and wary manoeuvring, his wonderful capacity to inspire confidence, still, at a remove of five centuries, it remains puzzling that he so often escaped the consequences of his betrayals. Part of the answer may be that Kings like Edward and Richard seem, paradoxically, to have been less sensitive—or more charitable—to treason than the impersonal governments of our day. The traitor was not then, as now, automatically seized by the machinery of law and condemned and executed for faithlessness to a concept called the state. In the fifteenth century treason was highly personal, the desertion of an oath made by a man to his lord, the breaking of an intimate compact. Because the offence was personal it was bitter, but it was forgivable; and medieval people were apparently more tolerant of human frailty and its effects than ourselves—as, for example, with bastards, who were by and large accepted as the inevitable fruit of man's weakness. The traitor did not disappear into the automatic jaws of law, his fate on no man's hands. He confronted the judgment of the King he had wronged, and might therefore—if the King were generous and he, artful—elicit mercy, play upon kindness, soften anger, to evade the penalty of his offence. It is also true that in the fifteenth century, when broken allegiance was endemic and monarchs were not settled in sanctity, political advantage often prompted a King to overlook a discreet treason, particularly when committed out of self-interest rather than incorrigible partisanship. After all, it was likely that the motive of interest might be touched to secure loyalty, as it had previously led to disaffection; and the expectation of good service, a commodity of which the King in these days always stood in need, could quench the desire to administer punishment, which punishment itself might lead to fresh trouble if the traitor were of a great house or had built himself a staunch following.

Such were the shifting courses of the Stanleys and such were the conditions of fifteenth century kingship which enabled Lord Stanley and Sir William to grow fat upon a diet that had brought mortal pangs to many. During these two and a half decades of Yorkist rule they had not only come to great power in the royal government but by assiduously cultivating their local authority and influence, they had made themselves masters of Cheshire, Lancashire, North Wales, and part of Shropshire. There now were few lords besides themselves whom men had served for a generation. Except for the Duke of Norfolk and the Earl of Northumberland, the Stanleys commanded the greatest seignorial power in England.

Of this power none was more aware than Richard, as he was aware too that the power was wielded over a territory contiguous to Henry Tudor's homeland of Wales, that if the Tudor triumphed Stanley would become the step-father of a King, that Stanley had made cause with Hastings against him in 1483 and remembered the scare Richard had given him in 1470, that Stanley would probably have betrayed him if Buckingham's rebellion had begun to prosper, and that the Stanleys had always tailored their allegiance to their advantage and their protestations of loyalty to the exigencies of the moment.

Had he not always known that Thomas, Lord Stanley would request permission to depart when the time had ripened and was come to its fullness? Glancing at his stout Yeomen of the Crown, Richard realized that he had but to move his hand and, whatever course the House of Stanley might take, the enigma of Lord Stanley himself would be solved by simply holding him in custody until the invasion had been mastered. No doubt John Kendall, Ratcliffe, Catesby, when they learned of Stanley's desire, begged him to refuse it. Would the King, having kept this cunningest of lords this long under his eye, permit him to depart in the very imminence of Henry Tudor's landing?

The King would. Lord Stanley must be allowed to ride away, in order that his allegiance be freely given, or in the critical hour Richard would be evading the test which he had set for himself and his rule. He had, in fact, boldly committed himself to his course six months before. On January 13 he had dispatched commands to the lords and gentry of Cheshire and Lancashire that when word came of the invasion they were to obey as their leaders Lord Stanley, his son Lord Strange, and his brother Sir William. Commander and captain though he was, Richard listened to another language than strategy and he was moved by a deeper compulsion than reason.

Yet, in the end, yielding to the demands of his councillors or unable to resist exposing to Stanley his awareness of Stanley's capacity for betrayal, he made a condition. Since decisive events were approaching and he needed men of experience about him, Thomas must send for Lord Strange to act as his deputy during his absence. Stanley gracefully acquiesced, sent for Strange, who promptly appeared. Then this accommodating lord, aware that his son had been demanded as a hostage and that Richard knew that he knew it, rode westward into his own country, where his wiliness was so much a by-word that two centuries later it was still being alluded to.[18]*

Richard must have realized that he had blunted the pure edge of his test. Not much but a little. It was a wedge of compromise that hardened him against allowing further compromises with his chosen destiny. Lord Strange he welcomed warmly, made him an intimate. But Richard's friends saw to it that he was watched by able men.

July was slipping away now. Richard probably received word from his agents in France that Henry was about to sail, for on the 24th he wrote to his Chancellor asking him to send the Great Seal at once by Thomas Barowe, Master of the Rolls. There is no reason to suppose that Richard had lost confidence in John Russell. He needed the Seal directly at hand; it was more fitting for the Bishop of Lincoln to remain at the head of the government in London than to be exposed to the rigours of the field. In the late afternoon of the first day of August, Thomas Barowe rode into Nottingham. At seven o'clock in the evening in the chapel of the castle he came before the King and there delivered up the Great Seal. Richard was attended by Thomas Rotherham, Archbishop of York, his heir John, Earl of Lincoln, Lord Scrope of Upsale, Lord Strange, John Kendall, and others.[19]

Now there was nothing to do but wait. England was as tense and thundery as the summer weather. The long continued, wearing threat of invasion had worked as an aid to the invasion itself. The realm had wearied of living with one hand upon the sword—but not the men of York. Merchants, artisans, 'prentices, they had left their occupations and their wives to accompany Richard into Scotland in 1482. In June of 1483 they had marched to London. Less than four months later they once more donned jacks and sallets* to follow the King all the way to Salisbury. Now they had again been commanded to hold themselves in readiness to march they knew not where in order to risk their necks in King Richard's quarrel. But the men of York were hardened to warfare, and they had long known Richard. Though there was plague in the city, they were alertly waiting to take up arms once more. The spirit of the men of York, however, did not animate all England.[20]

Still the days passed. The haze of late summer blurred the hills which ring Nottingham. And high on his rock, alone within his thoughts,

* tough leather coats and helmets.

King Richard waited in the Castle of his Care or went hunting in Sherwood forest. He had no army with him, only the Knights and Esquires of his Body and certain of his most intimate followers and their servants. Why did he wait thus, naked of arms? Perhaps pride compelled him so to affirm his disdain of Henry Tudor's challenge. Perhaps he shrank as long as he could from testing the loyalty of his subjects, that loyalty which he had stubbornly made the aim of his policy and the criterion of his reign.

On July 31, at the sign of the Red Pale within the precincts of Westminster Abbey, William Caxton had finished printing a redaction of famous chivalric tales composed by an obscure knight. Sir Thomas Malory's *Morte d'Arthur* fell upon a world in arms. On August 11 a messenger lashed his horse through Sherwood forest to Beskwood lodge in order to bring King Richard the tidings that at last the foot of Henry Tudor was on Britain's shore. Setting sail from Harfleur on the day Richard had received the Great Seal, the rebel host had landed at Milford Haven in South Wales on Sunday, August 7.[21]*

XI*

IN the spring Henry Tudor had received a message from John Morgan, a Welsh lawyer, that Sir John Savage, who was a man of authority in South Wales, and Rhys ap Thomas, its leading chieftain, were sworn to his cause. If Henry had had doubts about where he should land, they were dispelled by these tidings. The Stanleys sent word—or it was reported of them—that they would support Lord Stanley's wife's son. More encouragement came from the Lady Margaret's indefatigable servant Reynold Bray; he had gathered a considerable sum of money and was keeping in touch with adherents throughout the country. Henry sent secret messages to his followers in England promising to pass over the sea as soon as they had reported how many men they could assemble for the cause.[1]

He had left in Paris the Marquess Dorset and John Bourchier as pledges for the 40,000 livres which the government of King Charles had advanced. The French fleet of about fifteen ships, which was fitting at Harfleur, was to be commanded by Philippe de Shaundé. Now the court of France made its final contribution—a force of 2,000 men, but not regular troops or even mercenaries. They were the sweepings of the gaols of Normandy, offered their release on the condition that they would embark with the English adventurer. One could not find, Commynes remarks, a more evil lot.[2] Henry's commanders were his uncle Jasper Tudor, Earl of Pembroke, and John, Earl of Oxford; the chief figures among the band of English exiles were, except for Sir Edward Woodville, those who had fled to Brittany after the collapse of Buckingham's rebellion: John Cheyney, William Brandon, Thomas Arundel, Richard Guildford, William Berkeley, and a few others.

On the first of August Henry Tudor set sail from Harfleur with about 2,500 men to attempt the conquest of the English throne. It was a venture that certainly required courage, but Henry meant to be prudent in its expenditure, as he was to be prudent in expenditure of most kinds. He was probably spurred more by necessity than boldness; and his powerful ambition had perhaps persuaded him to believe, or to half believe, that he was indeed the heir of Cadwallader and the hope of England. More immediately pressing was his realization that this was the best, doubtless the last, opportunity he would ever have.

Weather sped the invaders. With a fair wind they sailed around Richard's fleet cruising off the southeastern ports, and on the afternoon of Sunday, August 7, they entered the great bay of Milford Haven at the tip of Pembrokeshire. Shortly before sunset they landed on the north shore of the bay near the village of Dale.[3] Henry knelt upon the sand and implored the favour of Heaven. 'With meek countenance and pure devotion,' says Fabyan, '[he] began this psalm: "Judica me Deus, et discerne causam meam . . ."' after which he kissed the ground and made the sign of the cross.[4] The rebel host remained that night at Dale. Next day Henry marched ten miles eastward to Haverfordwest, where he received some good, and some very bad, news. A delegation from Pembroke came in to promise that the town would serve Jasper Tudor, its 'natural' lord. At the same time tidings arrived that, contrary to their oaths, Rhys ap Thomas and John Savage were in arms to uphold King Richard's cause. Sending out scouts, Henry cautiously marched northwestward towards Cardigan; after he had gone only five miles he halted to await news. Suddenly a rumour blazed through his army that Sir Walter Herbert, whose headquarters were at Carmarthen, some thirty miles due east, was about to fall upon them with a mighty host. Panic ran through the ranks; Henry's commanders hastily sent out fresh scouts to search the roads. With vast relief Henry learned that the rumour was baseless and that the road to Cardigan was clear. Shortly after his force once more resumed its march, he was cheered by the arrival of the lawyer, John Morgan, with a band of followers. The small garrisons he now began to encounter were quickly overwhelmed or persuaded to submit. Halting in or near Cardigan, Henry learned that, somewhere to the northeast, Rhys ap Thomas was indeed in arms but giving no indication of what party he meant to espouse. Quickly Henry sent him word that the Lieutenantship of all Wales was his for life if he would come to the aid of his fellow-Welshman. Meanwhile, the host pursued a northeast course through Cardiganshire in order to pick up all possible followers in Wales and to screen their movements from King Richard as long as they could. The Tudor was marching under the dragon banner of Cadwallader. Here and there in the Welsh valleys the harps of bards were thrumming his descent from Celtic Kings or the coming again of Arthur—

> Jasper will breed for us a Dragon—
> Of the fortunate blood of Brutus is he—
> A Bull of Anglesey to achieve;
> He is the hope of our race.[5]

Onward he came, 'a train of Welsh myth streaming behind him and proclamations shooting out before'.[6] Only after he had crossed the mountains and was moving upon Newton did Rhys ap Thomas at last come in with his band of warriors.

Henry had in the meantime dispatched a stream of messages to his mother and Reynold Bray, to Sir William and Lord Stanley, to Sir Gilbert Talbot, to his kinsman John ap Meredith, and to others who had pledged their support, ordering them to join him at once with men and money and announcing that he meant to cross the Severn at Shrewsbury and march through Shropshire towards London. His letter to Meredith is headed 'By the King'; Richard is branded as a usurper of his right; and Meredith is sharply commanded to appear with all available forces 'as ye will avoid our grievous displeasure and answer it at your peril'.[7] The imperious tone of this communication betrays the tension and terrible sense of insecurity under which Henry was labouring. Since he had neither experience nor interest in warfare, he was in the hands of his commanders—and his exile had taught him to dislike being in anybody's hands. By temperament he distrusted the bloody chance of battle, and as he moved towards the fateful field, his risk showed no signs of diminishing. A number of Welshmen had swelled his ranks with their small bands of followers and the promise of the Lieutenantship had clinched Rhys ap Thomas's allegiance. But the people of Wales had not swarmed to his banners as he had expected, or hoped; there had been no popular rising to greet the heir of Cadwallader. These strains and disappointments caused him to be the more poignantly aware of all the uncertainties over which he had no command.

The most dangerous uncertainty was the Stanleys. With every mile that he moved away from the rugged country of Wales towards the Severn valley, the enigma of the Stanleys grew more portentous. Encamping near Shrewsbury on August 12, he entered the city the next day—it being the policy of townsmen in the fifteenth century to open their gates to any army. Several of his messengers now returned, bearing money from Reynold Bray and promises from the Stanleys. Sir William was encamped some miles to the northeast of Shrewsbury; Lord Stanley lay somewhere to the east of the town. Each had a large force of men at his back. They gave ready assurances of support but they did not find it convenient to join the invaders, yet. They strongly counselled Henry to abandon his plan of striking towards London. He should march directly to encounter King Richard. They would move eastward before him. Lord Stanley explained that his son Strange was in Richard's grip and hence he could not immediately show his hand.

It was becoming doubtful if the rebels could count on any considerable aid except from the men who had committed themselves to Henry's cause. The help of the Stanleys was indispensable. Besides, Oxford and Jasper Tudor must have been aware that to turn their backs on King Richard and head for London was a hazardous undertaking. If he overtook them on the march, theirs would be an evil plight. There would be no possibility of retiring to Wales after a defeat; disaster would be absolute. Though Henry and his commanders recognized that the course the Stanleys urged would permit them, if fortune turned against the dragon banner, to come in on Richard's side, there was nothing for it but to take their advice. Consequently, about August 14, the host advanced twenty miles eastward to Newport, where Sir Gilbert Talbot, uncle of the youthful Earl of Shrewsbury, brought in the following of his House, a contingent of four or five hundred men. The motive which prompted the Talbots to desert Richard for Henry was probably domestic and personal rather than political. The young Earl was married to a daughter of Lord Hastings; and the revelation of King Edward's pre-contract had exposed to the world the shame of his kinswoman, the Lady Eleanor Butler.[8]*

Moving more slowly now, Henry pushed forward to Stafford, a march of but thirteen miles. It was at Stafford that he at last met Sir

William Stanley. Sir William's retinue was small, however, and his sojourn brief. He reiterated his and Lord Stanley's assurances; in a short time, he promised, he would return for another interview and bring his brother; he himself was still gathering his forces and must therefore make a speedy departure. Henry was beginning to realize that the Stanleys, however well disposed towards him, might not commit themselves until the actual battle was joined.

The rebels' line of march was now changed. The advance from Shrewsbury to Stafford had pointed directly towards Nottingham. Perhaps Sir William had agreed, or suggested, that it might be well to make a feint towards London. Perhaps Henry, hoping for reinforcements, felt that he was approaching King Richard too rapidly. In any case, on leaving Stafford, Henry veered sharply southeast and marched on Lichfield, seventeen miles away. As the motley ranks of Frenchmen, Welshmen, and English appeared before the town, they were watched by mounted scouts whom the King had sent forth to learn their movements.

Henry had already reached the neighbourhood of Shrewsbury, when, on August 11, the news of his landing was brought to Nottingham. Richard at once sent word to Northumberland, Norfolk, Lovell, Brackenbury, and his other principal captains, commanding them hastily to assemble their men and join him at Leicester—the same rendezvous he had established on the outbreak of Buckingham's rebellion. Having no news beyond that of the landing itself, he probably supposed that Henry would emerge from Wales somewhere in Herefordshire or Shropshire, if he emerged at all. Sir William Stanley he did not summon; Sir William should be marching with the men of North Wales to intercept the invaders. To Lord Stanley, however, he sent orders to come immediately to Nottingham. He also dispatched 'scurriers'—mounted scouts—to seek news of the enemy's movements.

For himself Richard wanted nothing more than to meet with Henry Tudor, and would have set forth as early as Monday, August 15; but— the sacred festival of the Assumption of Our Lady falling on that day, which he would allow no rebel to distract him from observing—he determined to leave Nottingham on the morning following. So John Howard, Duke of Norfolk reported in haste, probably on Saturday the 13th, to his 'well beloved friend', John Paston. 'I pray you,' Norfolk went on, 'that ye meet with me at Bury [Bury St. Edmunds] for by the Grace of God I propose to lie at Bury as upon Tuesday night

[Aug. 16] and that ye bring with you such company of tall men as ye may goodly make at my cost and charge—beside [those] that ye have promised the King—and I pray you ordain them jackets of my livery and I shall content you at your meeting with me. Your lover. J. Norfolk.'[9]

By the flat roads of Norfolk, Suffolk, Essex, men at arms and yeomen archers began to converge upon Bury St. Edmunds in order to march beneath the Norfolk banner of the silver lion. But John Paston, and so John Paston's men, were not among them.

He preferred to remain peaceably on his acres than to play a part in the trial by battle for the English throne. He had had enough of wars and he would thrive equally well whether Richard retained his crown or Henry Tudor won it. He had sworn an oath to support his King in arms, but by the year 1485 that oath had lost its power to bind. John Howard he knew well; his father and Howard had quarrelled over local politics two decades before, but John might be considered to owe the Duke of Norfolk much. It was Howard and his cousin the Earl of Nottingham who had voluntarily given back to John Paston the great estate of Caister which a previous Duke of Norfolk had wrested from the Paston family. But even this was not enough.

John Paston's father, at odds with King Henry's favourites in Norfolk, had marched with King Edward to fight the bloody field ot Towton in 1461. Young John himself, taking service with the Duke of Norfolk, had participated in the sieges of the Lancastrian castles in Northumberland. His brother had been a popular courtier, had jousted with the King at Eltham. But in 1469 King Edward refused to interfere on the Pastons' side in their dispute over lands with the Duke of Suffolk. A few months later the Duke of Norfolk besieged Caister Castle and John Paston had to capitulate; George Neville, Archbishop of York, and the Duke of Clarence had, however, shown themselves sympathetic, if not very helpful, to the Pastons at the time Caister was lost. Hence, when Warwick put Henry VI back on the throne and John, Earl of Oxford, became the great lord of East Anglia, the Pastons gave him their hearty allegiance and were taken into his favour. The Yorkist Duke of Norfolk was now powerless; the Pastons looked to prosper. Upon Edward's return from Burgundy to reclaim his throne, John Paston and his brother took arms with the Earl of Oxford and fought for him at Barnet. Both were captured, but were shortly given pardons. The Duke of Norfolk was again the great man in East Anglia, and Caister seemed forever lost—until John Howard, becoming Duke, restored it. It was on local issues that the Pastons had taken sides in the warfare of Lancaster and York. Now John Paston would sit at home and let his armour rust.

There were many like him—commons, gentry, lords. It was not that they longed for King Richard's overthrow. It was that they were weary of alarums, marches, battles. It was that the feudal giving of allegiance was dead and the discipline of obedience to the throne had not yet been enforced, or demanded. The crown had changed hands so often that its sanctity, its magnetic power of attracting loyalty, was dulled. In taking it from his nephew, Richard had still further dimmed this lustre. Many a man who was content to see King Edward resume his sway in 1471 did not fight for him at Barnet. Now, many a man who had no desire for the triumph of an unknown exile named Henry Tudor refrained from calling up his men. The Duke of Suffolk, as had always been his wont, sat upon his estates, even though his own son, John of Lincoln, was Richard's heir to the throne. Doubtless there were a number who told themselves that the King had no need of them. Outside of Henry Tudor's partisans, there were probably not a great many who believed that the Welshman and his tail of followers could stand in battle against the King, the most famous warrior alive in England.

The gifts Richard had bestowed out of generosity rather than policy; the treasure he had dispensed to show his goodwill instead of withholding to toughen the sinews of his enterprises; the justice he had done at the risk of alienating powerful interests; the services he had performed for the weak—all these did little for him now. His kindness to the wives of rebels, his munificence to friends, his statutes to curb oppressions, his attention to the humble causes of commoners, would not stead him in the hour of mustering a steel host. In the Castle of his Care Richard was now collecting the consequences of his rupture of the royal succession, of his rule by desert, and of half a century's accumulation of broken loyalties.

It was probably on Monday the 15th that Richard received an answer to the message he had sent Stanley. Sly Thomas reported that he was suffering from sweating sickness and therefore could not join the King at this time. He perhaps also contrived to have instructions conveyed to his son that he should immediately slip away from Nottingham. Lord Strange, at any rate, made the attempt, but he had been well watched and he was apprehended in the act. Richard could feel the pattern of betrayal thickening around him—but had he not always known? had he not, indeed, so willed it? He sent some of his advisers to interrogate Lord Strange. Theirs was an easy task: the son of Stanley was not one to throw himself away for a cause, even his father's. And perhaps there was no need. He could reflect that what he had to reveal must inevitably come to light in a few days. Throwing himself on the King's mercy, he told all—or almost all—that he knew. He and his uncle Sir William and Sir John Savage had secretly plotted to betray their sovereign and join Henry Tudor. But his father, he swore, meant to—must—remain true. To make all sure, he begged to be allowed to send a message to his father. Richard doubtless put no trust in this assertion, but Strange was given ink and paper. He wrote of his terrible danger and implored Lord Stanley to come in at once to the King with all his forces. Meanwhile, Richard sent orders to the sheriffs of the realm that Sir William Stanley and Sir John Savage were to be publicly proclaimed as traitors.

Strange's confession was swiftly confirmed. On this same Monday Richard at last got more news of the invaders: three days before, they had entered Shrewsbury beneath spread banners 'without any annoyance received'. However much he was prepared for it, the revelation was bitter. It meant that not only Sir William Stanley and Sir John Savage but Rhys ap Thomas and other Welsh chieftains had betrayed him. It meant that Henry Tudor had penetrated, unmolested, well nigh to the centre of his kingdom. The pieces of the pattern were tumbling into position—yet, for a moment at least, he was struck to the heart. A cry of *treason!* escaped him; in one brief torrent of anger he inveighed against the men who had sworn to stand true. Then he locked away his feelings.

More scurriers soon came in with the news that the invaders had removed from Shrewsbury to Newport. Apparently, then, they were making straight for Nottingham, instead of heading for London. The Stanleys, Richard now learned, commanded separate forces which hovered to the east of the invaders, falling back before them. Sending out fresh scouting parties, he abandoned his plan of leaving Notting-ham next morning, Tuesday. If the rebels continued the direction of their march, he would summon his host gathering at Leicester to join him here. But in the meantime where was Northumberland with his Percy retainers and the levies of the East Riding? He had sent word that he was coming in all possible haste, but either he had not yet stirred or was moving very slowly. Richard realized that Henry Percy had per-haps been forewarned of the action the Stanleys were taking and meant to play a game of his own. It would not be surprising; Percy had begun playing the game in 1471. In any case, the intelligence of the rebels' approach was welcome news. He had spent his life in action. Now action would provide anodyne and fulfillment. Refusing to wait anxiously for the latest report or to be ever weighing possibilities with his advisers, he left his castle on Tuesday the 16th and rode northward a few miles, with a group of intimates, to spend the night at Beskwood lodge in Sherwood forest.[10]*

Next morning he was up early, horsed and ready for the chase, as if his kingdom were lapped in softest peace. Off he went, a-hunting, but his mind was doubtless brooding upon other game. It may have come to him that, in the critical casting of accounts, his crown had proved to cost too dear. The kingdom as a whole had not been unwilling, perhaps, to accept the price, but it had turned out, despite all his efforts, to be too steep for the standards of his own moral economy. The man whose life's motto was 'loyaulté me lie' had not been able to accommodate himself to the man who had taken a crown from his nephew. Like his father before him, who had groped for the throne so awkwardly because it was a role alien to his nature, he had, caught up in the coil of circumstance and character, assumed the sceptre; but he could not wield it comfortably because he could not assume with it the double conviction that he had done what he ought and that his one object must be to keep what he had got. To forestall his being betrayed by the Woodvilles when the boy King came of age, to redress what he deeply felt to be the betrayal of his brother Edward's greatness by these same Woodvilles and others, he had betrayed the son of Edward, who seemed only to be the son of Elizabeth. Now was he being betrayed by the Stanleys and perhaps Northumberland too, men whom he had cherished—instead of ruthlessly controlling—in the vain hope of ending at last the endless propagation of betrayal. Yet in his heart's history, these treacheries came late and light: he had first of all been betrayed by himself.

When Richard returned to Beskwood lodge during the afternoon there were conducted to him two men, sweat-soaked and dusty with travel, whom he knew well. They were John Sponer, Sergeant of the Mace, and John Nicholson, messenger, of York.

The morning before, an anxious deliberation had taken place in the council chamber of that city. Though the plague was still claiming victims, the Mayor and Aldermen felt impelled to grapple with a serious and puzzling issue: word had come that the rebels had landed some days before, but the city had received no instructions, about assembling an armed force, from the King or anybody else. 'It was determined,' records the scribe, 'that John Sponer, serjeant to the mace, should ride to Nottingham to the King's grace to understand his pleasure as in sending up any of his subjects within this city to his said grace for the subduing of his enemies late arrived in the parties of Wales.

'Also it was determined that all such aldermen and other of the council as was sojourning, for the plague that reigneth, without the City, should be sent for to give their best advices. . . .

'Also that there shall proclamations be made throughout this City, that every man fraunchest ['franchised', i.e., every man having citizenship] within this City be ready in their most defensible array to attend upon the mayor, for the welfare of this City, within an hour's warning, upon pain of imprisonment. . . .'

As Richard listened to John Sponer's tale, his mind must have leaped to the realization that the Earl of Northumberland intended to break his allegiance, probably not overtly but by managing to hold himself and his force neutral. It was Northumberland, Commissioner of Array for the East Riding, who should have called up the men of York. He would have an excuse of course, the plague; but it was obvious that the plague was not severe enough to prevent the city from marshalling a band of soldiers. Why he had not sent the summons was deadly clear—he wanted in his following a great preponderance of those who could be counted on to obey any order that he gave. Richard revealed none of these thoughts to Sponer and Nicholson but quietly bade them express his thanks to the city for its sturdy loyalty and inform the Mayor that he indeed had need of what men they could hastily assemble, for he intended very shortly to give battle to his enemies. John Sponer chose to remain in the Household of the King to accompany him on his wars; John Nicholson at once set forth to bring the King's word to York.

The moment he arrived, the officers of the city bent all their energies to answer the King's call. Plague or no plague, they meant to show their mettle. On the morning of Friday, the 19th, 'it was determined upon the report of John Nicholson, which was come home from the King's grace from Beskwood, that four score men of the City defensibly arrayed, John Hastings, gentleman to the mace, being captain, should in all haste possible depart towards the King's grace for the subduing of his enemies foresaid.' At two o'clock in the afternoon the council met at the Guildhall to pay out the soldiers' wages and towards evening,

or early the next morning, the mounted troop hastily set forth. Such
was the response of the men who knew the King best.[11]*

Richard, in the meanwhile, rode back this same evening, Wednesday,
August 17, through the forest aisles to Nottingham Castle. Though the
thought of Northumberland's defection doubtless weighed upon his
spirits, he must have realized—in the active, decisive part of his mind
which hived the long experience of the general and the governor of
men—that victory was probably yet his for the achieving. Even though
he had permitted the Stanleys to spring to arms against him, thus
opening the way for Henry Tudor to march so far unscathed and unchallenged, Sir William and Lord Stanley could be forced, by skilful
manoeuvring on his part, to abandon their dangerously ambiguous
positions and unite openly with the invaders, a move which might be
taken ill by some in their ranks and which would prevent them from
suddenly intervening by a flank attack to alter the complexion of battle.
As for Northumberland, the lord whose loyalty he had been wooing
for almost fifteen years, Richard stood between him and the rebels.
That ambiguous Earl could be compelled to take an unequivocal stand,
or, at worst, could be quietly put into custody; most of his Yorkshiremen would readily follow the King's banner if it became necessary to
deprive Percy of his command.

The royal host was not yet at full strength. Richard had ordered
a very hasty mustering; on all the roads leading to Nottingham and
Leicester men were moving to join him and others were still assembling
their retainers and supplies. Even from the little he knew about the
progress and numbers of the rebels, it did not appear that there had been
any popular rising, in Wales or England, in behalf of Henry Tudor; and
the passage of time was therefore not likely to bring him any great
accession of strength. Thus, by ruthlessly concentrating on the holding
of his throne, ruling himself entirely by the calculation of success,
conducting a campaign of whatever duration was advantageous, and
giving battle at last only when he had exploited every opportunity and
stood at the top of his resources, he could probably crush his enemies. He
might then look forward to a reign of peace, for Henry Tudor and
his partisans were the only disturbers of the realm. That which
he had been able, in two years, merely to initiate or to promise,
he could bring to proper fruition; and as his reign lengthened,
the faults of which he had been guilty in encompassing the crown
would be forgotten by his subjects and might even be forgiven by
Heaven. . . .

But he was Richard Plantagenet and none other. He would 'dree his weird', driving straight onward as he had long ago chosen.

When he arrived at Nottingham Castle he learned that the rebels, after advancing towards Nottingham as far as Stafford, had suddenly veered to the southeast as if they intended to move on London. Next day, Thursday, August 18, scouts brought word that Henry Tudor's host had lain outside the walls of Lichfield the evening before. Lord Stanley had evacuated that town three days earlier, ostensibly retiring before the invaders, and was now quartered at Atherstone, sixteen miles to the southeast and only twenty-one miles west of Leicester; Sir William Stanley was likewise between Lichfield and Leicester, somewhere to the north of his brother.

Richard instantly gave orders for his army to set out for Leicester early on the morrow. Norfolk should arrive there the same evening, having left Bury St. Edmunds on Wednesday, the 17th. He dispatched word to the Earl of Northumberland to overtake him at Leicester, if he could not come up before. Again he sent his scurriers forth to observe the movements of the enemy.

On Friday morning, August 19, Richard came down from his eyrie on the rock of Nottingham and took the southward road which wound across hills towards Leicester. His army moved in column of route— 'square battayll', Vergil calls it: a wing of cavalry ranging on each side, Richard and his Household men-at-arms in the van, the baggage in the middle, and a force of Northern lords, gentry, commons bringing up the rear. Lord Strange came too, under guard. No word had been received from his father.[12]*

Five other armies were now converging upon the neighbourhood of Leicester. In that town itself the levies of the Duke of Norfolk and men from the southern and Midland counties were gathering. Sir William and Thomas, Lord Stanley were approaching from the west, not many miles apart. Behind them moved Henry Tudor's army. Somewhere in Richard's rear came the mounted force of the Earl of Northumberland. King Richard and Henry Tudor had the most powerful armies; counting the men at Leicester, Richard's host was the larger. But the Stanleys and Northumberland, whose three forces were beginning to hover about the King's like birds of prey, commanded the decisive power if an immediate engagement were fought. It was the defection of the nobility, Vergil points out with surprising perception, which wrought Richard's fate. Actually, it was the defection of one baronet, one baron, and one earl. Because any field, however crucial, was decided in the latter half of the fifteenth century by small numbers, the fact that these men commanded strong local followings gave them, at the moment, an unusual power, a power which was no expression of the national will but only of their own interest. Richard was knowingly marching into an ambush which he had permitted these lords to set for him. But, indeed, he had already been ambushed by his own heart.

A little before sunset the King crossed the north bridge over the river Soar and entered the gates of Leicester. Up High Street (now High Cross Street) he rode, past All Saints' church, to dismount at an inn which exhibited his own device, the White Boar. The castle was probably untenanted, and besides, he was on campaign now and he did not mean to linger in Leicester. Faithful John Howard had already quartered his men of East Anglia in the town and was waiting to greet him. A message arrived from Northumberland that his contingent would reach Leicester the following evening. At a council of war that night Richard and Howard decided to wait the next day in Leicester for Northumberland and other captains to come in and to see if the rebels would now change the direction of their march.[13]

This same evening of August 19, Henry Tudor was undergoing one of the most dreadful experiences of his life. His army had left Lichfield that morning for Tamworth, but Henry, giving a vague excuse, had lingered behind with only a small bodyguard. At last he set forth, only to halt by the wayside, wrapped in moody thought; and when he again moved slowly forward, he was oblivious of everything but the ominous visions in his mind. His welling anxieties and doubts had suddenly crested in a terrible fear. The safety of Wales was far off; the Stanleys still refused to commit themselves. Though he had been assured that the King's power would collapse the moment he appeared, few men had joined his banners beyond those already pledged; and from his scouts he had just learned that 'nothing was more firm, nothing better furnished' than Richard's cause——

Suddenly he realized that it was growing dark. There was no sign of Tamworth or of his army. Fearfully he approached a small village, took shelter in a hut on the outskirts, forbade his men to show themselves. Tamworth, he learned to his relief, was only three miles distant. His army, the meanwhile, was shaken by his unaccountable disappearance, and Oxford and Jasper Tudor spent a haggard night. In the dawn of Saturday, August 20, Henry made his way to Tamworth. Assuming a mask of imperturbability, he declared that he had not lost his way 'but had withdrawn from the camp of set purpose to receive some good news of certain his secret friends'. Fortune began to smile a little. He was told that the Stanleys wanted him to come secretly to Atherstone for a conference. He complied at once, setting off with a small guard. Vergil is the only reporter of the scene: 'Here Henry did meet with Thomas and William, where taking one another by the hand, and yielding mutual salutation, each man was glad for the good estate of the others, and all their minds were moved to great joy. After that, they entered in council in what sort to darraigne battle with King Richard . . . whom they heard to be not far off.'

By the time the Stanleys had departed to their forces and Henry awaited the arrival of his at Atherstone, his great joy had evaporated. Lord Stanley had kept reiterating the danger in which his son stood; Sir William was full of reasons why he too must not yet join the rebel host. They would come in when the time was ripe: that was the essence of the interview. In the Stanleys' minds Henry read the reservation that the time might, just possibly, never *be* ripe. Even when the battle was joined, he foresaw, they would hold aloof, stationing themselves so that they could quickly, and mortally, intervene. If the dragon of Cadwallader raked the white boar, they would dash in to finish off the beast; or if the fight hung in the balance and they felt they could decide it, they would overthrow King Richard. But if Henry's army faltered and began to give way, the Stanleys would find excuses to associate themselves with the King in his triumph. They sincerely wished Henry to win, but, first of all, they meant to be on the victor's side. Henry never forgot the taste that the Stanleys left in his mouth during these feverish days.[14]

At Leicester on this Saturday, August 20, Richard was busy supervising, with John Howard and Howard's son Thomas, Earl of Surrey, and other captains, the orderly mustering of his host. Men were still streaming in from all directions who must be given quarters and assigned places in the ranks. Sir Robert Brackenbury, Constable of the Tower, arrived with a contingent from London. A little above Stony Stratford, he reported, Walter Hungerford and Thomas Bourchier had stolen away from his band, obviously with the design of joining Henry Tudor. Hungerford had been attainted for his prominent part in Buckingham's rebellion but Richard had been content to pardon him and restore much of his property.

By late afternoon Richard had learned from his scouts that Lord Stanley's army was at Stoke Golding, only about ten miles west of

Leicester, and that his brother Sir William had halted close by in the
vicinity of Shenton. Henry Tudor's host had occupied Atherstone, not
much more than nine miles to the rear. Though the movement of the
Stanleys made it appear that the rebels were headed directly eastward
towards Leicester, the town of Atherstone was on Watling Street, the
great Roman road which ran in a straight line southeast towards
London; and it was still possible that the rebels might strike down
Watling Street towards the capital, with the Stanleys manoeuvring to
mask this movement. Richard consequently sent out an advance party
to take up a position where they could keep Lord Stanley's camp under
observation.

Late in the evening the Earl of Northumberland at last arrived with
his men, who, he declared, were much wearied, their horses likewise,
from the speed with which they had come south. Richard gave no
sign that he was aware of anything suspicious in the Earl's conduct.
As he listened to Northumberland, however, he must have been con-
jecturing, from his long experience of the man, the thoughts that were
running in his mind.

Long ago Henry Percy had indicated his sentiments towards the
Crown. His great-grandfather had lost his life fighting against Henry
IV at Shrewsbury. His father had lost his life and the earldom fighting
against Edward IV at Towton. Restored to the dignity by Edward in
March of 1470, Henry, Earl of Northumberland had made up his mind
that he would remain aloof from any struggles for the English Crown.
Henceforth the House of Percy stood only for the House of Percy.
When Edward returned from Burgundy in March of 1471, Percy sat
upon his estates, neutral, content to accept Henry or Edward for his
sovereign.

His long association with Richard, Richard's courtesy and goodwill
when Duke of Gloucester, Richard's munificent gifts to him of estates
and offices when King, did not change his attitude. He had supported
Richard's assumption of the throne, but he had had no likely alternative.
He had marched with Richard in Buckingham's rebellion, but the
rebel cause had withered from the first and he had, besides, no reason
to love Buckingham. Despite Richard's generosity and favour he
nursed a resentment, grim and low-keyed—for he appears to have
been a colourless, low-keyed individual—against the man who had
won first place in the hearts of the North and against the King who
had established a royal council to dispense the King's justice and keep
the King's peace in Yorkshire. He could only look backward for his

M

cue, and he felt himself diminished in comparison with his ancestors, who had ruled the North as they pleased and dispensed their own justice as they saw fit.

By feeling as well as policy, then, he was disposed to break his oath to Richard and remain apart from the impending battle, knowing that if he could manage his neutrality with even moderate skill, the victor—whoever he was—would undoubtedly be content to accept his homage. But he preferred to see Richard vanquished. He probably had Henry's pardon in his pocket and he certainly supposed that the unknown exile would have his hands so full in London that he would be very glad to let Henry Percy rule the North as the Percies once had done. Now he was explaining to Richard that his soldiers had been slow in assembling and had therefore so hastened to reach Leicester that both men and horses needed rest. Perhaps it would be wise, he suggested, if his force should be the last to remain in the town and hence form the rearguard.

Richard concurred in this proposal. With the warning which the news from York had given him, it was not hard to sound the bottom of Henry Percy. He was too proud to make any last attempt to stir Percy's allegiance; he was too inflexibly committed to his ordained course—and perhaps too weary of spirit—to undertake any measures against Percy's obvious disaffection. That night the royal captains agreed with Richard that the host should march westward on the morrow to engage the enemy. Battle! Battle was the encounter, at long last, with Henry Tudor. Battle was the trial of loyalty and the answer to betrayal, the fulfillment of his reign and the registry of Heaven's judgment.

XII*

ON Sunday morning, August 21, the royal army formed in column of route. Trumpets resounded in the narrow streets of Leicester. Down the Swine's Market (now High Street) swung the troops, over the west bridge across the Soar, along the road to Kirkby Mallory, which lies almost in a direct line NE–SW between Atherstone and Leicester and roughly equidistant from them. The men-at-arms and archers of Norfolk and Surrey, protected by a cavalry screen, formed the van. Next came King Richard, riding with the Duke of Norfolk and the Earl of Northumberland at the head of the chief officers and knights and esquires of his household. There followed a great contingent, mostly of northern and midland men—among them, Lords Zouche and Scrope of Bolton and Scrope of Upsale and Dacre (he 'raised the North Countrye') and Greystoke ('he brought a mighty many') and Ferrers of Chartley and William Berkeley, Earl of Nottingham, and many baronets, knights, and esquires. Behind the centre division of the army rolled the baggage train; and then, issuing from Leicester after the van was well on its way, came the reVanguard, Northumberland's troop.

Richard was mounted on a white courser,[1] a slight figure even in the casing of full armour. He bore a golden crown upon his helmet, that friend and foe alike might know that the King was going forth to battle. The banners of England and St. George floated above him. In his train blazed the heralds in their tabard coats of arms and trumpeters and drummers, their instruments flaunting the leopards and lilies and the white boar.[2] So accoutred in all the panoply of knightly warfare, Richard rode without fear or hope, silent as was his wont, his general's eye scanning the country, noting the bearing of his soldiers, and picturing, as scouts brought their reports, the possible movements of the enemy.

When the van of the army reached Kirkby Mallory, Richard called a halt to permit his soldiers to eat a meal and to confer with his commanders. He had learned from his scurriers that the two Stanleys were holding their positions at Stoke Golding and Shenton. Henry Tudor's host was beginning to move down Watling Street from Atherstone. Whether it would turn aside to confront the royal army or try to slip past it to the south and continue on towards London there was yet no telling. Richard knew the country well. Only ten weeks before he had journeyed to Nottingham by Coventry and Leicester, on a road that skirted to the southeast the present terrain, a road down which he had marched from Leicester in October of 1483 and had travelled on previous occasions as well. He and his lieutenants quickly agreed that the royal army should take up a position which would bring the Stanleys, or at least Lord Stanley, under observation, block the approach of the invaders if they were marching to give battle, or serve as a springboard to come down upon their flank if they dared to follow Watling Street.

Commands rang out; the host resumed its march. Five miles west of Kirkby Mallory, the vanguard entered the village of Sutton Cheney, which stands upon the eastern end of a high ridge. The ridge extends westward for about a mile, like a crouched animal with head and hindquarters rising higher than its back. North of the ridge the land slopes upward to the town of Market Bosworth, some two miles distant. Looking across these slanted fields, the royal commanders at Sutton Cheney could see the encampment of Sir William Stanley, something more than a mile away, on low ground to the northwest of the ridge. Northumberland's sluggish rearguard was delegated to take up a position around Sutton Cheney in order to keep Sir William in view.

Meanwhile, Norfolk's vanguard, moving south out of the village, came down from the ridge on to a stretch of land called Redmore plain which slopes gently to the west as far as the eye can see. A road follows the plain, turning southwestward to join Watling Street. Here the vanguard, mainly composed of lightly armoured bowmen and billmen, halted to pitch camp. Richard led his division of heavily armed Household troops and men-at-arms of the North and Midlands on past Norfolk's station in order to bring them on to the high ground, now called Harper's Hill, which forms the southern boundary of Redmore plain before declining sharply into the plain itself. The wings of Richard's army were now separated but in close touch. The army could be pointed south towards Watling Street, some ten miles distant, or turned westward to block an advance up Redmore plain. From the headland on which he had halted to make camp Richard could see to the southwest, across a valley and a stream called the Tweed, the height near Stoke Golding on which Lord Stanley had stationed his force. To Stanley he sent a command to join the royal host at once. The messenger returned with an evasive answer.

It was now mid-afternoon, or later. Scouts had brought word by this time that the enemy had left Watling Street and were advancing up the road towards Redmore plain. As evening approached, the invaders appeared in the distance but shortly swung off the road to make camp. Soon lights began to twinkle in the dusk, like a cluster of fireflies, in meadows about three miles to the west of Harper's Hill and a little to the southwest of Ambien Hill, as the western extremity of the great ridge was called.

The terrain on which these four armies had halted is rolling, watered by numerous streams, with eminences which here and there crest into hills or hillocks. It was then open country, uncultivated and unenclosed, and well nigh treeless. Here the villages are built, not in the valleys which may be swampy, but on the hills or high ground. Market Bosworth and Stoke Golding, bounding the battleground to the north and south; Shenton and Sutton Cheney, facing each other east and west across the length of the great ridge, thrust themselves above the low lands like watch towers. They are all enclosed in an area of less than twenty square miles. The dominant feature of the landscape is Ambien Hill, which swells to a height of almost 400 feet and stands in the centre of the region. On the night of August 21, the opposing armies lay clustered about this hill—Henry Tudor and Sir William Stanley on low ground to the southwest and northwest, Lord Stanley on an eminence due south and the wings of the royal army extending in a north-south line from the eastern end of the ridge at Sutton Cheney across Redmore plain to Harper's Hill.

Doubtless Richard paced the outer reaches of his camp that night, surveying the lights of Lord Stanley's camp and Henry Tudor's, and Norfolk's fires stretching across the plain to Northumberland's, beyond. His mind was much upon the ridge, shrouded in darkness to the north, particularly the contours of Ambien Hill. From a part of its southern slope a marsh of perhaps a half hundred acres extended into the plain. The tilt of this slope, like that to the west, was considerable (about 1 in 20); on the northern side, he had learned, it was very much steeper (about 1 in 10). Perhaps by the time he reached Sutton Cheney, hours before, he had already conceived the plan which this night he outlined to the final council of his commanders.

His present position had halted the rebels' advance where he had chosen, and it was battleworthy. The Tweed river and the southwest declivity of Harper's Hill would help to protect his flank against Lord Stanley; from its western and northern crests he could assail the enemy advancing up Redmore plain against Norfolk. But Richard lacked the numbers to hold the hill in force and to provide Norfolk with the substantial addition of troops he would need to extend his line across the plain. Since Northumberland on the right must be counted a blank, Sir William Stanley might cross the ridge unopposed to swoop down on Norfolk's right.

Richard and his commanders therefore decided that the royal army should occupy Ambien Hill very early in the morning. It was a position of commanding advantage, its flanks protected against the treachery of the Stanleys and its limited extent minimizing the damage from Northumberland's probable refusal to join the conflict. These tactics were certain to bring the enemy to battle, and on terms that he had perhaps not foreseen. They also offered Richard the greatest possibility of getting at Henry Tudor, though this thought he likely did not bother to mention.

Having bidden his captains good-night, he doubtless paced again the

reaches of his camp, noting men's faces in the firelight, the condition
of their gear. As he gazed at Lord Stanley's fires across the darkness,
his grim content with his military dispositions gave way to sombre
thoughts about the treachery which had dictated them. It suddenly
seemed clear to him that it was not only the alternative of victory by
Henry Tudor which would change England, probably give her something like the cunning despotism that France had known under Louis
XI. His own triumph, too, must bring sharp changes. His present
experience of betrayal had poisoned his will to seek loyalty; henceforth,
if he conquered, he must be ruthless in demanding obedience and
compassing his own security. It was a prospect that served only to
deepen his depression of spirit.

Before it was light, officers moved among the sleeping soldiers
on Harper's Hill, bidding them wake and eat their breakfasts. The
chief men about the King gathered before his tent—Viscount Lovell
his chamberlain and Sir Robert Percy his comptroller, his advisers
Sir Richard Ratcliffe and William Catesby, John Kendall his secretary,
Sir Robert Brackenbury, Sir Thomas Mongomery, Sir Ralph Assheton
who was again Vice-Constable of England, and other councillors,
captains, and servants. Richard appeared shortly, an officer bearing his
helmet with the golden crown. In the greying darkness his face was
startlingly livid, attenuated. . . . He noticed their looks of concern. If
he appeared pale, he told them quickly, it was only because he had slept
little, troubled by dreams. He stood listening to the sounds of his stirring
camp—clash of harness, twanging of bowstrings, horses neighing and
stamping. It was grey in the east. In the west some lights flickered from
Henry Tudor's camp. The weather gave promise of being warm and
clear. Gloomily Richard looked at his faithful followers. There was
something, he said at last, that he must tell them. The battle this day—
no matter who won it—would prove to be the destruction of the
England they knew. If Henry Tudor was the victor, he would crush
all the supporters of the House of York and rule by fear. If he, Richard,
conquered, he would be equally ruthless and would use force to govern
the kingdom. A moment after he had ceased speaking, one of his
squires reported, falteringly, that there were no chaplains in the camp
to say divine service. Richard replied that it was as he intended. If their
quarrel were God's, they needed no last supplications; if it were not,
such prayers were idle blasphemy.[3]*

Word came from Norfolk that he was ready to march. Mounting
his white horse, Richard gave order for the army to set forth, and his

captains scattered to their detachments. He told John Kendall to dispatch a last message to Lord Stanley, commanding him to come in at
once if he valued the life of his son, a confessed traitor. While dawn
was yet reddening the sky, Richard's division streamed northward
down the slope of Harper's Hill in the fresh coolness of the August
morning. Ahead, the men of Norfolk, in column of route, were
ascending the rise into Sutton Cheney. Richard discovered when he
reached the village that Northumberland's men were only beginning
to form their ranks.

The troops were given a breathing spell. Norfolk, Surrey,
Northumberland, and the principal captains of the royal host gathered
about the King on a tumulus which stood on high ground between a
road fork north of the village. Scurriers brought word that the forces
of the Stanleys showed no signs of moving, but there was some
stirring in the rebel camp on the plain. Richard at once ordered a
detachment of mounted archers and men-at-arms to proceed along the
ridge to the crest of Ambien Hill. They were to make a show of force
and at all costs hold their position if attacked; they would soon be
reinforced. A blustering reply now arrived from Lord Stanley: he had
other sons and he was not, at the moment, of a mind to join the King.
Clearly, he counted on the King's mercy and on the King's hope that he
himself would yet prove true. In a blaze of anger Richard ordered
one of his squires to see at once to Strange's execution. Then,
controlling himself, he turned to his captains for their opinion. As he
listened to them, Richard suddenly perceived that, like everything else,
Lord Strange's fate must be decided by the wager of battle. He ordered
Stanley's son to be kept under close guard.[4*]

As the long column of men stood waiting—each detachment
marked by the livery jackets and the banners of its leader—Richard
quickly gave last instructions to his captains. Northumberland had
proposed that his mounted force hold a position on the ridge near
Sutton Cheney. Thus, the Earl averred, he would be able to fall on
Lord Stanley's flank if Stanley moved against Ambien Hill, and would
also be close enough to the King to provide quick reinforcement if
needed. Richard tersely agreed. Better for Northumberland to be
neutral in the rear than in the front of the line. Yet even in acceding
to the Earl's request, he must have realized that many a man beneath
the Percy standard had no idea of his lord's treachery and would have
followed the King with a will.

Norfolk's vanguard now resumed its march, flowing in a narrow column along the top of the ridge towards Ambien Hill with the Howard banner of the silver lion leading the way. As Richard mounted his horse to follow, some of his Household protested that he must not wear into battle the helmet with the golden crown, for it would mark him as the prime target for the enemy. Quietly Richard replied that he would live, and die, King of England. The Knights and Esquires of the Body gathering about him, he rode westward after Norfolk at the head of the centre of his host, turning his back with proud impassivity upon the Earl who had at last contrived to turn his coat.

As he approached the western extremity of Ambien Hill, Richard could see all three camps of his enemies. Both Lord Stanley's men and his brother's were standing to arms, motionless; but whereas Lord Stanley's were on foot, as was customary, Sir William's were mounted.[5]* Henry Tudor and his commanders had been taken by surprise. Their army was hastily moving eastward from its camp in order to interpose the swamp on the southern slope of Ambien Hill between it and the royal host occupying the summit. Norfolk was arranging his ranks a little way down the slopes in the shape of a bent bow pointing almost due southwest at the rebel camp, with a clump of archers on the left facing south towards the swamp, men-at-arms in the centre, and a clump of archers on the right facing west towards Shenton.[6]*

As Richard was disposing his division on the hilltop, the enemy trumpets rang out. It was they who would begin the battle—indeed, what was left for them? They came swinging around the western edge of the swamp led by John de Vere, Earl of Oxford, striding beneath his banner of a star with streams. Norfolk's archers assailed their ranks with a storm of missiles and were in turn galled by the arrow-fire of the advancing enemy and their reserve. Guns cracked; stone cannon balls bounded on the upper slopes.[7] The rebels had picked up some artillery at Lichfield and perhaps at Shrewsbury. The King's men replied with guns and serpentines, but they were few in number. The great arsenal in the Tower Richard had not drawn on. Cannon served to reduce castles, defend a city, or stiffen a defensive position. The invaders of his realm Richard had thought only of attacking. Still the mass of foot-soldiers poured around the swamp until they had reached a point almost half way across the western base of the hill. Their right rested on the swamp; their left flank was in the air—unless Sir William Stanley supported it with his cavalry, massed only a quarter of a mile away to the north. While the hot exchange of arrow fire continued, the rebels momentarily halted, their ranks shifting to face up the hill where the bent bow of Norfolk's line stood ready.

The respective numbers of the hosts can only be approximated. Henry Tudor had brought to the field about 5,000 men—2,000 French, 4 or 5 hundred exiles, 500 men of the Shrewsbury interest, 2,000 Welsh and English adherents—the former in the majority—who had joined him on his march. Of these, Oxford, trusting in the Stanleys, had committed about 4,000 men to his attack. The remainder were divided into two bodies, one remaining on the plain behind the right wing, the other taking its station on the rising ground opposite the west end of Ambien Hill (not many yards from the present railway station). Sir William Stanley mustered some 2,500 men; Lord Stanley counted perhaps 4,000 or 3,500.

Richard's host outnumbered Henry Tudor's almost two to one; it was smaller, however, than the combined forces of the rebels and the Stanleys. The King had led to Ambien Hill an army of perhaps 9,000 men—about the same size as that with which Edward had met Warwick at Barnet. Of these, 3,000 stood idly at the rear of the ridge under Northumberland's standard, leaving some 6,000 available troops. Norfolk's vanguard numbered approximately 2,500 men. From his centre, 3,500 strong, Richard had reinforced the Duke with about 1,500 soldiers to bring the vanguard up to the numbers of the enemy mass at the foot of the hill. Of his remaining 2,000 men, Richard had probably posted a few hundred on the southern brow of the hill, east of the swamp, to guard against a sudden attack by Lord Stanley, who had now advanced from his camp to a position on Redmore plain only half a mile from the hill. The King had sent another small detachment to the northwest brow of Ambien, in order to protect Norfolk's flank against assault by Sir William Stanley. Both forces were spread thin to mask their weakness. There remained probably 1,000 men for the general reserve, of whom some four score warriors in shining mail, the Knights and Esquires of the Body, were stationed close about the King and his standard.

As Richard scanned the battlefield, his glance turned often to the two bodies of the enemy reserve. Soon he called for men of specially keen sight who had some skill in heraldic bearings. Those who volunteered he dispatched forward with one brief injunction: find out where Henry Tudor has stationed himself.

The trumpets of the enemy rang out. A bedlam of commands in

M*

Welsh, French, English rose on the air. The mass of rebel troops began to climb the hill. Norfolk's trumpets sounded. Norfolk and Surrey, Lord Ferrers, Lord Zouche, and their captains shouted orders. With a yell the royal army plunged down the hill. The arrow fire and the banging of guns ceased. Midway down the slope the two hosts collided with a crash of steel and were instantly locked in combat. Norfolk's ranks were thinner than the enemy's. He had lengthened his line to cut round the flanks. In the centre his banner of the silver lion waved against Oxford's star with streams. Richard stood motionless on the

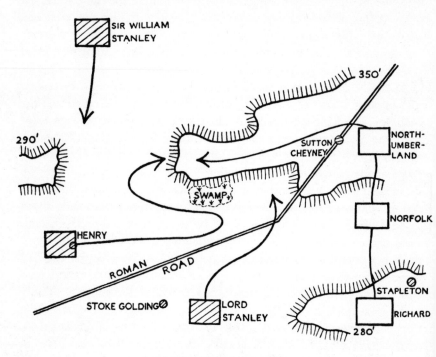

THE EVE OF BOSWORTH

hilltop, watching. The lines bulged, swayed like the throb of the sea, foaming with a surf of axes, swords, spears. Slowly, raggedly, the royal ranks gave a little ground. The pressure was greatest in the centre, where Oxford headed a massive phalanx. Norfolk's line bent backward, began to take the shape of a crescent. In one spot it was wearing dangerously thin; Richard gave a command; a knight moved forward with a detachment of the reserve to bolster the crescent. The centre held; and now Norfolk's tactics began to succeed. The horns of the crescent were goring the enemy flanks, driving them inward. The left flank which had no anchorage, was crumbling. Oxford's trumpets shrilled: retire to the standards! Welsh—French—English voices roared the commands above the din of battle. Oxford's men pulled back, massed themselves about the banners of their leaders. Momentarily bewildered by the manoeuvre, the royal army permitted them to disengage. A lull fell upon the field. A few feet apart, the forces glared at one another, panting for breath. Oxford's flanks, reinforced from the reserve, were now drawn inward; his army had taken on the

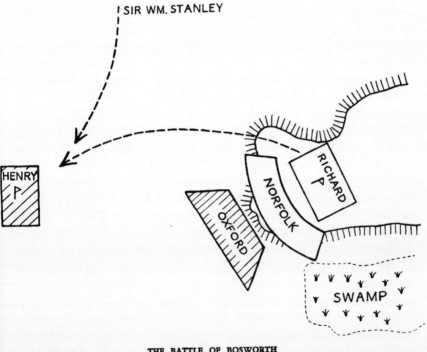

THE BATTLE OF BOSWORTH

shape of a wedge or rough triangle, the point aimed at the hill-top.

Norfolk stood looking along his line. His gruff and able son Surrey was waiting at his side. Zouche and Ferrers waved steel-gauntleted arms. As the Duke's trumpeters sounded the call to battle, his men hurled themselves once more upon the enemy. In the thickest of the press, Norfolk was showing himself worthy of the lion on his shield. A West country father and son, yeomen named Brecher, did such execution that Oxford's lieutenants marked them in memory. Zouche and Ferrers were pressing hard on the flanks.

One of the men of keen sight came running to King Richard——

He and his fellows had marked out him who must be Henry Tudor—there to the west on the rising ground opposite—the figure on horseback, close by the red dragon standard—he there in the centre of a mounted reserve of some twenty-five score men. Richard strode forward the better to see, straining his eyes against the dust of combat. At last he made out the figure, saw a messenger run up and do obeisance: it must be the Tudor.

A strange peace descended upon him, even as he instantly determined to exploit this opportunity which he had so long hoped for. He made no calculations of success; his mind had room only for decision. Yet, he was aware that to come down upon Henry Tudor in a surprise attack could clinch a quick and dazzling victory. If their Pretender were slain, the rebels had nothing to fight for; when the fatal word ran across the field, they would take to their heels or surrender, and the Stanleys would haste to include themselves among the victors. The risks were of course enormous. He would attack with only his devoted friends and servants, the men of his Household. They must ride directly across Sir William Stanley's front against a body of troops probably five times larger. And he himself must cleave his way to Henry Tudor before the rebels could rally or Sir William intervene. It was a desperate stroke, for failure meant absolute disaster, but it did hold a chance of brilliant victory. The blazing core of his purpose, however, was simply to slake his heart in the fierce joy of combat with the plotter who had poisoned his peace and racked his kingdom. But there must have been other motives, perhaps only dimly felt, inarticulate. The battle between two men for a crown should, by knightly standards, be a personal encounter, jeopardizing no lives beyond those of the men themselves or of their intimate servants. And when he struck at Henry Tudor he would put a quick end, one way or the other, to men's dying for what only Henry or he should die for. So too was there a mixture of impulses which prompted his decision to attack only with the small band of his Household. To lead a larger following might give brighter assurance of success, but these were his own fellowship of pledged comrades in arms, the sworn defenders of his body whose loyalty he had nurtured with his good lordship. None else would he ask to share this journey into peril. Yet it is also true that to ready more men would delay the enterprise and perhaps reveal it to the enemy.

Back he strode to the standard to give his orders. Attendants ran to the rear where a band of war steeds had been tethered. The men of the Household began to look to their weapons.

One of the King's squires cried out that John Howard was down. There, by the banner of the silver lion, was a swirl of fighting men. Surrey was laying about him furiously. A messenger raced up the slope to the King's standard: the Duke of Norfolk had been slain. As Richard ordered a detachment of the reserve to Surrey's aid, another messenger arrived with the news that Lord Ferrers had been cut off from his men and killed. Richard's eye was caught by a horseman galloping across Redmore Plain. He would be bearing Henry Tudor's tidings to Lord Stanley that Norfolk was no more. Richard summoned a pursuivant, bade him bear to the Earl of Northumberland the command to advance at once to the support of the royal army. Northumberland must be made to reveal to the world the colour of his allegiance.

The horses were led forward. The men of the Household quieted their mounts, tightened armour plate and saddles. The pursuivant returned. Perhaps with a grim smile Richard listened to his message: Northumberland felt it his duty to remain in the rear in order to guard against Lord Stanley. William Catesby came forward nervously, his face drawn with fear. He must urge the King to seek safety in flight while the way was still open . . . the Stanleys would advance at any moment against them . . . the loss of a single battle need not be serious. . . . The King shook his head impatiently, turning away; Catesby retired, but not to ride with his sovereign lord.

With the aid of his squires Richard mounted his white courser. Behind him, the Household swung into the saddle. He turned to look at them, the Knights and Esquires of his Body—Sir Richard Ratcliffe, Sir James Harrington, Sir Marmaduke Constable, Sir Thomas Burgh, Sir Ralph Assheton, Sir Thomas Pilkington, John Sapcote, Humphrey and Thomas Stafford. . . . They were all men who had done him good service in peace and war. Close behind him was his faithful Constable of the Tower, Sir Robert Brackenbury, and there, of no noble stock but in full armour to-day and ready to do knightly service, was his secretary, John Kendall. Beside him waited his friends, Francis, Viscount Lovell, and Sir Robert Percy.

The battle was scarcely half an hour old; the bulk of the royal reserve was uncommitted; the Stanleys still waited. . . . No matter.

Richard rose in his stirrups so that all might hear. 'We ride to seek Henry Tudor.' Their faces showed that they understood, and awaited only his command. He closed his visor. One of his squires put the battle-axe in his grip. He raised his gauntleted arm to signal his trumpeters. For the last time there sounded in the ears of men the battle-call of the fierce and valiant Plantagenets.

His horse moved forward at a walk, the men of the Household pacing close beside and behind him. Northwestward down the slope he rode to swing clear of the northern end of the battle line. Now the cavalcade gathered speed. At the head of less than a hundred men, the King of England, his golden crown flashing on his helmet, was charging the mass of the enemy reserve. Once he had reached the bottom of the hill, Richard urged his horse to a gallop, hooves thundering behind him. His mind was riveted upon the encounter to come, but he must have experienced a thrill of pride in the fellowship which rode like one man at his shoulder. They did not weigh the hazard he ordered them to dare. They did not ask him if his quarrel were good. *Loyaulté me lie.* . . . Perhaps now his mighty brother came to him, smiling, as he had smiled once upon a time, standing beneath the great sun banner in the moment of victory at Barnet. . . .

Straight across Sir William Stanley's bristling front King Richard galloped with his fellowship of steel. Through the eye-slits of his visor he caught a glimpse of hundreds upon hundreds of mounted men in bright red jackets, scarcely more than a bow-shot to his right, with Sir William's banner of the white hart at their head. Up a slight slope now Richard's courser raced, straight towards a milling mass of horsemen. The noise of the combat on Ambien Hill was dim, remote. Beyond, in the enormous silence of a kingdom waiting and wondering while the King charged upon the mightiest of his enemies, many hundred of soldiers, like the men of York, were moving along the roads to his support; hundreds of thousands more, like John Paston and the Duke of Suffolk, stayed at home indifferent to the issue.

Now Richard heard cries, volleys of shouted orders. Horses reared as their desperate riders forced them into a line. The steel ranks of Henry Tudor's guard surged forward. A mighty figure loomed up in Richard's path—Sir John Cheyney, noted for his girth and height. With a shock they crashed together, the giant and the frail King, Richard swinging his battle-axe in a flashing arc. The giant reeled, fell to the ground. Richard drove onward, cutting a path with his terrible axe. Around him steel crashed on steel; there was shouting; horses squealed in pain; dust swirled up from the earth like yellow fog. Lovell and Sir Robert Percy and others had forced themselves to his side.

Still forward thrust the troop, cleaving to the heart of the Pretender's guard. Richard was hewing his way towards the standard of the red dragon, borne by the stalwart William Brandon.

Behind, jerking his horse about, Henry Tudor precipitately recoiled. It was the most dreadful moment of his life. The slight figure wielding a battle-axe with the strength of Hercules was death itself; yet he dared retire not a foot farther lest his army see and lose heart from its leader's cowardice.

Richard caught one glimpse of him, then he had reached the red dragon standard and was whirling his axe against William Brandon's sword. A blow on the helmet he scarcely noticed. He struck again. . . . Down went the dragon of Cadwallader and Brandon rolled dead in the dust. In a tight arc about Richard his men were slashing their way onward. Only a few more yards now to Henry Tudor—— A squire seized Richard's bridle as Ratcliffe and Percy and others thrust their horses and their bodies before him.

The squire was shouting and pointing. . . . In the steel pocket his troop had forged for him Richard turned, made out through the dust the red jackets of Sir William Stanley's cavalry thundering upon him.

Another squire led up a fresh horse. Someone clutched his arm. Shaking his head, Richard shouted an order to Ratcliffe. A part of the little troop that remained swung round to meet the onslaught of Sir William Stanley. Forward again Richard spurred his white courser, forward towards the figure, so close now, who was Henry Tudor. But as he hewed his way, he became aware that all about him his men were falling, overcome by masses of weapons. 'Treason!' he shouted suddenly. 'Treason! Treason!' Swinging his battle-axe he thrust onward.

He heard yells . . . a shock of steel. Stanley's cavalry had crashed against his tiny fellowship. 'Treason!' he cried again, even as he struck with his axe, releasing his heart's anguish in one breath, crushing the predicament of his life into a word. None of his Household remained at his side. He was beating about him against a thicket of spears and swords, rocked by blows he could not feel. And still on his helmet shone—through the dust, through the flailing steel—the golden circlet of his crown. 'Treason!' he shouted, swinging his axe——

A dozen weapons smashed through his armour. In the midst of his foes, alone, he was beaten lifeless to the ground, leaving his kingdom and his fame to the hands of Henry Tudor.[8]*

He was thirty-two years old, had reigned two years, one month, twenty-eight days. The only language, it turned out, in which he had been able to communicate himself successfully to the world was the terse idiom of courage, and the chief subject he had been given to express was violence. It had begun for him as a child in violence and it had ended 'in violence; the brief span between had been a tale of action and hard service with small joy and much affliction of spirit. If he had committed a grievous wrong, he had sought earnestly to do great good. And through his darkening days he had kept to the end a golden touch of magnanimity. Men did not forget how the last of the Plantagenets had died. Polydore Vergil, Henry Tudor's official historian, felt compelled to record: 'King Richard, alone, was killed fighting manfully in the thickest press of his enemies.'

A handful of the King's companions managed to escape, including Viscount Lovell and Humphrey Stafford. When the word ran through the royal ranks on Ambien Hill that their sovereign had fallen, they knew there was no hope of anything but survival. Some broke away northeastward towards the hamlet of Cadeby; others plunged southward through the swamp to Redmore Plain, pursued by the rebel cavalry as far as Stoke Golding. Soon the victorious army gathered on a hill-top near that village. Sir William Stanley had managed to get his hands on the battered crown plucked from the dead King's helmet. While the troops cheered, the rescuer of Henry Tudor—or perhaps his brother, Lord Stanley—placed the crown on Henry's head and hailed him King.

Northumberland, all the while, sat still in Sutton Cheney until summoned to appear before the new-crowned monarch. Gravely he knelt in homage and gravely was his homage accepted; but he was taken into temporary custody, probably at his own request. He was the shame of the North, and four years later the North would avenge its shame by killing him. A few days after the battle, William Catesby, captured while fleeing, was hanged in a sweat of fear, and with him were hanged the Brecher father and son, West country yeomen.[9]* Norfolk and Ratcliffe, Brackenbury and John Kendall, and many others were beyond King Henry's reach.

From the first movement of Richard's army on to Ambien Hill, the battle had not lasted more than two hours; the actual combat, less than half that time. In the afternoon Henry Tudor and his host triumphantly entered the town of Leicester. A little after, arrived the last King of

England to die, or fight, in battle.[10]★ Stark naked, despoiled and derided, with a felon's halter about the neck, the bloody body was slung contemptuously across the back of a horse, which one of the dead King's heralds was forced to ride. As it was borne across the west bridge of the Soar, the head was carelessly battered against the stone parapet. For two days the body lay exposed to view in the house of the Grey Friars close to the river. It was then rolled into a grave without stone or epitaph.[11]★

The day after the battle, John Sponer galloped into York to bring news of King Richard's overthrow—the eighty soldiers of the city had not got as far as Leicester.

To the Mayor and Aldermen, hastily assembled in the council chamber, 'it was showed by . . . John Sponer . . . that King Richard, late mercifully reigning upon us, was . . . piteously slain and murdered, to the great heaviness of this City. . . .'[12]★

This is the unstudied epitaph of the men who knew him best.

Epilogue

Epilogue*

IN the late spring of 1487, Henry Tudor, now King Henry the Seventh, found himself, after almost the same length of rule, in much the same predicament that had confronted King Richard in the summer of 1485. A Pretender was about to invade the kingdom in order to claim his crown. He was a shabby Pretender at best—Lambert Simnel, the son of an obscure Oxford tradesman, who had been tutored in his role by a priest—and his assertion that he was the very son of Clarence, Edward Earl of Warwick, was a thin masquerade, for there were many who knew full well that the real Earl of Warwick was a prisoner in the Tower. But Henry recognized that the challenge to his shaky throne was formidable. The Irish, in their devotion to the House of York, had given Simnel an enthusiastic welcome, led by the Lord-deputy himself, the Earl of Kildare; the Earl of Lincoln, Richard's heir, had fled from Henry's council board and Francis, Viscount Lovell, Richard's chamberlain, had escaped from hiding, to seek aid for the cause from Richard's sister Margaret, Dowager Duchess of Burgundy. She provided them with the means of hiring 2,000 German mercenaries commanded by a redoubtable soldier, Martin Swart. On May 5, Lincoln and Lovell and their troops were triumphantly received at Dublin; Lambert Simnel was crowned King Edward the Sixth in Christ Church; a Parliament was summoned and coins were minted in his name; and large numbers of the Irish flocked to his standard. Some of his partisans apparently believed in his authenticity, but not Lincoln and Lovell. Since the conspiracy was thriving by the time Lincoln elected to join it, he had probably determined to act as Simnel's supporter until victory gave him the opportunity of assuming his position as the true heir of the House of York. On June 4, Lincoln and his army landed on the shores of Lancashire near Furness.

King Henry was not taken unawares. Since the beginning of the year he had been bending all his energies to meet the impending attack, for he was mistrustful of the issue and even of the loyalties of his supporters. Though the Queen Dowager was his mother-in-law, he seized the meagre estate he had allotted her and immured her in the convent of Bermondsey. What Richard had not done with Lord Stanley, Henry did with the Marquess of Dorset—clapped him into custody, with the comment that if the Marquess were a true friend, he should not resent a temporary spell of imprisonment for the good of the realm! As spring advanced, the King moved into East Anglia, anticipating an invasion from the Low Countries; but when it became clear that the blow would come out of Ireland, he emulated Richard and took his stance in the Midlands. Unlike Richard, he had by this time called up an army, composed of his surest followers. He made his headquarters at Kenilworth castle, while his host assembled at Coventry. Stringent orders were issued that the rest of his subjects were to be ready to join him at an hour's warning.

Five days after his enemies had landed, Henry was able to begin his northward march with perhaps 4,000 men. His journey to Nottingham was slow, apparently hampered by want of discipline and of enthusiasm in his troops and by rumours of disaster spread by rebel sympathizers. To his relief, Lord Strange appeared at Nottingham with the Stanley contingent of 5,000 men or more, which doubled the size of the King's army. Henry received few other additions to his strength; the kingdom, in no mood to rush to the support of its new King, was willing to wait and see. The Earl of Oxford led the royal host, with Jasper Tudor, now Duke of Bedford, second in command. The Earl of Northumberland was apparently sitting ambiguously upon his estates surrounded by a force of trusted retainers. Not long after Henry reached Nottingham, he learned from his scouts that his enemies were advancing southward by the eastern, rather than the western, route. On June 15 he moved nine miles eastward to the village of Radcliffe, preparing to march up the Fosseway in order to block the rebels' approach.

Lincoln's forces had soon been joined after their landing by Sir Thomas Broughton and other men of the Northeast, but there was no popular rising. It was Stanley territory, people disliked the 'wild Irish', and 'King Edward the Sixth' was a doubtful entity. Nevertheless, Lincoln advanced resolutely eastward across the Pennines, issuing strict orders against plundering or molesting the inhabitants. Richard still reigned in the hearts of Yorkshiremen; the North was discontented, restless. Lincoln could hope for a great accession to his strength. As he descended into the plain of the East Riding, however, he was confronted by a difficult decision. If he made for the city of York, he might have to fight Northumberland, but he was certain to swell the numbers of his army and he could probably stir a rising to his cause. On the other hand, having heard from his scouts that the King was beginning to move towards him, he saw that he must strike southward quickly if he hoped to force Henry to a battle before the royal army reached its full strength. Valiant and quick spirited, aware that the morale of his host was high, Lincoln chose to try the advantage of immediate attack. It was the sort of choice on which subsequent victory bestows the accolade of 'genius' and defeat, the reproach of 'rashness'. Lincoln swung his men boldly to the south and advanced by way of Doncaster, or Rotherham, to Southwell, where, on June 15, he turned eastward and crossed the Trent at Fiskerton ford, four miles south of Newark, in order to reach the great thoroughfare of the Fosseway. Hearing that the King was issuing from Nottingham, Lincoln pitched his camp that night not far beyond the ford on a ridge over which the Fosseway passed. Next morning he drew up his battle-line with his right flank resting strongly on a height above the river and his centre blocking the road. He had about 8,000 men, of whom at least half must have been Irish, eager for the fray but naked of armour and primitively armed. The power of the army was Martin Swart's 2,000 Germans and perhaps an equal number of English adherents.

Up from the south, a little before nine in the morning, came the forward wing of the royal army, mustering about 6,000 men—fully half of Henry's total strength—and deployed in line of battle beneath the standard of the Earl of Oxford. The centre and rear wings of the royal host were lagging well behind. As soon as Oxford's line reached the foot of the ridge, Lincoln and Lovell and Swart gave the signal to attack, and the invaders flung themselves down the hill upon their enemies.

Precisely what had happened in the royal army that morning and the night before remains obscure. After it reached Radcliffe, a disturbance of some sort occurred, and numbers of soldiers deserted in the night. The countryside round was buzzing with ominous rumours; some contingents marching towards the King were persuaded to disperse, so they afterwards averred, by rebel agents or sympathizers who spread reports that Henry had already lost the battle. To meet this crisis, uglier even than Richard's before Bosworth, Oxford concentrated the most trustworthy troops in his forward wing. The King, who had courage but knew how to lace it with prudence and was of no mind to risk all on a single engagement, chose to follow with the centre ward.

Since Oxford's division was the most zealous and no doubt the most soldierly, it deployed into line of battle on the morning of June 16 much more speedily than the centre and rear which had little will to fight for Henry's cause.

Thus it was that Oxford's **vangu**ard alone met the shock of Lincoln's attack. A long and savage struggle ensued. Oxford was outnumbered perhaps 3 to 4 but his soldiers were far better armed than the Irish half of the rebel host. In the first wild moments of the encounter the royal vanguard was badly shaken; men began a flight to the rear crying that the Tudor's cause was lost. But the superiority of Oxford's weapons gradually became evident, and when captains of the centre ward managed to bring up a few reinforcements, the royal line stiffened. Lincoln and Swart fought with a valour and skill that commended itself even to their enemies and the 2,000 Germans showed themselves peerless warriors. But the Irish, though they 'fought hardily and stuck to it valiantly', could not match their clubs and scythes against plate armour and swords, and they began to fall in numbers, slain 'like dull and brute beasts'. Gradually the weight of weapons told. With most of the Irish slaughtered or in flight, Oxford's men closed upon the diminishing band of English and Germans. Lincoln and Swart and Sir Thomas Broughton perished where they fought and most of the Germans with them. Lovell either was drowned trying to cross the Trent or later starved to death, somehow walled up in his own cellar. Half the rebel host was slain; Oxford's losses were almost as severe. King Henry, like his centre and rear, took no discernible part in the battle.

It had been a very close call for Henry. Except for his own party, the realm had given him little support and the contagion of treason had apparently run through a goodly part of his army. Had the Stanley interest not come in or had circumstances been but slightly altered, he probably would have been defeated by a challenge which, though spirited, had perhaps by no means mustered all the strength of its cause.

When Stoke was fought, Henry's reign had lasted almost as long as the full span allotted to Richard. Both men seized the crown, both were confronted with an insurrection a few months after ascending the throne, and both had summoned one Parliament. A survey of Henry's accomplishment during this period should provide, therefore, an apt comparison with Richard's.

Less than two weeks after Bosworth, Henry had entered London and was planning his coronation, for though many had accepted him for the sake of King Edward's daughter whom he had sworn to marry, he himself intended to appear as a King solely in his own right. He was crowned on October 30 with much pomp, but with a rather scanty attendance of the nobility. He signalled the occasion by taking the unprecedented step of creating a guard of yeomen to protect his person. Eight days later, Parliament assembled. The dubious question of the royal title was shrewdly solved by an act which declared, in effect, that Henry was true King of England by virtue of the fact that he was sitting on the throne. To put money in the treasury, a resumption of royal lands was passed and the usual subsidies and customs were granted the King. There were a few minor bills, among them one which made hunting in the royal forests a felony. Apart from these routine proceedings, there was but one enactment of importance, and it stunned the country. The late King and twenty-eight of his principal adherents were attainted of high treason—this startling measure being effected by the device of dating Henry's reign from the eve of Bosworth in order to transform the royal army into a band of rebels who had taken arms against their true King! The bill was so unpopular that men dared speak against it. The Croyland Chronicler was moved to cry out, 'O God! What security shall our Kings have henceforth that in the day of battle they may not be deserted by their subjects!' Thomas Betanson wrote to Sir Robert Plumpton that 'there was many gentlemen against it, but it would not be, for it was the King's pleasure'. At the end of the session, which lasted a little more than a month, the Commons petitioned the King to marry Elizabeth, and he gravely agreed to do, at his subjects' request, what he had two years before sworn to do in order to win the crown. On January 18, 1486, he married the eldest daughter of King Edward. While Parliament was meeting, Henry had begun a reorganization of the royal finances, on the lines initiated by Richard, and he had administered to his Household officers, Lords spiritual and temporal, and Commons an oath to eschew livery and maintenance and keep the peace. Such was the scope and quality of King Henry's legislative accomplishment and the executive action which accompanied it.

While he was spending his Easter (1486) at Lincoln, Henry learned that insurrections were being stirred around Worcester by Humphrey and Thomas Stafford and in the North by Viscount Lovell and other friends of King Richard. The North, it appears, would have risen to arms immediately after Bosworth to proclaim Lincoln, Richard's heir, as King, but Henry had published a false report of Lincoln's death and the men of York and the men of the moors, confused by the treachery which had encompassed their sovereign, found no immediate leader to follow and for the moment remained quiescent.

King Henry quickly gathered a small force under the command of Jasper Tudor and started north, proclaiming an offer of pardon to all who would submit. The Earl of Northumberland, but recently released from his 'imprisonment' in London, duly came in at the head of his retainers: the rebels were men who hated him for his treachery to Richard. By the time the King entered York, the rising had fizzled out, lacking a leader to challenge Henry's crown; and Lovell, after a vain attempt to seize the King, went into hiding. The Staffords likewise failed to rally Worcestershire to their standard and fled to sanctuary near Oxford. On the suddenly invented grounds that high treason could not merit sanctuary, the Staffords were dragged forth by the King's agents; Humphrey was promptly condemned and executed. After Henry had enjoyed the pageants which the city of York prudently exhibited for his pleasure, he was able to continue his progress through Worcester and Gloucester to Bristol. While the King was still in Yorkshire, however, there occurred in London itself a riotous attempt to depose him and set the imprisoned Earl of Warwick on the throne; and throughout the succeeding months before the battle of Stoke a series of similar risings and disorders troubled the kingdom. The North was hostile; other portions of the realm were restless, or sullen.

On September 20, 1486, Queen Elizabeth gave birth to a son. It had been carefully arranged that the child be born at Winchester, the ancient home of British Kings, in order to emphasize the antiquity of the royal house, and the infant was appropriately christened Arthur. Not much more than a month later, Henry got wind of Lambert Simnel's appearance in Ireland and set about preparing his defences.

His diplomacy during this period is unremarkable. He had quickly signed a year's truce with his friends the French, which, in January of 1486, was extended for three years. He made peaceful overtures to the Scots. He signed a commercial treaty with Brittany. But Edward's and Richard's all-important pact of amity and commerce with Maximilian was not renewed until January of 1487 and then only for a year.

Thus runs the record of Henry's achievement during the first two years of his reign. In stability of rule, establishment of order, vigour of diplomacy, development and execution of policy, and concern for the welfare of the people, the government of Henry Tudor hardly challenges comparison with the government of King Richard. It is true that Richard failed to keep his throne, whereas Henry kept his; but this difference in Henry's favour, overwhelming though it may seem, is not attributable to his popularity as a Pretender and it was certainly not the consequence of the greatness of his rule as a King. Only when government is viewed purely as a problem of power does Henry's *fact* of survival blot out the *terms* of Richard's failure to survive.

To read the panegyric of Polydore Vergil is to see Henry as only a little lower than an angel come from Heaven to rule over the English; to read such a representative modern work as *The Earlier Tudors* is to find Henry elevated to the lofty stature of having 'some claim to be regarded as the greatest of Tudors'. Seldom is the fox praised for swallowing down the grapes by being hailed as their 'rescuer'. Yet this is the accolade which has been bestowed upon Henry. Precisely from *what* he rescued England remains mysterious. From disorder, *The Earlier Tudors* remarks, rather as if the answer were self-evident. But the disorder of Henry's reign exceeded that of Richard's and the last half of Edward's. England as a whole neither needed nor wanted to be rescued. It doubtless learned of Richard's defeat with surprise, it accepted Henry's victory with apathy, and it afterwards resented Henry's harsh rule.

His 'shilling diplomacy', the remorseless fines by which he crushed the Commons, the extortions and oppressions of his rapacious agents Dudley and Empson—their books annotated by the King's own methodical hand—the treason trials and hangings, the menacing ubiquity of spies, the half a generation's span of insurrections and other disorders, the King's feverish accumulation of treasure mined from his hapless subjects' pockets—it is this record which explains Sir Thomas More's Latin verse hailing with joyous relief the advent of a new springtime in the accession of Henry VIII after the winter of his father's grim, oppressive reign.[1] In his acute analysis of the machinery of Henry's government, Kenneth Pickthorn observes—astonishingly enough—that the first duty of a government is to maintain itself. One might think that the first duty of a government was to rule well, but even by this amoral standard the record of the greater part of Henry's reign does not register more, despite his ruthless exercise of *Realpolitik*, than a shaky survival against challenges weaker than those the House of York had confronted and against domestic disaffection which was mainly the product of the very severities employed by Henry to maintain himself.

In the eyes of nineteenth century England, bustling with commercial success and proud of material accomplishment, Henry took on the appearance of an efficient company manager: shrewd, wary, his gaze unwaveringly on the main chance and his mind fixed on dividends. There was no nonsense about him; he showed a fat surplus which he thriftily passed on to the next managing director (who promptly spent it). How well he served the public, the actual quality of the obstacles he encountered, the help his predecessors had given him—these considerations were ignored. Since our present century has shown no decline in its respect for shrewd company managers, Henry's reputation has continued to grow. But perhaps his ultimate justification lies in the foresight he displayed in being the progenitor of the great *Gloriana*, the effulgence of whose reign is somehow reflected back upon his own. Seldom has a man, or a monarch, been given so much credit for being somebody's grandfather. Because Henry appears as the archetypic *entrepreneur*—Gairdner remarks approvingly that he ruled England by his cashbox—and because Queen Elizabeth was of his dynasty, he has fared considerably better than Sir Thomas More could have suspected.

Though of somewhat smaller stature as a King, Henry seems, however, to have been a much more interesting person than he is sometimes depicted. He was that vivid paradox, the unadventurous adventurer. If his dynasty happened to endure—thanks, in part, to the quantity of Henry VIII's marriages—for 119 years, he himself remained to the end of his days something of the exile, a freebooter who had tumbled into a fine nest and worked hard to remain in it. He based his title on the actuality of conquest, and he ruled England, with his guard and his secrecy and his iron self-interest, much in the manner of an alien conqueror. With Louis XI, governing France was the grand passion of his life. With Henry, governing was the means of remaining King of England, a position to which, in a grim yet half-humorous, cynical, detached, practical way, he was devoted. He had one standard of judging an act or policy—did it show a profit? Profit was anything that seemed to strengthen his rule. He was staggeringly objective; he permitted himself neither emotions, illusions, nor commitments to principle. Like the true adventurer he travelled without baggage; hence, he could use both hands to keep his crown on his head.

Such glimpses of Henry's private life as can be caught from his Privy Purse expenses show him as a man of lively interests in his hours of leisure, cultured and fond of princely pleasures. He surrounded himself with poets and Welsh bards and minstrels and harpers; he bought books and encouraged learning and the arts; he apparently enjoyed the antics of fools, for he had a stable of them. He once gave a woman five shillings for two glasses of water. 'To hym that founde the new Isle [John Cabot]' went a guerdon of £10, but a 'young damoyselle that daunceth' delighted him to the tune of thrice that amount. He was devoted to his mother, a most remarkable woman of learning, piety, and wit, to whom he owed much. His wife, Elizabeth of York, did not fare so well in his affections, perhaps, in part, because she was so much loved by his subjects. Bacon remarks, with grim understatement, that he was not uxorious. In the moment of being stricken by the news of his son Arthur's death (1502), he sought with great tenderness to comfort her, but she apparently had no share in the life of his heart. From the time she was married until she died, after childbirth, in 1503, Elizabeth was well nigh mute and almost invisible. Henry would not even permit her to be crowned till the intense dissatisfaction of his subjects with this slight made her coronation a matter of policy.

This ceremony itself was marred for her by a shocking stroke of violence. The cloth on which royalty trod from Westminster Hall to the Abbey was regarded, apparently, as the perquisite of the populace. As the Queen was walking in her coronation procession, a mass of people pressed forward, eager to snip their share of the cloth. In a sudden panic the guards drew their weapons and before the Queen's eyes killed several of the mob. So great was the commotion that 'the order of the ladies following the Queen was broken and distroubled'. From a stage hidden by lattices and arras, King Henry and his mother cozily watched Elizabeth's coronation, and in the same manner they afterwards surveyed the banquet in Westminster Hall.[2] It was Margaret Beaufort who, in the authority she wielded at court and in the affection the King gave her, was the true Queen. Both Ayala and the Sub-prior of Santa Cruz reported that she kept her daughter-in-law in subjection.[3] Elizabeth's own mother was immured for the rest of her days, except for rare visits to court, in the Bermondsey nunnery with a pension of £400.[4]*

Henry is not remarkable because, for the scope of his purposes and pursuits, he drew a large circle; actually, he drew a small circle, but he is remarkable because he filled it so completely, because he saturated it. This distinction Bacon suggests in his biography of Henry: 'If this King did no greater matter, it was long of himself: for what he minded he compassed'. He was not without his successes—in his own eyes the greatest perhaps was simply that he kept his throne. His management of finances was masterly; he improved the machinery of government and strengthened the force of law; he encouraged trade; he was an indefatigable negotiator with foreign powers and secured some advantageous treaties, notably the marriage alliance of his daughter Margaret with James IV of Scotland. But measured in terms of its effects, this accomplishment loses much of its lustre. He developed the machinery of government in order to rule as a tyrant; he gave force to the law that he might make it an engine of financial gain and political oppression; the limited view of his diplomacy permitted Brittany to be absorbed by France, commercial relations with the Low Countries to deteriorate, for a time, into a damaging trade war, and England to be drawn, to her future heavy cost, into the wake of Spain and Spanish interests. What he bequeathed to his son was some £1,500,000 and a despotism.

For the first two thirds of his reign there was disorder and for the last third, misery, because he lacked the magnanimity to win his subjects' hearts and the largeness of vision to seek their happiness and welfare. He was, says Bacon, who extravagantly admired his craft, 'a dark prince and infinitely suspicious and his time full of secret conspiracies'.

In 1495 the Milanese ambassador wrote his master, 'The King is rather feared than loved, and this was due to his avarice. . . . The King is very powerful in money, but if fortune allowed some lord of the blood royal to rise and he had to take the field, he would fare badly owing to his avarice; his people would abandon him'. In 1497 a mob of Cornishmen, driven to desperation by Henry's taxes, were able to march all the way to the gates of London without encountering any commons, gentry, or lords willing to stand against them for the King's sake. The following year, the Spaniard Ayala, an ambassador of a very friendly power, wrote that the customs revenues were diminishing because of the decay of commerce caused by the King's heavy impositions; 'another reason for the decrease of trade . . . is . . . the impoverishment of the people by the great taxes laid on them. The King himself said to me, that it is his intention to keep his subjects low, because riches would only make them haughty. . . . He is disliked, but the Queen is beloved, because she is powerless. They love the Prince [Arthur] as much as themselves, because he is the grandchild of his grandfather [King Edward]. . . . [Henry] would like to govern England in the French fashion, but he cannot. . . . Those who have received the greatest favours from him are the most discontented. . . . He likes to be much spoken of, and to be highly appreciated by the whole world. He fails in this, because he is not a great man'. There must have been numbers of men in England to whom the succeeding years had brought new reasons to regret the issue of Bosworth Field.[5]

What of those great lords whose treachery had given Henry this victory?

Thomas Stanley fared best. He was rewarded with the earldom of Derby. But Henry did not entrust him with the power he had enjoyed under Richard. He faded into the background of the reign, becoming, in effect, the King's mother's husband—but the King's mother forsook his bed under a vow of religious dedication. On one occasion Henry found a reason to squeeze from him a fine of £6,000.

Sir William Stanley, Henry's very rescuer, lived to regret that timely intervention at Bosworth. The King is said to have felt that though Sir William saved his life, he delayed long enough to endanger it. Henry bestowed lands upon his saviour, made him Lord Chamberlain, but gave him no title. Sir William, for his part, discovered that the change of Kings had not, after all, wrought a world more to his liking, even though he is reported to have become the richest commoner in England.

There appeared in Ireland in the autumn of 1491 a new Pretender to the throne, Perkin Warbeck, who was to trouble Henry for the next six years with the claim that he was Richard of York, the younger son of King Edward. In January of 1495 the kingdom was stunned to learn that Sir William Stanley had been arrested on a charge of treasonably conspiring with the Pretender. He was promptly sentenced to death and beheaded on February 5.

Without question, Sir William had become sufficiently embittered by his sense of Henry's ingratitude and disillusioned with Henry's rule to entertain the idea of overthrowing him; but whether he had engaged in the overt treason of which he was accused is uncertain. It was charged that in 1493 Sir Robert Clifford had joined Perkin in the Low Countries in order to concert the treason schemed by Stanley. It is possible, however, that Clifford was all along an *agent provocateur* of the King and that Stanley's disloyalty of thought had been deliberately magnified into a traitor's plotting. In any case, when Clifford returned voluntarily to England, Henry doled out to him the fat sum of £500 from the Privy Purse and Clifford then accused Sir William. Henry's Lord Chamberlain was said, among other things, to have declared that if Perkin were indeed the son of King Edward, he would never fight against him. Henry betrayed no interest in extending clemency to the man who had given him life and crown. 'Qualms he felt', says *The Earlier Tudors*, 'for he paid the expenses of the "traitor's" burial'.

Henry Percy, Earl of Northumberland, fared worst of all: he was of the North and the North could not forget that he had stood idly by while his lord King Richard had ridden to his death. For a time he thrived. He not only enjoyed his old offices of Lieutenant-General of the Marches, Captain of Berwick, Sheriff of Northumberland, but the King permitted Richard's regional council to lapse so that Northumberland might consider that at last he possessed his ancestors' sway and was Lord of the North.

Early in 1489, King Henry extracted from Parliament the staggering tax of £100,000 in order, he said, to levy war against the French—though, in fact, he did not go to war for many months after and when he did wage a very short campaign he spent far less than he had wrung from his subjects. The attempt to gather the tax provoked trouble in Yorkshire. The King promptly sent Henry Percy, and others, a commission to put it down. When Northumberland nervously urged his sovereign lord not to insist on the collection of the subsidy, Henry fired back a hard, curt demand that the tax be exacted to the uttermost farthing, whether the people could pay it or not, especially from those who 'whined most at it, lest it might appear that the decrees, acts and statutes made and confirmed by him and his high court of parliament should by his rude and rustical people be infringed, despised, and vilipended'.

Northumberland did not dare to disobey his master, though he was tensely aware of 'the continual grudge that the Northern men bare against him sith the death of King Richard whom they entirely loved and highly favored. . . .' Anxiously he sent word for his most trusted retainers to meet him at Thirsk, near which village he had halted with a small retinue of servants and followers. The very next day a force of the commons came upon him at Cocklodge not far from Thirsk. There was an exchange of angry words which led to a scuffle; then the commons fell upon the man they hated. In the moment of his greatest need Henry Percy's men deserted him. He was pulled from his horse and murdered. Thus did the North violently avenge its shame. King Henry evinced no sorrow for Northumberland's fate. He promptly reinstituted the council inaugurated by King Richard. He looted Henry Percy's son of £10,000 and Henry VIII swallowed down the whole earldom of *his* son.

But there was played a comedy, as well as a drama of revenge, in

he North. It was staged with danger ever in the wings by actors
unaccustomed to be venturesome. The solid burghers of York, despite
their townsman tradition of meddling not in the hazards of national
politics, were so staunch in their loyalty to King Richard that they
dared, though it would cost them dear, to sit spiritedly upon their
independence and mock Henry Tudor.

For weeks after Bosworth, York seethed; bitter language was used
against the new King and men openly showed their discontents. The
authorities worked to preserve order, for the safety of the city, at the
same time that they were beginning their duel with Henry. Only five
days after the fatal field, Robert Stillington, Bishop of Bath and Wells,
was haled a captive into the city by Windsor Herald and one Robert
Borow, who were on their way to London with him. The bishop was
afflicted in body and spirit, 'sore crazed, by reason of his trouble. . . .'
The council of York could not save the bishop, but they showed their
feeling by flatly informing his captors that he must be permitted to
continue still within the same city for four or five days for his ease and
rest'.

The action of the comedy proper sprang from the circumstance that
York imperturbably went on enjoying the services of Miles Metcalfe,
an ardent follower of King Richard, as its Recorder. On October 2
King Henry wrote the city that 'Miles Metcalfe . . . hath done much
against us which disables him to exercise things of authority. . . .' One
Richard Grene was the man the King wanted in the post. The council
duly informed Henry of its decision that Grene should occupy the
office of Recorder—'unto such time as it shall please the King's highness
to call Miles Metcalfe . . . unto his grace and favour'! Six days later, the
city received the King's proclamation of pardon to men of the North
Parts, which excepted eight of Richard's chief adherents, one of whom
was Miles Metcalfe.

On November 12, Henry tried again. He thanked the men of York
for what they had done for Grene but underlined the point that he
wanted his man made permanent Recorder 'in ample manner and form
as . . . of time passed'. The Earl of Northumberland wrote from London
four days later echoing the King's demand and referring to Grene as
his servant. The city council parried these thrusts by deciding to
postpone action on the Recorder question until their representatives
had come home from Parliament. On December 12 they received yet
another missive from King Henry, this time peremptorily ordering
them to heed no persuasions in Metcalfe's behalf and willing them to

give Grene permanent possession of the office. Grene himself wa present at the meeting in which this communication was read. When he had heard the council solemnly decide to continue the postponement of the issue until their colleagues returned from Westminster, Grene became so angry that he snatched the papers from the clerk and rushed from the chamber. The council had just the man to handle this situation. Three days later, Thomas Wrangwysh, King Richard's friend and the first soldier of the city, returned the papers to the clerk.

By that time the council was able to show the King's own writ of protection for Miles Metcalfe, which they immediately interpreted as giving them the right to reinstall him as their Recorder. When, however, the Earl of Northumberland returned to Yorkshire in January of 1486, he brought such pressure to bear on behalf of Grene that the city officers consented to make him a member of the council at twenty shillings a year, blandly promising that since Northumberland and King Henry had wished Grene to be Recorder, they would bear these requests in mind if Grene proved himself a satisfactory councillor. The city, in the meanwhile, had petitioned the King for a reduction in its fee-farm, boldly citing the relief which King Richard had given.

The second act of the comedy opened on the last day of February (1486), when it was learned that Miles Metcalfe was dying. Richard Grene immediately demanded the Recordership. The council, though it had promptly moved to reinstate Metcalfe in the absence of its parliamentary representatives, now declared that it could not act while they were out of the city. On March 7 the Mayor received a request from the Earl of Northumberland that he be granted the privilege of nominating the new Recorder. Without waiting for a reply, the Earl then sent a second letter, which the council received next day, asking them to elect his 'servant and councillor', Richard Grene. The council dispatched the polite answer that they would have to postpone decision until their colleagues returned. When, at last, these men came home from Westminster on March 11, with the report that they had 'laboured to the King' for the reduction of the fee-farm, the election of a Recorder was put off till the next Assizes. In a few days a new character appeared momently upon the stage, apparently as a friend of the city. It was no less than the Countess of Northumberland, who, the Mayor reported without comment on Tuesday, March 16, had called him and his aldermen before her the previous Sunday at the House of the Augustinian Friars and 'willed them nothing should be further attempted in the matter concerning the election of a new Recorder unto the next time f her return unto the same city, notwithstanding any writing to be made unto them in the meantime, shewing that she should be their warrant and defence in that partie'. Eleven days later arrived a letter from King Henry: having learned that Miles Metcalfe was dead, he wished the city to elect Thomas Middleton to the Recordership. By this time the city fathers were aware that a rising against the King was being stirred in Wensleydale and elsewhere and they were beginning their preparations for the impending visit to the city of Henry himself. Not many days before he arrived, they unanimously elected to the Recordership John Vavasour, an officer of King Richard who had probably been a member of his ducal council!

It was John Vavasour who delivered the oration of welcome to Henry when he arrived and it was John Vavasour who delivered the city's reply to a Lancastrian baron arrogantly presuming to exercise some authority within its walls. Shortly before the King reached York, Lord Clifford, who had been restored to his title and estates by the recent Parliament, wrote that in anticipation of the royal entry he intended to come to the city 'and there to minister as mine ancestors hath done heretofore in all things that accordeth to my duty. . . .' He requested the magistrates to provide a worthy welcome for the King and the rather at mine instance and desire to prepare all things there according to your old custom. . . .' Vavasour would not even dignify Clifford's demand with a written reply. He merely told the messenger of the baron that the Mayor possessed full authority to rule the city, that the citizens were fully aware of how a King should be received, and that though Clifford seemed to be labouring under the supposition that his ancestors hath had some manner of administration and rule in the said city in [respect to] the coming of the King unto the same', the magistrates find no record that his ancestors 'had any such administration or rule within the said city'. Vavasour ended by pleasantly commending the officers of York to Lord Clifford and desiring him 'to give his attendance of the King's grace according to his duty'!

The brief denouement of the comedy occurred the following June. It was provoked by yet another letter from King Henry in behalf of an office-seeker. Having heard that the Sword-bearer of York was about to retire because of age and illness, the King desired the city to appoint Robert Langston when the post fell vacant. The council had no trouble reaching a decision. Recalling that the King had promised them their ancient liberties, which included their right to elect whom they pleased, and recollecting that 'it had been of old time ordained' that whoever sought the King's favour for an appointment at the disposition of the magistrates should henceforth hold no office, they promptly determined that Robert Langston should not enjoy the position of Sword-bearer or any other post.

Comedy then gave way to the grim drama of Northumberland' murder and the insurrection that immediately followed it. The rebel stormed into the city of York, where they were joined by the Mayo and several gentlemen, for, says Bacon, the memory of King Richard still 'laid like lees at the bottom of men's hearts, and if the vessels were once stirred, it would rise'. But, the rest of the country remaining quiet the Earl of Surrey quickly came north with an armed force and pu down the insurrection. The North would continue to stir up rebellions culminating in the great rising against Henry VIII, the Pilgrimage o Grace. Its motives were religious and economic, but many of the leader must have remembered King Richard from their childhood and recalled what it had cost their fathers to remain loyal to him.

In the spring of 1491, meanwhile, just two years after they had had serious trouble with King Henry, the city magistrates learned tha John Burton, the schoolmaster of St. Leonard's hospital, was making mischief by saying that one John Payntor had called the Earl o Northumberland a traitor for betraying King Richard. When sum moned before them, Burton stuck to his story. According to John Payntor, however, who was then called in, Burton had said that King Richard was a hypocrite and a crouchback and was buried in a ditch like a dog; he, Payntor, had retorted that he lied—adding prudently that the King had buried him like a noble gentleman! Since the exchange had taken place in the house of William Plumer in the presence of three clerics of importance, they were then asked to give testimony. Al stoutly denied that Payntor had said anything treasonable, Richard Flint, a chaplain, deposing that Burton had called Richard 'caitiff' and used other 'unfitting language'. The most important of the ecclesiastics Christopher Wood, the Prior of Bolton abbey in Craven, was absen at this time from the city, but he made haste to send his deposition by messenger. According to the Prior, Burton said of King Richard tha 'he loved him never, and was buried in a dike. John Payntor said it made little matter neither of his love nor his —— and as for his burial, i pleased the King's grace to bury him in a worshipful place'. Payntor declared the Prior, had uttered nothing treasonable. He added that i was his opinion at the time that the schoolmaster was the worse fo drink. The Mayor ended the affair by commanding both men to keep

he King's peace on pain of forfeiture of 100 marks. However pleasing
hey might be to the King's ear, slurs upon Richard did not pass
nchallenged in the city of York.

Thus did he remain alive in many men's memories. But memories
re mute and the written word was dangerous. Henry had the writers,
nd what Henry's court said was all that counted. King Richard, such
s he was in life—confused and diligent and erring and earnest—was
uried beneath the black alluvial deposits of the Tudor historians, who
reated in his stead a simulacrum—an ogre, atop which King Henry was
lisplayed, rampant, rescuing England.

Appendices

Who Murdered the 'Little Princes'?*

THE fate of the 'Little Princes' is the most famous mystery in the annals of English history, and it has been acrimoniously debated for more than two centuries. Down to the present day the 'traditionalists' have maintained that King Richard the Third stands convicted of the crime, as asserted by the Tudor historians and blazoned to the world in Shakespeare's fine, bustling melodrama. The 'revisionists', insisting that the case against Richard is fraudulent, have either declared that the problem remains an enigma or fastened the guilt on other shoulders.

It will perhaps come as a surprise to the reader accustomed to the absolute assurance of history texts and guidebooks that there is no *proof* that King Richard murdered the two sons of King Edward IV. If we take 'evidence' to mean testimony that would secure a verdict in a court of law, there is no *evidence* that he murdered the Princes. Upon what materials, then, must an investigation be based?—upon rumours and hearsay, assertion from sources of demonstrable unreliability and inaccuracy, facts of disputed relevance, and inferences insusceptible to test drawn from events and acts. This is all that we have in the way of 'evidence', and it is a knotty, baffling, often contradictory complex of uncertainties.

The chief reason for the bitter disagreements that have raged around the problem of the Princes' murder is that the 'traditionalists' have ignored one or more of these disabilities inherent in the 'evidence'; whereas the 'revisionists' have tended to assume that these disabilities somehow gave them the licence to put forward a melange of speculation and wishful thinking at least as dubious as the traditional sources they scorn. On the one hand we have scholars clinging to 'evidence' which no jurist would dream of crediting—and no scholar either in any other context except the heated dispute over the fate of the Princes—while in refutation we behold writers unleashing as final revelation a farrago of conjecture. A plague o' both your houses! My purpose here is to present for the reader's judgment the materials which are available to

N*

elucidate the deaths of King Edward's sons, along with a commentary upon their ascertainable reliability and relevance.

This much can be advanced at way of a working hypothesis: the Princes were murdered by the instigation of one of three men. It is very possible that King Richard is guilty of the crime. If he is innocent, then it is well nigh inevitable that either King Henry the Seventh or Henry Stafford, second Duke of Buckingham, is guilty.

What is the case against King Richard?

Mancini, who left England at the time of Richard's coronation, July 6, 1483, has this to say: '. . . After Hastings was removed, all the attendants who had waited upon the king were debarred access to him. He and his brother were withdrawn into the inner apartments of the Tower proper, and day by day began to be seen more rarely behind the bars and windows, till at length they ceased to appear altogether. A Strasbourg doctor, the last of his attendants whose services the king enjoyed, reported that the young king, like a victim prepared for sacrifice, sought remission of his sins by daily confession and penance, because he believed that death was facing him. . . . I have seen many men burst forth into tears and lamentations when mention was made of him after his removal from men's sight; and already there was a suspicion that he had been done away with. Whether, however, he has been done away with [Mancini is writing in December of 1483], and by what manner of death, so far I have not at all discovered'.

The Great Chronicle, compiled some two decades later from London municipal records, echoes one part of Mancini's observations: 'And after this [death of Hastings] was the prince and duke of York holdyn more straight, and there was privy talk that the lord protector should be king'. This chronicle further reports that 'during this mayor's year [Edmund Shaa's], the children of king Edward were seen shooting and playing in the garden of the Tower by sundry times'. Since Shaa's year of office lasted from October 29, 1482 to October 28, 1483, this reference is too vague to be helpful. This same source records, however, that the first widespread rumour of the Princes' death did not come until after the following Easter (1484).

According to a recent discovery, which will be examined later, it appears that young Edward was suffering from a bone disease which had attacked his lower jaw. The boy's fears—as reported by Mancini—may have sprung as much from melancholia and ill health as any accurate apprehension of danger, beyond the realization that the lot of a deposed monarch is precarious.

It is not surprising that even before Richard's coronation some men suspected that the Princes might soon be killed. What then was the accustomed fate of deposed monarchs, even of men who had a measure of the blood royal in their veins? Edward the Second was murdered, perhaps by a red-hot spit thrust up his bowel. Richard the Second was starved, poisoned or hacked by steel in his cell at Pontefract castle. As recently as 1471 the feeble-witted Henry the Sixth had been put to silence. Shortly after this time, Henry the Seventh trumped up a charge in order to murder Clarence's son because he was of royal blood; and for the same reason Henry the Eighth executed Clarence's daughter, the Earl of Suffolk, the Duke of Buckingham, the Marquess of Exeter, and Lord Montagu. In this context of political practice it was inevitable that the moment Richard assumed the throne, there should be fears expressed for the future safety of the princes.

These suspicions recorded by Mancini, however, have small bearing upon the problem of the fate of the Princes. Whatever intentions Richard had regarding them, then or afterwards, considerations of policy dictated that they must be separated from their attendants—some of whom doubtless owed their appointments to the Woodvilles or Hastings, all of whom had served Edward when he was King, and some of whom might well be willing to undertake his escape—and that they must be withdrawn from sight lest their seeming accessibility stir men's minds to conspiracy. Mancini's statement about the replacement of the Princes' servants appears to be confirmed by a royal warrant of July 18, 1483, which authorizes payment of wages to thirteen men for their services to King Edward IV and 'Edward bastard, late called King Edward V' (Harl. 433).

Closest in time—and in more than time—to Mancini's testimony is a remarkable declaration by Guillaume de Rochefort, Chancellor of France, to the Estates General assembled in Tours in January of 1484: 'Regardez, je vous prie, les événements qui après la mort du Roi Édouard sont arrivés dans ce pays. Contemplez ses enfants, déjà grands et braves, massacrés impunément, et la couronne transportée à l'assassin par la faveur des peuples': the sons of King Edward butchered!—their assassin crowned by the people's will!

On what grounds the Chancellor based his declaration has long puzzled historians; Mancini has at last supplied the answer, as convincingly elucidated by his editor, C. A. J. Armstrong. Before he came to England, Mancini had addressed three poems to the French Chancellor, who had probably befriended him. 'It is remarkable that in the early days of December, 1483, when Mancini had just completed at Beaugency the *De Occupatione Regni Anglie*, the Chancellor was in the same neighbourhood presiding over the royal councils. . . . There was hardly an easier way for the Chancellor to have obtained the . . . information [concerning the murder of the Princes] than from the lips of Mancini' (*Usurpation*, p. 15). The Chancellor, then, knew only what Mancini could tell him: that at the time of the coronation in July some suspected that King Richard would soon kill the Princes.

It is not surprising that de Rochefort transformed the report of a suspicion into a fiery declaration of fact. England was the ancient adversary. In holding England up to scorn, the Chancellor could be sure of pleasing his audience, and at no risk, since she was now obviously incapable of going to war with France. Besides, Richard had been specially disliked by the French since 1475 when he had pressed King Edward to reject Louis XI's peace terms. Gairdner and others have pointed out that Richard was identified with the war party which for generations had made France bleed. The harsher things said of Richard, the better. In the early months of 1483 the French had pointedly arrested a servant of the Duke of Gloucester's at Tours, as Louis XI was unleashing his corsairs in the channel. But de Rochefort had a much more urgent and positive motive than these. France was now experiencing the perils of a minority reign. One of the principal purposes for the assembling of the Estates General which the Chancellor was addressing was to persuade the ambitious and quarrelsome princes to accept the government of the Regent, Charles VIII's sister, the Lady of Beaujeu. By transmuting the mere suspicions reported by Mancini into a certainty, the Chancellor secured just what he needed: a horrible example to the restless French nobles, a vivid warning of the direction their disaffection was tending, a plea not to follow the same reprehensible path taken by the hated English.

Next in time comes the evidence of the 'Second Continuation' of the *Croyland Chronicle*, compiled in the spring of 1486 from information in a large measure supplied, probably, by John Russell, Richard's Chancellor. Soon after Richard's coronation, this Chronicle records, the people around London and in the southern and southwestern counties began to conspire to free the Princes. Then 'public proclamation was made, that Henry, Duke of Buckingham . . . had repented of his former conduct, and would be the chief mover in this attempt, while a rumour was spread that the sons of King Edward had died a violent death, but it was uncertain how ("vulgatum est, dictos Regis Edwardi

pueros, quo genere violenti interitus ignoratur, decessisse in fata").'
The Chronicler nowhere else refers to the Princes, nor does he make any
comment upon the rumour which would suggest that he believed it
to be true. On the contrary, as Gairdner himself points out, the release
of the rumour was part of a prearranged plan. The revolt 'was not a
spontaneous result of popular indignation; it had been carefully
preconcerted several weeks before'. The rumour was deliberately
employed to divert the purposes of the rising to the ends of Buckingham
and Henry Tudor. Either the chronicler did not believe Richard guilty
of the murder, or he did not wish to accuse him, a possibility that seems
very unlikely. This much is certainly true: if it was indeed Richard's
Chancellor who supplied, early in the reign of Henry VII, the material
for this part of the chronicle, he did not choose to reveal what he knew,
or conjectured, concerning the Princes' fate.[1]

This is all the evidence furnished by the source materials most nearly
contemporaneous with Richard's reign: that as soon as he assumed the
sceptre some people began to suspect that he would make away with
his nephews (Mancini) and that a rumour of their deaths was loosed
for a special purpose by the chieftains of Buckingham's rebellion.

Between these sources and the Tudor historians, there are three
intermediate sources of some interest here. Two of these, Fabyan's
New Chronicles and The Great Chronicle, were compiled from London
municipal records about the same time that Vergil and More were
writing but are for the most part independent of them; the third, John
Rous's Historia Regum Angliae was composed a few years earlier. Rous's
flat statement, in a work dedicated to Henry VII, that Richard was
born with teeth and with hair streaming to his shoulders reveals the
valuelessness of his equally flat statements that Richard poisoned his
wife and killed the little Princes by means unknown; his testimony,
which is in general of little worth, seems to rest here upon no more than
rumour. Fabyan appears to record the hearsay of the early years of the
sixteenth century: 'As the common fame went, King Richard had,
within the Tower, put unto secret death the two sons of his brother
Edward IV'. The Great Chronicle, however, specifies, as we have seen,
that after Easter of 1484 'much whispering was among the people that
the King had put the children . . . to death'. Why 'after Easter'? It is
possible that, since Richard's little son died less than a week following
Easter Sunday, some folk saw in the boy's death a judgment of Heaven
which proved that the King had killed his nephews. This chronicle has
no more to add except for a catalogue of opinions of the possible ways

in which the Princes might have been dispatched—opinions which it seems to relate to the year 1485 but which more probably reflect the speculations of two decades later, historical perspective being unknown in this age. According to the chronicle, 'Some said they were murdered atween two feather beds, Some said they were drowned in malvesey [remaining no doubt from the execution of their uncle George of Clarence!] and some said that they were sticked with a venomous potion'. It seems safe to say that Fabyan, *The Great Chronicle*, and Rous have still nothing to contribute, two decades after Richard's reign, but rumour and that the rumours themselves are sprung from nothing more than suspicion. To suppose that the authentic details of the murder would naturally remain hidden even though a true report of the murder itself leaked out is to predicate the broad improbability that the very nucleus, the inner core, of the secret could somehow wriggle free without bringing a single shred of its attendant circumstances with it.

We come now to the Tudor tradition: it is a leap into another world, particularly in the case of Sir Thomas More's *Richard III*. The sparse and uncommunicative desert where grew only scattered shoots of suspicion that Richard was guilty suddenly blossoms into luxuriant certainty. The unreliability of More and Vergil I have demonstrated in the notes to the text and in Appendix II. More's story, and then Vergil's, must be examined, however, for what gleams of light they may cast upon the darkness.

In amazing contrast to what has preceded, More, writing about 1513, tells a brilliantly circumstantial story:

When Richard in his summer's progress of 1483 reached Gloucester, he suddenly decided that he must kill his nephews to secure his throne and so dispatched one John Grene 'whom he specially trusted' with a letter and credence to Sir Robert Brackenbury, Constable of the Tower, commanding Brackenbury to put the children to death. When Grene bore back the blunt answer of Brackenbury that he would never do the deed, Richard, now at Warwick, said to 'a secret page of his' that night as he brooded angrily on Brackenbury's refusal, 'Ah, whom shall a man trust. . . ?' The page had a ready answer: 'Sir . . . there lieth one on your pallet without, that I dare well say to do your grace pleasure, the thing were right hard that he would refuse'—meaning James Tyrell, a very ambitious man who was jealous of the favour which Ratcliffe and Catesby had won from the King. Richard at once summoned Tyrell to his chamber and 'brake to him secretly his mind in this mischievous matter'. Finding Tyrell instantly ready for the work, Richard armed him with a letter to Brackenbury, commanding that the keys of the Tower be delivered to Tyrell for one night. The Princes, according to More, were then in the exclusive charge of one William Slaughter, who, however, makes no further appearance in the story. As assassins Tyrell appointed Miles Forest, one of the four custodians of the Princes, 'a fellow fleshed in murder before time', and 'one John Dighton his own horsekeeper, a big broad square strong knave'. All the other attendants having been sent away, about midnight Forest and Dighton stole upon the sleeping Princes, 'suddenly lapped them up among the [bed] clothes', forced the 'featherbed and pillows hard unto their mouths', and so dispatched them. Tyrell had them buried at once 'at the stair foot, meetly deep in the ground under a great heap of stones'. When Tyrell apprised Richard of the deed, the King gave him great thanks 'and as some say there made him knight'. But Richard 'allowed not, as I have heard, the burying in so vile a corner. . . . Whereupon they say that a priest of Sir Robert Brackenbury took up the bodies again, and secretly interred them in such place, as by the occasion of his death, which only knew it, could never since come to light'.

The very incongruities and errors within this tale explode its claim on our belief.

1. It is inconceivable that any King, for the dispatch of business so desperately requiring secrecy, would employ letters such as Grene and Tyrell are supposed to have carried. The elaborateness of the dialogue alone, however, suggests that More's vivid imagination has considerably worked up whatever information he did receive.

2. James Tyrell needed no recommendation of a nameless page, nor did Richard for his dastardly deed 'as some say make him knight.' He had been a confidential servant of Richard's for at least a decade; he was knighted after the battle of Tewkesbury in 1471; and for his good service in the Scots campaign of 1482 Richard had made him knight banneret. By the time Richard set out on his progress Tyrrel was both his Master of the Henchmen and Master of the Horse.

3. Sir Robert Brackenbury cuts an impossible figure in the story. Having made his courageous and terribly dangerous refusal one week, he is, the next, confronted by Tyrell with a written notice to surrender the keys of the Tower for one night. Could he fail to guess Tyrell's business? And what of Will Slaughter and his assistants whom Tyrell did not employ? Abruptly turned out for a night and the next day finding the Princes gone, do they never let loose a word in an alehouse of this surprising circumstance? What does Richard, supposedly so ruthless, do about Brackenbury, hideously dangerous to him because he is so bold and honest? He bestows on Brackenbury a notable series of grants and offices as upon one who has served him faithfully and well—grants and offices which nobody ascribes to bribery. And how does honest Brackenbury express his horror of what the King has done? At Richard's call in August of 1485 he rushes north with all the men he can gather and dies fighting for his

master. Vergil likewise uses the incident of Brackenbury's stout refusal to do the evil deed. Apparently the Constable of the Tower, called 'gentle Brackenbury' by the *Chronicle of Calais,* was so well remembered for his integrity and charm of character that in order to make this tale of the murder of the Princes convincing, a clumsy device had to be invented in order to fit into it somehow this much admired man who was responsible for their custody. But so clumsy does the invention become that he is again involved in this deed so repulsive to him by the fact that a priest of his is said to have removed the bodies to another place—quite a task for a cleric to accomplish in a hurry, according to the description of how they were buried.

More's story is liberally sprinkled with names—John Grene, who bore the first mandate to Brackenbury; Miles Forest, one of the murderers, who afterwards 'at sainct Martens pecemele rotted away [an edifying spectacle!]'; and John Dighton, Tyrell's 'horsekeeper'. John Grene is of course a very common name, and at least two 'John Grene's' can be found in the register of Richard's grants. One John Grene was appointed Receiver of the Isle of Wight (a rather remote post in which to plant a man so dangerous on whom one would wish to keep a close eye); another John Grene, of Warwickshire, was issued, along with other men of the same neighbourhood, a pardon in September of 1483. A Miles Forest died sometime before September of 1484; an annuity of five marks was granted to his widow, one of many such grants to widows. Forest had been Keeper of the Wardrobe—the date of his appointment being unknown—at Barnard Castle, more than 200 miles from London. There is a John Dighton mentioned as the bailiff of the manor of Aytoun; another John Dighton was presented by Henry VII with the living of Fulbeck near Grantham in May of 1487. Neither of these men much resembles Tyrell's burly 'horsekeeper'. Since More's story presents so many inaccuracies and absurdities regarding its leading figures Brackenbury and Tyrell, there is no reason to suppose that it is any more accurate or reasonable in its use of minor figures like Grene, Forest, and Dighton, about whom almost nothing is known. It will appear, furthermore, from the circumstances under which this so-called information was secured, that it would not be very hard to come by a set of names.

The source More gives for his story is most impressive; it is nothing less than a confession of the murders made by Sir James Tyrell himself shortly before he was executed by Henry VII—for quite another crime —in May of 1502. The disparity between the authenticity of such a source and the incongruities of the tale will appear less puzzling when the circumstances of the 'confession' are examined.

Sir James Tyrell occupies a unique—in More's terms, a mordantly ironic—position in the history of his times. He is the only intimate officer of King Richard to continue a successful career under Henry VII.

When Bosworth was fought he was serving as the captain of Guisnes castle, one of the two fortresses protecting Calais. A month after the battle he was deprived of his sheriffdom of Glamorgan and Morgannok and a number of other offices in Wales, but he was not attainted in Henry's first Parliament. He sat tight in Guisnes, a strong position; and he soon began to climb into favour. In February of 1486 he was restored for life to the very offices he had lost the previous September. Continuing to hold Guisnes, he served on diplomatic missions of importance. He jousted at the tournament celebrating the creation of Henry VII's younger son Henry as Duke of York. Henry called him his faithful councillor. He eschewed the causes of the false Pretenders, Lambert Simnel and Perkin Warbeck. Interestingly enough, however, when a true scion of the White Rose crossed his path, his allegiance to Henry apparently faltered. After the Earl of Suffolk, Lincoln's younger brother, fled to the Continent in the summer of 1501, Tyrell was accused, perhaps by Sir Richard Nanfan, deputy lieutenant of Calais, of having given Suffolk treasonable aid. A spy's report to Henry VII about 1503 records that Nanfan once remarked 'how long was it ere his grace and his council would believe anything of untruth to be in Sir James Tyrell; and some said I did seek to do him hurt for malice'.

In the late winter or early spring of 1502 the garrison of Calais besieged Guisnes in an effort to arrest Tyrell for treason. He was finally lured from his stronghold by a safe-conduct given under the Privy Seal. The moment he came aboard ship to confer with Sir Thomas Lovell, Chancellor of the Exchequer, he was told that unless he sent a token to his son ordering the castle to be surrendered, he would instantly be tossed into the sea. When he had complied, he and his son Thomas were promptly clapped into the Tower. This is the story told by Suffolk himself only six days after Tyrell's execution; it is confirmed by a bitter remark Lord Sandys made in a letter to Cromwell of January, 1537: 'It appears that the privy seal was a ruse to induce Sir James Tyrell to come to England'.

On Monday, May 2, at Guildhall, Sir James was tried on a charge of high treason because of his association with Suffolk before a commission of *oyer and terminer* composed of some of the greatest officers and lords of the realm. With him were arraigned a servant of his, one Welles-bourne, a nameless 'shipman', Sir John Wyndham, and a few others. Condemned the same day, he and Wyndham were beheaded on Tower

Hill on Friday, May 6. The following day Tyrell's son Thomas was also condemned of treason; but he was not executed and he eventually secured the reversal of the attainders of his father and himself, which had been enacted, along with numerous other attainders, in the Parliament of 1503–04.

What says More? 'Very truth is it and well known', he concludes his tale, 'that at such time as Sir James Tyrell was in the Tower, for treason committed against . . . Henry the Seventh, both Dighton and he were examined, and confessed the murder in manner above written, but whither the bodies were removed they could nothing tell. . . . Dighton indeed yet walketh "on a live" in good possibility to be hanged ere he die'.

King Henry could have desired nothing more than to prove that the Princes were dead and that an intimate servant of King Richard had confessed to killing them upon Richard's command. Henry's baby son Edmund had died two years before; Arthur, his eldest son and husband of Katherine of Aragon, had suddenly died, to Henry's consternation, only a month before Tyrell was executed. The male succession of the Tudor dynasty now hung by one life, that of Prince Henry. His father knew that the hopes of the White Rose would soon be stirring, as indeed they did stir less than a year later.[2] Perkin Warbeck had been executed a few years before; there had been at least three other 'feigned boys'. When might not another Pretender, encouraged by the shakiness of the Tudor dynasty, blaze up in the guise of one of King Edward's sons to rally the following of York and the many men who were discontented with the asperities of Tudor rule? Ever since he had mounted the throne it had been of great importance to Henry to prove the Princes murdered; now it was of more pressing importance than ever. A confession by Tyrell would be a Heaven-sent piece of fortune. On the scaffold, as was customary, Tyrell would cry his confession aloud before he died. Copies of the document, signed by Tyrell, would be circulated through the court and the realm that all might know the truth. . . .

But nothing like this happened. Some time—an unknown time— after Tyrell's execution, King Henry simply let it be known that Tyrell and a servant of his had, upon being examined in the Tower, confessed to the crime. According to More, the King likewise remarked that this servant, Dighton, was still alive and at liberty. Apparently, however, neither More himself nor any other chronicler had ever actually talked with this man or heard his story. No John Dighton is recorded among those arraigned with Tyrell, or arrested. And what led Henry suddenly to suppose that Tyrell knew anything about the fate of the Princes? It seems clear that if the King had got anything resembling a confession from Tyrell he would have published it; there is no proof that he even *tried* to get anything from Tyrell. Considering the pressing need to confirm the Princes' death and Tyrell's well known connection with Richard's government, Henry had probably decided that he might gain some advantage by dropping the remark that Tyrell and a servant of his, still actually alive, had confessed to killing the Princes. The stratagem cost him nothing and might do some good, weak though it was.

Bacon's attitude towards this story is of interest. His source of information appears to have been More. Bacon had no doubt that King Richard had murdered the Princes, but here is his comment upon this version of the deed: 'Tyrell and Dighton agreed both in a tale (as the King gave out). . . . But the King nevertheless made no use of them [the examinations of Tyrell and Dighton] in any of his declarations; whereby (as it seems) those examinations left the business somewhat perplexed. And as for Sir James Tyrell, he was soon after beheaded in the Tower yard for other matters of treason. But John Dighton (who it seemeth spake best for the King) was forthwith set at liberty, and was the principal means of divulging this tradition'.

Bacon makes clear his incredulity. More himself handles this supposedly direct and circumstantial 'confession' in a curiously tortuous and uncertain manner. Though at the conclusion of his account he says that Tyrell's confession to the murder 'in manner above written' is 'well known', yet in his very next sentence he declares that this story 'I have learned of them that much knew. . . .' And at the beginning of his account he says, 'I shall rehearse you the dolorous end of those babes, not after every way that I have heard, but after that way that I have so heard by such men and by such means, as me thinketh it were hard but it should be true'. But why are there so many stories if the King's report of Tyrell's confession so neatly explains everything? These remarks of More are a succession of clods dropped into an already dim pool to muddy it still further. It appears that either (a) what Henry gave out was so meagre or vague that several different versions of what the King said have developed, from which More picks and chooses to assemble the tale that best pleases him; or (b) what Henry gave out was so meagre and vague that More felt he had to eke it out by making use of other tales and rumours as well.

But the thickest of the fog is yet to blow in upon this already obscure landscape. If Tyrell made a detailed confession of the murders, including, as More mentions, a revelation of the very staircase beneath which the Princes were buried, it is to be expected that Henry would at once have the bodies disinterred in order to secure incontrovertible proof of what he so much wanted the world to believe. Apparently no such operation was attempted. To explain this failure away, it seems, More tacks on the story that a priest, now conveniently dead, removed the bodies to another spot. In 1674, however, workmen removing a staircase attached to the White Tower and 'digging down' the foundations came upon the skeletons of two children buried in a wooden chest; as we shall see, there appears to be very good reason for believing that these indeed are the remains of the Princes. Gairdner thinks that this find somehow corroborates More's story. This appears to be a conclusion based on wishful thinking.

The discovery of the bones certainly throws no light upon why King Henry failed to exhume them, if Tyrell revealed the precise staircase beneath which they were buried, or why it was felt necessary to invent the tale of a priest's removing them, or why no writer of the time sees fit to retail this story except More. Further, the account of the burial of the Princes does not correspond very well with the circumstances of the actual burial as revealed by the discovery of 1674.[3]*

A comparison of Vergil's narrative with More's is instructive. Both men were seeking information at about the same time. More wrote his account in 1513; Vergil was completing his story of Richard's reign about 1517–18. As Henry's official historian, Vergil presumably enjoyed readier access to important people as he certainly did to documents of state. Whatever there was to be known of Tyrell's confession, Vergil would know it. If More, despite his muddling statements, had in fact reproduced what King Henry said that Tyrell said, Vergil can be expected to recount the same story.

He does nothing of the kind. He does not even regard Tyrell's 'confession' as worthy of mention. All he reflects of whatever King Henry said is that Tyrell was the murderer, and, like More, he is at pains to indicate Brackenbury's integrity. Though he pictures Richard as dispatching his first mandate from Gloucester, he seems to indicate that the King made his second attempt after he had reached York. Tyrell he portrays as no ready accomplice but as one compelled to act against his will. 'James Tyrell . . . being forced to do the King's commandment, rode sorrowfully to London. . . .' Interestingly enough, the

Wardrobe accounts indicate that, in fact, Tyrell did ride from York to London and back, or at least from London to York, about the time that Richard entered that city on his summer's progress of 1483: Richard had ordered a great array of raiment to be sent from the Wardrobe at Westminster to York for the ceremonial on September 8 of his son's investiture as Prince of Wales; and Tyrell is recorded in the Wardrobe accounts as having received cloth for himself and the royal henchmen of whom he was Master. It is possible that Vergil, coming across this record, decided to change the scene of Tyrell's agreement with Richard from Warwick to York—there apparently being little evidence, in his judgment, to locate the incident at Warwick. But what has happened to the anonymous page? to John Grene? to the jealous Tyrell ready for any desperate mission? Where is the murderous Forest and where is Dighton, so available for questioning? And where, indeed, is the vivid, circumstantial account of precisely how the children were murdered and how they were buried?—'With what kind of death these sely [innocent] children were executed it is not certainly known', says Vergil. It is a curious commentary upon the dogmatism which this long controversy over the murder of the Princes has engendered that Polydore Vergil, who was King Henry's personal historian and was therefore eager to fasten the blackest crimes upon his defeated rival King Richard, rejected (or never heard of) these embellishments of hearsay put forward by More, whereas certain historians even of our present day have continued to accept them![4]★

Vergil, it appears, establishes the essence of what King Henry 'gave out'—simply that Tyrell had confessed to the murder of the Princes. He contributes dubious colouring of his own, however. That Tyrell rode 'sorrowfully' to London would seem to be his or an informant's conjecture. In a similar vein he adds that 'King Richard . . . kept the slaughter not long secret, who, within few days after, permitted the rumour of their deaths to go abroad' in the hope that when the people knew that King's Edward's sons were gone beyond recall 'they might with better mind and good will sustain his government.' No other source makes such a statement and it has no show of probability to support it. For Richard to produce proof or the appearance of proof that the Princes were dead would at least put an end to restless speculation and attempts to rescue them; for Richard to spread such a rumour would only cause him to incur the odium without the advantages of their deaths. The *Croyland Chronicle*, it will be recalled, makes clear that the rumour emanated not from Richard, who knew nothing of it, but from his enemies who were plotting Buckingham's rebellion.

The later Tudor historians—Grafton, Hall, Holinshed—need not be examined; they merely echo or elaborate upon More and Vergil.

Since More's story is manifestly discredited by the circumstances of its origin, by its inaccuracies and incongruities, and by Vergil's rejection of it, the only 'evidence' for Richard's guilt which, it appears, had come to light by the time the Tudor tradition was established was (a) that during and after Richard's lifetime there were rumours, apparently based on no more than suspicion, that he had murdered the Princes; and (b) that King Henry VII, after Tyrell's execution, 'gave out' that Tyrell had confessed to dispatching the Princes.

Then, in 1933, new evidence was put forward pointing towards Richard's guilt. In 1674 workmen demolishing a stone staircase outside the White Tower which led up to a doorway, still visible, in its south face, discovered when they had excavated beneath the foundations of the stairs to a depth of ten feet a wooden chest containing the skeletons of two children. It being concluded that these were the very remains of the little Princes, the bones—somewhat damaged by the workmen's tools and by casual handling—were placed in an urn which was enshrined in Westminster Abbey, where it has ever since been displayed.

In July of 1933 the urn was opened and the bones were examined by an eminent physician and an eminent dentist.[5] The sum of their findings was that the elder skeleton was that of a child between the ages of twelve and thirteen; the younger, that of a child about ten years old. Since Edward V was born in November of 1470 and his brother in August of 1473, the ages at which the Princes met their deaths—if the bones are indeed those of the Princes—correspond closely with July-September of 1483, when they were rumoured to have been done away with. The anatomical evidence for the ages of the children and for death by smothering as indicated by a stain on one skull has been held, by subsequent authorities, to be unsound; but the dental evidence, according to authoritative opinion, is, in certain respects, beyond dispute.[6]* Yet the White Tower has stood for almost 900 years, in the course of which time many a secret bloody deed has been enacted there. It seems a pity that no anthropologist saw the bones; still an estimate of their age even today eludes us, dating by the carbon test being apparently impossible with material of so comparatively recent origin. If it could be established that the skeletons were between 450 and 500 years old, then it could be said with great positiveness that they were indeed the bones of the

Princes and that the Princes had died in the summer of 1483. As the matter stands, it can be asserted that (a) if these are the skeletons of the Princes, then the boys were killed in the summer of 1483; and (b) it is very probable that these are indeed the skeletons of the Princes.

Like the rumours already discussed, this very real evidence points towards the killing of the sons of King Edward during Richard's reign, but in itself it does not in any way illuminate the question of his guilt. It is now time to ask: are there any indications that Richard did not commit the deed?

There are, in fact, a number of such indications, of uncertain value.

Two documents in Harl. MS. 433 are of curious interest. One is a warrant to Henry Davy, dated March 9, 1485, 'to deliver unto John Goddesland footman unto the lord Bastard two doublets of silk, one jacket of silk, one gown . . . two shirts and two bonnets'. In the Wardrobe accounts the deposed Edward V is referred to as 'the lord Edward'; in a warrant to pay wages to his attendants he is called 'bastard Edward'. Richard, of course, had a bastard son John, who in March of 1485 was appointed Captain of Calais. Since John, however, was not a lord, he could not accurately be termed the 'lord Bastard'. But it is possible, as Professor A. R. Myers has kindly pointed out to me, that John was called 'lord Bastard' because he was a King's son.

The second reference occurs in the ordinances drawn up by King Richard for the regulation of the King's Household in the North (July, 1484): 'Item: my lord of Lincoln and my lord Morley be at one breakfast; the children together at one breakfast; such as be present of the council at one breakfast. . . . Item, that no liveries of bread, wine, nor ale be had, but such as be measurable and convenient, and that no pot of livery exceed measure of a pottle, but only to my lord [i.e., the Earl of Lincoln] and the children.'

One of these children was undoubtedly Clarence's son Edward, Earl of Warwick. I am indebted once more to Professor Myers for the suggestion that the others may have been Edward's sister Margaret and the younger daughters of King Edward. The following year Elizabeth, the eldest daughter, certainly became a member of this household. The children mentioned in the instructions are clearly of importance. Not only is a special breakfast arranged for them but only the Earl of Lincoln is to have a 'night livery' as grand as theirs. Apparently neither Lincoln nor Morley had offspring. It does not seem likely that these companions of Warwick were henchmen, because these children seem to be of greater importance than henchmen and because it is customary to find in household ordinances of the time specific regulations for henchmen. These two references can scarcely be said to weaken the strong probability that the sons of King Edward were killed in the summer of 1483, but the first, at any rate, *is* mysterious.

A statement in the *Croyland Chronicle*, which nowhere makes any reference to Richard's having murdered the Princes, can be instanced in support of his innocence. Catesby and Ratcliffe, says the *Chronicle*, were frantically opposed to Richard's marrying his niece Elizabeth out of fear that she might be able to revenge herself on them for urging Richard to take harsh measures against her kindred. Yet the measures the *Chronicle* specifies are the executions of Earl Rivers and Lord Richard Grey. If the chronicler believed Richard guilty of the Princes' death, could he have failed to mention the most obvious and poignant cause which Elizabeth would have to seek vengeance on the agents of the King's will?

Written sources yield nothing more. What else remains to be said in Richard's favour consists of inferences from actions and events.

What of the behaviour of the Queen Dowager, Elizabeth Woodville? In August or September of 1483 she secretly agreed to give her daughter Elizabeth to Henry Tudor, and on Christmas Day of 1483 Henry swore openly to make Elizabeth his bride. The Queen must have believed, at that time, that her sons were dead, or she would never have relinquished their rights to her daughter and a Lancastrian adventurer; and this belief seems to have been engendered by what the chieftains of Buckingham's rebellion told her. Yet six months later she accepted Richard's promise that he would treat her and her daughters well and surrendered them into his hands. That she came to terms with the man who had bastardized and deposed the Princes, driven her son the Marquess into exile, and executed her other son Grey and her brother Rivers is difficult enough to understand; but that she came to terms with Richard knowing also that he had murdered the Princes well nigh passes belief, or is at least incomprehensible. For in yielding her daughters not only had she shown herself amenable to Richard's request but she had delivered a blow to Henry Tudor's hopes and thus to her own hopes of some day seeing a descendant of hers upon the throne. She had done more: of her own volition she wrote to the Marquess, urging him to abandon Henry Tudor and put himself in Richard's hands. The Marquess was not a much tried, emotionally overwrought woman; there was no pressure upon him to return; indeed, it would be dangerous to make the attempt. Yet that is just what the Marquess did, only to be apprehended by Henry Tudor's agents in the act of flight and 'persuaded' to go back to Paris. This sequence of actions certainly suggests that Richard was able to offer the Queen—and the Queen to report to the Marquess—some proof or apparent proof or assurance that he was not guilty of the death of the Princes and that the Queen, her major cause of hatred thus removed, then accepted his offer. If this inference provides only doubtful support for Richard's innocence, the facts on which it is based unquestionably deepen the mystery surrounding the fate of the Princes.

An analysis of Henry Tudor's conduct likewise yields some reasons for acquitting Richard of the crime. In promising to marry the Princess Elizabeth, Henry emphatically rejected the position that King Edward's children were bastards; indeed he commanded all copies of the Parliament roll setting forth their bastardy to be burnt. As soon as Henry had won at Bosworth, he acted as a King in his own right. He had himself crowned on October 30; he summoned a Parliament which in November confirmed his title. Thus he minimized the danger that in making reference to the death of the Princes he would be giving too much emphasis to Elizabeth's position as next heir to Edward IV. In fact, it was of the greatest importance to Henry to prove that Richard had murdered Edward's sons in order to blacken his rival, discourage Pretenders, focus Yorkist feeling upon his bride Elizabeth, and establish his position in the hearts of the nation as the Heaven-sent avenger of those boys who, if alive, he must dispose of to hold the throne. He had the strongest motives for actively, openly and pressingly investigating the death of the Princes and publishing his proofs of Richard's evil dealing to the world.

This is precisely what he did not do.

The Parliamentary Bill of attainder accused Richard of 'unnatural, mischievous, and great perjuries, treasons, homicides and murders, *in shedding of infants blood* [my italics], with many other wrongs, odious offences and abominations against God and man and in especial our said sovereign lord. . . .' Clearly, by employing this insinuation he wished to suggest that Richard had murdered the Princes; it seems likely, however, either that he knew Richard was innocent or that he was unable to find proof of his guilt. Else why make use of mere innuendo? If Richard was guilty, to suppose that Henry, with all the resources of inquiry at his command, could elicit no damaging testimony from attendants at the Tower is scarcely credible. If Henry had secured strong evidence of Richard's guilt, to suppose that he would only hint at it in the bill of attainder instead of blazoning it to the world is almost as incredible. The actions and motives of Henry Tudor remain swathed in mystery—but we must remember that it is a mystery of his own making.

The passage of time only intensified Henry's motive for proving the Princes dead, as 'feigned boy' after 'feigned boy' arose to trouble his realm. Yet he said nothing about the death of Edward's sons until 1502; then he merely 'gave out', after Tyrell's execution, that Tyrell had confessed to the murders.

The circumstances under which Sir William Stanley was executed ten years after Bosworth tend to deepen the mystery. Sir William is said by Bacon to have been condemned for declaring that if Perkin Warbeck were indeed the son of Edward IV, he, Stanley, would never fight against him. If Sir William indeed made this remark, then, though he and his brother were most intimately connected with Richard's court, he must not have been certain that Richard killed the Princes. Royal children are rescued from death by kindly keepers and given into the hands of good shepherds only, it seems, in fairy tales. Stanley's remark would appear to have sprung not from his hope that, though Richard had doomed the Princes, one had managed to escape, but from his ignorance concerning their fate. This line of thought, however, is tenuous and tedious, and at best only casts still another veil about the enigma.

Considering the nature of the evidence for Richard's guilt, how strong a case does the sum of these inferences make for Richard's innocence? Strong enough, it would seem, to illuminate one rather obvious consideration which has largely been lost sight of in the quarrels over the worth of these 'evidences'. The most powerful indictment of Richard is the plain and massive fact that the Princes disappeared from view after he assumed the throne and were never again reported to have been seen alive. This fact is far more telling than any indications of his guilt that have been assembled and it weighs heavily against the indications of his innocence which have just been surveyed.

Indeed, it is reasonable to assert that only positive evidence that someone else murdered the Princes will tell against this indictment. It has been urged by Sir Clements Markham and Philip Lindsay, two of Richard's most recent defenders, that the Princes survived Richard's reign to be murdered by Henry VII. In the light of the very strong evidence, derived from the dental examination of 1933, that the boys were dispatched in the summer of 1483, this contention can hardly be any longer maintained, particularly since the case against Henry is itself weak. It rests upon a series of assumption: (a) that two pardons issued to Tyrell in the summer of 1486 reveal the interval in which, persuaded by Henry, he murdered the Princes; (b) that the Queen Dowager and the Marquess then sought to conspire with Lambert Simnel because they had discovered Henry's guilt; and (c) that after Henry managed to get rid of Tyrell in 1502, he noised abroad a true account of the murder but foisted responsibility for it upon Richard.

There is of course the possibility that the Princes died a natural death. Since Edward the elder was suffering from a chronic bone disease, he might well have succumbed; but that his brother Richard would conveniently follow suit is unlikely.

Is there any evidence that the Princes perished in Richard's reign but not by Richard's hand? Though hitherto largely ignored, a case, in fact, can be made out for the guilt of Henry Stafford, second Duke of Buckingham. It has been several times suggested that Buckingham was in collusion with Richard in the crime, or persuaded Richard to commit the crime or was aware of the crime; Gairdner, in *Letters and Papers*, reveals his belief in Buckingham's 'guilty knowledge'—' the circumstances of the revolt itself hardly admit of any other explanation.' They admit of one other explanation: that Buckingham himself contrived the murder of the Princes for his own ends.

There are indications among the chronicles of the time that in some men's minds Buckingham had at least a hand in the deed. A fragment of narrative (MS Ashmole 1448.60) says that Richard killed the Princes 'at the prompting of the Duke of Buckingham, as it is said ("initio concilio cum Duce de Bokyngham ut prefertur")'. The French chronicler Molinet, admittedly a very untrustworthy source for English affairs, puts forward the curious statement that 'on the day that Edward's sons were assassinated, there came to the Tower of London the Duke of Buckingham, who was believed, mistakenly, to have murdered the children in order to forward his pretensions to the crown.' Commynes, however, though in one passage he refers to Richard's having killed the Princes, declares in another passage that it was the Duke of Buckingham 'qui avoit faict mourir les deux enffans'—who had put the two children to death.

As Constable of England, Buckingham would find no doors shut to him. He had means of access to the Tower and to the Princes. It appears that he did not set forth with Richard on the royal progress, but, on the contrary, lingered a few days in London and then overtook Richard at Gloucester. And after he bade the King farewell, he rode away into Wales to begin plotting his overthrow. He had motives for murdering the Princes which were both stronger and more urgent than his sovereign's. Richard had assumed the crown without killing them and might maintain it without killing them, or until much time had passed and they had begun to be forgotten. Buckingham, on fire to claim the throne, or to help Henry Tudor claim it, must dispose of them at once because they were deadly rivals to his pretensions. By murdering the Princes, Richard risked stirring up a wave of hatred against himself. By murdering the Princes, Buckingham could further strengthen his cause, in spreading a rumour of their deaths, by blackening Richard's character and winning over the Woodville conspiracy to his own ends. Buckingham had scarcely less opportunity than Richard and he harboured stronger motives to perpetrate the crime.

Such motives explain why it was probably Buckingham who, before Richard assumed the throne, ordered preachers to insinuate the bastardy of Edward IV as well as of Edward's children: such odium cast upon the House of York he later hoped to profit by. Vergil makes a reference to these same motives: 'the multitude said that the duke did the less dissuade King Richard from usurping the kingdom, by mean of so many mischievous deeds, upon that intent that he afterward, being hated both of God and man, might be expelled from the same, and so himself [Buckingham] called by the commons to that dignity, whereunto he aspired by all means possible. . . .' It was undoubtedly Buckingham who supplied news of the Princes' death to the Woodville conspirators and, through the Countess of Richmond, to the Queen Dowager in sanctuary. Yet, according to all the hearsay, rumour, and allegation scraped together by More and Vergil, Richard did not give order for the crime until several days after Buckingham had left him. Only if Richard had dared to send word to Brecknock could Buckingham have learned, from the King, of the murders; and had he done so, Morton, Bishop of Ely, who was with Buckingham, would have known about the message too and reported it to More, if not previously to the world.

There is then a possibility well worth investigating that Buckingham, having murdered the Princes, dumped upon Richard—or left him to discover—a *fait accompli*.

It is quite possible, of course, that Henry Tudor sought to invade England in October of 1483 without enjoying any certainty that the

Princes were dead. He might reasonably conclude that this consideration was immaterial: Richard would not dare produce Edward's sons in any case, and if his invasion prospered, he would know how to deal with the boys when he found them. On the other hand, it seems somewhat more probable that he was furnished with some assurance of their demise; his boldness in proclaiming his promise to marry the Princess Elizabeth certainly reinforces this supposition. But it appears to be well nigh inevitable that only Buckingham could have furnished him with such assurances; yet Buckingham's fellow-conspirator and bitter enemy of Richard, Morton, Bishop of Ely, gives no indication, *via* More, that Buckingham possessed any evidence of Richard's guilt.

The agonized postscript which Richard appended to the letter he dispatched to Chancellor Russell on suddenly learning of Buckingham's rebellion sorts well with the supposition that Buckingham had saddled Richard and his government with the crime—'Here, loved be God, is all well, and truly determined, and for to resist the malice of him that had best cause to be true, the Duke of Buckingham, the most un-true creature living. . . . We assure you that there was never false traitor better purveyed for, as this bearer Gloucester shall show you.' When Buckingham was brought a prisoner to Salisbury, he immediately confessed all in order desperately to plead for one boon, an interview with Richard; both Vergil and Fabyan emphasize his feverish and 'importunate labour to have come to the king's presence' [Fabyan]. To beg Richard to forgive him because he had imperilled his soul for Richard's cause in dispatching the Princes—as he would certainly tell it—might well be the motive behind his wild desire to speak with the man he had betrayed. It is very possible, of course, that he had no other hope than to move Richard by his charm, as he had so often done in the past. Both these instances are but suggestive and may easily be otherwise interpreted; they do fit, however, this developing pattern.

The conduct of the Queen Dowager in yielding her daughters to Richard in March of 1484 and writing to the Marquess to abandon Henry Tudor ceases to be baffling on the supposition that Buckingham killed her sons. In their conferences with her, Richard's intimate counsellors would doubtless be able to provide evidences for the Duke's guilt—perhaps a statement from Brackenbury or from attendants at the Tower who had been menaced or duped into complying with his orders. Since Buckingham was clearing the way for Henry Tudor, it is small wonder that, despite her feelings against Richard, the passionate Queen should embrace the double purpose of securing her daughters' futures and dealing a heavy blow against the Pretender, Buckingham's partner and accomplice. This same supposition would resolve too what otherwise remains the contradiction of Brackenbury's integrity, so strongly established, and his continued zealous support of the King from whose bidding he recoiled in horror.

But we are not yet done with the Queen and the Marquess. On the assumption of Buckingham's guilt, an even more baffling example of their conduct likewise becomes understandable.

In the new reign of Henry VII the sun of fortune began to shine again upon the Woodvilles and they became once more figures of high consequence at court. Sir Edward Woodville was made Governor of the Isle of Wight; the Marquess Dorset, having served as a hostage for the money Henry owed the French, had returned to England and high station; and the Queen, too, had fared very well. The act of Richard's Parliament depriving her of her dignities and lands was repealed; and though Henry thriftily refrained from restoring her property, except for the meagre estate he allowed her as her widow's jointure, she enjoyed all the privileges, rights, and pomp both of a Queen Dowager and of a reigning Queen's mother. Her sons were no more, but her daughter was mantled in the purple and on September 20, 1486, she became the grandmother of England's heir, Prince Arthur. If fate and her own greedy machinations had cost her much suffering, she was now handsomely provided for, she was the progenitress of an incipient dynasty, and she might look forward to a proud and tranquil future.

Suddenly, the Queen's happy prospects were smashed, and it appears that it was she herself who wrought the ruin. Towards the end of 1486 Henry got word of Lambert Simnel's appearance in Ireland. After a council meeting held at Shene early in February of 1487, the King abruptly stripped Elizabeth Woodville of her modest possessions, her dearly beloved dignity and even her liberty. Her property was given to her daughter and she was shut away in a nunnery.

Henry gave out as the reason for this shocking action that the Queen Dowager had broken her promise to him and imperilled his cause when she surrendered her daughters to Richard in 1484. He offered no explanation why, although he knew all this when he took the crown, he had waited a year and a half before deciding that he must take revenge. 'This,' as *The Earlier Tudors* points out, 'was an old story, and that the council was really concerned with the new conspiracy [i.e., Lambert Simnel's] appears from the other measures which it took.' Bacon reports that it was considered dangerous, after the Queen

Dowager was immured in the nunnery, to attempt to see or talk with her. It is generally accepted that she was detected in the act of aiding Simnel's cause—Bacon even suggested that she coached the 'feigned boy'!—and this view is confirmed by the fact that, shortly after, the Marquess was clapped into custody, where he remained until the battle of Stoke was fought.

What possible motive impelled the Queen Dowager to aid a conspiracy which, if successful, would dethrone her own daughter, eradicate her proud position as the ancestress of Kings, and give the diadem to the son of Clarence, the man whose death she had sought, or to the Earl of Lincoln, the heir of her enemy Richard? What reason had Henry for thinking that the Marquess Dorset, a sybarite, might risk his newly recovered luxury of station and his life to support a rebellion inspired by men hostile to his family? The author of *The Earlier Tudors*, in a style that represents the usual handling of this problem, considers that the enigma is sufficiently resolved by characterizing the Queen Dowager as 'a flighty woman'. This, as Jeffrey wrote, with less cause, of Wordsworth's *Excursion*, this will never do! 'Flighty woman' is the very nadir of understatement. If this situation is squarely faced, it must be acknowledged to be an annoyingly important enigma, unless some overmastering motive can be found to account for the Queen's action. The supposition that Buckingham murdered her sons supplies the motive, as it supplied the motive for her yielding her daughters to Richard. Persuaded by Buckingham and the agents of Henry Tudor that Richard had killed the Princes, she then learns that the cause she has in consequence been led to adopt is the very cause in which her sons were sacrificed. In a woman of such passions as she harboured, this revelation would, it seems, be amply sufficient to drive her—at any cost—to revenge herself upon the man who had duped her to help him tread upon the bodies of her sons as stepping stones to the throne.

The supposition of Buckingham's guilt likewise offers an explanation of Henry Tudor's mysterious reticence, in despite of strong motivation, about seeking to establish Richard's infamy or even the mere fact of the Princes' demise. He could not declare the former without giving some solid evidence of the latter—which would, in turn, deny the declaration. Only after the passage of years and Tyrell's involvement with Suffolk gave him a likely opportunity did he venture to propagate by assertion what could otherwise not be propagated at all. Hence his use of insinuation in Richard's attainder and his failure, even in letters drumming up partisans for his invasion, to stir hearts to his cause by accusing Richard of murdering his nephews; 'homicide and tyrant' are the standardized epithets he uses in the missives that have survived.

As this pattern falls into place, it becomes apparent that all the 'evidence' for Richard's guilt, save the Tyrell story, is, in fact, equally applicable to Buckingham. This 'evidence', as we have seen, is the tissue of rumour, and the rumours appear to have been spun from mere suspicion arising from the disappearance of the Princes. It may have been Buckingham as well as Richard who brought about the disappearance; the rumours *assume*—doubtless with encouragement from Tudor adherents—the responsibility of Richard, but all they actually *attest* is the probability of the deed. It must, in addition, be remembered that, according to More and Bacon, Henry VII appears to have been as much, or almost as much, plagued by whispers that the sons of Edward were still alive as Richard by gossip that they were dead.

The evidence of character provides no more than an exercise in opinion; yet it is probably safe at least to remark that the rash, vain, ambitious, shallow Buckingham was not likely to be deterred by principles from performing a deed which might open up a glorious destiny and cast obloquy upon the wearer of the purple who had kindled his jealousy and his emulation.

An objection of some force, however, can be raised against this supposition of Buckingham's guilt. Why did not Richard attempt to still the attacks upon his fame by proclaiming that the crime was Buckingham's and publishing the story of what had actually happened?

If he learned of the deed only in parting from Buckingham at Gloucester or somewhat later on his progress, Richard had little time to meditate on the problem or penetrate the Duke's motive before he was suddenly confronted with the outbreak of Buckingham's rebellion. *Then* to accuse Buckingham would be to create a fire of speculation where none existed—save among the conspirators—and to risk being thought to have foisted his own crime on Buckingham in order to blacken an opponent of his crown. The same motive applies even more strongly after Buckingham's execution. His object must be to make the realm forget about, acquiesce in the disappearance of the Princes. To announce their deaths would be to remind his subjects of the dark consequence of his having seized the throne and would doubtless arouse as much suspicion against himself as conviction of the Duke's guilt, whatever evidence he advanced. It may well be too that in his uneasy mind he held himself ultimately responsible for the deed since Buckingham was his greatest officer and since he was enjoying the benefits of the act, even though the Duke had otherwise intended.

A very tenuous inference can be drawn that the news of the Princes' death at Buckingham's hands took Richard by surprise some time during August (of 1483). Though he had appointed his son Lieutenant of Ireland soon after he assumed the throne, he had had his wife and himself crowned and he had distributed the great offices of the realm without also elevating his heir to the dignity of Prince of Wales. Not until the boy joined his parents at Pontefract in late August was he made Prince; the hurried sending to London for ceremonial raiment shows that the investiture at York sprang from a sudden resolve. It is possible that, out of tortuous sentiment or superstition or the ramifications of conscience, Richard could not bring himself to assume the irrevocable position of announcing a dynastic establishment until the news of Buckingham's murdering the deposed Edward V led him to take the final step of creating his son Prince of Wales.

So run some answers that can be made to the objection; it must however, be taken into account.

Empirically, Buckingham appears more likely to have been the murderer of the Princes than Richard. On the supposition of the Duke's guilt, several instances of human behaviour, otherwise enigmatic and anomalous, become comprehensible: his guilt fits, if it is not required to explain, a complex pattern of actions which springs from Richard's assumption of the crown.

It is, of course, quite possible that Buckingham, to further his own purposes, persuaded Richard to acquiesce in the extinction of the Princes and himself accomplished the deed, probably while he tarried those few days in London in the middle of July. This final inter-relationship between Richard and Buckingham would thus bring to a mordant climax the history of Richard's incapacity to resist the blandishments of men of florid personalities and eloquent tongues. His failure to penetrate to the bottom of Clarence's shallow nature em-bittered his association with King Edward and hardened his mind against Edward's court. His inability to judge Buckingham's character served to push him along the road to the execution of Hastings and Rivers, and precipitated a rebellion against himself by causing him to load his weak and faithless ally with powers and posts. If indeed Richard consented to the death of the Princes because he succumbed to Bucking-ham's persuasions, he would find, in the reaches of his moral sense, no mitigation for his guilt as the responsible agent. This killing was a

o

grievous wrong—and grievously, whether or not he instigated or allowed it, has Richard paid for it.

It might be added that, in purely political terms, the dismissing of a King from the throne is but the first step in dismissing him from the world. A deposed monarch has nowhere to fall but into the grave, as, in English history alone, the usurpations of Mortimer and Isabella, of Henry IV, of Henry VII, and the triumph of the Round-heads abundantly testify. Though it seems unlikely that Richard, in deciding to take the crown, realized or was willing to face this fact, his assumption of power contained the death of the Princes within it. Horrible as their fate was, it is not a gratuitous or even an additional deed of violence; the push from the dais is itself the mortal stroke. In this sense it can be said that Richard undoubtedly doomed the Princes. The dark behavior of Henry Tudor, the ambitions and the opportunity owned by Buckingham give us reason to doubt, however, that he actually murdered them.

The available evidence admits of no decisive solution. Richard may well have committed the crime, or been ultimately responsible for its commission. The Duke of Buckingham may well have committed the crime, or persuaded Richard to allow its commission. What is inaccurate, misleading, and merely tiresome is for modern writers to declare flatly that Richard is guilty or to retail as fact the outworn tale of Thomas More. The problem owns more shades than are represented by the all-black or all-white which have hitherto usually been employed in attempts to solve this famous enigma. It eludes us, like Hamlet: we cannot pluck out the heart of its mystery. But at least we can do better than Rosencrantz and Guildenstern, who thought that there was no mystery at all.

APPENDIX II

Richard's Reputation[*]

THE history of Richard's reputation is a drama: it exhibits a cumulative plot, a powerful central conflict, and scenes of passion, scorn, vituperation, and ridicule. It begins more than 450 years ago, and it is not yet ended.

At the heart of the drama stands the Tudor myth, or tradition, a collection of alleged facts and attitudes and beliefs concerning the course of history in fifteenth century England, which was first propagated in the reign of Henry VIII and given its final expression in the three plays of *Henry VI* and the *Richard III* of William Shakespeare. The subsequent action of the drama consists in the series of attacks made upon the validity of this tradition and in the spirited counter-sallies of its defenders.

Actually, the drama begins off-stage, or before the curtain goes up, in the reign of Henry VII. At his court there existed among the men who had conspired against King Richard and brought about his overthrow a body of opinion, continually enlarged by tales and conjectures and anecdotal gossip, concerning the past which they had conquered. It was out of this amorphous mass of fact, reminiscence, hearsay, growing ever more colourful and detailed with the passing years, that the authors of Henry VIII's day fashioned the tradition. In the reign of Henry VII itself there were composed five works which contributed touches to the tradition and which therefore must be first noticed in this survey: John Rous's *Historia Regum Angliae*; Bernard André's *Life of Henry VII*; two works based upon the municipal records of London, Robert Fabyan's *New Chronicles* and *The Great Chronicle*; and the *Mémoires* of Philippe de Commynes.

Rous's history, completed about 1490, was written for the eye of Henry VII, and its treatment of Richard is fashioned accordingly. During Richard's lifetime Rous, a chaplain at Guy's Cliffe near Warwick, had written an account of the Earls of Warwick (the 'Rows Roll'), which included a ringing tribute to King Richard. This he had promptly expunged upon Henry VII's advent, but it remains in one copy of the Roll upon which, apparently, he was unable to lay his hands. His history actually contains very little about the House of York, being largely a tedious rigmarole of saints and miracles. Of Edward IV he says only that he was a great builder and captured Berwick. The few pages which he devotes to Richard exhibit details which seem authentic, and a number of stories of Richard's villainy then circulating at Henry's court he had never heard of; but his main purpose is to sketch for King Henry's gratification the picture of Richard as a 'monster and tyrant, born under a hostile star and perishing like Antichrist'.[1] It is Rous who begins the tale that Richard lay sullenly in his mother's womb for two years, and was born with teeth and with hair streaming to his shoulders.

Bernard André's *Life of Henry VII* adds little to the saga of Richard's evil deeds. It is, in fact, worth noting that André, who was Henry VII's poet laureate, historiographer royal, and tutor to Prince Arthur and who composed his work—mainly in the years 1500–03—directly at the King's wish, makes no mention of Queen Anne's death being due to poison, registers no suspicion that Richard had a hand in Clarence's execution, says that Henry VI's son Edward died in battle, and, though in one passage he mentions the gossip that Richard killed Henry VI himself, in another he declares that it was Edward IV who determined Henry's death. André's principal contribution is a deepening of the diabolic lines of Richard's portrait. Richard is a monster, delighting in deeds of blood from his babyhood. On the field of Bosworth, 'swollen with rage like a serpent that has fed on noxious herbs, like a Hyrcanian tiger or a Marsian boar ... [he] roars a wild command to his soldiers that he may slay Richmond [Henry Tudor] himself with new and unheard of tortures'! Henry, on the other hand is as saintly as Richard is evil. In this violent antithesis lies the germ of the Tudor tradition. It is André who inaugurates the humanistic method of historical writing in England, endowing his chief characters with long (and often preposterous) speeches.

The two 'city' chronicles, Fabyan's and *The Great Chronicle* represent, on the other hand, a continuation of the medieval tradition. These are much alike and may be considered together, particularly since the editors of *The Great Chronicle*, which was finished in 1512 but not printed until 1938, make out a convincing case for Fabyan's authorship of it. Fabyan, a member of the Draper's Company and an alderman of London, died in 1513. His *New Chronicles of England and France*, completed in 1504, was first published in 1516 in a version which ends with the death of Richard; the second edition of 1533, printed by William Rastell, adds the reign of Henry VII. These works contribute very little, of either myth or fact, to Richard's life—a detail here and there, that is all. Even their time scheme is confused, both picturing Buckingham's rebellion, for example, as taking place in 1484.

Though the *Mémoires* of Philippe de Commynes (1447–1511) were not published until 1524, the passages relating to England were written, as appears from internal evidence, between 1486 and 1489. Commynes contributed to the Tudor tradition in the very important work of Edward Hall. His evidence is of widely varying worth. Having been a councillor first of Charles, Duke of Burgundy, and then of King Louis XI, he speaks with great authority on Edward IV's flight to Burgundy and the invasion of 1475; but for events happening in England he had to depend on hearsay. His view of Richard's reign appears to have been largely determined by what Henry Tudor and Henry Tudor's followers told him while they were at the French court. Commynes was so much impressed by Henry that he pictures him as raised up by God to overthrow King Richard. When Commynes wrote, Henry VII had not yet gone to war with France nor secured the Spanish alliance.

The Tudor tradition proper begins with *The History of King Richard the Third* by Sir Thomas More. Written about 1513 when More was under-sheriff of London, it first appeared, in a corrupt copy, in Grafton's *Continuation* of 'Hardyng's Chronicle', 1543, then in Edward Hall's *The Union . . . of Lancaster and York*, 1548, and was finally published in an authentic edition by More's nephew William Rastell in 1557. Rastell adds certain passages translated from the Latin version of the work which was not printed until 1566. Because of the obvious animus which pervades this history and a conjecture put forward in the later years of Queen Elizabeth, it has often been maintained, particularly by those attacking the Tudor tradition, that the Latin version of *Richard III*, from which the English seems to be derived, was written by Cardinal Morton himself, in whose household Thomas More had been put to service as a boy. In the latest edition of More's work, however, R. W. Chambers has convincingly demonstrated that More wrote the history, deriving the greater part of his information from John Morton.[2]

The History of King Richard the Third created the portrait of Richard presented by the Tudor tradition. It can perhaps be called the first piece of modern English prose; in the vividness of its detail and the exuberance of its style it rivals anything in the Elizabethan age itself.

The *History* covers a period of less than four months, beginning with the death of Edward IV and breaking off in mid-flight with Morton's ensnaring the Duke of Buckingham at Brecknock. Why More failed to finish it is a mystery.

The opening description of Richard sets the tone of the work: he was 'little of stature, ill-featured of limbs, crook backed, his left shoulder much higher than his right, hard favoured of visage . . .; he was malicious, wrathful, envious, and from afore his birth, ever froward. It is for truth reported, that the Duchess his mother had so much ado in her travail, that she could not be delivered of him uncut: and that he came into the world with the feet forward . . . and (as the fame runneth) also not untoothed. . . . He was close and secret, a deep dissimuler, lowly of countenance, arrogant of heart, outwardly companionable where he inwardly hated, not letting to kiss whom he thought to kill: dispiteous and cruel, not for evil will alway, but after for ambition, and either for the surety or increase of his estate.'

It is from this work of More's that many of the leading elements in the Tudor tradition spring—Richard's repulsive appearance, his murdering King Henry by his own hand and bringing about Clarence's death, his plotting for the crown long before King Edward died, the invariable infamy of his motives, his stirring up hatred against the innocent Woodvilles in order to secure the protectorship, and, most of all, his glittering diabolism. All these elements are projected with rich and rhythmic phrases building into wonderfully dramatic scenes—the entrapping of Hastings at the Tower being the most famous—and also with a marvellous wit and an irony which, if obvious is nonetheless pungent. The dramatic power of the work is developed by extensive use of dialogue. Having quaffed the heady draughts of classical historians, More, in true Renaissance style, delivers more than one third of his *History* in the form of speeches by the chief characters.

The gross inaccuracies of this work, its apparently wilful distortions of fact and urgent bias, are not nearly so surprising as the positive virulence which informs it. Richard is entirely removed from the sphere of human life; he is evil incarnate, sheer monster, and as such he is reviled. Part of the explanation obviously lies in More's sources of information. Much of what he reports, he derived from John Morton, a bitter enemy of Richard's; other passages reflect the gaudy gossip of the Tudor court. But to say only this leaves out of account More's motive for writing the *History*. It is, as *The Earlier Tudors* points out, 'an attack upon the *Realpolitik* practiced by the princes of his day'.[3]

Like his friend Erasmus, and many other men of the New Learning, More was much concerned with the education of 'the Prince', that all-powerful head of the nationalist states then springing into bloom. Doubtless More and Erasmus had often discussed the matter and probably More was aware, in 1513, of Erasmus' plan to produce a book of precepts for the Christian Prince, which he published a few years later. To complement Erasmus' picture of the Good Prince, More saw in the horrible figure of the last Yorkist King which Morton and others had sketched for him the opportunity of creating the Bad Prince as an example and warning to the Kings of his generation. More's *History* is, in essence, a humanist tract. Ironically enough, it was perhaps Sir Thomas's intense dislike of Henry VII's dissimulation and dark dealings—openly attacked in his Latin verse celebrating the accession of Henry VIII—that led him so to emphasize these qualities in the Bad Prince as represented by Richard III! The animus of the work comes then not only from its sources but also from its purpose and is heightened by the stunning vitality of More's literary talent. His objective is not primarily to blacken Richard's character for the gratification of the Tudors, but to make the malign figure given him, even more malign in the good cause of humanist education.

More supplied the portrait of Richard III for the Tudors; Polydore Vergil created the ideological frame of the portrait. Vergil came to England in 1501 as the sub-collector of Peter's Pence for Pope Alexander VI; he already enjoyed a reputation as a humanist; he was a friend of Erasmus; he arrived with recommendations to Henry VII. About 1507 the King asked him to undertake a history of England. By 1517 he had completed the work down to the end of Richard's reign, and in this form his Latin history was first published in 1534; the second edition of 1546 carried the history down to the death of Henry VII in 1509; and the third edition of 1555, the year of Vergil's death, brought it to 1538. Most of this time Vergil spent in England, for though he incurred the enmity of Wolsey, he enjoyed the favour of the Tudors and received many ecclesiastical offices.

In his authoritative work upon Vergil, Denys Hay points out that 'Henry VII had more reasons that many other sovereigns for welcoming a defence of his dynasty which would circulate among the courts of Europe. The Italian historiographer was already at work in many trans-Alpine countries where no revolutionary change of rulers had occurred. . . . Henry VII had every reason to encourage Vergil to under-take a history of England which would justify the Tudors to the scholars of Europe. Vergil likewise could expect royal favours in return for the work.' Elsewhere Hay notes that Vergil 'thoroughly accomplished his task of interpreting English history in favour of the Tudors'.[4]

In his *Anglica Historia*, Vergil shows himself to be a thorough humanist, not only in his use of the stylistic mannerisms of the classical historians, but in the critical spirit with which he scrutinizes and employs his sources. He makes an attempt at characterization, he probes for motives, he establishes relationships of cause and effect. In all these respects he marks the change from medieval to modern historiography. He stirred up many enemies because he denied the cherished tale of England's being founded by the Trojan Brutus and was sceptical about other myths. He was called a liar; he was accused of burning waggonloads of source material. Though these charges probably represent no more than the outraged pride of his opponents, it is possible that, when he came to deal with the reign of Richard the Third, he did destroy evidence that showed Richard in too complimentary a light.[5]*

To the sixteenth century the really important part of the *Anglica Historia* lay in its picture of England from the usurpation of Henry IV to the reign of Henry VII; of which the portion dealing with the period from Henry VI to Richard III was soon translated into English. It is Polydore Vergil who creates for this piece of history the pattern which becomes the framework of the Tudor tradition. The pattern is both moral and theological, with a distinct beginning, middle, and end. The beginning is Henry IV's usurping the throne and taking the life of the luckless Richard II. By this act the divine concord of society is broken and England is eventually plunged into the horror of civil strife. This, in turn, is brought to its monstrous climax in the bloody career of King Richard, and the end of the drama is provided by Henry Tudor, God's Justicer and Vengeancer, who overthrows Richard to re-establish peace, concord and prosperity by uniting the Red Rose and the White. Heavenly retribution appears not only in the outline but in the details of the drama. Henry VI perishes because of the sin committed by his grandfather Henry IV; Margaret of Anjou pays the penalty for the murder of Duke Humphrey; the sons of Edward are the innocent victims of Edward's perjury in swearing to the men of York in 1471 that he had come only to claim his dukedom. The period of history from 1399 to 1485 is conceived as a separate and special entity; it is, essentially, a morality play. Richard, symbol of evil and discord, is eradicated by Henry Tudor, God's final agent of retribution and England's saviour.

Except for the information he supplies about Henry's plans and movements, Vergil has little to offer for the history of Richard's reign. Even though he is writing for Henry VII, he is too conscientious a historian to suppress all evidences of good rule on Richard's part; but he attempts to reconcile them to his audience and to his pattern by tortuous passages arguing that even Richard's worthy acts were performed from the basest motives. Vergil's great importance to the sixteenth century lay in the pattern that he created, a pattern into which later Tudor writers would snugly fit More's vivid portrait of Richard.

In fact, it can be said that subsequent Tudor historians simply reproduce, and sometimes embellish, Vergil and More, copying in varying degrees one from another. The following are the most important links in the chain:

The *Continuation* of Hardyng's 'Chronicle,' published in 1543 by Richard Grafton. Hardyng's verse history, which ended with the beginning of Edward IV's reign, is continued in prose to the year of publication. The *Continuation* leans heavily upon More and Vergil.

The Union of the Two Noble and Illustre Families of Lancaster and York by Edward Hall, published in 1548. This pictures the reigns of the eight kings who ruled after 1399, ending with 'The Triumphant Reign of Henry the Eighth.'

The *Chronicle* of Richard Grafton, published in 2 vols. in 1568; this follows More and Vergil, making use of Hall's additions.

The *Chronicles* of Raphael Holinshed, published in 1578. Shakespeare used the new edition of 1587. Holinshed follows Hall closely, though sometimes blurring his narrative, and makes some additions of his own.

The three parts of *King Henry the Sixth* by William Shakespeare, or perhaps a reworking by Shakespeare of earlier plays, and Shakespeare's *Richard the Third*.

Of these historical works, by far the most important is Edward Hall's, both because it was his history which Shakespeare used, probably directly as well as *via* Holinshed, and it is his history which finally welds together More and Vergil and permanently 'sets' the Tudor tradition.

Hall is himself an interesting character because he is so representative of his times. To the very depth of his being he believed in Protestantism and the new autocracy of the Tudors. Educated at Eton and Cambridge, he became a judge and a Member of Parliament during Henry VIII's reign, and Henry had no more loyal or passionate partisan than he.

Hall deepens and develops what he finds in More and Vergil. He actually succeeds in darkening the lines of More's portrait of Richard, and he makes Henry Tudor nothing less than an angelic deliverer. As E. M. W. Tillyard points out, 'for Hall these two are not so much

O●

historical personages as Good King and Bad King respectively'.[6] Similarly, the pattern sketched by Vergil is boldly developed—'as King Henry IV was the beginning and root of the great discord and division, so was the godly matrimony [of Henry VII and Elizabeth of York] the final end of all dissensions titles and debates'. The vehemence of Hall's viewpoint may be gathered from the fact that this wedding is compared to the union of godhead and manhood in Christ and no lesser power than the Holy Ghost informs the Duke of Buckingham that Henry Tudor is the lawful claimant of the throne. More's portrait and Vergil's pattern are not only merged but exaggerated and hallowed by Hall.

It is the substance and spirit of Hall that William Shakespeare worked to a still higher pitch of dramatic sensation to create *Richard III*. Written about 1593, this juicy melodramatic tragedy throbs with the youthful vitality of Shakespeare's genius; it also endorses the political attitude of the day which enjoyed contrasting the blessings of Tudor despotism with the preceding horrors of civil discord, and it reveals Shakespeare's indebtedness to the works of Christopher Marlowe. Marlowe had created the play of the super-man, a monolithic structure built about a colossal protagonist. In Hall's account of Richard, Shakespeare saw his opportunity of fashioning history into such a structure. As Barabas in Marlowe's *Jew of Malta* is a super-man of evil, so too is Richard a super-man, or rather a super-creature, in his ambition, 'Machiavellian' dissimulation, and absolute malice. Richard is 'this poisonous bunch-backed toad', a monster thrust beyond the pale of humanity, not only because of the crimes he commits but because he commits them with unbounded zest in ill-doing and is impervious to the appeals of human morality or emotions. Surrounded by heavy portents of coming retribution, harried by supernatural visitants, confronted at last by God's Knight, Henry Tudor, Richard is realized not as an arch-villain but the personification of arch-villainy; and so resourceful, exuberant, and unflagging in action is this bustling melodrama, that, though it cannot compare in profundity or subtlety of characterization with the later tragedies, it has justly remained one of Shakespeare's most popular plays: before the average person has come to any serious study of English history, he has once for all identified Richard III as a monster hunched of back, withered of arm, and twisted of countenance, who malignantly announces:

> I am determined to prove a villain
> And hate the idle pleasures of these days!

If it was the Tudor chroniclers rather than Shakespeare who led subsequent historians to make up their minds about Richard, it is Shakespeare who has led every one else to make up his imagination about Richard.

Created by More and Vergil, put into final form by Hall, and given irresistible expression in Shakespeare's *Richard III*, the Tudor myth—as Tillyard calls it—has, by and large, maintained its sway over scholars as well as the public until well into the twentieth century. Though those portions of it which have proved vulnerable to attack have been pruned or softened or swathed in qualifications, and it has here and there been stretched to admit certain incontrovertible facts, the tradition has retained its hypnotic hold—in part, at least, because the inroads made upon it have been strong enough to prick historians to its defence but not strong enough to force them to abandon it outright. It is significant that none of the heavy attacks has been made by a professional historian. With the notable exception of present-day scholars, the successive generations of historical writers since the Age of Elizabeth have been rather like a company of Roman legionaries who shake off indifferently the sporadic sallies of ill-armed barbarians or by the exercise of their martial disciplines mount a counter-attack which, in their estimation, completely disposes of the enemy. Yet it must be noticed that even before the middle of the nineteenth century there had been established a 'moderate' position between the hard-shelled 'traditionalists' and the zealous 'revisionists'.

Not long after the death of Elizabeth, the tradition was dared by *The Encomium of Richard III*, 'an oppressed and defamed King'; this slight work—a folio of eight leaves—was dedicated by its author, one William Cornwaleys, to no less a personage than 'his worthy friend Mr. John Donne'.[7]

The first substantial assault was delivered about the same time by Sir George Buc (died 1623), Master of the Revels to James I and a man of considerable learning and industry, one of whose ancestors had fought for Richard at Bosworth Field. His *History of the Life and Reign of Richard III*, in five books, first published in 1646 and then included in White Kennett's *Complete History of England*, 1710, is so desultory in organization as to make for grim reading; it is blundering and uncritical and as prejudiced in its direction as the tradition it attacks. Yet it is Buc who first makes use of the manuscript of the *Croyland Chronicle* to point out some of the inaccuracies of Vergil and More, who seeks sources more nearly contemporary with Richard than the Tudor writers, and who thus is the first to reveal that the tradition was not inviolable.

The next important challenge was delivered in the middle of the eighteenth century by a far more redoubtable controversialist, Horace Walpole. Employing fresh bits of material—not always wisely—and, in the style of his day, subjecting the Tudor myth to the scrutiny of 'enlightened reason', Walpole in his *Historic Doubts*, 1768, acquits Richard of the principal crimes with which he had been laden, from the stabbing of Henry VI's son Prince Edward to the dispatching of the Little Princes. This refutation he bases partly on an appeal to fifteenth century sources, partly on the argument of inherent improbability. He makes his best case in revealing a number of the inaccuracies and incongruities in More's tale of the murder of the Princes. Walpole's work suffers, however, from two great handicaps: he was not a scholar and he lacked source materials. Thus he was forced to attempt to break down the tradition from within, but he had nothing to put in the place of what he rejected. Furthermore, in his willingness to accept Perkin Warbeck as the veritable younger son of Edward IV and his tendency to dismiss traditional views simply by labelling them 'incredible', Walpole left obvious openings for subsequent rejoinders by the 'traditionalists'. Still, he demonstrated the manifest bias of the Tudor tradition, shook the credibility of some of More's testimony, and cast doubts upon the series of crimes attaching to Richard before he became King.

The nineteenth century witnessed a sharpening tempo of attack and defence. It opened with a fierce reaffirmation of every article of the tradition by the Roman Catholic ecclesiastic, John Lingard, the first three volumes of whose *History of England* (down to the death of Henry VII) appeared in 1819. Lingard may be called the last of the 'strict constructionists'.

Only eleven years later Sharon Turner, with the publication of his *History of England in the Middle Ages* (1830), created what might be called the 'moderate' position. He is the first professional historian to take his stand outside the Tudor tradition and to make use of its evidence in a detached and critical spirit as he is the first historian to view Richard's career in terms of its times. In fact, he is the first writer after the close of the fifteenth century to deal with Richard as if he had actually been a human being and to attempt some estimate of the characters and motives of the principal men who affected his life. If he supports the position that Richard was innocent of the earlier crimes attributed to him, he nonetheless holds him guilty of the murder of the Princes and is at pains to emphasize some of the weaknesses, as he sees them, of Richard's policy. Despite some errors of fact and an occasionally discursive style, Sharon Turner's history (vols. III and IV) offers a more measured and convincing view of Richard than is to be found in any subsequent full-length work.

Next come two briefs for the 'revisionists', neither of which has left very much impact upon the controversy, though both of them are earnest and lengthy: Caroline Halsted's *Life of Richard III*, 2 volumes, 1844; and Alfred O. Legge's *The Unpopular King*, 2 volumes, 1885. Though Miss Halsted did some valuable digging in Harleian 433, the registry of King Richard's grants and writs, and printed a number of the principal entries as well as other important source materials, her work is conceived rather in the vein of the Victorian Gift-book and, to this rude age, is almost unreadable. Richard is not far removed from one of the nobler figures in the *Idylls of the King* and the death of the Princes remains a mystery. Romantically enough, Miss Halsted married the rector of the church of Middleham, which had once been Richard's collegiate establishment. Legge's work is less impenetrable but it adds little to what Walpole had already said; it offers the suggestion that Buckingham, Catesby and Ratcliffe made away with the Princes without Richard's knowledge.

In 1892 appeared Sir James Ramsay's *Lancaster and York*, 2 volumes, which, like Hall's work and Shakespeare's two tetralogies of English historical plays, covers the period from the usurpation of Henry IV to the triumph of Henry VII. Ramsay has made use of all the sources at his command, printing much valuable information concerning finances, and his work, as a whole, occupies the moderate position; but in his account of the life and character of King Richard he remains, essentially, within the Tudor tradition.

In the meantime, the nineteenth century phase of the conflict had come to its climax; in 1891 attack and defence collided head-on in the pages of the *English Historical Review* (VI). Sir Clements R. Markham's 'Richard III: A Doubtful Verdict Reviewed', an ardent 'revisionist' tract which saddled Henry Tudor with the killing of the sons of Edward IV, was answered by James Gairdner, the most eminent of fifteenth century scholars, in 'Did Henry VII Murder the Princes?'; Markham issued a rejoinder, 'Richard III and Henry VII', to which Gairdner made a brief final reply. The attitudes of these two men can be most clearly perceived in the full-length work which each devoted to Richard.

Sir Clements Markham's *Richard III: His Life and Character*, 1906, has very little to do with either: it is almost entirely argument devoted to clearing Richard of all crimes and fastening the guilt for the death of the Princes on Henry VII. It must be confessed that it is difficult to take this work as seriously as it is intended. Markham's white and black are as intense as those of the Tudor tradition, only reversed. The Lancastrians are a pack of rascals; John Morton, who, Markham insists, wrote More's work, is 'a treble-dyed traitor and falsifier of history', and Richard, a sterling symbol of 'English pluck' . . . Richard is mantled in the airs which blow upon the playing fields of Eton and the glorious reaches of the nineteenth century British Empire. Morton, Fabyan and Henry VII are pictured as gleefully falsifying dates and Morton dashes about with unflagging vigour to plant a rumour or start a tale. The most interesting part of Markham's work, the case he builds against Henry VII as the murderer of the Princes, became outmoded with the exhumation of the skeletons in the Abbey in 1933.

But Markham has had his followers. In 1933 Philip Lindsay published a popular work, *King Richard III*, which is largely an emphatic restatement of Markham's arguments; recently Josephine Tey created an ingenious detective novel, *The Daughter of Time*, that likewise unravels the mystery of the Princes' deaths in Markham's terms; and the more popular elements of the Press still occasionally print articles 'revealing' the possibility of Henry VII's villainy.

So much for the 'revisionists'.

James Gairdner published in 1878 his *Life and Reign of Richard the Third*; in 1898 he issued a revised edition which takes into account some of the arguments set forth by Markham in their exchange in the *English Historical Review*. Gairdner's book is not only the 'standard' work upon King Richard—'the chief modern authority on the reign', as Lawrence E. Tanner phrases it[8]—but, with the exception of the 'revisionist' volumes referred to above, it is the last full-length study of Richard that has appeared.

Quite outside its historical value, Gairdner's *Life* is of psychological interest. It reveals an historian of great eminence, integrity, and industry desperately wrestling in public to reconcile the opposing forces of his scholarly conscientiousness and his emotional predispositions. Gairdner attempts to make use of all the new fifteenth century source material opened up by the researches of the nineteenth century and still to maintain the essential validity of the Tudor myth. It is a rather painful spectacle—a great historian beginning with a closed tradition instead of with an open mind. He is even driven to declare, in the preface to his revised edition (p. xi) that 'a minute study of the facts of Richard's life has tended more and more to convince me of the general fidelity of the portrait with which we have been made familiar by Shakespeare and Sir Thomas More'. What is astounding about this statement is not so much that Gairdner supposes the sensational protagonist of the melodramatic *Richard III* to be a portrait of the real Richard but that he supposes it to be, in any way, the portrait of a human being. This grotesque position Gairdner is led to adopt by his dependence upon tradition. Disregarding the obvious truth that, for the purposes of historical writing, traditions vary widely in worth and that any single tradition can only be so good as its proximity to truth, Gairdner insists upon an absolute value of tradition itself. This emotional, *a priori* approach involves him in endless difficulties as he reluctantly abandons those elements of the tradition which can no longer be defended but clings unhappily to the dominant tone and the remaining elements, which he strains to accommodate to the fresh evidence he has uncovered.

He finds it necessary to explain elaborately, for example, why Shakespeare's picture of Richard's plotting against George of Clarence cannot be accepted. Yet in flogging this dead horse, he is compelled by his devotion to the Tudor myth to find something vaguely sinister in the fact that after Clarence's death Richard founded two collegiate establishments; and because Clarence's execution was private, he cannot resist the inaccurate comment that it was an assassination. Similarly, though he must needs acknowledge the obvious incongruities in More's tale of the murder of the Princes and the suspicious origins of the story, he cannot give up the tale itself, remarking, almost wistfully, that 'it is not necessary to suppose More's narrative correct in all its details', and hopefully suggesting that Tyrell made a voluntary confession of guilt to ease his conscience! Again, whenever Gairdner is required to note beneficent qualities in Richard or his government, he follows the Tudor 'line' by automatically ascribing evil motives, adding passages of Victorian moralizing that are something less than enlightening. Finally, Gairdner is so immersed in his own intestine struggle that he pays scant attention to Richard's life up to the death of Edward IV, and in the marching and counter-marching of his arguments Richard's character is reduced to a mere arbitrary counter, 'black' or 'not-so-black' as the case may be.

Yet Gairdner's work makes clear that by the end of the nineteenth century sufficient contemporary source materials were available to reveal the inaccuracies, the distortions and the bias of the Tudor tradition and to create a *Life* of Richard or a history of the fifteenth century which did not depend upon the tradition as a primary source.

The last notable accession to these materials occurred in 1936 with the publication of Dominic Mancini's *Usurpation of Richard III*. Superbly edited and translated by C. A. J. Armstrong, this work is of first importance for events in England between the death of Edward IV and the coronation of Richard, since Mancini reports what he himself saw and heard and sets down his account in December of 1483. It must regretfully be pointed out, however, that though Mancini confirms or disposes of a number of doubtful issues and supplies some very valuable details of action and characterization, he is himself guilty of errors so considerable as to be baffling . . . until it is recalled that fifteenth century standards of scrupulous reporting and scholarly accuracy are far removed from those of our own age, dominated as it is by 'science', 'efficiency', and the pursuit of 'facts'. His work, then, is not quite the final answer to the problems of Richard's protectorship which might have been hoped for. Armstrong's notes admirably represent the 'moderate' position of most present-day scholars of this period, who take their stand upon contemporary sources and only make use of those details of the Tudor tradition for which some independent confirmation can be adduced.

There exists one more important narrative source for a life of Richard: the 'Second Continuation' of the *Croyland Chronicle*, first published in 1684. This is particularly valuable for the last half of the reign of Edward IV, Richard's protectorship, and the first part of his rule. There is considerable evidence to suggest that the materials, if not the actual writing, of most of this narrative, which appears to have been created at Croyland Abbey in the spring of 1486, is the work of John Russell, Bishop of Lincoln, one of Edward's most intimate advisers and Richard's Chancellor. Unfortunately Russell, it seems, lacked either the time or the inclination to complete his account of Richard's reign; for there is reason to believe that his monkish 'editor', —perhaps the Prior of the abbey—who inserted in their appropriate chronological places the annals of the monastery itself and can be shown to have intruded a number of his own naïve comments, likewise supplied the inaccurate and distorted account of Richard's last months which is in startling contrast to the authenticity of the preceding narrative.[9] Thus, though it is true that the medieval tradition of historical writing petered out about 1470, and such chronicles as exist throw almost no light upon Richard's earlier years, the 'Second Continuation' and Mancini's *Usurpation* provide information of unusual authenticity for the most significant parts of Richard's life. For the period of Richard's youth, Cora L. Scofield has uncovered a number of important facts in digging deep into the public archives for her *Life and Reign of Edward the Fourth*, 2 volumes, 1923; and her work has tremendously enlarged our understanding of the *milieu* in which Richard passed the critical years of childhood and adolescence.

For the rest, the researches of nineteenth and twentieth century scholars and successive publications by the Historical Manuscripts Commission and the Public Record office have made available an impressive array—emphatically belying the old assertion that fifteenth century sources are hopelessly meagre—of letters, wills, household regulations, financial records, and documents of state. And Harleian manuscript 433, of which only the most important items have been published, provides an intimate picture of the day-to-day workings of Richard's government. In addition, there have appeared in our century illuminating scholarly interpretations and special studies bearing upon Richard's life. C. H. Williams' essay, 'England: The Yorkist Kings' (Chapter XII), in the last volume of the *Cambridge Medieval History* (VIII)—in which, incidentally, the Tudor tradition is once for all relegated to its role of supplementary material—and Alec R. Myers' *England in the Later Middle Ages* (Penguin, 1952)* are good examples of the learned, judicious and impartial attitude which modern English scholars bring to a consideration of that inflammable subject, King Richard the Third.

And yet the Tudor myth is still flourishing. It is to be found not only in school textbooks and upon the lips of the present-day 'Beefeaters' in the Tower of London, but it continues to leave its mark upon the general histories, which by most people are regarded as the authoritative custodians of historical knowledge.[10] It even persists in certain works of scholarship. Lawrence Tanner, for example, in his scrupulously careful article in *Archaeologia* on the exhumation of the Princes' bones, cannot resist retailing, apparently as the authentic account of the murder, the out-worn yarn of Thomas More. While science is called in to examine the skeletons, myth continues to rattle them. Another example of the hypnotic hold the tradition somehow

* See also his 'The Character of Richard III,' *History Today*, August, 1954, which appeared too late for me to consult in the writing of this biography. This article offers, in my opinion, the best concise discussion of the sources available for an estimate of Richard's career and the essential qualities of his character.

retains, occurs in Angelo Raine's preface to the series of *York Civic Records*. Writing with much of the animus of More himself—and becoming so incensed as to fall into error—Raine argues that the city of York was not really devoted to Richard; whereas the records themselves, which Raine so admirably edits, eloquently testify to the eccentricity of this contention.[11]★

The forceful moral pattern of Vergil, the vividness of More, the fervour of Hall, and the dramatic exuberance of Shakespeare have endowed the Tudor myth with a vitality that is one of the wonders of the world. What a tribute this is to art; what a misfortune this is for history.

Notes

Notes

PROLOGUE
(pp. 15–23)

THIS sketch of England in the first half of the fifteenth century I have developed from a variety of sources. Since it would be tedious and probably of little profit to the reader for me to acknowledge my indebtedness in detail, I have chosen to list the primary and secondary sources which I have found most useful. Only those statements have been noted which appeared to require support or repay identification. Most of these materials I have likewise used extensively for my account of Richard's life 1452–71 (the thirteen chapters of 'Richard, Duke of Gloucester').

PRIMARY SOURCES:

Chronicles of London, ed. by C. L. Kingsford, Oxford, 1905.

An English Chronicle of the Reigns of Richard II, Henry IV, Henry V, and Henry VI, ed. by J. S. Davies, Camden Society, 1856.

Excerpta Historica, London, 1831.

Gregory's Chronicle: The Historical Collections of a Citizen of London, ed. by James Gairdner, Camden Society, 1876.

'Historiae Croylandensis', *Rerum Anglicarum Scriptorum*, I, ed. by W. Fulman, Oxford, 1684; there is an English translation: *Ingulph's Chronicle of the Abbey of Croyland*, trans. and ed. by Henry T. Riley, Bohn's Antiquarian Library, London, 1854. All page references to the *Croy. Chron.* are to this translation, unless otherwise noted.

Letters and Papers Illustrative of the Wars of the English in France during the Reign of Henry the Sixth, ed. by J. Stevenson, 2 vols., Rolls Series, 1864 (especially William Worcester's *Annales Rerum Anglicarum*, II, pp. 743–93).

Letters of Queen Margaret of Anjou, ed. by Cecil Munro, Camden Society, 1863.

Original Letters, ed. by Henry Ellis: 3 series, London, 1825, 1827, 1846; vol. I in each of the three series.

The Paston Letters, ed. by James Gairdner (Library Edition), London, 1910.

Six Town Chronicles of England, ed. by R. Flenley, Oxford, 1911.

Three Fifteenth Century Chronicles, ed. by James Gairdner, Camden Society, 1880.

Polydore Vergil, *History*, ed. by Henry Ellis, Camden Society, 1844; a 16th century translation of the *Anglica Historia*.

Jehan de Waurin, *Anchiennes Chronicques d'Engleterre*, ed. by Mlle. Dupont, Paris, 1858–63 (vols. II and III).

John Whethamstede, *Registrum Abbatiae Johannis Whethamstede*, ed. by Henry T. Riley, Rolls Series, 1872–73.

SECONDARY SOURCES:

J. J. Bagley, *Margaret of Anjou*, London, 1948.

Mabel E. Christie, *Henry VI*, London, 1922.

C. L. Kingsford, *Prejudice and Promise in Fifteenth Century England*, Oxford, 1925.

A. Lecoy de la Marche, *Le Roi René*, 2 vols., Paris, 1875.

K. B. McFarlane, 'Bastard Feudalism', *Bull. Inst. Hist. Research*, XX, pp. 161–180.

C. Oman, *The History of England from the Accession of Richard II to the Death of Richard III*, London, 1906.

C. Oman, *Warwick the Kingmaker*, London, 1893.

E. Power and M. M. Postan, *Studies in English Trade in the Fifteenth Century*, London, 1933.

James H. Ramsay, *Lancaster and York*, 2 vols., Oxford, 1892.

Cora L. Scofield, *The Life and Reign of Edward the Fourth*, 2 vols., London, 1923.

K. H. Vickers, *England in the Later Middle Ages*, London, 1926.

DOCUMENTS OF STATE:

Rolls of Parliament: *Rotuli Parliamentorum*, Vols. V and VI.

Calendar of the Patent Rolls, Henry VI, 1452–1461, London, 1910.

NOTES:

[1] Suffolk, it seems, wrote verses to the Queen; see H. W. MacCracken, 'An English Friend of Charles of Orleans', *PMLA*, XXVI (1911), p. 159, pp. 168–69.

[2] *Paston Letters*, I, p. 378.

[3] It seems probable that he was murdered or treated so harshly that he succumbed to apoplexy.

[4] *Paston Letters*, I, pp. lx–lxi; York's protest to Henry VI appears in Holinshed.

[5] York's protest: *Paston Letters*, I, pp. lx–lxi.

[6] *Idem.*

[7] John Stow, *The Annales or Generall Chronicle of England*, London, 1615, p. 393; *Paston Letters*, I, lxxii.

[8] York's oath appears in Exchequer Miscellanea, 8/19, 8/20, 8/21 (Scofield, I, p. 17).

THE KING'S BROTHER

RICHARD, DUKE OF GLOUCESTER

(pp. 27–30)

[1] King Henry's progress to Stamford and Peterborough in the early fall of 1452 is established by the dates of privy seals; see *Paston Letters*, I, p. lxxxvi.

[2] The information about the family of the Duke of York is drawn from the *Annales* of William Worcester, as annotated by Gairdner, who also quotes the contemporary rhyme: James Gairdner, *History of the Life and Reign of Richard III*, rev. ed., Cambridge, 1898, pp. 3–5.

[3] See H. K. Bonney, *Historic Notices in Reference to Fotheringhay*, Oundle, 1821. Only the mound on which stood the keep remains today, but the general scene has probably undergone little change.

[4] That George was Margaret's favourite brother is indicated by the whole course of their relationship; see Scofield, I, p. 562. It seems safe to infer from George's character and career that he was spoiled as a child.

[5] McFarlane, 'Bastard Feudalism'; for an illustration, see *Paston Letters*, I, pp. 350–52; Oman prints a typical indenture of this kind (*Warwick*, pp. 36–37).

[6] *Paston Letters*, I, pp. 106–08; 207–08; see also pp. xxx–xxxii and pp. lxviii–lxix.

[7] Quoted from the modernized version in Bagley, *Margaret of Anjou*, p. 62; see John Hardyng, *Chronicle*, ed. by Henry Ellis, London, 1812.

II
(pp. 30–32)

It appears that Richard, Duke of York was neither aiming at the crown nor seeking more of a voice in the government that he was entitled to. He represented, to many Englishmen of the day, the only hope of rescue from the swamp of disorder and evil rule in which the realm was floundering. See, for example, the *Paston Letters*, I, pp. 152–54; 521–22; compare Oman, *Warwick*, pp. 41–44. Popular bitterness against the Queen's government fires many a song and ballad: see Wright, *Political Poems*, II and *Excerpta Historica*, p. 162.

[1] Christie, *Henry VI*, p. 232 and note 3.

[2] *Cal. Milanese Papers*, I, p. 58.

[3] *Rot. Parl.*, V, pp. 280–81.

[4] *Croy. Chron.*, p. 418.

III
(pp. 33–38)

[1] There is no record of when Richard was moved from Fotheringhay to Ludlow or by what route. Since he was sickly and the time perilous, it seems likely that he remained at Fotheringhay till the spring of 1459. All that is definitely known of Richard's first years is that he was born at Fotheringhay on October 2, 1452, and captured at Ludlow on October 13, 1459.

[2] For York's principal supporters, see *Rot. Parl.*, V, p. 348.

[3] Hearne's *Fragment*, in *Chronicles of the White Rose*, p. 5. It is reported that Cicely and her two boys were found in the village. Since she was a woman of spirit and was apparently trying to protect her villagers, I have conjectured that she took her stance at the market cross. See Scofield, I, p. 37 and note 2.

[4] On the strength of Gairdner's interpretation of a reference in the *Paston Letters*, it seems to have been generally assumed (see, for example, Scofield, I, p. 37, note 2) that it was to one of Buckingham's manors in Kent that Cicely and her two boys were brought. The letter in question—P.L., I, pp. 504–05—derisively mocks Lord Rivers by reporting that Rivers, his son, and others have won Calais 'by a feeble assault made at Sandwich' by John Dynham (it was, in fact, Dynham who had captured Rivers; see p. 36). The letter continues, 'But my lady Duchess is still again received in Kent'. Gairdner, for no apparent reason, identifies 'my lady Duchess' with Cicely, Duchess of York. Rivers' wife, however, was the Dowager Duchess of

Bedford. Since she was taken to Calais with her son and husband (see Scofield, I, p. 51) and since the sentence clearly continues the subject of their capture, the reference must be to Rivers' wife, not York's. That is, Rivers' wife had been permitted to return to Kent. On what estate Cicely and her two sons were kept in the custody of the Duchess.of Buckingham is unknown.

5 Davies, *Eng. Chron.*, p. 83.

6 Whethamstede, I, pp. 367–68; *Chronicle o London*, ed. by E. Tyrell and Sir H. Nicolas, London, 1827, p. 140.

7 P.L., I, p. 506; see note 4 above.

8 Davies, *Eng. Chron.*, pp. 91–94.

9 More than a decade after this time, Edward IV, formerly Ear of March, bestowed a grant upon the Archbishop of Canterbury because 'in time past and at the King's request he supported the King's brothers the Dukes of Clarence and Gloucester [George and Richard] for a long time at great charges' (*Cal. Pat. Rolls*, 1467–77, p. 296, Dec. 10, 1471). Before the flight from Ludlow in Oct., 1459, and from Sept. to Dec. of 1460, it would certainly have been the Duke of York, rather than his son Edward, who would have made such a request of the Archbishop. After the return of George and Richard from Burgundy in June of 1461, there appears to be no interval during which they might have been placed under the Archbishop's tutelage. George acted as Steward for Edward's coronation; he met the King at Leicester the following May (Scofield, I, p. 245, note 5); the preceding January (1462) it was rumoured that he and the Duke of Suffolk would head a commission of *oyer and terminer* for Norfolk (P.L., II, p. 82). These activities suggest that he was not in the Archbishop's charge. Furthermore, it appears that Richard went north to enter the household of the Earl of Warwick in the fall of 1461 (see p. 45). It is most unlikely that at any time after this the boys would be considered still young enough for such tutelage. By a process of elimination it would seem that the Archbishop must have assumed charge of George and Richard early in 1460, shortly after their mother left Coventry in the Duchess of Buckingham's custody, and maintained them until they rejoined her in September of 1460.

10 It rained all summer, rotting the crops, washing away bridges and houses. Whethamstede, I, 381, 384–85; *Chronicle of John Stone*, p. 78; *Three Fif. Cent. Chrons.*, p.154; compare Scofield, I, p. 120.

11 P.L., I, p. 525.

IV
(pp. 38–42)

1 Hall, pp. 250–51; Clifford probably never said this, but he undoubtedly thought it.

2 *Croy. Chron.*, pp. 422–23; the chronicler vividly depicts the fear and hatred which Margaret's march aroused in the hearts of southerners and midlanders. 'Blessed be God!' he exclaims in wild relief, 'who did not give us for a prey unto their teeth!'

3 On Oct. 16, 1461, King Edward granted John Skelton, esq., for good service to the King and his brothers, the Dukes of Clarence and Gloucester, the office of surveyor of the scrutiny in the port of London (*Cal. Pat. Rolls*, 1461–67, p. 52). I have conjectured that the service Skelton performed was to escort the two boys across sea.

[4] *Cal. Milanese Papers*, I, pp. 73–74; see also p. 67 and p. 72. Hearne's *Fragment*, p. 6.

[5] See Caxton's prologue to his *Life of Jason*; for a description of the court of Burgundy: *Mémoires d'Olivier de la Marche*, ed. by H. Beaune and J. d'Arbaumont, Paris, 1883; or for brief modern accounts, J. Calmette, *Autour de Louis XI*, Paris, 1947, pp. 132–38, or D. B. Wyndham Lewis, *King Spider*, London, 1930, pp. 109–24.

[6] The news reached Bruges on April 12: *Cal. Milanese Papers*, I, pp. 67–68.

[7] Jehan de Waurin, *Anchiennes Cronicques d'Engleterre*, II, pp. 305–06.

V

(pp. 43–45)

[1] The Croyland chronicler says that Edward was 'a person of most elegant appearance, and remarkable beyond all others for the attractions of his person' (pp. 481–82).

According to Vergil, 'King Edward was very tall of personage, exceeding the stature almost of all others, of comely visage, pleasant look, broad breasted, the residue even to his feet proportionably correspondent' (p. 172).

Thomas More, in his *Richard III*, describes Edward: 'He was of visage lovely, of body mighty, strong, and clean made. . . .' (p. 3).

Du Clerq, a contemporary Burgundian chronicler, calls Edward the handsomest young knight in all England (J. du Clerq, *Mémoires sur le Regne de Philippe le Bon*, ed. by M. le Baron de Reiffenberg, Brussels, 1835–36, liv. IV, c. xvii).

Commynes, meeting Edward for the first time in 1470, declared that he was 'fort beau prince, plus que nul que j'aye veu jamais en ce temps là, et très vaillant' (*Mémoires de Philippe de Commynes*, ed. by B. de Mandrot, 2 vols., Paris, 1901, I, p. 201). Describing the interview five years later between the Kings of England and of France at Picquigny, he remarked that Edward was 'ung très beau prince et grand . . et l'avoye veu autresfoiz plus beau, car je n'ay pas souvenance d'avoir jamais veu ung plus bel homme qu'il estoit quant monsieur de Warvic le feist fouyr d'Angleterre' (I, p. 316). Edward's height has been precisely determined: 'when his coffin was opened in 1789, his skeleton was found to measure six feet, three inches and a half' (Scofield, I, p. 127, note 2.).

[2] My account of Richard's initiation is based upon a minute description of the ritual in 'The Manner of making Knights after the custom of England in time of peace, and at the coronation, that is to say, Knights of the Bath' from 'Stowe's Historical Memoranda' printed in *Three Fif. Cent. Chrons.*, pp. 106–13. See also Hearne's *Fragment*, p. 10.

[3] *Reports Touching the Dignity of a Peer*, V, p. 327.

[4] Scofield, I, p. 216.

[5] See, for example, *A Relation of the Island of England*, written by an Italian visitor of a generation later: 'everyone, however rich he may be, sends away his children into the houses of others. . . .' (p. 23).

[6] *Cal. Pat. Rolls*, 1461–67, p. 66.

See note 9 of chapter 3 above.

VI
(pp. 45–53)

[1] In the fall of 1465 King Edward granted Warwick £1,000 to defray the costs and expenses he had incurred in maintaining Richard, Duke of Gloucester (Tellers' Roll, Mich. 5 Edw. IV (no. 36), m.2.; quoted by Scofield, I, p. 216, note 6).

The precise times at which Richard entered and departed from Warwick's household are unknown. In view of the sum granted the Earl, Richard's attaining the age of thirteen in the fall of 1465, the break between Edward and Warwick following the announcement in September of 1464 of Edward's marriage, and a record of Richard's being at court in May of 1465, it seems likely that he entered Warwick's household in November of 1461, following his appointment as Commissioner of Array for the North, and that he had left it by the early spring of 1465.

Davies (York Records, p. 48) declares that Middleham was 'the favourite retreat of . . . Warwick'. It had been the chief residence of his father, the Earl of Salisbury. The Countess of Warwick was certainly here in the late spring of 1462 (see York Records, p. 15).

[2] Sir Charles R. Peers, Middleham Castle, H.M.S.O., 1943 (reprinted, 1951); though in ruins, the castle is still impressive.

[3] See, for example, York Records, p. 15.

[4] York Records, p. 58; Miles Metcalfe became one of Richard's councillors (see below, p. 129), and other Metcalfes were in his favour (Harleian MS. 433).

[5] Ibid., p. 194, note; though the DNB says that Lovell was one of Richard's companions at Middleham, the statement should be phrased as a probability rather than a certainty. The £1,000 that Warwick received for Richard's maintainance came from the profits of Lovell's wardship and marriage (see note one, above), and this alone proves that Lovell was not then Warwick's ward. Not until 1467 was the Earl granted Lovell's lands during his minority and his custody and marriage (Cal. Pat. Rolls, 1467–77, p. 51).

[6] See the following note (7); compare H. F. M. Prescott, Mary Tudor, London, 1952, pp. 8–9.

[7] See Scofield, II, pp. 451–55, for the sort of books King Edward read, and for the general upper class reading of the time consult the Paston Letters.

This account of the training and daily regimen of Richard is based upon the household regulations of Edward IV (the Liber Niger) and the household regulations of George, Duke of Clarence, published in Ordinances and Regulations for the Government of the Royal Household. The former (p. 45) includes the duties of the 'Maistyr of Henxmen' (noble pages and apprentices in knighthood) to Edward IV. Warwick undoubtedly had his 'Master of Henchmen' too. The 'livery' I have used is that issued to a gentleman in the household of the Duke of Clarence (p. 91); Warwick's would be similar. Compare the 'livery' of a baron in the royal household (p. 31).

[8] For a discussion of Richard's appearance, see note 9, p. 458.

[9] The ceremony at Fotheringhay: the information is drawn from the enrolments of Wardrobe Accounts and from the Issue Rolls, as cited by Scofield, I, p. 268.

For the Neville interment at Bisham, see Ordinances and Regulations, p. 131.

10 That Richard was in London in the late spring of 1463 is indicated by his witnessing, along with his brother George, Warwick, and Hastings, the confirmation of a borough charter (*Cal. Pat. Rolls*, 1461–67, pp. 307–08). Though the patent was sealed June 23, it must have been drawn up at least three weeks earlier because Warwick left London on June 3 (see Scofield, I, p. 288). Since he was in London in the late spring, it seems likely that Richard accompanied Edward south in January to honour his father's memory and that he returned to the North with Warwick. He paid a brief visit to Canterbury in late August of 1463 (*Chronicle of John Stone*, ed. by W. G. Searle, Cambridge 1902, p. 88).

Richard was apparently not summoned to Parliament until 1469, when he received a writ for Warwick's Parliament that never met (*Dignity of a Peer*, IV, pp. 966–70).

11 *Cal. Pat. Rolls*, 1461–67, p. 391. For Richard's holdings of land, see next note.

12 Clarence's and Richard's grants: see *Cal. Pat. Rolls*, 1461–67.

According to the *Dignity of a Peer* (II, p. 112), the grant of the county, honour, and lordship of Richmond did not carry with it the dignity of the earldom of Richmond, Clarence—to whom Edward soon made over the grant—never having assumed the dignity. Though it is true that in a patent of April, 1463 (*Cal. Pat. Rolls*, 1461–67, p. 270), he is called 'Duke of Clarence and Lord of Richmond', the fact is, however, that he did assume the title. In a proclamation which he issued during the re-adeption of Henry VI, 1470–71, he styles himself 'George, Duke of Clarence and Earl of Richmond' (*Original Letters*, series 2, I, p. 139). It was not beyond Clarence, though, to appropriate a dignity which did not belong to him. In 1471, Henry VI confirmed to him the grant of Richmond (*Dignity of a Peer*, II, p. 112). As part of the division of estates between Clarence and Richard in 1474, Clarence was confirmed in the possession of the county, honour, castle, town, and fee-farm of Richmond, but he was not given the *lordship*. This omission suggests that, whether or not he had in the past rightfully born the title of Earl of Richmond, the dignity was now withheld (*Cal. Pat. Rolls*, 1467–77, p. 457). Only the castle and the fee-farm of the town of Richmond passed to Richard after Clarence's death (*Cal. Pat. Rolls*, 1476–85, p. 90). It appears that in the fifteenth century there was no clearly established distinction between the grant of an authority or an estate and the grant of the corresponding dignity. Practice seems to have varied according to the circumstances of each particular case (see *Dignity of a Peer*, II, *passim*).

13 See, for example, the comment of Fabyan (p. 654). Almost two decades later a foreign visitor was told that when Edward put a dagger to her throat, she still would not yield her virtue! (Mancini, p. 73). For rumours about Warwick's quarrelling with Edward, see *Cal. Milanese Papers*, I, p. 116.

14 *Cal. Milanese Papers*, I, p. 100.

VII
(pp. 53–63)

1 Richard was with the court at Greenwich on May 23, 1465, when Nucelles pursuivant reported to the King that the Bastard of Burgundy had accepted Lord Scales' challenge to a joust (*Excerpta Historica*, p. 172).

2 Cust, *Gentlemen Errant*, pp. 36–39; see also Scofield, I, p. 397, note 1.

3 P. 238.

[4] For Anthony Woodville's literary accomplishments, see, below, p. 171. For Worcester and George Neville as scholars, see R. Weiss, *Humanism in England during the Fifteenth Century*, London, 1941; R. J. Mitchell, *John Tiptoft*, London, 1938 (for Tiptoft's death, see pp. 142–43); James Tait, 'Letters of John Tiptoft, Earl of Worcester, and Archbishop Neville to the University of Oxford', *Eng. Hist. Rev.*, XXXV (1920), pp. 570–74; P. S. Allen, 'Bishop Shirwood of Durham and His Library', *Eng. Hist. Rev.*, XXV (1910), pp. 445–56.

[5] Scofield, I, p. 310.

[6] Cust, *Gentlemen Errant*, p. 40; of the choir of the royal chape the Bohemian knights had said that 'there are no better singers in the world' (pp. 41–42).

[7] It was common opinion on the Continent that Warwick was a coward. So Commynes indicates, and Chastellain writes bluntly, 'Warwyc . . . estoit laiche et couard. . .' (See, further, George B. Churchill, 'Richard the Third up to Shakespeare', *Palaestra*, X (1900), Berlin, p. 58).

[8] Leland, *Collectanea*, VI, pp. 1–14.

[9] *Cal. Venetian Papers*, I, p. 117; *Cal. Milanese Papers*, I, pp. 118–20.

[10] As late as 1469, it is true, rumour was still coupling Richard's name with Anne Neville's. In August of that year an Italian observer in London mistakenly reported that Warwick had married his two daughters to the King's two brothers (by which time Clarence had married Isabel), *Cal. Mil. Papers*, p. 131.

[11] Jean de Waurin, *Anchiennes Cronicques d'Engleterre*, II, pp. 333–34; Oman accepts this story without giving its source (*Warwick*, p. 169); C. A. J. Armstrong also seems to accept it (Mancini, p. 134, note 14); the fact is, however, that the court of France in these years abounded in absurd rumours regarding the course of events in England (see *Cal. Milanese Papers*, I, *passim*).

[12] See, for example, Mancini, pp. 79–81.

[13] *Cal. Pat. Rolls*, 1461–67, p. 530.

VIII
(pp. 63–71)

[1] *Cal. Mil. Papers*, I, p. 122.

[2] *Excerpta Historica*, p. 198; for a detailed account of the tournament see pp. 197–212.

[3] There is no record of his participation in any of the great jousts of King Edward's reign. See Scofield, I and II, *passim*.

[4] Fabyan, pp. 655–56.

[5] Scofield, I, pp. 456–57.

[6] *Great Chronicle*, p. 205.

[7] *Ibid.*, pp. 207–08.

[8] See Scofield, I, pp. 436–39; compare *Great Chronicle*, p. 213 and Mitchell, *John Tiptoft*, pp. 113–121.

Confirmation for the story appears in a documentary source which has not, apparently, been hitherto cited. Many years later Richard sent word to the heir of the murdered Earl of Desmond that those responsible for his father's death were the same ones who had wrought the ruin of the Duke of Clarence (i.e., the Queen and her kindred)—Harl. MS 433, f. 265. For a further consideration of this document, see, below, note 7 of chapter 3, 'The Lord of the North'. William Worcester states flatly (p. 789) that 'the King was at first displeased' by the news of Desmond's execution.

IX
(pp. 71–77)

[1] *Croy. Chron.*, p. 444.

[2] For more about Brampton, see, below, p. 187.

[3] See the *Paston Letters*, II, pp. 355 and 358; among those of the royal entourage whom young John Paston entertained one day to dinner were 'John of Par' and 'Perse (P.L., II, p. 358). The latter would seem to be Robert Percy, though the identification cannot be positively established. The former I conjecture to be a squire of Richard's because of Richard's close association with the Parre family: Hutton, *Bosworth*, p. xxxiii, says that Thomas a Par and John Milwater, two of Richard's squires, were slain at his feet in the battle of Barnet; Sir William Parre was later a member of Richard's council (*Cal. Pat. Rolls*, 1476–85, p. 343: commission of *oyer and terminer* for York; Reid, *King's Council in the North*, p. 44).

For Richard's shortage of money, see his letter, p. 73 below (printed in *Original Letters*, 2nd series, I, p. 143). This financial difficulty suggests that the King included him at the last minute.

[4] The whole story is vividly unfolded in a letter which young John Paston wrote to his brother, Sir John (P.L., II, pp. 355–58).

[5] 2nd paragraph of note 3, above. Though the letter bears no year date, and though none has apparently been hitherto suggested, it must have been written in 1469. Privy seals show that Edward was at Walsingham on June 22 and at Lynn on June 26 (P.L., II, p. 355, headnote to letter 612); Castle Rising lies between them; and on no other occasion is Richard known to have been in Norfolk with Edward in June before accompanying him northward.

[6] *Croy. Chron.*, p. 445.

[7] *Chronicles of the White Rose*, pp. 219–224.

[8] P.L., II, pp. 360–61.

[9] Scofield, I, p. 497.

[10] Scofield (I, p. 500), following the *Croy. Chron.*, says that the Archbishop of York conveyed Edward to Middleham; but it is clear from a letter written at London by Sir John Paston on Sept. 10 (P.L., II, pp. 367–71) that the Archbishop had been in London for a considerable time and had, only one or two days before, started northward. It appears very unlikely that he took Edward to Middleham towards the latter part of August, rushed back to London to carry on the business of the council, and went northward again on Sept. 8 or 9. Warwick, on the other hand, was in Yorkshire at the beginning of September (Scofield, I, p. 501). It was probably he, therefore, who conveyed the King. Vergil, p. 123, indicates that it was the Earl who accomplished Edward's removal, and an Italian in London reported, on August 16, that Clarence and the Archbishop were expected in the City (*Cal. Mil. Papers*, pp. 131–32).

[11] Vergil, p. 125.

[12] Contemporary sources tell confused and conflicting stories about the end of Edward's captivity. On the Continent it was reported that, under the colour of going hunting, Edward gave Warwick the slip and made his way to London (*Cal. Mil. Papers*, I,

p. 133). Commynes says that with the help of the Duke of Burgundy, who found means of getting in touch with him, Edward escaped from Warwick (*Mémoires*, I, p. 197). Vergil declares that after he had corrupted his guards, Edward escaped first to York and then into Lancashire, where Hastings had gathered a force which brought the King safe to London (Vergil, pp. 123-24). The most authentic information, which is all too meagre, occurs in a letter written by Sir John Paston from London in October, 1469 (P.L., II, pp. 389-90):

> The King is come to London, and there came with him, and rode against [to meet] him, the Duke of Gloucester, the Duke of Suffolk, the Earl of Arundel, the Earl of Northumberland, the Earl of Essex, the Lords Harry and John of Buckingham, the Lord Dacres, the Lord Chamberlain [Hastings], the Lord Mountjoy, and many other Knights and Squires, the Mayor of London, 22 Aldermen, in scarlet, and of the Craftsmen of the town to the number of 200, all in blue. The King came through Chepe, though it were out of his way, because he would not be seen, and he was accompanied in all people with 1,000 horse, some harnessed and some not. My Lord Archbishop came with him from York, and is at the Moor [his great manor in Hertfordshire], and my Lord of Oxenford rode to have met the King, and he is with my Lord Archbishop at the Moor, and came not to town with the King; some say that they were yesterday three miles to the Kingwards from the Moor, and that the King sent them a messenger that they should come when that he sent for them. I wot not what to suppose therein; the King himself hath good language of the Lords of Clarence, of Warwick, and of my Lords of York and of Oxenford, saying they be his best friends; but his household men have other language, so that what shall hastily fall I cannot say.

From this letter Scofield draws the positive conclusion that Edward 'was brought to London voluntarily by the Archbishop' (I, p. 505, note 5), apparently leaning heavily on the statement, 'My Lord Archbishop came with him from York'. What follows, however, suggests quite a different interpretation: that though Edward, to suit his own purposes, was content to have the world believe that he and the Nevilles were, and had been, friends, and though the Archbishop of York may have come south at the same time as the King—i.e., riding close behind his party—Edward had, in fact, asserted his independence without seeking his captors' permission; and when George Neville sought to overtake him, in order to keep up appearances by entering London with him, the King made clear by his message that he was his own master. The fact that the Archbishop was under the necessity of overtaking the King certainly suggests that he had not come south with the royal entourage. The implications of this letter, coupled with the widespread reports of an escape, lead me to suppose that Edward, realizing Warwick's powerlessness to hold him longer, openly threw off his shackles; that is, he escaped simply by choosing the right moment to declare his independence.

About the middle of September a certain 'Master Writtill', a servant of the Duke of Clarence's who was attempting to negotiate in the Pastons' behalf with the Duke of Norfolk, observes in a letter that 'divers of my Lords [of the council] . . . be at the King's high commandment hastily departed unto His Highness' but he expects 'to have hearing in brief time of their hasty coming again' (P.L., II, p. 377). Certainly Warwick, Clarence and the Archbishop had no desire to strengthen Edward's hand by summoning his advisers to his side. It seems probable that Edward himself had boldly commanded their attendance without Warwick's knowledge or consent, so that he might return to his capital in royal state surrounded by the chief lords of his court. It is this summons, coupled with Hastings' and Richard's probable providing of an armed escort, that accounts for the train of lords and soldiers with which the King entered London. According to news received at the French Court, 'Lords and military commanders have fled from the earl and gone to meet the King' (*Cal. Mil. Papers*, pp. 133–34).

My version of Richard's share in his brother's 'escape' from Warwick is necessarily conjectural. The rewards, and particularly the responsibilities, which Edward immediately after thrust upon his young brother (see *Chapter* 10), suggest that in this crisis Richard had demonstrated to the King not only his loyalty but his bravery and skill in handling affairs as well.

X
(pp. 78–84)

[1] Grant to Richard of the Constableship: *Cal. Pat. Rolls*, 1467–77, p. 178; grant to Earl Rivers of the same: *ibid.*, p. 19. Compare *Excerpta Historica*, p. 241. For a discussion of the authority of the Constable, see S. B. Chrimes, *English Constitutional Ideas in the Fifteenth Century*, Cambridge, 1936, and R. J. Mitchell, *John Tiptoft*.

[2] Grants of lands to Richard: *Cal. Close Rolls*, 1468–1476, p. 102; *Cal. Pat. Rolls*, 1467–77, p. 179; Cotton Julius B XII, f. 111 *et seq.* (Brit. Mus. MSS.).

Disaffection in Wales: Cotton Vespasian F XIII, f. 38.

[3] The commission of array: *Cal. Pat. Rolls*, 1467–77, p. 195. Chief Justiceship of North Wales: *ibid.*, p. 178. Steward, approver, etc.: *ibid.*, p. 179. Authority to recapture the castles etc.: *ibid.*, p. 180. Richard's success is indicated by the fact that nothing more is heard of difficulties with the castles of Carmarthen and Cardigan.

[4] Richard's return to London: he was witness to the creation of George Neville, son of John, Earl of Northumberland, as Duke of Bedford, which charter was sealed on January 5, 1470 (*Cal. Charter Rolls*, VI, p. 238). Commission of *oyer and terminer*: *Cal. Pat. Rolls*, 1467–77, p. 198. Chief Justice and Chamberlain of S. Wales and Steward etc.: *ibid.*, p. 185.

Warwick as former holder of these offices: *Foedera*, XI, p. 647; at the same time— i.e., during Edward's captivity—Warwick had also been made Constable of Cardigan castle and Steward of other Welsh lands, offices which, like the Chief Justiceship and Chamberlainship of S. Wales, had belonged to his slain enemy, Herbert, Earl of Pembroke (*Foedera*, XI, pp. 647–48). Edward ended Warwick's short-lived attempt to become the great power in Wales by conferring that power on his brother Richard.

[5] Pp. 125–26.

[6] My account of the events which follow is based principally on the *Chronicle of the Rebellion in Lincolnshire*, a detailed contemporary narrative, and on the confession of Sir Robert Welles (*Excerpta Historica*, pp. 282–84). Compare Scofield, I, pp. 509–14.

[7] *Cal. Pat. Rolls*, 1467–77, p. 205.

[8] P.L., II, p. 395.

[9] *ibid.*, p. 396; *Dignity of a Peer*, V, p. 380 (Edward's proclamation at Nottingham, March 31, 1470, in which he explains that he was forced to give over the pursuit of Clarence and Warwick for lack of victuals) and also *Cal. Close Rolls*, 1468–1476, p. 137 and pp. 135–36.

[10] *Dignity of a Peer*, V, p. 379; P.L., II, p. 396; *Cal. Pat. Rolls*, 1467–77, p. 206. Percy had been released from the Tower on October 27, 1469, and had sworn an oath of allegiance to the King (*Cal. Close Rolls*, 1468–76, p. 100).

[11] So far as I know, Richard's part in this campaign has been hitherto unnoticed; it must, in fact, be largely conjectured. My reconstruction has been developed from the following evidence: (1) the King's proclamation to the Sheriff of York on March 25 (see text, p. 84; *Cal. Close Rolls*, 1468–76, p. 138; also Signed Bills, file 1501, 46—renumbered from 4339 as given by Scofield, I, p. 516, note 3—). (2) The foregoing proclamation provides a motive—Richard's advance from Wales—for Stanley's sudden decision to desert Warwick and Clarence; since he entered London with them the following October (*Chronicles of London*, p. 182), he probably was able to show good reason for having failed to aid them. (3) It is well established that Richard did not set out from London with King Edward and that he was not with the King at York (an enumeration of the nobles who accompanied Edward makes no mention of the Duke of Gloucester: *Six Town Chronicles*, p. 164; and Richard did not witness the charter, issued March 25 at York, creating John Neville Marquess of Montagu: *Dignity of a Peer*, V, p. 379).

[12] *Cal. Pat. Rolls*, 1467–77, p. 219.

[13] On April 17, at Exeter, Richard was given a commission of array for Cornwall and Devon (*Cal. Pat. Rolls*, 1467–77, p. 221).

XI
(pp. 84–93)

[1] Richard received commissions of array of June 2 for Gloucestershire, Somerset, and Hereford (*Cal. Pat. Rolls*, 1467–77, p. 220) and a commission of *oyer and terminer* of July 11 for the city and county of Lincoln (*Cal. Pat. Rolls*, 1467–77, p. 221).

[2] *Cal. Pat. Rolls*, 1467–77, p. 221.

[3] *Foedera*, XI, pp. 658–60.

[4] P.L., II, pp. 409–10.

[5] For Warwick in France see 'The Manner and Guiding of the Earl of Warwick at Angers' in *Original Letters*, 2nd series, I, p. 132 or in *Chronicles of the White Rose*, p. 229; *Cal. Milanese Papers*, I, pp. 136–42; Commynes, I, pp. 201–06; compare the accounts in Scofield, I, pp. 523–36 and in Bagley, *Margaret of Anjou*, pp. 196–204.

[6] See W. I. Howard, 'Economic Aspects of the Wars of the Roses in East Anglia', *Eng. Hist. Rev.*, XLI (1926), pp. 170–89. Hearne's *Fragment*, p. 29.

[7] For King Henry's re-emergence from the Tower, see Fabyan, p. 659.

[8] P.L., II, p. 412.

[9] For Edward and Richard in Burgundy, see Commynes, I, pp. 207–216; also Waurin, III, p. 56; compare Scofield, I, pp. 562–68.

[10] My account of Edward's invasion is mainly based on the *Historie of the Arrivall of Edward IV in England*, an official report of his reconquest which was composed by one of his servants who was an eyewitness of most of the events he describes. Despite its obvious Yorkist bias, it is a narrative of inestimable value.

[11] The *Arrivall* gives an interesting but not altogether convincing analysis of Montagu's motives; compare Vergil, p. 140; see also Scofield, I, pp. 570–71.

[12] Historical Manuscripts Commission, *Rutland*, I, pp. 2–5.

[13] Letters which Clarence wrote to Vernon establish his movements (HMC, *Rutland*, I, pp. 2–5).

[14] The *Arrivall* says that Clarence spoke 'in his best manner', which would indicate that his eloquence was already well known. Compare his appearance before the royal council in the fall of 1471 (*Croy. Chron.*, p. 470) and Mancini, p. 77 and note, p. 134.

[15] *Great Chronicle*, p. 215.

[16] Wright, *Political Poems and Songs*, II, p. 274.

[17] *Great Chronicle*, p. 216.

XII
(pp. 93–99)

I have reconstructed the Battle of Barnet from my own inspection of the ground, which I pursued in the light of three authoritative but unfortunately sketchy accounts, all of which were composed very shortly after the engagement: the narrative in the *Arrivall*; a letter which Richard's sister Margaret, Duchess of Burgundy, wrote to the Dowager Duchess Isabel (quoted by Mlle. Dupont, the editor of Waurin's *Anchiennes Cronicques*, III, p. 213); and a report sent home by an Easterling, Gerhard von Wesel (*Hanserecesse*, Leipzig, 1890, VI, pp. 415–18). Not only the *Arrivall* but the *Chronicles of London* and Vergil (pp. 143–47) describe the field as being 'upon the plain without Barnet town' (*Chrons. of London*, p. 184); and, writing four days after the battle, in which he took part, Sir John Paston places it 'upon the field, half a mile from Barnet' (P.L., III, p. 4).

Ramsay's *Lancaster and York* (II, p. 370 *et seq.*) presents a confused and obviously inaccurate account, upon which Scofield has too heavily leaned (I, pp. 578–81). The most stimulating and helpful version, to which I am indebted, is given by Col. A. H. Burne in his *Battlefields of England*, London, 1950, pp. 108–16.

So far as I know, however, no one has attempted to explain why it was that King Edward's battle line was not drawn up directly in front of Warwick's. The answer to this question, I believe, provides the master clue to the precise positions of the two armies.

On the afternoon before the battle, Warwick had plenty of time to survey the ground and choose the best position it would yield. 'Dead Man's Bottom' offered a splendid anchor for the left wing; the hollow is less than a mile north of Barnet (see map in text, p. 94); it drops away only about 150 yards east of the St. Albans–Barnet Road down which Warwick was advancing. If Warwick placed his left so that the 'Bottom' protected its flank, then his line would extend a far greater distance to the west, than to the east, of the road. It is thus, I believe, that he disposed his army; because this arrangement explains why King Edward, assuming in the darkness that the Lancastrians were in equal strength on both sides of the road, drew up his line accordingly, and so greatly overlapped the Lancastrians on the east as he was overlapped on the west. Thus Richard, in command of the van or right wing, occupied the high ground of Hadley Common which directly faces the 'Bottom'. Warwick's line ran roughly east and west about 250 yards south of the monument which today stands in the fork of the roads leading to St. Albans and Hatfield. By taking the right-hand, Hatfield, road, one may

P

look eastward down into the 'Bottom'. Westward, Warwick's line extended beyond the modern St. Albans–Barnet Road, probably along a hedge which Col. Burne has ingeniously re-discovered straggling across a golf links that now occupies the ground (the *Arrivall* declares that Warwick assembled men 'under an hedge-side').

[1] *Arrivall*, p. 18.

[2] For an interesting account of English battle tactics written only a dozen years after Barnet by an Italian visitor, see Mancini, pp. 103–05.

[3] From the general fierceness of the fighting it does not seem unlikely that two of Richard's squires might have been slain fighting at his side. The only authority for this supposition, however, is Hutton's *Bosworth*, p. xxxiii, where no source is given for the statement.

[4] P.L., II, pp. 411–13 and III, p. 4; for the Pastons' relations with Norfolk and Oxford, see II, *passim*.

[5] Duchess of Burgundy's letter (see headnote, above).

[6] *Arrivall*, pp. 19–20.

[7] See Vergil, pp. 143–47; *Arrivall*, p. 20; Warkworth's *Chronicle*, p. 16; Fabyan, p. 661 compare Scofield, I, p. 580.

[8] Sir John Paston reported that more than 1,000 men had been killed in the battle (P.L., III, p. 4); Commynes (I, p. 218) and Fabyan (p. 661) both give 1,500 as the number of slain.

For King Edward: Lord Say, Lord Cromwell, and Sir Humphrey Bourchier fell on the field and Lord Mountjoy's son died of his wounds; Richard and Earl Rivers were slightly wounded. On the other side, Warwick and Montagu were the only great lords slain; the Duke of Exeter was severely wounded, left for dead on the field, and carried off to safety by one of his men; the two Paston brothers were both captured, young John suffering a wound in the hand (Warkworth, pp. 16–17; *Arrivall*, p. 20; von Wesel's letter, see headnote, above; P.L., III, pp. 3–5).

XIII
(pp. 99–104)

[1] This and subsequent quotations are from the *Arrivall* (pp. 27–28). I have reconstructed the battle from its wonderfully vivid, though patchy, account, the only contemporary narrative, and from my own study of the field. The best modern account is that of Col. A. H. Burne, *Battlefields of England*, pp. 117–136, which I have found most helpful.

[2] No less than seven contemporary sources offer unanimous testimony that Prince Edward 'was slain on the field,' i.e., in the pursuit.

(1) The *Arrivall*, admittedly Yorkist in viewpoint, says simply that 'Edward, called Prince, was taken, fleeing to the townwards, and slain, in the field' (p. 30).

(2) The Croyland chronicler, though a councillor of King Edward's, was a learned churchman and he wrote his account after the death of Richard, when he was free to say what he pleased (for the identity of this chronicler, see Appendix II, p. 432). Although his statement is not couched in the clearest terms, he indicates that the Prince, as the *Arrivall* declared, was slain in the field. Gairdner supports this interpretation (*Hist. Croy. Chron.*, p. 555).

(3) Warkworth, a contemporary chronicler who cannot be accused of Yorkist bias, says that the Prince was overtaken in the pursuit and slain even as 'he cried for succour to his brother-in-law, the Duke of Clarence' (p. 18).

(4) Clarence himself, who would not be likely to feel any scruples in reporting to a friend exactly how the Prince died, wrote, two days after the field, that 'Edward, late called Prince,' and 'other estates, knights, squires, and gentlemen were slain in plain battle' (HMC, Rutland, I, p. 4).

(5) Commynes says that Prince Edward was 'killed on the field.' (I, p. 220).

(6) A paper written, apparently, immediately after the battle lists as 'Ded in the Feld' a number of lords headed by 'Edward that was called Prynce' (P.L., III, pp. 8–9).

(7) The Tewkesbury Chronicle—of which Professor Myers has kindly reminded me— 'in an account of the battle probably written soon afterwards, and in a spirit rather hostile to Edward IV, merely states that Prince Edward was slain in the field' (Myers). See C. L. Kingsford, English Historical Literature in the Fifteenth Century, pp. 376–78.

I have followed Warkworth in attributing the Prince's death to Clarence, because Warkworth's statement accords well with the character of Clarence and the nature of the battle. Since Richard and the King were leading the assaults against the centre of the Lancastrian line, it seems likely that Clarence, perhaps commanding the reserve, would be in a better position to mount a horse and lead the pursuit than his brothers who were in the thick of combat.

[3] The author of the Arrivall declares openly that, although Edward gave free pardon to the rebels in the abbey, he later had Somerset and the other Lancastrian leaders brought forth to stand trial. The author seems to imply that the King's pardon was never meant to extend to other than the rank-and-file.

As for the quality or degree of sanctuary offered by the abbey; 'All churches,' Professor Myers notes, 'were, by canon law, sanctuaries; but they were not really safe unless they had a royal charter or a papal bull, and Tewkesbury had neither.'

[4] The Arrivall's ascription of Henry VI's demise to 'pure displeasure and melancholy' (p. 38) cannot be given a great deal of weight since it proceeds from King Edward's official reporter. For an examination of Henry VI's bones by W. H. St. John Hope, see Archaeologia, LXII, pp. 533–42; the appearance of Henry VI's skull suggested that Henry had died a violent death. Since the Lancastrian King's disappearance was obviously convenient to the House of York and since suspicion that he was put to death was widespread, the weight of probability certainly inclines to this supposition. That Richard was responsible for Henry's death is, however, very unlikely. True, Commynes implicates Richard (I, p. 219). Fabyan (p. 662) and Vergil (pp. 155–56) both make clear that the accusation against Richard which they report is the product of later gossip and hearsay. The Croyland chronicler, with no reason to shield Richard, simply reports, and deplores, Henry's taking off. Warkworth says that on the night Henry was killed, the Duke of Gloucester 'and many other' were at the Tower (p. 21).

Gairdner (Richard III, pp. 16–19) points out that it must have been King Edward and his council who determined upon Henry's death. In his capacity as Constable of England it would officially fall to Richard to bear their mandate to the Tower and receive notification that it had been carried out. The Milanese ambassador to the French court reported to his master that King Edward 'has caused King Henry to be secretly assassinated in the Tower. . . . He has, in short, chosen to crush the seed' (*Col. Mil. Papers*, p. 157).

THE KING'S BROTHER

THE LORD OF THE NORTH

I

(pp. 105–113)

The three principal contemporary sources for the second half of Edward the Fourth's reign (1471–83) are the *Croyland Chronicle* ('2nd Continuation'), the *Paston Letters*, and documents of State. My study of Richard's life during this period is mainly based on these sources and on Davies, *York Records* and the more recent *York Civic Records*, which provide a mine of information concerning Richard's activities as Lord of the North. The most detailed modern account of this period is offered by the second volume of Scofield's *Life and Reign of Edward the Fourth*, in which appear many documents and much diplomatic correspondence unearthed by Miss Scofield's monumental industry.

[1] Commynes, I, p. 198; the 'Rows Rol', par. 58; compare Scofield, I, pp. 519–20.

[2] *Cal. Mil. Papers*, I pp. 117–18.

[3] J. Calmette and G. Périnelle, in *Louis XI et L'Angleterre*, have proved that Anne and Prince Edward were married: see p. 133 and *Pièces Justicatives*, # 39, p. 319.

[4] It seems a safe conjecture that Anne spent the summer in the London household of her sister since Clarence, in the fall, hid her within the city (see, below, note 8).

[5] Richard had acted as Constable at Tewkesbury (see, above, p. 103); for further proof that Richard was again Constable and Admiral, see *Ancient Correspondence*, XLIV, # 61.

Grant of the Great Chamberlainship: *Cal. Pat. Rolls*, 1467–77, p. 262. Grant of the Stewardship of the Duchy of Lancaster: Cotton Julius B XII, f. 109.

Richard's resignation of Welsh offices and their assumption by Pembroke: *Cal. Pat. Rolls*, 1467–77, p. 275.

A few years later Herbert exchanged the earldom of Pembroke for that of Huntingdon: *Dignity of a Peer*, II, p. 219.

[6] *Cal. Pat. Rolls*, 1467–77, p. 319, p. 439; HMC, VI, p. 223.

[7] *Ibid.*, p. 260 and p. 266.

[8] I have developed this episode from the bald statement in the *Croyland Chronicle* (pp. 469–70) that Clarence 'caused the damsel [Anne] to be concealed, in order that it might not be known by his brother where she was; as he was afraid of a division of the earl's property, which he wished to come to himself alone in right of his wife, and not to be obliged to share it with any other person.' Richard, however, 'discovered the young lady in the city of London disguised in the habit of a cookmaid; upon which he had her removed to the sanctuary of St. Martin's.'

[9] *Cal. Pat. Rolls*, 1467–77, p. 297.

[10] *Croy. Chron.*, p. 470.

[11] Clarence was not Anne's guardian, and he had no claim to the estates remaining to the Countess of Warwick; see Gairdner, p. 20 and Scofield, II, pp. 6–7.

[12] P.L., III, p. 38.

[13] *Cal. Pat. Rolls*, 1467–77, p. 330, p. 262, p. 338; *Dignity of a Peer*, V, p. 390; *Cal. Charter Rolls*, VI, p. 238, p. 240.

[14] *Rot. Parl*, VI, p. 100 (where the possibility of their having to remarry because the marriage was irregular is indicated); compare Gairdner, pp. 21–24 and Scofield, II, p. 27. As with Clarence and Isabel, a papal dispensation was necessary because Anne and Richard were cousins, Richard's mother and Anne's grandfather being sister and brother.

[15] P.L., III, p. 88 and p. 92.

[16] HMC, VI, p. 223.

[17] P.L., III, pp. 92–93; HMC, 11th Rep., VII, p. 95.

[18] P.L., III, p. 102 and see Scofield, II, p. 89 and note 3; *Rot. Parl*, VI, p. 173; *Cal. Pat. Rolls*, 1476–85, p. 192; Harl. MS. 433, f. 53b.

[19] *Cal. Pat. Rolls*, 1467–77, p. 408.

[20] P.L., III, p. 98.

[21] P.L., III, p. 102.

[22] *Croy. Chron.*, p. 477 (the chronicler misdates the act of resumption as occurring after Edward's invasion of France); *Rot. Parl.*, VI, p. 75.

[23] *Rot. Parl.*, VI, p. 100, pp. 124–25 and *Cal. Pat. Rolls*, 1467–77 p. 457, p. 466. The precise division of lands between Richard and Clarence is not on record. Richard received all of Warwick's estates in the North and Clarence was given only those noted in the text. Clarence, on the other hand, apparently, received very much the larger share of the Countess of Warwick's Despenser-Beauchamp lands; Richard secured of the Countess's inheritance certain grants in Wales such as the lordship of Glamorgan and Morgannok (see *Cartae et Munimenta de Glamorgan*, V, Talygarn, 1910, p. 1725), the possession of Barnard Castle (see, below, note 13 of chapter 3) and such rights as the bestowal of certain advowsons, etc. (*idem*).

II
(pp. 114–121)

For the story of Edward's French expedition I have drawn heavily upon Commynes (I, pp. 283–323), who, as one of Louis XI's most trusted advisers, was in the thick of events.

[1] *Foedera*, XI, pp. 844–48; compare F. P. Barnard, *Edward IV's French Expedition of 1475*, Oxford, 1925.

[2] *French Expedition*, pp. 10–12.

[3] Scofield, II, p. 117, note 2; *Cal. Pat. Rolls*, 1467–77, p. 549, p. 485, p. 556.

[4] *Croy. Chron.*, p. 472; see Scofield, II, p. 132 and note 2.

[5] *Cal. Mil. Papers*, I, pp. 189–90.

[6] *Cal. Pat. Rolls*, 1467–77, p. 560; compare Commynes, I, pp. 302–03.

[7] *Cal. Pat. Rolls*, 1467–77, p. 560.

[8] Gairdner, *Richard III*, p. 28.

[9] *The Stonor Letters and Papers*, II, pp. 6–8.

[10] *Croy. Chron.*, p. 473.

[11] *Lettres de Louis XI*, IX, p. 276.

[12] Fabyan, p. 663.

[13] *Croy. Chron.*, pp. 473–74.

[14] Apparently, he came south only once during this period, to escort the bodies of his father and his brother Edmund from Pontefract to Fotheringhay, where they were interred in the collegiate church after a splendid ceremony which lasted two days (Harl. MS. 48, ff. 78–91; *Cal. Pat. Rolls*, 1467–77, p. 592; compare Scofield, II, pp. 167–68).

III

(pp. 121–127)

[1] P.L., III, p. 173.

[2] *Cal. Pat. Rolls*, 1476–85, p. 137.

[3] *Rot. Parl.*, VI, pp. 173–74; *Cal. Pat. Rolls*, 1476–85, pp. 72–73.

[4] *Croy. Chron.*, p. 479; *Cal. Pat. Rolls*, 1476–85, p. 115: a grant to Earl Rivers 'in consideration of the injuries perpetrated on him and his parents by George, late Duke of Clarence'; Mancini, pp. 75–77.

[5] *Croy. Chron.*, p. 480; *Rot. Parl.*, VI, p. 409; *Cal. Pat. Rolls*, 1476–85, p. 102; for Clarence impugning the validity of Edward's marriage, see below, pp. 215–18.

[6] *Louis XI et L'Angleterre*, p. 377 (Pièce Justificative ǂ 72).

[7] Clarence was sent to the Tower about the end of June. At this time Richard was, in all probability, in the North: during this year Richard and Anne became members of the Corpus Christi Guild of York and undoubtedly walked in their celebration, which fell, in 1477, on Friday, June 6, the day after Corpus Christi Day. Richard must have returned to London before the end of October, for on October 21 the magistrates of York addressed a letter to him there, to which he replied from London on November 15 (*York Records*, pp. 89–90).

[8] Mancini, writing less than six years later, declares that Richard was bitterly opposed to Clarence's execution: '[he] was so overcome with grief for his brother, that he could not dissimulate so well, but that he was overheard to say that he would one day avenge his brother's death' (p. 77). Even More admits, though with gratuitous suspicion, that Richard begged King Edward to spare Clarence (p. 10). There exists independent documentary testimony to the fact that Richard not only profoundly resented his brother's execution but held the Woodvilles responsible. Among the instructions which, some years later, he gave his councillor, the Bishop of Enachden, for conferring with the Earl of Desmond, there occurs this passage: 'Also he shall show that albeit the father of the said earl . . . was extorciously slain and murdered . . . by certain persons then having the governance and rule there [in Ireland, i.e., Earl of Worcester] . . .; yet notwithstanding that *the semblable chance was and happened sithen, within this realm of England, as well of his brother the Duke of Clarence*, as other his nigh kinsmen and great friends. . . .' (Harl. MS. 433, f. 265b: in Gairdner, *Letters and Papers*, I, p. 68). The italics are mine. It was the Queen who had prompted Worcester to murder the foregoing Earl of Desmond's father (see, above, pp. 70–71); Richard is reminding the Earl that he too has suffered heavy personal loss at the hands of the Woodvilles.

For Clarence's dangerous assertions see note 5, above.

[9] 'Narrative of the Marriage of Richard, Duke of York' in W. H. Black, *Illustrations of Ancient State and Chivalry*, Roxburghe Club, 1840, pp. 27–40.

[10] *Rot. Parl.*, VI, p. 409.

[11] Mancini says flatly that everybody considered the Woodvilles responsible for Clarence's death (p. 83).

[12] *Cal. Pat. Rolls*, 1476–85, p. 115: a grant of certain manors for six years to Earl Rivers 'in consideration of the injuries perpetrated on him and his parents by George, late Duke of Clarence, and because the said duke on the day of his death and before intended that he should be recompensed.'.

This statement indicates that Clarence was duly informed of his approaching end and was given the customary opportunity to make last requests and, no doubt, to shrive his soul.

This supposition is confirmed by an addition Stowe made to *The Great Chronicle* in which he noted that 'the Duke of Clarence . . . offered his own mass penny in the Tower of London and about twelve of the clock at noon made his end in a rondelet of malvesey. . . .' (p. 226).

The execution of the Duke of Clarence, though private, followed formal and prescribed procedure.

The story of Clarence's demise in malmesey wine is so widespread and persistent that it cannot be discounted. Of the two best contemporary sources, the Croyland Chronicler is uncertain or unwilling to say how Clarence met his death: 'the execution, whatever its nature may have been. . . .' (p. 480); Mancini, however, retails the story (p. 77). It appears on the Continent (Scofield, II, p. 209, note 5). Vergil says cautiously that Clarence 'was drowned (as they say) in a butt of malmesey' (pp. 167–68). Stowe (quoted above) echoes the tale. See the excellent summary of the evidence given by Armstrong, who accepts its validity (Mancini, pp. 134–35).

Despite its inherent improbability, the tale is very likely true. Throughout his life the improbable seems to have been Clarence's habitual *milieu*.

[13] *Cal. Pat. Rolls*, 1476–85, p. 67 and p. 90; *ibid.*, p. 139 and compare Ramsay, II, p. 425.

Gairdner declares that after Clarence's execution Richard 'obtained by grant from the Crown undivided possession of the lordship of Barnard Castle, of which he had hitherto held only a moiety in right of his wife' (pp. 36–37). The fact is, no such grant exists, and the absence of such a grant would itself indicate that Richard's full possession of Barnard Castle, in right of his wife, dates from the division of the Countess's property in 1474. Gairdner based his conclusion upon a confused, and unsupported, statement in Robert Surtees, *The History and Antiquities of the County Palatine of Durham*, London, 1823, 4 vols. (in 2), IV, p. 66, that although the parliament of 1474 transferred the Countess's inheritance to her two daughters and though Clarence's attainder could not destroy his wife's title or, if it could, would cause her half to be vested in the crown, yet Richard obtained individual possession of Barnard Castle. Surtees possibly entertained the curious notion that the two brothers divided each of the Countess's manors between them, or he may have been confused by a private bill of the Parliament which met to attaint Clarence, in which Richard was granted permission to use, for the establishment of a college and twelve priests (which *Cal. Pat. Rolls*, 1476–85, p. 67 proves to have been the college at Barnard Castle), *advowsons* (my italics) which had come to him in the partition of the

Countess's estates. (*Rot. Parl.*, VI, p. 172). Surtees' evidence is no evidence at all. It seems clear that Barnard Castle, lying close to Richard's other Yorkshire estates, had come to him in the division of property (see, above, note 23 of chapter I, 'The Lord of the North.')

[14] *Cal. Pat. Rolls*, 1476–85, p. 67.

IV
(pp. 127–137)

My account of Richard's relationship with the city of York is based upon Davies, *York Records* and Raine, *York Civic Records*, I. Unless otherwise noted, the correspondence and other documentary information relating to the city cited in this chapter are drawn from YR, pp. 39–99, 108–127, 140–42, 227–49 and from YCR, I, pp. 5, 8, 26, 53–54, 48–52, 56.

[1] During March a delegation from the city of York rode to Middleham to confer with the Duke of Gloucester (YR, p. 59).

[2] For proof that Richard was in London during the early part of April, 1481, and departed from the city before April 16, see *Stonor Letters*, II, pp. 122–24.

[3] P. 77.

[4] The mummings: Harl. MS. 433, f. 118; the fairs: *Cal. Pat. Rolls*, 1476–85, p. 154; for glimpses of Richard's minstrels and players as they travel about England performing for a great lord or the burgesses of a town, see, for example, *Household Books of John Howard, Duke of Norfolk*, p. 70, p. 207; HMC, V, p. 527, p. 547; HMC, 9th rep., I, p. 143.

[5] *Cal. Pat. Rolls*, 1467–77, p. 184, p. 495, p. 307, p. 511, p. 591, etc.

[6] For Richard's duties and powers as Warden, see *Foedera*, XI, pp. 658–60.

[7] In Henry VIII's time, Lord Dacre, Warden of the West March, kept writing plaintively to Wolsey that he shouldn't be expected to equal the accomplishment of Richard, Duke of Gloucester (*Letters and Papers of the Reign of Henry VIII*, ed. by J. S. Brewer, London, 1864–76, I, 2, p. 1054 and p. 1260). Wolsey replied severely that Dacre must provide the same kind of effectual rule (*ibid.*, IV, i, p. 52).

[8] For the composition of Richard's council, see YR, p. 41 and Reid, *The King's Council in the North*, pp. 44–46.

[9] YR and YCR, *passim*; Reid, pp. 52–59; for Holy Trinity Priory: YCR, I, p. 26.

[10] See, above, p. 111; the indenture: HMC, VI, p. 223; Reid, p. 43.

[11] See remainder of chapter; also *Cal. Close Rolls*, 1468–76, p. 365 and YR, p. 59 and p. 63.

When one George Willaby declared that he had discovered rich silver mines, both the Duke of Gloucester and the Earl of Northumberland received a commission to inquire into this interesting report, which turned out so promising that Richard and Percy and two merchants secured a grant to work four silver mines for fifteen years (*Cal. Pat. Rolls*, 1467–77, p. 464, p. 505, and p. 513).

[12] YCR, I, p. 42.

[13] Harl. MS. 433, f. 68b.

[14] YR., pp. 140–41. I have, in the text, edited the reported conversation—without altering the language—by choosing from conflicting testimony what seems to be the essential flow of the dialogue.

V

(pp. 137–144)

[1] *Cal. Pat. Rolls*, 1476–85, p. 205, pp. 213–14; YR, pp. 106–07; H. Hatcher, 'Old and New Sarum' in R. C. Hoare, *History of Modern Wiltshire*, London, 1843, pp. 198–200.

[2] Northumberland's letter of October 13 (YCR, I, p. 36) provides a neat explanation for the delegation which the city sent to Richard on October 14, 1480 (YR, p. 108; YCR, I, p. 36). The Earl's letter, however, omits the year and it may possibly have been written in October of 1481, though this does not seem likely.

Edward to the city of York: YCR, I, p. 42.

[3] YCR, I, pp. 40–41; *Stonor Letters*, II, pp. 122–24; Scofield, II, p. 303, p. 305 and note 3; YCR, I, p. 42.

[4] *Cal. Venetian Papers*, I, p. 145.

[5] Scofield (II, p. 316 and note 3) lists a number of indentures for this year, but there is no indication that, the King having failed to take the field, the men proceeded northward. For Richard's attempt this summer to win over Scots to his service, with the help of the Earl of Douglas, see *Calendar of Documents Relating to Scotland*, IV, p. 300. The men of York apparently saw no service this summer (YCR, I, p. 46).

[6] Northumberland's letters of Sept. 7 to the city of York (YCR, I, 35) and to Robert Plumpton (*Plumpton Correspondence*, p. 40) omit the year, as does Richard's letter of Sept. 8 to York. Since, however, the men of the city were making hasty preparations for 'this viage against the Scots' on Sept. 8, 1481, and on Sept. 9, 1481, changed the date of their departure from Monday until Tuesday (YCR, I, p. 47), it seems almost certain that Northumberland's and Richard's letters belong to 1481. In the early days of Sept., 1480, Richard and Northumberland had already led a carefully planned expedition northward (see, above, p. 137).

[7] Richard's visit to Nottingham is not definitely established. While Edward was at Nottingham, however, he received the gift of a horse from Richard and in a letter he wrote on Oct. 19 spoke of the good report he had received from his brother of the city's loyal disposition (Scofield, II, p. 320 and note 1; YCR, I, p. 36). It seems more likely that Richard himself appeared than that he sent a messenger.

[8] Licence for food: *Cal. Pat. Rolls*, 1476–85, p. 254.

Pardon for Tynedale and strife in the Duchy of Lancaster: Scofield, II, p. 334.

Commission of *oyer and terminer*: *Cal. Pat. Rolls*, 1476–85, p. 343; see also, Reid, p. 44.

[9] YR, pp. 127–28; YCR, I, p. 59.

[10] This year, the city fathers of Canterbury noted, upon seeing the King, that his health was not good (HMC, 9th rep., I, p. 145).

[11] YR, pp. 128–30.

[12] YCR, I, pp. 58–59.

[13] The *Croyland Chronicle* (in a comment made, apparently, by the monk who edited the true author's material for the '2nd cont.': see, below, Appendix II, p. 432) deplores Richard's humanity in 'leaving that most opulent city untouched' (p. 481). See also Edward's letter to the Pope, *Cal. Venetian Papers*, I, pp. 145–46.

[14] Vergil, pp. 170–71; *Foedera*, XII, p. 160; Hall, pp. 332–33 (which seems to draw on documents of state: compare Scofield, II, pp. 345–49).

P*

[15] HMC, III, p. 113.

[16] *Croy. Chron.*, p. 497; *Cely Papers*, p. 113; *Cal. Venetian Papers*, I, pp. 45–46.

[17] Richard's presence in London during the Christmas season of 1482 is shown in a payment he later made for New Year's gifts which he purchased from the goldsmith Shaa (Harl. MS. 433, f. 148).

VI

(pp. 144–150)

[1] *Richard III*, p. 4.

[2] For Edward's entertaining the citizens of London, see More, p. 3 and Fabyan, p. 667. The *Croy. Chron.* (pp. 483–84), Mancini (pp. 79–83), More (pp. 2–6), and Vergil (p. 172) all give vivid character sketches of Edward which exhibit striking similarities. A brief account of Edward's capacity to charm money from his subjects is given by an Italian visitor to England in 1475: *Cal. Milanese Papers*, I, pp. 193–94.

[3] This profound motif or theme of Richard's life I have inferred not only from the relations between Richard and Edward and Richard's attitude towards Edward's court, as recounted in the six chapters of this section, 'The Lord of the North', but also from Richard's actions and the manifestations of his character after King Edward's death.

[4] More, p. 84 *et seq.*; his account of Jane Shore is surely the most charming piece of prose that had yet been written in England. Protection for Wm. Shore: *Cal. Pat. Rolls*, 1476–85, p. 9. For Hastings' and Dorset's subsequent relations with Jane Shore, see below, note 6 of Chapter 5, 'Protector and Defensor'. Richard's attitude towards Jane: there was a streak of the Puritan in Richard, a strong preoccupation with personal morals, which becomes broadly manifest in his last years (see, below). It seems a likely conjecture that he would be as impervious to her charm as she would be repelled by his earnestness and sobriety.

[5] Scofield, I, p. 378, p. 397; II, p. 26, p. 38 etc.; More, p. 77 and p. 13; Mancini, p. 85; *Croy. Chron.*, p. 479.

[6] Although Armstrong follows the contention of Calmette and Périnelle (*Louis XI et l'Angleterre*, p. 251–54) that 'at the time of Edward's death the scene was set for an immediate war between England and France, which only failed to break out seriously when Louis XI perceived that England was effectually crippled by internal troubles' (Mancini, p. 145); Armstrong himself, however, shows that Louis had launched an intense guerilla warfare at sea (p. 144), which was his only possible mode of attack.

The taxes Parliament voted to Edward, the agreement the King signed with the Duke of Albany in February, 1483, and the tenour of the parliamentary grant to Richard all indicate that England's chief immediate effort was to be directed against Scotland (see Scofield, II, pp. 360–64, and this chapter, below).

[7] John Wode became Richard's Treasurer (see, below, p. 184). For the enactments of this Parliament, see *Rot. Parl.*, VI, pp. 197–98 and pp. 204–05.

[8] YR, p. 142.

[9] I have based my description of Richard upon the portrait in the Royal Collection at Windsor castle, painted by an unknown artist who was almost certainly a contem-

porary of Richard's—perhaps a visiting Flemish painter. The painting in the National Portrait Gallery is a copy, probably by the artist.

The consensus of contemporary descriptions bears out the evidence of these portraits that Richard had no noticeable bodily deformity, and establishes him as a thin, frail man of a little less than normal height. Neither the author of the '2nd Continuation' of the *Croyland Chronicle*, who knew Richard well, nor Dominic Mancini, who must have seen him several times and wrote his book but a few months after he had last seen him, mentions any physical irregularity; and Stowe talked to old men who, remembering Richard, said 'that he was of bodily shape comely enough, only of low stature' (Buc in Kennett's *History of England*, p. 548). A German traveller, Nicolas von Poppelau, who spent ten days in Richard's household in May of 1484, describes Richard as 'three fingers taller than himself . . . also much more lean; he had delicate arms and legs, also a great heart' (Mancini, pp. 162–64). C. A. J. Armstrong, who prints von Poppelau's observation in an appendix of his invaluable edition of Mancini, concludes that since von Poppelau, being noted for immense strength, was likely to be sizable, Richard was 'a tall and emaciated man, who not improbably stooped as well'. Though it is an ingenious suggestion, von Poppelau was quite possibly squat and barrel-shaped, a short, wide fellow; it seems most likely that Richard was not quite so tall as the run of mankind. The evidence of Stowe is strongly supported by a Latin oration, delivered before Richard in September of 1484 by Archibald Whitelaw, one of the Scots envoys, in which he said of Richard that nature never enclosed within a smaller frame so great a mind or such remarkable powers (Buc in Kennett, p. 572).

Ten years after Richard's death, an ill-wisher of his in York (YR, pp. 220–22)—whose remarks were resented by the company in which he made them—said that Richard was a 'crouchback', but no one else in the 15th century says so. It may well be, however, that the speaker was exaggeratedly describing an actual inequality in Richard's shoulders, perceptible but not sufficiently so to be labelled a deformity or to intrude itself upon the beholder's notice. An inequality of shoulders is mentioned —though without agreement as to which shoulder was the higher!—by Rous, More, and Vergil. In inuring his slight frame to bear easily the weight of armour, in practising assiduously when still a boy with his sword arm (see, above, p. 48), in forcing his frail body to become strong, Richard probably developed an unusually powerful right shoulder and a torso ribbed with muscle, which, in contrast with his thin arms and legs and a less prominent left shoulder, produced a vague, general suggestion of lack of bodily proportion or symmetry.

The monster created by Shakespeare in his *Richard III* represents the zestful elaboration of the zestful elaborations of the later Tudor chroniclers (see Appendix II).

THE KING

PROTECTOR AND DEFENSOR

I

(pp. 153–162)

By far the most important single source for a study of Richard's protectorship and reign is Harleian MS. 433, a register or docket book in which Richard's secretariat recorded—sometimes in abbreviated form but often in full—the warrants issued to the Chancellor for grants, writs, pardons, proclamations, etc., under the Great Seal; instructions to ambassadors and other state papers, including a number received from foreign envoys; and Richard's correspondence. The first of these documents was registered on May 3 (though later dated May 5), the day before Richard entered London with Edward V, and the last, only a few days before Bosworth Field. J. G. Nichols has edited a compilation of all the entries in the docket book which fall within the reign of Edward V (April 9–June 26, 1483), *Grants, etc., from the Crown*. Most of the important diplomatic correspondence can be found in *Foedera*, XII, James Gairdner's *Letters and Papers of the Reigns of Richard III and Henry VII*, 2 vols., or Ellis' *Original Letters*. Many documents of great value have never been printed, however, and the register remains yet to be edited. A catalogue of the contents, Brit. Mus. Additional MS. 11, 269, 2 vols., is of limited worth.

For the period of Richard's protectorship, Mancini's record of these months, which he composed so early as December of 1483, is of first importance: Dominic Mancini, *The Usurpation of Richard III*, edited by C. A. J. Armstrong, who discovered the manuscript not much more than two decades ago and whose notes are admirable. The only other reliable contemporary source is the *Croyland Chronicle* ('2nd Continuation'). Vergil and More are occasionally useful, but they must be regarded, at best, as only secondary, or supplementary, sources—as C. H. Williams points out in his essay on 'The Yorkist Kings' in the *Cambridge Medieval History*, VIII. For a fuller discussion of sources, see Appendix II.

Principal sources for this chapter: Mancini, pp. 71–85; *Croy. Chron.*, pp. 481–84; Vergil, pp. 171–72 and pp. 164–66; More, pp. 1–18.

[1] The precise nature of Edward's fatal illness remains a mystery. Commynes (I, p. 454; II, p. 63) and Mancini (p. 71) believe that the Treaty of Arras cast him into a profound melancholy from which he never recovered. For the immediate cause of death I have followed Mancini's story of the fishing trip (p. 73). Commynes twice mentions that Edward died of apoplexy (II, p. 63 and p. 91). The account of the Croyland Chronicler reveals that the court was baffled by Edward's illness: when the King took to his bed, he was 'neither worn out with old age nor yet seized with any known kind of malady, the cure of which would not have appeared easy in the case of a person of more humble rank' (p. 483). Vergil says that he 'fell sick of an unknown disease' (p. 171), later adding an Italianate touch by hinting at poison (p. 172). For the unreliable suppositions of French chroniclers and later Tudor historians, see Armstrong's summary of the evidence, Mancini, p. 3, note 5.

The false report of his death which reached York: YR, pp. 142–43.

[2] *Croy. Chron.*, pp. 481–82; Mancini, pp. 71–73.

[3] More, pp. 18–19. For the ordinances and composition of Prince Edward's household and council at Ludlow, see Halliwell, *Letters of the Kings of England*, I, pp. 136–44; *Grants*, pp. vii–viii; I. D. Thornley, *England under the Yorkists*, p. 149; Armstrong in Mancini, p. 139, note 37.

[4] P. 173.
Concerning Henry's Welsh lineage, J. D. Mackie, *The Earlier Tudors*, sums up cautiously, 'The obvious "necessity" of magnifying Henry VII's ancestry after his accession makes the account of Meredith's descent a little uncertain. . . .' (p. 47, ft. 2).

[5] P. 211.

[6] *Cal. Pat. Rolls*, 1461–67, p. 114 (Feb. 3, 1462, and Feb. 12, 1462). See also Scofield, I, pp. 202–03.

[7] Pp. 164–66. Vergil is the only source for most of the information about Henry Tudor's life before 1483.

[8] More's circumstantial account of how Edward sought to reconcile the two factions cannot be accepted as a literal transcript of what was said (pp. 12–18), but that Edward made the attempt is confirmed by Mancini, who says that the reconciliation took place two days before Edward died (p. 85). Though Mancini's statement is to be preferred, I have taken the liberty, in order to develop the scene, of placing the reconciliation, as More does, only a few hours before Edward died. See also *Croy. Chron.*, pp. 483–84.

[9] *Croy. Chron.*, pp. 483–84. *Ex. Hist.*, p. 378 for Edward's will of 1475; *Collection of Wills*, pp. 345–48 for the executors of Edward's last will, which has disappeared, perhaps destroyed by the Woodvilles. That Edward appointed Richard Protector of the Realm is firmly established: Mancini, p. 73 and p. 85; C.C., pp. 485–86; Vergil, p. 171 and p. 175; Bernard André in *Memorials of King Henry VII*, ed. by James Gairdner, Rolls Series, 1858, p. 23.

[10] *Household Books of Howard*, p. 383.

[11] A contemporary account of Edward's obsequies appears in *Letters and Papers*, I, pp. 3–10, taken from MS. I, 7, f. 7. College of Arms. See also *Household Books*, p. 386.
The cost of Edward's funeral services amounted to £1,496 17s 2d (*Collection of Wills*, p. 348).

II
(pp. 162–173)

The primary sources for this chapter are Mancini, pp. 79–91 and *Croyland Chronicle*, pp. 484–87; I have, as usual, drawn on Vergil, pp. 173–76 and on More, pp. 18–34 and 134–35, as well as on Fabyan, p. 668, for details which conform to the pattern of events developed by the primary sources and which seem to derive from information rather than conjecture.

[1] Mancini (p. 85) says that Richard was on his Gloucester estates, by which he undoubtedly means that Richard was at home. None of the other sources specifies Richard's whereabouts. Most authorities agree that he was at Middleham.

[2] Vergil, p. 173; Mancini, p. 87.

[3] Bearing in mind the limits of time and the speed of travel, I have reconstructed the

order of messages which Richard received and sent by a comparison of the sources, which are far from precise on this subject. For Richard's writing Rivers, see Mancini, p. 91, where, however, the time element is confused. It seems reasonable to suppose that the rendezvous at Northampton was arranged by an inquiry from Richard and a response from Rivers.

4 Mancini, p. 89. For the sake of clarity, I have slightly rearranged the order of topics as given by Mancini. In his paraphrase we seem to be very close to the actual wording of the letter. Though Mancini does not mention Richard's writing to the Queen, the C.C. makes a point of it (p. 486); compare Vergil, pp. 173–74.

5 Compare Pickthorn, *Early Tudor Government*, pp. 2–5.

6 Mancini, p. 101; Fabyan, p. 668; More, p. 135; C.C., p. 486.

7 Though the city records make no mention of the oath-taking at York described by the C.C., neither do they mention Richard's arrival in the city. The entry in the records for April 23 that John Brackenbury was to go to London with Richard (YR, p. 143) does not necessarily mean that Richard had already left York. All that is known about the earlier stages of his journey is that he reached Nottingham on April 26 (see next note).

8 W. H. Stevenson, *Records of the Borough of Nottingham*, London, 1882, II, p. 394; More, p. 135.

9 See notes 2 and 3, above.

10 Mancini, p. 83; compare Armstrong, Mancini, p. 140, note 41.

11 Mancini, p. 79.

The success with which the Marquess at first swayed the council, itself suggests that he and the Queen had been at work behind the scenes. Only two days after hearing the first word of Edward's death, the new King wrote to the city of Lynn that he was coming to London for his crowning 'in all convenient haste' (HMC, 11th rep., III, p. 170). This statement almost certainly reflects orders from the Queen which accompanied the news. Received at Ludlow on April 14, the dispatch must have been written not more than 36 hours after Edward's death and therefore *before* any council meeting (Mancini, p. 87, says the council first assembled 'at the completion of the royal obsequies'). She must have considered that the reins of power were already safely in her hands.

12 Turner, *History of England*, III, pp. 394–97, translated by Turner from Brit. Mus. Cotton Cleopatra E III, pp. 106–16.

13 *Ibid.*, p. 394; compare *Grants*, p. xxxviii.

14 See note 11, above.

15 *Cal. Pat. Rolls*, 1476–85, p. 350 (April 21).

16 Mancini, p. 99, p. 103, p. 105; More, pp. 26–27. For Richard's action against Sir Edward's fleet, see, below, p. 186. On June 9 it was reported that Richard was still trying to recover portions of the treasure seized by the Marquess (below, p. 200).

Louis XI recommended 'Lord Cordes' (Philippe de Crevecoeur) to his son as the ablest French commander (Molinet's *Scandalous Chronicle* in vol. 2 of *Memoirs of Philippe de Commines*, ed. and trans. by Andrew R. Scoble, London, 1907, p. 393). For Cordes' harrying English commerce, see *Letters and Papers*, I, p. 18.

17 Compare Pickthorn, pp. 28–34 *et seq.*

18 *Cal. Pat. Rolls*, 1476–85, pp. 352–53 (April 27).

Because Gairdner (*Richard III*, p. 55) found two documents, one dated April 21 and the other May 2, which styled Richard as Protector of England, he assumes that the Protectorship was acknowledged in London before Richard arrived there. In the first document, however—Commissions of the Peace on the patent roll (see *Grants*, p. xxxii)—all the commissions save Richard's are dated no earlier than May 14, and from the weight of evidence cited above it seems likely that the date 'April 21' is a clerical error for 'May 21'. The second document—from MS. 433, 265b—itself contains proof that its date of May 2 must be an error since it relates to the disposition, by Richard, of certain of Earl Rivers' lands and must therefore have been drawn up after Richard established his government in London. The date undoubtedly should be 'June 2'.

[19] Mancini, p. 89; *Croy. Chron.*, pp. 484–85.

[20] Mancini reports the debate concerning the Protector's powers (p. 87); the C.C. reports the debate concerning the limitation of the King's escort (pp. 484–85). Each doubtless remembered what seemed to him the most important of the council's conflicts. Put together, the two versions would appear to supply an account of the council's principal business.

[21] P. 89.

[22] *Ibid.*, pp. 89–91; since Mancini rarely permits himself a direct quotation, it seems probable that he had first-hand information that the Marquess had said these very words.

[23] See Caxton's prologue to Rivers' *Dictes and Sayings of the Philosophers* and his epilogue to the Earl's translation called *Cordyal. Ex. Hist.*, pp. 240–45, offers a considerable sketch of Rivers' life.

[24] See note 11, above.

[25] Rous, *Historia Regum Anglie*, p. 212, gives the date of departure from Ludlow as April 24. This source is unreliable, but since it is known that Edward and Rivers reached Northampton on April 29 and since the journey with a cumbersome waggon train would be slow, April 24 seems a reasonable date to assign for their departure.

III
(pp. 173–182)

For the story of what happened at Northampton on April 29–30, at Stony Stratford on April 30, and in London when the news reached there, I have followed principally the accounts of Mancini (pp. 71–101) and the *Croyland Chronicle* (pp. 485–87), which are very similar. More (pp. 23–34) appears to have secured authentic information regarding these events: his version corresponds remarkably with Mancini and the C.C. I have therefore drawn on him for certain details which are in accord with the Mancini-C.C. pattern. Since Mancini and More agree that Rivers returned from Stony Stratford to Northampton, I have adopted that version rather than the C.C.'s statement that Rivers did not leave Northampton with the King. Vergil, Fabyan, and *The Great Chronicle* all give sketchy and inaccurate accounts.

[1] There exists no precise documentary proof that Richard had a rendezvous with the King and Rivers at Northampton. Mancini (p. 91) clearly indicates, however, that he had sent Rivers an inquiry about the King's itinerary in order to join him *en route*.

The actions of Rivers and the King, the actions of Richard and Buckingham, make it all but absolutely certain that such a rendezvous was arranged. Why, for example, should Rivers ride back from Stony Stratford to Northampton—evidently prepared to stay the night—unless he thought to find Richard halted there in expectation of meeting the King?

[2] Exactly why Rivers took the King on to Stony Stratford nobody could know except Rivers and, no doubt, the Queen and Marquess. Their eagerness to crown the King and to circumvent Richard's Protectorship provides an obvious motive: to see that he reached London before Richard. Mancini (p. 95) says that Lord Richard Grey had ridden from London shortly before to join the King's cavalcade—bearing a message, it seems likely, that the King must press on to the capital and not wait for the Protector to join him.

What Mancini and the C.C. say seems to be speculation; Mancini, that the King sent Rivers back 'to deserve well of his paternal uncle by extreme reverence', and the C.C., 'to submit the conduct of everything to the will . . . of his uncle'. In the light of what had happened in London, the latter statement is certainly incorrect. More gives no reason at all. Both Mancini and More, however, report that most of the King's train was sent still further on towards London from Stony Stratford in order to make room for the Protector's men. More pictures the movement as occurring in the early morning of April 30. The matter of moving on, allegedly to make room, does not, however, fit Stony Stratford. The King's household at Stony Stratford knew that Rivers was spending the night of April 29 in Northampton with Richard. Consequently, there would be no reason for them, next morning, to make room for Richard's men at Stony Stratford; Richard would have no wish to halt at Stony Stratford on the 30th since it is only a fourteen mile journey from Northampton. It seems likely, therefore, that the excuse concerning lodgings was used by Rivers to justify to Richard the King's failure to wait for him at Northampton, for it was this failure that needed an explanation; and it seems equally likely that the King's men were streaming out of Stony Stratford, southward, early in the morning of April 30 and the King himself was in the saddle ready to depart, not to make room for anybody, but to hurry on towards London as fast as possible. Compare Armstrong, Mancini, p. 141, note 45.

Of all the sources, only Mancini reports that the Queen and the Marquess made frantic efforts to raise a force, before they took sanctuary. It would not require much time for the Marquess to learn from hastily dispatched messages that the lords would not support him against the Protector. I have therefore accepted Mancini's version but reconciled it to the time scheme of the C.C. and the other sources. Compare Armstrong, Mancini, p. 144, note 51.

[4] See James R. Scott, *Memorials of Scott of Scotts Hall*, pp. 154–58 and Campbell, *Lives of the Lord Chancellors*, I, pp. 390–400; compare David MacGibbon, *Elizabeth Woodville*, London, 1938, p. 144 and note.

[5] More, pp. 28–31; the essential facts and the spirit of his narrative both accord with Mancini's and the C.C.'s brief accounts. Doubtless the scenes at the Chancellor's palace and in the sanctuary are enhanced by More's imagination but they cannot be far wrong.

[6] Mancini, pp. 99–101; again, Mancini seems to paraphrase the actual letter.

[7] *Ancient Correspondence*, XLV, no. 236.

[8] *Grants*, p. 1.

[9] The parchment is on display at the British Museum; it is from Cotton, Vespasian F XIII.

[10] *Grants*, p. 1, undated but given at St. Albans. Since Richard and the King were still at Northampton on May 2 (see note 7, above), they undoubtedly spent the night of the 3rd at St. Albans. John Geffrey, however, did not receive the benefice; less than a month later Thomas Langton, Bishop-elect of St. David's, was granted a licence to seek papal provision to hold it *in commendam*, as a means of augmenting the meagre revenues of his see (*Cal. Pat. Rolls*, 1476–85, p. 348; *Grants*, p. 37).

[11] Fabyan, 668; *Great Chronicle*, p. 230; Mancini, p. 101; C.C., p. 487; More, pp. 33–34.

Though Mancini says that the exhibition of Woodville armour 'exceedingly augmented' distrust of the Protector, his narrative of events that followed does not bear this out. The cry of the crowd I have taken from More; his guess, or hearsay evidence, that only a few were moved to distrust seems, in the light of Richard's undoubted popularity during the next month (see, below, p. 183), to be more plausible.

IV
(pp. 183–200)

For the period embracing May and the early days of June, 1483, contemporary historical narrative is scanty and confused (see headnote to the notes on chapter 5 for further discussion of this subject). The *Croyland Chronicle* is reticent and terse; Mancini sees events mostly from the outside and, though writing only six months later, omits much of importance and does not always recollect events clearly. Vergil is at his least helpful here; like him, More leaps from Richard's entry into the city on May 4 to the delivery of little York from sanctuary on June 16; Fabyan and *The Great Chronicle* are no better. The fact is, this was a confusing period, of much movement but no great events, of increasing political activity which went on behind the scenes, of bewildering diversity in the functioning of government—with the King at the Tower, Richard at Crosby's Place, and the council splitting into committees and shifting their meetings from place to place. Small wonder that men did not remember clearly, and often did not perceive, what was really happening, particularly since the period was brought to an abrupt close by a stroke of violence, which was quickly followed by events of profound importance. Fortunately, documentary sources—the Patent Rolls and Harl. 433—make it possible to recover a good deal of what was going on, to establish a pattern which gives a clue to what is of value in the confused accounts of the chroniclers. A matter of the greatest significance, the inception and the early development of the rift between Hastings and the Protector, can only be conjectured; I have inferred it from biographical data, discernible traits of character, subsequent and past events, and the evidence of grants. Even Gairdner accepts Hastings' break with the Protector as being rooted in a dissatisfaction with his share of power which antedates any knowledge on his part, or supposition, that Richard might aim at the throne (*Richard III*, pp. 71–80). Evidence for Hastings' developing a party hostile to the Protector is discussed in the next chapter.

Principal sources for this chapter: *Cal. Pat. Rolls*, 1476–85; *Grants* (Harl. 433); C.C., pp. 487–88; Mancini, pp. 103–113; *Household Books of Howard, passim*; and details from More, pp. 34–35 and 65–67 and from Vergil, pp. 176–79.

[1] *Household Books*, p. 390.

[2] *Collection of Wills*, pp. 345–46.

[3] Vergil says that Edward bequeathed to Richard the 'tuytion' of Edward V as well as the protectorship of the realm (p. 171, p. 176). 'Tutele and oversight, etc.' is quoted from a draft of the speech Chancellor Russell intended to deliver before the Parliament of June 25, in which Russell writes as if Richard already possessed the authority of Tutor as well as Protector, both of which powers the Chancellor is asking Parliament to continue (*Grants*, pp. xlvii–xlix). See J. S. Roskell, 'The Office and Dignity of Protector of England', *Eng. Hist. Rev.*, LXVIII (1953), pp. 193 *et seq*.

Both Vergil (p. 176) and More (pp. 38–39) picture Richard as declaring that he will abide by the will of the council.

In documents of state Richard first appears as 'Protector of England' ('carissimo avunculo nostri Ricardo duci Gloucestrae protectori Angliae') in the commissions of peace issued on May 14 (*Grants*, pp. xxxi–xxxii and p. xiii). The formula varies slightly from one document to another (see *Grants*, *passim*, beginning May 12, p. 12). Attempts have been made to distil significance from the fact that Richard is not named Protector on a document until May 14 and that an occasional writ does not bear this title. These inferences seem to rest on the assumption that clerks of the 15th century had the same regard for consistency and accuracy as our present day civil servants.

[4] Appointments—Gunthorpe: *Grants*, p. 72.

Wode: *Grants*, p. 13; *Cal. Pat. Rolls*, 1476–85, p. 349; see, *ibid.*, p. 315.

[5] Writs in Harl. 433 show the King at the palace of the Bishop of London as late as May 9 and settled at the Tower by May 19 (*Grants*, p. 1 and p. 15).

The summons to Parliament was dispatched to the Archbishop of Canterbury on May 13 (*Collection of Wills*, p. 347); on May 17 Howard paid 3s 4d 'to a man that brought a writ of the parliament' (*Household Books*, p. 393); the summons was read to the council of the city of York on June 6 (YR, p. 144).

Convocation: *Grants*, p. 13.

[6] *Collection of Wills*, pp. 345–48.

[7] Since the only partisans of the Woodvilles in the council were certain of the spiritual lords, I infer that opposition to beheading Rivers sprang from them. The clerical members in general were probably ranged against the proposal.

Negotiations with the Queen: London, Guildhall MS Journal 9, fol. 23vo; compare MacGibbon, p. 148.

[8] *Grants*, p. 2, p. 3; for Cobham's expedition, see HMC 9th rep., I, p. 145.

[9] For Fulford's activities, see Scofield, I and II.

[10] Brampton's services to Edward: *Cal. Pat. Rolls*, 1467–77, p. 357; compare Scofield, II, p. 87 and note 3 and p. 88; also see, above, p. 72.

Household Books, p. 12.

A not altogether satisfactory sketch of Brampton appears in Cecil Roth, 'Perkin Warbeck and His Jewish Master', *Transactions of the Jewish Historical Society*, IX, pp. 143–62.

[11] Mancini relates this story in vivid detail (pp. 103–07). On July 25 Brampton was

granted an exemption from customs and subsidies of £350 (*Cal. Pat. Rolls*, 1476–85, p. 366).

[12] *Grants*, p. 2, p. 11, pp. 67–68.
For John Davy: *Household Books*, p. 388 and p. 405.

[13] *Cely Papers*, p. 129.

[14] *Grants*, pp. 19–22.

[15] Only the Mastership of the mint and the exchange was expressly confirmed to Hastings by patent: *Cal. Pat. Rolls*, 1476–85, p. 348; there is no reason to doubt, however, that he retained the governorship of Calais and the lord chamberlainship: More says that 'the Lord Chamberlain and some others, kept still their offices that they had before' (p. 35).

    Grants—Catesby: *Grants*, pp. 3–4.
           Dynham: *ibid.*, p. 24.
           Howard: *ibid.*, p. 4.
           Arundel: *Cal. Pat. Rolls*, 1476–85, p. 349.

Though Lord Stanley received no immediate rewards, his brother Sir William was given the lucrative custody and marriage of an orphan (*Grants*, p. 50). As in the case of Hastings, it seems likely that Lord Stanley was continued in the office which he had held in the reign of Edward IV, Steward of the Household.

[16] In addition to the evidence of Mancini and the C.C., it is to be noted that a letter of June 9 which mentions a council meeting specifies only Buckingham's name (see below, p. 201).

[17] I have inferred Buckingham's flashy personality from his remarkable eloquence, his vanity, his meteoric rise and ignominious end (see below, *passim*). His resemblance to Clarence seems striking. That Richard was attracted to two men of weak character but vivid personality appears to be more than coincidence.

[18] *Grants*, pp. 5–7, pp. 7–11, p. 13, pp. 34–35, p. 35; compare also p. 12, p. 36, pp. 49–50. *Cal. Pat. Rolls*, 1476–85, p. 356, pp. 349–50.

[19] Lovell is a shadowy figure; Colyngbourne's distich probably provides the most direct indication of his importance in Richard's government (see below, p. 300). I infer Lincoln's early adherence to Richard from his later career (see below, *passim*) and from the fact that, having attended Edward's funeral (*Letters and Papers*, I, p. 1 *et seq.*), he was probably now in London. Stillington's support of Richard is indicated by his revelation of the pre-contract (see below, p. 215). Sir Richard Ratcliffe left London on June 11 on an important errand for Richard (see below, p. 206). I infer the presence of Tyrell and Brackenbury from their later importance in Richard's government (see below, *passim*). Catesby's future prominence implies an early shift from Hastings to the Protector; More's evidence on the point is doubtful but interesting. That Catesby betrayed Hastings in supporting Richard is by no means necessary to believe; Catesby's later career would probably be sufficient to stimulate More's conjecture (pp. 67–69).

[20] The *Paston Letters* give only the Pastons' view of this trouble. As Sheriff of Norfolk, John Howard reported quite a different story. See C. H. Williams, 'A Norfolk Parliamentary Election, 1461', *Eng. Hist. Rev.*, XL (1925), pp. 79–86.

[21] See *Household Books*, *passim*.

[22] In the autumn of 1479, Howard, at Swansea castle in S. Wales, was in communication

with Richard about some matter; and Richard may have spent some time with Howard at Swansea (*Household Books*, pp. iii–iv).

²³ *Household Books*, p. 399.

²⁴ See 'Observations on the Wardrobe Account for the Year 1483', *Archaeologia*, I, pp. 361–83.

²⁵ *Original Letters*, 2nd series, I, p. 147; compare *Foedera*, XII, p. 181. According to the C.C., the date was first set for June 24 (p. 487), but this may be an error. Stallworthe's letter of June 9 (see below, p. 200) places the date, with some uncertainty, as June 23, which seems likewise to be a slip. June 22 fell on a Sunday, and Sunday was the coronation day of the House of York (Edward IV: Sunday, June 28, 1461; Richard III: Sunday, July 6, 1483).

²⁶ *Orig. Letters*, 2nd ser., I, p. 147 (Harl., 433, f. 227).

²⁷ YR, pp. 144–45. Much has been made of the fact, particularly by Gairdner, that, according to the entry for June 6, 'the writ of our Lord the King' called for 'four cocitizens of this city to be sent to Parliament' (p. 144). The very next entry, however, that of June 13, makes clear that York chose, as usual, only two parliamentary representatives and that therefore either the city clerk had carelessly written 'four' when he meant 'two' or that a mistake in the official writ had been quickly corrected by the dispatch of a second writ. Compare YCR, I, p. 72.

²⁸ See note 3, above.

²⁹ See, for example, Pickthorn, p. 132 *et seq.*

³⁰ *Grants*, pp. xxxvii–xlix.

³¹ Anne's arrival is recorded in Stallworthe's letter of June 9 (see below, p. 200); for the delicate health of Richard's son, see below, p. 257. Since Anne was undoubtedly welcomed by the Mayor and Aldermen when she passed through York and since Richard wrote his letter to the city on the same day she arrived in London, it seems likely that Anne reported the anxiety of the citizens to her husband.

³² YR, pp. 146–47.

V

(pp. 200–213)

The Monday-to-Monday, from June 9 through June 16, a cluster of days of first importance to an understanding of Richard's life, is miserably reported by the chroniclers. With the exception of the *Croyland Chronicle*, their accounts are hopelessly distorted by a major error in chronology: they picture the delivery of York from sanctuary as occurring before, rather than three days after, the execution of Hastings on Friday, June 13. The accuracy of the C.C. is established not only by Simon Stallworthe's letter of June 21 but also, as Armstrong has pointed out, by an entry in the *Household Books of Howard* showing payment for eight boats up and down from Westminster on Monday, June 16 (p. 402; Mancini, pp. 149–50, note 72). In More, Vergil, Fabyan, *The Great Chronicle*, and even in Mancini, little York's delivery from sanctuary is recounted as the first important business on which the Protector embarked after he reached London (May 4). So profound a rupture of chronology at so important a period not only confuses the order of events but makes it likely that individual events themselves have been distorted or misinterpreted in order to fit them into a scheme in which they do not belong. As for the *Croyland Chronicle*, it unfortunately offers only the briefest account for this period. A few important letters have survived, however, and there are a number of documents of great value. In the context of happenings that these establish, reliable scraps of information from the chroniclers can sometimes be chosen with confidence, but I have nonetheless been forced, for this period, to attempt a much bolder reconstruction of events than has hitherto been necessary, or defensible.

Perhaps the most disturbing element in the situation is that Mancini proves, in a matter so significant, to be no more reliable than More and Vergil. How, writing only six months after these events, can he possibly confuse chronology so memorable? It is possible that he was constructing his account upon a basic assumption which led him, unconsciously, to confuse his recollections. The assumption he makes is that the moment Richard entered London, he began to aim for the throne. It seems reasonable that Mancini, a foreigner, trying to understand the rush of events that swept Richard to supreme power less than two months after his entry into the capital, should have taken it for granted that the Protector had made up his mind to seek the crown as soon as he saw how things stood in London. Dominated by this assumption, Mancini may well have decided—against the evidence of his notes or his memory—that Richard must have got little York into his power before overtly showing his hand by executing Hastings; and he completed the circle of this deduction by deciding that Richard had Hastings killed because the Lord Chamberlain then remained the only obstacle in his path to the throne. As will be seen in the next chapter of notes, this conjecture is supported by another astonishing lapse on Mancini's part, this time of omission, a lapse which, again, appears to derive from this same dominant assumption.

That Mancini had, unconsciously, to falsify the order—and thus, in some measure, the value and the context—of events in order for them meaningfully to fit his assumption throws suspicion on the assumption itself, particularly since Tudor writers like More and Vergil, who make the same assumption—for more interested reasons—commit precisely the same error of chronology. The assumption, of course, may be true: there is no absolute evidence to disprove it, as there is none to support it. On the other hand, the egregiousness of the error suggests that the thinking which led Mancini to his assumption was more decisively conditioned by the bewildering speed of events and, particularly, by their *dénouement* than by the significance of each successive event in the series. Mancini may well have committed the common fallacy of supposing that because, in the end, Richard assumed the throne, he must have been planning to assume it throughout his protectorship.

There is no direct evidence pointing to any one day or week in which Richard first contemplated the possibility of dispossessing his nephew. There are, however, a number of pieces of evidence which suggest that, although Richard was probably apprised of the pre-contract before June 13, he did not actively entertain the idea or set about sounding men's opinions on the subject until after the delivery of York on Monday, June 16:

The forthright preparations for the coronation of Edward V.

Richard's decision to submit to Parliament the proposal that the protectorship be continued. That this plan was not discarded a great many days before June 25 is suggested by the fact that the Chancellor, Russell, had time to finish the draft of his speech for the opening of Parliament. On the other hand, Russell's undoubted ignorance of the scheme to eliminate Hastings indicates that he was not a member of the inner circle of Richard's advisers.

The evidence that Hastings' conspiracy was directed against the continuance of the protectorship rather than against a possible usurpation (see below). Had Hastings feared that Richard would take the crown, it does not appear likely that he would have acted so unwarily as he did.

The hasty call for military aid which Richard dispatched on June 11. Since Richard, after he *had* decided to seek men's opinions about his possible assumption of the throne, saw to it that no troops arrived in London until his elevation had taken place, it may well follow that when he ordered the troops, he was not contemplating this step but only the possibility of an upheaval consequent upon his crushing the Hastings-Woodville conspiracy.

The developing pattern of events. This, the subtlest, most tenuous, least satisfactorily 'objective' piece of evidence, is nonetheless, in my opinion, the strongest. I suggest that it was the 'following on' and cumulation of circumstances themselves, rather than any *a priori* designs on his part, that determined the direction of Richard's protectorship; that the actions of his opponents played a considerable part in shaping his course; and that, either early or late, there was no one 'moment of decision'. Sources: Mancini, pp. 107–13; C.C., pp. 488–89; Fabyan, pp. 668–69; *Great Chronicle*, pp. 230–31; More, pp. 69–87 and 35–63; Vergil, pp. 176–82.

[1] *Stonor Letters and Papers*, II, pp. 159–60; *Ex. Hist.*, p. 16. The letter is addressed to Sir William Stonor.

[2] The action Richard took against Hastings, Stanley, Morton, and Rotherham (and Edward's secretary, Dr. Oliver King: see below, p. 214) corroborates Mancini's, More's, and Vergil's identification of the group. Mancini's evidence is somewhat ambiguous: he supposes that Richard proceeded against them 'for fear that the ability and authority of these men might be detrimental to him'; yet he adds, 'for he had sounded their loyalty through the Duke of Buckingham and learnt that sometimes they foregathered in each other's houses'. This comment suggests that if they were not actively conspiring, they had drawn close for their own private purposes. It is a common experience that the secret of an abortive conspiracy dies with it. Mancini saw events only from the outside; the Croyland chronicler limits himself to a very bare sketch of the protectorship. Hence it is to be expected that only faint traces of Hastings' purpose will survive. More pictures the association of Hastings, Stanley and Co., assigning, as might be anticipated, fear of Richard's designs as the motive for their meetings. The ascertainable reasons why this quartet was likely to become dissatisfied with the Protector's government (see text, below) offer, it seems to me, a more likely motive. Gairdner is convinced that Hastings and his friends entered upon an active conspiracy, which led them to unite with the Woodvilles in order to secure the King. One basis for his conclusion, however, is untenable. He alludes to Polydore Vergil's statement that at a meeting in St. Paul's, Hastings and a group of lords considered violent measures to secure the person of Edward V (Vergil, pp. 175–76); but this meeting is clearly narrated by Vergil as occurring the morning after the news of the *coup* at Stony Stratford reached London, and therefore provides no evidence for Hastings' conspiracy which developed weeks later. Mancini, More, and the C.C. all make a reference of some sort to this meeting. Sharon Turner's

view of Hastings' plot against the Protector, though outmoded in some details, seems fundamentally sound (*History of England*, III, pp. 370–448).

One of the strongest indications that Hastings was preparing to take action against Richard is that Richard was apparently able to present convincing evidence of this action to the meeting of council which was held shortly after Hastings' execution and which proceeded to agree that little York must be delivered from sanctuary. Why did Mancini and the rest reverse the order of events if not, in part, on the assumption that the Archbishop of Canterbury could not have pleaded so strongly with the Queen for her son if he believed that Hastings had been put out of the way because he was an obstacle to Richard's ambition?

[3] See *Grants*, pp. 68–69: authorizing payments to men who are to inquire about and resist 'our rebels'.

[4] In his early obscure days Morton apparently had had at least one brush with the law; in March of 1455 the Chancellor sealed a pardon of outlawry in favour of John Morton, clerk, late of Greenwich (*Ordinances of the Privy Council*, VI, p. 358).

[5] The pre-contract is discussed in the following chapter (6).

[6] What happened to Jane Shore immediately after Edward's death must, like so much else, be inferred from scattered, though apparently reliable, pieces of evidence. Neither Mancini nor the C.C. makes any mention of her, but it is probable that by the beginning of June she was intimately connected with the activities of Hastings' faction. In Stallworthe's letter of June 21 the imprisonment of Mistress Shore is reported directly following an account of what has happened to the rest of Hastings' faction (see below, p. 213). Out of More's potpourri of probable fact and undoubted fiction (see note 11, below) can be translated three tenable conclusions: Richard charged Jane Shore with serving as a go-between for Hastings and the Woodvilles, imprisoned her on this charge, and compelled her to do penance as a harlot. Gairdner (pp. 87–90) accepts this view, but he confuses the order of events in her life. Whose mistress Jane was must be inferred from evidence which appears to be, but is not necessarily, conflicting. In his proclamation of October 23, 1483, Richard states that she had become the mistress of the Marquess of Dorset (*Cal. Pat. Rolls*, 1476–85, p. 371; *Foedera*, XII, p. 204). According to More, Richard proclaimed on June 13 that she was the mistress of Hastings, and unless she were the mistress of Hastings, it would not be likely that she acted as his go-between. More's statement is confirmed by *The Great Chronicle* (p. 233): 'And shortly after [the coronation], was a woman named . . . Shore, that before days, after the common fame, the lord chamberlain held, contrary his honour, called to a reckoning for part of his goods and other things [which refutes More's absurd statement that Richard, out of greed, plundered her of her possessions and illustrates the kind of embellishment that constantly obscures what truth there is in his narrative: doubtless the goods of Hastings which were recovered were restored to his widow Katherine, whom Richard took under his protection—see below, p. 209]. In so much that all her moveables were attached by the Sheriffs of London, and she lastly as a common harlot put to open penance, for the life that [she] led with the said Lord Hastings and other great estates'. The last phrase provides a clue to the compatibility of Richard's October proclamation with the evidence of More and *The Great Chronicle*: I assume that on, or before, Edward's death, Jane Shore became the mistress of the Marquess and that after he disappeared from the scene on May 1, she was happy to accept the protection of Hastings.

⁷ YR, pp. 148–50.

⁸ *Ibid.*, pp. 144–52; Ratcliffe's halt at Leconfield is conjecture: it is possible that Richard had sent Northumberland an earlier message.

⁹ *Paston Letters*, III, p. 306.

¹⁰ C.C., p. 488.

¹¹ More's famous account of the scene, the information for which was doubtless supplied to him by Morton himself, evaporates when compared with contemporary sources. Since Richard had no withered arm (see above, p. 150), he could scarcely accuse the Queen and Mistress Shore of having withered it. In Vergil, only the Queen is accused of sorcery. To substitute the charge of sorcery for the real accusation was easy: Morton would certainly not be likely to confess to young More than he and Hastings *had* been in the thick of a conspiracy. No doubt, with the passage of years the octogenarian Morton came to believe in his own story.

Neither *The Great Chronicle*, nor Fabyan, nor the *Croyland Chronicle*, nor Mancini makes any mention of sorcery. All they know is that some charge of treason was brought by Richard against Hastings and his friends, before the armed crew rushed in to arrest Hastings.

¹² More's account of the herald's proclamation is supported, in general, by Mancini.

¹³ The political situation at Hastings' death is commented upon in an anonymous communication, so cautiously veiled that it remains a riddle. See *The Cely Papers*, p. 132.

¹⁴ I have inferred the citizens' attitude towards Edward's *amours* from the fact that though they were well known, the King remained very popular; and I find no evidence that his popularity was achieved in despite of his licentiousness.

¹⁵ Richard's indenture with Katherine Hastings: Harl. 433, fs. 108b–109. Richard's treatment of Ralph Hastings: *Cal. Pat. Rolls*, 1476–85, p. 363, p. 365, p. 462; Harl. 433 f. 55 (granting him an annuity of £40), f. 159, and f. 239 (in *Original Letters*, 2nd, I, p. 150), and f. 243 (in *Letters and Papers*, I, p. 46 et seq.).

¹⁶ Grafton's statement, followed by Gairdner (p. 100) that Richard released Stanley on July 4 is incorrect. Stanley was one of the councillors who witnessed, on June 27, the delivery of the Great Seal to Bishop Russell (*Foedera*, XII, p. 189). Since Stallworthe's letter of June 21 (see below, p. 213) does not mention Stanley, it is likely that he was freed before that date. So soon, it seems, was he restored to favour that Mancini does not even note that he was arrested.

¹⁷ Mancini says that Richard ordered these executions 'of his own authority as protector' and I have followed him. He says, however, that the Protector came to this decision 'when by means of the council [he] could not compass the execution'. It may be that he is confused by the council's earlier decision not to put Rivers *et al.* to death and is unaware of a later decision. I doubt if it was necessary or likely for Richard to proceed against the wishes of the council at so ticklish a moment when he needed their support. (See Mancini, p. 113).

¹⁸ *Ex. Hist.*, pp. 246–48.

¹⁹ There seems to be no reason to doubt Rous's ascription of this ballad to Rivers, particularly since Caxton mentions that Rivers composed ballads (see above, p. 171). Rous gives only two stanzas (pp. 213–14); the others have been recovered and printed in Ritson, *Ancient Songs*, II, p. 3, and by Percy in some editions of his *Reliques*; compare Gairdner, pp. 90–95.

20 Rous, p. 213; *Ex. Hist.*, pp. 240–48; *Grants*, pp. xviii–xix; Cotton Faustina B VIII f. 4b: compare Gairdner, pp. 90–95. Since Rous is a very unreliable source, the story of the hairshirt which he alone gives is doubtful, but in character. Rous says that Northumberland, who was then at Pontefract, served as president of the court which formally sentenced Rivers.

Fabyan reports that Sir Richard Haute, cousin to the Woodvilles and treasurer of Prince Edward's household, was arrested and executed along with Rivers, Grey, Vaughan. No other contemporary source mentions Haute, however, and the subject is doubtful and confused. According to J. G. Nichols (*Grants*, p. xvi, note a), there were two Richard Haute's, both from Kent, Sir Richard and a Richard Haute, esq., of Ightam. Rivers in his will proposed Richard Haute as one of his executors. Richard Haute was attainted in Richard's parliament for taking part in Buckingham's rebellion and his attainder was reversed in the first parliament of Henry VII. Meanwhile, however, Richard, circa March of 1485, issued a pardon to 'Sir Richard Haute' (Harl. 433, f. 99b).

21 That is, 'tragedie' in the medieval sense of describing a pattern of life in which the protagonist ascends to great place and pride only to be whirled upon fortune's wheel and cast into the depths.

VI
(pp. 213–223)

Of all the narrative sources, only the *Croyland Chronicle* correctly reports the story of Edward's pre-contract with Lady Eleanor Butler, which is officially set forth in an enactment of Richard's Parliament of January, 1484, rehearsing and confirming the bill drawn up by the 'informal' Parliament of June 25, 1483. If the inaccuracies of More and Vergil are ever due to deliberate falsification on their part, rather than to faulty sources or exuberant imagination—a debatable thesis—they certainly falsified the claim which Richard made to the throne. The pre-contract with Lady Eleanor, which More, writing about 1513, perverts and which Vergil, writing a few years earlier, expressly attempts to deny by branding it a false rumour, was well known to the ambassador of a foreign power in the year 1533 (see below, note 14). It is here that Mancini commits his second major lapse (see headnote to previous chapter of notes); he is, in fact, as inaccurate as More or Vergil. True, he mentions a pre-contract, but he says that when Edward married Elizabeth 'he was contracted to another wife, whom the duke [*sic*] of Warwick had given him. At Edward's command the duke had previously crossed the seas and betrothed the other lady by word of proxy....' Yet, though he is somehow led to substitute for the truth this stale rumour, which had probably been current eighteen years before, he mentions with only a slight confusion in chronology the events leading up to Richard's assumption of the throne, and even alludes to certain statements in the bill which the assembly or Parliament of June 25 enacted (p. 119). Similarly, he makes the inaccurate observation that at this time (June 25) Richard's and Buckingham's power was supported by a 'multitude of troops' (p. 119); yet, later (p. 121) he reveals his own error by stating that Richard summoned troops 'as the day appointed for the coronation approached', and Fabyan confirms the fact that Richard's military force from the north did not appear in London until 'a little before his coronation' (p. 669). How can these bewildering inconsistencies and errors be accounted for? I suggest that, as in the case of his major mistake in chronology, the root of the trouble was the dominant assumption which shaped Mancini's memories that Richard, from the beginning of his protectorship, sought to force his way to the throne.

Sources: Mancini, p. 109, pp. 117–21; C. C., pp. 488–89; Fabyan, pp. 669–70; *Great Chronicle*, pp. 131–32; Vergil, pp. 182–87; More, pp. 87–90, pp. 99–126. Fortunately, the uncertain evidence of the chroniclers is supplemented by Commynes, the Rolls of Parliament and a few documents of great value.

[1] I have omitted from my paraphrase the sentence which follows this one because it cannot be clearly read. Bentley, the editor of *Ex. Hist.*, transcribes it, 'As soe feste he is in hold and mene for hys lyffe.' That is, Richard will not yet release Rotherham and Morton because he is taking no chance of an attack upon his life and so holds all his prisoners fast. C. L. Kingsford, however, the editor of the *Stonor Letters*, renders the sentence, 'As for Foster he is in hold and meue fer hys lyffe.' That is, Foster is in prison and pleads for his life. Kingsford's reading must be given preference . . . but who is Foster?

[2] *Stonor Letters*, II, p. 161; *Ex. Hist.*, pp. 16–17.

[3] Mancini, p. 115; *Great Chronicle*, p. 234.

[4] *York Records*, p. 154, reveal that on June 21 a writ of *supersedeas*—postponement of Parliament—was received. This entry has led to considerable speculation, by Gairdner and others, about the possibility that, since York was friendly to the Protector, Richard's enemies must have issued the *supersedeas*. The town of New Romney, however, likewise received a *supersedeas* and a writ postponing the coronation (HMC, V, p. 54). Grafton, *Chronicles*, II, p. 102, says, for what it is worth, that the coronation was postponed until November 2. The comments of the chroniclers in general and the bill setting forth Richard's title enacted by the Parliament of January, 1484 (*Rot. Parl.*, VI, p. 240) indicate that the Parliament or quasi-Parliament of June 25, 1483, was well attended (see also Armstrong, Mancini, p. 154, note 91). Apparently only a few writs of *supersedeas* were dispatched before Richard discontinued them, having decided that Parliament should assemble, after all.

[5] The question of the cognizances seems only to indicate the uncertainty of the men of York as to whether Richard would wish them to emphasize, by wearing his badge, their personal loyalty to him. The time-table of preparations at York shows that the Northern troops could have arrived in London several days before they actually appeared about July 1–3. Probably Richard's order to Northumberland to sentence and execute Rivers, Grey, and Vaughan also contained a request to delay the march south. YR, pp. 152–56. It seems likely that the rumour Stallworthe had heard about the imminent arrival of the troops (as of June 21) was not very widely known. No mention is elsewhere made of it; Mancini, indeed, was under the impression that the men were not even summoned until after June 26 (p. 121).

[6] *Paston Letters*, II, pp. 347–53; pp. 363–66, p. 389.

[7] See, for example, Mancini, pp. 81–83.

[8] II, p. 64.

[9] The main surviving facts about the Lady Eleanor Butler can be found in the *Inquisitions Post Mortem* and the *Calendar of the Patent Rolls*.

From the *Inquisitions Post Mortem* (8 Edward IV, # 39; see also *Cal. Inq. Post*

Mortem, p. 344, and G.E.C., XII, p. 422): Eleanor, wife of the deceased Thomas Butler, knight, and sister of Sir John Talbot, died on June 30, 1468, possessed of the manors of Grove (or Greve) and Great Dorset in Warwickshire.

John Talbot, first Earl of Shrewsbury, had a son John by his first wife and one of the same name by his second. The former, inheriting his father's earldom, fell at Northampton in 1460. The latter was created, in 1444, Baron and Viscount Lisle and died at Chatillon with his father in 1453. It seems likely that the 'Sir John Talbot' named in the *Inquisitions Post Mortem* is the son of the second marriage and that, in 1468, he was referred to as 'Sir John' to distinguish him from the deceased second earl, his half-brother. Thus, Eleanor would be identified as a daughter of old Talbot's second marriage.

From the *Calendar of the Patent Rolls, 1467–77*, p. 133 (Feb. 6, 1469): 'Whereas by an inquisition taken before William Moton, esquire, late escheator in the county of Warwick, on the death of Eleanor, late the wife of Thomas Butteler, knt., it was found that Ralph Butteler, knt., lord of Sudeley, was seised of the manors of Greve and Great Dorset, county Warwick, in his demesne as of fee and in the year 28 Henry VI granted them to the said Thomas his son and the said Eleanor and the heirs of the body of Thomas [which probably indicates the time of Eleanor's marriage], and the said Thomas died without issue and Eleanor was seised of the manors for her life and in the year 39 Henry VI surrendered her estate in the said manor of Greve to the said Ralph, and the said manors were taken into the King's hands because the grant and acquisition of them and the entries thereon were without license; the King pardons these trespasses and grants to the said Ralph that he may enter into and hold the said manors . . . from the time of the death of Eleanor. . . .'

10 *Stonor Letters*, II, p. 42. *Foedera*, XII, p. 66.

11 C.C., p. 470. Alcock was President of the council of the Prince of Wales which was dominated by Woodvilles. For Henry VI on Stillington, see Scofield, I, p. 94.

12 *Rot. Parl*, VI, p. 256.

13 *Ibid.*, pp. 240–41.

14 Stillington was of so much importance to Henry that on the very day of Bosworth Henry issued a warrant for his arrest, and five days later he had been hunted down and captured (YCR, I, p. 122). Deprived of the Deanery of St. Martin's, he was pardoned by act of Henry's first Parliament, for of what offence could he have been accused, save one which Henry apparently had no wish to be publicly examined? The pardon declared him guilty, however, of nothing less than 'horrible and heinous offences imagined and done' against the King—the offences being unspecified. When Lincoln and Lovell invaded England in 1487 under the banner of Lambert Simnel, Stillington rushed to espouse their cause. After the defeat at Stoke, he took refuge at the University of Oxford, which surrendered him to the King with great reluctance. He was immured in a cell at Windsor Castle and there died four years later. It seems clear that Henry thought him a dangerous man.

Henry saw to it that his first Parliament passed an act ordering all copies of the enactment of Richard's Parliament of 1484 to be seized and burnt.

Neither More nor Vergil says a word of Lady Eleanor or the Bishop of Bath and Wells. More (pp. 99–101) declares that Shaa's sermon of June 22 (see below, p. 220) accused Edward of entering into a pre-contract with Elizabeth Lucy—thus making the accusation absurd by substituting the name of a wanton at court for that of a noble lady. Vergil goes even further (pp. 182–85). That Shaa declared Edward's children to be bastards he dismisses as 'common report', which he declares emphatically to be 'void of all truth'. Yet twenty years later, Chapuys, the ambassador of Charles V, knows about the pre-contract revealed by the Bishop of Bath and Wells (*Letters and Papers of the Reign of Henry VIII*, VI, p. 618). Not until Sir George Buc in the seventeenth century reported the accurate version given in the *Croyland Chronicle* and a copy of the roll of Richard's Parliament was discovered to confirm the C.C., did the true story come to light.

[15] Buckingham's urging Richard to take the crown seems to me to be substantiated by the general picture of these days which the chroniclers have left us, his hold upon Richard as indicated by the favours he enjoyed, and his subsequent actions (see below, *passim*, and Appendix I).

[16] The fact that to believe in the truth of Stillington's story presented Richard with an immense opportunity cautions us to scrutinize the evidence for the truth or falsity of the story with as much care as possible. The fact itself, however, cannot be regarded as evidence telling against the truth of the pre-contract. No such evidence exists (the statement in *The Earlier Tudors* (p. 49) that the falsity of the pre-contract is a *fact*, being unsupported, must be regarded as in error). The issue, then, resolves itself into the single question: how convincing is the evidence which testifies to the truth of Stillington's revelation?

The first indication that it was the Bishop of Bath and Wells who disclosed the secret comes from Commynes, who twice refers to the subject (I, p. 455; II, pp. 64–65). The second time he discusses it in some detail but in ambiguous and bizarre terms. It is fortunate that there is corroborative evidence. On Dec. 16th, 1533, Chapuys, Charles V's ambassador to the English court [see note 14, above], wrote his royal master that people 'say you have a better title than the present King [Henry VIII then being unpopular for having put aside Katherine of Aragon to marry Anne Boleyn], who only claims by his mother, who was declared by sentence of the Bishop of Bath a bastard, because Edward had espoused another wife before the mother of Elizabeth of York' [in the same vein, see also *Letters, etc. of Henry VIII*, VII, # 1368].

That the story of the pre-contract is true is supported by an inference drawn from the circumstances of Clarence's execution and from the inevitable inference that springs from Henry VII's attempt to suppress all knowledge of such a pre-contract. The supposition that Edward did enter into an engagement with Lady Eleanor Butler explains why Edward IV in 1477–78 was persuaded by the Woodvilles that Clarence posed an intolerable threat to Edward's heir, Clarence having been informed of the secret by his friend the Bishop of Bath (see, above, p. 217); it also explains why Henry VII, needing to secure his title on the lineal descent of his wife, who was Edward's daughter, went to such lengths to eradicate all knowledge of the pre-contract by commanding the destruction of the roll of Richard's Parliament; and why both Henry VII and Henry VIII were so dangerously sensitive to criticisms of their royal claims. It seems to be more than coincidence that both Edward IV and Henry VII charged Stillington with offences against themselves but refrained from stating on what grounds the charges were made.

The sum of the evidence by no means amounts to proof; it seems to me, however, to establish, in the absence of evidence to the contrary, the strong possibility that

Stillington's revelation was true. Gairdner is inclined to accept it. The rumour that Edward had once wronged a lady of Warwick's house may represent a distorted version of the pre-contract; after Warwick's quarrel with Edward, it would be natural for those who had heard some faint whisper of the truth to assume that the lady must have been a relative of the House of Neville rather than of the House of Talbot (Vergil, p. 117).

When did Richard decide, on the basis of Stillington's revelation, to sound men's opinions on the subject of his assuming the throne? The writ postponing parliament, which was received at York on June 21, must have been dispatched during the week-end which began with the death of Hastings and ended with the delivery of little York from sanctuary (June 13-16). Richard's decision to halt the sending out of these writs and to hold a parliamentary assembly probably coincides with his decision to sound men's opinions, and would seem to have been made about Tuesday or Wednesday, June 17-18, since only a few writs of postponement were apparently sent out.

[17] Mancini, p. 75; Commynes, I, p. 305; see Armstrong, Mancini, p. 133, note 12, and, above, p. 124.

It seems to be of some significance that Fabyan, the city chronicler, records that Shaa declared the bastardy of Edward's children but makes no mention of an attack on Edward's legitimacy (p. 669). Mancini (p. 117) says that preachers spread the story that Edward was a bastard; only a few lines further on, however, he reports that Buckingham based his appeal to the lords on the illegitimacy of Edward's children. It is possible that an emphasis on Richard's being the only son of the Duke of York to be born in England—a statement made in the parliamentary declaration of Richard's title, where it appears to be little more than the kind of non-sequitur which often embellishes the enactments of the 15th century—was construed by Mancini and others as an attack on Edward's legitimacy. It seems probable, however, that Richard's lieutenants did seek to make some political capital of the old scandal of Edward's bastardy; but in the light of Fabyan's evidence and Mancini's using of the plural 'preachers', it does not seem likely that Friar Shaa's 'official' sermon referred to Edward's bastardy. Since Buckingham made himself the chief mover in Richard's affairs and might have a motive of his own for slurring the Duchess of York's character (see below, p. 412)—as Richard had none—I see no reason to doubt that if preachers were encouraged to attack Edward's legitimacy, it was Buckingham who directed the campaign. For Richard's relations with his mother, see, below, p. 320.

[18] Fabyan, p. 669; *Great Chronicle*, p. 232.

[19] See note 4, above.

[20] *Rot. Parl.*, VI, pp. 240-42. Apparently Stillington himself drew up the bill (Ramsay, II, p. 488 and note 2).

[21] Mancini, the C.C., and the secondary sources offer a mosaic of conflicting details and vague assertions regarding the order of events of June 23-26. Fortunately, a writ of June 28 establishes beyond doubt that the parliamentary assembly met on June 25 to draw up 'a bill of petition, which the lords spiritual and temporal and the commons of this land solemnly porrected unto the King's highness at London the 26th day of June. Whereupon the King's said highness, notably assisted by well nigh all the lords spiritual and temporal of this Royaume, went the same day unto

his palace of Westminster, and there in such royal honour apparelled within the great hall there took possession and declared his mind that the same day he would begin to reign upon his people' (Harl. 433, f. 238, printed in *Letters and Papers*, I, pp. 11–16 and in *Original Letters*, 2nd series, I, pp. 148–49).

[22] Fogge's name appears in Commissions of the Peace for the country of Kent in three patents of June 26, July 28, and July 30 (see Appendix to *Cal. Pat. Rolls*, 1476–85, pp. 562–63).

VII

(pp. 223–226)

This picture of Richard's mind, in the moment of his most crucial decision, I have developed by inference from the events narrated in the previous chapter and from all that I have been able to discover about his life and character.

VIII

(pp. 227–231)

This chapter is based almost entirely on the evidence of documents; the chroniclers offer very little.

Sources: C.C., pp. 489–90; Mancini, pp. 121–23; Vergil, pp. 185–87; More, pp. 125–26; Fabyan, pp. 669–70.

Documents: 'Observations on the Wardrobe Account for the year 1483', *Archaeologia*, I, pp. 361–83.

A detailed, contemporary description of Richard's coronation, printed in *Ex. Hist.*, pp. 379–84.

Cal. Pat. Rolls, 1476–85. Harl. 433.

[1] Russell made Chancellor: *Foedera*, XII, p. 189; Catesby: *Cal. Pat. Rolls*, p. 360 (the appointment was enrolled on Monday, June 30); Peter Curteys: 'Wardrobe Account'; dignities of Berkeley and the Howards: *Cal. Charter Rolls*, VI, p. 258; commission to Dynham, Harl. 433, f. 238 (in *Letters and Papers*, I, pp. 11–16 and *Foedera*, XII, p. 191).

[2] Estimates of the numbers vary surprisingly little: generally from 4 to 5 thousand. Chroniclers tend to exaggerate the size of armies. Compare Armstrong's summary of the evidence, Mancini, p. 156, note 101.

[3] Mancini, for example (p. 121).

[4] For the names of those who were made Knights of the Bath, see *Ex. Hist.*, p. 384. Richard's proclamation: Harl. 433 f. 239b (in *Letters and Papers*, I, pp. 16–17).

[5] 'Wardrobe Account'. I have no better authorities for Buckingham's splendour than Grafton, pp. 799–800 and Hall, p. 375. That he would strive to outshine all others, however, is completely in character.

[6] Though Howard was created Earl Marshal (*Call. Pat. Rolls*, p. 358) and appointed to execute the office of Steward of England for the King's coronation (*ibid.*, p. 360), the Wardrobe account speaks of Buckingham as 'having chief rule and devising of the ordinance for . . . the King's . . . coronation' (p. 374); and the coronation narra-

tive says he bore a white wand—i.e., the Wand of High Steward—during the ceremonies (*Ex. Hist.*, p. 380).

[7] Stanley's bearing of the Constable's Mace was an honorific office only. Richard, who had himself been Constable, had not yet bestowed the post. It was shortly given to Buckingham (see below, p. 250).

[8] So I infer from what is known of preceding coronations as far back as Richard II's, which was notably splendid but could not have matched the material resources of Richard III's.

THE KING

RICHARD, BY GRACE OF GOD . . .

I
(pp. 232–249)

This chapter is developed from such a variety of sources that it would be impossible for me to acknowledge my indebtedness in detail without immersing the reader in a morass of notes. A few works of the fifteenth or early sixteenth century I have drawn on very heavily:

A Relation of the Island of England, ed. by C. A. Sneyd, Camden Society, 1870.

Mancini, *Usurpation*—particularly for a description of London; Armstrong's notes are very helpful. In an appendix, Armstrong prints an extract from von Poppelau's diary (pp. 162–64).

Mrs. Henry Cust, *Gentlemen Errant*, London, 1909—extracts from the journal kept by one of a group of Bohemian knights who visited England in 1465–66.

Paston Letters.

Stow, *Survey of London.*

J. Leland, *Collectanea* (*De rebus britannicis Collectanea*), ed. by T. Hearne, London, 1715.

II
(pp. 249–260)

For the period from Richard's coronation to the end of his reign the narrative sources contract in number and seriously decline in importance. Mancini left England within a few days of the coronation. More's *Richard the Third* comes to an abrupt end before the outbreak of Buckingham's rebellion in October of 1483. Vergil is of little use except for certain events in the life of Henry Tudor. Even the *Croyland Chronicle* shows signs of deterioration, as the monastic editor more and more intrudes himself to fill out with his own opinion the increasing scantiness of the author's material (see below, headnote to Chapter 12 and Appendix II, p. 432).

Consequently the remainder of this biography is based largely on state papers, letters, and other contemporary documents.

[1] Harl. 433, f. 107b.

[2] Harl. 433, f. 107b; *Cal. Pat. Rolls*, 1476–85, p. 361; Harl. 433, f. 22.

[3] Norfolk: *Cal. Pat. Rolls,* 1476–85, p. 362, p. 363, p. 365, p. 359. He was also given the castle and lordship of Farley (Harl. 433, f. 24b) and made Chief Steward of the Duchy of Lancaster south of Trent (*ibid.,* 23b).

Northumberland: *Cal. Pat. Rolls,* 1476–85, p. 462.

[4] Brackenbury: *Cal. Pat. Rolls,* 1476–85, p. 364 and p. 463.

Lovell: *ibid.,* p. 365.

Prince Edward: *ibid.,* p. 403.

[5] *Great Chronicle,* p. 233; Stanley remained in Richard's entourage throughout the rest of 1483 and, apparently, all of 1484. It is likely that Richard wished to keep an eye on this baron, whose past had shown him to be anything but a pillar of trust; it is furthermore probable that Stanley was Steward of the Household, though no record of his holding the office has survived. It is true that in the contemporary account of Richard's coronation banquet (*Ex. Hist.,* p. 382) the Earl of Surrey is designated as 'Steward . . . with a white staff in his hand', but the office appears to have been an honorary one, for this occasion only, since there is no indication that Surrey was afterwards a member of Richard's Household. Stanley had been Edward IV's Steward, was probably continued in the office under the protectorship—as Hastings was continued as Lord Chamberlain—and restored to it, as he was to the council, shortly after his brief imprisonment following Hastings' execution. See note 15 of Chapter IV, 'Protector and Defensor'.

[6] *Great Chronicle,* p. 233.

[7] Harl. 433, f. 265b (in *Original Letters,* 2nd series, I, pp. 123–24). These instructions for the Earl of Desmond doubtless reflect the exhortation Richard delivered to all the lords.

[8] William D. Macray, *Register of Magdalen College, Oxford,* London, 1894 (new series), I, pp. 11–12.

[9] Vergil (p. 194) and More (p. 137) say that Buckingham accompanied Richard to Gloucester, Buckingham then going on to Wales. The C.C. omits the episode. There is some reason to believe, then, that the Duke and the King parted at Gloucester, but the Register of Magdalen College shows that Buckingham was not with Richard during the visit to Oxford of July 24–25. Hence, I have conjectured that he did not leave London until a few days after Richard had departed on his progress and, riding directly to Gloucester, overtook the King there.

[10] Rous, p. 216; Harl. 433, f. 110.

[11] Richard's itinerary is established by writs in Harl. 433. YR, pp. 162–64, Rous, p. 216. Langton: *Christ Church Letters,* ed. by J. B. Sheppard, Camden Society, 1877, p. 64.

[12] Harl. 433, f. 235 (in *Original Letters,* 2nd series, I, pp. 152–54 and *Letters and Papers,* I, pp. 21–23); *ibid.,* f. 241 (in *L. and P.,* I, 23–25); *ibid.,* f. 244b (in *L. and P.,* I, pp. 48–51); *Foedera,* XII, pp. 193–94 and pp. 198–202.

[13] Duke Maximilian: Harl. 433, f. 236b (in *L. and P.,* I, pp. 26–30).

Scots: Harl. 433, f. 246b (in *L. and P.,* I, pp. 51–52).

Richard and James: Harl. 433, f. 247 (in *L. and P.,* I, p. 53); *Christ Church Letters,* p. 46.

Douglas and Albany: Harl. 433, f. 51b; Rous, p. 217.

[14] Coinage: Harl. 433, f. 233 (in *L. and P.,* II, pp. 286–87 and *Original Letters,* 3rd series, I, pp. 103–05).

Kildare: Harl. 433, f. 242 (in *L. and P.*, I, pp. 43–46).

Desmond: Harl. 433, f. 265b (in *Original Letters*, 2nd series, I, pp. 122–23).

[15] Louis to Richard: Harl. 433, f. 236b (in *L. and P.*, I, p. 25).

Richard to Louis: Harl. 433, f. 237 (in *L. and P.*, I, pp. 34–35); two days later, Richard wrote Louis a brief note, in the same casual vein, asking for licence to ship a supply of wines.

Richard's fleet: Harl. 433, f. 113b.

[16] Vergil, pp. 190–91; *Foedera*, XII, p. 194; Harl. 433, f. 241 (in *L. and P.*, I, pp. 22–23).

[17] Movements of the King: Harl. 433, ff. 109b–111.

Summonses: Harl. 433, f. 111b.

[18] YR., pp. 157–67.

Prince Edward: Harl. 433, f. 118; *Cal. Charter Rolls*, VI, p. 260.

Richard's train: Rous, p. 217; *Register of Magdalen*, pp. 11–12; YR., p. 176.

[19] Order to the Wardrobe: Harl. 433, f. 126 (transcribed with some inaccuracies in Halliwell, *Letters of the Kings of England*, I, pp. 252–53); see also YR., p. 283. Apparel for Tyrell: 'Observations on Wardrobe Account,' *Archaeologia*, I, p. 363.

Mayor entertains: YR., p. 176.

Creed Play: YR., pp. 171–72 and p. 282.

Investiture of Prince: As Davies has shown (YR., p. 285), this ceremony was not a second coronation. It is described in the patent conferring knighthood on Sasiola (*Foedera*, XII, p. 200); Vergil, p. 190.

Remission of fee-farm: YR., pp. 173–75; compare *Cal. Pat. Rolls*, 1476–85, p. 409.

Royal household in North: Vergil, pp. 187–88. This indicates only that the Earl of Warwick went to live at Sheriff Hutton, but it seems probable that Lincoln did likewise in view of their later association. Though Vergil says that Warwick was 'in ward', there is evidence to show that this statement is false (see below, p. 312 and *York Records*, pp. 210–13).

[20] Commissions of *oyer and terminer*: *Cal. Pat. Rolls*, 1476–85, p. 465.

Mission of Mainbier: Harl. 433, f. 247b (in *L. and P.*, I, pp. 37–43). Mainbier left Nantes about August 26.

[21] Harl. 433, ff. 115, 120; *Stonor Letters*, II, p. 163.

III

(pp. 260–268)

[1] C.C., pp. 490–91.

[2] *Rot. Parl.*, VI, p. 244; Agnes E. Conway, 'The Maidstone Sector of Buckingham's Rebellion,' *Archaeologia Cantiana*, XXXVII (1925), pp. 106–14; *Stonor Letters*, II, p. 70, pp. 122–24 and intro.

[3] C.C., p. 491.

[4] Hall, pp. 388–89.

[5] Vergil, pp. 193–97.

[6] More, pp. 135–43.

[7] C.C., p. 491.

[8] P. 195.

[9] P. 195.

Q

[10] HMC., VI, p. 244; Gairdner, pp. 107–08.

[11] Rous, p. 216; the source is untrustworthy but the remark is certainly in character.

[12] P. 137.

[13] *Rot. Parl.*, VI, p. 244.

[14] *Paston Letters*, III, p. 308.

[15] Harl. 433, f. 3.

IV
(pp. 269–277)

[1] *Stonor Letters*, II, p. 163. On Oct. 11, Richard set the rendezvous for Oct. 20; next day he requested the men of York to be at Leicester by Oct. 21 (YR., pp. 177–78).

[2] *Original Letters*, 2nd series, I, pp. 159–60. This letter reveals that Richard had already sent a message to Russell.

[3] YR., pp. 179–80; *Close Roll*, I Rich. III, 100^r and *Foedera*, XII, p. 203; *Stonor Letters*, II, p. 163.

[4] *Plumpton Correspondence*, pp. 44–45; *Cal. Pat. Rolls*, 1476–85, p. 476—grant to Lords Stanley and Strange for good service against the rebels.

[5] *Household Books of Howard*, pp. 412–479; *Paston Letters*, III, p. 308; *Rot. Parl.*, VI, p. 244 and Conway, 'Maidstone Sector', p. 106 *et seq.*; C.C., p. 492.

[6] Harl. 433, f. 120 (Richard at Melton Mowbray on Oct. 21); YR., p. 178; *Foedera*, XII, p. 204; Vergil, p. 200. That Dr. Hutton returned from Brittany to warn Richard of Henry Tudor's invasion seems probable.

[7] *Cal. Pat. Rolls*, 1476–85, p. 368.

[8] C.C., pp. 491–92; *Rot. Parl.*, VI, p. 244.

[9] *Rot. Parl.*, VI, p. 244; C.C., pp. 491–92; Vergil, p. 206.

[10] Vergil, pp. 199–200. The precise date on which Richard entered Salisbury is unknown. He left Coventry on or after Oct. 24 and was in Salisbury, at the latest, on Nov. 1.

[11] Vergil, p. 201; Fabyan, p. 671. C.C. (p. 492) confuses the date of Buckingham's execution and is apparently mistaken about his capture. See grants to Ralph Bannaster and Thomas Jebbe for their taking of Buckingham: *Cal. Pat. Rolls*, 1476–85, p. 482 and p. 484; *Original Letters*, 3rd series, I, pp. 101–02.

[12] C.C., pp. 492–95; Vergil, pp. 201–02; *Great Chronicle*, p. 235; Richard's movements are established by *Cal. Pat. Rolls*.

[13] Vergil says Henry left Brittany on the '6th ides of October'—i.e., on October 9— but since he misdates even the year of Buckingham's rebellion this much too early date can safely be dismissed. Much more disturbing is the statement in the bill of attainder drawn up by the Parliament of January, 1484, that Henry touched at Plymouth on October 19 (*Rot. Parl.*, VI, p. 244), a date which also seems too early since Richard was still at Grantham and the rebellion was only a day old. It accords well, however, with Vergil's date; if Henry did indeed touch on the south coast this early, the hostile reception he received, before Richard had gathered his army, testifies eloquently to the weakness of the rebel cause. There is evidence, however, for a much later date and Oct. 19 may be an error for Oct. 29.

Henry Tudor received a loan of 10,000 crowns from the Duke of Brittany on October 31 at Paimpol, on the channel (Brit. Mus. Add. MS. 19,398, f. 33). This loan must have been made either on Henry's return from his abortive invasion or just before he sailed. At Nantes on November 22 Henry was lent another 10,000 crowns by Duke Francis (*L. and P.*, I, pp. 54–55), which—considering the previous loan—would appear to be a sum advanced to meet the needs of Henry and his followers on his return. Furthermore, if Vergil's story of soldiers lining the coast at Poole, in Dorset, is true, these troops would seem to be among those whom, according to Vergil, Richard dispatched to the seaside after he reached Salisbury (around Oct. 28). Finally, the C.C. (p. 495) says that it was while Richard was at Exeter that Henry touched at Plymouth, and Richard reached Exeter some time between Nov. 5 and Nov. 8 (*Cal. Pat. Rolls*, 1476–85, p. 370). The sum of the evidence indicates that Henry probably sailed on Oct. 31 from Paimpol.

[14] Commissions: *Cal. Pat. Rolls*, 1476–85, p. 375, p. 370, p. 371.

Bodiam: *ibid.*, p. 370.

Rebels executed: Fabyan, p. 671 (he says 'Roger' Clifford in one edition, 'Robert' in others); *Great Chronicle*, p. 235 (which gives 'William' Clifford). A 'Robert Clifford', however, was granted a pardon by Richard in April, 1485 (Harl. 433, f. 101).

[15] Richard's movements established by Harl. 433 and *Cal. Pat. Rolls*.

Lord Cobham: HMC, 9th rep., I, p. 177.

Richard redelivered the Great Seal to Russell on November 26 at Westminster (*Foedera*, XII, p. 203).

[16] *Rot. Parl.*, VI, p. 244; for pardons, see *Cal. Pat. Rolls*, 1476–85 and Harl. 433. Bray's pardon: *Cal. Pat. Rolls*, 1476–85, p. 411.

[17] All references in this note are to *Cal. Pat. Rolls*, 1476–85, or to Harl. 433:

Huddleston: p. 369 and p. 372; Tunstall: p. 368; Tyrell: f. 75; Stanley: f. 120b (Kymbellton), p. 367 and p. 381 (Constable); Sir William Stanley: p. 368 and f. 45b; Herbert: p. 367; Northumberland: p. 367 and p. 409, f. 124b and f. 30b; small annuities: f. 29b; Rhys ap Thomas: p. 406 and f. 36.

[18] Since Richard returned the Great Seal to Russell on Nov. 26 (*Foedera*, XII, p. 203), it is likely that he reached London the day before. Fabyan (p. 671) and *The Great Chronicle* (p. 235) give this account of Richard's welcome as of Nov. 9, 1484. However, both ascribe Buckingham's rebellion to 1484 and describe this entry as following the rebellion. The fact that Richard is said to be coming from Kennington shows that he approached London from the south, which would fit his arrival in Nov. of 1483, rather than from the north, as he did on his return to the capital in Nov. of 1484.

V
(pp. 277–286)

[1] C.C., p. 495; Harl. 433, f. 136b; HMC, I, p. 50; *Great Chronicle*, p. 233 and p. 235; Fabyan, p. 671; Harl. 433, f. 165, f. 130, f. 55b.

Both *The Great Chronicle* and Fabyan place Buckingham's rebellion in 1484 and, as a result, confuse the borrowing Richard resorted to in December of 1483 with that of the end of 1484.

[2] Harl. 433, f. 39.

Q*

[3] Harl. 433, ff. 140, 134, 149b, 164, 135, 136, 136b, 139b, 146 (*Letters and Papers*, II, p. 287), 159b, 180; *Cal. Pat. Rolls*, 1476–85, p. 426, p. 465, p. 402.

[4] Harl. 433, ff. 150, 127, 127b, 138b, 138.

[5] Harl. 433, ff. 141, 141b, 142, 144.

[6] Harl. 433, f. 128b (in Gairdner, pp. 343–44).

[7] For the enactments of Richard's Parliament, petitions and statutes, see *Rot. Parl.*, VI, pp. 237–62 and *Statutes of the Realm*, London, 1816, II, pp. 477–98.

[8] Gairdner, p. 153. *Grants*, l–lxiii.

[9] *Cal. Pat. Rolls*, 1476–85, p. 494.

VI
(pp. 286–291)

[1] Vergil, p. 210; C.C., p. 496; *Statutes*, II, p. 498.

[2] Harl. 433, f. 308 (in *Original Letters*, 2nd series, I, p. 149).

[3] Nesfeld: C.C., p. 491 and p. 497; *Cal. Pat. Rolls*, 1476–85, p. 448, p. 485.
   Marquess: Vergil, p. 210, p. 214.

[4] All of the following citations are in Harl. 433:
   Creditors of Buckingham: f. 67b and f. 97; Prior of Carlisle: f. 166; Bailiff of Huntingdon: f. 166b; Combe: f. 20; Filpot: f. 148b; Creyke: f. 153b; Bentley: f. 158; Green and Hawkins: f. 46; John Kendall: ff. 30b, 59b, 83b, 164, 166; bear-ward: f. 139; St. James of C.: ff. 145b, 171, 171b, 172b, 174b, 175.

[5] C.C., p. 496.

[6] *Foedera*, XII, pp. 214–23; *Cal. Pat. Rolls*, 1476–85, p. 423 and p. 477; Cotton MS. Faustina III, p. 405; Harl. 433, ff. 31, 68b, 96b; *Cal. Pat. Rolls*, 1476–85, p. 387.

[7] C.C., pp. 496–97.

[8] Although Rous (pp. 217–18) says that Richard first appointed Warwick as his heir, there is no evidence to support this statement. Lincoln's maturity and good service (*Cal. Pat. Rolls*, 1476–85, p. 388) and his being chosen by Richard to head the Council of the North suggest that the King never had any other choice in mind. There is no proof, however, that Warwick was a 'retarded' child. It may be that it was only the long imprisonment to which Henry VII subjected the unfortunate son of Clarence, before putting him to death, which enfeebled his mind. See Davies, YR., p. 211.

VII
(pp. 291–302)

[1] C.C., p. 497.

[2] *Cal. Pat. Rols*, 1476–85, p. 385, p. 448, p. 405, p. 163. See also *ibid.*, p. 483 and Harl. 433, f. 139b and f. 145.

[3] *Cal. Pat. Rolls*, 1476–85, pp. 397–401.

[4] *Lists and Indexes*, XLIX, p. 59.

[5] Harl. 433, f. 170; *Cal. Pat. Rolls*, 1476–85, p. 355, p. 356, p. 362, p. 493, etc.

[6] *Cal. Pat. Rolls*, 1476–85, pp. 370–71, p. 425, p. 446, pp. 517–18, p. 520, p. 544, etc. See especially *ibid.*, p. 493, pp. 391–92 and HMC, II, p. 91.

[7] C.C., pp. 497–98.

[8] *Foedera*, XII, p. 253.

[9] Forssa: Harl. 433, f. 75. Portugal: *Foedera*, XII, p. 228.

[10] *L. and P.*, II, pp. 3–51; *Cal. Pat. Rolls*, 1476–85, p. 446, p. 518; *Foedera*, XII, p. 231, pp. 248–49.

[11] Traders: Harl. 433, f. 170. Langton: *Foedera*, XII, pp. 221–23; Safe-conducts: *ibid.*, p. 234. See also Gairdner, pp. 171–72.

[12] *Foedera*, XII, pp. 226–27 and p. 229; also *Cal. Pat. Rolls*, 1476–85, p. 517 and p. 547; Vergil pp. 205–06.

[13] Vergil (pp. 206–08) is our only authority for these passages in Henry's life. Gairdner (pp. 169–70) prints a memorandum of the French council, dated Oct. 11, 1484, ordering the governor of Limousin to meet Henry, the council having heard that Henry has left Brittany. This evidence is not incompatible with the supposition that Henry escaped from Brittany about June, for the court of France may not have wished to welcome Henry or found the opportunity to notice him for some months after his appearance on French soil. Richard's signing a treaty with Brittany in June and preparing to send Francis 1,000 archers was almost certainly the signal for Landois' attempt to commit Henry to custody. The instructions which Maximilian drew up for his envoys to England in 1484 are undated, but internal evidence (*L. and P.*, II, pp. 44–49) indicates that they were composed shortly after Richard announced his truce with Brittany on June 8. In these instructions reference is made to Henry's departure from Brittany.

[14] *Foedera*, XII, p. 255, pp. 260–61; *Lists and Indexes*, XLIX, p. 60.

[15] *Foedera*, XII, p. 207; *Original Letters*, 3rd series, I, pp. 111–13; *L. and P.*, I, pp. 55–56.

[16] *Foedera*, XII, pp. 230–32, pp. 235–43; *L. and P.*, I, pp. 59–63.

[17] *L. and P.*, I, pp. 64–67; *Foedera*, XII, pp. 236–43.

[18] While in London, Richard had the body of Henry VI moved from Chertsey Abbey and reinterred in St. George's Chapel, Windsor.

[19] Richard's movements are established from Harl. 433.

[20] Turburvyle: Sir John Turburvyle was a shipowner; he is recorded as securing gear in 1486 for two of his vessels (R. C. Anderson, 'The Grace de Dieu of 1446–86', *Eng. Hist. Rev.*, XXXIV (1919), p. 586).

Colyngbourne as an officer of Duchess Cicely: Harl. 433, f. 2b (in *Original Letters*, 2nd series, I, pp. 161–62).

Indictment: printed by Holinshed; see Gairdner, p. 186 *et seq.*

Commission: *Cal. Pat. Rolls*, 1476–85, p. 519.

Fabyan: p. 672; see also *Great Chronicle*, p. 236; in a patent of Feb. 1, 1485, Colyngbourne is 'now dead' (*Cal. Pat. Rolls*, 1476–85, p. 510).

Gairdner insists that Colyngbourne must have committed his treasonable acts in July of 1483, but his argument is tortuous and unconvincing. The fact that on July 10 Colyngbourne asked Yate to go to Brittany, whereas by that time in 1484 Henry had escaped to France, is far easier to explain than the incongruities which arise if it supposed that this proposal was made in 1483. It is quite probable that Colyngbourne had not yet learned of Henry's departure from Brittany. There is no reason to believe that the Marquess of Dorset, mentioned as being with Henry at this time, was in Brittany in the summer of 1483, and the reference to Richard's trifling with the French ambassadors fits only the summer of 1484, when Langton was negotiating with the government of Charles VIII (see, above, p. 296). Louis XI neither sent nor showed any intention of sending envoys to England in July of 1483. Colyngbourne advised Henry to invade England *before* St. Luke's day (October 18), but that is something quite different from Henry's having agreed with Buckingham and the Woodvilles in 1483 to land *on* St. Luke's day; and though Colyngbourne counselled Henry to disembark at Poole, there is no reason to suppose that he would not suggest a landing where a landing had been attempted before. The absence of any reference to the Woodville conspiracies in the southern counties does not necessarily clinch the case for 1484, since July 10 is only four days after Richard's coronation; but the sum of the evidence appears to support the accuracy of the date of the indictment. Gairdner's citation of Richard's allusion to Colyngbourne as a former officer of his mother's in a letter of June, 1484, in no way supports the thesis that Colyngbourne's activities took place in 1483; it indicates only that Colyngbourne had been known for a rebel for some time before he was apprehended and had probably been in hiding.

[21] Vergil, p. 213.

[22] Cora L. Scofield, 'The Early Life of John de Vere, 13th Earl of Oxford,' *Eng. Hist. Rev.*, XXIX (1914), pp. 244–45; Harl. 433, f. 83; *Cal. Pat. Rolls.*, 1476–85, p. 526; Harl. 433, f. 201. Mountjoy had been ill at least since August (*Foedera*, XII, p. 232).

Siege of Hammes: occurred on Dec. 15, according to MS. Chronicle cited in *Letters and Papers*, I, p. xxvi.

Vergil (pp. 212–13) says that Oxford returned with a band of soldiers to help the besieged garrison of Hammes and was thus able to secure terms whereby the garrison and Blount's wife were freely permitted to depart with bag and baggage, Thomas Brandon and thirty men entering the castle through a marsh to help the besieged. Fabyan (p. 672), however, does not support the tale. There is no record of Richard's sending a fresh garrison to Hammes, as he did to Guisnes (Harl. 433, f. 201). Twice in November Richard offered pardons to James Blount and the garrison (Harl. 433, f. 83); the final pardon of January 27, however, which was apparently accepted, omitted James Blount, as would be expected, but included Blount's wife and Thomas Brandon. The pardon for Blount's wife may have been offered in kindness, and may not have been accepted; but there is no reason to suppose that Richard would single out, among the exiles already in France, Thomas Brandon for pardon, if he had actually performed the feat attributed to him by Vergil.

[23] Harl. 433, f. 273b; *Cal. Pat. Rolls*, 1476–85, p. 488; Harl. 433, f. 198. See also Harl 433, f. 1986—instructions to ready the defenses of Harwich, Dec. 22, 1484.

VIII
(pp. 303–306)

[1] YR., p. 206; C.C., p. 498.

[2] C.C., p. 499; I infer tuberculosis from the fact that Richard's physicians forbade him to share Anne's bed, the prohibition indicating a contagious disease; the Croyland chronicler implies that by Christmas of 1484 the Queen's illness was known to be mortal. See discussion of the Queen's death, note 2 of chapter 10, below. Again, there is no precise information concerning the fatal illness of Isabel, Duchess of

Clarence; she may have died because of complications following childbirth. Both Anne and Isabel, however, succumbed before they reached the age of thirty, a fact which would seem to make tuberculosis a likely cause of both their deaths.

[3] The story of John Stafford is told in the entries of YR., pp. 200–05.

[4] Margery's letter: *Paston Letters*, III, p. 314; for the courtship, see *ibid.*, III, pp. 158–60; pp. 169–72, *et seq.*

[5] C.C., p. 498.

IX
(pp. 306–324)

All references to grants, patents, etc. are taken from Harl. 433 or *Cal. Pat. Rolls*, 1476–85; passages relating to the city of York are based upon *York Records*.

Also from Harl. 433: Regulations for the King's Household in the North, f. 265 (in Halsted's *Life of Richard III*, II, pp. 524–25); Richard's Instructions to the Council, f. 264b (in *Letters and Papers*, I, pp. 56–59); Richard's Letter to the Bishops, March, 1484, f. 281 (in Halliwell, *Letters of the Kings of England*, I, pp. 153–55); Richard's Letter to his Mother, f. 2b (in *Original Letters*, 2nd series, I, p. 161); Richard's Letter to his Chancellor about Lynom and Shore, f. 340b (in Halliwell, *Letters of the Kings of England*, I, pp. 160–61).

[1] See below, p. 313 and note 7 of this chapter.

[2] *Year Books*, 2Riii, ff. x, xi; see Pickthorn, *Early Tudor Government*, I, p. 54, note 3.

[3] *Coventry Leet Book*, ed. by Mary D. Harris, EETS, 1907–13, pp. 523–24.

[4] See A. F. Pollard, 'The Council under the Tudors,' *Eng. Hist. Rev.*, XXXVII (1922), pp. 343–45; and A. F. Pollard, 'The Growth of the Court of Requests,' *Eng. Hist. Rev.*, LVI (1941), pp. 301–03.

[5] *Chronicle of Calais*, ed. by J. G. Nichols, Camden Society, 1846, p. 1.

[6] See A. P. Newton, 'The King's Chamber under the Early Tudors,' *Eng. Hist. Rev.*, XXXII (1917), pp. 348–72.

[7] *York Records*, pp. 190–99.

[8] David Wilkins, *Concilia*, III (4 vols.), London, 1737, pp. 614–16.

[9] *Complete Peerage*, II, Appendix B, p. 545.

[10] Considerable obscurity attends the identity and life of Richards Secretary, John Kendall, since no less than four distinct John Kendalls make their appearance in documents of the 15th and early 16th centuries, with one or more of whom our John Kendall has been confused. Davies, in his notes to the *York Records*, confuses him with an elder John Kendall, and Nichols, in his preface to *Grants, etc.*, confuses him with a John Kendall who was Turcopolier of Rhodes and lived for years after Bosworth Field.

There is proof that the elder John Kendall is not our John. He appears in several patents of Edward IV, two of which are particularly significant for our purposes. The first, of March 20, 1481 (*Cal. Pat. Rolls*, 1476–85, p. 275), bestows a 'grant for life to John Kendall, esq., who spent the days of his youth in the service of the king's father and the king and by continued attendance and his great labours and charges in that service has come to old age and debility, and Nicholas Geddyng, esq., for his good service to the king and to Edward, Prince of Wales, of the office of comptroller of the king's Works within the realm. . . .' The second patent, of almost exactly a year later (March 21, 1482, *ibid.*, p. 296) clearly refers to this same man: 'Grant for life to John Kendall, esq., for his good services to the king's father and the king and because he has come to old age and debility, that he shall be one of the knights of the king's alms within the College of St. George within the castle of Windsor.' But a few days before this last patent was issued, *our* John Kendall received a grant (March 6, 1482: *ibid.*, p. 324): 'Grant for life to John Kendall, servant of the king's brother Richard, duke of Gloucester . . . of the office of clerk of all returns of writs in the castle of York within the city of York. . . .'

Final proof that these John Kendalls are two different men occurs in Harl. 433, f. 16b: 'a petition of Richard Tilles Clerk, Comptroller of the King's most honourable household, for the office of Comptroller of his Majesty's Works within this realm, now being made void by the death of Sir John Kendall late one of the Alms Knights within the College of Windsor'. This establishes that the elder John Kendall died some time during Richard's reign while our John Kendall was flourishing.

It can also be shown that Richard's Secretary, who undoubtedly died at Bosworth—the last heard of him is his attainder in the first Parliament of Henry VII and the *Croyland Chronicle* mentions him in terms that indicate his death in the field (see headnote to Chap. XII)—is not the John Kendall who was Turcopolier of Rhodes and later Grand Prior for England of the Order of St. John of Jerusalem. *This* John John Kendall was involved in intrigues against Henry VII (see *Letters and Papers*, I, pp. 318–26); he also addressed a letter on one occasion 'before 1503', to Sir John Paston (*Paston Letters*, III, p. 397). This Turcopolier was commissioned, along with John Sherwood, Bishop of Durham, and Thomas Langton, Bishop of St. David's, by Richard on December 16, 1484, to offer the King's obedience to the new Pope, Innocent VIII (*Foedera*, XII, p. 253). Consequently, the Turcopolier of Rhodes, then in Rome, and Richard's Secretary, then in London, are manifestly two different persons.

One other John Kendall occurs, but offers no difficulty: a man of that name, about 1503 or later, addressed a letter to the Pastons begging for money and signing himself 'your poor servant and beadman.' (*Paston Letters*, III, p. 402).

[11] P. 495. For the censorious monk, see Appendix II, p. 431.

[12] See *Grants*, p. xxxiv.

[13] HMC, 3rd Rep., p. 188; G. F. Warner and J. P. Gilson, *Catalogue of Western Manuscripts in the Old Royal and Kings' Collections*, 1921, II, p. 267, pp. 372–74.

[14] See article in DNB.

[15] C. A. J. Armstrong's appendix to Mancini, *Usurpation*, pp. 162–64.

X
(pp. 324–339)

Narrative sources: C.C., pp. 498–501; Vergil, pp. 211–15; *Great Chronicle*, pp. 234–37; Commynes, II, pp. 65–66.

[1] *Foedera* XII, p. 265 (in Latin). The authority of appointing subordinate officers was reserved to the King until the boy should come of age.

[2] Sir George Buc in his history of Richard III (in Kennett, *History of England*, I, p. 568)

paraphrases a letter he declares to be extant in which the Princess Elizabeth, writing to the Duke of Norfolk, expresses, while the Queen is dying, her impatience to marry Richard, 'her only joy and maker in the world'. Since no one else has apparently ever seen this letter, it can scarcely be entertained as evidence. That the Dowager Queen Elizabeth, incorrigibly ambitious, was scheming to marry her daughter to Richard, however, does not seem unlikely (see further, Appendix I, p. 413). For a judicious consideration of the weight that can be attached to Buc's citation, see Gairdner, pp. 203–04.

Rous, *The Great Chronicle*, and, of course, Vergil accuse Richard of poisoning Anne. Most authorities agree in rejecting this rumour; it is clear, from the *Croyland Chronicle*, that the Queen had been ailing for some time. The age was fond of showing its new Italianate sophistication by attributing the demise of the great to poison: Vergil even mentions such a rumour regarding Edward IV.

3 Harl. MS. 787, f. 2; Gairdner, pp. 193–94.

4 Harl. 433, f. 214: commissions of March 8 and March 11 and March 29.

5 *York Records*, pp. 208–10.

6 *Mémoires*, II, pp. 65–66.

7 Harl. 433, ff. 275b–76; compare Gairdner, pp. 196–97.

8 *Cal. Pat. Rolls*, 1476–85, p. 545; see also p. 544 (May 30).

9 See above, p. 317.

10 Harl, 433, f. 205.

11 Richard's itinerary is established from Harl. 433.

12 Richard to his Chancellor, June 21, 1485, 'to prepare the following proclamation', in *Original Letters*, 2nd series, I, pp. 162–66 (imperfect in Harl. 433, f. 220b); the proclamation, as addressed to the Sheriff of Kent, appears in *Paston Letters*, III, p. 316–20; the December proclamation is given in Harl. 433, f. 273b.

13 *Original Letters*, 2nd series, I, p. 146 (Harl. 433, f. 220). On June 22 all sheriffs were commanded to keep residence in their shire towns so that they might be ready at once to execute the King's orders (Harl. 433, f. 220b).

14 Fabyan says that, for defence against Henry's invasion, 'king Richard, for so much as he feared him little, made but small provision' (p. 672). Fabyan's evidence on the point cannot, however, be considered very reliable.

15 So he appears in the Knowsley portrait (see DNB).

16 See note 5 of Chap. 2, 'Richard, by Grace of God. . . .'

17 Stanley received a pardon in June of 1470 (*Cal. Pat. Rolls*, 1467–77, p. 211). His besieging Hornby Castle: *Cal. Pat. Rolls*, 1467–77, p. 241.

18 Though the C.C. (p. 501) says that Richard asked Stanley to send Lord Strange to him after Stanley had been some time absent, Vergil's report that Stanley did not depart until Strange arrived seems much more likely, in the circumstances.

Writing in 1688, one Roger Fleming refers to the reticent, perplexing conduct of the Earl of Derby, Lord Stanley's descendant, and adds, 'I cannot understand it unless he is as cunning as his predecessor in crookback Richard's time' (HMC, 12th Rep. (Le Fleming), VII, p. 221).

19 *Foedera* XII, pp. 271–72.

20 *York Records*, pp. 213–14.

21 Richard's letter to the Vernons, written August 11 from Beskwood lodge, announces that 'our rebels and traitors . . . are landed at Nangle [Angle] beside

Milford Haven on Sunday last past [August 7]' (HMC, Rutland, I, p. 7). Angle is on the south side of the bay. Dale, on the north shore, where Vergil says Henry landed, gives so much readier access to Haverfordwest, the town to which the rebels first marched, that it seems likely that Richard's first hasty information was in error.

XI
(pp. 339–354)

The marching itinerary of Henry Tudor's army is given in detail by Vergil, but I have had to infer the time scheme and the relationship between Henry's movements and Richard's decisions.

Narrative sources: C.C., pp. 500–02; Vergil, p. 212, pp. 216–22.

[1] Halliwell, *Letter of the Kings of England*, I, pp. 161–62.

[2] *Mémoires*, II, p. 66.

[3] See note 21 of previous chapter (X).

[4] P. 672.

[5] W. Garman Jones, *Welsh Nationalism and Henry Tudor*, pp. 32 and 33, quoted in *The Earlier Tudors*, p. 52.

[6] Charles Williams, *Henry VII*, London, 1937, p. 28.

[7] Wynne, *History of the Gwydir Family*, pp. 55–56; quoted in Gairdner, *Richard III*.

[8] Yet the young Earl of Shrewsbury is listed in Harl. 542, f. 34 (cited in William Hutton, *The Battle of Bosworth*, ed. by J. Nichols, London, 1813) as present at Bosworth in King Richard's army and according to *The Chronicle of Calais* (ed. by J. C. Nichols, Camden Society, 1846, p. 1), the Earl was captured by Henry's forces after the battle. It seems probable, therefore, that he was loyal to the King despite his uncle's holding with Henry, but the evidence is so doubtful that I have not included him as one of Richard's supporters.

Except for those few already outlawed or committed in advance to Henry's cause, no peer of England joined the invaders.

[9] *Paston Letters*, III, p. 320.

[10] I conjecture this from the fact that messengers from York found him at Beskwood lodge next day, the 17th (see the following note (11) and the text, p. 347 *et seq.*).

[11] The significance of Sponer's and Nicholson's mission appears to have been hitherto unnoticed (*York Records*, pp. 214–16; for Sponer accompanying Richard, YR., p. 218). The fact that Richard replied to their query by asking for men indicates that it was not fear of the plague which had prevented him from sending a military summons to the city. Apparently he did not make a stringent effort to call up soldiers, as the C.C. indicates (p. 501); only one letter, that to the Vernons of August 11, seems to have survived. But it is hard to believe that he would neglect to summon adherents so trusty and sturdy as the men of York. The only remaining alternative which appears reasonable is that he expected Northumberland, his Commissioner of Array for the East Riding of Yorkshire, to send them word. Northumberland's failure to do so, in view of his subsequent conduct at the battle (see below, p. 358), is almost certainly a sinister indication of his desire to surround himself with as many men of his own persuasion and as few of the King's as possible; this failure also

represented perhaps a kind of revenge for the times in the past when Northumberland had summoned the men of York, only to discover that they had obeyed Richard's call instead.

[12] I have inferred the date of Richard's leaving Nottingham from the total military picture. He does not appear to have stayed long at Leicester (see the act of attainder of Henry's parliament, *Rot. Parl.*, IV, p. 276); it seems likely that news of Henry's advance towards Nottingham would cause him to postpone his departure, which he had originally intended for Tuesday, Aug. 16, until word came that the rebels had turned southeast towards Leicester or London. No one seems hitherto to have noticed that Henry's march from Shrewsbury to Stafford aimed directly at Nottingham; only after he veered southeastward towards Lichfield would Richard have had any reason to proceed to Leicester.

[13] I am indebted for information about Leicester in King Richard's day to Professor Jack Simmons, of the University of Leicester; see John Nichols, *The History and Antiquities of the County of Leicester*, VI, part II, London, 1811; William Kelley, *Royal Progresses and Visits to Leicester*, Leicester, 1884; *Transactions of the Leicestershire Architectural and Archaeological Society*, II, Leicester, 1870.

[14] As will appear in the *Epilogue*; see p. 383.

XII
(pp. 354-369)

There exists no satisfactory contemporary, or even near contemporary, account of the battle of Bosworth. Vergil is the only source which provides any details; these I have followed closely, except for his statement that by swinging around the marsh, Henry's men 'kept the sun upon' their backs. The lie of the land reveals that, without question, this is an error, doubtless arising from Vergil's having confused what one of his informants told him. It has betrayed subsequent writers like Ramsay, who apparently did not visit the field, into arranging the armies in fantastic positions. A survey of the ground, in conjunction with a perusal of Vergil's narrative, shows, almost beyond a doubt, that Richard occupied Ambien Hill (probably from the Old English 'ana beame', one tree) and that the invaders swung northward around the marsh created by the spring called 'Dickon's Well' in order to attack Norfolk's line. The term used by the *Chronicle of Calais*, 'at Bosworth heath', would seem to confirm Ambien Hill as the locus of the battle. The location of the opposing camps the night before, I have inferred from details in Vergil and the terrain itself. Hutton, in the eighteenth century, asserted that he had discovered earthworks where I have placed Henry's and Richard's camps, but this evidence is doubtful at best; no trace of these earthworks now remains. After I had gone over the ground, I came upon Col. A. H. Burne's spirited account in *The Battlefields of England* and I was happy to learn that his 'reconstruction' was very much like my own, except for the conjectural conclusion to the battle which he devises. Richard's actions in the struggle are narrated by Vergil in considerable detail, which I have followed. He alone estimates the size of the armies, assigning 'scarce 5,000 men' to Henry, 'twice so many and more' to Richard, 3,000 men to Sir William Stanley and, by giving no figure for Lord Stanley's force, seeming to imply that it was still larger than that of his brother. Vergil keeps a discreet silence,

Q**

however, on the 'neutrality' of Northumberland, which is attested by later writers as well as by the *Croyland Chronicle*, which credits the Earl with 'a large and well-provided body of troops'. I have conjectured Northumberland's behaviour on the eve and on the early morning of the battle. The *Croyland Chronicle* supplies a few details about Richard during the early hours of August 22, which seem to me to represent authentic information. For the battle itself, however, the *Chronicle* offers an account which brings to its nadir an increasing unreliability as, apparently, the data supplied by the well-informed author came to an end and the monkish editor filled out the narrative with his own opinions. Though he writes too early to learn from the later Tudor court that Richard's army put up little fight and thus records that the struggle was 'of the greatest severity', he falsifies the action by asserting that Henry Tudor charged upon the King, instead of the other way round as even Vergil frankly reveals, and apparently out of his obsessive hatred of Northerners he retails the gross untruth that the chief men of Richard's army, who in actuality were killed—as was well and widely known—'took to flight without engaging' together with 'many others, chiefly from the North'. This account is so perversely false as to be inexplicable.

Vergil gives the captains of Henry's force. Richard's principal supporters are listed in Harl. 542, f. 34 (quoted in Nichols' edition of Hutton's *Bosworth*), which is probably not altogether reliable; and the chief casualties of the King's army are noticed, with a few variations, by Vergil, the *Chronicle of Calais*, the *York Records*, the *Croyland Chronicle* (if the reader substitutes 'killed' for 'fled'!), and by a proclamation issued shortly after the battle by Henry Tudor, in which, however, the Earls of Lincoln and Surrey and Viscount Lovell, all of whom survived the battle, are listed as slain, probably in an attempt, which was successful, to prevent the North from rising, by picturing all the Yorkist leaders at Bosworth as having been killed. I have made no reference to Richard's heir, the Earl of Lincoln, as taking part in the battle; his name is not given in Harl. 542 and he was not attainted. Lovell and Surrey, however, were both undoubtedly at Bosworth (act of attainder and Vergil). Vergil's reference to the sun indicates that the weather was clear. A few details such as the red coats of Sir William Stanley's horsemen and the rebel guns secured from Lichfield I have taken from *The Song of the Lady Bessy*, a ballad composed some two decades after by a servant of Lord Stanley's (Harl. MSS. 367 and 542; paraphrased in an appendix to Gairdner's *Richard III* and cited in Nichols' edition of Hutton's *Bosworth*). It appears that a few Scots fought for Henry Tudor: see Mackie, *The Earlier Tudors*, p. 51 and note 1.

Narrative sources: C.C., pp. 501–05; Vergil, pp. 222–27; *Great Chronicle*, pp. 237–38; Hutton's *Bosworth* (for some interesting local 'traditions' regarding the battle).

[1] So says later tradition. Harl. 433, f. 4, records the names of some of Richard's horses, one of which is 'White Surrey'.

[2] I infer these details; one of Richard's heralds was attainted (*Rot. Parl.*, VI, pp. 75–78).

[3] Richard's pallor, his mordant comment, the lack of chaplains, are taken directly from the C.C.; all these seem to me to be convincing details. The comment is wonderfully suggestive of the movement of Richard's mind on this critical morning.

[4] All that is known of Lord Strange is that, despite Stanley's refusal to join the royal army, Richard did not have him executed. In view of the *Croyland Chronicle*'s gross inaccuracy regarding the battle and the likelihood that Richard's intimate

servants were completely trustworthy, the *Chronicle*'s statement that those whom Richard ordered to behead Strange, seeing that the issue of the battle was doubtful, left Strange to his own devices and rushed into the fray on Richard's behalf, seems very improbable. Stanley apparently counted on Richard's mercy; he guessed correctly.

[5] I conjecture that Lord Stanley's men were on foot, since this was the customary mode of fighting (see, for example, *Mancini*, p. 123), but they may have been mounted, as Sir William Stanley's men certainly were.

[6] I assume this arrangement of archers and men at arms, since such had been the usual—but not invariable—disposition of troops by English commanders for the past century.

[7] Hutton in his *Bosworth* reports the finding of stone cannon balls on Ambien Hill.

[8] Richard's repeated cry of 'Treason!' as he battled the overwhelming numbers of his enemies is specifically reported by John Rous (p. 218). It seems to me likely that Rous, an otherwise very untrustworthy source, must have heard this from one who took part in the battle.

[9] Catesby's will, which he wrote just before he was executed at Leicester three days after Bosworth, exudes his feverish terror in every line. Doubtless in the vain hope of winning a last-minute pardon, he forgoes all dignity by abjectly declaring that he has 'ever loved' Henry Tudor. 'My lords Stanley, Strange, and all that blood!' he rushes on, 'help! and pray for my soul for ye have not for my body as I trusted in you' (Dugdale, *Warwickshire*, p. 789).

[10] Henry VIII's slight encounter with the enemy in the 'Battle of the Spurs' can scarcely be counted as fighting in the sense in which Henry V, Edward IV, and Richard fought in battle. After Bosworth, Kings sometimes went to the wars, but they did not lead their men into the fray.

[11] Some years after, Henry disbursed £10 1s for a tomb of sorts for Richard's grave ('Privy Purse Expenses' in *Excerpta Historica*, p. 105). At the dissolution of the monasteries the Grey Friars' was plundered; Richard's tomb was destroyed, his body thrown into the river Soar.

[12] *York Records*, p. 218. The city records show that the soldiers of York were gone for 4½ days (Drake's *Eboracum*, p. 121). It would have taken them the better part of three days to reach Sutton Cheney from York. They probably got no farther than Nottingham. John Sponer must have ridden night and day to reach York the day after the battle. Perhaps he remained in Leicester, waiting to guide the city troop to the field. This supposition is supported by the fact that he reports the Duke of Norfolk as betraying Richard, rather than the Earl of Northumberland. This lapse suggests either that he got his first word of the battle from an adherent of Northumberland's who thus sought to conceal his master's treachery from the North, or that the city clerk, out of caution, was ordered to substitute the name of Norfolk for Northumberland.

EPILOGUE
(pp. 373–389)

By its very baldness, Robert Fabyan's *New Chronicles of England and France* (in the continuation including the reign of Henry VII first printed by Rastell in 1533), suggests the darkness of Henry's reign. The yearly entries are for the most part brief and grim: money extorted and traitors executed.

I have principally relied for the chapter upon the following materials:

PRIMARY SOURCES AND COLLECTIONS OF PRIMARY SOURCES:
Calendar of the Patent Rolls, 1485–1509, 2 vols.
Rotuli Parliamentorum, VI.
Statutes of the Realm, II and III.
William Campbell, *Materials for the Reign of Henry VII*, 2 vols., Rolls Series, 1873, 1877.
Croyland Chronicle, 'Third Continuation'.
'Extracts from the Privy Purse Expenses of King Henry the Seventh' (1491–1505), *Excerpta Historica*, pp. 87–133.
Robert Fabyan, *New Chronicles of England and France* (the continuation of 1533).
James Gairdner, *Letters and Papers Illustrative of the Reigns of Richard III and Henry VII*, 2 vols., Rolls Series, 1861.
James Gairdner, *Memorials of King Henry VII*, Rolls Series, 1858 (containing Bernard André's life of Henry VII, *Vita Henrici VII*).
A. F. Pollard, *Sources for the Reign of Henry VII*, 3 vols., London, 1913.
Polydore Vergil, *Anglica Historia*, ed. and trans. by Denys Hay, Camden Series (RHS), 1949.
C. H. Williams, *England under the Early Tudors*, London, 1925.
York Civic Records, vol. I, ed. by Angelo Raine, The Yorkshire Archaeological Society, 1939. (I have drawn exclusively on this for my narrative of events in the city, except for the account of the Payntor-Burton controversy, which is taken from *York Records*, pp. 220–24).

SECONDARY SOURCES:
Francis Bacon, *The Life of Henry VII* (too remote from Henry's time and too derivative to be considered a primary source).
A. H. Burne, *More Battlefields of England*, London, 1952 (I am indebted to Col. Burne for his spirited and convincing account of the battle of Stoke in this volume).
W. Busch, *England under the Tudors*, London, 1895.
J. D. Mackie, *The Earlier Tudors*, Oxford, 1952 (Oxford History of England Series).
Kenneth Pickthorn, *Early Tudor Government*, I, London, 1934.
R. R. Reid, *The King's Council in the North*, London, 1921.
C. H. Williams, *The Making of the Tudor Despotism*, London, 1928.
Charles Williams, *Henry VII*, London, 1937.

ARTICLES OF SPECIAL VALUE:
W. A. J. Archbold, 'Sir William Stanley and Perkin Warbeck,' *English Historical Review*, XIV (1899), pp. 529–34.
C. H. Williams, 'The Rebellion of Humphrey Stafford in 1486,' *English Historical Review*, XLIII (1928), pp. 181–89.

[1] *Epigrammata*, published 1520.
[2] Leland, *Collectanea*, IV, pp. 222–27.
[3] *Cal. State Papers, Spain*, I, p. 164, p. 178.

Her will, executed on April 10, 1492, shortly before she died, is pathetic: 'Item, where I have no wordly goods to do the Queen's Grace, my dearest daughter, a pleasure with, neither to reward any of my children, according to my heart and mind, I beseech Almighty God to bless Her Grace, with all her noble issue, and with as good heart and mind as is to me possible, I give Her Grace my blessing, and all the foresaid my children.' (*Collection of Royal Wills*, p. 150).

[5] *Cal. Milanese Papers*, I, p. 299.

NOTES TO APPENDIX I
(pp. 393–418)

Appendix II, *Richard's Reputation*, includes a brief study of the Tudor tradition. Both there and in the notes for the text (see especially those for the section 'Protector and Defensor') I have discussed its general unreliability. In this appendix, therefore, my analysis of the value of More and Vergil is confined to their accounts of the murder of the Princes. Since the worth of a source as a whole casts light upon the worth of any single piece of testimony it advances, the reader may prefer to read Appendix II before this appendix.

[1] For a brief account of the authorship of the 'Second Continuation' of the *Croyland Chronicle*, see Appendix II, p. 432.

[2] See the report of one of Henry VII's spies in *Letters and Papers*, I, pp. 231–40.

[3] The method of judging More's tale, in the light of its suspicious origins and manifest inaccuracies, which is illustrated by Ramsay and Gairdner and cited approvingly by Lawrence Tanner as late as 1934 (see note 5, below) is to concede all that can be demonstrated to be false or unsatisfactory but to insist that the story is fundamentally true because *every* detail has not been proved inaccurate! It is a method foreign to logical analysis and to law, and it apparently springs from a rooted predilection for the Tudor tradition. Gairdner's rather painful attempt to square this tradition with the unanswerable objections that can be raised against it sometimes involves him in contradictions. For example, in the preface to *Letters and Papers*, I, he put forward his belief that Buckingham had a 'guilty knowledge' of the Princes' death; yet in his *Richard III* he clings to More's tale of the murders, which excludes the possibility of Buckingham's having any such 'guilty knowledge'.

Even the one apparent parallel between More's tale and the truth as it can be ascertained—the discovery in 1674 of two skeletons beneath a staircase within the precincts of the Tower—of which Gairdner *et. al.* have made so much, is by no means an established parallel. In the first place, to bury bodies secretly beneath stairs seems to be a method of disposal on which the imagination of the time often seized, as it likewise loved to suppose that those in high station met their ends by poison. In a later, embellished Tudor version of the crime, for example (John Rastell, *The Pastime of People*, published 1529, which offers a bizarre collection of rumours about the Princes' fate), the bodies were first interred at the foot of a staircase and then dug up and flung into the sea; the hole, incidentally, had been excavated in advance and the Princes had been lured into the chest so that they could be buried alive. Can it be seriously argued that the discovery of the skeletons vouches for the essential reliability of this tale, or More's, simply because one detail seems to correspond with the truth? There were many staircases in the Tower. The correspondence may well be coincidence (which is often a weakness in fiction but is even oftener a condition of real life). Why is More, why are the later Tudor writers at such pains to append the statement that the bodies were later disinterred? Why, except to account for the intransigent fact that the remains had not been exhumed even though Tyrell was supposed to have indicated their precise place of burial? Either the bodies had not been searched for or they had not been discovered. Both alternatives suggest that the staircase instanced in the tale which More heard and the staircase outside the White Tower beneath which the bodies were discovered have no actual connection.

Indeed, the circumstances of the burial recorded by More do not show much correspondence with the conditions of the actual disinterment. More believed a single priest capable of digging up the bodies in secret haste; no single priest could have so disinterred the bodies in their true hiding place. 'At the stair foot, meetly deep in the ground under a great heap of stones' is a more accessible location than ten feet deep in the ground beneath the foundations or within the foundations of a staircase, as the skeletons were actually discovered.

The surviving 17th century accounts of the exhumation are exasperatingly vague. Against the south wall of the White Tower there stood a 'forebuilding' which housed a stone staircase leading up to a door which may be seen today about fourteen feet from the ground. This door 'opens on a small landing of a now blocked spiral stair-case', which mounts to the chapel of St. John within the White Tower. The private way from the royal lodgings to the chapel led through the forebuilding, up the stone stairs built against the south wall of the White Tower, through the door and on up the interior spiral staircase, which is hewed out of the thickness of the eleventh century wall. In July of 1674, workmen had torn down the forebuilding and the stairs leading up to the door and were excavating the foundations of these stairs when they came upon the chest containing the bones. Four contemporary accounts use almost identical phraseology to describe the discovery: (1) 'digging down the stairs . . . were found the bones'; (2) 'in digging down a pair of stone stairs'; (3) 'in digging some founda-tions in the Tower'; (4) 'I saw . . . working men dig out of a stairway'. The first two accounts seem to indicate that the stairs were those within the forebuilding running up to the door; the third account simply says that the foundations were 'in ye Tower'; the fourth says that the stairway was 'in the White Tower'.

As Tanner points out, however, it is almost impossible to believe that the bones were dug out of the spiral staircase *within* the Tower. If they were, though, these bones can scarcely be those of the Princes. In all likelihood the skeletons were dis-covered just beneath or within (why dig lower than the bottom of the foundation?) the foundation of the staircase leading up to the door in the south wall.

In order to bury the bodies, therefore, a hole had to be dug downward about ten feet, and then an excavation made *inward*, under that is, or within, the foundations of the staircase. This Herculean operation can not be said to be described by More's words, 'At the stair foot, meetly deep in the ground under a great heap of stones'. It seems likely that the gossip which More—and no one else—retails, accidentally happened to approximate the actual mode of burial. See Lawrence E. Tanner and Prof. William Wright, 'Recent Investigations regarding the Fate of the Princes in the Tower', *Archaeologia*, LXXXIV (1934), p. 1 *et seq.*

[4] The rumour that Tyrell committed the murders reached the city of London. Fabyan

does not use it but *The Great Chronicle* does, doubtingly. 'Sir James Tyrell was reported to be the doer, but others put that weight upon an old servant of King Richard's named ———' [name omitted from *Chronicle*]. What King Henry 'gave out' was evidently so doubtful that many people preferred other versions of the murders. Concerning the circumstances of the deed, the *Chronicle* gives only a catalogue of possible murder methods—smothering, drowning, slaying by a poisoned dagger. As for Bernard André, Henry VII's official biographer and poet laureate, who was apparently completing his *Life* about 1503 when the news about Tyrell should have been very fresh, he says nothing on the subject of who killed the Princes, merely remarking that Richard ordered them to be put to death secretly by the sword. Where, again, is More's fine circumstantial tale?

5 Tanner and Wright, 'Recent Investigations, etc.', *Archaeologia*, LXXXIV (1934), p. 1 *et seq.*

6 Since the conclusions of science are not static, it seemed to me wise to submit the anatomical and dental evidence set forth in Tanner and Wright's article (see preceding note) to authoritative scrutiny. I am deeply indebted to Dr. W. M. Krogman, Professor of Physical Anthropology in the Graduate School of Medicine of the University of Pennsylvania, and to Dr. Arthur Lewis, Orthodontist, of Dayton, Ohio, for their kindness in patiently discussing this evidence with me; to Dr. Richard Lyne-Pirkis of Godalming, Surrey; and to Professor Bertram S. Kraus of the Department of Anthropology, the University of Arizona.

Dr. Krogman summarizes his conclusions regarding the evidence as follows: 'The ages as given are, in my opinion, a little too precisely stated. The dental evidence for age is, I think, the soundest. The evidence of age from the bones is limited because of the absence of most of the centers of ossification of the long bones. All things considered, the total age range of all the material is such that both children could have met their death as historically stated [i.e., in August of 1483].

'The so-called staining of the facial bones, attributable to the suffusion of suffocation, is not borne out by experience. Unless there were a rupturing of vessels, the suffusion would be limited to facial tissue and would not register itself upon the bones.'

On the basis of the dental evidence, Dr. Arthur Lewis gave his opinion that the elder child might be anywhere from 11 to 13 years of age but that he most probably appeared to be about 11½, according to the description of the dentition set forth by the article, the terminology of which was not altogether clear.

Professor Bertram Kraus writes, in part: '... the conclusion that the two skeletons were those of male sex was not substantiated (indeed it would be difficult to establish sex on pre-pubertal skeletons), and the terminology with regard to the dentition is somewhat questionable.

'Two points lead me to the conclusion that the individual [the elder child] is not over nine years of age. First assuming that there is correspondence between skeletal age and chronological age, the status of eruption of the permanent dentition would place the individual at nine years of age and definitely under twelve. Secondly, it is stated that there were no signs of epiphyseal union at the proximal end of the humerus. Complete union at this point generally occurs at the age of eighteen and if union has not occurred there is no accurate way of assessing age by degree of incompleteness of union. I notice that the apex of the odontoid processes of the axis was not fused, which ... "makes it possible to say with confidence that it belonged to a child who had not yet attained the age of thirteen". This, unfortunately, is not a correct statement. Fusion of the apex to the odontoid process takes place between four and six years of age. This would merely indicate that the child is under four years of age.'

Dr. Lyne-Pirkis, of Godalming, Surrey, who kindly discussed with me the anatomical evidence relating to the elder skeleton, likewise declared that the inference drawn from the odontoid processes of the axis was incorrect; and, like Dr. Krogman, he was of the opinion that the so-called stain upon the facial bones of the skeleton was not a blood stain resulting from the suffusion of suffocation.

While it appears, then, that a major conclusion of Tanner and Wright's article is correct—that if the bones are indeed the skeletons of the Princes, the boys were certainly dead by the end of the year 1483 and therefore could not have been dispatched by Henry VII—it also appears that other conclusions drawn in the article are not substantiated by certain present-day scientific authorities. The anatomical evidence for the age of the elder child is not sustained, and the conclusion that the stain on the facial bones upholds the story that the children were smothered is likewise not borne out. Most disturbing of all is the possibility that the elder child was *too young* to have been Edward V.

The sum of these findings and the circumstances under which the bones were discovered (see preceding note 3) indicate that the skeletons inurned in Westminster Abbey cannot be flatly and incontrovertibly identified with the sons of Edward IV. Until or unless the urn is reopened in order to attempt an estimate of the age of the bones, it must be acknowledged that their identification with the Princes, can only be expressed in terms of probability.

NOTES TO APPENDIX II
(pp. 419–434)

The testimony of More and Vergil is analyzed, for specific instances and assertions, in the notes—see particularly the notes for the chapter 'Richard, Protector and Defensor' —and also, for the murder of the Princes, in Appendix I.

For my sketch of the development of the Tudor tradition I am especially indebted to George B. Churchill's analysis, 'Richard the Third up to Shakespeare' in *Palaestra*, X (1900), Berlin; to Denys Hay's authoritative *Polydore Vergil*, London, 1952; and to E. M. W. Tillyard's *Shakespeare's History Plays*, New York, 1946. My account of the tone and substance of the Tudor tradition is in general accord with the conclusions of these authorities.

[1] Churchill, p. 51.

[2] W. E. Campbell and A. W. Reed, *The English Works of Sir Thomas More*, London, 1931, pp. 24–41. Compare A. F. Pollard, 'The Making of Sir Thomas More's Richard III', *Historical Essays in Honour of James Tait*, Manchester, 1933, pp. 223–38.

[3] P. 258.

[4] P. viii and p. 9.

[5] In a letter which Professor Hay was kind enough to write me concerning this issue, he considers it conceivable that Vergil burnt records 'which might have tended to

prejudice Tudor origins', but he doubts 'very much whether Vergil and his English contemporaries would have felt the historical relevance of such documentation'. This judgment clearly establishes the unlikelihood that Vergil deliberately destroyed documents relating to Richard's reign.

[6] P. 48.

[7] HMC, 3rd Rep., p. 43.

[8] 'Recent Investigations etc.', *Archaeologia*, LXXXIV (1934), p. 2.

[9] See 'Bishop Russell and the *Croyland Chronicle*', by J. G. Edwards, George Lam, and Paul M. Kendall (as yet unpublished but shortly to appear in the *English Historical Review*).

[10] See, for example: J. D. Mackie, *The Earlier Tudors*; Kenneth H. Vickers, *England in the Later Middle Ages* (4th ed., London and New York, 1926—vol. 3 of 'A History of England' in 7 vols.); C. Oman, *The History of England* (1377–1485) (London and New York, 1906—vol. 4 of the 'Political History of England' series); and a representative general history recently produced in America, Walter P. Hall and Robert G. Albion, *A History of England and the British Empire* (2nd ed., London and New York, 1946).

[11] *York Civic Records*, I, ed. by Angelo Raine, introduction. Raine says, p. vi, that Richard was distrusted and disliked by many of the commons, and, p. vii, that there is no evidence that the city council loved Richard. He continues, p. vii, 'The delay in sending soldiers from the City to take part in Bosworth fight does not show love, but rather anxiety to keep out of it and to join the winning side'. It is apparently the Tudor tradition which leads Raine into this indefensible position and also into an outright error. 'The most unpopular thing Richard ever did in York', he says, 'was to ask for and receive from a compliant council some common pasture near St. Nicholas' Hospital' (p. viii). Actually, the common pasture was to be enclosed for the benefit of the hospital, as *York Records* makes abundantly clear: '17th March, 1484: At the which day the letter of our sovereign lord the King, by the which our said sovereign desired to have a close belonging to the hospital of Saint Nicholas, the which is common from the feast of St. Michael to Candelmas, to have it closed and several to the behove of the said hospital. . . .' (p. 186).

BIBLIOGRAPHY

This list contains only those works and manuscript sources which I have cited most frequently and found most valuable. Books or manuscripts to which I have referred only once or twice are described in the notes in which they are mentioned.

Those sources, books, and articles which were mainly useful for the Prologue and the section 'Richard, Duke of Gloucester', dealing with Richard's earlier years, I have listed at the head of the notes on the Prologue; principal sources for the Epilogue (the reign of Henry VII) I have listed in the notes to that section; studies in Tudor historiography are indicated in the notes to Appendix II; and the works which make up the Tudor tradition of history from Rous to Shakespeare I have discussed in Appendix II.

MANUSCRIPT SOURCES:
British Museum: Cotton MSS.
            Harleian MS. 433.
Public Record Office: Chancery Records, Edward IV and Richard III.
            Exchequer Records, Edward IV and Richard III.

PRIMARY SOURCES, PRINTED:
Calendar of the Close Rolls, 1461–68; 1468–76; 1476–85.
Calendar of the Patent Rolls: 1452–61; 1461–67; 1467–77; 1476–85.
Calendar of State Papers and Manuscripts, relating to English affairs, existing in the Archives and Collections of Milan, I, ed. by A. B. Hinds, London, 1912.
Calendar of State Papers and Manuscripts, relating to English affairs, existing in the Archives and Collections of Venice and in other Libraries of Northern Italy, I, ed. by Rawdon Brown, London, 1864.
Foedera, etc., compiled by Thomas Rymer, vols. XI and XII, London, 1727.
Rolls of Parliament: Rotuli parliamentorum, V and VI.
Statues of the Realm.
Cely Papers, ed. by H. E. Malden, Camden Society, 1900.
Chastellain, Georges. Oeuvres, ed. by M. le Baron Kervyn de Lettenhove, Brussels, 1863–65.
Chronicles of London, ed. by C. L. Kingsford, Oxford, 1905.
Chronicle of the Rebellion in Lincolnshire, 1470, ed. by J. G. Nichols, Camden Society, 1847.
Chronicles of the White Rose of York, London, 1845.
Chronique Scandaleuse. Journal de Jean de Roye connu sous le nom de Chronique Scandaleuse, 1460–83, ed. by B. de Mandrot, Paris, 1894–96.
Collection of all the Wills now known to be extant of the Kings and Queens of England, etc. Society of Antiquaries, London, 1780.
Collection of Ordinances and Regulations for the Government of the Royal Household, London, 1790.
Commynes, Philippe de, *Mémoires de Philippe de Commynes*, ed. by B. de Mandrot, Paris, 1901–03.

Coventry Leet Book, ed. by M. D. Harris, Early English Text Society, 1907–13.

Croyland Chronicle: Historiae Croylandensis in Rerum Anglicarum Scriptorum, I, ed. by W. Fulman, Oxford, 1684. English translation: Ingulph's Chronicle of the Abbey of Croyland, trans. and ed. by Henry T. Riley, Bohn's Antiquarian Library, London, 1854.

Cust, Mrs. Henry. *Gentlemen Errant*, etc., New York, 1909.

Dignity of a Peer: Reports from the Lords' Committees touching the Dignity of a Peer of the Realm, 1829.

Devon, F. *Issues of the Exchequer*, London, 1837.

Drake, F. *Eboracum*, etc., London, 1736.

Ellis, Henry. *Original Letters*, in three series (Vol. I of each series), London, 1825, 1827 1846.

Excerpta Historica, London, 1831.

Fabyan, Robert. *The New Chronicles of England and France*, ed. by Henry Ellis, London, 1811.

Fortescue, Sir John. *The Governance of England*, etc., ed. by C. Plummer, Oxford, 1885.

Grants of King Edward the Fifth, ed. by J. G. Nichols, Camden Society, 1854.

The Great Chronicle of London, ed. by A. H. Thomas and I. D. Thornley, London, 1938.

Halliwell, J. C. *Letters of the Kings of England*, London, 1846.

Historie of the Arrivall of Edward IV in England, etc., ed. by John Bruce, Camden Society, 1838.

HMC: Historical MSS. Commission. Reports of the Royal Commission on Historical Manuscripts.

Household Books of John, Duke of Norfolk, and Thomas, Earl of Surrey, 1481–90, ed. by Payne Collier, Roxburghe Club, 1844.

La Marche, Olivier de. *Mémoires d'Olivier de la Marche*, ed. by H. Beaune and J. d'Arbaumont, Paris, 1883.

Leland, J. *Collectanea: De rebus britannicis Collectanea*, ed. by T. Hearne, London, 1715.

Letters and Papers Illustrative of the Reigns of Richard III and Henry VII, 2 vols., ed. by James Gairdner, Rolls Series, London, 1861–63.

Lettres de Louis XI, roi de France, ed. by Jos. Vaesen and others, Paris, 1883–1909.

Mancini, Dominic. *The Usurpation of Richard III*, ed. by C. A. J. Armstrong, Oxford, 1936.

Manners and Household Expenses of England in the Thirteenth and Fifteenth Centuries, ed. by T. H. Turner, Roxburghe Club, 1841.

Molinet, Jean. *Chroniques, 1476–1506*, ed. by J. A. Buchon, Paris, 1827–28.

More, Thomas. *The History of King Richard III*, ed. by J. R. Lumby, Cambridge, 1883.

The Paston Letters, ed. by James Gairdner (Library Edition), London, 1910.

Plumpton Correspondence, ed. by T. Stapleton, Camden Society, 1839.

Political Poems and Songs relating to English History, II, ed. by T. Wright, Rolls Series, London, 1861.

A Relation of the Island of England, ed. by C. A. Sneyd, Camden Society, 1870.

Rous or Ross, John. *Historia Regum Angliae*, ed. by Thomas Hearne, 2nd ed., Oxford, 1745.

Rous or Ross, John. *The Rows Rol*, ed. by W. Courthope, London, 1845.

Stonor Letters and Papers, 1290–1483, 2 vols., ed. by C. L. Kingsford, Camden Society, 1919.

Stow, John. *The Annales or Generall Chronicle of England*, London, 1615.

Stow, John. *A Survey of London*, ed. by C. L. Kingsford, Oxford, 1908.

Vergil, Polydore. *Anglica Historia*, 3rd ed., London, 1555. An English translation of those Books of the Anglica Historia which relate to the fifteenth century: Polydore Vergil, History, ed. by Henry Ellis, Camden Society, 1844 (a sixteenth century translation).

Wardrobe Accounts of Edward IV, ed. by Sir H. Nicolas, London, 1830.

Warkworth, John. *A Chronicle of the First Thirteen Years of the Reign of King Edward the Fourth*, ed. by J. O. Halliwell, Camden Society, 1839.

Waurin, Jehan de. *Anchiennes chronicques d'Engleterre*, ed. by Mlle. Dupont, Paris, 1858–63 (vols. II and III).

Wilkins, David. *Concilia*, etc., III (4 vols.), London, 1737.

York Records: Extracts from the Municipal Records of the City of York, ed. by R. Davies, London, 1843.

York Civic Records, I, ed. by Angelo Raine, The Yorkshire Archaeological Society, 1939.

SECONDARY SOURCES:

Anstis, J. *The Register of the Most Noble Order of the Garter*, London, 1724.

Baldwin, J. F. *The King's Council in England during the Middle Ages*, Oxford, 1913.

Blades, W. *The Life and Typography of William Caxton*, 2 vols., London, 1861–63.

Burne, Col. A. H. *The Battlefields of England*, London, 1952.

Calmette, J. and Périnelle, G. *Louis XI et L'Angleterre*, Paris, 1930.

G.E.C. *Complete Peerage*.

Chrimes, S. B., *English Constitutional Ideas in the Fifteenth Century*, Cambridge, 1936.

Dugdale, William. *The Baronage of England*.

Gairdner, James. *History of the Life and Reign of Richard III* (rev. ed.), Cambridge, 1898.

Hay, Denys. *Polydore Vergil*, Oxford, 1952.

Hutton, W. *The Battle of Bosworth Field*, Birmingham, 1788; also, the revised edition ed. by J. G. Nichols, London, 1813.

Kingsford, Charles L. *English Historical Literature in the Fifteenth Century*, Oxford, 1913.

MacGibbon, David. *Elizabeth Woodville*, London, 1938.

Mitchell, R. J. *John Tiptoft*, London, 1938.

Myers, Alec R. *England in the Late Middle Ages*, Penguin, 1952.

Pickthorn, Kenneth. *Early Tudor Government*, I (2 vols.), Cambridge, 1934.

Ramsay, Sir James. *Lancaster and York*, 2 vols., Oxford, 1892.

Reid, R. R. *The King's Council in the North*, London, 1921.

Scofield, Cora L. *The Life and Reign of Edward the Fourth*, 2 vols., London and New York, 1923.

Turner, Sharon. *History of England during the Middle Ages*, 4 vols., London, 1825.

Weiss, R. *Humanism in England during the Fifteenth Century*, London, 1941.

Williams, C. H. *England: The Yorkist Kings*, Chapter XII of the Cambridge Medieval History, VIII, Cambridge, 1936.

Index